KW-763-899

Clinical Practice in
Sexually Transmissible Diseases

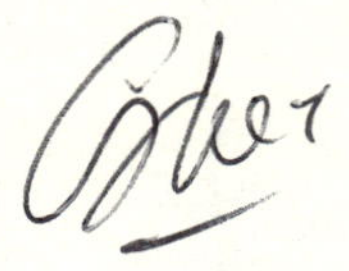

Clinical Practice in Sexually Transmissible Diseases

D H H Robertson, MB, CHB, FRCP(Ed), DTM&H
Head of University Department of Venereal Diseases
Consultant Physician, Department of Sexually Transmitted Diseases
Edinburgh Royal Infirmary

A McMillan, BSc, MB, ChB, MRCP(Ed)
Consultant Physician, Department of Sexually Transmitted Diseases, Glasgow
Honorary Senior Lecturer, University Department of Venereal Diseases, Edinburgh Royal Infirmary

H. Young, BSc, PhD
Lecturer, Department of Bacteriology
University of Edinburgh and Edinburgh Royal Infirmary

PITMAN MEDICAL

First published 1980

Catalogue Number 21 3227 81

Pitman Medical Limited
57 High Street, Tunbridge Wells, Kent TN1 1XH

Associated Companies
Pitman Publishing Pty Ltd, Melbourne
Pitman Publishing New Zealand Ltd, Wellington

British Library Cataloguing in Publication Data

Robertson, D H H
Clinical practice in sexually transmissible diseases.
1. Venereal diseases
I. Title II. McMillan, A
III. Young, H
616.9'51 RC200

ISBN 0-272-79568-2

Set in 11 on 12 pt IBM Journal by
Gatehouse Wood Limited, Cowden
Printed by offset-lithography and bound
in Great Britain at The Pitman Press, Bath

Contents

Foreword

I entertain the hope that the Foreword may help to introduce this volume to a much broader readership than just those already committed to the specialty of Sexually Transmissible Diseases. The increased opportunities for the transmission of infection by sexual contact which contemporary patterns of living promote, and the widening spectrum of organisms of all genera involved, have enhanced the relevance of this volume's subject matter to many areas of medical practice.

Sexual health problems, regrettably, are ignored or deliberately avoided by many doctors. I believe the reasons for their unease with these topics are linked with influences operating in the formative years of their medical careers. During their early professional training, doctors unconsciously acquire a necessary indifference to the nudity and intimate touching inseperable from clinical practice. Often their continuing comfort in the face of this physical closeness is only maintained if the patient's sexuality is excluded from thought or discussion.

However, it is impossible to practice medicine competently wearing sexual blinkers, for many important problems of physical and mental health originate from sexual function or dysfunction. A new specialty—'Sexual Medicine'—has been adumbrated, but I wonder if it is the wisest course to attempt to segregate all sexual aspects of health in this way: they are too much an integral part of the general fabric of health care. I believe, therefore, that the information which Dr Robertson and his colleagues have brought together in this volume will be of value to many health professionals, but the book bears its own commendation in the blend of scientific erudition, humane concern and sound practical guidance which is so clearly evident throughout.

Philip R. Myerscough,
MB, ChB, FRCOG, FRCS(Ed),
Senior Lecturer,
University Department of
Obstetrics and Gynaecology,
Edinburgh Royal Infirmary

Preface

This book has been written primarily for those who are actively engaged in the increasingly demanding clinical practice of venereology and who, by so doing in the United Kingdom at least, now tend to undertake so large a part of the primary care of adolescents and young adults. We have attempted to bring together information which is widely scattered in the literature and to present an appreciation of clinical and laboratory aspects of the various subjects in a way which we believe will be useful to our colleagues. It is our hope that the book will be of value, as a reference in teaching and also to the wider range of clinicians, for instance gynaecologists and urologists, who participate as we do in the practice of sexual and reproductive medicine and will therefore often require to consider the full range of sexually transmitted diseases. General practitioners and other clinicians, who are involved in clinics set up for counselling and for giving contraceptive and kindred advice, will find some answers to their questions, and physicians, who may not ordinarily look after adolescents and young adults, may find the inclusion of sexually transmissible infections in their differential diagnosis a rewarding exercise. It is clear that when precise information about the organisms involved is regarded as an essential discipline in the diagnosis of genito-urinary and pelvic inflammatory disease, the importance of transmission by sexual intercourse will become better appreciated and the application of isolation methods, more searching than conventional bacteriological investigations, will help in developing more rational care of patients.

Although this book is primarily for medical readers it is hoped that those involved in nursing or counselling patients, tracing contacts or in health education will be able to obtain some of the factual information which they require. Barriers between disciplines are tending to become inappropriate and those who share objectives in patient care will require to pool their knowledge to obtain the best results possible.

There is more to be achieved by those concerned than a technical understanding of one aspect of clinical medicine and microbiology because psychological and social barriers intrude and hamper at every level. Some aims of this text are primarily intellectual and are fundamental to practice in a subject which involves deep personal feelings to such an extent that patient, doctor and society may appear not infrequently to be bewitched. The reader will be encouraged to adopt a logical attitude essential in clinical practice and an approach to the subject based on an acceptance of human diversity.

Acknowledgements

The authors wish to thank colleagues, scientists, technologists, librarians and others in the National Health Service or in the Faculty of Medicine of the University of Edinburgh for their help, advice and discussion. In addition the authors acknowledge with thanks the valuable help of colleagues and publishing houses, who have allowed inclusion of tables and diagrams, which add so much to the illustration of the text. The origins of such contributions are acknowledged individually as they appear within the book.

The authors wish to acknowledge particularly the help and advice of Dr J F Peutherer and Dr I W Smith in connection with the chapters on virus diseases and the electron micrographs and other illustrations.

The contribution of members of the Department of Medical Illustration of the University of Edinburgh is gratefully acknowledged.

The authors wish to thank Mrs J M Gilbertson for her skill in typing the manuscript and for her patience and help given in its preparation.

Finally the helpfulness and courtesy of the staff of Pitman Medical Publishing Co, Ltd, is much appreciated; particularly that of the Editor, Mr G W Smith.

CHAPTER 1

Introduction

A. Social change
B. Evolutionary and biological background to human sexual behaviour
C. Sexual habits of young people
D. The social impact of sexually transmitted disease
E. Personal prophylaxis
F. Facilities for diagnosis and treatment
G. Tracing of contacts and the case against compulsion
H. People with high risks
I. Companionship, marriage and divorce
J. Medical secrecy
K. Education
L. The dilemma of a name—publicity

A. Social change

The medical responsibility for diagnosis, treatment and control of sexually transmitted diseases (STD) in a community requires cultivation of new skills, new attitudes and a sense of realism. These will be dependent not only upon medical knowledge but also upon a comprehension of human sexual behaviour, an insight into one's own personality and a wish to care for patients whose situation may have rendered them particularly vulnerable. Insofar as the United Kingdom, although varying geographically in its prevailing attitudes, is representative of a rapidly changing western society it is worth-while to consider some important milestones in its recent social history.

In the BBC Reith Lectures for 1962, entitled *'This Island Now'* Carstairs [1] outlined many of the points of change which were occurring at that time and among these he included the profound decline in the influence of the Church as a tradition-centred authority for moral values, the extension of materialism and credulity among the masses. He touched on the changing role of women and the abandonment of chastity as a supreme moral value. Here he recognized that sexual experience before marriage with precautions against pregnancy would become a recognized preliminary to marriage. As in the early 1960s, modern advertising, films, television and popular reading have continued through the seventies to constantly expose the young to sexual stimulation.

What has made a deep impact in society is the counter-culture [2] about which Carstairs was well aware. There are a number of main themes which permeate society and which can be readily recognized in day-to-day life and which require appreciation by clinicians, particularly those involved in the care of the adolescent or young adult. There are attitudes which tend to favour perhaps a spontaneous rather than a manipulative and possessive use of sex. There has been an extinction of social formalities which promotes an uninhibited approach of one young person to another. With spontaneity of expression and the search for ecstasy, whether homosexual or heterosexual, the dangers of sexually transmitted infections are obvious. With the breaking of taboos concerning sex [3], habits of oral and anal intercourse, whether on a homosexual, heterosexual or bisexual basis, have increased the complexity of the clinical situation. Such sexual adventuring may be continuous but it may also be sporadic when it is confined to holidays, when restraints are abandoned. In all this and in the rejection of sexual exclusiveness, the doctor has to keep an open mind, otherwise his efficiency and relevance will suffer. The risks of individuals are enhanced by travelling and mixing with people often in parts of the world with poorer access to medical care than in this country.

Although a setback to mingling and holidaying occurred in 1973, it is still a major activity insisted upon by all classes and by the young particularly, and unlikely to be given up willingly. The cultural attitudes of the older generation (say those over 40 years of age!) are different and their views emphasize the importance of work, economics and power. The counter-culture tends to develop at first in minorities but it colours the whole and it leaves long-lasting effects.

By the late 1960s there was a shift of people out of industry into the service sector, offices, tourist activities and above all into the social services. With new riches there has been more intermingling, and inflation has effectively redistributed wealth from the thrifty to the spender, from the old to the young. The 1972–1973 boom produced even greater expectancies broken, however, by the devastating effect of the increase in oil prices in autumn 1973 [4]. This jolt to rising expectancy has reduced materialistic ambition and the risks of promiscuous sexual behaviour are likely to be more restricted geographically as a result.

Edinburgh, for example, has been one focus for the developing counter-culture in Scotland and there have been incidents which form evidence of its presence. There was, for example, the announcement, from the pulpit of St Giles, by Mr Muggeridge of his resignation as Rector of Edinburgh University. This episode followed the resolution of the Students' Representative Council that the Students' Health Service should provide contraceptive pills for students if they wanted them. The doctors of the University Health Service at that time hopefully asserted their right to prescribe as they thought fit as doctors and particularly their right to prescribe or to refuse to make the pill available on request. Again in 1967, in the Family Planning Centre in Edinburgh, unmarried girls were excluded unless they were intending marriage. An escape from this restriction was however possible and a progressive private organization, the Edinburgh Brook Advisory Centre, provided it. This facet of the counter-culture has led to alteration in Government Policy as in 1974 the Brook Centre became an agent for contraceptive services of the Lothian Health Board (National Health Service (Scotland) Act, 1972). The counter-culture too has affected profoundly the policy of the Family Planning Centre in Edinburgh where in the early part of 1976 it was recorded that two-thirds of its new patients were unmarried in comparison to the situation in 1967 when only one-third were in the unmarried category and these patients claimed that they were 'about to be married'.

The jolt to expectancies produced by economic recession and an oil crisis led to a reduction in the amount of movement in the population and this was probably a factor in producing a reduction in the rate of increase of sexually transmitted disease in Scotland where the average annual rate of increase of 12 per cent between 1964 and 1973 was reduced to 0.3 per cent. This reduction is in line with Musgrave's hypothesis which predicts a flourishing of the counter-culture in times of expanding opportunities and wealth and a retrenchment in times of restriction to these opportunities.

Although the counter-culture diminishes in its extent it will have long-term effects and in terms of premarital sexual expression, at least, there has been a deep impact, although there may be a general disapproval of casual sexual expression. In England, in a survey by Bone [5], for example, she found that somewhere between 33 per cent and 38 per cent of single women aged 16–35 were at least from time to time exposed to unprotected intercourse. She found also that 63 per cent of single women did not reject premarital intercourse and also that there was no evidence of any difference between the social classes in attitudes towards premarital intercourse. Such attitudes obtain also in Scotland where it was found that although 75 per cent of young people (494 people aged 16–20) disapproved of casual sex, 61 per cent approved if the couple were in love and 73 per cent approved if the couple were engaged. As large a percentage as 16 per cent approved of casual sexual expression (*Scotsman,* 28 April 1976).

Men and women now expect to have opportunities of achieving personal happiness, unfettered by the views of others. Such concepts, derived from the human rights movement [6] have repercussions on the professions which have tended to adapt by altering an authoritarian stance to one where the views of the individual patient play an influential part.

B. Evolutionary and biological background to human sexual behaviour

There is no aspect of human existence that has been so prone to cultural influences as human sexual behaviour and reproduction. This social overlay has obscured what might be termed the natural history of our species which needs to be defined if we are to understand both the causes and consequences of the recent explosive increase in the human population [7] and for the purposes of this discussion, possibly to alter attitudes to behaviour leading to unwanted effects such as the increases in the incidence of sexually transmitted diseases reported throughout the world.

From the point of view of sexual behaviour and reproduction, Short [7], has summarized important biological differences in man in comparison with other mammals. In *Homo sapiens,* females are potentially attractive and receptive at any time from adolescence to old age and apparently, alone among primates, may receive added gratification from sexual intercourse in the form of orgasm. Much behaviour, including sexual, is culturally adapted but it would be rash to assume that man has no unlearned or innate behaviour [8]. For reasons based, for example, on differences in body size between the sexes in primates including man, insight can be gained, in evolutionary terms at least, into man's marked incapacity (particularly in the male) to adhere to a monogamous path [9]. Within communities of the developed world individuals tend generally to be directed towards monogamy to secure pair-bonding, for the benefit of children who require, in comparison with other mammals, a long time to mature. Within modern urban society, for example, serial monogamy (often non-reproductive) is often a usual form of relationship among the unmarried [10], particularly as effective contraception is readily available and may represent one compromise between a polygamous nature and monogamy. When, however, the compromise produces relationships that tend to be of short duration and more numerous or even casual, sexually transmitted disease becomes an important cause of morbidity with effects which will depend on the accessibility of medical care. The implications of mankind's evolutionary and biological background are inescapable.

AGE OF PUBERTY

In developed countries there has been a spectacular decline in the age of the menarche (Figure 1.1) although more recent evidence suggests that this downward trend has come to a halt [11, 12] to give a mean menarchal age of 12.6–13.5 years. During the period 1830–1960 secular

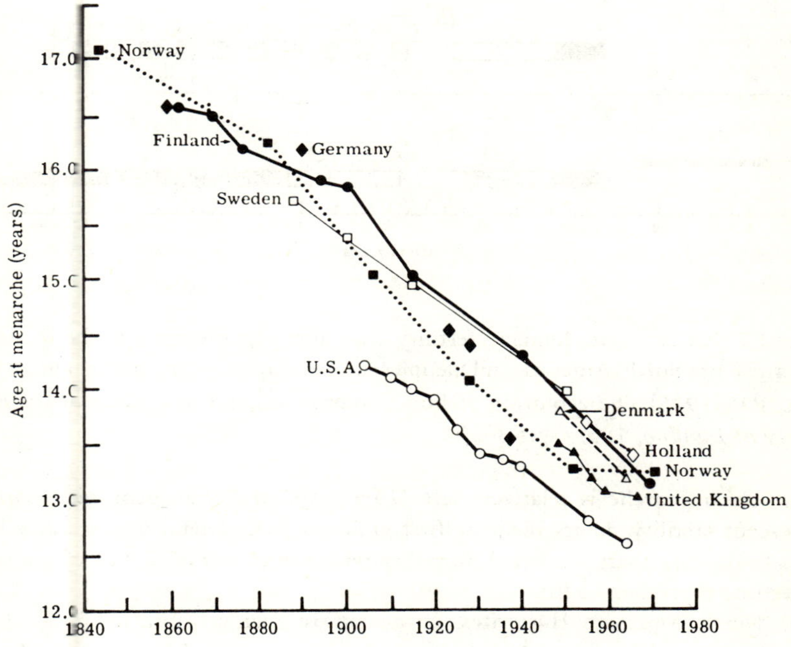

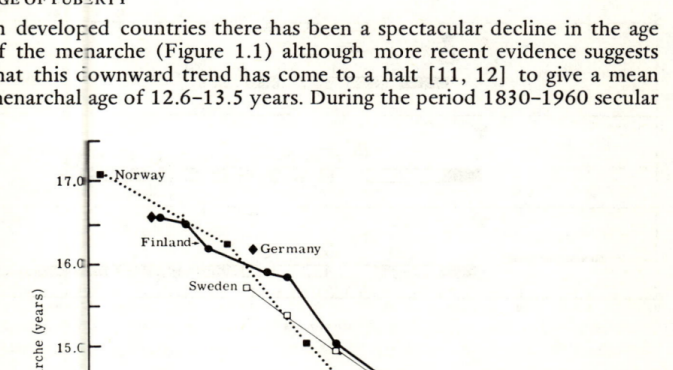

Figure 1.1 Secular trend in age at menarche from 1840 (Marshall, WA and Tanner, JM (1974) *Scientific Foundations of Paediatrics* (Ed) Davis, JA and Dobbing, J. Heinemann, London).

diminution in age of menarche was calculated to be about 3–4 months per decade. The highest menarchal ages are now to be found among the poorest countries and the trend towards earlier maturation is occurring in many countries where improved nutrition, particularly an increase in the protein content of a child's diet, has been shown convincingly to be

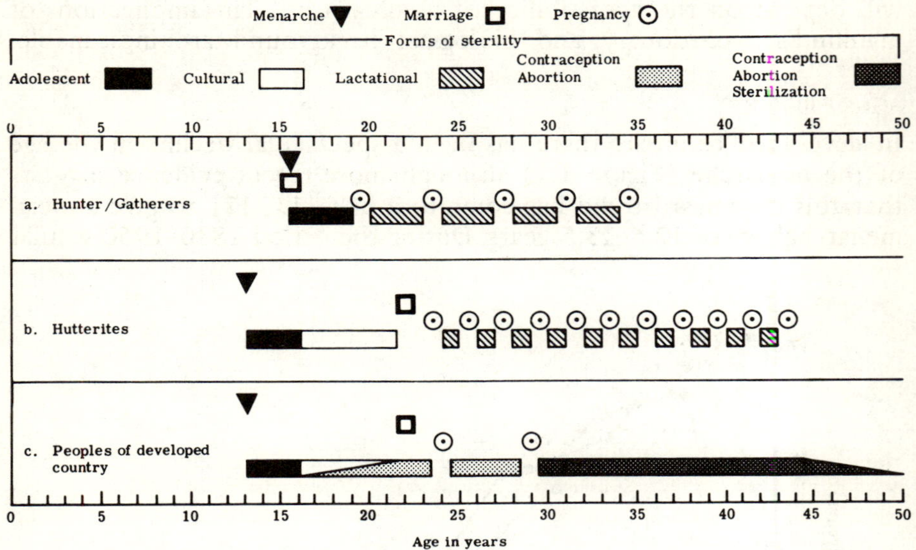

Figure 1.2 Patterns of human fertility in hunter/gatherers of the Kalahari, Hutterites of North America and peoples of developed countries (adapted from Short, RV (1976) The evolution of human reproduction. *Proceedings of the Royal Society of London*, 195, pages 3–23).

(a) The menarche is relatively late (15½ years) and coincident with marriage. Adolescent sterility defers birth of first child to 19½. Lactational sterility keeps births four years apart. Maternal mortality results in family of 5, 3 of whom would survive into reproductive life.

(b) North American Hutterites, an anabaptist sect, practise no form of contraception. Menarche is at 13 and taboo prevents premarital intercourse. Marriage occurs at age of 22. Lactational amenorrhoea is short and births occur every 2 years to give a family size of 11. Sexually transmitted disease cannot thrive in such a situation.

(c) Menarche is at 13; taboo against premarital intercourse breaks down in late teens and this requires the use of contraception and abortion. Lactation is so short in duration that it does not induce amenorrhoea and if the desired family size is 2, contraception, abortion or sterilization is necessary for 20 years with an enormous increase in number of menstrual cycles in comparison with *(a)* and *(b)*. Sexually transmitted disease can thrive under these circumstances, where sexual maturity occurs long before marriage and where taboo against premarital or extramarital intercourse or divorce diminishes or becomes ineffective.

the cause. In Britain the rich and poor are now beginning to reach the limit of the genetic potential as the latest English and Scottish data show no differences which reflect differences in their family income. In Hong Kong, however, the data show a difference of nine months between rich and poor, presumably because the poor are much worse off than the poor in Britain. A most convincing argument for nutritional causes is the example of the Lapps who had practically the same age of menarche, 16½ years, from 1780 to 1930 while maintaining their pastoral nomadic way of life. During the same period the neighbouring Norwegians, being settled farmers, became two years earlier in their age at menarche [12].

Although boys become fertile before girls they are at a very early stage in their pubertal development and are still physically immature. There is little information about the secular changes in the time of onset of male puberty but evidence for both sexes suggests that psychosexual development is determined by nutritional events which control the time of onset of puberty. Short rightly emphasizes that the social consequences of lowering the age of puberty are more important than the demographic impact of prolonging the life span and to regard premarital intercourse and contraceptive advice for present-day school children as stigmata of decadence is to miss the point about the biological nature of man (Figure 1.2). Tanner [13] emphasizes also that the two facts of human growth which are important in their repercussions on and within the culture are the great range of chronological ages at which adolescence occurs and the advancement in maturity of girls over boys. In girls, although their period of adolescent infertility, between 12 and 14 years of age [14], with about 60 per cent of menstrual cycles being anovular, will be protected to this extent against pregnancy, STD risks will remain.

Facts given in discussion of the evolutionary and biological background to human behaviour need not be taken as an absolute threat to the point of view that man has a capacity to make personal choices but more that it gives weight to argument about probabilities rather than necessities [15] and therefore the data deserve to be taken into account by those involved in making decisions on, say, education for healthy living in its widest sense or on community health needs.

C. Sexual habits of young people in western society

A broad picture of the sexual habits of young people in England is indicated in Schofield's diagrams reproduced here (Figures 1.3 and 1.4) which summarize his findings by questionnaire as to the incidence of deep-

Table 1.1 Results of interviews in 376 individuals aged about 25 years giving data on number of sexual partners in the previous year [18]

	Status, marital or other						
Number of partners in previous year	*Married*	*Divorced or separated*	*Living together*	*Steady partner*	*Not Steady*	*Number*	*Percentage*
Only one partner	240	5	3	23	6	277	74
One other, once	2	0	0	1	0	3	1
One other, several times	2	3	0	2	0	7	2
Several, once each	1	0	0	3	3	7	2
Several people, many times	12	1	2	14	17	46	12
No sexual intercourse	0	1	0	9	26	36	9
Total	257	10	5	52	52	376	100

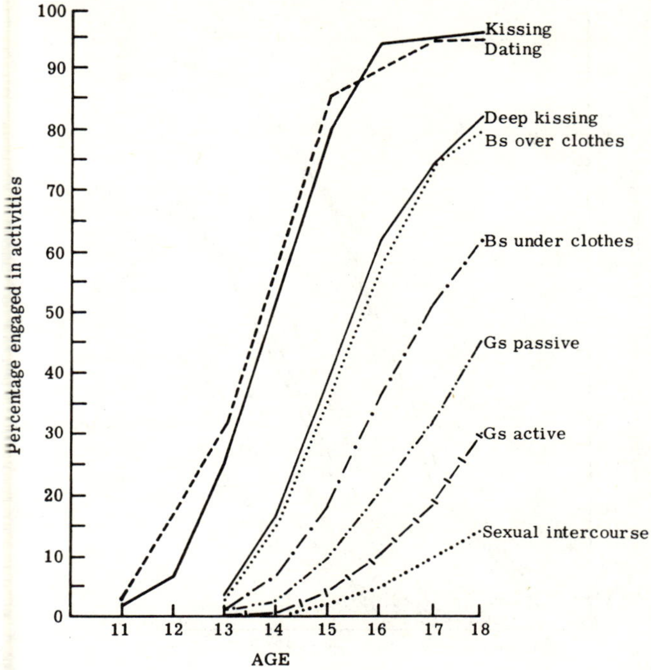

Figure 1.3 Accumulative incidence curves of eight activities for girls. Bs = breast stimulation; Gs = genital stimulation (Schofield, M, 1965, *The Sexual Behaviour of Young People*, Longmans, London, page 36).

kissing, breast stimulation (Bs) and genital stimulation (Gs) among girls and boys at different ages as well as full intercourse. In an enquiry on such a delicate subject there may well have been incomplete disclosure and therefore an underestimate of the amount of sexual activity in teenagers and a survey as long ago as 1964 [16] is likely to be out of date now. Davies [17] points out that in the United Kingdom attitudes to sex have changed very rapidly since the 1960s.

In Schofield's second book [18] the follow-up seven years after his original study gives an indication of the extent of sexual intercourse and of the degree of mixing or 'promiscuity' of young adults (Table 1.1). Many married men and women who are now quite faithful to each other may have had several partners before they married and although the various percentages in a survey will vary it is important to recognize that many thousands behave in this way. Restricting the definition of

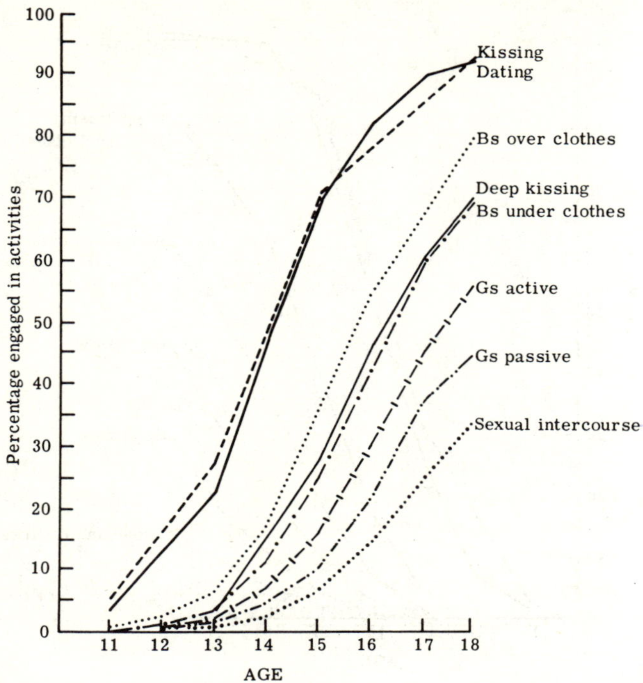

Figure 1.4 Accumulative incidence curves of eight activities for boys. Bs = breast stimulation; Gs = genital stimulation (Schofield, M, 1965, *The Sexual Behaviour of Young People*, Longmans, London, page 35).

'promiscuity' to refer to those who in the course of the year had several different sexual partners Schofield found that 14 per cent of the whole group were 'promiscuous' and 5 per cent of those who were married were promiscuous in this sense. Davies [17] has drawn attention to a study by Wright and Cox of teenagers, but restricted to grammar-school sixth formers in England, which shows that a remarkable change has taken place in attitudes towards premarital sex during the 1960s. Wright and Cox asked their boys and girls to rate various activities on a scale according to whether they thought them wrong. The percentage change of the sample who endorse the different rating categories for premarital intercourse in 1963 and 1970 is shown in Table 1.2. There has been a massive shift in attitudes especially among girls. The view that premarital intercourse is wrong is rapidly disappearing, although in attitudes to other activities such as gambling, smoking, stealing and

Table 1.2 Opinion on premarital intercourse

Year		*Percentage opinion on premarital intercourse*				
		Wrong				*Undecided*
		Always	*Usually*	*Sometimes*	*Never*	
1963	Boys	28.6	27.6	20.5	10.2	13.1
	Girls	55.8	25.2	6.6	2.4	10.0
1970	Boys	10.3	12.8	30.4	33.7	12.8
	Girls	14.6	19.5	30.0	17.7	18.2

the colour bar there had not been anything like the shift in opinion as on the issue of premarital sex. Studies elsewhere have tended to confirm that the change in sexual attitudes has a close relationship with the change in sexual behaviour [17]. Eysenck [19] recently referred to the pressure on young people to behave in a manner contrary to their personality make-up and value judgements.

An even more massive shift in sexual attitudes is apparent in some localities as recorded in a small city in the Rocky Mountain region of the United States [20]. Here it was found that in one group studied over the four years of high school (ages 16–19 years) the proportion of non-virgins in males was, for consecutive years, 8, 16, 22 and 33 per cent and in females 5, 13, 46 and 55 per cent. Later, in the four years at college rates for males were 46, 65, 74 and 82 per cent and for females the corresponding percentages were 51, 70, 80 and 85 per cent. In this study it did not seem that a radical change in attitudes to sexual intercourse had occurred in high school as the function of intercourse most strongly endorsed was a close relationship and love rather than a casual encounter. In college, however, 64 per cent of the males and 44 per cent of the females thought it was acceptable for two young people to engage in sexual intercourse if they both want to, when they hardly know each other and have no special feeling for each other. These are clearly potentials for change which have profound implications for the provision of STD facilities at least, although again needs will vary geographically according to prevailing attitudes.

Within Europe as a further indication of more mixing and hence increasing relevance of STD as a factor to be considered on a lifetime basis there have been big increases in divorce at younger ages and shorter durations of marriage, and corresponding increases in the numbers remarrying. This remarried group has become an increasingly important demographic and social group. For example, in an analysis of family structure, in England and Wales there has been a marked increase in the number of remarried women aged under 50 from 300,000 in 1971 to 465,000 in 1976 [21]. Marriage patterns are being profoundly altered and in Sweden, for example, illegitimate births constituted one-third of all births in 1975, reflecting large declines in marriage rates and substantial proportions of couples cohabiting outside marriage. To a lesser extent Denmark follows the same path [22].

D. The social impact of sexually transmitted diseases

In the United Kingdom the social impact of venereal disease [23] in the era before the discovery of arsenicals and antibiotics was daunting even to the most courageous. It had an immediate effect by interfering with ability to earn a livelihood and might well lead to destitution. Later, in gonorrhoea for example, when antiseptic treatment was introduced it brought the prolonged misery of urethral irrigations and the anxiety of uncertain cure. If a man infected his wife the guilt, shame and doubt about the prospects of cure devastated a marriage. If syphilis occurred and involved a wife there was also the spectre of congenital syphilis which could kill or stigmatize their children with disabilities such as blindness, deafness or juvenile dementia paralytica. In developing countries, particularly those in which medical services are very poor or disrupted by strife, severe effects are likely to become more common.

Congenital syphilis has virtually disappeared as a cause of death in infants under the age of one year (Figure 1.5) although fear of it as a menace justifiably remains. The death rate started to decline when arsenical treatment became widely available in the clinics which were established during World War I*. A short rise in incidence followed the outbreak of World War II but the infant death rate declined even more sharply with the advent of penicillin. Some sixty years ago 1,200 infants died each year from congenital syphilis; today the recognition of this disease in the newborn is a very rare event. Congenital syphilis accounted for 12 per cent of the blindness in the United Kingdom in the 1930s but by the mid 1950s it accounted for less than one per cent and the numbers have continued to fall.

In the case of gonorrhoea, ophthalmia neonatorum (conjunctivitis of

*These clinics were established throughout the United Kingdom after the enlightened recommendations of the Royal Commission on Venereal Diseases (Cd. 8189 & 8190 [24]. As a result of these the Local Government Board developed an organization providing for the free diagnosis and treatment of persons suffering from venereal disease [25].

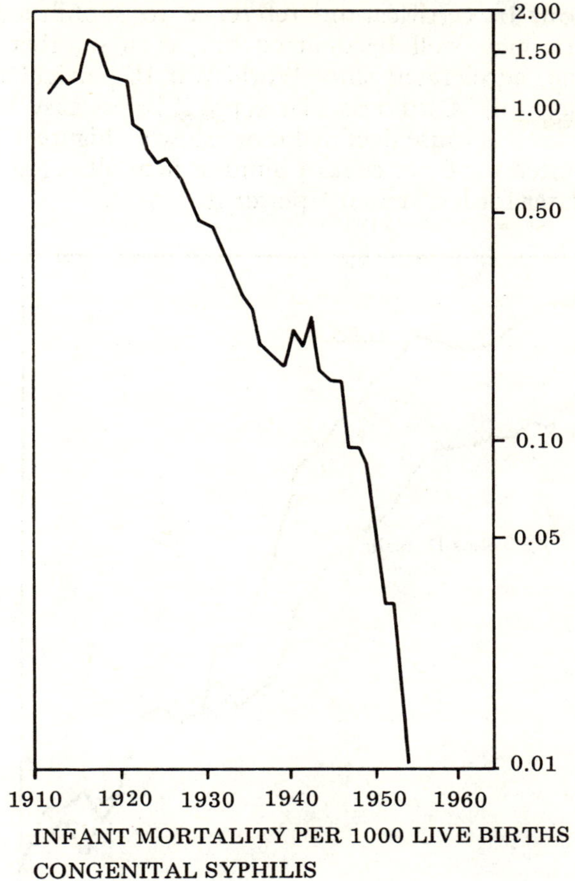

Figure 1.5 Cases of congenital syphilis. Ages 0–5 years, England and Wales 1911–1954. (Office of Health Economics (1963) *The Venereal Diseases,* Office of Health Economics, London, page 23).

the newborn) was the largest single cause of blindness. In 1922 it accounted for one-third of all cases entering schools for the blind; since 1955 there have been no cases of blindness from this cause.

Syphilis affected about 10 per cent of the total population in 1913. In this infection the serious aftermath showed itself. About 40 per cent of those infected developed, if untreated, gummatous, cardiovascular or neurosyphilis. These late effects might not show till 30 years after the initial infection. In certification, reference to syphilitic effects as a cause of death may well be omitted but, even so, there occurred a striking decline, accelerated since World War II, particularly in neurosyphilis (Figure 1.6). Cardiovascular syphilis is less easy to detect and death rates from this cause declined more slowly (Figure 1.7). Acquired syphilis accounted for 6 per cent of blindess in adults aged 30–49 years, but 30 years later for less than 0.1 per cent.

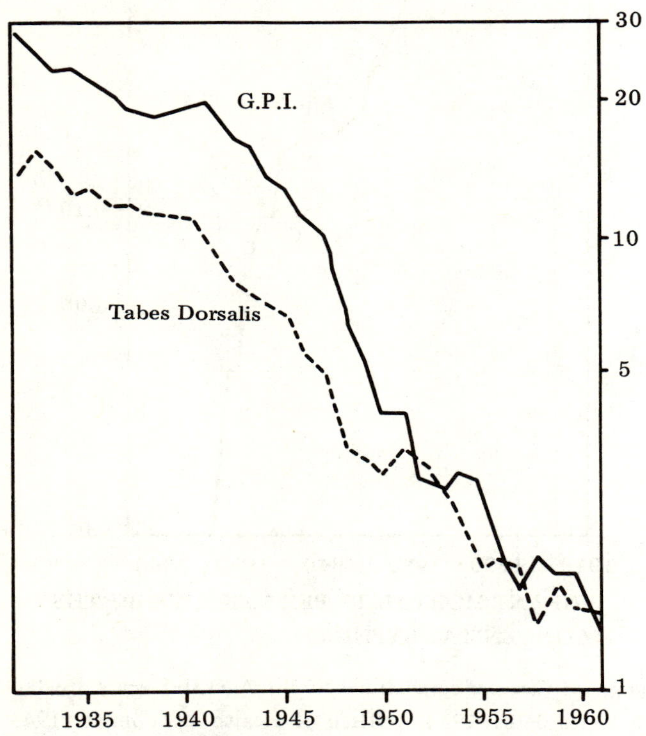

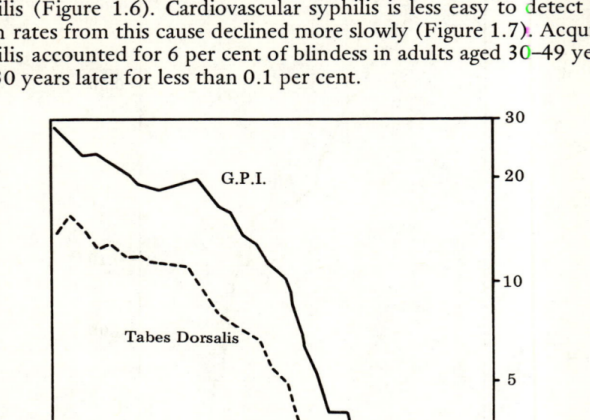

Figure 1.6 Death rates per million population for neurosyphilis. England and Wales 1931–1961 (Office of Health Economics (1963) *The Venereal Diseases,* Office of Health Economics, London, page 26).

Although the miraculous effects of antibiotics and chemotherapy on the devastations of the important venereal diseases (gonorrhoea and syphilis) are a marvel of the age these diseases continue to produce impacts exceeding their purely medical effects. The occurrence of an infection, although curable, engenders fear and upsets close personal relationships both within and outside marriage. Patients continue to look to their doctor for reassurance and support; he may, also, act usefully as a conciliator in a conflict between partners. Television programme or newspaper headline not infrequently provoke anxiety and bring patients to the clinic seeking reassurance. Non-gonococcal urethritis in men, uncertain in its aetiology, with its tendency to show post-coital relapses, can disturb a sexual relationship and bring un-

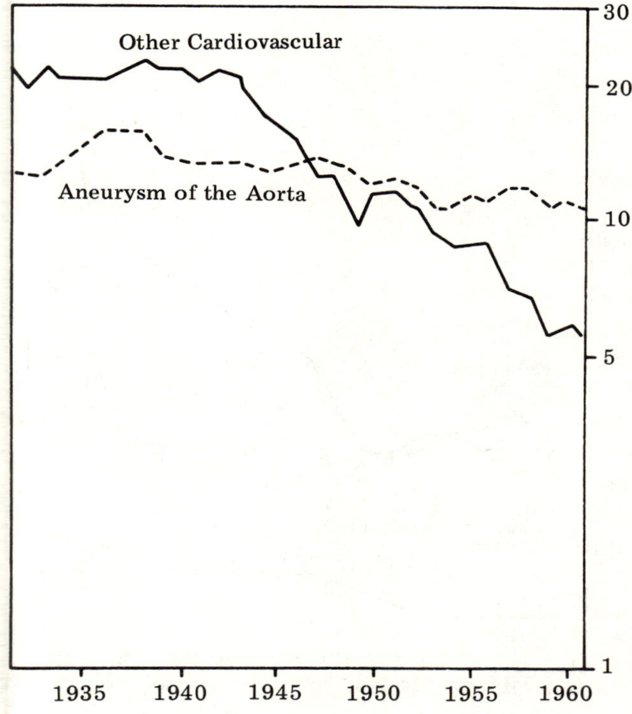

Figure 1.7 Death rates per million population for cardiovascular syphilis. England and Wales 1931–1961. (Office of Health Economics (1963), *The Venereal Diseases*, Office of Health Economics, London, page 27).

happiness to a honeymoon or to a marriage. Genital warts may appear in partners, engendering suspicion, anxiety and unhappiness. Similarly, genital herpes can cause a very unpleasant vulvitis or balanitis and the data suggesting a possible relationship of this virus to carcinoma of the cervix may cause patients much anxiety. Now that infections such as non-gonococcal urethritis, as yet incompletely understood, and genital herpes simplex are becoming more common their social impact involves increasingly large numbers of people. The doctor's function is to relieve and to lessen the stress which results from such anxieties and he or she should be careful not to add to them. Patients may suffer from guilt and may be reluctant to come for help. The doctor's function is to make facilities as accessible as possible and to discourage patients from any tendency to hide such problems.

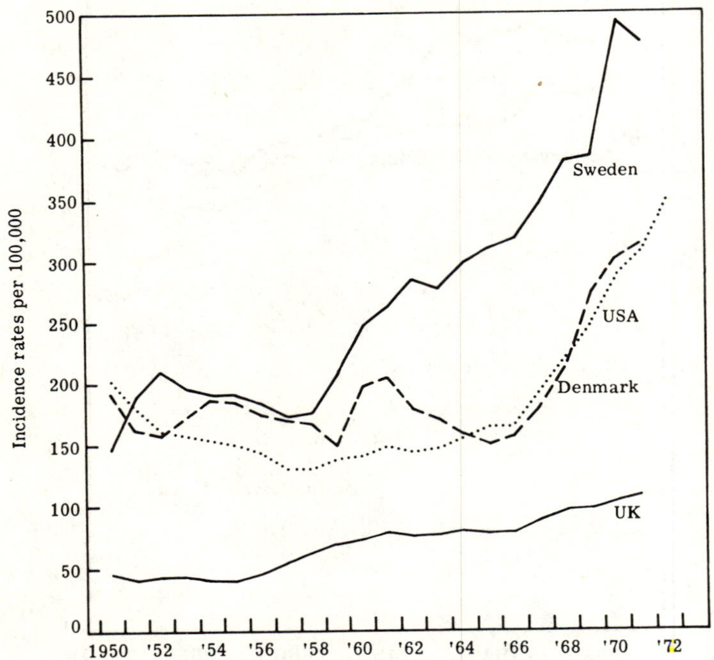

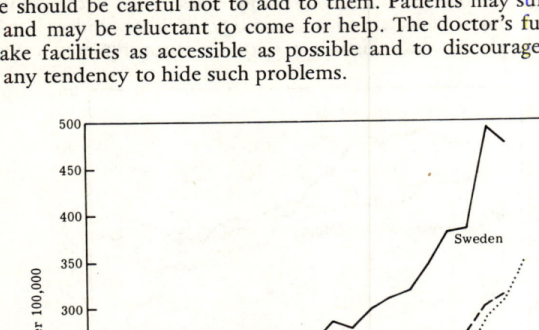

Figure 1.8 Reported cases of gonorrhoea 1950–1972. Incidence per 100,000 population. (Idsoe, O, Kiraly, K and Causse, G, *World Health Organization Chronicle 1973,* 27, 414).

The increase in the occurrence of STD in recent years (Figures 1.8 and 1.9) and the not infrequently poor facilities and inadequate staff for this work have caused difficulties in meeting the demand. The diseases dealt with in the clinics show a different pattern from that of the past and as time passes it is likely that more and more will seek advice and help (Figure 1.10). Changing attitudes together with changing patterns of sexual behaviour and reproduction (*see* sections B and C) together with increasing realization of the medical importance of sexually transmissible organisms require the involvement of all responsible for patient care.

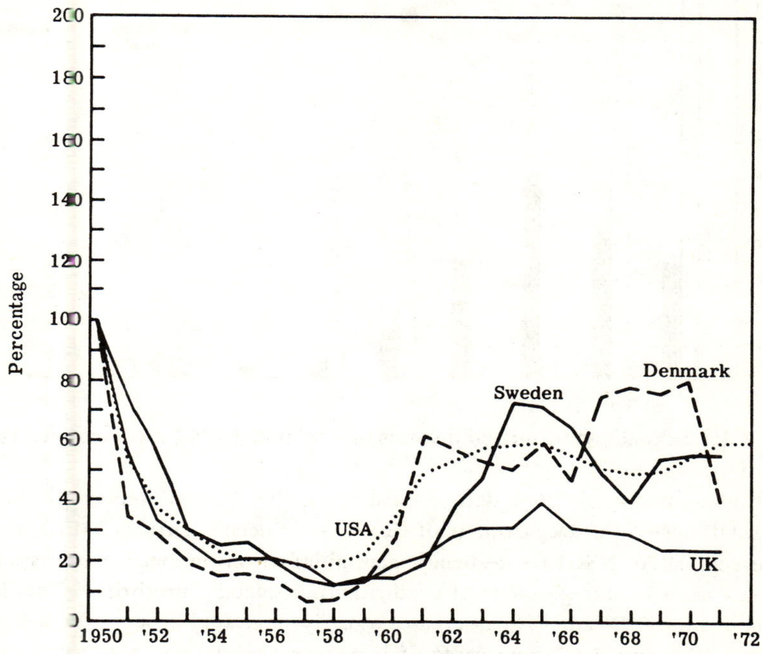

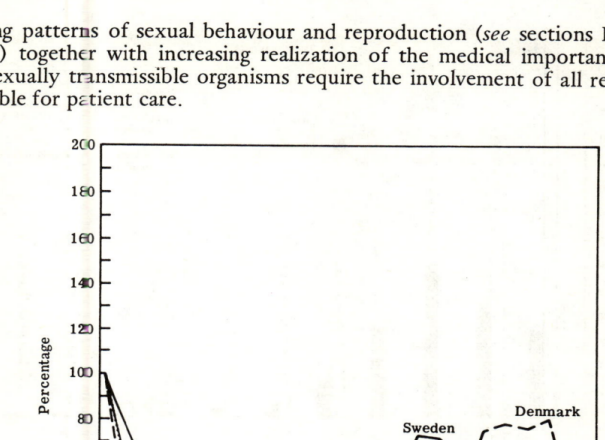

Figure 1.9 Reported primary and secondary syphilis 1950–1972. Yearly percentage variations in incidence per 100,000 population, taking 1950 as reference year (100%). (Idsoe, O, Kiraly, K and Causse, G, *World Health Organization Chronicle, 1973*, 27, 413).

E. Personal prophylaxis

When personal prophylaxis is discussed in public critical reactions take a predictable form. The moralists will say that promiscuity will be encouraged and that chaste living outside marriage and fidelity within should be promoted instead. The deterrent effect of STD may be given prominence and the efficacy of the measures advocated will be questioned. Methods may be effective in the control of diseases such as gonorrhoea and syphilis particularly if applied under conditions re-

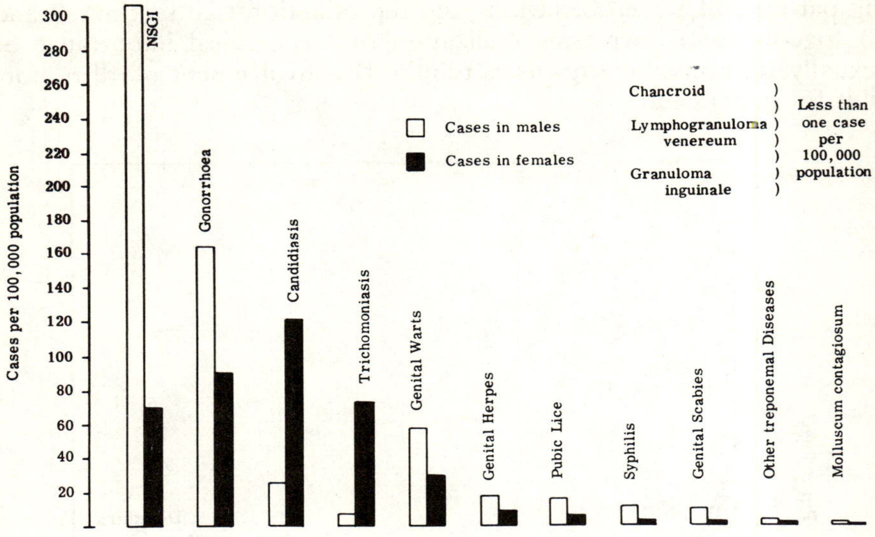

Figure 1.10 Sexually transmitted diseases in England, 1975 (new cases per 100,000 population).

Histogram prepared from data published in the Annual Report of the Chief Medical Officer of the Department of Health and Social Security (HMSO, London) for the year 1976. NSGI (Non-specific genital infection) in males comprises for the most part cases of non-gonococcal urethritis (non-specific urethritis). The data for syphilis include 8.52 and 1.41 new cases of early-stage syphilis per 100,000 population and 3.54 and 1.67 new cases of late-stage syphilis per 100,000 males and females respectively. The discovery of latent syphilis will vary geographically according to the sensitivity and specificity of the serological tests used routinely.

sembling those of an animal farm but it is usually on the actuality of individual behaviour that proposals will founder. It is necessary however to have a clear understanding of the present position [27, 28].

Abstinence or sexual fidelity to another uninfected person is a prescription for the primary prevention of venereal disease which fails because human behaviour is not sufficiently stereotyped to conform to such a pattern and shows no likelihood of becoming so. Risks are reduced when the amount of sexual mixing (promiscuity) is restricted.

Mechanical prophylaxis in the form of a condom is effective if used, undamaged, throughout all phases of sexual activity. Use of the diaphragm offers little protection because the gonococcus can survive longer than the barrier remains in place and is able to involve the urethra and rectum in spite of it. In the case of the condom education regarding its use and promotional activity to ensure its availability may increase sales but reluctance to use it tends to restrict its value.

The value of local agents which affect the micro-organisms and are applied post-coitally are difficult to assess experimentally in the human situation. Long ago Professor Metchnikoff and Roux [29] showed that primary lesions of syphilis did not develop if the skin of chimpanzees inoculated with treponemes was rubbed for five minutes with calomel ointment (one part calomel to two of lanolin). Figures for men have been given relating to several thousand exposures which showed that only 0.08 per cent of infections occurred after disinfection (with a 1 in 2000 solution of potassium permanganate) and inunction (30 per cent calomel ointment) within one hour, 0.65 per cent after from 2 to 4 hours, but 7.80 per cent after 10 hours or a reduction of nearly 100 per cent by very early disinfection [30].

To provide controls in such an investigation is difficult but interest in such methods has been renewed. Orthoiodobenzoic acid in an oil base which foams on contact with the vagina has been tried in the brothels of Nevada but, although there was less gonorrhoea in the women who used the product than those who did not, vaginal drying and irritation was sufficiently troublesome to terminate the study.

In World War II prophylactic kits and condoms for individual use were issued to the men of the United States armed forces. A 'V packet' unfortunately produced a chemical urethritis but this was followed by the issue of a PRO-KIT which provided a non-greasy, non-irritating ointment containing sulphathiazole and calomel. The product was acceptable to the men and appeared to be associated with low rates of venereal disease although adequately controlled trails were not possible. Foaming vaginal tablets containing penicillin produce high local levels of penicillin which persist for 24 hours and in a group of Japanese prostitutes this appeared to reduce the incidence of gonorrhoea and syphilis. Once again the difficulty of such an investigation and the absence of controls makes interpretation difficult. The serious risks of sensitization cannot of course be discounted in such a scheme.

Post-coital use of antibiotics, taken systemically, clearly may not prevent all STD from emerging but there are some situations in which this form of treatment may be justifiable, particularly in early syphilis and possibly occasionally in gonorrhoea when the precise diagnosis in the contact is known. Doses which are effective prophylactically are difficult to determine and full therapeutic doses should be used if this course of action is considered to be justified together with the high standard of follow-up customarily practised. There is a principle involved too, when a disease manifests itself in an acute form which, although noticeable by the patient or detectable by careful and repeated examinations, is not seriously damaging as in gonorrhoea or in very early syphilis. In such cases the preferred practice in those able to comply with medical instructions is to treat the infection, when it is recognized and diagnosed precisely, with the effective treatments available.

F. Facilities for diagnosis and treatment

The policy in clinics in the National Health Service in the United Kingdom has evolved from principles laid down by the Royal Commission on Venereal Diseases [31]. These principles included:

1. Voluntary attendance for investigation and treatment, without any system of notification or compulsory powers to secure attendance.
2. Investigation and treatment available to everyone free of charge.
3. Laboratory facilities for diagnosis available to all practitioners free of charge.

(i) OUTPATIENTS

The majority of patients can be investigated and treated as outpatients. Clinics should be as accessible as possible to patients and although an appointment system may be necessary, patients should not be excluded by a rigidity which will tend to exclude high-risk groups. Essentially the staff must function as a team. Whether the patient attends on his own account or is referred by his general practitioner or other doctor it is the skills available and facilities (clinical, microbiological, counselling and contact-tracing) of the clinic which justify the existence of the specialty. The ever increasing number of patients requiring attention confirms its importance although the method of securing such attention may have to change and be improved. Reception of patients is always important but particularly so in a department dealing with sexually transmitted diseases. Receptionists should be taught, like others in the health services, to recognize the effects of their own attitudes and behaviour upon patients, particularly the newly arrived. In some patients their feelings of being looked at or of being in some way made to feel humiliated may be due to projection in the Freudian sense. History-taking and examination must be methodical but considerate and diagnosis must be backed by the results of careful microbiological investigation. Treatment must be given under supervision and its effectiveness monitored. Whether the clinic is for males or females the nurse's skills are an integral part of clinical work. All this will fail unless counselling can take place in a relaxed manner and unless there is a systematic effort to trace contacts.

(ii) INPATIENTS

The need for inpatient facilities has greatly diminished. Young women are admitted for salpingitis, refractory gonococcal infections or because supervised treatment is advantageous. In some cases patients with severe herpetic vulvitis or genital warts merit admission and on occasions social disadvantage, such as homelessness or a social crisis, can be relieved in this way. In early syphilis, particularly in secondary cases, admission is advantageous at least for a day or two as treatment may cause an unpleasant Jarisch-Herxheimer effect. It may be necessary to admit those with extensive anal or genital warts or when there is subpreputial sepsis and phimosis. Patients with arthritis associated with urogenital infections such as in Reiter's disease, benefit by admission. Men with strictures and recurrent urinary infection, rare now in the United Kingdom, are reminders of intractable problems and suffering of the past or of the present situation of neglected people in impoverished countries of the third world.

G. Tracing of contacts and the case against compulsion

Although males may have an asymptomatic gonococcal infection, the majority (85–90 per cent) tend to develop an obvious urethral discharge with makes them seek medical help. In contrast, in females the infection is frequently inapparent or asymptomatic (75 per cent) so it is essential to ensure that the female consort is investigated and treated. The process of securing the attendance of a sexual contact is known as contact-tracing and to be successful depends upon the trust of the patient and contact(s) in the confidentiality of the process.

The necessary interviewing of the index patient is a matter of great delicacy, it is time-consuming and it must be carried out in privacy. It depends essentially upon the regard and respect of the interviewer for the patient. There is no place for hostility and everything must be done to encourage rapport. Gently, the patient must be persuaded that he or she is the only person who can ensure that the one or more consorts are treated. It is explained how effective treatment is and how helpful it would be for all concerned if the sexual partner could attend. Irrespective of the length of the list of recent consorts, irrespective of the varied character of those involved and irrespective of the form of sexual behaviour, the patient must not be allowed to feel stigmatized or allowed to feel unworthy. If the patient's memory is faulty and the relationship has been casual, details are often hazy. At the best a note giving the Index Case Number, date, diagnosis in code (understood for example in all clinics in the United Kingdom: *see* Table 2.1 in Chapter 2) and clinic address, can be delivered by the patient to a consort to bring as an introduction to the clinic. If the patient fears to make the approach, the person responsible for contact-tracing, say a health visitor, involved also in the clinic with counselling and health education, will do it for him. Sometimes, but not often, the description of a tattoo, a scar or a dress may help in the tracing. Information about haunts, about friends or about work may also be of value. The patient must be assured of the tact and experience of the staff involved and of their skills in avoiding embarrassing situations.

In Edinburgh in recent years, it has been found generally that about half of the female contacts, acknowledged by male patients with gonorrhoea as possible sources of infection (source contacts), are unknown and therefore untraceable. About half of source contacts are known or accurately described and most are traced and treated without great difficulty unless they belong to a floating population or change their address frequently. The secondary contacts (wives, consorts, girl friends, fiancées) whom the patient had himself involved, and possibly infected, are traced and treated in nearly every case. In spite of the nature of the careful approach needed in contact-tracing and the few, known insufficiently to be described, who are missed, some still feel that legal compulsion is necessary. The history of the effect of such compulsory measures, used at one time in the United Kingdom, and still advocated and practised in some countries, deserves scrutiny as the activities have tended, in the case of gonorrhoea particularly, to be directed against women rather than men.

In the British Army of the middle of the 19th century, more than 90 per cent of the soldiers were unmarried as they were not permitted to marry until they had seven years service and had one good conduct badge. Working classes married early but breakdown due to poverty was common. Women were particularly vulnerable as it was generally impossible for them to find employment and, if a servant, for example were sacked without a 'character' because she became pregnant, prostitution was often the only alternative to destitution or the oppressive environment of the workhouse. There was, too, an excess of women over men because of the higher death rate of the male children.

In 1860 about 25 per cent of soldiers in London suffered from syphilis, and the Contagious Diseases Acts (1864, 1866 and 1869) were introduced with the object of checking the spread of disease in the Armed Forces. These Acts applied to garrison towns and provided for the examination of prostitutes and their detention in hospital if diseased. The regulations, oppressive and extraordinarily bureaucratic in form, listing the certificates required for every move in the appalling process, were administered by officers drawn from the Metropolitan Police.

Josephine Butler opposed and vigorously campaigned against these Acts, forming a Ladies National Association for the repeal of the Contagious Diseases Acts. Her case was based on the fact that certain women, usually poor, were robbed of their civil rights and that this violated the constitution. Among other objections she showed how these Acts were designed for the benefit of soldiers or sailors but applied only to civilian women who could be unjustifiably persecuted by officials administering the Acts. Although medical opinion of the day supported the legislation it provided no evidence that the diseases were checked in any way. Mrs Butler's main attack was directed also against the double standard of morality in a male dominated society which condoned the sexual activities of the male and persecuted the female, applying legislation against the prostitute but ignoring her client. The evils of prostitution, including recruitment of girls to the trade, was under attack at a time when a virgin could be bought for a few shillings and the age of consent to sexual intercourse (up till 1885) was only 12 years [32, 33]. The Acts were finally repealed in 1886.

Further attempts to introduce coercive Acts have been made in the United Kingdom. In 1917 a Criminal Law Amendment Bill was introduced in the House of Commons by which it was proposed to make it penal for a person suffering from venereal disease in a communicable form to have sexual intercourse with any other person. The maximum penalty provided was two years imprisonment with hard labour. Power was to be given to the court to order a medical examination of the person charged. As the existence of the infection could only be provable by medical evidence it was a matter of close concern to doctors. By November the opposition to the Bill in the House of Commons, which preferred a policy of persuasion to a policy of penalty, led to its being abandoned

As the Criminal Law Amendment Bill failed to reach the statute book because of opposition inside and outside Parliament and as there was a demand from Dominion Armed Forces' representatives, the Army Council in May 1918 passed Regulation 40D (Defence of the Realm Act [34]) imposing punishment for the offence of communicating venereal disease to soldiers, although the Regulation did not proceed as far as to make it compulsory for women arrested for this offence to subject themselves to a medical examination. The basis of the Regulation was similar to that of the Contagious Diseases Acts of 1864, 1866 and 1869, in that it was directed against civilian women with the intention of protecting soldiers (Venereal Disease and the Defence of the Realm Act [34]).

The Regulation was not effective as a public health measure and women against whom no charge had been established were arrested, imprisoned and remanded for examination (201 prosecutions, 101 convictions). By the end of 1918 Regulation 40D was suspended as valueless and other more helpful measures were being suggested by a Royal Commission (*see* section F), at a time when an estimated 300,000 men, still infectious, of the Navy and Army were actually under treatment and might be due to return to their homes.

Compulsory powers were sought unsuccessfully by the Edinburgh Corporation Bill, 1928 (Statement for the Corporation [35]). The proposers believed that it was those who discontinued treatment while still infective who were the chief cause for the failure of medical control of these diseases.

Regulation 33B (Defence Regulations, 1939) was brought in during the fourth year of World War II. It extended its compulsion, as a war time measure only, to a group of persons, small in number, who refused to attend voluntarily. In this Regulation specialists were required to pass on to the Medical Officer of Health the name of the contact thought by a patient to be responsible for passing on the venereal infection. The Medical Officer of Health would serve a notice on the contact if he received two or more notifications relating to him (or her) requiring him (or her) to attend a specialist and submit to an examination. If infected, he (or she) would be required to have treatment.

Inevitably the Regulation restarted the controversy which raged at the time of the Contagious Diseases Acts and its inefficiency was shown by a reply given by the Minister of Health in Parliament* [36, 37].

Again in 1962 and in 1967 attempts were made to restore the provisions of Regulation 33B in Bills introduced by Mr Richard Marsh and Sir Myer Galpern respectively.

Propositions of this kind are no doubt well meaning but legislation of

* 'In England and Wales 36 men and 475 women had been reported to a Medical Officer of Health as alleged sources of venereal infection, of which 1 man and 27 women have been the subject of more than one report. Of these 28 persons two women have refused treatment, one expressly, and one by default, and have been prosecuted and imprisoned. No civilian voluntarily undergoing treatment for venereal disease is subject to complusion to complete it.'

this kind is an ineffective, discredited public health measure. It is the policy of persuasion backed up by a humane approach, careful techniques in clinics and good antibiotic and chemotherapy with contact-tracing that is the mainstay of control. Apart from the infringement of individual liberty which coercive legislation entails, the atmosphere of the clinics would be profoundly altered. To examine and treat reluctant patients is clinically unsatisfactory as well as interference with the autonomy of doctor and patient.

In practice, a very small proportion, less than one per cent, who are found, refuse or fail to attend and about half of female contacts of men attending with gonorrhoea cannot be traced due to a genuine lack of information. In the case of homosexually acquired infection the proportion of contacts seen is very low (14 per cent), probably because the hostility of society makes the individual fearful to surface for help.

Although international action is envisaged by Resolution (74)5, adopted by the Committee of Ministers at Strasbourg in 1974, the greater the distance involved and the larger the number of administrative, political or geographical barriers the less effective is contact-tracing. The concept of international contact-tracing would, to be effective, depend upon confidence that a humane system free from threats would be used to secure the necessary high standard of medical investigation and treatment. In the case of early syphilis and gonorrhoea, efforts to achieve these aims on an international basis are laudable [38], but when a patient knows a contact sufficiently to give an adequate description more can often be achieved at a personal level by letter.

H. People with high risks

Special attention is needed by individuals who are particularly exposed to risk [39]. In some, exposure is related to occupation as in the armed forces, seafarers, immigrants, refugees, workers separated from their families, tourists, hotel staff and professional travellers such as long-distance lorry drivers. In others the risk may be more restricted to adolescence or young adulthood, where taboos against premarital intercourse are weakening and patterns of sexual behaviour may vary from that of a series of partnerships to multiple casual relationships. Multiple casual contacts are also a problem in those male homosexuals who are promiscuous and in men and women involved in prostitution. Patterns of behaviour will vary widely but in so far as medical care is concerned it is particularly important to befriend and assist so that individuals may be encouraged to attend rather than to seek legal

Table 1.3 Medical support required by an individual female patient between her first attendance at the age of 18 years and a few weeks before her death

	Sexually transmitted diseases					*Gynaecology*		*Accident & emergency*	*Self-poisoning*		*Psychiatry*		*Ophthalmology*	
Year	*Out-patient visits*	*Cultures taken*	*Gonococcus isolated*	*In-patient days*	*General practitioner visits*	*Out-patient visits*	*In-patient days*	*out-patient visits*	*Incidents*	*In-patient days*	*Out-patient visits*	*In-patient days*	*Out-patient visits*	*In-patient days*
1969	–	–	–	–	4	1	–	–	–	–	–	–	–	–
1970	29	16	2	6	5	1	–	–	–	–	–	–	–	–
1971	65	38	12	–	–	–	–	1	–	–	–	27	–	7
1972	45	40	3	–	7	1	3	4	3	5	2	13	–	–
1973	34	25	4	–	1	2	6	–	–	–	–	–	–	–
1974	24	16	1	–	10	–	9	2	1	1	2	56	–	–
1975	18	17	2	–	12	–	3	3	3	5	–	36	–	–
Total	215	152	24	6	39	5	21	10	7	11	4	132	–	7

powers and compulsion to enforce medical examination and treatment (*see* Tracing of contacts and the case against compulsions p.21).

Rates for illness in different parts of a city show marked differences and there is a relationship to social difficulties such as delinquency in juveniles and overcrowding. In cities, as for example in Sydney and Edinburgh, it has been found that areas with the highest concentrations of gonorrhoea and syphilis can be recognized, although no particular area may claim immunity [40, 41, 42]. Within some large cities a mobile population and chaotic living may make the collection of such data difficult.

(a) PROSTITUTION IN FEMALES

In the legal framework of Scotland as well as in that of England and Wales it is not a common law crime for a woman to use a house she occupies for her own habitual prostitution, but more extensive organization of prostitution is likely to be an offence. Essentially private behaviour is not the concern of the law.

A severe disorder of personality may be an important source of difficulty in the control of sexually transmitted infections. An indication of the problems in supplying medical care in such cases is given in Table 1.3 which lists the attendance of one patient from her appearance at the age of 18 years until her death a few weeks before her 25th birthday. Statistics of this nature are a poor reflection of the work involved in the care given within the National Health Service to a patient whose personality disorder can be categorized as psychopathy [43] and whose illnesses were associated with alcoholism and prostitution and grossly disruptive behaviour. As an extreme example it places difficulties in reaching ethical conclusions on the right approach as there is a conflict between the patient's needs, the rights of other patients and the limitations to freedom. The clinician, however, will generally conclude that insofar as sexually transmitted disease alone is concerned the advantage of a legal restraint is short lived and to use such methods poses ethical problems which discredit them as methods of control.

(b) HOMOSEXUAL BEHAVIOUR IN MALES

According to Kinsey *et al* [44] in the total male population, between adolescence and old age, 6.3 per cent of the total number of orgasms is derived from homosexual contacts. In a considerable proportion of the male population homosexual psychosexual relations co-exist with heterosexual and males who are more than incidentally homosexual are most numerous in pre-adolescence and through the teens, becoming less numerous with advancing age.

It is useful for clinicians to consider the scale of psychic or physical erotic responses in the manner of Kinsey *et al* although the anatomical sites liable to infection will depend upon individual preferences in physical contact and risks will vary depending upon whether mutual masturbation, anal intercourse or oro-genital activities are practised:

0. Exclusively with individuals of the opposite sex.
1. Predominantly heterosexual only incidentally homosexual.
2. Predominantly heterosexual but more than incidentally homosexual.
3. Equally homosexual and heterosexual (no strong preferences).
4. Predominantly homosexual but more than incidentally heterosexual.
5. Predominantly homosexual but incidentally heterosexual.
6. Exclusively homosexual.

The hostility of society's reaction to homosexuality appears to have dated from the middle of the 1st century AD when the sin of Sodom (*Genesis* XIX,5) became closely identified with this form of sexual behaviour [45]. The laws of Justinian admonished homosexuals in the 6th century and a thousand years later in the reign of Henry VIII of England a statute classed buggery as a felony with death as the penalty. In 1562, after repeals and re-enactments Queen Elizabeth fixed death as the penalty which remained on the statute book till 1861, when it was replaced by imprisonment for 10 years, a term liable to be extended to penal servitude for life. In 1885 a member of parliament, Mr Labouchère, introduced as an amendment into the Criminal Law Amendment Act a penal clause against those convicted of homosexual behaviour. A new and enlightened approach developed gradually and this was defined in the Report of the Committee on Homosexual Offences and Prostitution, known as the Wolfenden Report [46]. The most important recommendation 'that the homosexual behaviour between consenting adults in private be no longer a criminal offence' was opposed by only one of the thirteen distinguished members of the committee, a Scottish procurator fiscal, who strongly objected to the removal of the prohibition.

The Wolfenden Report raised an important issue in jurisprudence, namely that unless society made a deliberate attempt to equate the sphere of crime with that of sin, there must remain a realm of private morality which is, in brief and crude terms, not the law's business. The issue became the subject of a great debate in which Devlin [47] contended that the law should indeed enforce morality and Hart [48] maintained that deviations from sexual morality such as homosexuality did not harm others and are therefore not a matter for the law. The latter argument followed the philosophy of John Stuart Mill [49] given in his famous essay 'On Liberty' which is a logical and reasoned defence of individualism as an element of permanent importance to society and opposed coercion to enforce moral values.

In England and Wales a new Act (Sexual Offences Act, 1967) came into force ten years after the publication of the Wolfenden Report [46]. An enormous amount of time was spent on the subject of the Act (11 days of parliamentary time and 135 speeches). The main features of the Act were as follows:

The Sexual Offences Act, 1967, provided that a homosexual act in private shall not be an offence 'provided that the parties consent thereto and have attained the age of twenty-one years'.

A discriminatory clause, introduced by those who opposed the Bill, defined 'privacy' in the context of the Act as follows:

(2) An act which would otherwise be treated for the purposes of this Act as being done in private shall not be so treated if done—
   (a) when more than two persons take part or are present; or
   (b) in a lavatory to which the public have or are permitted to have access, whether on payment or otherwise.

There are important exceptions to these provisions:

(i) If one of the individuals is suffering from severe mental subnormality (Mental Health Act, 1959) then his consent in law cannot be valid.
(ii) If one of the individuals is on the staff of the hospital having responsibility of the other then he would be excluded.
(iii) Members of the Armed Forces are excluded.
(iv) The homosexual acts among individuals on Merchant Ships are excluded also.

Punishment:

Maximum 10 years—In this case if one individual over the age of 16 did not consent.

Maximum 5 years—In this case if one individual is over 21 and the other under 21 and did not consent.

Maximum 2 years—If both are over 21 and one did not consent.

Other definitions are given and punishments are defined for living on earnings of male prostitution and for using premises for homosexual practices.

In Scotland, with her separate legal system, the reaction to homosexual acts, such as anal intercourse, was hostile. In the 17th century Sir George Mackenzie [50] thought that 'they are crimes extraordinary and rarely committed in this Kingdom' and recorded that the ordinary punishment was burning. In present times the law, which is less dependent on statutes than in England, was not formally changed and anal intercourse is still a crime; the Sexual Offences Act, 1967 does not apply [51]. The effect of the Act is, however, persuasive and prosecutions of consenting adults for acts in private are not likely to occur. The Lord Advocate who alone initiates prosecutions has given this assurance but the Scottish Minorities Group feel that the ill-defined state of the law indirectly encourages social discrimination and prejudice against homosexuals.

Pleas [52] against discrimination today rest their case on the fact that in England, for example, something like two million mature men and women frequently indulge in sexual acts with the same sex [53], that in embryonic life males and females cannot be told apart and that the mechanisms determining the direction the embryo is to go are extremely complex and open to error. Many such effects have been described in human subjects as clinical entities with clear functional and physical differences from the normal range. From the social point of view homosexual attachments, often short of physical interaction, are often as acceptable as heterosexual and sometimes more so; sometimes also, homosexual tendencies are fostered by segregation of the sexes. The persistence of exclusive homosexuality is most often unassociated with anatomical or physiological abnormality and this orientation is often as immutable as a developmental anomaly. The numerous studies on human subjects reveal a scene that is entirely in keeping with observations which have also been made in mammals and primates in particular, and lead to a conclusion that homosexuality is no more than one of several manifestations that might be expected. To regard the practice as immoral and deserving public censure, it is submitted, is unfair and unjust.

In young boys homosexual behaviour may not persist into adult life. It may be restricted to mutual masturbation and this act carries little risk of communicating disease. In the case of the close mucosal contact in oral or anal intercourse it is a different matter and the involvement of boys at puberty has led to infection with syphilis and gonorrhoea. Generalizations about homosexuality from knowledge of those attending STD clinics are unwise but homosexuals who are promiscuous, as in the case of heterosexuals, may only know their sexual contacts by their forenames when the sex contact is merely a means of obtaining relief from sexual tension. Such tendencies make tracing contacts difficult and promiscuity, reticence and reluctance to attend for help produces dangerous reservoir effects. The doctor should be alert to the existence of these problems which tend to be more common in larger cities. Patients ordinarily heterosexual may also have episodes of homosexual behaviour and this overlap of sexual activity makes the homosexual reservoir of infection a matter for concern in the community, heterosexual and homosexual alike.

In the City of Edinburgh it has been found that more than one-third of homosexual patients belonged to Social Class I and II and included highly trained and professional groups. The majority tended to reside in central areas of the City and in the case of gonorrhoea tracing of contacts was successful in only 14 per cent in contrast to an estimated success rate of 40 per cent in heterosexuals. Similar difficulties were encountered in tracing contacts in early syphilis which occurred in 34 per cent of cases (n = 110) in homosexuals in the period 1970–1976 [42]. In the United States of America, Webster [54] estimated that in 1968 homosexual contacts comprised 25.4 per cent of venereal disease. In the United Kingdom the proportion of infections with primary and secondary syphilis known to have been contracted homosexually rose from 42.4 per cent in 1971 to 54.5 per cent in 1977. The largest concentration was noted in London, particularly the West End (British Co-operative Clinical Group [55]). To encourage a reduction in social hostility to homosexuality may reduce the effects of alienation; a change in the law is but a first step.

(c) GIRLS CONFINED TO INSTITUTIONS FOR DELINQUENCY

The conventional wisdom that delinquency in young girls is inevitably or at least frequently associated with sexual promiscuity has been challenged [56] as the view has been based on studies of institutionalized samples. In Aberdeen, a city characterized, until the recent introduction of the oil industry, by homogeneity and a low rate of mobility, it was found that sex-related offences formed an insignificant part (1.3 per cent) of female delinquency dealt with by the courts. It seemed, however, that in cases of girls of 14 years or more, or where the girl was perceived to be in some kind of moral danger, the courts would tend to place her under supervision or confine her to an institution. It was found in this study that the prevalence of delinquency leading to court appearance was about six times greater in boys than girls. In the case of girls about 70 per cent of offences recorded against girls was theft whereas breaking and entering and vandalism were mainly male prerogatives [56].

Among those, however, who are sent to institutions sexual promiscuity of a casual nature may be common and such girls may have suffered from a grossly disturbed family life (Cowie *et al* [57] ; Timms [58]). Investigation for sexually transmitted disease will therefore be one of the requirements of medical care [59] so individuals will need careful and considerate enquiry into their sexual attitudes and relationships. In the case of a girl who has these difficulties it is important to obtain her confidence and trust as she will require care and advice in connection with STD and contraception probably for many years. It is clear that the medical examinations involved should not be compulsory nor backed by threats; co-operation should be obtained by explanation and reassurance as it is paramount that the individual should perceive her own needs in this context.

I. Companionship, marriage and divorce

It is clearly important for the doctor to avoid adding to a patient's difficulties by an approach which might upset the relationship between one partner and the other. The doctor must not divulge the confidences of one partner by giving information to the other although there are clearly difficulties, not insurmountable, when he is responsible for the medical care of both. An attempt must be made to elicit what one partner has told the other and to determine the attitudes of the patient to his or her situation. An individual patient has a right to know the nature of any infection discovered and if asked directly the doctor should not prevaricate further but tell the truth, although he can do this in a reassuring and conciliatory way emphasizing the good parts of a relationship. Often a patient will convey without words an attitude to the situation and the doctor should try to interpret his patient's feelings and match his approach to them.

In divorce proceedings the acquisition of gonorrhoea or syphilis has implications regarding adultery and as such the doctor should know something about the law of marriage and divorce and, as in both England and Scotland, its recent changes [60, 61]. In companionate relationships, as well as in marriage, sexually transmitted diseases including gonorrhoea and syphilis may contribute to a breakdown and the doctor should not feel he is entitled to be more considerate to married partners and less to those who are not.

Essentially marriage is maintained by the continued consent of each partner. The law itself does not necessarily help in maintaining such person-to-person relationships and in childless marriages the interest of the secular state is clearly more limited than in those with children.

Tensions and difficulties are common and counselling and family services are more important than legalities provided there is a willingness to use such services. In Scotland, at least, where safeguards to individual rights are necessary, in companionate childless relationships, so common among young people today, recognition might become possible by the Scottish method where 'by habit and repute' the legal validity of such marriages can be established [62].

The grounds for divorce in Scotland until 1st January 1977, were adultery, cruelty, desertion, incurable insanity, sodomy and bestiality. In the case of the first four grounds the courts were in effect looking to see whether 'matrimonial offences' had been 'committed'. In recent times attempts have been made to get away from ideas of fault and guilt and the new Act allows divorce by consent after two years separation [61]. There is still a clear difference between Scotland and England at the present time in regard to divorce. In England and Wales (Divorce Reform Act, 1969) 'irretrievable breakdown' of marriage is the only reason for dissolving it. Although such a description has a complex meaning the lawyer tends to look for evidence or a clear definition. For example, if the respondent has committed adultery and the petitioner finds life with the respondent intolerable as a result then this is a ground for divorce. A petitioner cannot now have an impulsive divorce on sole proof of adultery.

In the case of Scotland, Divorce (Scotland) Act, 1976, although 'irretrievable breakdown' of marriage is the sole ground for divorce, proof of adultery establishes this 'irretrievable breakdown' and it is therefore still possible for an 'impulsive divorce' in Scotland.

From the point of view of the events leading up to divorce proceedings solicitors may seek information from STD clinics to be used as evidence of adultery. Generally such an imputation from the legal point of view may be made only in the case of gonorrhoea or syphilis, acquired after marriage. The doctor is required to give whatever information a solicitor may ask for on behalf of the client regarding the client's medical findings. He is not entitled to be given information about the client's partner without the consent of the party concerned unless the doctor receives an order by the Court, that is, in Scotland, the Court of Session at Edinburgh. It is important to maintain these safeguards and to avoid passing on information which the doctor is not entitled to give. Records on contact-tracing information are probably a separate issue to be excluded from case records.

Medical evidence in the United Kingdom is not privileged and the doctor must divulge his information if ordered to do so in court. Where litigation is imminent, however, between a husband and wife, as soon as a doctor or other counsellor is asked by either the wife or husband to act as an intermediary between them with a view to reconciliation any statement written or oral made by either party is privileged. The law favours reconciliation and a person acting as a conciliator will not be compelled to give evidence as to what was said in the course of negotiation [63].

J. Medical secrecy

Confidences are only privileged in a Court of Law when they are part of a discourse between a person and his advocate or solicitor in connection with legal proceedings [64, 65]. The one exception is that privilege is accorded to those acting as conciliators in a matrimonial dispute, whether doctor, priest, banker or social worker [66]. In the case of venereal diseases, although Ministerial Regulations, relating only to England and Wales (see appendix to this section), demand confidentiality, they do not confer privilege [67].

The presence of gonorrhoea or early syphilis in an individual may be used as evidence of recent adultery (*see* Section I on Companionship, marriage and divorce). In the case of non-specific urethritis, trichomoniasis, candidiasis and other conditions, these are unreliable indicators of a recent sexual contact and would not be valid as evidence of this. In late or latent syphilis the duration of the infection may be such that meaningful conclusions cannot be reached.

The clinic is not a court of law but it is an everyday occurrence to look after couples who may or may not be married. It is important not to divulge the nature of an infection in one partner to the other in precise terms without consent. When looking after a partner infected by the other, indefinite terms may be used such as 'an infection' but individuals have an absolute right to know their diagnosis if they insist. It is probably wise to avoid giving the organismal diagnosis until confirmed by the laboratory.

Young people must be encouraged to attend if they have run risks of acquiring STD. If they are under the age of 16 years it is important to ask them if they have told one or other parent and to suggest to them that they should do so. If they decline to confide in parents their confidences must be kept although they may agree to have a letter sent to their general practitioner. At no age should legal rules prevent the doctor from examining the patient in the manner indicated by the history or from treating an infection. If a girl is under 12 years of age then the doctor has the responsibility of reporting what may have been a serious crime. In all cases the doctor's acts should be governed by what he considers to be best for his patient and his attitudes should be protective, avoiding disclosures which may be damaging.

In so far as different skills are involved in the care of patients the clinic staff must work as a team and the importance of confidentiality should be understood by all concerned. In some cases the patient may wish his secrets to be restricted to the doctor or another of the health staff. A patient should be encouraged nevertheless to accept that all the staff are concerned and involved in his or her care. If a computer-assisted record system is used access to the system must be restricted and a number can be recorded instead of a name in the system used.

In some clinics patients' case numbers are used to call a patient rather than his or her name. At present times this appears to be expected by only a few and, in Edinburgh for example, the case number is used to label laboratory specimens leaving the clinic but the patient's name is used normally in an unrestricted manner within the clinic. Undue secretiveness is seldom necessary within the clinic where an open relaxed manner is preferred. Problems of secrecy are complicated [68, 69] and tact is always essential.

APPENDIX TO INTRODUCTION (J)

1. *NATIONAL HEALTH SERVICE (VD) REGULATIONS (Applicable only to England and Wales). 1968: (1968 No. 1624) National Health Service (Venereal Diseases) Regulations 1968 (coming into operation December 1, 1968).*

The Minister of Health, in exercise of his powers under Section 12 of the National Health Service Act 1946 and of all other powers enabling him in that behalf, hereby makes the following regulations:

(3) Every Regional Hospital Board and every Board of Governors of a teaching hospital shall take all necessary steps to secure that any information obtained by officers of the Board with respect to persons examined or treated for venereal disease in a hospital for the administration of which the Board is responsible shall be treated as confidential except for the purpose of communicating to a medical practitioner, or to a person employed under the direction of a medical practitioner in connection with the treatment of persons suffering from such disease or the prevention of the spread thereof, and for the purpose of such treatment or prevention.

2. *1974: (1974, No. 29 National Health Service (Venereal Diseases) Regulations 1974 (coming into operation April 1, 1974)).*

Confidentiality of information

(2) Every Regional Health Authority and every Area Health Authority shall take all necessary steps to secure that any information capable of identifying an individual obtained by officers of the Authority with respect to persons examined or treated for any sexually transmitted disease shall not be disclosed except:

(a) for the purpose of communicating that information to a medical practitioner, or to a person employed under the direction of a medical practitioner in connection with the treatment of persons suffering from such a disease or the prevention of the spread thereof, and,

(b) for the purpose of such treatment or prevention.

K. Education

In the United Kingdom since the 1960s profound changes in attitudes to sex and other matters has led to a clash between the younger and older generations. Parliament has freed homosexuals from persecution, legalized abortion, made contraceptives easily available and made it easier to get a divorce. Today the arguments for and against forbidding any activity are very different from those in the past and are based on comparing the consequences of legalizing an activity with the consequences of not doing so. If more harm is done by forbidding an activity than by allowing it then Parliament will permit it. This reasoning has been termed a causalist approach whereas in the past the decision to punish was taken on moralist grounds when those in favour of forbidding an activity would argue that the activity was wrong or wicked [70]. The growth of the human rights movement too has emphasized the right of an individual to human happiness unfettered by the views of others.

Against this background there is clearly a need for young people to be armed with the facts of life before they run risks to their health and happiness. The Swedish approach to sex education has been usefully described [71] and suggestions for improvements [72], include the following:

1. Acquire knowledge about anatomy, physiology, psychology, ethics and sociology.
2. Acquire an objective and comprehensive orientation about various

norms and attitudes of importance for sexual life, both the accepted and controversial.

3. Develop the ability to perceive sexuality as an integrated part of human life

4. Acquire increased consciousness and thereby a better chance for personal judgement on different levels of maturity and sexual experience.

The principles of democracy, equality and respect for the individual are stressed. Education must avoid traditional double standards of morality by which certain sexual modes of behaviour are acceptable for males but condemned for females. Tolerance and an understanding view of the various forms of sexuality is encouraged, as well as an acceptance of the right to a sexual life for the handicapped, the elderly and the mentally ill. Different life forms are discussed objectively but the risks in a too early sexual debut emphasized, namely unwanted pregnancy, venereal disease, superficial and disharmonious relationships.

In respect to VD or STD the following should be stressed:

1. Duty to protect yourself and others against STD or VD.
2. Hasty sexual contact can lead to infection.
3. Avoid casual sexual relationship.
4. Consult a doctor or clinic (make sure that the facilities in each locality are well known) if infected or a risk has been taken.
5. The sooner the condition is treated the sooner cured.
6. A condom, properly used, offers a reasonably good defence.
7. Do not let a sense of shame deter you from such help.

The possibility that sex education might encourage recruitment to the sexually active minority is a question that is posed [73] but equally evidence that the minority increases in size, particularly with increasing maturity and age, should not be ignored. The propositions outlined in the Swedish theme aim to help the individuals to reach their own decisions and to make their own judgements; others would prefer the prescription of a code of rules. Goals and objectives differ although the aim is human happiness. A basic goal of health care [74] and presumably that of health education is the enhancement of relationship capacities. Among causes of breakdown of such relationships STD are prominent.

In order to reach the population at large different forms of communication have been tried. On television, for example, 'Kojak' attracts audiences of 20–25 million, whereas documentaries on public health issues only reach about 5 million. Documentaries on VD have an effect in increasing the numbers of patients attending clinics but the effect is short-lived. In one follow-up of a documentary it was discovered that not more than half of the groups studied knew where to find a clinic in their locality and it was noted that very few clinics had an entry in the telephone directory [75].

In the United Kingdom the Health Education Council has a role to conduct national and regional campaigns based on research. Data on epidemiology tends to be collected by others but the Council's work relates to methods of communication and to the establishment of base lines of knowledge on attitudes and behaviour before and after a campaign. There are indications that efforts should be concentrated on people with special risks [76], although changes in attitudes have increased the numbers of those at risk.

With respect to medical undergraduate education, it is important to those involved in the care of patients to come to terms with the fact that western society has become openly pluralist and to be careful not to assume that sexual behaviour of a patient is a stereotype of one's own. It is necessary also to recognize that a patient has a right to sexual expression and be prepared to open the subject about this in a kindly way. If the facilities for taking history in private are poor then they should be improved.

In girls and young women with symptoms such as lower abdominal pain, dysuria or vaginal discharge, or whenever an infection of the urogenital tract is suspected, make sure that the tests which are necessary for diagnosis are, in fact, done. Do not take a circuitous route by avoiding the sexual issue by referring a patient to a gynaecological outpatient department where the necessary facilities for STD exclusion are not generally available. The subject may be opened by saying: 'Have you got a boy friend?' 'Are you on the pill?' 'When did you last have intercourse?'. If it is thought that questions like 'Have you had sex with anyone else?' are too delicate at the time then these questions can be postponed but not forgotten. Think of patients as individuals and have regard to their feelings whatever is done but do not avoid taking the steps to reach a diagnosis.

In the case of elderly patients who have been discovered to have positive serological tests for syphilis then it may be assumed that the infection has been there for a long time, the patient is not infectious and has not been so for decades. It is not right to withdraw sympathy from the patient and it is best not to spell out the diagnosis unnecessarily. If advisable to examine his or her partner try to do this without giving away secrets. Do not question the elderly about their early sex life although it is important to try, in a humane manner, to obtain their confidence.

Complaint has been made that the medical profession shows a moral indifference [77] and that undesirable social practices are being unconsciously legitimized. The views of the medical profession tend, however, to follow those of society at large but it could be said that insufficient interest is displayed in education and discussion of the complex factors involved. With regard to sexually transmitted disease medical undergraduates tend to get too little experience in talking to patients about their sexual difficulties and in dealing with STD clinically.

L. The dilemma of a name - publicity

One of the first questions asked by medical students may be: 'Why are there no notices to your department in the Royal Infirmary?' The reply is generally to ask another question: 'What would you call the department and where would you put the notices?' The problem of a name is not new and those interested will find that in 1914 in the illuminating minutes of evidence given to the members of the Royal Commission on Venereal Disease [78], men of eminence such as Sir William Osler and Lord Sydenham, were numbered among those who could not come to a satisfactory conclusion. There are references to the words Genito-urinary and Venereal and Sir William Osler refers to the latter as being more or less tabooed as a name. At the present time discussions are often still heated as 'venereal disease' has become value-laden as a term. The words Genito-urinary Medicine, Genital Medicine and Sexually Transmitted Disease have been offered as replacements for Venereal Disease on the grounds that the latter (legally defined as gonorrhoea, syphilis and the now rare chancroid) may comprise less than 20 per cent of clinic work. There is a stigma to the letters VD, there are taboos to sex and new names will not resolve these difficulties. Attitudes to the name and to notices will vary geographically according to the prevailing attitudes of the population and the degrees of tolerance within a society with conflicting moralities. It is essential to ensure that information reaches all young people who should know where they can obtain help. The solution will be imperfect but it is best perhaps for governments to place obligations on local authorities to ensure that information is made available and constantly kept up to date with notices being renewed and kept fresh. At all events the subject must not be allowed to be closed by a moralistic silence.

In this locality water-slide transfers are used as notices. They are small (14 x 9cm) with white letters against a blue background and they are difficult to deface or to spoil with graffiti. The notice reads: '*V.D. and Sexually Transmitted Disease.* Confidential specialist advice and treatment are available. For clinic times Tel. 225-4471.' In this way a notice can stay unaltered for years as the telephone number gives a recorded message which can be changed as service circumstances change.

Other pamphlets headed *'VD, sexually transmitted diseases:* Are you worried?' (Health Education Centre, Edinburgh) or again 'Straight Facts about Sex and Birth Control' (Family Planning Association, London) are available and can be given to doctors for their surgeries, to contraceptive clinics and to those responsible for teaching adolescents or young adults.

The name of the speciality remains a problem. Oriel [79] writes 'Genito-urinary medicine is an appropriate term, but it is not synonymous with venereology; it symbolizes a different and it might be thought, more mature and realistic view of the speciality which now includes so much more than the legally designated venereal diseases.' Perhaps stigma and anxiety will persist as long as sexual behaviour continues to be associated with guilt and its variations to cause overt hostility. A change in name tends, perhaps, to make the obligations of the speciality more diffuse and the responsibilities less clear cut.

REFERENCES

A. Social change

1 Carstairs, C M (1963) *This Island Now. The BBC Reith Lectures, 1962.* Hogarth Press, London

2 Musgrave, F (1974) *Ecstasy and Holiness. Counter Culture and the Open Society.* Methuen, London

3 Martin, B (1975) *The Mining of the Ivory Tower.* Black Paper, 1975 (Ed. Cox, C B and Boyson, R). Dent, London

4 Cairncross, F and McRae, H (1975) *The Second Great Crash.* Eyre Methuen, London

5 Bone, M (1973) *Family Planning Services in England and Wales.* Office of Population Censuses and Surveys, London. HMSO

6 Scarman, Sir Leslie (1974) *English Law—The New Dimension,* Stevens and Son, London

B. Evolutionary and biological background to human sexual behaviour

7 Short, R V (1976) The evolution of human reproduction, *Proceedings of the Royal Society of London,* 195, pages 3–23

8 Herbert, J (1972) in *Behavioural Patterns in Reproduction in Mammals. Book 4 Reproductive Patterns* (Ed. Austin, C R and Short, R V). University Press, Cambridge, page 34

9 Short, R V (1978) in *Reproduction and Evolution* (Ed. Calaby, C and Tyndale-Biscoe, C H) (Opening Address 4th International Symposium on Comparative Biology of Reproduction, December, 1976) Australian Academy of Science, Canberra, page 3

10 Cole, J B, Beighton, F C L and Jones, I H (1975) *British Medical Journal,* 2, 220

11 Dann, T C and Roberts, D F (1973) *British Medical Journal,* 2, 265–267

12 Marshall, W A and Tanner, J M (1974) in *Puberty in Scientific Foundation of Paediatrics* (Ed) Davis, J A and Dobbing, J. Heinemann, London, page 146

13 Tanner, J M (1962) in *Growth at adolescence, 2nd ed.* Blackwell Scientific Publications, Oxford, page 153

14 Doring, G K (1969) *Journal of Reproduction and Fertility,* suppl. 6, 77

15 Campbell, A V (1975) in *Moral Dilemmas in Medicine.* Churchill Livingstone, Edinburgh, London and New York, pages 116–125

C. Sexual habits of young people in western society

16 Schofield, M (1965) in *The Sexual Behaviour of Young People* Longmans, London, pages 34–36

17 Davies, C (1975) *Permissive Britain: Social change in the sixties and seventies.* Pitman Publishing, London

18 Schofield, M (1973) in *The sexual behaviour of young adults. A follow-up study to the sexual behaviour of young people.* Allen Lane, London, page 179

19 Eysenck, H J (1978) in *Sex and Personality.* Abacus edition. Sphere Books, London, page 247

20 Jessor, S L and Jessor, R (1975) *Developmental Psychology,* **4**, 473

21 Leete, R (1977) Changing marital composition. *Population Trends,* **9**, page 18. Population censuses and surveys, HMSO, London

22 Pearce, D and Farid, S (1977) *Population Trends,* 9, page 20. Population censuses and surveys, HMSO, London

D. The social impact of sexually-transmitted diseases

23 Office of Health Economics (1963) *The Venereal Diseases.* Office of Health Economics, London

24 Cd. 8189 & 8190 (1916) *Final Report and Appendix. Royal Commission on Venereal Disease.* HMSO, London

25 Leading Article (1917) The control of venereal disease *Lancet,* **i**, 309

26 Idsoe, O, Kiraly, K and Causse, G (1973) *WHO Chronicle,* **27**, 410

E. Personal prophylaxis

27 Barrett-Connor, E (1975) *American Journal of Medical Sciences,* **269**, 4

28 Darrow, W W and Wiesner, P J (1975) *Journal of the American Medical Association,* 233, 444

29 Metchnikoff, E L and Roux, E M (1906) in *Attempts at preventive treatment. Selected Essays on Syphilis and Small-pox,* The New Sydenham Society, London, page 129

30 Anonymous (1918) *Lancet,* **ii**, 471

F. Facilities for diagnosis and treatment

31 Cd. 8189 & 8190 (1916) *Final Report and Appendix Royal Commission on Venereal disease,* HMSO, London

G. Tracing of contacts and the case against compulsion

32 Bell, E M (1962) *Josephine Butler, Flame of Fire,* Constable, London

33 Rover, C (1967) *Love, Morals and the Feminists,* Routledge and Kegan Paul, London

34 Venereal Disease and the Defence of the Realm Act (1917) *Lancet,* **ii**, 23

35 Statement for the Corporation (1928) Edinburgh Corporation Bill 1928 (Venereal Diseases). City and Royal Burgh of Edinburgh

36 Results of Regulation 33B (1943) *British Journal of Venereal Diseases,* **19**, 92

37 Shannon, N P (1943) *British Journal of Venereal Diseases,* **19**, 22

38 Willcox, R R (1973) International contact tracing in venereal disease. *WHO Chronicle,* **27**, 418

H. People with high risks

39 Public Health Paper No. 65 (1977) *Social and Health Aspects of Sexually Transmitted Diseases. Principles of control measures;* Study based on the Technical Discussions held during the Twenty-eighth World Health Assembly, 1975. World Health Organization, Geneva
40 Adams, A (1967) *Medical Journal of Australia,* **1**, 145
41 Robertson, D H H and Hosie, D D (1970) *British Journal of Venereal Diseases,* **46**, 488
42 McMillan, A and Robertson, D H H (1977) *Health Bulletin,* **35**, 266
43 Barrett, B J (1977) in *Dictionary of Medical Ethics.* (Ed) Duncan, A S, Dunstan, G R and Welbourn, R B Darton, Longman and Todd, London, pages 257–260
44 Kinsey, A C, Pomeroy, W B and Martin, C E (1948) *Sexual Behaviour in the human male.* Saunders and Co., Philadelphia
45 Bailley, D S (1955) *Homosexuality and the Western Christian Tradition,* Longmans, London
46 Wolfenden Report (1957) *The Report of the Committee on Homosexual Offences and Prostitution,* Cmnd, 247. HMSO, London
47 Devlin, P (1959) in *The Enforcement of Morals.* Oxford University Press, London, pages 1–25
48 Hart, H L A (1963) *Law, Liberty and Morality,* Oxford University Press, London
49 Mill, J S (1859) in *On Liberty, Representative Government and the Subjection of Women, 1912.* The World's Classics, Oxford University Press, page 15
50 Mackenzie, Sir George (1678) in *Lawes and Customes of Scotland in Matters Criminal.* Brown, Edinburgh, page 161
51 Gordon, G H (1967) *Criminal Law.* Green, Edinburgh, page 836
52 Austin, C R (1978) *Journal of Medical Ethics,* **4**, 132
53 Schofield, M (1965) in *Sociological Aspects of Homosexuality,* Longman, London, page 160
54 Webster, B (1970) *British Journal of Venereal Diseases,* **46**, 406
55 British Cooperative Clinical Group (1977) *Homosexuality and Venereal Disease in the United Kingdom, a second study.* unpublished
56 May, D (1977) *Medicine, Science and the Law,* **17**, 203
57 Cowie, J, Cowie, V and Slater, E (1968) *Delinquency in Girls.* Heinemann, London
58 Timms, N (1968) *Rootless in the City.* National Institute for Social Work Training, London
59 Robertson, D H H and George, G (1970) *British Journal of Venereal Diseases,* **1**, 46

I. Companionship, marriage and divorce

60 Grant, B and Levin, J (1973) *Family Law,* Sweet and Maxwell, London
61 Keith, R M and Clark, G B (1977) *The Layman's Guide to Scots Law, Vol.* **2**, *Divorce,* Gordon Bennett, Edinburgh
62 Willock, I D (1974) *Journal of the Law Society of Scotland,* page 223
63 Henley *v* Henley (1955) *Law Reports Probate.* Incorporated Council of Law Reporting in England and Wales, London, page 202

J. Medical secrecy

64 Birkenhead, Viscount (1922) in *Points of View.* **2**, *should a doctor tell?* Hodder and Stoughton, London, pages 33–76
65 Riddell, Lord (1929) in *The law and ethics of medical confidences. Medico-Legal Problems,* H K Lewis, pages 45–69
66 Henley *v* Henley (1955) *Law Reports Probate,* Incorporated Council of Law Reporting in England and Wales, London, page 202
67 Garner *v* Garner (1920) *British Medical Journal,* **1**, 135

68 Bernfield, W K (1967) *British Journal of Venereal Diseases,* **43,** 53
69 Bernfield, W K (1972) *Cambrian Law Review,* **3,** 11

K. Education

70 Davies, C (1975) *Permissive Britain: Social Change in the Sixties and Seventies.* Pitman, London
71 Lenner, B (1967) *Sex and Society in Sweden.* Jonathan Cape, London
72 Bergstroöm-Walan, M (1977) *British Journal of Sexual Medicine,* 4, 18
73 Dalzell-Ward, A J (1977) in *Dictionary of Medical Ethics* (Ed) Duncan, A S, Dunstan, G R and Welbourn, R B Darton, Longman and Todd, London, pages 287–288
74 Campbell, A V (1975) in *Moral Dilemmas in Medicine.* Churchill Livingstone, Edinburgh, London and New York. page 190
75 Goodchild, P (1976) in *Sexually transmitted diseases* (Ed) Catterall, R D and Nicol, C S, Academic Press. pages 245–250
76 Dalzell-Ward, A J (1976) in *Sexually Transmitted Diseases* (Ed) Catterall, R D and Nicol, C S, Academic Press, London, pages 239–240
77 Habgood, J S (1976) in *Sexually Transmitted Diseases* (Ed) Catterall, R D and Nicol, C S, Academic Press, London, pages 256–261

L. The dilemma of a name – publicity

78 Cd. 8189 & 8190 (1916) Final Report and Appendix Royal Commission on Venereal Disease HMSO, London
79 Oriel, J D. (1978) *British Journal of Venereal Diseases* **54**, pages 291

CHAPTER 2

Clinical Investigation of the Patient

The central importance of attitudes and behaviour of medical and other staff towards patients, often too vulnerable to complain, has been discussed and emphasized. As Fluker has pointed out in the film 'Gonorrhoea, the persistent paradox' (Pacesetter Productions, 1974), the most modern techniques may be set at nought should a patient be offended enough not to wish to return.

Under the circumstances of rising demand for clinical, laboratory and other services clear objectives require to be defined. A structured approach to history taking and examination is necessary to obtain the initial relevant details particularly as there is in most cases involvement of the lower urogenital tract. When appropriate, extension of history taking and physical examination will not be different from that required in a general medical examination [1] .

The quality of reception is important and peremptoriness is to be deplored at all stages. Privacy while giving personal details required for registration is appreciated by patients and confidentiality can be explained when early reassurance is necessary.

Objectives of clinical investigation

In any clinic in any locality priority should be given to *the first two main objectives,* which are:

1. To detect or exclude early syphilis and to trace contacts.
2. To detect or exclude a gonococcal infection and to trace contacts.

A *third objective* is one of making a clinical and microbial diagnosis of a wide variety of lesser conditions, based on the isolation and detection of the organism considered to be causative. This is a laudable aim of venereologists, but, insofar as technical resources are limited in the case of, for example, certain viruses, ureaplasma, or chlamydiae, barriers may be set in practice to such an aspiration. Within this objective contact-tracing will be considered when useful and appropriate.

To secure the first *two specific objectives* is mandatory in all clinics as syphilis and gonorrhoea are potentially so serious to the individual and to the community. A very high standard of serological testing for syphilis and cultural detection of the gonococcus is the *sine qua non* of every clinic. In these two diseases specific treatment is effective and cheap and tracing of contacts is as essential for the patient as for the community.

The *fourth objective* will cover the detection of other medical problems in the patient together with their resolution. To encourage contraception in those at risk; to detect pregnancy (see appendix for note on pregnancy tests); to coax individuals into obtaining necessary antenatal care and to assist those seeking termination of pregnancy, are objectives which will fall naturally into the clinical responsibilities of those in STD clinics. Within this fourth objective will fall also a wide area of medicine as STD clinics may tend to become involved with primary medical care for adolescents or young adults. Within a hospital or polyclinic these activities will tend to encourage close team work with colleagues in departments of gynaecology and obstetrics in the case of the female; in departments of urology, more particularly in the case of the male with persistent signs or symptoms and in microbiology laboratories where studies in serological and isolation methods have enhanced the value of this speciality. Clinics for contraceptive advice should be readily accessible.

The *fifth objective* involves the clinic in medical social work; a particularly close association with the medical social worker being necessary to detect and to relieve or remedy homelessness, marital stress and poverty, which, together with deviancy and difficulties in establishing and maintaining relationships, are matters of special concern to the clinician. As reservoir effects are significant and particularly common in those groups, in which fear of, or hostility to, 'The establishment' is found, there is a special duty to offer help as a means of securing confidence.

History taking

History taking is an extension of clinical skills required in any branch of medicine. A patient attending a clinic on his own account, on advice from a sexual contact, or after an explanation and referral by his general practitioner, will generally expect a series of questions relating to his or her recent sexual contacts: in some cases, however, the doctor will ask first about his or her main complaints and their duration or, in the case of females, begin to consider and record the menstrual history and contraceptive practice of the patient. Information on antibiotic or chemotherapy received during the last month or longer will be relevant.

Data about sexual intercourse are best obtained after the doctor has obtained *rapport* with the patient. The date of the last coitus is noted. Record this as LC in the unmarried, as last marital coitus (LMC) or as last extramarital coitus (EMC) in the married. Fuller details of a more complex and detailed nature can be obtained later and recorded separately on say, a coloured sheet, for convenience by health personnel responsible for tracing contacts.

For convenience and to ensure that the main medical objectives are secured in every case a proforma may be drawn out for history taking in males and females: examples of these proforma are shown in Figures 2.1 and 2.2 respectively. Such proforma will be sufficient in the average case so that the main details will be rapidly apparent to the doctor involved with the follow-up of a case, who will not be necessarily the same on every occasion.

In connection with the past history, information should be obtained about previous sexually transmitted diseases as well as previous illness of a medical or surgical nature. A history of hepatitis should be noted. Overseas visits whether recent or remote are relevant. The patient should be asked about blood donations.

Family history is often restricted in the male to those questions of sexual relationships unless more detail on social background is required. Narrowing of the scope of the investigation is often a result of limited time and a patient's apparent wish to be cured quickly with the least possible intrusion into personal affairs. In the case of the female, children's needs may make her attendances difficult. Judicious questions will often elicit symptoms of family stress.

Clinical examination: special features

Initial examination in both male and female can conveniently include inspection of the skin surface above the waist. This can be carried out having due regard to the patient's sense of privacy and feelings. Examine the cervical, axillary and epitrochlear lymph nodes. The axillary region and scalp should be inspected. Careful examination of the wrist creases, the webs between the fingers and on the back of the elbow is necessary for the detection of scabies. The presence of old self-inflicted scars, tattoo marks and uncleanliness should be noted.

EXAMINATION OF THE MALE

In the inspection of the skin surface below the waist and of the anogenital region in particular, attention should be paid to the following:

The abdomen and inguinal lymph nodes

Penis

Retract the prepuce and note the extent it can move freely over the glans. Examine in particular, the urethral meatus (note if there are meatal warts, sore or stricture), glans, frenum, coronal sulcus, prepuce and shaft.

Scrotum and contents

Testes, epididymes and spermatic cords and coverings.

Pubic region

Look for evidence of the crab louse (*Pthirus pubis*), the lesions of molluscum contagiosum. Examine the inguinoscrotal fold for tinea cruris, for example.

Anus and peri-anal skin

Look for warts, anal chancre or fissure.

Examination of the anogenital region with gloved hands is the correct procedure and is mandatory where moist infective or potentially infective lesions are present. Disposable vinyl examination gloves are satisfactory.* An attempt should be made to milk any discharge from the penile urethra. If a discharge is present, the urethral meatus should be cleansed with a saline-soaked gauze swab and the discharge obtained by means of a disposable plastic inoculating loop. The 10 μl loop, blue in colour (Nunc products, Kamstrup, DK - Roskilde, Denmark), is inserted past the everted lips of the meatus and gently passed for 2–3 cm within the urethra. Where even minor urethral symptoms are present in the male a scraping should be taken and plated directly on to a selective medium for the gonococcus even if there is no visible discharge. If direct plating is impossible transport medium should be used (Chapter 11). It is a useful procedure in such cases to ask patients to return the following morning after retaining urine overnight. The patient should empty his bladder late at night before retiring and come to the clinic in the early morning. Such early morning urethral smears, examined by microscopy and culture, are useful in the detection of minimal degrees of urethritis whether non-gonococcal or gonococcal. To avoid missing asymptomatic cases, there is a strong case for the routine culture of urethral scrapings in all cases where there has been a risk of acquiring gonorrhoea. Facilities may, however, be restricted, in which case contacts should be examined in this way.

In contacts of gonorrhoea or in those with gonorrhoea, a cotton-

*E.g. Triflex, Travenol Laboratories Ltd, Thetford, Norfolk, England.

wool swab should be passed over the pharynx and both tonsils or tonsillar beds and plated directly on medium selective for the gonococcus.

Visual examination of the urine is necessary in every case, but particularly so in the male as the urine will contain exudate from the urethra in the case of urethritis. In anterior urethritis, the initial 20ml of urine passed will contain many pus cells, causing a turbidity, not cleared by the addition of 10% acetic acid, which will be less in the second portion of urine passed. This crude test has value in detecting obvious urethritis. In subacute or chronic urethritis, casts consisting of mucopus from urethra and urethral glands, may sink as threads and deposits in the specimen. In anterior urethritis exudate will tend to be passed mainly in the first urine voided; in posterior urethritis or prostatitis the first and second specimens may contain such deposit.

Examination of urine for protein, sugar and blood are essential. The most widely used test for these are the stick tests;

Glucose*	Qualitative tests practically specific for glucose.
Protein*	Simple semi-quantitative tests but their sensitivity as tests for Bence-Jones protein is poor.
Haemoglobin*	All detect haemoglobin but do not differentiate between haematuria and the true (but much rarer) condition of haemoglobinuria. A false-positive result can be seen when the urine is contaminated (1/1000) with povidone-iodine (Betadine).

A specimen of venous blood is taken in every case for serological tests for syphilis (STS) (Chapter 4). Venepuncture is conveniently carried out when the patient's examination is completed.

EXAMINATION OF THE HOMOSEXUAL MALE

As in cases of gonorrhoea among homosexuals the urethra may be involved in 60 per cent, the ano-rectum in 40 per cent and the pharynx in about 7 per cent, sampling from *all* these sites should be a routine in every case (Chapter 11). In gonococcal urethritis there are generally, but not always, symptoms; in ano-rectal gonorrhoea symptoms may be present only in one-third of cases and in the pharynx the infections tend to be asymptomatic. It is recommended that samples are taken from these sites as follows:

*Fuller details are given in Whitby, Percy-Robb and Smith [2].

(*a*) Urethral smear and culture.

(*b*) Ano-rectal cultures. Because the lubricants used contain anti-bacterial agents proctoscopy should be postponed until after the ano-rectal culture has been taken by passing a swab, moistened with sterile saline, through the anal canal towards the rectum. On proctoscopy, when there is evidence of inflammation with erythema, mucosal oedema, mucopus and blood, it may be possible to obtain a sample of pus in which the gonococcus can be seen on microscopy although diagnosis will require confirmation by culture.

(*c*) Pharyngeal cultures. Cultures are taken but not smears for microscopy.

Three sets of samples should be taken from ano-rectal and pharyngeal sites before a gonococcal infection is discounted.

Venepuncture for STS should be carried out at the first visit after the culture tests have been taken. Serological tests for hepatitis B (*see* Chapter 24) should be carried out also in homosexuals.

EXAMINATION OF THE FEMALE

As the initial examination above the waist may be carried out while the patient is seated the taking of a throat culture and venepuncture for STS may be conveniently taken at this stage. Examination below the waist may be completed when the patient is in the semi-lithotomy position.

The abdomen should be examined first by inspection and palpation. The female ano-genital region can only be examined properly for inflammatory disease in the semi-lithotomy position. Disposable plastic gloves should be worn by the examiner.

Inspection and palpation, where necessary, of the anus and external genitalia should be systematic and include:

Mons veneris and pubic hair

Inguinal lymph nodes

Perineum and anus

Vulva—labia majora; labia minora; vestibule and fourchette

External urethral meatus

A finger should be inserted into the vaginal orifice and the contents of the urethra and its para-urethral glands massaged towards the orifice. Smears and cultures are taken from this site in all cases.

ROYAL INFIRMARY OF EDINBURGH

Referred by	Age	Diagnosis	First Attendance	Case No.
			M S D Sep.	

Date of recent contact
if married L.M.C. 1) 2) 3)

HISTORY

Homosexual	Yes	No

Contraception

Previous History

Eczema

Previous Penicillin Penicillin Reaction Asthma Hay Fever Other Sensitivity

Examination P. pubis

Skin S. scabiei

Abd.

Urethra

Testes Scrotum

Penis Anus

Inguinal g Proctoscopy

Glucose

Urine 1) 2) Hours held Protein

Provisional diagnosis	Tests	Results	Treatment	Next attendance

1. Primary Contact Known Unknown Prost. Consort M.C.

Contacts	Relationship	No.	Diagnosis	Date	Notes
	1				
	2				
	3				

Locality acquired	HV
	Referred
	Not referred

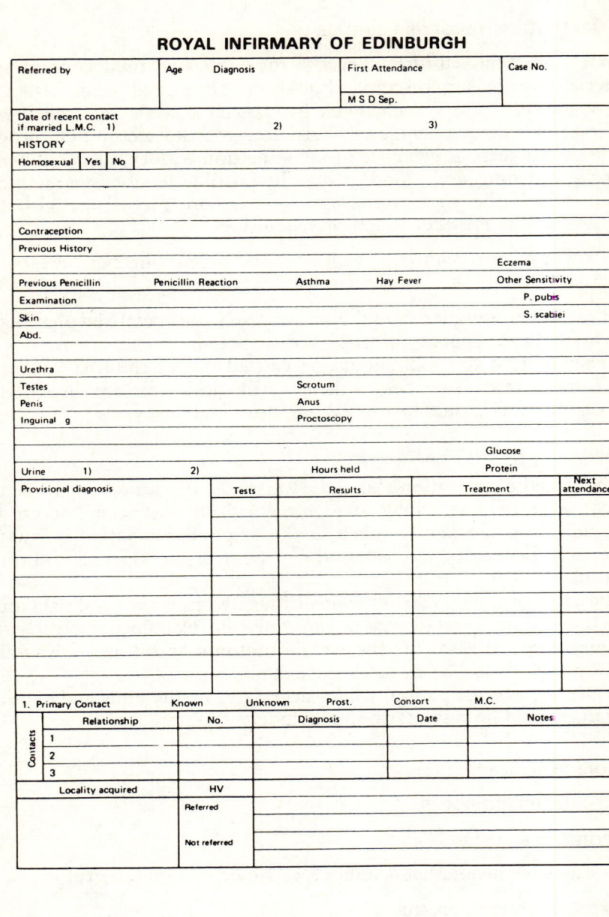

Figure 2.1 Sheet giving framework for initial history and examination in the male.

ROYAL INFIRMARY OF EDINBURGH

Referred by	Age	Diagnosis	First Attendance	Case No.
			M S D Sep.	

Date of recent contact
if married L.M.P. 1) 2) 3)

HISTORY

Menarche Sanitary protection Contraception

L.M.P.

Menstruation

Previous History

Attendances Eczema

Previous Penicillin Penicillin Reaction Asthma Hay Fever Other Sensitivity

Pregnancies	E D C.

Examination P. pubis

Skin P. capitis

S. Scabiei

Abdomen

Vulva Vagina

Cervix

Urethra

P.V.

Introitus

Bart R. L.

Anus

	Cultures		Locality acquired	HV
Herpes isolation				
Herpes CFT		T		referred
		Ur		Not referred
		Cx		
		R		

Contacts	Relationship	No.	Diagnosis	Date	STS		Cy-tology
	1						
	2						
	3						

Provisional diagnosis

Figure 2.2 Sheet giving framework for initial history and examination in the female.

Orifices of a pair of para-urethral glands open on either side of the urethral meatus (Skene's glands)

Smears and cultures can be taken from this site specifically or added to the urethral swab when pus is seen at the duct orifice.

Orifices of the greater vestibular glands

The orifices of the greater vestibular glands (Bartholin's gland) open external to the hymen on the inner side of the labia minora. The gland (1–1.5cm in diameter) may be examined by passing a finger into the vagina and hooking it behind a point in the substance of the labium majus at the junction of the anterior two-thirds and posterior one-third. It cannot be palpated unless enlarged or fibrotic. By gently massaging the gland and expressing the mucus secretion towards the duct orifice material may be collected in a loop or cotton-wool applicator for the immediate preparation of a smear and culture.

The next step in the pelvic examination is to pass a self-retaining bivalve speculum of the Cusco type gently into the vagina so that the vaginal walls and cervix may be inspected. The presence and character of any vaginal discharge is noted and a record made concerning its odour, appearance and consistency. A swab is swept along the posterior fornix to collect the vaginal discharge. Specimens are taken routinely from this site as follows:

(*a*) Vaginal film (dry) for Gram-staining is taken to describe the appearance of the bacterial flora and to detect *Candida.* Culture methods may be available to the clinician (Chapter 17).

(*b*) Vaginal film (wet). The discharge is suspended in a drop of saline and covered with a cover-slip for immediate microscopic examination (x40 objective) for *Trichomonas vaginalis.* Again culture methods may be available to the clinician (Chapter 18).

Discharge is removed from the upper vagina and the external os is cleansed with a pledget of wool held in dressing forceps. A plastic bacteriological loop or suitable cotton-wool applicator is passed into the endocervix to obtain endocervical secretions from which a smear is made; this is stained with Gram stain and further secretions obtained with a second swab for plating on selective medium for the gonococcus.

Further samples of secretions and scrapings may be required from the endocervical canal, the os or the vaginal portion of the cervix for the isolation of *Chlamydia* (Chapter 13) or herpesvirus (Chapter 20). When appropriate a swab may be inserted into the cervical canal and swept across the upper part of the vagina, particularly the posterior fornix, to obtain secretions for examination for bacteria which can be isolated by special methods (e.g., *Corynebacterium vaginale* (Chapter 13), or routine methods, e.g., *Bacteroides* (Chapter 13).

Before withdrawing the speculum it is convenient to take a cervical smear for cytological examination. Using Ayre's method, a special wooden spatula is then used to scrape the superficial cells from the external os and lower end of cervix. The scrapings are taken throughout an arc of 360 degrees and a slide prepared and fixed immediately in 95 per cent industrial methylated spirit. The detection of carcinoma of the cervix is discussed later (Chapter 32).

After withdrawing the Cusco speculum, a swab is passed into the ano-rectum to obtain a sample for immediate plating on selective medium. If skin tags or haemorrhoids make this process difficult a child's proctoscope may be slightly lubricated with saline and passed into the rectum. The swab may now be passed beyond the tip of the proctoscope which is then itself withdrawn and the swab withdrawn gently afterwards. A bimanual vaginal examination should be carried out gently. The lubricated (K-Y water-soluble lubricating jelly) index and second finger of the right hand are used to separate the labia and are then passed into the vagina. Gently pressing backwards the fingers are gradually passed towards the anterior fornix when the uterus can be palpated by the fingers of the left hand placed well above the symphysis pubis. The fundus of the retroverted uterus can be felt through the posterior fornix. The uterine appendages may be examined through the lateral fornix and a swelling outlined between the fingers of the two hands.

Tenderness in the fornices, with or without swelling of the Fallopian tubes or on movement of the cervix are signs elicited in inflammatory disease such as in gonococcal infections of the upper genital tract. Inflammatory swellings may also be felt in the rectovaginal pouch (pouch of Douglas).

In the case of the female the urine may be examined after the pelvic examination. Pronounced dysuria or frequency tends to be more often associated with a urinary tract infection due to coliform organisms, than to the gonococcus. Pregnancy tests are often required and a clear understanding of these tests is important (Appendix to Chapter 2).

Examination of ulcers (see Chapter 33)

Syphilis must be excluded as a cause of any sore in the anal or genital region. After cleansing the surface with a swab soaked in sterile saline, serum is squeezed by gentle pressure from the depth of the lesion. This serum may be collected directly on a coverslip or if this is difficult, in a capillary tube. If collected in a glass capillary, one end of the capillary can be sealed in a gas microburner: the column of air beyond the seal is then heated to expel fluid neatly on to the centre of a coverslip, which is then positioned on a slide. After firmly pressing the glass coverslip and slide between pieces of filter paper, the preparation can be examined by dark-ground illumination. It is useful in a clinic to have the microscope arranged with an automatic focusing device so chances of damaging the oil-immersion lens may be minimized, and rapid examination made easy (the Zeiss research microscope with automatic focusing handle gives excellent service in a busy clinic).

Dark-ground examination of serum from all ulcers on genital mucosa or at mucocutaneous junctions is a policy which should be adopted routinely so that a diagnosis of early syphilis may not be missed. Three sets of tests should be taken if syphilis is suspected. The administration of sulphadimidine 2g. initially followed by 1g. 6-hourly will often reduce sepsis sufficiently, without affecting the treponeme, to achieve reduction of the phimosis and to obtain direct access to the ulcer. Lymph node puncture may occasionally yield *Treponema pallidum.*

In homosexuals, typical anal chancres are uncommon although dark-ground examination of radial linear anal fissures, seen in early syphilis in such cases, will often reveal *T. pallidum.*

Culture of fluid from sores may yield herpesvirus although such a finding does not exclude the possibility of syphilis.

Tracing of contacts

It is essential that personnel involved in the tracing of contacts are adequately trained for their task. It is the authors' view that this aspect of the clinical task should fall on those who have had training as nurses as well as training in community health. In the interviewing of patients a deep appreciation of the medical and social consequences of the various sexually transmissible diseases is essential. An ability to give reasoned explanations about health matters which the doctor may have omitted or which the patient has been unable to comprehend is one of the essential educational priorities of this type of work. An open mind and an awareness of the varied nature of human sexuality are essential. Experience in the local community and in the homes of patients are the leavening of experience which will help to prevent or mitigate the sometimes serious social catastrophes. Where appropriate, conciliation should be possible in difficult situations which arise between

Table 2.1 Reference numbers for diagnosis

Condition	*Ref. No.*	*Description*
SYPHILIS	A1	Acquired, primary.
	A2	Acquired, secondary.
	A3	Acquired, latent in first 2 years of infection.
	A4	Acquired, cardiovascular.
	A5	Acquired, neurological.
	A6	Acquired, all other late or latent stages.
	A7/A8	Congenital.
GONORRHOEA	B1.1	With lower genito-urinary tract infection.
	B1.2	With mouth and throat infection.
	B1.3	With eye infection.
	B1.4	With upper genital tract complications.
	B1.5	With systemic complications.
	B3	Gonococcal ophthalmia neonatorum.
OTHER	C1	Chancroid.
	C2	Lymphogranuloma venereum.
	C3	Granuloma inguinale.
	C4	Non-specific genital infections.
	C5	Non-specific genital infections with arthritis.
	C6	Trichomoniasis.
	C7	Genital candidiasis.
	C8	Scabies
	C9	Pubic lice (*Pthirus pubis*)
	C10	Genital herpes simplex.
	C11	Warts (Condylomata acuminata).
	C12	Molluscum contagiosum.
	D1	Other treponemal diseases.
	D2	Other conditions requiring treatment in the centre.
	D3	Other conditions NOT requiring treatment.
	D4	Other conditions referred elsewhere.

1. Syphilis - latent in first 2 years of infection (A3), this applies to cases presenting no clinical sign of syphilis but considered (e.g. by rapid reversal of positive blood findings on treatment or on epidemiological evidence) to have contracted this disease within the preceding 24 months.

2. Syphilis, acquired, cardiovascular (A4). To include patients with cardiovascular syphilis who are also suffering from syphilis of any other system.

3. Congenital syphilis: elsewhere in the United Kingdom where age-groups are not used, A8 refers to those aged 2 years and over.

4. Gonorrhoea. In this form the total of B1.1 to B1.5 is equivalent to items B1 (post-pubertal gonorrhoea) and B2 (pre-pubertal gonorrhoea) in returns used elsewhere in the United Kingdom. Proctitis is included as B.1.1.

5. Non-specific genital infections, should include all chlamydial infections - genital or ophthalmic.

Table 2.2 Some priorities in tracing contacts

Diagnosis	*Degree of danger to a sexual contact*	*Degree of priority for rapid contact-tracing*	*Comment*
Acquired early-stage syphilis	Very high	Very high	Essential.
Acquired late-stage syphilis	None	None	Exception possibly in a long-term partner.
Non-gonococcal urethritis in the male and non-specific genital infection in the female	Low	Low	In regular partner examination and treatment may be justified.
Lymphogranuloma venereum	Moderate	Moderate	In regular partner examination is justified.
Trichomoniasis	Low	Very low	In regular partner examination and treatment may be advised.
Candidiasis	Low	Very low	In regular partner examination and treatment may be advised if patient has recurrent infection.

Scabies	Low	Moderate	Examination of all family advisable.
Pthirus pubis	Low	Low	In partner examination and treatment may be advised.
Herpes genitalis	Uncertain	Low	Steps to ensure that regular cervical smears are being examined are justified. If partner is pregnant examination is justified. Isolations important in six weeks before term.
Cytomegalovirus infection	Low	Low	Primary infection in pregnancy may be a danger to the fetus.
Genital warts	Low	Low	In regular partner examination and treatment may be justified.
Hepatitis B virus infection	High	Moderate	Tracing of contacts is justifiable in some cases, in regular partners and particularly in pregnancy.
Molluscum contagiosum	Low	Low	In regular partner examination and treatment may be justified.
Marburg Disease, Lassa and Ebola Fever	Very high	Very high	Essential to prevent spread of this rare epidemic disease with a high mortality. Sexual intercourse is not the main method of spread.

partners, whether married or not. The diagnosis of gonorrhoea and syphilis and by implication the diagnosis of other STD may be regarded as defamatory so there are legal and social obligations requiring the exercise of care and consideration. It is the patient's cooperation which must be sought and everything should be done to mitigate not only the medical but the social consequences arising from the diagnosis.

In the tracing of contacts, as in the United Kingdom, it is useful to have some procedures common to all clinics in the country although methods of approach acceptable in one city may not be appropriate in another. At its simplest a patient may be asked to give his or her consort a personal note, usually called a contact slip, to bring to the clinic. This note may be headed with the name of the clinic and contain a record of the patient's case number, his or her diagnosis in code (Table 2.1) and the date of the diagnosis. Such a personal note can be readily interpreted in any clinic although the patient's anonymity is secure in the event of its loss.

If a contact is to be looked for in another part of the United Kingdom then a special Contact Tracing Form (Special Clinic Contact Report; Department of Health & Social Security) may be sent to the physician in charge of the clinic serving the area concerned. When the name and address of the contact is known, limited additional details of description are needed. If only a forename is known and descriptions are inadequate successful contact-tracing is rare. Recognizing that these forms together with the searching to be undertaken may be regarded as defamatory, personnel responsible for the process, including the medical staff, must exercise care and judgement in every case. In the process of tracing contacts the patient may be persuaded to help but it is not permissible to use any form of trick or coercion to obtain information. In the search for contacts it is essential to treat individuals with respect and make sure that confidential information is not communicated to others. Threats are never justified; the exercise demands persuasion by explanation, kindness and tact. Initial failures may be rewarded by patience, and delays are preferable to the harmful effects of threats.

In the context of this chapter an attempt has been made to put together a working guide as an indicator of priorities in the tracing of contacts (Table 2.2).

Medical social work

Access to a medical social worker (MSW), as the fifth objective in a clinic should be freely available to patients and referral should be a regular feature of STD clinical work. It is important that the clinician and health visitor or counterpart remain alert to the needs of patients which are best considered by an MSW. In particular, all patients of 16 years of age or less should be seen in every case and an endeavour made to allow young patients to reconsider their life-style in relation to the risks that are taken. It gives opportunities to individuals to express their anxieties and problems.

APPENDIX

Pregnancy tests

Tests for pregnancy [3] are required when there is a need for immediate information concerning the existence or otherwise of pregnancy. Early diagnosis makes it easier to secure the social and medical support required in antenatal care. If pregnancy exists termination may be necessary for social or therapeutic reasons and the earlier in the pregnancy this is undertaken the less danger there is to the woman. The tests are carried out on urine and immunological methods have replaced the earlier biological tests.

Immunological tests for pregnancy (IPT) react positively when chorionic gonadotrophin (HCG) is present in the urine. A positive result indicates the secretory activity of trophoblastic tissue usually associated with the presence of a viable fetus. HCG is produced before the missed but expected menstrual period and in increasing amounts until a peak is reached about 8 weeks after conception. There is a dramatic fall after this peak but the hormone is excreted throughout normal pregnancy and into the postpartum period. IPT do not distinguish between pituitary luteinizing hormone (LH) and HCG. Pregnancy tests are correctly positive in the absence of a fetus when a hydatidiform mole, chorioadenoma or choriocarcinoma is present. Similarly, urine from men with testicular tumours containing trophoblastic tissue will evoke a positive reaction. In addition to the value in the diagnosis of early pregnancy these tests can be useful in excluding pregnancy as a cause of secondary amenorrhoea, particularly in women approaching the menopause. Such women may excrete enough LH to produce a false positive result with the ordinary test, and if a woman is known to be near the menopausal age the test can be modified. In disturbed or ectopic pregnancy the results of the tests may either be positive or negative indicating the secretory activity of the trophoblast and not necessarily the viability of the fetus.

The majority of false negative results are due to tests being done too soon after the missed but expected period or during the second or third trimester of pregnancy when urinary HCG is low.

False or inconclusive results are more likely to occur in latex agglutination tests than in the preferred haemagglutination inhibition tests (e.g. Pregnosticon). False positive results have occurred with non-specific agglutinins, glassware contaminated with detergents, proteinuria, haematuria, bacteriuria, as well as with some drugs. The easy to do, unreliable tests are likely to create more problems than they solve. Any home test kit or do it yourself kit must be simple, be accompanied with explicit instructions, and give a positive course of action for the woman to take regardless of whether the results are positive or negative.

Interactions between oral contraceptives and other drugs

Impairment of contraceptive efficacy can arise through interactions between oral contraceptive steroids and other drugs which stimulate the formation of hepatic microsomal enzymes. These enzymes increase the rate of metabolism of the oral contraceptive so that the plasma concentration of steroids falls to levels inadequate for the control of conception. Breakthrough bleeding and spotting are common warning signs of this phenomenon [4]. Many specific agents used in therapy, such as rifampicin, phenytoin, phenobarbitone and phenylbutazone, as well as those present in the environment, can induce enzymes which metabolize steroids, although the specific pattern of induction may vary according to the compound and the genetic constitution of the individual [5].

Risks appear to be particularly associated with rifampicin, but pregnancies have also been reported in women treated with ampicillin whilst taking oral contraceptives [6].

Although the number of interaction reports is still very low, widespread use of the lower hormone pill may reveal more interactions than previously. It is possible too that antibiotics other than ampicillin may also have similar interactions. Although temporary abstinence from sexual intercourse will ordinarily be advised for a patient being treated for a sexually transmitted disease such as gonorrhoea, and although regimens of treatment tend to be brief, the use of the condom may be advised during and for a week after treatment if abstinence is not possible.

REFERENCES

1 Macleod, J (1976) (Ed) *Clinical Examination,* Churchill Livingstone, Edinburgh

2 Whitby, L G, Percy-Robb, I W and Smith, A F (1975) in *Lecture Notes on Clinical Chemistry,* Blackwell Scientific Publications, Oxford, page 35

3 Hobson, B M (1974) Bibliography (with review) on Advances in human pregnancy testing. *Bibliography of Reproduction,* **24**, 111

4 Robertos, Y R and Johnson, E S (1976) *Current Medical Research and Opinion,* **3**, 647

5 Buss, W C (1979) *Journal of Antimicrobial Chemotherapy,* **5**, 4

6 Dossetor, J (1975) *British Medical Journal,* **4**, 467

CHAPTER 3

Syphilis: Introduction

Syphilis is an infectious disease caused by the bacterium *Treponema pallidum*. It is spread principally by sexual intercourse but may also be acquired congenitally, that is to say, by the fetus infected *in utero* by the mother. The disease is systemic from the onset and the natural course of infection may span several decades.

Syphilis is conveniently divided into stages, early infectious and late non-infectious (Figure 3.1). In the early infectious stage of the disease lesions occur on the moist mucocutaneous parts of the body, particularly the genitalia. These lesions contain many treponemes and

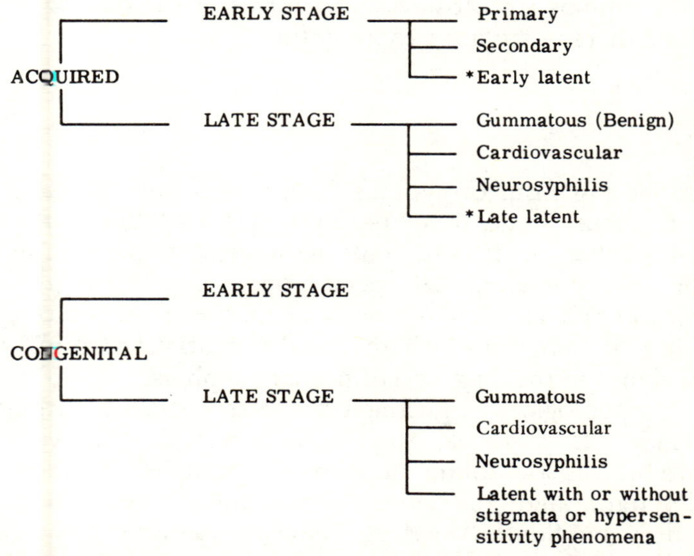

Figure 3.1 Classification of stages of syphilis. A patient* whose serological tests for syphilis are positive, but in whom there are no clinical signs of the disease, no abnormality of the cerebrospinal fluid, and no past history of treatment of syphilis, is said to be suffering from latent syphilis. The distinction between early latent and late latent syphilis is an arbitrary one. Early latent syphilis refers to infection, diagnosed on serological grounds, and acquired within the preceding two years.

enable transmission to occur by sexual intercourse. Even if untreated, these lesions tend to heal but may recur during the first 2–4 years, after which they heal and the disease becomes latent or hidden. The latent form or the non-infectious late stage of the disease may persist for decades without producing obvious clinical changes, but a proportion of patients will unpredictably develop active involvement of the cardiovascular system (about 10 per cent), the central nervous system (about 10 per cent), or localized gummatous destructive lesions which can affect the musculo-skeletal system, the viscera and mucous membranes (about 15 per cent).

In both early and late stages of syphilis an infected mother can communicate the disease to her unborn fetus. Although the disease can be transmitted to the fetus transplacentally long after a mother has ceased to be sexually infectious the longer she has had the disease the less likely is this to occur.

If treated in the early stage clinical cure can be achieved by penicillin treatment and with certain other antibiotics. In the late stages curative effects are often spectacular in some forms of neurosyphilis and in gummatous syphilis. In cardiovascular forms of the disease the effects of antibiotic therapy are not easy to define.

Aetiology

The causative organism of syphilis, *Treponema pallidum* is a delicate spiralled filament, some 6 to 14μm by 0.1 to 0.2μm with 6 to 12 regular coils (Plate 1). It is the only pathogenic treponeme indigenous to Britain. Many commensal species occur in the mouth (e.g. *T. macrodentium* and *T. microdentium*) an on the mucous surfaces of the genitalia (e.g. *T. calligyrum*) where their differentiation from *T. pallidum* is of importance in the diagnosis of primary syphilis.

Other morphologically indistinguishable treponemes, pathogenic for man, include: *T. pertenue,* the cause of yaws, a non-venereal but communicable disease found in tropical countries; *T. carateum,* the cause of pinta, a mild contagious disease similar to yaws but confined to the Central and South Americas. These diseases caused by treponemes are referred to collectively as the treponematoses (*see* Chapter 9).

The term, spirochaete, is often used to describe treponemes and organisms of similar spiral morphology belonging to the genera *Borrelia* and *Leptospira; Borrelia* spp. are commonly found in the subpreputial discharges and must be distinguished carefully from *T. pallidum; Leptospira* spp. transmitted from rodents to man cause leptospirosis, the clinical features of which range from a mild febrile illness to a fatal condition associated with liver and kidney failure.

TREPONEMA PALLIDUM

T. pallidum is feebly refractile and too narrow to be seen well by ordinary light microscopy. Dark-ground illumination is normally used to examine the organism and this was the technique used by Schaudinn and Hoffmann in 1905 to demonstrate that *T. pallidum* was the cause of syphilis details relating to this discovery can be found in a brief biography of Schaudinn [1]. Special techniques such as silver impregnation may be used to demonstrate the organism, particularly in tissue, but this tends to alter the morphology. Immunofluorescent techniques can now be used to demonstrate the organism in tissues and body fluids.

T. pallidum is actively motile although lacking flagella. There are three movements that propel it: slow undulation, corkscrew-like rotation, and a sluggish backwards and forwards motion. It often displays a characteristic tendency to bend at right angles near its mid point.

T. pallidum is feebly viable outside its host. It cannot be cultured *in vitro* either in artificial media or by cell culture although viability may be maintained for several days. Recently an increase in *T. pallidum* equivalent to approximately three cell generations has been reported using cultured baby hamster kidney tissue cells [2]. This work has not been corroborated so far [3]. Pathogenic strains can grow in the testicular tissue of rabbits and this is the normal way of maintaining the organism in the laboratory. Apart from ethical considerations intratesticular inoculation and weekly passage is a difficult, expensive, and time-consuming process. These factors have limited basic studies on the biology of *T. pallidum.* It divides by binary fission approximately once every 30 hours when environmental conditions are favourable. Mucopeptide is probably an integral part of the cell wall and accounts, in part, for the organism's sensitivity to penicillin. Cardiolipin, present in the lipid fraction of treponemes, causes the production of an antibody which cross-reacts with host-tissue antigens. This is important in the diagnosis of treponemal infection (Chapter 4).

Origin of syphilis

The first recognizable epidemic of sexually-transmitted syphilis in

Europe occurred at the end of the 15th century. There are two main theories regarding the appearance of the disease.

COLUMBIAN THEORY

The outbreak is attributed to the importation of syphilis to Spain in 1493 by the crews of Christopher Columbus on their return from the West Indies where they acquired the infection. Some members of the crew later became mercenaries in 1494 at the siege of Naples where a great epidemic broke out. It was not called syphilis* at that time but referred to as the 'French disease' by the Italians and the 'Italian disease' by the French.

Social conditions, the abundance of wars and resulting mobility of armies and associated camp followers largely contributed to the spread of the infection throughout Europe. Protagonists of the Columbian theory base their arguments on the lack of description of any disease that can be clearly identified as syphilis, in Europe prior to this period. The Columbian theory does not take account of the origin of syphilis on a world-wide scale.

UNITARIAN THEORY

This evolutionary theory put forward mainly by Hackett [4] suggests that all the present-day treponemal diseases (treponematoses) have a common ancestor, a free-living saprophytic treponeme. The free-living organism came to be carried commensally by man as are the dental treponemes today. Disease syndromes then developed as natural selection favoured the survival of mutants most likely to produce the lesions best suited to transmission from host to host in the prevailing environment [5].

According to this theory, pinta was the first treponematosis to evolve within the Afro-Asian land mass, from where it gained world-wide distribution, finally persisting among the underprivileged people in the remoter areas of the Central Americas and the Northern part of the South American continent.

Yaws evolved from pinta as a humid warm environment developed in Afro-Asia: the local moisture from sweating favoured the production

*The name syphilis was not generally used until about 1850, some three centuries after Frascatorius of Verona wrote his famous poem 'Syphilis sive Morbus Gallicus'. This poem tells of one 'Syphilus' a shepherd who was afflicted first by the disease because he had uttered blasphemy against the sun (Glendening, G L (1942) *Source Book of Medical History*, Hoebner, London, pages 120–121).

of exuberant skin lesions containing vast numbers of treponemes characteristic of yaws. The absence of clothes and person-to-person contact of sweaty skins in a topical environment facilitated its spread amongst primitive communities making it a disease predominantly of childhood.

Endemic syphilis (called bejel in the Middle East) probably evolved in a warm dry climate with colder nights: the wearing of clothes would prevent skin-to-skin transmission and only organisms producing lesions of the mucous membranes could survive, presumably due to transfer by kissing and sharing of eating and drinking utensils. Infection would tend to occur before puberty and sexual spread would be rarely noted.

Venereal syphilis develops from endemic syphilis as social advance limits transmission between children; as the children grow up they become susceptible to the infection as a result of sexual transmission. Endemic syphilis was probably widespread in Europe prior to the 15th century.

This theory is attractive since there are overwhelming similarities in the treponematoses. In fact, it has been suggested that there is really only a single disease (*treponematosis*) of which the variants are determined by differences in climate and domestic environment. The organisms are considered to be indistinguishable bacteriologically and all produce similar antibody response: using certain strains of treponemes there may be subtle differences in the symptoms produced experimentally in rabbits and hamsters [6].

Whichever theory is favoured it is fact that an epidemic of syphilis swept through Europe in the late fifteenth and early sixteenth centuries. By the eighteenth century it was widely known that syphilis and gonorrhoea were transmitted by sexual intercourse but they had not been recognised as separate entities: many thought that gonorrhoea was the early symptom of syphilis. In 1797 this view gained apparent scientific credibility from the famous experiment in which John Hunter was alleged to have inoculated himself with gonococcal pus. The patient from whom the pus was obtained had syphilis as well as gonorrhoea and the allegation was made that Hunter developed both diseases. This story, hallowed by repetition, is probably untrue although the experiments were probably carried out on another individual [7]. In 1793, Benjamin Bell in Edinburgh maintained the view that syphilis and gonorrhoea were different diseases. This view was later confirmed in 1837 by Philip Ricord of France who is usually credited with the separation of gonorrhoea and syphilis: the causal organisms were finally identified in 1879 (Albert Neisser) and 1905 (Schaudinn and Hoffmann) respectively.

Transmission of infection

SEXUAL

T. pallidum is so feebly viable outwith its host that syphilis is ordinarily acquired by sexual intercourse. The organism has little intrinsic invasiveness and usually gains entry to its new host through minute abrasions in the epithelial surfaces which come into contact with the moist mucocutaneous lesions of an infected partner. An infected person usually ceases to be sexually infectious 2–4 years after acquiring the disease. Some individuals appear resistant to infection since not everyone exposed to early syphilis acquires the disease.

ACCIDENTAL

Acquisition by means other than sexual intercourse usually involves direct contact. In such cases the organisms may gain entry through a small skin abrasion. Accidental inoculation has occurred under the following circumstances: in doctors and nurses who have examined a syphilitic lesion without wearing gloves; in laboratory workers by needle prick when inoculating pathogenic *T. pallidum* into rabbits or when handling large numbers of treponemes during isolation and purification procedures; in patients being transfused with blood from a donor suffering from early syphilis. The risk of accidental infection by infected blood is highest when fresh blood is used. In usual practice when infected blood is stored at 5°C in citrate anticoagulant, infectivity is lost in 96 hours or less. Treponemes are not viable after storage for a few days to a few weeks at –10°C to –20°C. Treponemes are, however, viable when stored for extended periods at –45°C and infectious for an indefinite period when stored at –78°C. Freezing followed by desiccation kills the organism [8].

CONGENITAL

Although it had previously been considered that *T. pallidum* was not transmitted to the fetus before the fourth month of gestation, possibly through the protective effect of the cytotrophoblastic (Langhan's) layer, recent studies have clearly demonstrated that infection of the fetus can occur before the tenth week [9]. A woman can transmit syphilis to her fetus long after she has ceased to be sexually infective, although the longer she has had syphilis the less likely this is to occur; transmission to the fetus is almost inevitable in the early stage.

NON-VENEREAL

Endemic treponematosis is transmitted by direct or indirect non-venereal contact in early childhood, e.g., in playing, in sharing eating or drinking utensils and in close skin contact. It usually occurs in communities living in overcrowded and unhygienic conditions. Once common in parts of Europe, e.g., Yugoslavia, it is seen mainly in Africa as yaws, and in the Middle East as bejel and in certain parts of Central and South America as pinta (Chapter 9). There is no certain evidence of transmission from an infected mother to the fetus *in utero*.

Course of untreated syphilis

The natural course of infection may span many decades and present a variety of clinical forms. The classification shown in Figure 3.1 represents the main stages of the disease.

ACQUIRED INFECTION

Clinical features are dealt with in detail in the following chapters but the infection, if untreated, may run courses outlined diagrammatically in Figure 3.2.

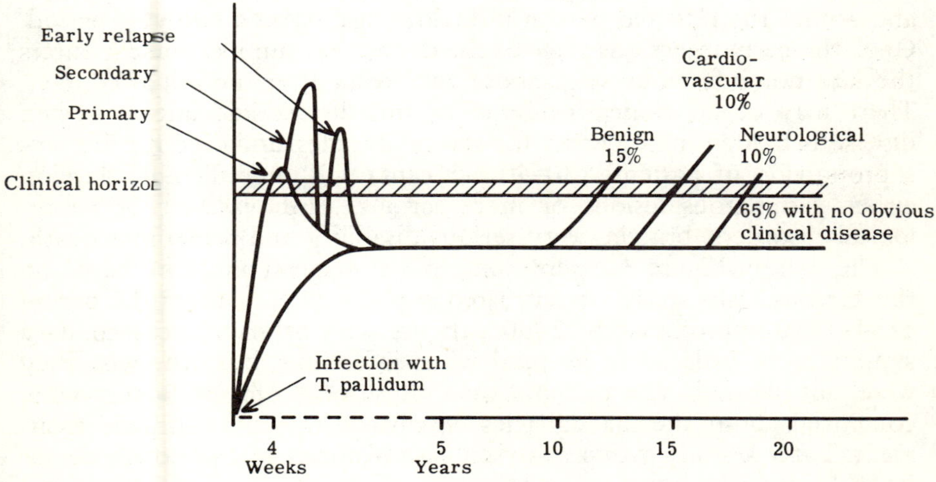

Figure 3.2 Progress of untreated syphilis (percentage of effects will vary). (Modified from Kampmeier, R H (1964) *The Medical Clinics of North America*, **48**, 667).

The clinical horizon in this figure separates the stages when clinical features are absent from those when these are present. The period before the disease shows itself (prepatent or incubation period) is usually about 25 days (range 9–90 days). The primary lesion or chancre (page 94) tends to appear at the site of entry of treponemes. Owing to local multiplication of the organism, treponemes are present in the fluid that can be expressed from the depth of the chancre. The time taken for a chancre to appear depends to some extent on the number of treponemes in the initial inoculum. In men the chancre is usually penile and noticeable, but in women a chancre on the cervix uteri could pass unnoticed in the same way as anal chancres in homosexual men. Chancres in other sites occur uncommonly (less than one per cent). These primary lesions are painless and tend to heal spontaneously in three to eight weeks, falsely reassuring the individual that all is well.

If the disease is not detected and treated in the primary stage, it progresses to the secondary stage, usually six to twelve weeks after contact but occasionally this process may take up to 12 months. Secondary syphilis, characterized by a variety of macular, papular, papulosquamous, and other skin lesions, results from the generalized spread and multiplication of *T. pallidum* throughout the body; the treponemes may be carried to virtually every organ and tissue.

After the primary or secondary stage and probably also *ab initio* the infection becomes latent but mucocutaneous relapses may recur and render the infected person infectious again over a two-year period. Once the early infectious stage of the disease has run its course it enters the late non-infectious stage about two years after the initial contact. There may be no clinical evidence of this disease and latency, when disease is hidden, may persist for several decades, and even for life, but a proportion of patients (30–40 per cent) will unpredictably develop either gummatous lesions or more serious, cardiovascular or neurological disorders, bringing very serious disability and sometimes death.

The data in Figure 3.2 pertaining to late stage syphilis are based on the famous Oslo study of untreated syphilis [10]. During the period 1891–1910 approximately 2000 patients with primary and secondary syphilis were isolated in hospital when infectious, but otherwise they were not treated. The patients were those of Professor Boeck, who, convinced about the inadequacies of current therapy, withheld treatment. Later a study group analysed case histories of 1404 of Professor Boeck's original admissions to hospital.

As shown in Figure 3.2 infection may not run the typical course and remains below the clinical horizon. Patients are diagnosed with latent infection who are completely unaware of having experienced primary or secondary symptoms. Symptoms are often suppressed during pregnancy. Antibiotics prescribed for other conditions may abort or delay early stage infection, minimizing or abolishing early symptoms.

CONGENITAL INFECTION (CHAPTER 8)

In congenital syphilis resulting from blood-borne infection of the fetus via the placenta there is no stage analogous to primary acquired syphilis. Congenital infection is divided clinically into the early stage, the late stage and the late latent stage with or without stigmata: the division between early and late stage is an arbitrary one.

Early stage pertains to the first two years of life and produces infectious lesions similar to those in the secondary stage of acquired syphilis. Lesions of late-stage congenital infection generally occur from two to three years of age and include gummata identical with those of benign tertiary acquired syphilis. The stigmata are scars and deformities of early or late lesions which are no longer active: these include the saddle-shaped nose, interstitial keratitis, Hutchinson's teeth and eighth nerve deafness.

Epidemiology

Syphilis has a world-wide distribution, but, as in the case of gonorrhoea, it is difficult to compare the incidence rates of the disease from one country to another due to marked variations in reporting.

Figure 3.3 shows the incidence of syphilis in England and Wales during the period 1945 to 1975. The incidence fell sharply in the first four years after the war, and has remained fairly constant in recent years in contrast to the rise in cases of gonorrhoea. In the United States of America the situation is much different; after the post-war fall the incidence has been slowly rising since the late 1950's. In 1974 the incidence of early syphilis in the United Kingdom was 3.5 per 100,000 population compared with 11.9 reported cases per 100,000 in the USA [11]. Although the control of syphilis may be attributable to better facilities for diagnosis, treatment and contact-tracing, since the incidence of the disease had been falling since the mid-1800's, it is more likely that improving socio-economic factors have played the major role. In recent times the widespread use of antibiotics in Britain is likely to have reduced the spread. During times of stress, e.g. war, the incidence rises, although in those whose sexual behaviour is very promiscuous, e.g. many male homosexuals, the incidence is high.

Figures 1.6 and 1.7 show the reduction of mortality rates for neuro-

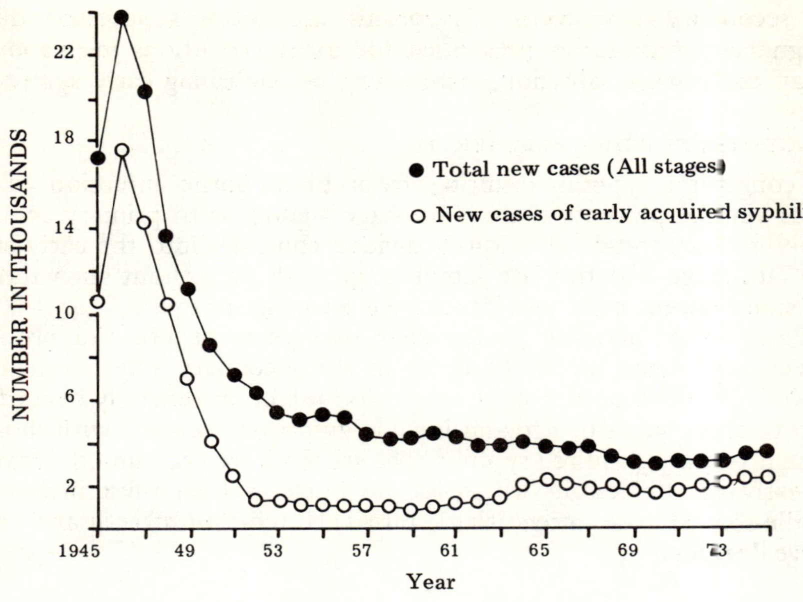

Figure 3.3 Syphilis in England and Wales (1945–75 inclusive).

syphilis and cardiovascular syphilis respectively since the 1930's. These stages of late syphilis are now seldom seen in the United Kingdom.

The marked reduction in infant mortality from congenital syphilis is shown in Figure 1.5. This remarkable achievement has resulted from improved socio-economic conditions, better antenatal care including routine screening of the serum of pregnant women for syphilis, and particularly treatment of infected persons with penicillin. In developed countries, congenital syphilis should not occur, but occasionally an infected woman does not seek medical advice, for a variety of reasons, until very late in pregnancy.

In this country, early syphilis is a disease of young adults, most infections occurring between the ages of 20 and 24 years. More males are infected than females, e.g. the sex ratio in 1975 being about 3:1.

It has become apparent in the past years that the proportion of infections acquired by homosexual contact has increased. For example, in Edinburgh in 1976, 21 of 30 cases of early syphilis (70 per cent) had been acquired by homosexual activity. As a considerable number of males with syphilis are bisexual, females may also be involved in an outbreak of the disease in a community.

Syphilis is still prevalent in many parts of the world, and with modern transport, infections can be spread rapidly. Seafarers and other travellers, associating with prostitutes in less-developed countries, still contribute to the number of cases recorded in the United Kingdom.

REFERENCES

1 Thorburn, A L (1971) *British Journal of Venereal Disease,* **47,** 459
2 Jones, R H, Finn, M A, Thomas, J J and Polger, C (1976) *British Journal of Venereal Disease,* **52,** 18
3 Foster, J W, Kellogg, D S, Clark, J W and Balows, A (1977) *British Journal of Venereal Disease* **53,** 338
4 Hackett, C J (1963) *Bulletin of the World Health Organisation,* **29,** 7
5 Willcox, R R (1974) *British Journal of Venereal Disease,* **50,** 169
6 Kiraly, K (1973) WHO VDT/RES Document 73, 169
7 Dempster, W J (1978) *Lancet,* **i,** 316
8 Chambers, R W, Foley, H T and Schmidt, P J (1969) *Transfusion,* **9,** 32
9 Harter, C A and Benirschke, K (1976) *American Journal of Obstetrics and Gynecology,* **24,** 705
10 Gjestland, T (1955) *Acta dermato venereologica,* Stockholm, **35,** Supplement 34
11 Annual Report of the Chief Medical Officer at the Department of Health and Social Security for the year 1974 (1976) *British Journal of Venereal Disease,* **52,** 351

CHAPTER 4

Diagnosis of Syphilis

In syphilis the social and medical implications are so serious that a clinical diagnosis must be confirmed in the laboratory either by:

(1) demonstrating antibodies in the serum and/or

(2) finding *Treponema pallidum* in the exudate obtained from the depth of early lesions.

During treponemal infection, whether in syphilis or in the endemic treponemal diseases such as yaws or pinta, a variety of antibodies are produced. In Figure 4.1 these are classified into non-specific anti-treponemal antibodies and antibodies specific for pathogenic treponemes: tests currently used to detect the different antibodies, and

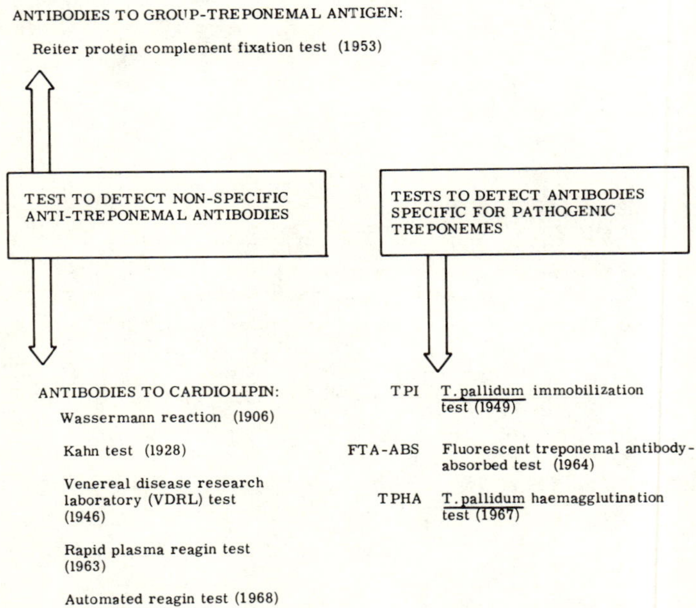

Figure 4.1 Tests to detect antibodies produced during treponemal infection. The year of introduction of each test is given.

their year of introduction, are also shown. In the following section these tests and their history are outlined and discussed as a background to a rational approach to syphilis serology.

Serological tests

A. TESTS TO DETECT NON-SPECIFIC TREPONEMAL ANTIBODIES

Cardiolipin antigen tests

These tests are suitable for routine screening and usually become positive 10 to 14 days after the appearance of the chancre, the titre gradually increasing. The titre tends to diminish and the test tends to become negative after treatment. In late or latent syphilis the cardiolipin antigen tests are often negative.

1. *Wassermann reaction (WR)*

The complement fixation test introduced by Wassermann in 1906 was the first serological test for the diagnosis of syphilis: the historical background to this work can be found in a brief biography of August von Wassermann [1]. The antigen in the original WR consisted of a saline extract of syphilitic tissues obtained from still-born fetuses with congenital infection. It was assumed that *T. pallidum* present in the infected tissue was responsible for the positive reactions obtained in patients with syphilis. Later it was shown that the same results were obtained with an alcoholic extract of heart muscle. In 1941 the diphospholipid cardiolipin was identified as the active component in beef heart extract [2] and this led to new chemically defined lipoidal antigens being produced in the form of pure cardiolipin supplemented with lecithin and cholesterol. In laboratories where the WR is still performed a chemically pure cardiolipin antigen is used and the test is referred to as the cardiolipin Wassermann reaction (CWR).

Complement fixation depends on the ability of antibody to fix complement in the presence of its specific antigen. Fixation of complement is detected by an indicator system comprising sheep erythrocytes coated with anti-sheep cell antibody: in the presence of complement the erythrocytes lyse. In the CWR patient's serum, previously heated at 56°C for 30 minutes to destroy its own complement, is mixed with cardiolipin antigen in the presence of a predetermined quantity of complement. If the patient's serum contains anticardiolipin antibody, complement is used up when this combines with the antigen, and, on adding the sensitized erythrocytes, no lysis takes place. A positive reaction is therefore indicated by no lysis whereas in the absence of antibody, complement is not fixed and a negative reaction is indicated by haemolysis. The test must be strictly controlled, is fairly time-consuming and requires skilled personnel. A control tube without antigen must be set up for each serum tested. Occasionally sera are found which inactivate complement in the absence of antigen. Such a serum is referred to as anti-complementary and the test is invalid and must be either repeated with another specimen of blood or, preferably, an alternative cardiolipin test used.

Flocculation tests can be used in place of complement fixation to detect anti-cardiolipin antibody.

2. *Kahn test*

Flocculation tests are simpler and more rapid to perform than complement fixation. The patient's serum is mixed with antigen and shaken vigorously. Positive sera form large floccules, i.e. visible aggregates of antibody–antigen complexes in suspension. In the Kahn [3] test, which is mainly of historical interest and rarely used nowadays, the reaction is carried out in a tube and flocculation assessed macroscopically.

3. *Venereal Disease Research Laboratory (VDRL) test*

Because it is easy to standardize, simple and reproducible, the VDRL slide test [4], introduced in 1946, is the preferred cardiolipin antigen test in most laboratories.

The test is usually performed as a slide test in which the patient's serum, previously heated to inactivate complement, is mixed with a freshly prepared suspension of cardiolipin-lecithin-cholesterol antigen on a glass slide. The mixture is rotated, usually mechanically, and after a few minutes flocculation is detected microscopically using a low power objective. Quantitative tests with serial dilutions of patient's serum are easily carried out.

The VDRL test is versatile and can be modified for testing unheated serum or plasma either by automated or manual techniques.

4. *Rapid plasma reagin (RPR) test*

VDRL test antigen suspended in choline chloride can be used to test plasma or unheated serum. By adding a chelating agent to remove metallic impurities the antigen remains stable for up to 6 months when stored at 4°–10°C. In the RPR test [5] finely divided carbon particles are added to the above antigen: results can be read with the naked eye instead of microscopically. The test can be performed with disposable equipment and plastic cards marked in circular areas. This makes the RPR test particularly suitable for use in field studies in developing countries. Unfortunately, the reagents are more expensive than simple VDRL slide test antigen.

5. *Automated reagin* test (ART)*

This test [6] uses the same antigen as the RPR test. Unheated serum or plasma are sampled automatically using Auto-Analyser equipment and passed through mixing and settling coils. The resultant mixture is deposited on a moving strip of filter paper. Positive reactions show clumping of the carbon particles while negative sera give a uniform grey suspension. The ART is particularly useful in laboratories serving blood transfusion centres.

There are other cardiolipin antigens, e.g. in Price's precipitation reaction, but these are rarely used nowadays.

Cardiolipin is widespread in nature and can be isolated from many mammalian tissues: it is a component of the inner membrane of the mammalian mitochondrion which accounts for the success of beef heart, which is rich in mitochondria, as a source of antigen. Historically the type of antibody reacting in the Wassermann reaction was termed reagin at a time when little was known of the nature of the reactions involved. The antibody is now generally considered to be directed against cardiolipin present in treponemes, i.e. it is antibody against a non-specific antigen shared by treponemes and mammalian tissues. Previously, it was considered that these antibodies were produced against host tissue cardiolipin released during treponemal infection.

Due to the widespread nature of cardiolipin, antibodies reacting with it are occasionally found in the sera of healthy individuals (less than 1 per cent of the population) or patients without any clinical evidence of syphilis. These reactions are termed Biological False Positive (BFP). BFP reactions are classified as acute if they disappear spontaneously within 6 months and chronic if they persist longer (page 90). Acute BFP reactions are usually associated with acute febrile infectious diseases while chronic BFP reactors show a high incidence of auto-immune and related disorders. Other tests are required to distinguish between positive cardiolipin antigen tests resulting from BFP reactions and those resulting from treponemal infection.

B. TEST TO DETECT GROUP-SPECIFIC TREPONEMAL ANTIBODIES

Reiter's protein complement fixation (RPCF) test

The antigen used in this test [7] is a protein extract produced by dis-

*Reagin is an obsolete and confusing term and should no longer be used: unfortunately the term was used in naming certain currently used tests and reagin tests are widely referred to in the literature and in clinical practice. The preferred terms are cardiolipin antigen, or lipoidal antigen tests.

ruption of Reiter treponemes*: the Reiter treponeme shares a common group specific antigen with both pathogenic and commensal treponemes. Although false-positive reactions occur with the RPCF test, the antibody detected by the RPCF test is distinct from that detected by cardiolipin antigen tests and differs from that causing false-positive reactions with the latter tests. The RPCF test can be used for screening purposes and a positive reaction in both this test and a cardiolipin test is strongly suggestive of treponemal infection. Unfortunately, the RPCF test is often negative in cases of late syphilis.

C. TESTS TO DETECT ANTIBODIES SPECIFIC FOR PATHOGENIC TREPONEMES

The antigen used in these tests is derived from Nichols strain of *T. pallidum.* This strain, isolated in 1913 from the cerebrospinal fluid of a patient with neurosyphilis, is still virulent for man and is maintained in rabbits by intratesticular inoculation and weekly passage. Tests using pathogenic *T. pallidum* as antigen tend to remain positive following treatment. These tests have been used as verification tests to confirm the treponemal nature of a positive cardiolipin antigen test.

1. *The* T. pallidum *immobilization (TPI) test*

In this test [8] live treponemes are incubated with heat-inactivated serum in the presence of complement and the number of organisms immobilized is determined by dark-ground microscopy; if 50 per cent or more treponemes are immobilized the result of the test is positive. The antibody detected by the TPI test is slow to develop and the test is often negative in untreated primary syphilis but usually positive in all other stages of the disease.

Following its introduction in 1949, the TPI test served for many years as the only reliable verification test for treponemal infection available to the clinician. The test, which is complicated, technically difficult to perform, expensive in animals and reagents, was restricted to a few reference laboratories. The development of microtechniques facilitated the introduction of new specific tests using immunofluorescence of haemagglutination techniques for the detection of antibody. The TPI test is rarely used now. The specificity of the TPI test has been accepted as absolute although it may rarely give false-positive results.

*The Reiter treponeme is reputed to be an adapted strain of *T. pallidum* isolated from a patient in 1920 at the Kaiser Wilhelm Institute in Berlin. It can be grown in relatively simple media, is avirulent for man and is considered by many authorities not to be *T. pallidum* (Wallace, AL and Harris, A (1967) *Bulletin of the World Health Organisation,* **360,** Supplement No. 2.)

2. *The fluorescent treponemal antibody absorbed (FTA-ABS) test*

In the FTA-ABS test [9] the patient's serum is absorbed with a sonicate of Reiter's treponemes in order to remove group-specific antibody. Binding to *T. pallidum* of antibody specific for pathogenic treponemes is then demonstrated by the indirect immunofluorescence technique*. The FTA-ABS test is an accepted reference test and is highly specific and sensitive at all stages of syphilitic infection although a small percentage of false-positive reactions occur.

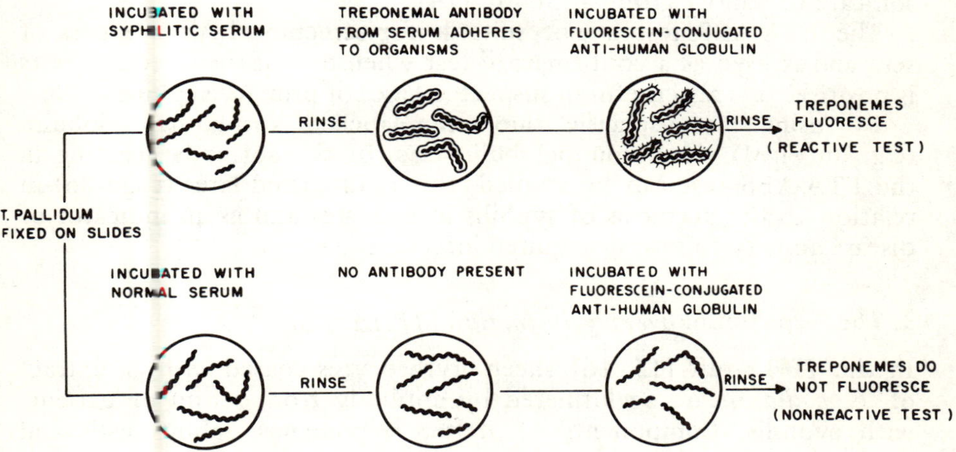

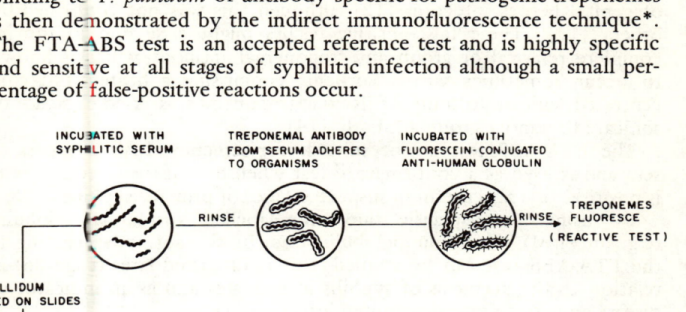

Figure 4.2 Diagram of the mechanism of the FTA-ABS test (from Newman, R B (1974) CRC *Critical Reviews in Clinical Laboratory Sciences*, 5, 1.)

False-positive results have been reported in patients with systemic lupus erythematosus and other connective tissue diseases [10]. These false-positive results can be differentiated from positive FTA–ABS tests due to treponemal infection since the sera from patients with collagen disorders also give fluorescence with *Trypanosoma cruzi* and *Toxoplasma gondii* - absence of fluorescence with organisms pre-treated with deoxyribonuclease demonstrates that cross-reaction is probably due to anti-DNA antibodies in patients with collagen disease [11].

*The indirect immunofluorescence technique is carried out in two stages. In the first stage a mear of *T. pallidum* is incubated with patient's serum: any anti-treponemal antibody in the patient's serum reacts with the treponemes on the slide. In the second stage fluorescein-labelled anti-human immunoglobulin is added to reveal any antibody which bound in the first stage. Treponemes are located by dark-ground microscopy and then examined by ultra-violet illumination. If the serum is positive the treponemes give bright apple-green fluorescence.

Excessive growth of commensal treponemes in the oral lesions of patients with ulcerative stomatitis produces high levels of group anti-treponemal antibody which may give a false-positive FTA-ABS test. Recently, transitory false-positive results were reported in some cases of genital herpes infection [12] although this was not confirmed by others [13]. These false-positive results might arise due to the incomplete removal of group anti-treponemal antibody which is known to occur sometimes when 'Sorbent' comprising a heated and concentrated culture filtrate of Reiter treponemes is used instead of sonicate to remove group antibody [14].

The FTA-ABS test is not suitable for screening large numbers of sera and is used as a confirmatory test when one of the screening tests is positive. It is also useful in suspected cases of primary syphilis.

By using mono-specific fluorescein-labelled anti-human globulin (e.g. anti-IgM) the immunoglobulin class of the antibody reacting in the FTA-ABS test can be studied; this is discussed later (page 86) in relation to the diagnosis of syphilis in neonates and as an indicator of disease activity following acquired infection.

3. *The* T. pallidum *haemagglutination (TPHA) test*

In the TPHA test [15, 16] sheep erythrocytes coated with an extract of *T. pallidum* are agglutinated by antibody from serum of patients with syphilis. Components of Reiter treponemes, rabbit testis and erythrocyte membranes are used to absorb test sera in order to eliminate haemagglutination due to antibody against any of these agents. Any serum giving a positive reaction is tested against control erythrocytes (i.e. not coated with *T. pallidum* antigen) to check the specificity of the agglutination. In spite of the absorption procedure about 0.1 per cent of specimens agglutinate erythrocytes in the absence of antigen: this non-specific agglutination makes the individual test result invalid. The use of fowl erythrocytes in the TPHA test [17] may decrease the number of non-specific agglutination reactions.

The TPHA test is simple to perform and as reagents based on sheep and fowl† erythrocytes are available commercially, it has become the first of the specific tests suitable for routine screening: because of the expense of reagents, tests are normally carried out by a micro-method [18]. It is often negative in untreated primary syphilis but otherwise has a sensitivity and specificity comparable with the FTA-ABS test.

*Fujizoki Pharmaceutical Company, Tokyo, Japan.
†Don Whitley Scientific, 4 Wellington Crescent, Shipley, West Yorkshire, England.
†Wellcome Reagents Ltd, 303 Hither Green Lane, Hither Green, London.

Occasionally false-positive haemagglutination may result from heterophil antibody in the serum of patients with infectious mononucleosis; this only occurs if the control cells fail to agglutinate, otherwise a non-specific agglutination reaction would be recorded. In certain tropical countries a small percentage of BFP reactors have given apparent false-positive results: these positive results, due to the sensitivity of the TPHA test, could represent the residue of previous infection by endemic treponematosis [19].

4. *Enzyme-linked immunosorbent assay (ELISA)*

ELISA is a relatively simple and new serological technique. Patient's serum is allowed to react with antigen coated on the inside surface of small plastic tubes or wells in a micro-haemagglutination plate. Specific antibodies binding to the antigen are then quantitated by means of anti-immunoglobulin conjugated to an enzyme, e.g. alkaline phosphatase. The enzyme remaining in the tube after washing provides a measure of the amount of specific antibody in the serum: the bound enzyme is detected by the addition of p-nitrophenyl phosphate. The reaction product (p-nitrophenolate) possesses a yellow colour which is measured spectrophotometrically at a wavelength of 400nm. This is an advantage over the FTA-ABS test in which the reading of the test is subjective.

Veldkamp and Visser [20] using an ultrasonicate of *T. pallidum* as antigen concluded that ELISA was simple, reliable, and relatively quick and that its sensitivity in all stages of syphilis was equal to that of the FTA-ABS test. ELISA has the potential for mechanization of all stages; for large scale application alkaline phosphatase can be replaced by peroxidase. The technique requires further investigation as a first-line screening procedure for syphilis. Among other factors, the widespread adoption of the technique will depend on commercial availability of suitable antigen.

2. Microscopy

DEMONSTRATION OF T. PALLIDUM IN THE PRIMARY OR SECONDARY LESIONS

1. *Dark-ground microscopy*

After cleansing the surfaces of the primary or secondary lesions with a swab soaked in physiological saline, serum is obtained from the depth of the lesion as described (page 53), and examined by dark-ground microscopy using the oil-immersion objective. *T. pallidum* is recognized by its slender structure, characteristic slow movements and angulation.

It must be carefully distinguished from the many other treponemes that may occur in genital ulcers (e.g. *T. calligyrum*) but these tend to be surface organisms and are not found in the depth of lesions. If the initial test is negative the procedure should be repeated daily for at least three days: antibiotics should be withheld during this period although sulphadimidine in an oral dose of 1g. 6-hourly and local saline lavage may be used to reduce local sepsis. Many commensal treponemes occur in the mouth and therefore dark-ground illumination is not suitable for examining oral lesions. Organisms are not easily found in skin lesions of secondary syphilis except those in moist skin areas.

Identification of *T. pallidum* requires a microscope with dark-ground illumination and an experienced observer. In circumstances in which there is a lack of experience in dark-ground investigation of lesions, recently introduced fluorescent techniques may prove useful.

2. *Fluorescence microscopy*

A smear of the material to be tested is made on a glass slide, fixed and sent to the laboratory. In remote areas the specimen can be posted. On receipt in the laboratory the smear is stained with fluorescein-labelled antibody specific for *T. pallidum* and examined by fluorescence microscopy. Although the technique requires further study it has obvious advantages and would be the method of choice in examining suspected oral or rectal lesions, which may harbour commensal treponemes [21].

Rationale of serological screening and clinical interpretation of test results

The demand for serological tests parallels the recent overall increase in STD and far exceeds the present incidence of the disease. Since syphilis can be acquired concomitantly with any other STD all patients attending the clinic should be screened to exclude syphilis. As syphilis may mimic a variety of dermatological, medical and surgical conditions serological tests are of value in excluding this disease. Serological screening of all antenatal patients and blood donors is carried out to prevent congenital and transfusion-acquired infection respectively (page 66).

The large numbers of specimens to examine and the long duration of the infection dictate that a suitable serological tests should be: sensitive at all stages of infection; specific for syphilis and not react with sera from patients with other conditions, reproducible, simple and rapid to perform and preferably inexpensive. Unfortunately no single serological test meets these requirements and as outlined in Figure 4.1, many tests have been developed over the years. The efficiency of some of these tests in detecting all stages of untreated syphilis is shown in Figure 4.3: the tests are divided into accepted screening and verification tests; the TPHA test is placed intermediate between these two groups as its role is not yet universally accepted.

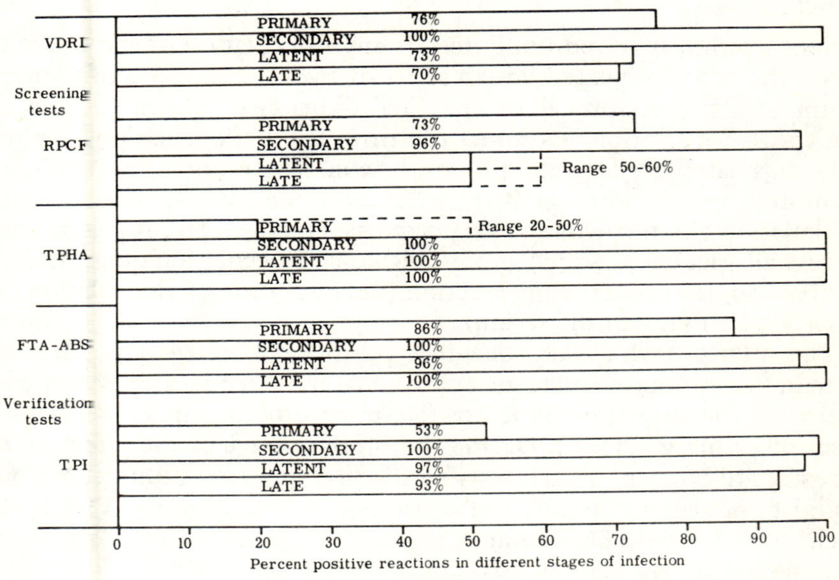

Figure 4.3 Comparative sensitivity of serological tests in different stages of untreated acquired syphilis.

SCREENING WITH A COMBINATION OF VDRL AND TPHA TESTS

This is the screening schedule favoured by the authors [18, 22]. Any of the cardiolipin antigen tests can be used for routine screening and all behave in a similar manner with respect to stage of infection, effect of treatment etc. Because it is easy to standardize, simple and reproducible, the VDRL test is the preferred cardiolipin antigen test in most laboratories. It is clear from Figure 4.3 that the traditional verification tests which detect antibodies against pathogenic treponemes are more efficient in the diagnosis of late and latent syphilis whether treated or untreated. It was not possible to introduce such a test into a screening schedule until the introduction of the TPHA in 1967.

When used together, the VDRL and TPHA tests provide a highly efficient screen for the detection or exclusion of treponemal infection; their activity is complementary, both are simple to perform and can be readily quantitated. The VDRL test is more sensitive than the TPHA in the detection of very early syphilis while the TPHA is more sensitive than the VDRL in the detection of latent and late infection [18, 22].

THE VDRL TEST

Patient's serum is tested undiluted. If any flocculation of the antigen is noted the test is repeated with a series of twofold dilutions of patient's serum and the reciprocal of the final dilution of serum causing unequivocal flocculation is termed the titre, e.g. if flocculation occurred only with undiluted serum the result would be reported as 'Positive—undiluted serum' whereas if 1 in 16 was the last dilution showing flocculation the test would be reported as 'Positive—16'. It is important to test all specimens showing any degree of flocculation quantitatively in order to detect a prozone reaction (i.e. inhibition of flocculation due to excess antibody in the serum).

The VDRL test usually becomes positive 10 to 14 days after the appearance of the chancre or approximately three to five weeks after acquiring the infection. It is positive in approximately 75 per cent of cases of primary syphilis. During the primary stage of the infection the titre rises to 8 or 16. VDRL tests with a titre of 16 to 128 are commonly found in secondary syphilis. After the secondary stage the VDRL titre declines and eventually becomes negative in approximately 30 per cent of untreated latent and late cases.

VDRL TEST IN EVALUATION OF TREATMENT

All cardiolipin antigen tests tend to become negative after treatment particularly in early syphilis. Serial quantitative tests should be carried out for up to two years following treatment for early acquired syphilis and for up to five years in late stage infection. In interpreting a fall or rise in titre in early-stage syphilis a fourfold change is considered significant but a twofold change is not. Fluctuating antibody levels are sometimes found in treated late and congenital syphilis. These do not necessarily indicate a need for further treatment.

THE TPHA TEST

Patient's serum is screened at a final dilution of 1 in 80: if any haemagglutination is noted the test is repeated with a series of twofold dilutions from 1 in 80 to 1 in 5120. The reciprocal of the final serum dilution resulting in marked haemagglutination is termed the titre. TPHA titres are reported as Positive–80, Positive–160, etc. Each specimen is also tested against control cells (no antigen) at a serum dilution of 1 in 80: if the control cells agglutinate the serum is reported as 'non-specific agglutination – test invalid'.

The TPHA is usually negative in early primary syphilis but may become positive at low titre (80 to 320) towards the end of the primary stage. The TPHA titre may give some indication of the duration of the infection. Titres rise sharply during the secondary stage and commonly reach 5120 or greater. The TPHA titre declines during the latent stage but invariably remains positive at low titre (80 to 640).

The only stage of syphilis likely to escape detection by screening with a combination of VDRL and TPHA tests is early primary syphilis, although repeated tests over a 3-month period will detect such an infection. Most such cases of sero-negative primary syphilis should be detected by a careful clinical examination and dark-ground investigation. Since the FTA-ABS is normally the first test to become positive following infection it is a useful aid in the diagnosis of primary syphilis. Although it cannot be applied to all specimens the test can be carried out and should be requested in cases of suspected primary syphilis.

The FTA-ABS test should be used as a verification test in the case of specimens showing reactivity in the VDRL and/or TPHA tests during screening. When such a system is employed the pattern of results obtained (Table 4.1) may give valuable information as to the stage of

Table 4.1 Pattern of results of serological tests in different stages of acquired syphilis

(In endemic treponemal diseases, such as yaws, bejel or pinta, patterns are similar to syphilis)

VDRL	*TPHA*	*FTA-ABS*	*Likely diagnosis*
+	–	–	False-positive reaction. Repeat to exclude primary.
+	–	+	Primary. Dark-field investigation of lesion may be positive.
+	+	+	Untreated (or recently treated). Probably beyond primary stage.
–	+	+	Treated or partially treated at any stage. Untreated latent or late.
–	+	–	History of treated syphilis.

+ = positive – = negative

infection. This figure is only a guide: each case must be interpreted individually in the light of available clinical and epidemiological data.

Patterns of serological results

BIOLOGICAL FALSE-POSITIVE REACTION

Sera positive only in the VDRL test are most likely to be biological false-positive reactions. A further specimen of blood should be taken and the test repeated to exclude technical error or an atypical primary pattern. In screening for early syphilis tests should be repeated over a period of at least three months. If the VDRL test remains the only test positive for longer than six months then investigations should be instigated to exclude the various conditions often associated with a chronic biological false-positive reaction (page 90).

PRIMARY SYPHILIS

A typical pattern of primary syphilis is VDRL and FTA-ABS positive but TPHA negative. Very early in the infection the FTA-ABS may be the only test positive while towards the end of the primary stage the TPHA may be positive at low titre. Dark-ground examination of serum obtained from the depth of mucocutaneous lesions may also be positive at this stage.

SECONDARY SYPHILIS

When quantitative VDRL and TPHA tests are positive to high titre and the FTA-ABS is also positive the most likely diagnosis is secondary syphilis or early latent syphilis. The same pattern of results can be obtained in late syphilis or in recently treated secondary syphilis so it is clear that interpretation of syphilis serology is dependent on the history and clinical findings.

LATE-STAGE SYPHILIS

When quantitative VDRL and TPHA tests are positive regularly over a period of time at low titre in patients without signs then the infection is likely to be beyond the early latent stage and may have been modified by coincidental curative or subcurative antibiotic treatment. In patients with clinical signs of late syphilis the titres may be higher but they are not invariably so. In those with gummatous lesions titres are high.

In many cases of treated or partially treated syphilis and in approximately 30 per cent of cases of untreated latent and late symptomatic syphilis or other treponematoses such as yaws, bejel or pinta the VDRL test is negative. The TPHA and FTA-ABS tests invariably remain positive in such cases. Although the TPHA test is often negative in untreated primary syphilis the test may become positive at low titre following treatment.

When the TPHA is the only positive test it is usually of low titre and a history of syphilis, treated as many as 20 to 40 years previously, may be obtained. Sometimes there is merely a hint of some half-forgotten incident.

CONGENITAL SYPHILIS

Early-stage congenital syphilis is a rarity in the United Kingdom and there are few up-to-date serological data available. The use of the FTA-IgM test in the diagnosis of early-stage congenital syphilis is discussed in the following section. In late-stage infection, either treated or untreated, test results tend to fluctuate over a period of months or years. The VDRL test often remains positive at low titre in association with a low TPHA titre and positive FTA-ABS test.

DIFFERENTIATION OF TREATED, PARTIALLY TREATED OR UNTREATED SYPHILIS

The TPHA test remains positive for life even in those who have been fully treated with adequate doses of penicillin. In such cases, the detection of a positive TPHA, perhaps later in life, is not an indication for further treatment and investigation, provided the patient has been adequately treated in the past and provided he has not been at risk since. The TPHA test presents the clinician with the problem of differentiating between treated and untreated or partially treated infection. However, the reliable detection of latent and late syphilis by the TPHA test is very important since, if untreated, a proportion of these patients will unpredictably develop the clinical manifestations of late infection. The widespread use of antibiotics for many other conditions, often trivial, has produced a situation where untreated infections are now a rarity. The clinical and pathological features of partially treated or suppressed infection require further study and screening by the TPHA test is of value in this respect.

The detection of anti-treponemal antibody of the IgM class with mono-specific fluorescein-labelled anti-human immunoglobulin in the FTA-ABS test has been investigated as an aid in assessing 'activity' of the disease and as an indicator for prescribing anti-treponeme treatment.

FTA-IgM test in early-stage syphilis

IgM anti-treponemal antibody is consistently present in untreated primary or secondary syphilis. Following treatment for primary syphilis a positive FTA-IgM test persists for three to six months while infections treated at the secondary or early-latent stage remain positive for eight months on average after treatment. Arrest of disease may be associated, therefore, with disappearance of anti-treponemal IgM while its persistence may reflect recent or inadequate treatment or relapse [23].

FTA-IgM test in late-stage syphilis

The situation with regard to late-stage syphilis is less clear. In one report [24] only 23 per cent of patients with untreated latent syphilis gave a positive FTA-IgM test while another study [25] found that half of a series of latent infections treated thirteen years previously were FTA-IgM positive. The continued presence of anti-treponemal IgM may reflect persistence of the antigen in the host. Treponemes or treponeme-like forms have been observed in tissues and intra-ocular and cerebrospinal fluid of patients with treated late syphilis (page 39). False positive FTA-IgM reactions may also occur due to rheumatoid factor (IgM antibody) in the serum reacting with treponemes already coated with anti-treponemal IgG [26]. Any serum giving a positive FTA-IgM test should be re-tested after absorption with precipitated globulin to remove anti-IgG antibody [24].

FTA-IgM test in congenital syphilis

Since IgM antibodies do not cross the intact placenta, the presence of anti-treponemal IgM in cord blood should indicate active infection of the neonate. The FTA-IgM test may, however, be negative at birth and take up to nine weeks to become positive [27]: this could be due either to suppression of IgM synthesis in the neonate due to circulating maternal anti-treponemal IgG or to competition between IgG and IgM for binding sites on the treponeme during the actual test. The latter problem can be prevented by fractionating the serum and performing the test with the IgM fraction. False-positive FTA-IgM results can also occur in neonates due to the production of a rheumatoid factor-like antibody capable of reacting with treponemes which have united with passively transferred maternal IgG [26].

At present, careful clinical scrutiny and serological testing constitute the best management. If a baby has been infected, titres will rise whereas in the absence of infection, say when a mother has been treated during the pregnancy, passively transferred antibody detected by the VDRL will decrease in titre and the test will become negative in approximately three months. In the case of the TPHA the titre will become low and the test negative in six to twelve months. It is also of value to compare antibody levels in mother and infant: higher titres in the infant are suggestive of infection. The FTA-IgM test requires further study before it can be reliably used in the management of both the neonatal and adult patient.

SCREENING SCHEDULES OTHER THAN A COMBINATION OF VDRL AND TPHA TESTS

Many laboratories screen with Reiter's protein complement fixation test in combination with either the cardiolipin Wassermann reaction or the Automated reagent or VDRL tests. These screening schedules will detect almost all cases of untreated syphilis apart from a few patients with untreated or partially treated late-stage infection. It is prudent to maintain the FTA-ABS test in all instances but particularly in situations where typical clinical findings are absent. The automated 'reagin' test alone provides adequate screening for blood transfusion centres: all sera giving positive reactions must, of course, be sent for further investigation.

Whichever screening system is used human and technical errors may result and *a diagnosis of syphilis should never be made on the results of a single blood specimen.*

Examination of the cerebrospinal fluid

The cardiovascular changes of late-stage syphilis cannot be detected until clinical or radiological signs develop, whereas invasion of the central nervous system (c.n.s.) can be discovered early by the examination of the cerebrospinal fluid (c.s.f.) obtained by lumbar puncture. Because of this and because the effects of syphilis on the c.n.s. can often be reversed by penicillin treatment, c.s.f. examinations are important in the assessment of patients with the disease. In the case of early syphilis it is traditional policy to carry out a lumbar puncture 12 months after treatment as part of the test of cure. In the case of patients with syphilis of uncertain duration or in the late symptomatic or late latent-stage, c.s.f. examination is an essential part of the investigation necessary before treatment. When there is evidence of clinical relapse or a fourfold rise is noted in the titre of the serological tests, in the follow-up of a patient, c.s.f. examination is necessary [28].

Investigation of the c.s.f. should include: (i) a cell count; (ii) estimation of total protein; (iii) estimation of IgG and IgM. The Lange colloidal gold test is useful when these estimations cannot be made; (iv) serological tests such as VDRL, TPHA, FTA-ABS on the c.s.f. A total volume of 8–10ml is generally sufficient for the tests required which should be carried out as soon as possible after collection.

CELL COUNT

Cell counts are carried out in a Fuchs-Rosenthal haemocytometer. The total and differential white blood cell counts are performed. Normally there are less than 3 leucocytes per mm^3 (3×10^6 per litre) and the first indication of involvement of the c.n.s. by syphilis may be a count of 10 lymphocytes or more per mm^3 (10×10^6 per litre).

After treatment with penicillin in cases of neurosyphilis or asymptomatic neurosyphilis, the leucocyte count in the c.s.f. reverts rapidly towards normal; with tetracycline and erythromycin, given to those who are allergic to penicillin, more careful c.s.f. follow-up with retreatment would be wise as confidence and experience with these antibiotics in the treatment of neurosyphilis is less than with penicillin.

TOTAL PROTEIN AND IMMUNOGLOBULINS

The total protein is normally 10–40mg per 100ml (100–400mg per litre) and in neurosyphilis the increase may be only slight or may reach levels of 100–200mg per 100ml (1000–2000mg per litre). Total protein tends to revert towards normal after treatment more rapidly than more complex qualitative changes such as those detected by the Lange test and by electrophoresis. In the absence of virus disease, an increase in immunoglobulin (IgG) above 13 per cent of total protein is supportive evidence of neurosyphilis or multiple sclerosis [29]. In such cases c.s.f. protein should be submitted, where possible and practicable, to polyacrylamide gel electrophoresis at pH 8.8 as a quantitative analysis of these immunoglobulins may help in the assessment of c.s.f. activity. In neurosyphilis IgM may be elevated in the c.s.f. and it tends to fall rapidly after treatment [30]. In paretic (first zone) curves in the Lange test (*see* below) there is a striking increase in slow gamma globulin when the c.s.f. is examined by a polyacrylamide gel electrophoresis [31].

The Lange colloidal gold test is a traditional test used over many years to indicate alterations in the albumin/globulin ratio. Colloidal-gold activity resides in the gamma globulin fraction; gamma globulins are more positively charged in solution and have a greater tendency to precipitate negatively charged gold sol.

In the test, twofold serial dilutions of c.s.f. in saline are made beginning with a 1 in 10 dilution in tube 1 and reaching a final dilution of 1 in 5120 in tube 10. Gold sol is added to each dilution and the tubes left overnight. After 24 hours any colour change and precipitation are noted and the tubes scored as follows: 0 = red (no precipitate); 1 = reddish blue; 2 = lilac; 3 = blue; 4 = pale blue-grey; 5 = colourless (complete precipitation with blue precipitate). Values of one or below are normal. Abnormal readings fall into 3 main patterns: early zone or paretic curve, e.g. 5555432100; mid-zone or luetic curve, e.g. 0124321000; and end-zone or meningitic curve, e.g. 0000123431. The Lange colloidal gold test is not specific for syphilis. Although early zone curves are typically associated with patients with neurosyphilis they are also usually found in patients with multiple sclerosis. The colloidal gold test has fallen out of favour because laboratory control of the test is difficult and results unreliable. There is, however, a correlation between the paretic (first zone) curve and a striking increase in slow gamma globulin [31] although other qualitative differences in gamma globulins influence the test.

SCREENING FOR NEUROSYPHILIS

The use of the VDRL and the TPHA on CSF as routine screening tests for syphilis on patients in whom there is no clinical suspicion of syphilis, is unjustified, as a negative TPHA test on the blood will virtually exclude active neurosyphilis and is a better screen for the detection of all forms of late syphilis [32].

In cases selected on clinical grounds and backed by a positive TPHA test on blood, however, the VDRL, TPHA and FTA-ABS should be performed on the c.s.f. as they may also be positive. In the interpretation of the results of tests on the c.s.f. it is necessary to make comparisons with the results in the first specimen obtained. Follow-up and comparison of a sequence of the results of such tests provide useful data on response to treatment. Any accidental contamination of the c.s.f. specimen with a small amount of blood can give false and misleading results. In the absence of such contamination false-positive reactions are very rare.

In cerebrospinal and ocular fluids treponemes indistinguishable from *T. pallidum* may be found sometimes after treatment, in late syphilis. The presence of these treponemes is of uncertain clinical significance and they are not necessarily associated with progression of the disease nor are they indicators that the patient can transmit his disease at that stage [33]. The search for such treponemes in the centrifuged deposit of the c.s.f. and by inoculation of experimental rabbits with c.s.f. are research procedures rather than routines required in day-to-day clinical practice.

Biological false-positive (BFP) reactors

BFP reactors are those patients whose serum gives a positive cardiolipin antigen test but negative specific treponemal antigen tests in the absence of past or present treponemal infection [34].

There are several possible reasons for obtaining a BFP reaction. It may be the result of tissue destruction and liberation of cardiolipin from mitochondria. Infection with micro-organisms containing cardiolipin, or serum protein disturbances may also result in BFP reactions. Anticardiolipin antibody is present in small quantities in the sera of healthy individuals where it is normally inhibited by a globulin known as the inhibitor. If the amount of inhibitor is reduced a positive cardiolipin antigen test can result [35].

The frequency of BFP reactions depends upon the test used and appears to be lower with the VDRL test than with the Wassermann reaction. The lower the incidence of treponemal infection within the community the higher the relative frequency of BFP reactors among positive cardiolipin screening tests. Chronic BFP reactors are seen more frequently in the female and in the elderly as a result of tissue wear and tear. A high frequency of BFP reactions also occurs among drug addicts although the significance of this is not clear at present. The BFP reaction may sometimes have a genetic basis.

The acute or transient BFP may occur shortly after an acute febrile infectious disease (e.g. infectious mononucleosis, infective hepatitis, measles, upper respiratory tract infection) or be provoked by strong immunological stimuli such as vaccination and pregnancy. The acute BFP disappears within a few weeks or months after the acute illness has subsided. Approximately 60 per cent of acute BFP reactors are under 30 years of age.

In contrast, the chronic BFP reaction persists longer than six months and approximately 60 per cent of reactors are over 30 years of age. Chronic BFP reactions are also more common in women than men. They may be associated with auto-immune and related diseases, e.g. rheumatoid arthritis, systemic lupus erythematosus, Sjogren's disease, auto-immune thyroiditis and auto-immune haemolytic anaemia.

Antibody of class IgG giving rise to a BFP reaction may cross the placenta and be detected in the neonate. On serial testing the antibody should disappear and the tests become negative in two to three months.

Repeated serological tests are necessary in order to differentiate between acute and chronic BFP reactors and cases of treponemal infection. Great care should be exercised in the interpretation of results to prevent misdiagnosis. By mechanisms quite distinct from the BFP reaction patients with systemic lupus erythematosus may give a false-positive FTA-ABS test. Similarly, a proportion of patients with infectious mononucleosis may give a false-positive TPHA test due to high levels of heterophile antibody. The TPI test is less sensitive than either the FTA-ABS or TPHA tests in late syphilis and if relied upon patients with treponemal infection could be falsely classified as BFP reactors. Since the chronic BFP reaction may precede the clinical manifestations of systemic lupus erythematosus or other auto-immune disease the diagnosis of chronic BFP reactor may eventually have serious implications for the patient. About 20 per cent of women and 5 per cent of men who are chronic BFP reactors may give a history of hypersensitivity to penicillin, underlining the importance of accurate diagnosis of this group [34].

RE-INFECTION

The natural course of syphilis indicates that immune mechanisms are involved in the host-treponeme relationship. An initial attack does not give complete immunity but the majority of patients maintain a level of immunity sufficient to limit the disease to such an extent as to remain latent, i.e. a balance is struck between the infecting organisms and the specific cellular immune process; the relative importance of humoral and cell-mediated responses requires further investigation [36]. In early syphilis there is a partial inhibition of the cell-mediated response which could account for the persistence of infectiousness and for the ease of demonstrating treponemes in tissues. Immunity is not always beneficial: tissue hypersensitivity develops to the treponemes or their destruction products and subsequent invasion of these sensitized tissues causes massive destruction characteristic of the gumma.

Humoral mechanisms of immunity do exist in syphilis but appear to be relatively inefficient and of uncertain protective value. It is a well known clinical finding that patients with early acquired syphilis may have high levels of circulating antibody yet become re-infected after treatment. The series of results of serological tests in a patient re-infected after treatment for secondary syphilis is shown in Figure 4.4.

Case history

The patient, a homosexual male, attended the clinic in late October 1974. Although there was no history of syphilis the FTA-ABS test was positive, the VDRL titre was 8 and the TPHA titre 1280. The rise in

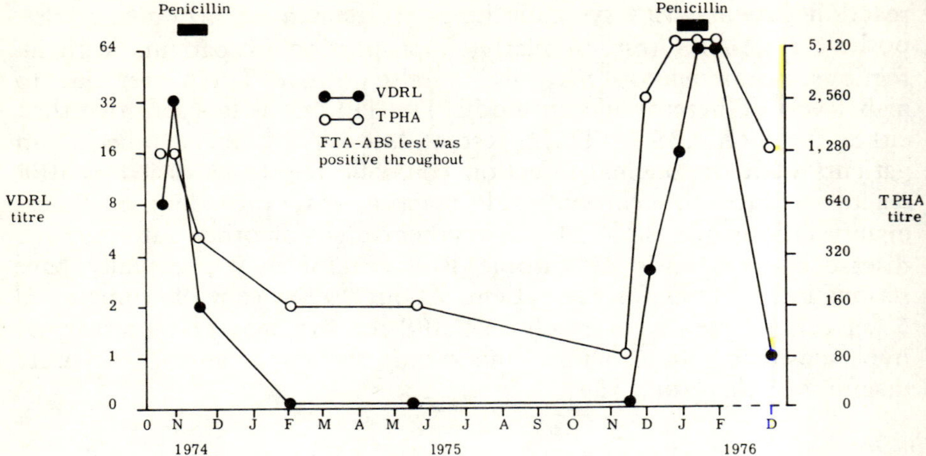

Figure 4.4 Re-infection with syphilis: *see* case history in text.

VDRL titre from 8 to 32 in the next seven days suggested an early secondary infection. Following a course of penicillin treatment the VDRL titre decreased and became negative by February 1975, again indicating an early infection. Although the TPHA titre decreased to 80 by mid-November, characteristically it did not become negative. In mid-December the VDRL had risen to 4 and the TPHA titre to 2560 suggesting re-infection. By mid-January the VDRL titre was 64 and the TPHA 5120. On clinical examination the patient had a maculopapular rash and an anal chancre abounding with treponemes. Following the second course of penicillin therapy titres again declined.

A degree of natural immunity to venereal syphilis results from other treponemal infections. In areas where yaws is prevalent venereal syphilis is uncommon. The eradication of yaws has had remarkable benefits but the population will be more susceptible to infection with *T. pallidum*.

Although the search for a syphilis vaccine is progressing the difficulties associated with growing pathogenic *T. pallidum* endow the work with many problems. If used widely, diagnostic difficulties would arise as it would be impossible to distinguish between vaccinated and infected individuals by existing serological tests. The effectiveness of penicillin in the treatment of early syphilis and its great value in some forms of late syphilis has lessened the need for a vaccine in the western world. The assessment of the effectiveness of the vaccine would be very difficult as even in syphilis itself a high proportion of patients may develop the disease in a latent form only.

REFERENCES

1 Editorial (1968) August von Wassermann (1866–1925) *Journal of the American Medical Association,* **204,** 1000
2 Pangborn, M C (1941) *Proceedings of the Society for Experimental Biology and Medicine,* **48,** 484
3 Kahn, R L (1922) *Archives of Dermatology and Syphilology,* **5,** 570
4 Harris, A, Rosenberg, A A and Riedel, L M (1946) *Journal of Venereal Disease Information,* **27,** 169
5 Portnoy, J, Brewer, J H and Harris, A D (1962) *Public Health Report, Washington,* **77,** 645
6 McGrew, B E, DuCros, M J F, Stout, G W and Falcone, V H (1968) *American Journal of Clinical Pathology,* **50,** 52
7 D'Alessandro, G and Dardanoni, L (1953) *American Journal of Syphilis, Gonorrhea and Venereal Diseases,* **37,** 137
8 Nelson, R A and Mayer, M M (1949) *Journal of Experimental Medicine,* **89,** 369
9 Hunter, E F, Deacon, W E and Meyer, P E (1964) *Public Health Report, Washington,* **79,** 410
10 McKenna, C H, Schroeter, A L, Kierland, R R, Stilwell, G C and Pien, F D (1973) *Mayo Clinical Proceedings,* **48,** 545
11 Wright, D J M (1973) *Journal of Clinical Pathology,* **26,** 968
12 Wright, J T, Cremer, A W and Ridgway, G L (1975) *British Journal of Venereal Diseases,* **51,** 329
13 Chapel, T, Jeffries, C D, Brown, W J and Stewart, J A (1978) *British Journal of Venereal Diseases* **54,** 299
14 Wilkinson, A E and Johnston, N A (1975) *Annals of the New York Academy of Sciences,* **254,** 395
15 Rathlev, T (1967) *British Journal of Venereal Diseases,* **43,** 181
16 Tomizawa, T and Kasamatsu, S (1966) *Japanese Journal of Medical Science and Biology,* **19,** 305
17 Sequeira, P J L and Eldridge, A E (1973) *British Journal of Venereal Diseases,* **49,** 242
18 Young, H, Henrichsen, C and Robertson, D H H (1974) *British Journal of Venereal Diseases,* **50,** 341
19 Manikowska-Lesinska, W, Linda, B and Zajac, W (1978) *British Journal of Venereal Diseases,* **54,** 295
20 Veldkamp, J and Visser, A M (1975) *British Journal of Venereal Diseases,* **51,** 227
21 Daniels, K C and Feryneyhaugh, H S (1977) *Health Laboratory Science,* **14,** 164
22 Robertson, D H H, McMillan, A, Young, H and Henrichsen, C (1975) *British Journal of Venereal Diseases,* **51,** 79
23 O'Neill, P and Nicol, C S (1972) *British Journal of Venereal Diseases,* **48,** 460
24 Wilkinson, A E and Rodin, P (1976) *British Journal of Venereal Diseases,* **52,** 219
25 Logan, L C, Norins, L C, Atwood, W G and Miller, J L (1969) *Journal of Investigative Dermatology,* **53,** 300
26 Wilkinson, A E (1976) In *Sexuall Transmitted Diseases* (Ed) Catterall, R D and Nicol, C S. Academic Press, London, pages 214–218
27 Johnston, N A (1972) *British Journal of Venereal Diseases,* **48,** 464
28 Catterall, R D (1977) *British Journal of Hospital Medicine,* **17,** 585
29 Millar, J H D (1975) In *Recent Advances in Clinical Neurology* (Ed) Matthews, W B. Churchill Livingstone, Edinburgh, page 220
30 Oxelius, V A, Rorsman, H and Laurell, A B (1969) *British Journal of Venereal Diseases,* **45,** 121
31 Thompson, E J, Norman, P N and MacDermot, J (1975) *British Journal of Hospital Medicine,* **14,** 645
32 Leading Article (1977) *Lancet,* **ii,** 595
33 Collart, P Borel, L J and Durel, P (1962) *Annales de l'Institut Pasteur,* **102,** 596
34 Catterall, R D (1972) *British Journal of Venereal Diseases,* **48,** 1
35 Kiraly, K (1973) WHO/VDT/RES Document 73. 304
36 Wright, D J M and Grimble, A S (1974) *British Journal of Venereal Diseases,* **50,** 45

CHAPTER 5

Acquired Syphilis: Early Stage

Primary syphilis

Following a prepatent period of about three weeks (range 10 to 90 days), the primary lesion or chancre develops at the site of inoculation of *T. pallidum.* It should be clearly understood that by the time the chancre appears, dissemination of the organism throughout the body has already occurred. In all probability the primary lesion results from a complex immunological reaction at the site of entry of the organism into the body.

The initial lesion noted in primary syphilis is a dull red papule, resulting from infiltration of the dermis with lymphocytes and plasma cells. As the disease progresses, thrombotic obstruction of blood vessels, whose walls show marked inflammatory changes (endarteritis obliterans), leads to necrosis of overlying epidermis, and hence ulceration.

The chancre is typically a single ulcer, well demarcated from the surrounding tissue, with a smooth, flat, dull-red surface, which may be covered by a thin yellow or brown crust. Characteristically the ulcer is painless, not tender and on pressure serous fluid, but no blood, exudes from the lesion. Induration of the ulcer is often marked giving it a cartilaginous consistency. Occasionally there may be considerable oedema of the adjacent tissues.

Many lesions of primary syphilis are atypical [1]. The patient may complain of painful tender ulceration, a result of secondary bacterial infection. Multiple chancres may occur. In the anal region, primary lesions may resemble slightly indurated anal fissures. In any patient with an ulcer in an oral or anogenital site, particularly, it is essential to exclude syphilis by dark-ground examinations when appropriate and by serological tests repeated over a three-month period (Chapter 4).

Within a few days of the appearance of the chancre there is usually regional lymph node enlargement. When the chancre is on the genitalia, bilateral inguinal lymphadenitis is usual, but when the lesion is extra-genital, it is more common to find unilateral enlargement. The enlarged lymph nodes are discrete, rubbery and, unless the chancre is secondarily infected, painless. Without treatment, the primary lesion heals within three to eight weeks, leaving a thin atrophic scar.

SITES OF PRIMARY LESIONS IN THE MALE

The chancre may be found on any part of the external genitalia, but especially in the coronal sulcus, on the inner surface of the prepuce, on the glans, or on the shaft of the penis. Rarely an intra-urethral chancre may occur, producing symptoms of urethritis. In male passive homosexuals, the chancre may be found at the anal margin, or less frequently in the rectum [2] where it may be mistaken for carcinoma. Primary lesions in the latter sites may produce no symptoms, and as a result the patient may first present with manifestations of secondary syphilis.

Chancres may also occur on the lips, buccal cavity, tongue, tonsil and pharynx, particularly in homosexual patients. Lesions of the tonsil and pharynx may be painful. In these sites the diagnosis by dark-ground microscopy may be difficult because there are often saprophytic treponemes. Lesions elsewhere, such as on a finger, are rare.

SITES OF PRIMARY LESIONS IN THE FEMALE

Chancres may occur on the labium majus, labium minus, fourchette, clitoris or cervix. Lesions of the cervix usually produce no symptoms and as the lymph drains to the iliac nodes, these may be found to be enlarged on abdominal examination. Extragenital chancres are uncommon.

Secondary syphilis

Signs of secondary syphilis usually appear seven to ten weeks after infection or six to eight weeks after the appearance of the primary lesion which may not have been noticed by the patient (*see* above). In about a third of patients with early secondary syphilis a primary lesion will still be present.

Lesions of secondary syphilis result from the spread of *T. pallidum* throughout the tissues of the body and the immunological reactions of the host. Without treatment, the features of secondary syphilis may appear and regress spontaneously at intervals over a period of about two years. During such relapses mucocutaneous lesions in the anogenital area contain *T. pallidum* enabling further transmission during sexual intercourse. After the secondary stage, or after the chancre or even in the absence of these stages the infection persists as a hidden disease, that is, as latent syphilis.

Over the last decade, many atypical cases of early syphilis have been described, and although this may be due to a change in the disease itself, it is as likely that clinicians have become more aware of the possibility of syphilis and have access to more sensitive and more specific diagnostic tests. Widespread use of antibiotics may have a modifying effect and produce more atypical cases.

Clinical features of secondary syphilis

SYMPTOMS

The patient often feels generally unwell, with mild fever, malaise, headache and anorexia. He may complain of a non-itchy skin rash, patchy loss of hair, hoarseness, swollen lymph nodes, bone pain and, rarely, deafness or other evidence of neural damage.

SIGNS

(a) Skin lesions (syphilides) and their histopathology

Skin lesions are seen in over 80 per cent of patients with secondary syphilis. Mucocutaneous lesions, particularly, contain many treponemes and are infectious.

Skin eruptions are often polymorphic (several types of eruption appear simultaneously) during the course of secondary syphilis and although early skin lesions are usually symmetrically distributed, later lesions are not always in this pattern. Pruritus is not a feature of the skin eruption.

The classical description of the histopathology of secondary syphilis is that of swelling and proliferation of the endothelium of the superficial and deep dermal blood vessels, and of intense perivascular infiltration with plasma cells and lymphocytes. Recent studies suggest, however, that the histological appearances are more variable [3, 4].

The dermis shows some abnormality in all cases. Infiltration with lymphocytes and plasma cells in both the superficial and deep dermis is usual, particularly near dermal blood vessels. Vasodilatation is common but evidence of endothelial damage is usually limited to swelling of these cells. Endothelial proliferation is rare.

Considerable emphasis has been placed, when making a histological diagnosis of syphilis, on the presence of plasma cells in the dermal infiltrate. In at least 25 per cent of biopsies, however, these cells are either inconspicuous or absent.

Oedema of the epidermis can be observed in about 75 per cent of biopsies, and acanthosis, that is, an increase in the number of cells in the Malpighian layer, is found in about 30 per cent of cases. Exocytosis, that is, the presence of inflammatory cells within the epidermis, is seen in at least 80 per cent of biopsies; there are polymorphonuclear leucocytes but lymphocytes usually predominate. Variable degrees of hyperkeratosis and parakeratosis may be observed.

The diagnosis of secondary syphilis usually depends upon clinical and serological findings but, when biopsies have been taken in a histological approach to the diagnosis of skin disease, the pattern of changes seen on microscopy may suggest such a diagnosis. Except in condylomata lata, *T. pallidum* is only occasionally found in histological sections [5].

Macular syphilide (roseola)

These lesions are usually the earliest to appear, but are often overlooked, being faintly coloured. The individual macules are rose-pink in colour, about 1cm in diameter, discrete and with indistinct margins. Pressure obliterates the lesion. The rash progresses daily, becoming more widely distributed, but occasionally may last only a few days. It is common to find macules or papules in the generalized eruption.

Papular and papulosquamous syphilide

These are the commonest lesions to be detected in secondary syphilis. Papules are dull red lesions variable in size, distributed symmetrically (during the early stages of secondary syphilis) over the body, and especially prominent on flexor aspects. They are firm to touch and initially have a shiny surface. Later, as the papule ages, scaling is noted on the surface. When scaling papules predominate in the eruption, the term papulosquamous syphilide is applied.

Although papules may be found anywhere on the body, the following sites require special mention:

Face. This is often affected, papules being especially prominent in the naso-labial folds and on the chin. Occasionally a group of papules may be noted on the forehead just below, and parallel to, the hairline, sometimes described as 'corona veneris'.

Scalp. When a hair follicle is involved in the inflammatory changes in the skin, hair growth is arrested and shedding of the contained hair occurs. Hair loss in secondary syphilis is characteristically irregular, the scalp having a 'moth-eaten' appearance (syphilitic alopecia).

Occasionally as a non-specific reaction to a systemic disease there may be a more diffuse hair loss (*telogen effluvium*) after recovery from the secondary stage. This results from interference with hair growth at the time of the illness, the abnormal hair being lost three to five months afterwards as the new hair starts to grow.

Palms and soles. (Palmar and plantar syphilide). Papular lesions on these sites do not project much above the surface of the skin, but appear as firm lesions, dull red in colour, associated with thickening and peeling of the overlying epidermis. Frequently a collar of scales surrounds individual lesions (Plate 5).

Genitalia. On moist areas such as the vulva and peri-anal region, papules may become hypertrophied, forming broad-based, flat-topped, moist, wart-like lesions—condylomata lata (Plates 2 and 3). The surface is often eroded, the exudate from the erosion containing large numbers of *T. pallidum.* Such lesions are highly contagious. Commonly papules encircle the free margin of the foreskin, and, as a result of moisture, trauma and secondary infection, deep painful fissures develop. Papulosquamous lesions are often found on the shaft of the penis and on the scrotum.

In the later stages of secondary syphilis, papules become fewer in number and asymmetrical in distribution. Nummular lesions, 1–3 cm in diameter, are commonly found at this time and are frequently surmounted by a thick layer of scales, resembling the plaques of psoriasis. Coalescence of papules in the later secondary stage may produce annular lesions, especially in dark-skinned people. Occasionally, a large papule may be found, surrounded by smaller satellite lesions – corymbose syphilide. Such lesions may be the only ones noted in late secondary syphilis.

Nail growth may be affected, usually in the late secondary stage. The nail loses its lustre, becomes brittle and may be shed.

Pustular syphilide

Rarely papules become pustular due to necrosis of the upper dermis and epidermis as a result of occlusion of the lumen of blood vessels. Multiple pustular lesions are very seldom found in western countries [6] but may be seen in patients suffering from some concomitant debilitating disease such as tuberculosis.

With the exception of pustular syphilide, the skin lesions of secondary syphilis heal without leaving scars. Areas of faint pigmentation may persist for months. Occasionally, depigmentation of the skin of the neck may be noted, particularly in dark-haired women – *leucoderma colli.* This residual depigmentation lasts for life.

(*b*) *Lesions of the mucous membranes*

Such lesions are found in about 30 per cent of patients with secondary syphilis. The characteristic lesion is the so-called 'mucous patch' which appears at the same time as the skin rash. Both skin and mucosal lesions have similar histological appearances.

The mucosal lesions appear as round or oval grey areas surrounded by a narrow zone of erythema. Shedding of the grey necrotic membrane reveals superficial ulceration and if several patches coalesce, a 'snail-track ulcer' may result (Plate 4).

Mucosal lesions are generally painless and resolve within a few weeks, or, less commonly, within a few days.

The following sites may be involved in secondary syphilis:

Tonsils: Usually the mucous patches are symmetrically arranged.

Cheeks, palate and lips: Lesions appear as grey-white patches.

Tongue: Mucous patches on the tongue appear as round or oval, smooth areas, sharply demarcated from the surrounding epithelium. The smoothness of the lesions is a result of loss of filiform papillae.

Larynx: Lesions are most often found on the epiglottis and aryepiglottic folds Surrounding tissue oedema produces hoarseness, a common symptom of secondary syphilis.

Nasal mucosa: Mucous patches of the nasal mucosa may produce serous nasal discharge.

Mucous membranes of the genitalia: Patches may be found on the glans penis, subpreputial surface of the prepuce, vulva, fourchette and cervix.

(*c*) *Lymph node enlargement*

Generalized lymph node enlargement is found in at least 60 per cent of cases of secondary syphilis. Cervical, suboccipital, axillary, epitrochlear and inguinal nodes are often palpably enlarged. The glands are discrete with a rubbery consistency and are not tender. Not uncommonly, the spleen is enlarged in secondary syphilis.

(*d*) *Periostitis*

This is said to be an uncommon manifestation of secondary syphilis, although bone pain may occasionally be the presenting feature of the disease [7]. Periostitis is usually a localized process most commonly affecting the anterior tibia. Localized bone pain, especially at night, relieved by movement and exacerbated by immobilization is the chief symptom and localized tenderness may be noted on examination. Radiological examination usually reveals no abnormalities although osteolytic foci may be seen. Bone scanning, using technetium-99, may show areas of increased bone uptake [8].

(*e*) *Arthritis and bursitis*

Painless effusion into joints and bursae occurs rarely during the course of secondary syphilis. Arthralgia, however, either localized or generalized, is more common, affecting at least 6 per cent of patients.

(*f*) *Hepatitis*

Rarely, jaundice may be associated with secondary syphilis. It may be difficult to differentiate between jaundice due to syphilis and hepatitis B, both diseases being encountered in homosexual patients more commonly than in heterosexual patients (Chapter 24). A fairly regular feature of biochemical tests of liver function in this form of hepatitis is a disproportionately elevated serum alkaline phosphatase (of hepatic origin) in comparison with only a moderate elevation of the alanine aminotransferase level. These serum enzyme abnormalities may also be noted in patients with secondary syphilis who are not jaundiced. Usually within 6 weeks of treatment the results of these tests revert to normal [9].

(*g*) *Glomerulonephritis and the nephrotic syndrome*

Patients with secondary syphilis frequently have mild albuminuria, possibly as the result of immune complexes trapped by the glomeruli setting up an inflammatory reaction there. Usually such changes are mild and transient, but rarely a membranous glomerulonephritis results, being manifest as the nephrotic syndrome. Nodular lumps on the epithelial side of the basement membrane are found on electron microscopy of glomeruli in renal biopsy specimens, and immunofluorescence studies show deposition of IgG and complement component (C3) in these lumps. Anti-treponemal antibody can be demonstrated in affected glomeruli by using elution techniques. These findings suggest that the glomerulonephritis of secondary syphilis is due to the presence of treponemal antigen–antitreponemal antibody complexes from the circulation being deposited within the glomeruli [10].

If untreated, the nephrotic syndrome appears to resolve spontaneously.

(h) *Iridocyclitis and choroido-retinitis*

Iritis, usually discovered late in secondary syphilis, is now a rare complication in western countries (less than 1 per cent of cases). Uveitis and choroido-retinitis may be precipitated by the use of corticosteroid preparations for some other complication (e.g. glomerulonephritis) or for some intercurrent illness.

Treponeme-like forms have been identified in the aqueous humour of patients suffering from iridocyclitis [11].

(i) *Neurological abnormalities in secondary syphilis*

Headache, especially noticeable in the morning, is a common complaint and probably reflects meningeal inflammation. Although transitory abnormalities of the cell count and protein content in the cerebrospinal fluid (c.s.f.) occur in only about 5 per cent of patients with secondary syphilis, frank meningo-encephalitis may rarely be encountered [12].

Peripheral neuritis may be a rare complication. Perceptive nerve deafness with or without vestibular dysfunction, is another uncommon complication. It is usually associated with tinnitus and the c.s.f. tends to show some abnormality. Improvement, both subjective and objective, occurs following antibiotic treatment [13].

DIFFERENTIAL DIAGNOSIS OF SECONDARY SYPHILIS

The appearance of the rash of secondary syphilis is variable and as a result many dermatological conditions have to be considered in the differential diagnosis. Table 5.I indicates the more common conditions which require to be considered; the problem is generally resolved by the serological tests for syphilis and by the generally rapid response to antibiotic treatment.

Early latent syphilis

The lesions of early syphilis may heal and the disease may become latent. During this stage, known as early stage latent syphilis, recurrence of infectious mucocutaneous lesions may be seen. Latency may, however, persist, and early stage latent syphilis is arbitrarily taken to last for two years.

Table 5.1 Differential diagnosis of secondary syphilis

Lesions		*Diseases to be differentiated*
Macular syphilide	Drug eruptions	History of intake; pruritus present in drug eruptions.
	Measles, Rubella	May be difficult clinically to differentiate from secondary syphilis.
	Pityriasis rosea	'Herald patch'. Lesions of generalized eruption, discrete, oval, dull pink with collarette of fine scales. Usually on trunk, proximal areas of limbs. Palmar/plantar lesions exceptional.
Papular syphilide	Psoriasis	
	Lichen planus	
	Pityriasis lichenoides	Lesions are small firm lichenoid papules, reddish-brown in colour. On detaching overlying scale, shiny brown surface revealed.
	Condylomata acuminata	On vulva, peri-anal region.
	Ulcerated haemorrhoids, Herpes simplex infection	May resemble mucous patches, but herpes lesions are usually painful.
	Impetigo contagiosa	Facial papules of syphilis may resemble impetigo.
	Tinea pedis	Plantar syphilide and hypertrophic papules between toes require differentiation from tinea.
	Trichophytides	Micro-papular syphilides may resemble these.
	Keratotic eczema	Resembles plantar or palmar syphilide.
Mucosal lesions of syphilis	Aphthous ulcers, Herpetic gingivo-stomatitis	Generally painful and tender.
	Infectious mononucleosis	May be difficult to differentiate clinically from secondary syphilis – macular rash, tonsillar/palatal lesions, lymph node and splenic enlargement; occasionally jaundice. Cardiolipin tests (VDRL) may be positive.

REFERENCES

1 Chapel, T A (1978) *Sexually Transmissible Diseases,* **5**, 68
2 Marino, A W M (1964) *Diseases of the Colon and Rectum,* **7**, 121
3 Jeerapaet, P and Ackerman, A B (1973) *Archives of Dermatology,* **107**, 373
4 Abell, E, Marks, R and Wilson Jones, E (1975) *British Journal of Dermatology,* **93**, 53
5 Lomholt, G (1972) in *Textbook of Dermatology* (Ed) Rook, A, Wilkinson, D S and Ebling, F J G. Blackwell Scientific Publications, Oxford. Second edition, page 637
6 Miller, R L (1974) *British Journal of Venereal Diseases* **50**, 459
7 Waugh, M A (1976) *British Journal of Venereal Diseases,* **52**, 204
8 Tight, R R and Warner, J F (1976) *Journal of the American Medical Association,* **235**, 32
9 McMillan, A, Anderson, J R and Robertson, D H H (1977) *British Journal of Venereal Diseases,* **53**, 295
10 Gamble, C N and Reardan, J B (1975) *New England Journal of Medicine,* **292**, 449
11 MacFaul, P A and Catterall, R D (1971) *British Journal of Venereal Diseases,* **47**, 159
12 Parker, J D J (1972) *British Journal of Venereal Diseases,* **48**, 32
13 Vercoe G S (1976) *Journal of Laryngology and Otology,* **90**, 853

CHAPTER 6

Treatment of Syphilis: General Considerations

Among the kaleidoscopic changes that have come to medical practice since 1946 when penicillin first became easy to obtain, the effect of this antibiotic in microbial disease [1] has nowhere been more spectacular than in syphilis where it continues to be the antibiotic of first choice for the treatment of all stages of the disease [2] and effectively replaces arsenicals and bismuth. The persisting susceptibility of *Treponema pallidum* to penicillin over an extensive period of time suggests that this organism, in distinction from many other pathogens, does not appear to have the genetic capacity to develop resistance to this antibiotic [3].

Principles of penicillin therapy in syphilis

One layer of the cell wall of the treponeme consists of a complex macromolecule, peptidoglycan. Peptidoglycan is the component of the cell walls of bacteria, responsible for their mechanical strength [4]. It is a fortunate fact for the development of chemotherapy that peptidoglycan is unique to the prokaryotic cell wall as are its characteristic monomer components, N-acetyl muramic acid, diaminopimelic acid and some D-amino acids.

The final cross-linking stage in peptidoglycan synthesis involves a transpeptidation reaction between adjacent peptide chains with the elimination of a molecule of D-alanine per linkage. The cross-linking results in the production of a vast sponge-like macromolecule of considerable strength, but penicillin inhibits this final stage. If synthesis of the peptidoglycan is inhibited by penicillin whilst synthesis of other cell components and the action of autolysins (enzymes which bring about minor removal of wall substances necessary for remodelling of the cell wall in the course of growth) continue, then gradually increasing numbers of weaknesses appear in the cell wall until the hydrostatic pressure within causes the organism to rupture.

It is important to appreciate that penicillin* is only effective against

*Penicillin is thought to be a structural analogue of D-alanyl–D-alanine; this would explain its effect on the final transpeptidation reaction involving the two terminal D-alanines on the pentapeptide.

actively growing bacteria, the optimum effect being achieved when there is unhindered and rapid multiplication. It follows that penicillin will be most effective against the treponeme during early syphilis where there is rapid multiplication of the organism. Treponemes, like other bacteria, can exist in a resting phase when there is minimal cell wall synthesis and when penicillin effects are minimal [5].

In rapidly growing bacteria, such as gonococci, the organism will be particularly sensitive to the action of penicillin many times over a 24-hour period. In organisms with a longer generation time these phases of optimal sensitivity are correspondingly less frequent as in the case of *Treponema pallidum* in the experimentally infected rabbit testicle, where the generation time is given as 33 hours [6]. During a treatment period of 10–14 days, for example, these phases might well occur 7–10 times; as the treponemes do not reproduce synchronously in the infected host these phases of maximum sensitivity to penicillin are conceivably spread diffusely over the period of treatment [5]. It is, therefore, an important determinant for therapeutic success to ensure that effective plasma concentrations are maintained over an adequate time [7].

T. pallidum is one of the most penicillin-sensitive micro-organisms known. However, for penicillin to be effective in the therapy of syphilis, two requirements are essential: a minimal concentration of 0.03iu of penicillin per ml of serum, which gives several times the serum and tissue levels needed to kill *T. pallidum,* should be maintained for at least 7–10 days in early syphilis; and penicillin-free or subtreponemicidal intervals during treatment should not exceed 24–30 hours in order that treponemes still surviving can be prevented from remultiplying [2].

Experience has shown that huge intravenous doses of the aqueous penicillin, available at that time, over a single 24-hour period gave very poor results in early syphilis [8] and it has been observed that ampicillin 2g + probenecid 1g by mouth, an effective treatment for gonorrhoea, may not abort early syphilis during the incubation period [9].

Although *T. pallidum* is extremely sensitive to penicillin, healing of lesions occurs rapidly and treponemes disappear from early-stage lesions; biological cure, that is eradication of treponemes, is difficult to prove as *T. pallidum* cannot be cultured *in vitro.*

Although lesions of early-stage syphilis heal spontaneously, the disease can remain as a latent (concealed) infection for many years, even for a life-time, while a proportion, unpredictable in the individual, develop overt forms of late syphilis. The passage of time has, however, given confidence that individuals treated for early syphilis will not suffer ill effects due to late syphilis provided that they have had a course of penicillin which gives adequate blood levels over a sufficient length of time.

After treatment of some early, but especially of latent or late-stage syphilis with penicillin or indeed after treatment with any anti-treponemal agent, the *T. pallidum* immobilization test (page 76) positive before treatment remains positive afterwards and remains thus often for life [10], although cardiolipin antigen tests, such as the VDRL, become negative. The explanation of this persistence of immobilizing antibody in these circumstances was sought for by a French team, Collart, Borel and Durel [11]. This team came to the conclusion that the persistence of immobilizing antibody was due to the persistence of treponemes in the tissues after treatment.

Their conclusions were based on careful experimental work in which testes of rabbits were inoculated with *T. pallidum.* In most of these rabbits a syphiloma developed and in the others a persistently positive *T. pallidum* immobilization test (TPI) indicated latent syphilis. A popliteal lymph node was removed from some of the rabbits 18–24 months after inoculation and implanted subscrotally into other uninfected rabbits. After 40 days approximately 75 per cent (29/38) of these rabbits developed a syphiloma. The experiment and its continuation showed that in experimental syphilis there is a progressive lessening of virulence of the treponeme with the duration of the infection. It was clear, however, that lymph node transplants alone could not be relied upon to confirm sterilization of a treponemal infection.

In rabbits infected with *T. pallidum* two years previously and then treated with penicillin, the titre of the TPI dropped faster than in the untreated controls but in no animal, however, did the TPI become negative. Collart *et al* [11, 12], found that in both untreated controls and in those treated with penicillin two years after infection, occasional treponemes could be found in histological sections. In the treated group, however, lymph-node transplants were seldom successful in producing a syphiloma. The authors concluded from their experiments that viable treponemes, particularly if long resident in the host, persist after treatment, although these organisms appear to have lost their virulence.

Continuing their study in humans, they examined 10 patients (three with latent syphilis, six with tabes dorsalis and one with taboparesis). All but one had had different treatments including penicillin over periods varying from 1 to 16 years. All showed a positive TPI test. Treponemes were seen in the lymph nodes from all cases, in six cases the treponemes were typical and in four they were considered atypical.

Lymph nodes transplanted to healthy rabbits produced syphilomas with spiral organisms considered to be *T. pallidum*.

With careful search, too time-consuming to apply in clinical practice, tests of aqueous humour, cerebrospinal fluid and other sites for treponeme-like forms have given a small yield in undoubted cases of late syphilis. In a few cases these organisms have been shown to be *T. pallidum* but in many their nature is uncertain [13]. The finding of treponemes, apparently avirulent and incapable of causing further clinical disease, persisting after treatment of late syphilis, does not alter the fact that the treatment of early syphilis produces a clinical cure and prevents the emergence of late effects and that it is only in early syphilis with moist lesions that transmission can occur by sexual contact.

World-wide experience in the use of penicillin in the treatment of syphilis over three decades has been fully and valuably considered by Idsoe *et al* [2] in a World Health Organization publication. There are a multiplicity of empirically developed treatment plans but in spite of these variations in the case of long-acting penicillins results have been good [5]. Imperfections in the understanding of penicillin effects in late and latent syphilis and more particularly in the long-term value of alternative antibiotics leave some questions unanswered. Recommendations by the Venereal Disease Control Advisory Committee in the USA [14] (marked*) form a valuable basis when considering therapy:

TREATMENT OF EARLY (PRIMARY, SECONDARY, LATENT SYPHILIS OF LESS THAN ONE YEAR'S DURATION)

1. *Benzathine penicillin G, 2.4 million units given intramuscularly once, OR

2. *Aqueous procaine penicillin G, 4.8 million units total. 600,000 units by intramuscular injection daily for 8 days, OR

3. *Procaine penicillin G in oil with 2% aluminium monostearate (PAM†), 4.8 million units total by intramuscular injection. Dose given is 2.4 million units at the first visit and 1.2 million units at each of two subsequent visits three days apart.

In early latent syphilis it is difficult to obtain direct information regarding it's duration and it is advisable in cases of doubt to examine the cerebrospinal fluid, because when it is abnormal a diagnosis of asymptomatic neurosyphilis can be made and treatment with aqueous

(†PAM, available in some countries, is no longer available in USA and is not included in the British National Formulary, 1976–1978.)

procaine penicillin G can be given daily over a 21-day period. Kern in Berlin [5] sets the desirable duration of the long-acting penicillin course at 15 days in the case of all forms of early-stage syphilis and at 30 days for later stages.

In the authors' practice, in early syphilis the daily dose of aqueous procaine penicillin G given is higher (i.e. 0.9–1.0 million units) and the duration 10–15 days. Single dose benzathine penicillin is not used, except when interruptions in treatment are unavoidable.

In patients with secondary syphilis admission to hospital is advisable, at least for the first one or two days of treatment. The patient can then receive care during the Jarisch-Herxheimer Reaction [15] and the opportunity can be taken to give explanations, to help with social problems, and to interview deeply regarding possible sexual contacts. Kern [5] emphasizes the value of admission to ensure also continuous and correct treatment which in Germany has to conform to certain legal requirements.

Patients who are hypersensitive to penicillin (see also pages 109–113*)*

1. *Tetracycline hydrochloride, 500mg four times a day by mouth for 15 days, OR

2. *Erythromycin (stearate, ethylsuccinate or base), 500mg four times a day by mouth for 15 days.

These antibiotics appear to be effective but results have been evaluated less fully than in the case of penicillin therapy. Oxytetracycline may be used in the same dosage as an alternative to tetracycline. Serological follow-up (pages 115–116) is therefore all the more important.

SYPHILIS OF MORE THAN ONE YEAR'S DURATION

(Latent syphilis of indeterminate or more than one year's duration, cardiovascular, late benign, neurosyphilis)*

1. *Benzathine penicillin G, 7.2 million units total. 2.4 million units by intramuscular injection weekly for three successive weeks, OR

2. *Aqueous procaine penicillin G, 9.0 million units total. 600,000 units by intramuscular injection daily for 15 days.

Optimal schedules for syphilis of greater than one year's duration are less well established than those for early syphilis. Cerebrospinal fluid (c.s.f.) examinations are mandatory in suspected symptomatic neurosyphilis and desirable in other patients with syphilis of greater than one year's duration.

Although blood-levels are maintained penetration of penicillin into the normal central nervous system is low, about 0.5–2.0 per cent of the blood concentration being found in the c.s.f. [16] . In neurosyphilis the authors would not use the weekly single dose regime of benzathine penicillin given above. In neurosyphilis Mohr *et al* [17] treated 13 patients with 3.6 million units of benzathine penicillin G once weekly for four weeks. In twelve there was no detectable penicillin in the c.s.f.; in one patient there was 0.1mg/ml c.s.f. Mohr *et al* [17] obtained encouraging c.s.f. values in two patients after giving 5 and 10 mega units daily intravenously in divided doses. At present it may be said that a daily intramuscular dose of aqueous procaine penicillin (0.6–1.0 million units) for 21 days is probably adequate in neurosyphilis. Although larger doses of benzyl penicillin given intramuscularly or intravenously each day at four- to eight-hourly intervals would clearly give higher c.s.f. levels there is no evidence that better results will be obtained clinically. When the response is in doubt clinicians tend to give repeated courses and some use parenteral benzyl penicillin to give the c.s.f. levels considered desirable.

Patients who are hypersensitive to penicillin
(In those with syphilis of more than one year's duration)

In the circumstances of out-patient clinics for sexually transmitted disease it is wise to avoid penicillin injections particularly in those with a history of penicillin hypersensitivity, asthma, eczema or other illnesses due to hypersensitivity. In conditions such as neurosyphilis penicillin should be given wherever possible. Alternative antibiotics recommended by the Centre for Disease Control, USA [14] , are as follows:

1. *Tetracycline hydrochloride, 500mg four times daily by mouth for 30 days, OR

2. *Erythromycin stearate, ethylsuccinate or base, 500mg four times daily by mouth for 30 days.

Oxytetracycline in the same dose may be used as an alternative to tetracycline.

C.s.f. examinations and follow-up are important in patients being treated with these regimens as their efficacy in the long term is not yet clear.

Syphilis in pregnancy

With the increasing number of reported cases of transplacental (congenital) syphilis in the USA for example, although not yet observed in the United Kingdom, the proper treatment of pregnant women is a matter of major importance.

Penicillin is recommended in dosage appropriate for the stage of syphilis. The authors would prefer to use benzyl penicillin 1 million units eight-hourly for the first five days in the case of early syphilis in pregnancy, followed by 10 days of aqueous procaine penicillin. Aqueous procaine penicillin alone for 15 days is preferred in late or latent stages in pregnancy.

Pregnant women should be followed up carefully and have monthly quantitative cardiolipin antigen serological tests, e.g. VDRL, for the remainder of the current pregnancy. A fourfold rise in titre is an indication for retreatment.

It is the authors' practice to give a single 10-day course of aqueous procaine penicillin during early pregnancy in any patient who has had syphilis even if adequately treated in the past. This 'insurance course' is justified on the grounds that treponemes appear to persist in the host in spite of treatment and might be transmitted transplacentally. It is difficult, however, to test the validity of this argument.

Alternative antibiotic therapy in pregnant women with a history of hypersensitivity to penicillin

In the gravid woman allergic to penicillin, tetracyclines should not be used. Erythromycin has been offered as a suitable alternative to penicillin and Spence [18] employs this in an oral dose of 500mg four times daily for 20 days. If gastrointestinal symptoms preclude its use he advises admission to hospital for desensitization before giving penicillin treatment. With oral erythromycin however serum levels may be unsatisfactory and even after multiple maternal doses the average fetal blood level may only be 0.06μg/ml. As placental transfer is unpredictable and the problem of patient compliance very serious, the evidence suggests that oral erythromycin is not an appropriate agent in the treatment of *in utero* syphilis [19]. In the case reported by these authors a 24-year-old gravid woman with syphilis was treated with erythromycin stearate 750mg four times daily for 12 days; during her pregnancy her serum VDRL titre declined from 16 to 2. Notwithstanding this apparently satisfactory response in the mother the female infant, apparently normal on physical examination at birth, developed an ill-defined rash on the face at seven weeks and florid effects of early congenital syphilis (papulosquamous skin lesions, stuffy nose, adenopathy and osteochondritis of the right index finger) at 11 weeks. The VDRL at birth, seven weeks and 11 weeks showed titres of 2, 1 and 256 respectively.

South *et al* [20] first recorded this problem in a pregnant woman who was treated for secondary syphilis with erythromycin estolate in an oral dose of 500mg thrice daily for 10 days; her syphilis was apparently controlled but the infant had severe congenital syphilis.

In view of the unpredictable placental transfer of erythromycin during treatment of the pregnant woman for syphilis with this antibiotic full treatment of the infant with penicillin, beginning at birth, is an essential precaution [19] and it is clear that admission to hospital is desirable to ensure that the prescribed dosage is in fact taken at the required intervals. Estimations of serum erythromycin levels [21] are desirable.

Fenton and Light [19] suggest that in cases of suspected hypersensitivity to penicillin in maternal syphilis the use of intravenous erythromycin should be investigated and that the history of allergy to penicillin, often vague, should be closely scrutinized and practical methods should be applied to predicting penicillin reactions.

Cephaloridine crosses the placenta to achieve levels in the cord or fetal blood approximately 60 per cent of that in the maternal circulation. Holder and Knox [22] recommend for this reason intramuscular cephaloridine as a reasonable alternative and refer to doses of 0.5g daily for 10 days as a possible course; more data are required on dosage and possible teratogenic effects.

There is, of course, a calculated risk, which these authors recognized, as there is a cross allergenicity between penicillins and cephalosporins. The incidence of allergic reactions to cephalosporins in patients not allergic to penicillin is given as 1.7 per cent and in those who are so allergic 8.2 per cent [23]. From a wide study of the literature, Dash [24] concluded that 91–94 per cent of patients with a history of penicillin allergy have not reacted to a cephalosporin.

In the case of syphilis in the pregnant woman who gives a history of hypersensitivity to penicillin, treatment is problematic. The situation deserves discussion, weighing the various risks in the individual patient. Treatment with erythromycin may control the infection in the gravid patient but it may fail to prevent or cure the infection in her fetus. Experience with cephaloridine is limited but a hypersensitivity reaction is to be expected in nine per cent of those with a history of hypersensitivity to penicillin, and preparations (appendix to this chapter) should therefore be made to deal with a reaction, particularly if a Type 1 systemic reaction (anaphylactic sensitivity) should occur [25].

Green [26] has discussed the problem in relation to optimal antibiotic therapy for patients with a history of penicillin allergy who have a life-threatening infection such as bacterial endocarditis. About 60 per cent (34/56) of Green's patients with bacterial endocarditis who gave a history of hypersensitivity to penicillin were treated with this antibiotic without incident. Four patients reacted severely enough to discontinue treatment and one had a severe, although not fatal, anaphylactic type reaction. It is through the fear of the latter reaction that physicians tend to avoid giving penicillin to all who give a history of penicillin allergy.

Type 1 hypersensitivity reactions (anaphylactic sensitivity) are very rare indeed and occur in about 3 in every 100,000 cases and fatalities in less than 2 in every 100,000. The rare and fatal reactions occur mainly in those known to have had a prior reaction to penicillin or an allergic diathesis [26]. Skin testing is not useful in detecting those liable to develop the serious and feared Type 1 hypersensitivity reaction and indeed fatal anaphylactic reactions have been reported in patients with a negative skin test to penicillin.

It appears therefore that penicillin is withheld from many individuals who could tolerate it because of the fear that they may develop the rare anaphylactic Type 1 reaction.

It is wholly justifiable in a life-threatening condition such as bacterial endocarditis to give penicillin, when it is considered to be the best antibiotic, to patients who give a history of allergy to this antibiotic, although its administration should be in hospital under the guidance of a physician knowledgeable in the handling of acute allergic states [26]. These special facilities include: (1) giving subcutaneously suitable freshly prepared dilutions of aqueous penicillin G by the doctor into the arm of the patient distal to a sphygmomanometer cuff placed on the arm for recording blood pressures and, if necessary, for temporarily occluding the circulation to reduce the amount of penicillin reaching the systemic circulation; (2) the dosage would be of the order of 1.0iu; 2.0iu; 5.0iu; 10.0iu; 20iu and 50iu at intervals of not less than 15 minutes; (3) should no reaction occur larger doses are given, say, 100iu; 1000iu and 10,000iu before giving the larger dose required to begin for the course of treatment; (4) during the time-consuming administration of treatment the facilities listed in the appendix to this chapter (including adrenaline injection B.P., already in the syringe and hydrocortisone sodium phosphate 100mg ampoules) should be available as well as the supporting facilities for the very serious reaction outlined in fuller detail by Green [26]. Consultation with those skilled in intensive medical care is desirable.

Although the scheme may be justified in life-threatening bacterial endocarditis, is it justified to put the life of a pregnant woman at risk, even if remote, to protect or cure with certainty a fetal infection *in utero*? The infection in the fetus might or might not be seriously damaging and would be treatable effectively with penicillin at birth although damage already sustained would not necessarily be reversed.

The problem is not wholly solved and deserves thought. The clinician requires a test to recognize liability to systemic anaphylactic sensitivity (Type 1 hypersensitivity) and a means of preventing it. These questions, of an immunological nature, have not yet been answered.

Congenital syphilis

Congenital syphilis is considered more fully elsewhere (Chapter 8). The discovery of congenital syphilis is an indication of defective antenatal care or failure of antibiotic treatment, e.g. as with erythromycin, (*see* page 110).

The Venereal Diseases Control Advisory Committee [14] advise that the cerebrospinal fluid should be examined before treatment in congenital syphilis and that infants with abnormal c.s.f. particularly, require:

1. Aqueous crystalline penicillin G, 50,000 units/kg intramuscularly or intravenously daily in two divided doses for a minimum of 10 days, OR

2. Aqueous procaine penicillin G, 50,000 units/kg intramuscularly daily for a minimum of 10 days.

After the neonatal period the dose should be the same dosage used for neonatal congenital syphilis. For larger children the total dose need not exceed the dosage advised in adult syphilis for more than one year's duration. If hypersensitive to penicillin, erythromycin may be used. Tetracycline or oxytetracycline should not be used in those under 12 years of age [27].

FOLLOW-UP AFTER TREATMENT
(Early and congenital syphilis)

The Venereal Diseases Control Advisory Committee [14] advise that quantitative non-treponemal tests (e.g. VDRL) should be taken after three, six and twelve months. If disease is of more than one year's duration serological tests for syphilis should be repeated 24 months afterwards. Follow-up is especially important in patients treated with antibiotics other than penicillin. C.s.f. is examined at the last follow-up after treatment with alternative antibiotics. In neurosyphilis a follow-up is advised for at least 3 years, clinical revaluation at 6-month intervals when the c.s.f. may be examined.

In the authors' practice case holding tends to continue for longer than outlined in the preceding paragraph. In the case of early syphilis a 2–3-year follow-up is maintained where possible.

FOLLOW-UP AFTER TREATMENT
(Late-stage syphilis)

In the authors' practice in the case of late syphilis follow-up over a life time is maintained except in latent syphilis. In the case of cardiovascular syphilis follow-up by a cardiologist is also advisable. In the case of neurosyphilis a life-time follow-up is best. Liaison with the general practitioner responsible for primary care is essential particularly in late-stage cases where re-investigation may be started unnecessarily if the patient is admitted to hospital for investigation of some possibly unrelated complaint.

RETREATMENT

Reinfection with syphilis (page 91) is a possibility particularly in the promiscuous who have casual relationships and where contacts, as in the case of some homosexuals particularly, may fear or neglect to surface for medical help. A cerebrospinal fluid examination should be carried out before retreatment unless reinfection and a diagnosis of early syphilis is clearly established.

Retreatment should be considered under the following circumstances:

1. If clinical signs or symptoms persist or recur.
2. If there is a sustained fourfold increase in the titre of a non-treponemal test.
3. If an initially high titre non-treponemal test fails to show a fourfold decrease within a year.

When a patient is retreated one retreatment course is indicated and the course used will be that recommended for syphilis of more than one year's duration.

TREATMENT ON EPIDEMIOLOGICAL GROUNDS

The authors consider that patients, who have clearly been exposed to infectious syphilis and who are not willing or likely to cease sexual intercourse for three months, or to attend for surveillance, should be considered for treatment and followed up; the regimen advised is that for early syphilis. It is our practice to treat husband and wife simultaneously, if possible, if one partner develops early syphilis. Every effort is made, however, to establish a diagnosis in such cases.

In the case of early-stage syphilis rapid therapeutic or preventive treatment for the infected person or potentially infected contacts will interrupt a possible chain of infection. Although about one-third of recently exposed persons will develop syphilis and two-thirds will not, the United States Public Health Service has advocated 'epidemiologic' treatment (preventive) of all contacts because of the inability to identify quickly those who will develop the disease [28]. In the authors' practice this is not generally applied as early syphilis is still not common in this city and is sporadic in appearance. In favour of the concept of 'epidemiologic' treatment it must be said that on occasions contacts of early syphilis, particularly in those who are homosexual and promiscuous have been lost to follow-up. They have not infrequently defaulted from the prolonged serological testing necessary for the exclusion of syphilis.

Response to treatment and assessment of cure

(*a*) RESPONSE TO TREATMENT: EARLY STAGE SYPHILIS

Penicillin in sufficient dosage causes disappearance of *T. pallidum* from early surface lesions within 6–26 hours [2]. Infectivity appears to be lost very soon and lesions heal often within a few days. Obviously induration, depth, size and number of lesions will vary in relation to the duration of the disease and healing may be correspondingly longer. The infection can no longer be transmitted by sexual contact and relapse after adequate treatment is exceedingly rare, recurrences being usually due to reinfection.

In addition to careful clinical assessment of the patient, serological tests must be performed serially over a period of time to ensure that treatment has been satisfactory. These tests should be carried out immediately after completion of treatment, monthly for the first 3 months and thereafter 3-monthly in the first year and twice in the second year.

Following satisfactory treatment, quantitative tests for cardiolipin antibody (e.g. VDRL) gradually become negative, usually within 3 to 6 months, unless the initial titre was high, in which case positive results may be obtained, at lower titres, for a much longer period (*see*, for example, Figure 4.4, which shows the changes in titres of serological tests taken after treatment of a patient who is later re-infected).

The RPCFT, like tests for cardiolipin antibody, usually becomes negative within 6 months of treatment of early syphilis.

The TPHA which detects mainly IgG antibody, remains positive for years after treatment, unless this was given very early in the course of the disease when the titre in the serum was low (e.g. 1 in 80). Unlike the cardiolipin antibody tests, the TPHA is therefore of very little value in assessing efficacy of treatment and like the *T. pallidum* immobilization test remains positive often for years, or even for life. The FTA-ABS test and probably the ELISA also remain positive for many years after treatment. More experience is required in the use of the FTA-IgM test before it can be used routinely.

To ensure that treatment of secondary syphilis has been adequate it is generally considered good practice, even after penicillin therapy, to examine the cerebrospinal fluid (cell count, total protein content, IgG content, VDRL, TPHA and FTA-ABS test) about a year after treatment. Such examinations are essential after treatments with antibiotics other than penicillin.

Abstinence from sexual intercourse is advised in a patient being treated for early syphilis until the disease cannot be transmitted. This is usually achieved within a few days but it is wise for the patient to abstain until after the course of antibiotic when all lesions will be healed and possibly for one month after treatment if resumption of intercourse with an uninfected partner is to take place. If one partner is infected and has put the other at risk simultaneous treatment of both is advisable as reinfection of the treated by the untreated can occur. Such treatment on epidemiological grounds in a person at very high risk will call for the same follow-up and assessment of cure as in the patient in whom a diagnosis is established.

(*b*) RESPONSE TO TREATMENT; LATE-STAGE SYPHILIS

Response to treatment is discussed elsewhere for gummatous syphilis (page 127), neurosyphilis (page 134) and cardiovascular syphilis (page 140). Titres of cardiolipin antigen tests tend to diminish over the years in some but persistence of a high titre does not necessarily indicate a need for further treatment. If penicillin has been given in an adequate dosage further courses are not necessarily indicated. In cases of neurosyphilis the advisability of higher penicillin dosage is under consideration as levels in the cerebrospinal fluid after doses of long-acting penicillin preparations may be very low (page 109).

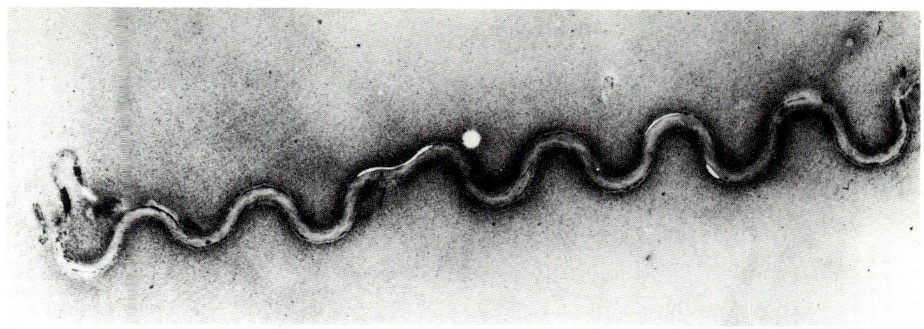

1

Plate 1 Electron micrograph of *Treponema pallidum* from exudate of a primary chancre (stained with phosphotungstic acid): magnification x 60,000. Reproduced by kind permission of Dr R. H. A. Swain.

Plate 2 Condylomata lata of the vulva.

Plate 3 Perianal condylomata lata in homosexual male.

2

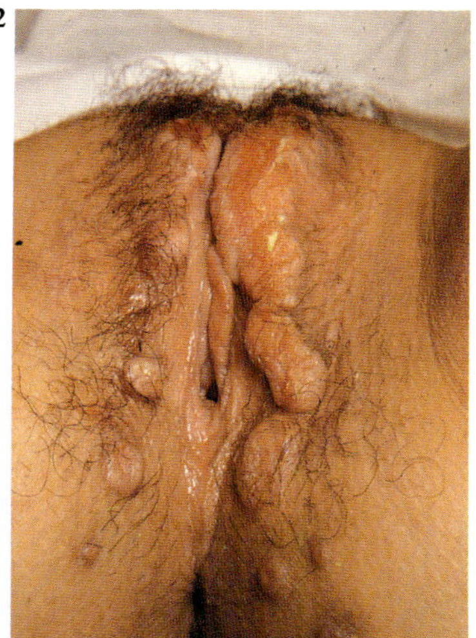

3

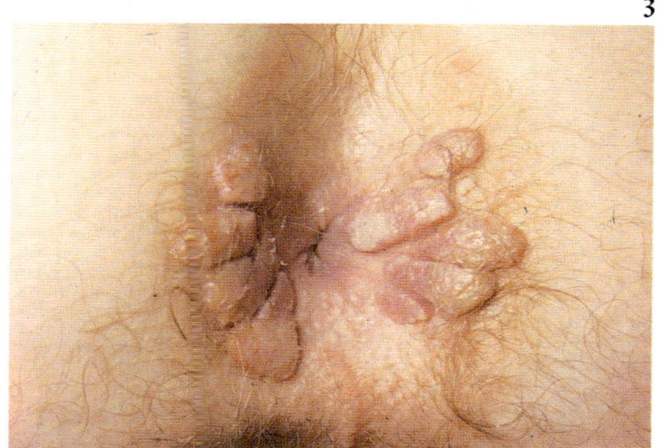

4

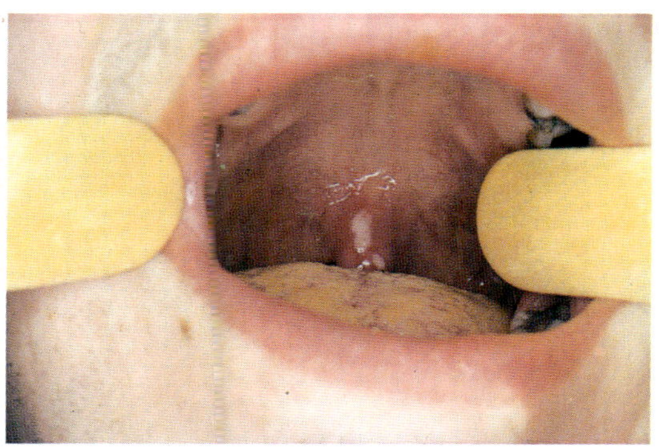

Plate 4 Mucous patch on uvula in secondary syphilis.

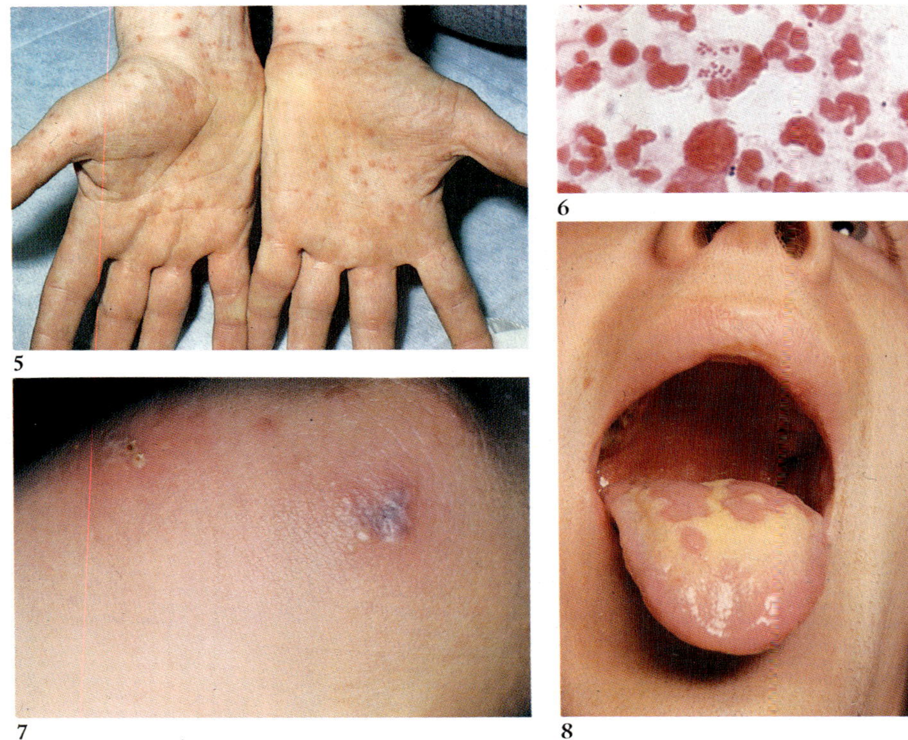

Plate 5 Palmar syphilide in secondary syphilis.

Plate 6 Gram-stained smear of urethral discharge in a male with gonorrhoea.

Plate 7 Haemorrhagic vesicles and pustules on the elbow in disseminated gonococcal infection.

Plate 8 'Bald' patches on dorsum of tongue in Reiter's disease.

Plate 9 Pocks due to Herpesvirus Type 1 on the chorioallantoic membrane of a developing chick embryo. Compare with Plate 10.

Plate 10 Pocks due to Herpesvirus Type 2 on the chorioallantoic membrane of a developing chick embryo. Compare with Plate 9.

Plate 11 Electron micrograph of vesicle fluid showing a herpesvirus The envelope is present, although broken, and the individual capsomeres can be seen on the capsid (100nm). Phosphotungstic acid preparation x 100,000.

Plate 12 Herpesvirus Type 1. Electron micrograph showing intranuclear array of naked virions and margination of host-cell chromatin (Ultrathin section stained with uranyl acetate and lead hydroxide x 17,600).

Plate 13 Herpesvirus Type 2. Electron micrograph showing intranuclear and cytoplasmic filaments and a few virions. The nuclear membrane is not preserved. (Ultrathin section stained with uranyl acetate and lead hydroxide x 40,000).

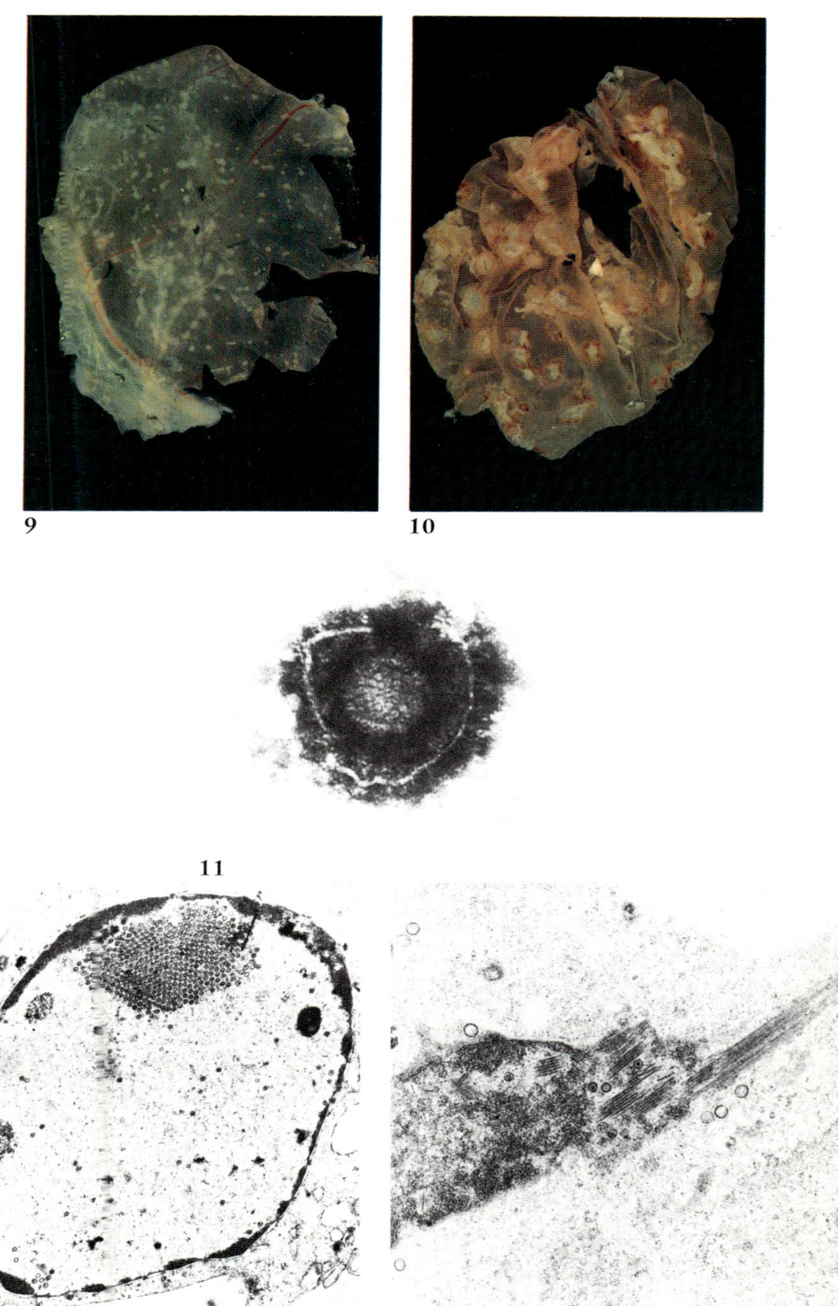
9
10
11
12
13

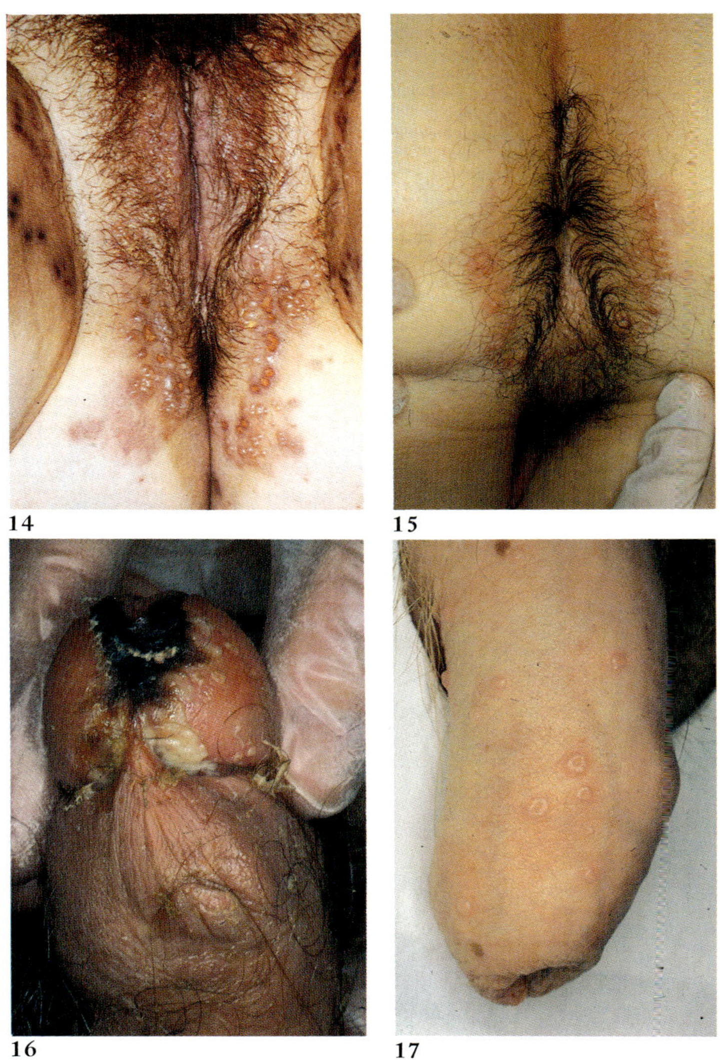

Plate 14 Herpes simplex of the vulva.

Plate 15 Perianal herpes simplex in homosexual male.

Plate 16 Necrotizing balanitis in a case of primary herpes genitalis with herpes lesions also disseminated elsewhere in the body

Plate 17 Molluscum contagiosum, penile lesions.

JARISCH–HERXHEIMER REACTION (JHR)

This reaction is a complication that usually follows within a day of the initial treatment of a number of organismal diseases, including syphilis, and it is characterized by fever and an aggravation of existing lesions together with their attendant symptoms and signs [29, 30, 31].

In 1895 Jarisch recorded the fact that the spots of roseolar syphilis became clearer and more numerous after treatment with mercury. Later, in 1902, Herxheimer and Krause pointed out that the reaction followed soon after an adequate dose of mercury and was accompanied by a rise in temperature. The reaction is generally confined to the first day of treatment and it occurs also after treatment with antibiotics such as penicillin; it can be evoked twice in the same patient if the first injection of penicillin is only 10–20iu per kg body weight [32]. The JHR develops in about 55 per cent of cases of VDRL negative primary syphilis, also in 95 per cent of VDRL positive primary and secondary cases. In 75 per cent of patients with general paralysis of the insane, particularly in those with high c.s.f. cell counts, the JHR may be expected to occur after treatment when there may be exacerbation of mental signs or symptoms. Generally no reaction is noted following treatment of very early and late-stage latent syphilis. The JHR may occur in early-stage congenital syphilis, most frequently in children under the age of 6 months, but is rare after treatment of late-stage congenital syphilis.

The salient features of the JHR are as follows [33]:

1. A rise and then a fall in body temperature: the rise is accompanied by a chill and the fall by sweating.
2. Aggravation of pre-existing lesions and their attendant symptoms and signs, e.g., flaring of the rash in syphilis and acute myocarditis in louse-borne relapsing fever.
3. Characteristic physiological changes, which include early vasoconstriction, hyperventilation and a rise in blood pressure and cardiac output, and later a fall in blood pressure associated with a low peripheral resistance.

In 1895 Jarisch postulated that the cause of the reaction was a toxin liberated from degenerating treponemes but it was not until 1961 that endotoxin-like activity was detected in a spirochaete, *Borrelia vincentii* [31] and only in 1973 was a lipopolysaccharide, resembling that of Gram-negative organisms, identified in *T. pallidum* [34]. In louse-borne relapsing fever, due to *Borrelia recurrentis*, the JHR is much more severe than in syphilis and in an investigation Bryceson *et al* [33] found that in one case out of the four examined the plasma taken from a patient during the JHR induced fever 60 minutes after transfusion into that patient on the following day. In addition endotoxin has been detected by the limulus amoebocyte lysate assay in the plasma of patients at the time they were undergoing the JHR and this was accompanied by depression of the third component of complement [35]. Findings of Fulford *et al* [36] suggested activation of the classical pathway resulting from antigen–antibody interaction, rather than the alternative pathway, although some alternative pathway antibody by treponemal endotoxin could not be excluded. Polymorphonuclear activation may lead to pyrogen release and resulting fever. These authors also found that levels of IgM fluorescent treponemal antibodies (FTA) were higher in patients who developed reactions than in those who did not. Combination of these antibodies with newly available antigenic sites could lead to complement binding. They suggested that antigenic determinants, particularly those corresponding to FTA antibody, placed deeply within the treponemes, may be released after death and breakdown of treponemes by treatment.

In neurosyphilis exacerbation of signs may occur in patients treated with penicillin [37, 38] and this may resemble but be less severe than the reactive encephalopathy seen in patients with *Trypanosoma brucei rhodesiense* or *T.b.gambiense* meningo-encephalitis treated with melarsoprol [39]. In neither general paralysis of the insane nor in secondary syphilis, however, are these JHR as severe as in louse-borne relapsing fever. In a number of instances a possible flare-up of local lesions is feared as for example in acute labyrinthitis of early syphilis when irreversible deafness is a threat [40]. In the now rare gummata of the brain and larynx, which contain numerous treponemes, treatment has proved on occasions fatal [41]. In local lesions of the aorta involving the coronary ostia [15] a JHR may give rise to anxiety (page 141).

The late lesions of syphilis described are rare. The use of prednisolone in high initial dosage is advised on rather limited evidence in acute labyrinthitis and may be considered, again on limited evidence of its efficacy, in late forms of disease where exacerbation of local inflammation is feared. In the louse-borne relapsing fever model of the JHR, high dose hydrocortisone infused before and during the JHR reduced the patient's base line temperature but did not mitigate the febrile, physiological or local inflammatory features of the JHR in any way [42]. The clinical value of steroids remains unproven, although prednisone may reduce pyrexia [32].

CLINICAL PHASES OF THE JARISCH-HERXHEIMER REACTION (JHR)

There are four clinical phases and the effects are greatest in secondary syphilis and in general paralysis of the insane. In primary syphilis the effects are usually mild. The reaction develops within four hours of starting treatment, becomes most intense at six to eight hours and resolves within 24 hours.

The clinical phases are:

(*a*) *Prodromal phase* with aches and pains.

(*b*) *Rigor* or *chill.* Temperature rises by an average 1°C. (Range 0.2°–2.7°C) four to eight hours after treatment.

(*c*) *Flush.* Temperature reaches a peak usually at about eight hours after the first injection and is associated with hypotension.

(*d*) *Defervescence,* which lasts up to 12 hours.

Other clinical and physiological observations

The patient may feel discomfort in the local lesions which become more pronounced and show an acute transient inflammatory reaction. Histologically it is found that neutrophil and mononuclear cells appear and migrate through the swollen vascular endothelium into the surrounding oedematous tissue.

There is a leucocytosis and a fall in the lymphocyte count. The metabolic rate is increased and peaks with the rigor. Pulmonary ventilation and cardiac output exceed metabolic requirements and pulmonary oxygen uptake is impaired.

During the rigor phase there is early hyperventilation; the systemic arterial blood-pressure rises due to vasoconstriction, but falls in the flush phase due to decrease in vascular resistance as a result of vasodilatation.

The reaction to specific treatment, whether antibiotic or not, is seen in diseases other than syphilis, namely in louse-borne relapsing fever, rat-bite fever, leptospirosis, yaws, brucellosis, tularaemia, glanders, anthrax and in African trypanosomiasis, particularly in that due to *T.b.rhodesiense.* In relapsing fever and leptospirosis the reaction is much more severe than in syphilis and it can be fatal.

ADVERSE EFFECTS OF PENICILLIN

Penicillins are virtually non toxic in the doses discussed but by far the most serious reactions are due to hypersensitivity—Type 1 anaphylactic sensitivity—(Appendix to this chapter) and penicillin is one of the most common causes of other forms of hypersensitivity. There appears to be no completely safe and reliable practical method of detecting sensitivity to penicillin but inquiry concerning reactions to previous treatment should always be made. Patients who suffer from sensitivities to other agents are more liable to react adversely to penicillin and sensitivity induced by one penicillin may lead to similar reactions to others. Reactions are more severe when penicillin is given parenterally but may be fatal after even oral administration. Reactions include skin rashes of all types, fever, arthralgia, lymphadenopathy, stomatitis and glossitis but Type 1 hypersensitivity (anaphylactic reactions) with hypotension, bronchospasm, prostration, cardiac arrest and death may occur.

Occasionally very serious reactions and even death occurring during or shortly after an injection of penicillin may result from accidental intravenous injection with subsequent pulmonary embolism. Some of these reactions may simulate anaphylaxis. Some patients may experience extreme anxiety and a sensation of impending death after aqueous procaine penicillin. Acute psychotic behaviour may occur. These attacks are self-limiting, subsiding after 15–30 minutes and it appears that they are due to direct procaine toxicity [43].

In syphilis the Jarisch-Herxheimer reaction (page 117) occurs within the first twenty-four hours of treatment and it is particularly prominent in secondary syphilis.

ADVERSE EFFECTS OF TETRACYCLINES

As tetracyclines are selectively taken up by the growing teeth and bones of fetus or child the use of tetracyclines should be avoided in pregnancy or in childhood. Tetracyclines other than doxycycline should be avoided in patients with impaired renal function as acute renal failure may be precipitated. Doxycycline, in particular, commonly induces photosensitization and patients should be warned regarding the risks of sun-bathing if receiving this treatment.

Gastrointestinal side-effects of tetracycline therapy such as nausea, vomiting and mild diarrhoea, are common. Less commonly there is suppression of normal microbial flora leading to superinfection of skin and mucous membrane with organisms such as *Candida* spp, *Staphylococcus aureus*, *Proteus* spp. Rarely a fulminating staphylococcal enterocolitis results.

ERYTHROMYCIN

Erythromycin, given orally, as the stearate, is well absorbed from the gastrointestinal tract, peak levels being obtained two to four hours after ingestion. Erythromycin estolate is hepatotoxic, and the stearate ester (ethylsuccinate or base) should be used in the treatment of syphilis. The dosage recommended is not toxic, nausea and vomiting are uncommon side effects, occurring in less than 5 per cent of cases.

Erythromycin although apparently safe to use in pregnancy is unpredictable in its effects on the fetus in *in utero* syphilis (page 110).

Appendix to Chapter 6
Reactions to penicillin

Hypersensitivity reactions (Instructions for out-patient clinic)

PRECAUTIONS

1. Avoid penicillin in those with a history of:

   Previous penicillin reactions
   Bronchial asthma
   Tendency to allergic reactions
   (Biological false-positive reactors).

2. The injections should be given to the patient in the lying down position or a couch should be nearby.

3. The patient should have rested for 5 minutes before the injection and he/she should wait for 25 minutes afterwards.

4. Avoid unintentional intravenous injections by observing the following technique:

   (*a*) Use one needle for drawing up the contents of the ampoule.
   (*b*) Use another needle for the injection.
   (*c*) Insert the needle into the upper and outer quadrant of the buttocks.
   (*d*) Patient should be in the prone position.
   (*e*) Leave the needle for 30 seconds after insertion and suck back before injection.
   (*f*) If a vein is entered withdraw the needle and reinsert.

Emergency kit

Adrenaline injection BP .... Ampoule 1ml 3
Disposable syringe (2ml + needles) 3
Chlorpheniramine maleate (Piriton) ...... Ampoule 10mg 3
Aminophylline injection BP (250mg in 10ml) 3
Disposable syringes (10ml) 3
Hydrocortisone sodium phosphate
(Efcortesol, Glaxo 100mg) Ampoules 3
Oxygen and means of administration
Sphygmomanometer

PROCEDURE

1. On appearance of signs of reaction patient should lie down—(head down and feet up position). Call the doctor.
2. Take blood pressure.
3. If BP is low give 0.5–1.0ml adrenaline intramuscularly into upper arm.
4. If no response give 100mg of hydrocortisone sodium phosphate i.m. or i.v.
5. If angioneurotic oedema give i.m. or i.v. chlorpheniramine (Piriton).
6. If cough, dyspnoea, respiratory distress give aminophylline i.v.

TYPE I HYPERSENSITIVITY REACTIONS (ANAPHYLACTIC-TYPE REACTIONS)

After a penicillin injection patients should be observed for 30 minutes, particularly after the first injection. The serious and life-threatening complication of penicillin which is feared is a Type 1 hypersensitivity reaction (anaphylactic-type reaction) and this calls for an immediate intramuscular injection of adrenaline (*see* above).

The signs and symptoms of a Type 1 hypersensitivity reaction (anaphylactic-type) include generalized pruritus, particularly of the palms of the hands and soles of the feet. Hyperaemia develops with facial flushing, bronchospasm, laryngeal oedema, hypotension, tachycardia and shock [44]. Early intramuscular adrenaline BP 0.5–1.0ml is the most important form of therapy.

Additional facilities which may be required in hypersensitivity reactions (*see* Green for fuller details [26]).

Equipment for intravenous infusion and tracheostomy, including tourniquet, venous cutdown equipment and 5% glucose; oxygen supply with means of administering it and endotracheal tube.

REFERENCES

1 Hare, R (1970) *The birth of penicillin and the disarming of microbes.* Allen and Unwin Ltd

2 Idsoe, O, Guthe, T and Willcox, R R (1972) *Penicillin in the Treatment of Syphilis: The experience of three decades.* Supplement to Vol. 47 of the Bulletin of the World Health Organization. World Health Organization, Geneva

3 Lamanna, C, Mallette, M F and Zimmerman, L (1973) *Limits of mutation.* in *Basic Bacteriology, its biological and chemical background.* Williams and Wilkins Company, Baltimore, page 626

4 Duguid, J P, Marmion, B P and Swain, R H A (Eds) (1978) *Mackie and McCartney Medical Microbiology. British Journal of Venereal Diseases* 13th ed. **1** Churchill Livingstone Edinburgh, page 15

5 Kern, A (1971) *Medicamentum,* Berlin *12,* page 194

6 Turner, T B and Hollander, D H (1957) in *Biology of the treponematoses* Wld. Hlth. Org. Monograph Series No 35, page 43

7 Goodman, L S and Gilman, A (1975) *The Pharmacological Basis of Therapeutics.* Bailliere Tindall, pages 1130–1140

8 Willcox, R R (1953) in *Progress in venereology,* Heinemann, London, page 97

9 Wright, J J (1975) *British Journal of Venereal Diseases,* **51**, 410

10 Moore, J E and Mohr, C F (1952) *Journal of the American Medical Association,* **150,** 467

11 Collart, P, Borel, L-J and Durel, P (1962) *Innales de l'Institut Pasteur de Lille,* **102,** 596; 693

12 Collart, P, Borel, L-J and Durel, P (1964) *British Journal of Venereal Diseases* **40,** 81

13 Dunlop, E M C (1972) *British Medical Journal,* **2,** 557

14 Center for Disease Control (1976) Syphilis *Journal of Infectious Diseases* Chicago, **134,** 97

15 Leading Article (1977) The Jarisch-Herxheimer reaction. *Lancet* **i,** 340

16 Garrod L P and O'Grady, F (1971) in *Antibiotic and Chemotherapy,* 3rd Edition. Livingstone, Edinburgh, page 326

17 Mohr, J A, Griffiths, W, Jackson, R, Saadah, H, Bird, P and Riddle, J (1976) *Journal of the American Medical Association,* **236,** 2208

18 Spence, M R (1977) *Medical Clinics of North America* **61**, No 1 139

19 Fenton, L J and Light, I J (1976) *Obstetrics and Gynecology,* **47,** 492

20 South, M A, Short, D H and Knox, J M (1964) *Journal of the American Medical Association,* **190,** 182

21 Ryden, E (1978) in *Erythromycin in Laboratory methods in antimicrobial chemotherapy.* (eds) Reeves, D S, Phillips, I, Williams, J D and Wise, R. Churchill Livingstone, Edinburgh, page 208

22 Holder, W R and Knox, J M (1972) *Medical Clinics of North America* **56,** 1151

23 Petz, L D (1971) *Postgraduate Medical Journal,* Supplement vol. 47, page 00

24 Dash, C H (1975) *Journal of Antimicrobial Chemotherapy, 1* (Suppl) 107

25 Roitt, I (1977) in *Essential Immunology.* Blackwell Scientific Publications, Oxford, page 151

26 Green, G R (1975) in *Penicillin Allergy: Clinical and immunological aspects* Stewart, G T and McGovern, J P (Eds) C C Thomas, Sprinfield, Illinois USA, page 162

27 McAllister, T A and Arneil, G C (1978) in *Textbood of Paediatrics* (Eds) Forfar, J O and Arneil, G C. Churchill Livingstone, Edinburgh, page 1615
28 Kaufman, R E, Blount, J H and Jones, O G (1974) *Public Health Reviews,* **3,** 175
29 Warrell, D A, Perine, P L, Bryceson, A D M, Parry, E H O and Pope, H M (1971) *American Journal of Medicine,* **51,** 176
30 Bryceson, A D M (1976) *Journal of Infectious Diseases,* **133**, 696
31 Leading Article (1977) *Lancet,* **i,** 340
32 Gudjonsson, H and Skog, E (1968) *Acta Dermato-venereologica,* **48,** 15
33 Bryceson, A D M, Cooper, K E, Warrell, D A, Perine, P L and Parry, E H O (1972) *Clinical Science,* **43,** 343
34 Jackson, S W and Pinina, N Z (1973) *Journal of Bacteriology,* **114,** 838
35 Gelfand, J A, Elin, R J, Berry, F W and Frank, M M (1976) *New England Journal of Medicine,* **295,** 211
36 Fulford, K W M, Johnson, N, Loveday, C, Storey, J and Tedder, R S (1976) *Clinical and Experimental Immunology,* **24,** 483
37 Tucker, H A and Robinson, R C V (1946) *Journal of the American Medical Association,* **132,** 281
38 Hoekenga, M T and Farmer, T W (1948) *Archives of Internal Medicine*, **82,** 611
39 Robertson, D H H (1963) *Transactions of the Royal Society of Tropical Medicine and Hygiene,* **57,** 122
40 Vercoe, G S (1976) *Journal of Laryngology and Utology,* **90,** 853
41 Moore, J E, Farmer, T W and Hoekenga, M T (1948) *Transactions of the Association of American Physicians,* **61,** 176
42 Warrell, D A, Pope, H M, Parry, H O, Perine, P L and Bryceson, A D M (1970) *Clinical Science,* **39,** 123
43 Kucers, A and Bennett, N McK (1975) *The use of antibiotics.* Heinemann Medical Books, London
44 Drusin, L M (1972) The diagnosis and treatment of infectious and latent syphilis. *Medical Clinics of North America,* **56,** No. 5, 1161

FURTHER READING

Kucers, A and Bennett, N McK (1975) *The use of antibiotics.* Heinemann Medical Books, London

Stewart, G T and McGovern, J P (1970) *Penicillin Allergy. Clinical and immunological aspects.* C C Thomas, Springfield, Illinois, USA

CHAPTER 7

Acquired Syphilis: Late Stage

In the early years of a syphilitic infection the lesions already described (chancre, mucous patch, condyloma latum) are infectious and there is evidence of a recurrent spirochaetaemia and recurring mucocutaneous lesions. In pregnant women also infection of the fetus *in utero* is inevitable in early untreated syphilis. Syphilis then enters a subclinical stage of latency, in which the only readily detectable evidence of infection is serological and this latency may persist for years or even for life. Transmission of the disease by sexual intercourse does not occur although in the case of pregnancy the woman can infect her fetus long after she has ceased to be infectious sexually. Further activity of the disease may, at any time during latency, cause profound effects [1] and lead to death as long as three decades or more after infection. The main forms of late-stage syphilis are described below although the protean manifestations call for the consideration of syphilis in the differential diagnoses of many diseases involving particularly the cardiovascular or central nervous system.

The decline in the incidence of late-stage syphilis [2] and of neurosyphilis and cardiovascular syphilis in particular has been discussed in relation to the changes in the social impact of STD (page 12). By 1969, for example, deaths in England and Wales from these two main causes declined further to 73 and 148 respectively and in 1973 to 38 and 85.

Late-stage latent syphilis

The diagnosis rests on the finding of positive specific serological tests for syphilis (Chapter 4), and the absence of other evidence of disease. Before reaching this diagnosis the cerebrospinal fluid (Chapter 4) should be examined and the heart and aorta screened by fluoroscopy to exclude changes due to involvement of the aortic valve and the first part of the aorta particularly. In the absence of obvious stigmata of congenital syphilis, corneal microscopy should be carried out in patients with latent syphilis, as the finding of traces of a healed interstitial keratitis will assist in differentiating a congenital infection from an acquired (page 148). Latent syphilis is the commonest manifestation of late syphilis, probably made more common because the patient will have had courses of antibiotics for other conditions which will have prevented the emergence of the late effects such as neurosyphilis.

In syphilis of longer than two years' duration longer courses and sometimes higher doses of penicillin are considered necessary (Chapter 6). Clear cut demonstration of the value of treatment is not always so apparent as in early syphilis except perhaps in gummatous skin lesions and in some cases of neurosyphilis. In late-stage latent syphilis the prognosis with treatment is good. The differentiation between early-stage latent and late-stage latent is an arbitrary distinction but treatment prevents the emergence of late effects although it cannot reverse damage already sustained. This general rule appears to be sound clinically although it should be noted that only careful examinations will detect the cardiovascular changes and the methods currently used to detect involvement of the central nervous system (c.s.f. examination) may not be entirely sensitive.

There are problems too in the diagnosis of reinfection and present serological tests may not give clear answers. Clinical judgement must be used therefore in deciding whether to re-treat a patient whose life style brings him into continuous risk of reinfection.

Late-stage gummatous syphilis

This is now very rare. It is characterized by gumma formation (syphilitic granulation tissue) which may develop because there is reactivation of residual treponemes in sensitized persons who have been untreated or inadequately treated. Possibly re-exposure may induce gumma formation in sensitized persons who have been adequately treated [3].

Serological tests are positive (Chapter 4). Gummatous lesions tend to be solitary or few in number. They are asymmetrical, indurated and indolent. On the skin late-stage lesions tend to be arcuate in outline because without treatment, they tend to heal partially in the centre and extend peripherally. Atrophic or hyperpigmented scars form. Gummatous lesions respond rapidly to treatment. A gumma may form a nodule in the subcutaneous tissue which increases in size, breaks down and may produce a gummatous ulcer, often described as 'punched out' as it tends to have vertical walls. The granular floor of such an ulcer may have a 'wash leather' appearance due to slough. The sites commonly involved are the upper part of the leg below the knee, the scalp, face, sternoclavicular region or the buttocks.

The mouth and throat are much less frequently involved by a gummatous lesion than the skin and bones. The submucosa is involved first but either the soft or hard palate may be affected, leading to perforation. A gumma of the tongue can develop but a diffuse lesion with infiltration and a chronic superficial glossitis is more common. In such a case the patchy epithelial necrosis and the leukoplakia which develops, produces white areas of adherent epithelium on the tongue. Mouth lesions should be biopsied always as malignant change is not uncommon and a careful life-long follow-up is necessary. Infiltration of the laryngeal mucosa may occur with or without ulceration.

Two main types of late syphilis of bone are recognized. Gummatous periostitis without destruction but with bony proliferation may lead to the development of 'sabre tibia'. Gummatous osteitis may cause a destructive lesion. Clinically, in late syphilis of the bone, the patient may have boring pain and localized redness or swelling.

In congenital syphilis of the acute form, many treponemes are found in the liver, and a pericellular fibrosis results. Gummata of the liver may occur in late syphilis. A gumma of the testis produces a smooth painless swelling; the testis must be removed surgically to exclude malignant neoplasm (Chapter 14). Lesions of the oesophagus, stomach and intestine have been reported. An opacity, however, detected in a chest X-ray of a patient with syphilis is nearly always due to a carcinoma as a gumma is very rare [4].

Gummatous lesions generally respond rapidly to treatment although when fibrosis is marked resolution will be slow. Reference has already been made to the importance of biopsy and a careful follow-up in cases of mouth lesions where malignant change is a recognized hazard.

Neurosyphilis

Although *Treponema pallidum* may invade the central nervous system and involve particularly the meninges during early syphilis causing minor changes in the cerebrospinal fluid (c.s.f.), overt manifestations may occur only in about 5 per cent of cases. If not clinically inapparent, meningeal symptoms or signs may appear abruptly (headache or drowsiness, amaurosis with papilloedema, cranial nerve palsies or hemiplegia). Neurological abnormalities in early syphilis have been referred to in Chapter 5.

Neurosyphilis of the late stage is uncommon although its sporadic appearance and often very good response to antibiotic therapy makes it vitally important to make a diagnosis as early as possible. It may appear in a form with more localized and less striking clinical effects [5, 6] than was seen in the classical forms of parenchymatous neurosyphilis which were so much commoner in times before antibiotic and chemotherapy, when the wards of every mental hospital were crowded with cases in various stages of mental and physical deterioration. Although late-stage neurosyphilis can be classified into various forms there may be considerable overlap.

It is clearly important in all hospital departments to consider syphilis in diagnosis and to use treponemal serological tests (e.g. TPHA, FTA-ABS; *see* Chapter 4) as non-treponemal tests (e.g. VDRL; *see* Chapter 4) are sometimes negative in late syphilis. In recent years early infectious syphilis has been commoner in homosexual males and in recent series of 17 cases of neurosyphilis, one occurred in a woman and 16 in men, of whom seven were homosexual [5].

PATHOLOGY OF NEUROSYPHILIS

In all forms of meningovascular syphilis there is a widespread often diffuse thickening of the pia-arachnoid and infiltration with lymphocytes and plasma cells. The basal meningitis of the secondary stage may be carried into the late stage with increased fibrosis and the formation of small miliary gummata. This can lead to hydrocephalus and papilloedema. The basal meningitis may be continued over the upper cervical segments of the spinal cord or a diffuse spinal arachnoiditis may reveal its presence by root signs and symptoms. Meningeal gummata are very rare.

Lesions of the cerebral vessels may accompany any form of neurosyphilis but syphilitic vascular disease is not a common cause of cerebral vascular accidents. The classical lesion is endarteritis obliterans with fibroblastic and eventually collagenous thickening of the intima.

In tabes dorsalis the lesions are concentrated on the dorsal roots and columns, most often at the lumbosacral and lower thoracic levels. In classical paretic dementia (general paralysis of the insane) in a patient who dies demented after several years of illness the brain is shrunken and covered with opaque thickened arachnoid. Microscopical examination at any stage shows the lesions to be concentrated in the cerebral cortex, corpus striatum and hypothalamus. In the cerebral cortex, particularly in the prefrontal cortex, all cellular elements are involved with a striking loss of cortical architecture. The meningeal and perivascular infiltrations, microglial and astrocytic hyperplasia and the degeneration and disappearance of nerve cells are similar to those found in other forms of subacute or chronic encephalitis such as African trypanosomiasis (due to *Trypanosoma brucei rhodesiense* or more particularly in that due to *T. b. gambiense*) and subacute sclerosing panencephalitis.

Although neurosyphilis is classified as parenchymatous or meningovascular, overlapping processes are found. The classification of tabes dorsalis among the parenchymatous forms of neurosyphilis is justified by the concentration of the lesions in the dorsal roots and columns. In most cases of tabes dorsalis in which cerebral symptoms appear and which are diagnosed clinically as taboparesis the cerebral lesions are those of meningovascular syphilis. Again, primary optic atrophy is commonly associated with tabes dorsalis and sometimes with meningovascular syphilis but rarely with general paralysis of the insane [8].

CLINICAL FORMS OF ACQUIRED LATE-STAGE NEUROSYPHILIS

ASYMPTOMATIC NEUROSYPHILIS

The diagnosis rests on c.s.f. findings, indicative of syphilis of the c.n.s. in the absence of clinical symptoms or signs. It is reasonable to conclude that the inflammatory process is more restricted than in those forms of the disease with overt signs and symptoms. The investigation in such a case should not be restricted to serological tests for syphilis and c.s.f. examination but should include a full clinical examination and fluoroscopic chest examination to exclude signs of syphilis in other systems.

MENINGOVASCULAR SYPHILIS

Symptoms and signs of meningovascular involvement may develop even during the secondary stage when the effect is predominantly meningeal with signs discussed already.

Meningovascular syphilis of the late stage may produce headache associated with cranial nerve palsies, particularly of the third and sixth; the auditory or vestibular nerves may also be affected. The optic nerves or chiasma may be involved in a basal meningitis. If cerebral vessels are affected mental deterioration and focal signs such as aphasia or hemiplegia will occur. If the gummatous infiltration involves the spinal cord progressive paraplegia can develop and occasionally there is a transverse myelitis due to occlusion of the anterior spinal artery. In meningovascular and indeed all forms of late-stage neurosyphilis pupillary abnormalities are common and the fully developed sign is the Argyll Robertson pupil.

Argyll Robertson pupil

In December 1868 at a meeting of the Edinburgh Medico-Chirurgical Society [9], Douglas Argyll Robertson described reflex pupillary paralysis to light in a case of spinal disease and later he defined the sign now known by his name:

'Although the retina is quite sensitive, and the pupil contracts during the act of accommodation for near objects, yet an alteration of the amount of light admitted into the eye does not influence the size of the pupil.'

In all forms of late neurosyphilis, overt or latent, pupillary abnormalities in the presence of good vision are common. In more than 80 per cent of cases and in tabes in particular, pupil abnormalities develop in the course of time. The fully developed condition already described and known as the Argyll Robertson pupil is a valuable sign although not pathognomonic of neurosyphilis, as it has been described as a curiosity in conditions such as diabetes, hypertrophic polyneuritis, sarcoidosis and injury to the orbit [10].

Earlier manifestations of reflex iridoplegia (failure to react to light) may be found in neurosyphilis and during neurological examination the eye should be examined carefully to discover whether:

1. Reaction to light is reduced in amplitude.
2. Reaction to light is not sustained.
3. Latent period is longer than usual.
4. Reaction may be brisker in one eye.
5. Consensual reflex may be brisker than the direct.
6. Rarely a dilatation may occur in response to light.

In addition, oculosympathetic paralysis may be seen with no dilatation of the pupil in response to a scratch on the neck. Ptosis with compensatory wrinkling of the brow may also occur. Patchy depigmentation of the iris may give it a watery blue colour. Both pupils are usually affected but unequally.

The fully developed Argyll Robertson pupil may best be described as 'small, constant in size and unaltered by light or shade; it contracts promptly and fully on convergence and dilates again promptly when the effort to converge is relaxed; it dilates slowly and imperfectly to mydriatics.'

The method of testing is important.

The light reflex

1. Ask the patient to look at a distant object.
2. Cover the other eye to eliminate the consensual reaction.
3. Test by shining light into the eye and look for contraction of the pupil.

Accommodation reflex

1. Ask the patient to look at distant object.
2. Then, ask him to look at examiner's finger which is brought gradually to within 2 inches of the eyes. The reaction consists of contraction of the medial recti muscles and contraction of the pupil.

The site of the lesion continues to excite controversy and is not entirely settled although the reflex paths in the midbrain are the most popular site for the causal injury although a peripheral lesion in the iris has been suggested.

General paresis
(Dementia paralytica, general paralysis of the insane or GPI)

This can develop 7–15 years after a primary infection. The clinical syndrome now encountered is often one of simple mental deterioration, sometimes with depression, not distinguishable from the commoner and less specific presenile dementia. In the classical form of GPI the disease is insidious in its development and is characterized by episodes of strange behaviour at variance with the previous good character of the individual. Comprehension and aesthetic feelings are dulled and the alterations in the patient's personality distress his friends and relatives. Grandiose delusions and euphoria used to be commonly seen but are rare now. Writing may be tremulous and tremors of the tongue, hands and facial muscles may develop. Pronunciation difficulties may distort words beyond recognition. Epileptic fits and transient attacks of hemiplegia and aphasia are frequent. Tremor of the hands and a slow slurred speech are characteristic as the disease progresses. Spastic weakness of the legs develops and the final stage is that of paralysis and dementia [10].

Neurosyphilitic psychosis most commonly presents now as a depressive illness or a simple dementia and patients presenting with grandiose delusions are very rare [11].

Tendon reflex abnormalities are common and degrees of iridoplegia, irregularity and inequality of the pupils are valuable signs. The fully developed Argyll Robertson pupil may be found in 25 per cent of cases.

Tabes dorsalis

The lesions in tabes dorsalis are concentrated on the dorsal spinal roots and dorsal columns of the spinal cord most often at the lumbosacral and lower thoracic levels. The dorsal roots are thin and grey and contrast with the thick white ventral roots. The dorsal columns show shrinkage although the dorsal root ganglia show less definite atrophy. The reasons for this selective degeneration are not understood.

Among the subjective manifestations are lightning pains, so called from their sudden brief stabbing quality. A brief jab of severe pain striking a localized point of one leg may make the patient wince. Such pains can be felt as girdle pains around the trunk or in the area supplied by the trigeminal nerve. The patient may complain of paraesthesiae saying that he feels as if he is walking on cotton wool. He may have defects in his sensation of the need to defaecate or to empty his bladder.

Various paroxysmal painful disorders of the viscera known as tabetic crises, probably reflecting irritation of the dorsal roots, may occur as a result of spasm of smooth muscle. In gastric crises attacks of epigastric pain and ceaseless vomiting may mimic the 'acute abdomen' and last for several days. Laryngeal crises present with dyspnoea, cough and stridor. Tenesmus and bladder and penis pain occur in rectal and vesical crises respectively.

Other symptoms and signs are explained in terms of loss of sensory function. The patient is ataxic as there is loss of position sense, he tends to walk on a broad base, staggering and lifting his feet with a stamping gait. In Romberg's sign the patient demonstrates his inability to keep his balance with his eyes closed and his feet together. Muscles are hypotonic, the tendon reflexes diminished or absent. Vibration sense, deep pain sense and position sense are all diminished or absent.

Trophic changes may be seen. In the neuropathic joint (Charcot's joint) affecting a knee, a wrist, or other joints, there is bone destruction with osteophyte formation. The joint is swollen and deformed with marked crepitus but quite painless. Collapse of the lumbar spine can cause nerve root compression. Perforating trophic ulcers may develop on the soles of the feet.

Charcot's joints are not pathognomic of syphilis, being found in other neurological conditions such as syringomyelia, subacute combined degeneration of the cord, diabetic neuropathy, or following intra-articular injections of corticosteroids [12].

Optic atrophy and a bilateral ptosis with compensatory wrinkling of the brow is common in tabes.

Optic atrophy

Optic atrophy as an isolated condition occurs as blindness in a third form of late-stage neurosyphilis. The discs are small and pale. The atrophy may progress to cause complete blindness in about one-third of patients even with penicillin treatment. Atrophic fibres cannot regenerate whatever treatment is given. Recognition of syphilis at an early stage and penicillin therapy is vital in the prevention of these serious late-stage effects.

Modified late-stage forms of neurosyphilis

In countries of the west since the introduction and widespread use of antibiotics the classical clinical picture of late-stage neurosyphilis is seldom seen but the disease may appear as modified neurosyphilis [13] with more isolated, localized and less striking signs. The diagnosis is backed by the sensitive and highly specific serological tests such as the FTA-ABS and/or TPHA tests (Chapter 4). In such modified forms the differential diagnosis needs careful thought.

1. OPHTHALMOLOGICAL SIGNS INDICATIVE OF NEUROSYPHILIS

Argyll Robertson pupil or an irregular, unequal fixed pupil sometimes with synechiae of the iris and with positive serological tests for syphilis is indicative of neurosyphilis.

2. OPTHALMOLOGICAL SIGNS IN WHICH POSITIVE SERUM TREPONEMAL ANTIBODY TESTS MAY BE COINCIDENTAL

Such findings [14] should not be attributed automatically to syphilis although full treatment for late-stage syphilis is nevertheless mandatory.

(*a*) *Chorio-retinitis*

This is a manifestation of posterior uveitis and is now more commonly due to *Toxocara* or *Toxoplasma* infestation than to syphilis.

(*b*) *Secondary pigmentary degeneration of the retina*

This may be a sequel to syphilitic neuroretinitis and resemble retinitis pigmentosa, an entity where there is a family history of the condition and the patient will complain of night blindness. There is concentric constriction of the visual fields and pigmentation obscures the choroidal blood vessels which are narrowed.

(*c*) *Ptosis*

In bilateral ptosis consider also myasthenia gravis or a rare localized ocular myopathy. If the ptosis is unilateral a neoplasm or aneurysm in the chest or neck or diabetes are possibilities as well as syphilis.

(*d*) *Optic atrophy*

This may be associated with an insidious glaucoma, multiple sclerosis or the result of injury or retro-orbital neoplasm or inflammation. In cases of optic atrophy associated with temporal arteritis the patient is ill, has continuous headache and a high erythrocyte sedimentation rate.

3. NEUROLOGICAL FEATURES ATTRIBUTABLE TO LOCALIZED INFLAMMATORY LESIONS OF SYPHILIS

In this group patients may present with epileptiform fits or as incomplete tabes with tendon reflex changes such as absent ankle jerks or a Babinski sign. Some may have a sensory abnormality and in some the signs of cervical spondylosis are due to syphilitic pachymeningitis rather than arthropathy.

4. PSYCHIATRIC DISORDERS

Here it may be difficult to attribute depression, mania, personality disorder or dementia, to syphilis unless there are definite c.s.f. changes.

Treatment of neurosyphilis

The question of dosage of penicillin is considered in Chapter 6. There is little evidence that more clinical benefit is obtained by using doses higher than that recommended or by giving more than one course. There does not appear to be any correlation between the size of the penicillin dosage and the likelihood of developing new symptoms and it has been found that in 40 per cent of cases of general paresis new neurological signs may develop. Such progression of the disease occurs in the absence of a deterioration in the c.s.f. and it may be due to irreversible cerebrovascular disease before treatment [15].

The first principle of effective treatment of neurosyphilis is early diagnosis. This is a matter of great importance as the effectiveness of treatment will depend upon how much irreversible damage to the central nervous system has occurred before treatment has begun. The appearance of neurosyphilis is a result of a failure to detect syphilis at the early stage when treatment will prevent the emergence of late-stage effects. In late-stage forms of neurosyphilis modified by previous courses of antibiotics given for other reasons, both the recognition of the disease and the detection of objective signs of improvement after treatment will be difficult.

Any case thought to be neurosyphilis should be regarded as one of medical urgency and the patient should be assessed within 24 hours. A careful examination of the patient will include an examination of the c.s.f., an investigation which is essential in every case of late-stage syphilis except in those over 60 years of age, when its omission in the absence of neurological signs may be justified. Having established the diagnosis, treatment with penicillin should be started immediately.

A Jarisch-Herxheimer reaction with pyrexia occurs in over 90 per cent of patients with general paresis with grossly abnormal cerebrospinal fluids but in other forms of neurosyphilis it is much less frequent (less than 40 per cent). Clinical reactions are of special importance in general paresis when 10 per cent of patients may be expected to develop a sudden intensification of somatic or psychotic symptoms (convulsions, coma, focal vascular accidents, excitement, confusion, mania, hallucinations or paranoid delusions [16].

TREATMENT, FOLLOW-UP AND PROGNOSIS OF NEUROSYPHILIS

The prognosis and follow up after treatment depends upon the type of neurosyphilis [17] and the amount of permanent damage caused before treatment is started.

Syphilitic meningitis

With the predominantly meningeal involvement, which occurs in early-stage syphilis beyond the primary stage, treatment is very effective. When there is an acute labyrinthitis with eighth cranial nerve dysfunction recovery may be slow and deafness can persist. Where there is a labyrinthitis, prednisolone in a high initial dosage together with penicillin is justified as an attempt to reduce the chance of an irreversible deafness [13]. Recovery from other meningitic effects is usual.

Meningovascular neurosyphilis

In late-stage meningovascular neurosyphilis the effects are due to foci of ischaemia due to the syphilitic arteritis and although there is often considerable recovery after penicillin and an arrest of the disease process, ischaemic effects will persist and together with gliosis will cause persistent focal neurological effects such as aphasia, hemiplegia and cranial nerve involvement. In patients with predominantly psychiatric disorders differentiation from other psychosis is most important. Early treatment produces often remarkable improvement but complete recovery is not to be expected.

General paresis (Dementia paralytica, general paralysis of the insane)

Early diagnosis and the rapid institution of treatment is vital. In patients who have an acute onset of symptoms and are seen within weeks treatment can be spectacular in its effect. Patients have been able to resume the practice of a profession within weeks of treatment and have remained efficient subsequently.

In those with a greater degree of damage recovery is often remarkable and the patients will feel much better, wishing to return to work as soon as possible. Sometimes their enthusiasm is not matched by the return of their intellectual ability and psychological assessment is a necessary prelude to retraining for an occupation requiring less intellectual effort and less responsibility.

In patients who have become demented over a few years and in whom the disease has presented with a more insidious course there is often a serious loss of cortical neurones. Although treatment will arrest part of the disease process further neurological signs will tend to develop [15] which do not seem to be limited by further courses of penicillin or by larger amounts of this antibiotic.

Tabes dorsalis

This condition is rare and may present in an incomplete form. In some patients the disease is recognized as a result of a chance medical examination or because they seek advice for ataxia or lightning pains. Treatment with penicillin sometimes appears to halt the progress but deterioration often occurs in spite of treatment. Lightning pains, tabetic crises, bladder dysfunction, Charcot's arthropathy, and optic atrophy, may progress after treatment. In the follow-up of a case of tabes dorsalis there are particular points to consider.

The paroxysmal painful disorders of visceral function known as crises can be cut short by an injection of pethidine hydrochloride, 100mg. If this fails morphine and atropine may be given. In the case of a gastric crisis the patient should have a barium meal as the failure to diagnose a gastric ulcer in a tabetic may be more disastrous for the patient than to mistake a gastric crisis for an organic lesion of the stomach [19].

The loss of circulatory reflexes and orthostatic hypotension may result from interruption on the afferent side of the reflex arc from baroreceptors as part of the deep sensory loss characteristic of tabes. Such patients learn that they can rise to their feet only slowly if they are to avoid fainting but few have more than an occasional loss of consciousness [20].

Tabetic pains can be controlled sometimes by analgesics although the assessment of the value of individual drugs in the relief of the characteristic lightning pains is notoriously difficult in this now rare condition. In some cases analgesics are effective and their use should follow the principles of analgesic medication [21]. If the antipyretic analgesic, acetyl salicylic acid (as aspirin soluble tablets BP) in a dose of 0.6g (up to 0.9g) every four to six hours is ineffective or unsuitable, because of gastrointestinal side-effects paracetamol (as tablets BP) 0.5g repeated every four to six hours may be tried. Mefenamic acid in a total daily dose of 1.0g (each capsule contains 250mg) may be used as an alternative; repeated changes within this group will delay tolerance and minimize side-effects. If the pains are very intense one of the weak narcotics, dihydrocodeine tablets BP (e.g., DF 118, Duncan Flockhart and Co. Ltd.) in an oral dose of 30mg can be tried or alternatively the narcotic antagonist with analgesic activity, pentazocine (as tablets BP) in the oral dose of 25–50mg may be given after food.

The pains of tabes are paroxysmal, brief and often very intense and this similarity to the pains of trigeminal neuralgia suggested the use of carbamazepine. It appeared to be effective when given as an initial dose of 200mg twice daily, increasing to a maximum maintenance dose of 400–800mg daily [22].

In tabes the bladder becomes atonic and distended because there is damage to the posterior roots and ganglia which give loss of both deep pain and deep postural sensation including that of the bladder [20]. If there is no evidence of hydronephrosis the patient should be instructed to empty the bladder every three hours during the day by the clock before retiring and again early in the morning. Attempts may be made to empty an atonic bladder by giving an anticholinesterase (e.g., distigmine bromide (Ubretid, Berk Pharmaceuticals), 5 mg by mouth half an hour before breakfast or by an intramuscular injection of 0.5mg for the first few days), or by reducing the resistance at the bladder neck with a transurethral resection. Manual compression can be dangerous as more urine may pass up the ureter than is expelled. Permanent drainage with a urethral or suprapubic catheter may be necessary or the urine can be diverted to the skin. Urine must not be diverted in to the colon in tabes as it will leak from the anus which is supplied by the same nerve roots as the bladder [23].

In Charcot's arthropathy attempts are made to reduce the weight carried by the joint and improve its stability. Various calipers are available for the patient to use while walking. Perforating ulcers should be prevented by wearing well-fitting socks and shoes and by careful treatment of corns on the feet. When ulcers do develop, rest, clean dressings and antibiotic treatment will aid healing [24].

Ataxia may be improved by careful exercises which give confidence, supervised by a physiotherapist.

Optic atrophy

Acute optic neuritis in secondary syphilis will respond well to penicillin and the visual prognosis is good when there is acute visual loss. In optic atrophy the prognosis is poor although prednisone 30–60mg daily with penicillin therapy may be given in an attempt to halt its progress. The help of an ophthalmologist should be sought in all such cases.

Cardiovascular syphilis

Reference has already been made to the decline in the numbers of deaths from cardiovascular syphilis (page 15) in England and Wales, a decline shared by all forms of late-stage syphilis although the improvement in incidence has been much more apparent in its neurological than in its cardiovascular forms.

Gummata tend to occur in the interatrial septum or in the upper portion of the interventricular septum. Because of their proximity to the atrioventricular node, they may disturb the conducting system of the heart and provide one of the rare causes of the Stokes-Adams syndrome (complete heart block).

The second category of cardiac lesions in acquired syphilis are those which lead to aortic valve insufficiency. In all stages of syphilis arteritis is a constant feature. There is an endarteritis obliterans with a cellular reaction which radiates at some distance round the lesion in the form of a cuff within the periarterial tissues. This form of arteritis is important in two situations—the aorta and the brain. Involvement of the aorta is the commonest manifestation of late-stage syphilis. The severest lesions are usually in the aortic ring and the ascending part of the aorta, possibly because the vasa vasorum with their circumvascular lymphatics are most numerous in these portions of the vessel. The elastic tissue and muscle of the tunica media are destroyed and hence, there is weakening of the aortic wall and loss of its elastic recoil. As the vessel becomes unable to withstand the force of the blood pressure it dilates. The dilatation often affects the root of the aorta and hence widens the ring of the aortic valve. This is not the only cause of incompetence for the cusps suffer damaging changes of a distinctive kind. There is an ingrowth of fibroblasts from the intima of the aorta along the free margin of the valve which is given a cord-like or 'rolled edge' deformity.

Granulomatous lesions often involve the openings of the coronary arteries particularly in those patients in whom, as a developmental anomaly, the vessels arise above the level of the aortic sinus and are consequently nearer to the region of the greatest damage to the aorta.

Weakening of the media in syphilis often leads to general dilatation of the aorta and in addition localized dilatation may occur almost always in the ascending thoracic aorta. Such an aneurysm may press on neighbouring structures including the vertebrae, sternum and ribs which can be eroded by continuing pressure. The recurrent laryngeal nerve may be stretched and the oesophagus compressed. Rupture of the aneurysm is a common cause of death.

The coronary ostial stenosis coupled with the low diastolic pressure accompanying the valvular insufficiency gravely lessens the blood supply to the myocardium. The ischaemia may cause angina and sudden death due to infarction.

Aortic lesions in syphilis are maximal in the first part of the aorta and the arch; they are absent below the diaphragm. In contrast, in atheroma the lesions increase progressively from the arch to the bifurcation. In syphilis an aneurysm is usually thoracic and the aortic valve incompetent; in atheroma, the aneurysm is usually abdominal and if the aortic valve is involved it is stenosed [25].

CLINICAL FEATURES

Compensation for aortic regurgitation is so efficient that patients may live for many years with minimal symptoms. They may be aware of the heaving cardiac impulse in bed and may notice transient dizziness following changes in posture. The compensation is achieved because the refluxing blood augments that which enters the left ventricle through the mitral valve to produce increased stretching and hence more powerful contraction of the ventricle. Gross hypertrophy and dilatation of the left ventricle has produced some of the largest hearts to be found at autopsy.

The symptoms and signs depend upon the site and the anatomical nature of the lesion. Coronary ostial stenosis will cause angina. Dilatation of the aorta may cause an aortic systolic murmur and a characteristic loud aortic component of the second sound. Aortic regurgitation is responsible for an early diastolic murmur, often best heard in the second right intercostal space with the patient leaning forward and holding his breath.

An aortic aneurysm may cause pulsation of the anterior chest wall or occasionally obstruction of the superior vena cava, causing facial oedema. Pressure of the aneurysm on the bronchi can cause a tracheal tug felt by the examiner as a downward pull on the thyroid cartilage. Hoarseness, dysphagia and bone pain are other symptoms.

Electrocardiogram changes may show evidence of myocardial ischaemia or signs of left ventricular hypertrophy. The radiograph of the chest shows dilatation of the aorta and linear calcification of the surrounding portion is a useful early sign. The most useful diagnostic measure is an injection of radio-opaque dye into the ascending aorta by catheterization which demonstrates the degree of reflux into the ventricle in diastole. As long as compensation is maintained cardiac catheterization will show that the end diastolic pressure in the left ventricle and the left atrial pressures are normal.

DIAGNOSIS

In any case of aortic regurgitation or aneurysmal dilatation syphilis should be suspected. Syphilis seldom causes ischaemic heart disease alone without producing aortic regurgitation. In any form of late-stage syphilis the chest should be examined by fluoroscopy as when the aorta is involved there is a loss of parallelism of its walls and often calcification of the first part before aneurysmal changes are pronounced [26]. Serological tests for syphilis will indicate the aetiology (Chapter 4).

TREATMENT OF CARDIOVASCULAR SYPHILIS

Treatment with penicillin should take the form advised for late-stage syphilis other than neurosyphilis (Chapter 6) although objective evidence of cardiovascular improvement can seldom be obtained [27]. None the less such a course of treatment should be given and it should be remembered that neurosyphilis may coexist with cardiovascular syphilis, when a longer course is advised.

In uncomplicated syphilitic aortitis diagnosed on the basis of fluoroscopic detection of dilatation of the aorta in the absence of aortic incompetence, there is no appreciable threat to life during the first seven years after the discovery. Progression to aortic incompetence occurs in about a third of patients within four years and the quantity of penicillin treatment given does not appear to influence these changes [28].

The progression of uncomplicated aortitis to aortic incompetence is not certainly halted by antibiotic treatment. Compensation for aortic regurgitation is so efficient that patients may live for many years with minimal symptoms such as an awareness of the heaving cardiac impulse in bed or transient dizziness following sudden changes in posture. Failure of compensation is indicated by angina and shortness of breath. As life expectancy is so good and the long term effects of valve replacement are still unpredictable, physicians may be reluctant to refer patients for surgery until they develop symptoms. This excessive conservatism has its disadvantages as the results of surgery will be adversely affected if the operation is deferred until the ventricle has become irreparably damaged.

In surgery of aneurysm of the ascending aorta a mortality as high as 40 per cent may be expected. Resection of an aneurysm of the aortic arch is the most demanding operation in surgery and carries a very high mortality [29].

In coronary ostial stenosis surgical intervention can produce dramatic relief and although antibiotic treatment is given as in other forms of cardiovascular syphilis a decision about the advisability of surgery will require a cardiological assessment including a coronary arteriogram.

REFERENCES

1 Kammeier, R J (1964) *Medical Clinics of North America,* **48,** 667
2 Martin, J P (1972) *British Medical Journal,* **2,** 159
3 Olansky, S (1964) *Medical Clinics of North America,* **48,** 653
4 Morgan, A D, Lloyd, W E and Price-Thomas, Sir Clement (1952) *Thorax,* **7,** 125
5 Joffe, R, Black, M M and Floyd, M (1968) *British Medical Journal,* **1,** 211
6 Heathfield, K W G (1968) *British Medical Journal,* **1,** 765
7 Luxon, L, Lees, A J and Greenwood, R J (1979) *Lancet,* **i,** 90
8 Harriman, D G F (1976) In *Greenfield's Neuropathology, Bacterial Infections of the Central Nervous System,* (Ed) Blackwood, W and Corsellis, J A N, Arnold, London, pages 238–268
9 Robertson, D M C L, Argyll (1869) (a) *Edinburgh Medical Journal,* **14,** 696 (b) *Edinburgh Medical Journal,* **15,** 487
10 Matthews, W B and Willer, H (1972) In *Diseases of the Nervous System,* pages 188–193
11 Dewhurst, K (1969) *British Journal of Psychiatry,* **115,** 31
12 Boyle, J A and Buchanan, W W (1971) In *Clinical Rheumatology,* Blackwell Scientific Publications, Oxford, pages 359–360
13 Hoosmand, H, Escobar, M R and Koff, S W (1972) *Journal of the American Medical Association,* **219,** 729
14 Duke-Elder, Sir Stewart (1971) In *System of Ophthalmology, Neuro-ophthalmology,* Vol. XII, Kimpton, London, page 660
15 Wilner, E and Brodie, J A (1968) *Lancet,* **ii,** 1370
16 Moore, J E, Farmer, T W and Hockenga, M T (1948) *Transactions of the Association of American Physicians,* **61,** 176
17 Kelly, R (1964) *The Practitioner,* **192,** 90
18 Vercoe, G S (1976) *Journal of Laryngology and Otology,* **90,** 853
19 Walton, J N (1977) In *Brain's Diseases of the Nervous System,* Oxford University Press, New York, page 476
20 Spalding, J M K (1974) In *Disorders of the Autonomic Nervous System.* Blackwell Scientific Publications, Oxford, pages 96; 235
21 Mehta, M (1973) In *Intractable pain: Treatment,* Saunders, London, page 61
22 Ekbom, K (1972) *Archives of Neurology* (Chicago), **26,** 374

23 Newsam, J E and Petrie, J J B (1975) In *Urology and Renal Medicine,* 2nd edition, Churchill Livingstone, Edinburgh, page 251

24 Catterall, R D (1977) *British Journal of Hospital Medicine,* **17,** 585

25 Symmers, W St C (1976) (Ed) In *Systemic Pathology,* Vol. 1. Churchill Livingstone, Edinburgh, pages 39; 136

26 McCann, J S and Porter, D C (1956) *British Medical Journal,* **1,** 826

27 Macfarlane, W V, Swan, W C A and Irvine, R E (1956) *British Medical Journal,* **1,** 827

28 Irvine, R E (1956) *British Medical Journal,* **1,** 832

29 Collis, J L, Clarke, D B and Smith, R A (1976) In *d'Abreu's Practice of Cardiothoracic Surgery,* 4th edition, Edward Arnold, London, pages 431–435; 516–518

CHAPTER 8

Congenital Syphilis

Introduction

Congenital syphilis is an uncommon disease in the United Kingdom; for example, in England during the 12 months ending in June 1976 there were 141 cases reported and a case rate of 0.36 per 100,000 population was reported for 1975 [1]. Antenatal examination routinely includes serological tests for syphilis and this screening, together with adequate treatment of infected mothers, accounts for the low incidence of the disease in this country. In Africa and South America, congenital syphilis is still common although where yaws is endemic an immune effect may modify the consequences of syphilis in the adult females and its transmissibility to the fetus. It can be prevented *in utero* by treatment of the infected woman with penicillin during early pregnancy, or cured later in pregnancy; its occurrence in a community is an indicator of defective antenatal care and the result of insufficient primary medical care.

Transmission of infection

Although it had long been considered that involvement of the fetus did not occur before the fourth month of gestation, recent studies have clearly demonstrated that infection may occur within 10 weeks of conception [2]. Any infection before 20 weeks gestation will not stimulate immune mechanisms because the fetal immune system is not as yet well developed and thus no histological evidence of fetal reaction to infection will be seen [3]. The theory that the cytotrophoblastic layer (Langhan's layer) of the early placenta protects until its disappearance at 18–20 weeks gestation, against transmission of the organism from the maternal to the fetal circulation [4], has now been discounted. Electron microscopic studies have shown that this layer of cells does not completely atrophy [5].

Infection of the fetus is more likely to occur when the mother's infection is in the early stage, as at this time considerable numbers of organisms are present in the circulation. During the first year of infection in an untreated woman there is an 80 to 90 per cent chance that the infection will be transmitted to the fetus. The probability of fetal infection declines rapidly after the second year of infection in the mother and becomes rare after the fourth year. In general, the greater the duration of syphilis in the mother, the less chance there is of the fetus being affected.

In pre-antibiotic days it was common for a mother of a child with congenital syphilis to give a history of previous miscarriages succeeded by a premature stillbirth, then a stillbirth at term, and later an apparently healthy child at birth. The widespread use of antibiotics for concomitant infection has completely altered this pattern of events, and such an obstetrical record is now virtually unknown.

Although uncommon, a woman with late syphilis, however, may give birth to a child with syphilis, although the child of a previous pregnancy had been apparently healthy. This may be explained by the speculation that there is an intermittent release of treponemes from lymphoid tissue into the circulation in late syphilis. Should such an event occur the fetus may become infected.

If a mother with early-stage syphilis is not treated, 25 to 30 per cent of fetuses die *in utero,* 25 to 30 per cent die after birth, and of the infected survivors 40 per cent develop late symptomatic syphilis [6].

Clinical features

The manifestations of congenital syphilis may conveniently be divided into two stages, early and late; the end of the second year of life is the arbitrary point of division between the two stages. Fuller details of the clinical features of congenital syphilis may be found in Nabarro's book [7] and in a review by Robinson [8] as well as by reference to individual papers quoted.

Early congenital syphilis

When congenital syphilis was common it was rare to find acute signs of syphilis in the newborn and in cases that occurred, death usually followed within a few days. Infants were often born prematurely or, if full term, were often of low birth weight. The skin was wrinkled and there was a bullous skin rash (syphilitic pemphigus), particularly on the soles and palms. The clear or purulent fluid from the bullae contained large numbers of *T. pallidum* and was highly infectious. Other skin lesions, most often maculo-papules, were usually present and were found around the body orifices. Rhinitis produced a mucoid or mucopurulent nasal discharge, and a hoarse cry resulted from laryngitis.

Abdominal distension was common, and hepatic and splenic enlargement almost invariably found. Haemorrhagic manifestations occasionally occurred. This has been shown to have been due to thrombocytopenia and macroglobulinaemia [9]. The majority of infants infected with syphilis appear healthy at birth, as the characteristic clinical features do not develop until between 2 and 12 weeks. After a period of normal development, the child fails to thrive and the clinical picture of congenital syphilis becomes apparent.

It is convenient to describe the manifestations according to the particular part of the body affected.

CUTANEOUS MANIFESTATIONS

Skin rashes of varied character are found in 70 to 90 per cent of infants with congenital syphilis. The rash is symmetrical in distribution and erythematous macular, papular and papulosquamous lesions may exist together in different parts of the body. On the face the eruption is particularly prominent around the mouth. Where the skin is moist, for example on the buttocks and external genitalia, the rash appears eczematous. In these sites hypertrophic lesions resembling condylomata lata (page 98) may appear, usually as a manifestation of a recurrence following resolution of the initial rash. Deep fissures develop round the body orifices, and healing of these lesions leaves characteristic scars (rhagades).

The skin of the palms and soles may show peeling. In severe cases, the hair becomes scanty and brittle and involvement of the nails leads to shedding, and replacement by narrow, atrophic nails.

In addition to the eruptions described, the skin may show wrinkling from weight loss and there is café-au-lait pigmentation.

If an infant is not treated, or is inadequately treated, the skin lesions usually heal within a year, but there may be recurrences during the second year. Recurrent lesions usually differ from those seen in the original rash and include condylomata lata.

MUCOSAL LESIONS

Clinical evidence of rhinitis is found in 70 to 80 per cent of infected infants. There is nasal obstruction and a mucoid nasal discharge which becomes mucopurulent and occasionally blood-stained (syphilitic snuffles). Numerous treponemes may be demonstrated in the discharge which is highly infectious. Arrested development of nasal structures, and continued pressure changes within the nose as a result of obstruction lead to deformities of the nose (saddle nose).

Mucous patches resembling those seen in secondary acquired syphilis may occur in the mouth and pharynx. Laryngitis produces a hoarse or aphonic cry.

LYMPHADENITIS AND SPLENIC ENLARGEMENT

Although not a constant accompaniment of early congenital syphilis, moderate generalized enlargement of the lymph nodes is common. The spleen is enlarged in at least 60 per cent of infected infants.

BONE AND JOINT MANIFESTATIONS

Bone disease, diagnosed by clinical or radiological examination, or both, occurs in at least 85 per cent of infected infants under the age of 1 year [7].

In only about 40 per cent of cases is there clinical evidence of bone involvement. Bones are usually affected symmetrically, but one side may be more involved than the other. The child cries when adjacent joints are passively moved and he moves affected limbs rarely (Parrot's pseudo-paralysis).

Radiological examination of infected infants under the age of 12 months, who have no clinical evidence of bone involvement, demonstrates abnormalities in at least 75 per cent of cases. Multiple long-bone involvement is most commonly found, the metaphyses being particularly affected.

Variable degrees of calcification at the growing ends of the bone result in a variety of radiological changes. Most commonly there is an irregular (saw tooth) dense zone of calcification overlying an osteoporotic area at the metaphysis. Peripheral osteoporosis of the metaphysis is less often observed, as is the appearance of dense bands sandwiching such zones.

Irregular patchy areas of loss of bone density are commonly found in both metaphyses and diaphyses. A characteristic sign is loss of density of the upper medial aspect of the tibiae (Wimberger's sign). In severe cases there may be a fracture at the site of bone destruction in the metaphysis, with impaction or displacement of the epiphysis.

Periostitis, appearing on the radiograph as a single layer, or multiple layers of new-bone formation along the cortex of the shaft of the bone, is the most frequent radiological abnormality found in early congenital syphilis. Although any long bone may be affected, the distal femur and radius and the proximal tibia and humerus are the most often involved. The changes described are not specific for syphilis, similar radiological findings being encountered in rubella, cytomegalovirus infection, rickets and haemolytic disease of the newborn [10]. Occasionally in early congenital syphilis lens-shaped areas known as Parrot's nodes appear around the anterior fontanelle on the frontal and parietal bones. These nodes are probably due to periostitis. Usually the changes described resolve within the second 6 months of life, but periostitis persists and may become more pronounced.

During the later stages of early congenital syphilis, dactylitis, manifest clinically as painless, spindle-shaped swelling of the fingers, may occur in a small number of cases (less than 5 per cent). Radiographic examination shows that up to 25 per cent of all infected children under the age of two years have dactylitis.

HEPATIC AND PANCREATIC INVOLVEMENT

The liver is almost invariably enlarged, usually in association with the spleen, in congenital syphilis appearing in the neonatal period, and in at least 60 per cent of older infants. Jaundice is an uncommon feature, but its presence in the neonate should alert the physician practising in areas where syphilis is common, to the possibility that syphilis may be the cause of the jaundice.

Although not clinically apparent, pancreatitis is a common finding at autopsy of infants dying of congenital syphilis in the neonatal period [11].

RENAL INVOLVEMENT

The nephrotic syndrome may rarely be associated with early congenital syphilis, and is thought to be the result of deposition of soluble complexes of treponemal antigen and anti-treponemal antibody in the glomeruli [12]. Acute nephritis is a rarity [13].

BRONCHO-PULMONARY INVOLVEMENT

In the aborted fetus and stillborn infant, the lungs are always affected, as bronchi and lung parenchyma have developed abnormally.

NEUROLOGICAL INVOLVEMENT

Although meningitis is common in early congenital syphilis, particularly during the exanthem stage, clinical signs relating to the nervous system are uncommon. Epileptiform seizures, irritability and bulging of the anterior fontanelle may occur. There may be focal changes in the cerebral tissue due to thrombotic occlusion of blood vessels affected by a panarteritis. These cerebral lesions may produce hemiplegia, monoplegia and cranial nerve palsies.

In about a third of infants under the age of 12 months, the cerebrospinal fluid is abnormal with respect to cell content and protein levels, and gives positive results when examined by the serological tests for syphilis.

OCULAR MANIFESTATIONS

Iritis is rare in early congenital syphilis. Choroido-retinitis is considerably more common during the first year of life. Examination with the ophthalmoscope shows small spots of pigment surrounded by yellow areas (salt and pepper fundus). If untreated the inflammatory process progresses and if the macular or optic disc regions are involved, blindness may result.

HAEMATOLOGICAL ABNORMALITIES

Anaemia of varying severity occurs in at least 20 per cent of infants with congenital syphilis. Normocytic, normochromic anaemia reflects depression of haematopoiesis in the bone marrow as a result of the chronic infection. Increased haemolysis probably plays a small part in the development of the anaemia. Secondary iron deficiency produces a microcytic, hypochromic anaemia. Occasionally a leuco-erythroblastic anaemia occurs.

Thrombocytopenia, associated with a bleeding disorder during the first few weeks of life has been described [14]. Macroglobulinaemia may be associated with the bleeding diathesis [9].

In early congenital syphilis, the white cell count is usually elevated, with lymphocytosis.

Late congenital syphilis

Infected and untreated children are said to have entered the late stage of syphilis after their second birthday. In at least 60 per cent of affected children there are no clinical signs of the disease, the only abnormal finding being positive serological tests, that is latent congenital syphilis.

INTERSTITIAL KERATITIS

This is the most common clinical manifestation of late congenital syphilis, occurring in about 40 per cent of affected children. Interstitial keratitis appears to be the result of immunological reaction in the cornea to the treponeme, penicillin treatment having no influence on the course of this manifestation. In most cases this develops between the ages of 6 and 14 years, but it may occur earlier or very much later (even over the age of 30 years). Although commencing in one eye, both become involved in more than 90 per cent of cases; the second eye shows features of the condition a few days to several months after the first. The patient complains of pain in the affected eye, photophobia with excessive lacrimation and dimness of vision. A diffuse haziness near the centre of the cornea of one eye is the earliest clinical sign, but within a few weeks the whole cornea becomes opaque. This is usually associated with circumcorneal sclerotic congestion.

Examination by slit-lamp microscopy shows that these corneal changes are attributable to blood vessels extending into the cornea from the sclera, and to exudation of cells from these vessels.

The condition gradually improves over a period of 12 to 18 months, leaving a variable degree of corneal damage which may lead to blindness or be only detectable by slit-lamp examination. This latter investigation may show empty blood vessels (ghost vessels) within the cornea of patients who have had interstitial keratitis earlier in life, but have had no apparent residual scarring [15].

After resolution of the initial episode of interstitial keratitis, 20 to 30 per cent of patients suffer a relapse of this condition.

BONE LESIONS

The essential bone lesion in late congenital syphilis is hyperplastic osteoperiostitis, a process which may be diffuse, resulting in sclerosis of bone, or localized (periosteal node or gumma). Gumma formation may lead to necrosis of underlying cortex with softening of the bone. The tibiae are most commonly affected by these changes.

Usually bone lesions develop between the 5th and 20th year of life, when the patient complains of pain in the affected bone. Palpation may reveal nodules on the anterior surface of the bone, and rarely ulceration may be observed where a gumma has involved skin and bone. In older children, thickening of the anterior surface of the tibia may result in forward bowing of that bone (sabre tibia).

Painless gummatous lesions may be found on the hard and soft palates or in the pharynx. These are often extensive, with considerable necrosis of tissue. Perforation of the palate, absence of the uvula and scarring about the oropharynx may be the result.

Destructive gummatous lesions of the nasal septum may cause perforation of the septum with or without deformity of the lower part of the nose.

JOINT LESIONS

The commonest type of joint lesion (Clutton's joints), seen in about 20 per cent of untreated children, is bilateral effusion into the knee joints [16]. This condition, like interstitial keratitis, is unaffected by antibiotic treatment, and appears to be an immunological reaction to *T. pallidum*. Less commonly, other joints are similarly affected. Although most frequently occurring in children between the ages of five and 10 years, joint involvement may be seen at any age from three years to the mid-twenties.

The onset of the arthritis starts acutely often with a history of antecedent trauma. Although most commonly painless, the affected joints may be acutely painful, particularly at the onset. Radiological examination reveals no specific changes in the joint.

There is gradual resolution of the arthritis over many months, with recovery of full function.

NEUROSYPHILIS

In about 20 per cent of infected children over the age of one year neurosyphilis is latent or hidden and diagnosis depends upon the detection of abnormalities in the cerebrospinal fluid.

As a late result of the meningitis of early stage congenital syphilis, epileptiform seizures, mental deficiency and cranial nerve palsies may be found in children over the age of two years. Parenchymatous involvement produces two main clinical conditions, juvenile general paralysis of the insane and tabes dorsalis.

JUVENILE GENERAL PARALYSIS (JUVENILE GPI)

This occurs in about one per cent of affected children appearing about the age of 10 years, but occasionally much earlier, or much later as in middle age. The sexes are affected equally (in contrast to the GPI of acquired syphilis in which males are more often affected than females). There is usually a gradual onset of symptoms, the child becoming dull, irritable, apathetic and forgetful. Later, delusions, usually paranoid in type, occur and speech becomes disturbed. The voice is monotonous, articulation becomes stumbling and tremulous and speech is eventually lost. There is generally tremor of the lips, hands and legs. Handwriting becomes indistinct. Epileptiform seizures are common at a late stage of the disease.

Pupillary abnormalities are seen in over 90 per cent of cases; the pupils are of the Argyll-Robertson type (page 129) or immobile and dilated. Optic atrophy occurs in between 10 and 35 per cent of cases.

Other physical findings resemble those found in general paralysis of acquired syphilis.

JUVENILE TABES

This is much rarer than general paralysis. The onset of the condition is generally between the ages of 10 and 17 years. Failing vision and paraesthesiae are the most common symptoms; lightning pains and ataxia are rare. Later in the course of the disease headaches, photophobia and diplopia occur frequently. Sphincter disturbances are uncommon although enuresis may be found. Clinical examination may detect nystagmus, pupillary abnormalities, optic atrophy, and absent or diminished tendon reflexes. Trophic disturbances are rare and it is unusual to find evidence of loss of cutaneous sensation.

EAR DISEASE

The middle ear may be affected by a painless otolabyrinthitis, showing as a slight purulent aural discharge. Conduction deafness may result without treatment.

Even after what has been considered adequate penicillin treatment, treponemes have been demonstrated in endochondral bone, a dense structure into which antibiotics do not readily diffuse.

Subjective hearing impairment is commonly a late manifestation often not occurring until adult life, although it can occur in childhood. In addition the patient may not be seen first till middle age, when the diagnosis of congenital syphilis may not come readily to mind unless there are other stigmata of the disease.

Complaints may include episodes of tinnitus, dizziness or rotational vertigo. There is progressive deterioration of deafness although spontaneous fluctuation may occur. The most severe difficulty is in discrimination of speech. It is usually an isolated finding, bilateral, although one side is often more severely affected than the other. There are usually no abnormalities in the cerebrospinal fluid [17].

SKIN LESIONS

Gummata similar to those occurring in late acquired syphilis may be found.

CARDIOVASCULAR LESIONS

Myocarditis may be found in children dying of congenital syphilis, but aortitis is exceedingly rare.

LIVER DISEASE

Gummata of the liver are rarely found.

PAROXYSMAL COLD HAEMOGLOBINURIA

This rare condition occurring in less than 1 per cent of patients with late congenital syphilis, may be seen also in acquired syphilis. Large quantities of haemoglobin are excreted in the urine after exposure to cold. Shivering or a rigor heralds the attack and this is rapidly followed by fever, headache and pains in the back or limbs. A generalized urticarial rash may also develop. Within the next few hours the urine becomes dark brown in colour and contains haemoglobin, methaemoglobin, but few red blood cells. In most cases, the clinical features described resolve within several hours, but occasionally mild jaundice may develop and persist for some days. This condition is liable to recur periodically when the patient is exposed to cold of varying severity.

Cold haemolysins are found in the blood, and demonstrated by the Donath Landsteiner test. The basis of this test is the ability of the haemolysin to unite with red cells when the blood is chilled; when the blood is then warmed to 37°C, these sensitized cells are lysed in the presence of complement.

Stigmata of congenital syphilis

Lesions of early and late congenital syphilis may heal leaving scars and deformities characteristic of the disease. Such scarring and deformities constitute the stigmata of congenital syphilis, but only in some 40 per cent of patients do they occur.

STIGMATA OF EARLY LESIONS

1. Facial appearance

The 'saddle-nose' deformity may result from rhinitis (page 145). The palate may appear high-arched as a result of underdevelopment of the maxilla.

2. Teeth

The tooth germs of deciduous teeth are fully differentiated by the 10th week of gestation before tissue reaction to treponemes appears to occur; hence these teeth are usually unaffected. Teeth which develop later may, however, be affected. Two groups of teeth bear the brunt, the upper central incisors and the 1st molars.

Typically the affected upper incisor is smaller than normal, and darker in colour and peg-like, instead of being flat, with the sides converging to the cutting edge which classically has a notched centre, the so-called Hutchinson's incisor [18]. Affected incisors do not always show this typical appearance but may often be thickened anteroposteriorly, with rounding of the incisal angles; they may have a shallow depression on the incisal edge rather than a notch.

The typically affected molar, Moon's molar, shows a constricted occlusal surface and rounded angles. The cuspules of the molar are poorly developed and appear crowded together. Such teeth are prone to dental caries and as a result are lost early.

In one series [19], in 45 per cent of patients with congenital syphilis the upper central incisors were affected, and in about 20 per cent the first molars were involved. The incidence of dental changes is high in patients who also develop interstitial keratitis.

3. Rhagades

The deep cutaneous lesions around the orifices of the body heal producing scars radiating from the orifice known as rhagades.

4. Nails

Atrophy and deformity of the nails may be seen in adult life as a result of nail-bed inflammation in infancy.

5. Choroidal scarring

Healing of choroido-retinitis produces white scarred areas surrounded by pigmentation on the retina.

STIGMATA OF LATE LESIONS

1. Corneal lesions

Opacities of the cornea and ghost vessels observed on slit-lamp examination are the result of interstitial keratitis [15].

2. Bone lesions

Sabre tibia resulting from osteoperiostitis may be observed, as may the scars of destructive lesions of the oropharyngeal and nasal regions. Broadening of the skull may result from osteoperiostitis of the frontal and parietal bones.

3. Optic atrophy

This may occur as a single entity without iridoplegia (e.g. Argyll Robertson pupils) [8].

4. Nerve deafness

Diagnosis

It is important to ascertain that a child born to a mother who has been apparently adequately treated for syphilis, is not infected. An infected infant may appear healthy at birth. Blood from the neonate should be examined at birth, using VDRL and TPHA tests. As a result of transplacental passage of maternal antibody, those tests which are positive in the mother are also likely to be positive in the infant and at a similar titre. Within 6 months, however, these maternal antibodies will have disappeared from the infant's serum and, if the child is not infected, the tests will have become negative. Persistently positive serological tests, or a rising titre, suggests congenital infection and the need for treatment.

The use of the FTA-ABS test, using monospecific antisera to detect specific IgM antibodies in the infant's blood has been described (page 86). It is important to remember that this test may be negative at birth in a child with active infection and may not become positive until the age of 3 months. Serial serological tests up to 6 months are therefore required in apparently healthy babies born to mothers with positive serological tests for syphilis particularly if untreated or suspected to be so.

In western industrialized countries, the discovery of positive serological tests in an otherwise healthy person often raises the question as to whether syphilis has been acquired before birth or later. This problem is difficult as stigmata appear to be rare now. A family history may be misleading (page 144). Patients should, however, be carefully examined for the presence of obvious stigmata and slit-lamp microscopy of the cornea should be included in the investigation to search for ghost vessels, as a trace of previous interstitial keratitis [15]. Nerve deafness may be obvious or, if mild, demonstrable by audiography. In doubtful cases, serological examination of parents or brothers and sisters may be helpful, and to avoid serious social upset consultation and collaboration with the general practitioner is advised.

Treatment of congenital syphilis

EARLY CONGENITAL SYPHILIS

Although infants with massive infection may still die in the neonatal period, the majority will be cured by adequate penicillin treatment. Stigmata, particularly dental, will, however, be detectable.

Prior to instituting treatment, the c.s.f. should be examined to detect neurological involvement. Benzyl penicillin in an intramuscular dose of 50,000 units per kg should be given daily in two divided doses. Alternatively procaine penicillin (50,000 units per kg per day) may be used [20]. Treatment should be continued for at least 10 days, and preferably longer if the c.s.f. is abnormal. Further details on prevention, treatment and the problem when erythromycin has been used for treatment of the pregnant woman with syphilis are discussed in Chapter 6.

LATE CONGENITAL SYPHILIS

The dosage of procaine penicillin required for the treatment of late congenital syphilis is similar to that used in the therapy of late acquired syphilis (page 108). Treatment, however, does not prevent the development or course of interstitial keratitis, hydrarthrosis and neural deafness.

(*a*) *Management of interstitial keratitis*

Patients with interstitial keratitis should be managed in hospital, in consultation with an ophthalmologist.

Topically-applied corticosteroids rapidly suppress the inflammatory reaction in the cornea and anterior uveal tract, and their use, until spontaneous cure occurs, has revolutionized the management of this condition. Although the infiltration of the cornea by inflammatory cells resolves, scarring from previous episodes of keratitis is not affected.

Betamethasone eye drops, B.P.C. 0.1 per cent, instilled into the affected eye(s) every 1 to 2 hours, is a useful preparation. Treatment should be continued until the corneal inflammatory infiltrate has cleared, and visual acuity restored to the patient's normal level. Slit-lamp examination is essential before steroid treatment is discontinued, as mild degrees of keratitis may not be apparent otherwise. Regular examination is required after cessation of treatment, as corneal scarring may result from continuing mild inflammation.

During steroid treatment, mydriatics such as atropine eye drops B.P.C., 1 per cent, may be useful adjuvants by reducing ciliary muscle tension.

Corneal grafting may be required in patients with corneal scarring acquired during attacks of interstitial keratitis.

(*b*) *Hydrarthrosis (Clutton's joints)*

This is a self-limiting disorder, and does not require any specific therapy.

(*c*) *Nerve deafness*

Despite previous treatment of congenital syphilis with what has been regarded as adequate doses of penicillin, progressive neural deafness may develop at any age, most commonly in middle age. This may be the result of failure of the drug to reach adequate concentrations in the perilymph or endolymph.

In advanced cases where there has been considerable tissue damage, no response to medical treatment occurs. Where there has been less damage, the use of large doses of antibiotics such as benzyl penicillin with corticosteroids may produce some improvement [17].

Ampicillin in a dosage of 1.5g six-hourly for four weeks, together with prednisolone 30mg daily for 10 days, tailing off over the succeeding 10 days has been used in the management of this condition [21]. Audiometry may give useful information regarding response to treatment. If improvement does not occur or if a satisfactory initial response is not maintained, weekly intramuscular injections of ACTH (40 units) may be used indefinitely.

The value of treatment has not been fully assessed. In some cases, the disease process may be arrested, but in others, improvement in hearing may only be temporary.

REFERENCES

1 Department of Health and Social Security (1977) in *On the State of the Public Health for the year 1976*, London, HMSO, page 63

2 Harter, C A and Benirschke, K (1976) *American Journal of Obstetrics and Gynecology*, **124**, 705

3 Silverstein, A M (1962) *Nature*, **194**, 196

4 Curtis, A C and Philpott, O S (1964) *Medical Clinics of North America*, **48**, 707

5 Benirschke, K (1974) *American Journal of Diseases of Children*, **128**, 1–2

6 Thomas, E W (1949) *Syphilis: Its Course and Management*, Macmillan Co, New York

7 Nabarro, D (1954) *Congenital Syphilis*, Edward Arnold Ltd, London

8 Robinson, R C V (1969) Congenital Syphilis. Review Article, *Archives of Dermatology*, **99**, 599

9 Marchi, A G, Pambussi, A M and Famularo, L (1966) *Minerva Pediatrica*, **18**, 1155–1158

10 Cremin, B J and Fisher, R M (1970) *British Journal of Radiology*, **43**, 333

11 Oppenheimer, E H and Hardy, J B (1971) *John's Hopkins Medical Journal*, **129**, 63

12 Yuceoglu, A M, Sagel, I, Tresser, G, Wasserman, E and Lange, K (1974) *Journal of the American Medical Association*, **229**, 1085

13 Taitz, L S, Isaacson, C and Stein, H (1961) *British Medical Journal*, **2**, 153

14 Freiman, I and Super, M (1966) *Archives of Diseases in Childhood*, **41**, 87

15 Dunlop, E M C and Zwink, F B (1954) Incidence of corneal changes in congenital syphilis. *British Journal of Venereal Diseases*, **30**, 201

16 Scott Gray, M and Philp, T (1963) Syphilitic arthritis. *Annals of the Rheumatic Diseases*, **22**, 19

17 Hahn, R D, Rodin, P and Haskins, H L (1961) *Journal of Chronic Diseases*, **15**, 395

18 Hutchinson, J (1858) *Transactions of the Odontological Society*, **2**, 95

19 Putkonen, T (1962) *Acta Dermato-venereologica* (Stockholm), **42**, 44

20 Hager, W D (1978) *Sexually Transmitted Diseases*, **5**, 122

21 Kerr, A G, Smyth, G D L and Cinnamond, M J (1973) *Journal of Laryngology and Otology*, **87**, 1

CHAPTER 9

Endemic Treponematoses

In 1905, Castellani, working in Ceylon, discovered the causative organism of yaws, and Schaudinn discovered and characterized *Spirochaeta pallida** in syphilis and confirmed that the causative organisms of yaws and syphilis were morphologically identical [1, 2, 3]. Since the very time of this discovery the biological and epidemiological relationships of the treponemes of venereal syphilis and the non-venereal treponemal diseases, such as yaws and pinta have continued to fascinate for there are clinical, epidemiological and immunological similarities which continue to defy attempts to separate and distinguish the organisms. The various biological differences appear, rather, to illustrate the remarkable adaptability of the treponeme and its ingenuity for survival. A number of other morphologically identical treponemes are known in mammals also and cannot yet be clearly distinguished from *Treponema pallidum* in the laboratory. These include *T. cuniculi* which causes a venereal disease in rabbits, and a treponeme found in the popliteal lymph nodes of the feral *Cynocephalus* (dog-headed ape) or baboon of Guinea. It is better to regard these treponemes as varieties or adaptations to secure survival than as distinct species.

The treponematoses of man have developed in differing geographical and epidemiological situations as parasite and host and have evolved a *modus vivendi.* The non-venereal diseases tend to exist among primitive peoples in rural communities, where transmission occurs by skin contact in childhood with other younger or older children who, themselves, have relapsing crops of infective skin lesions. If infected in childhood susceptibility to venereal syphilis later as adults is diminished.

Syphilis, on the other hand, probably evolved as a venereal disease as a result of social and climatic change as in those who began to wear clothes and, apart from sexual contact, tended to live more separate existences. The survival and transmission of the treponeme under these circumstances became possible only when susceptible adults, escaping yaws in childhood, became infected by contact with genital lesions at sexual intercourse.

*Translated 'pale spiral hair'; later the name was changed to *Treponema pallidum.*

Pinta

This is a disease affecting the skin (blue-stain disease) and it is the least damaging of the human treponematoses. The organism *Treponema carateum,* the most attenuated of the pathogenic treponemes, has a localized distribution amongst primitive peoples in certain rural and jungle areas of Central America and the northern part of the South American Continent, being most prevalent in Mexico, Venezuela, Columbia, Peru and Ecuador [4]. Throughout its course the disease is confined to the skin, where pigmented and achromic lesions may remain infective for years, permitting spread by direct skin to skin contact.

CLINICAL FEATURES

The primary or initial lesion develops after one to three months, often on an uncovered part of the body as a lenticular and slightly scaly papule which enlarges to form a plaque. At first the primary lesion is reddish but it becomes pigmented or hypochromic to a variable degree as it enlarges. After two months or up to a year later, secondary lesions develop, some on occasions appearing on the same site as the initial lesion. At first erythematous and afterwards copper coloured they become pigmented to a varying degree and areas of erythema, hypopigmentation and leucoderma develop. The polychromic lesions become keratotic. In late-stage pinta residual areas of hyperchromia and achromia develop in isolated patches to form multicoloured lesions. Adenopathy occurs in both early and late-stage pinta. The organism *T. carateum* is detected by dark-ground illumination microscopy in serum obtained from the base of a lesion after abrading the surface [5].

Yaws

Yaws is a contact disease of childhood, caused by *Treponema pertenue,* [6] and is characterized by crops of highly infectious and relapsing skin lesions in the first five or six years of the natural course of the infection. The nomenclature for the lesions of yaws is that established in an illustrated monograph of the World Health Organization [7] and the bone lesions are discussed more fully by Hackett [8].

The most characteristic lesion in early yaws is the papilloma and in the exudate of all early lesions, which may be macular, maculopapular or papular, treponemes are numerous. The early papule enlarges to form a papillomatous lesion being some resemblance to a raspberry (the disease has been called framboesia). There may also be adenitis. After two to six months the initial lesion heals, often without scarring. Further papillomata develop most often around the body orifices, near the nose, mouth, anus and vulva. Hyperkeratotic lesions occur on the soles of the feet and palms of the hands. On the feet plaques develop which are painful and walking becomes difficult (crab yaws). A periostitis may affect long bones or cause a polydactylitis affecting the phalanges and metacarpals. An osteitis of the nasal processes of the maxilla produces paranasal swellings (goundou) and is common in Africa. The tibia may become sabre-shaped.

Ganglions, particularly at the wrist, and hydrarthrosis can also occur in early yaws. There is also an early latent stage which may be interrupted by relapses of active early lesions.

Late lesions develop five or more years after the infection and the characteristic late lesion is a destructive ulcer, which may involve skin, subcutaneous tissue, the mucosae and the bones and joints. Deep destructive lesions are typified by the hideous mutilation of the central part of the face (*rhinopharyngitis mutilans*) called gangosa in which there is destruction of cartilage and bone structures of the septum, palate and posterior part of the pharynx [9]. It is probable, however, that there is no bone lesion that occurs in yaws that does not also occur in syphilis [8].

There is no certain evidence of transplacental or congenital infection in yaws. Serologically it cannot be distinguished from syphilis.

Endemic syphilis

Endemic syphilis occurs in a number of countries in the Middle East and in Africa, bordering on the Sahara desert in the north and around the Kalahari desert in the south [10].

In the Middle East endemic syphilis is known as bejel and it presents with a mucocutaneous eruption and exuberant papules predominantly around the genitalia and anus. Mucous patches appear on the lips, in the mouth and in the fauces. Symptoms such as hoarseness, dysphagia or dyspnoea have been attributed to extension of the mucous patches to the larynx. Periostitis also occurs [11].

Late lesions are destructive and the nose and its bony structure, the oral cavity and the hard palate and larynx are favourite sites. Hudson [11] remarks that in his time 'cleft palate voices were common in the market place'. Destructive skin ulcers, plantar keratosis, juxta-articular nodes and depigmented lesions are common late manifestations.

Control of endemic treponematoses

Although the treatment of whole communities with long-acting penicillin preparations for the control of endemic treponematoses of childhood was followed initially by a remarkable regression of the community disease, early clinical yaws has not been eliminated in large endemic areas where transmission continues and periodic focal outbreaks tend to occur [12].

In the 1950s, on the basis of pilot studies in yaws in Haiti, endemic syphilis in Yugoslavia and pinta in Mexico, mass-treatment campaigns with penicillin were undertaken in 46 countries in the context of the World Health Organization Treponematoses Campaign. Up till 1970 some 160 million people had been examined and 50 million clinical cases, latent cases and contacts had been treated. In Western Samoa, for example the prevalence of clinically active yaws was about 11 per cent in 1955 with about 3 per cent with infectious lesions. On re-survey of the population after mass treatment a year later clinically active yaws was found in only 0.06 per cent and infectious cases in 0.02 per cent. In Bosnia, Yugoslavia, the prevalence of endemic syphilis varied from district to district and was highest in north-eastern Bosnia, where about 14 per cent of the population were infected. Of all those found during the campaign to have the treponemal disease about 10 per cent had early infectious lesions, 0.2 per cent congenital, 85 per cent latent and 5 per cent late [13]. During the follow-up period after mass-treatment it soon became evident that the chief risk of perpetuating the disease lay, not in treatment-failures, but rather in infected persons escaping examination, in migrants from other districts with early lesions, in those with latent infections or those incubating the disease at the time of examination. In Yugoslavia the careful campaign and follow-up reduced the rate of endemic syphilis to nil.

In Haiti, more than 1.3 million clinical cases, latent cases and contacts were treated and surveys showed steady progress to low infectious levels of 0.01 per cent in 1961.

Techniques of surveillance have now changed to a strategy that relies on the extensive use of immunological methods made available by WHO research teams [14]. The original indices were clinical but field teams could not remain on treponematoses survey alone when the prevalence had become very low. Age-specific sero-reactor rates are now used to define areas as hyperendemic, mesoendemic and hypoendemic and in surveys after mass treatment such profiles demonstrate the age at which infections are occurring. In areas where very well conducted campaigns have been carried out an occasional sero-reactive child is discovered with no evidence of past or present clinical disease so there is a possibility of persisting subclinical infection. If the proportion of the population examined and treated is too low then sero-reactors will be common in early age groups of a sample and a further mass campaign will be necessary.

False sero-reactions in cardiolipin tests (biological false-positives) become relatively important when the sero-reactor rates are declining and particularly so in childhood. Special techniques of storing serum in liquid nitrogen [15] and other facilities have been developed to ensure that reliable specific FTA or other treponemal antibody tests can be carried out for those working in the field.

It is clear that in no large area has infectious clinical yaws been eliminated. Only in Yugoslavia where progressive environmental changes have favoured the host has early clinical endemic syphilis been eliminated. Possibilities, however, of subclinical infections remain. It will be necessary to discover how important are subclinical infections and the effect in a community of those, escaping yaws in childhood, but by doing so, remaining susceptible to venereal syphilis after puberty [12].

Antibiotic treatment in endemic treponematoses

In mass treatment campaigns it is proper to ensure that the long-acting penicillin preparation used conforms to WHO standards [16]. Procaine benzyl penicillin in oil with aluminium monostearate (PAM) or benzathine benzyl penicillin G (DBED) in single intramuscular doses of 2.4 megaunits is to be regarded as the minimum curative dose for early infections, for incubating syphilis (epidemiological treatment), as well as preventive if given before exposure.

Adults who may have acquired yaws in childhood may be seen in the clinics of western countries, when the results of serological tests will not differentiate from syphilis; in such cases, treatment appropriate for syphilis is advised (*see* Chapter 6).

Tetracyclines or erythromycin can be used as alternatives if patients give a history of reaction to penicillin, asthma or other allergy or eczema. Tetracyclines should not be used in pregnant women or in children under the age of twelve (page 120).

REFERENCES

1 Castellani, A (1905) *British Medical Journal,* **2,** 1280

2 Castellani, A (1906) On the prevalence of spirochaetes in yaws. In *Selected essays on syphilis and smallpox* (Ed) Russell, A E. New Sydenham Society, London, page 80

3 Schaudinn, F and Hoffman, E (1906) A preliminary note upon the occurrence of spirochaetes in syphilitic lesions and in papillomata (English translation of 1905 paper) in *Selected essays on syphilis and smallpox.* (Ed) Russell, A E. New Sydenham Society, London, page 2

4 Medina, R (1967) *Dermatologia Iberolatino-Americana* (English edition), **1**, 121

5 Marquez, F (1975) Pinta. In *Clinical tropical dermatology,* (Ed) Canizares, O. Blackwell Scientific Publications, London, page 86

6 Chambers, H D (1938) *Yaws (framboesia tropica).* Churchill, London

7 Hackett, C J (1957) *An international nomenclature of yaws lesions.* World Health Organization, Geneva

8 Hackett, C J (1951) *Bone Lesions of Yaws in Uganda.* Blackwell Scientific Publications, Oxford

9 Vegas, F K (1972) Yaws. In *Textbook of Dermatology,* (Ed) Rook, A, Wilkinson, D S and Ebling, P J G. Blackwell, London, page 668

10 Willcox, R R (1969) The treponematoses. In *Essays on Tropical Dermatology.* (Ed) Simons, R D G Ph and Marshall, J. Excerpta Medica Foundation, Amsterdam, page 35

11 Hudson, E H (1958) *Non-venereal syphilis.* Livingstone, Edinburgh

12 Guthe, T, Ridet, J, Vorst, F, D'Costa, J and Grab, B (1972) Methods for surveillance of endemic treponematoses and sero-immunological investigations of 'disappearing' disease. *Bulletin of the World Health Organization,* **46**, 1

13 Grin, E I (1953) Epidemiology and Control of Endemic Syphilis. *World Health Organization. Monograph Series* No. 11. Geneva

14 WHO Scientific Group (a) (1970) Multipurpose serological surveys and WHO Serum Reference Banks, *World Health Organization Technical Report Series,* No. 454

15 WHO Scientific Group (b) (1970) Treponematoses Research, *World Health Organization Technical Report Series,* No. 455, page 61

16 WHO Expert Committee (1964) WHO Expert Committee on Biological Standardization. 16th Report. *World Health Organization Technical Report Series,* No. 274, page 41

CHAPTER 10

Gonorrhoea: Aetiology, Pathogenesis and Clinical Features

Gonorrhoea, an infection of the mucosal surfaces of the genito-urinary tract with the bacterium, *Neisseria gonorrhoeae,* is mainly transmitted by sexual intercourse. In men the infection is associated with an acute purulent urethritis in approximately 90 per cent of cases, but the organisms may spread also to the epididymis and the prostate. In women the urethra and cervix are infected in 65–75 per cent and 85–90 per cent of cases respectively and the rectal mucosa in 25–50 per cent. Occasionally (about 10 per cent) infection extends from the cervix to the endometrium and fallopian tubes. Infection of the fauces may occur in both sexes (2–5 per cent); eye infections are seen rarely in adults. In homosexual men, who act as passive partners in anal intercourse, rectal infections also occur. In a small percentage of untreated cases, systemic spread gives rise to an entity known as disseminated gonococcal infection, characterized clinically by arthritis with or without skin lesions.

Aetiology

The causative organism, *Neisseria gonorrhoeae,* commonly referred to as the gonococcus, derives its generic name from Albert Neisser who described it in 1879.

The gonococcus is a delicate organism with exacting nutritional and environmental requirements. Media containing blood or serum, a temperature of 36°C to 37°C and a moist atmosphere, enriched with carbon dioxide (10 per cent) must be provided to ensure growth. The organism is liable to die if separated from its host and it is also readily killed by drying, soap and water, and many other cleansing or antiseptic agents.

The bacteria are small Gram-negative cocci, kidney-shaped and arranged in pairs (diplococci) with the long axes in parallel and the opposed surfaces slightly concave; the organisms are typically intracellular.

By microscopy it is impossible to differentiate the gonococcus from *N. meningitidis* or from other non-pathogenic or potentially pathogenic neisseriae commonly found in the upper respiratory tract. Commensal neisseriae can also be found on the mucous surfaces of the genito-urinary tract, particularly in the female.

In nature, *N. gonorrhoeae* is a strictly human pathogen although experimental infections have been induced in the urethra of the chimpanzee [1, 2].

In 1963 Kellogg and his co-workers [3] described four distinct colony types of gonococci, referred to as T1 to T4. Later an additional colony type (T5) was recognized [4]. Bacteria from colony types 1 and 2 are virulent for human volunteers [3] and possess pili [5] whereas colony types 3 and 4 are essentially avirulent and lack pili. Freshly isolated strains from clinical specimens are predominantly colony type 1, but on sub-culture in the laboratory the avirulent colony types become established. Gonococci with pili attach to epithelial cells more readily than do organisms without pili [6, 7]. Pili may also make gonococci more resistant to phagocytosis [8]. The precise relationship between pili, other surface antigens and virulence is not clear at present. Gonococci studied in urethral pus possess relatively few pili [9].

Gonococci are antigenically heterogeneous and no widely accepted method of typing strains has yet been developed. A system of classifying gonococci on the basis of their nutritional requirements, known as auxotyping, has been used to show that gonococci that require arginine, hypoxanthine, and uracil ($Arg^{-}Hyx^{-}Ura^{-}$) for growth are usually highly sensitive to penicillin G and are associated with disseminated gonococcal infection [10]. The heterogeneity in pilus protein, in major outer membrane protein, and in gonococcal susceptibility to bactericidal typing sera has been employed to demonstrate the identity of isolates from sexual consorts. Geographical differences, also, have been described in the distribution of the 16 gonococcal outer membrane protein immunotypes described so far [11]. Recently, *N. gonorrhoeae* has been classified into immunotypes by the micro-immunofluorescence method [12], which may be used in studies on epidemiology. The absence, however, of a simple method of strain differentiation of gonococcal isolates is a major handicap in studying the epidemiology and immunology of the disease. A method of strain differentiation based on the sensitivity of gonococci to pyocines, the name given to bacteriocines produced by *Pseudomonas aeruginosa,* has been investigated [13].

Pathogenesis

Primary infection commonly occurs in the columnar epithelium of the urethra and para-urethral ducts and glands of both sexes, of greater vestibular glands (Bartholin's) of the cervix, the conjunctiva and of the rectum. Primary infection may also occur in the soft stratified squamous epithelium of the vagina of young girls: involvement of this type of epithelium in other parts of the body such as the skin of the glans penis, cornea and mouth is extrememly rare.

During acute gonococcal urethritis, by the third day of infection, gonococci have penetrated the mucosal lining of the urethra and have become established in the subepithelial connective tissue [14]. The capillaries are dilated, and there is an exudation of cells and serum. Dense cellular infiltrations consisting of polymorphonuclear leucocytes, plasma cells and mast cells soon make their appearance beneath the columnar epithelium, being particularly numerous in the region of Littré's glands and ducts. The inflammatory reaction involves the deep tissue of the corpus spongiosum and may extend into the corpora cavernosa. Gonococci are thought to penetrate the intact mucosal surface by invasion through the cells rather than by passing between cell junctions; the intracellular penetration of gonococci into mucosal cells desquamated from the cervix and urethra of infected patients, has been demonstrated [15].

According to one concept, gonococcal pathogenicity may be based primarily on internal disorganization of human macrophages [16]. Gonococci in pus appear in specific clusters in which they are surrounded by organelles and granules derived from the host cells in which they multiplied. These clusters are called infectious units because:

1. the cocci multiply within them,
2. the whole complex makes contact with epithelial cells,
3. the cocci in units are not recognized by polymorphs as long as the coating of granules is dense enough, and
4. the cocci are probably protected against humoral defence mechanisms.

Gonococci phagocytosed by polymorphonuclear leucocytes are killed. Those phagocytosed by macrophages, however, interfere with the cells' regulatory processes, survive and form a cluster of multiplying gonococci surrounded by granules and remnants of macrophages, i.e., the infectious units; the host cell remnants are utilized, the gonococci become less and less coated and are rephagocytosed, and the cycle is repeated. Depending on the nature of the phagocytic cells involved, an abortive infection or a self-cure of gonorrhoea may occur.

Transmission of infection

Owing to the poor viability of the gonococcus away from the mucosal surfaces of the host, gonorrhoea is ordinarily acquired by sexual intercourse with an infected person. There are so many variable factors that it is difficult to assess the risk of acquiring an infection from a single exposure. However, gonorrhoea is regarded as being of high infectivity, the risk for a female having intercourse with an infected male being higher, 60–90 per cent [17, 18, 19] than that for a male with an infected female, 30–50 per cent [20].

The incubation period in the male tends to be about three to five days (range two to 10 days). In the female a precise incubation period is difficult to determine since approximately 70 per cent or more of infections may cause no symptoms. Such asymptomatic infections make it possible for individuals to remain as sources of infection within the community whilst at risk themselves of developing pelvic inflammatory disease or disseminated infection.

The gonococcus can be transmitted to the pharynx by oro-genital contact. Transfer of gonococcal pharyngitis by kissing appears to be a rare occurrence.

In males, rectal infection results from anal intercourse. Colonization of the rectal mucosa in the female is common (25–50 per cent) [21] and ordinarily results from backward extension of the infection due to contamination by infected vaginal secretions.

Vulvo-vaginitis in young children under the age of puberty is caused more commonly by organisms other than *N. gonorrhoeae,* but such infections can result from accidental contamination of the child with discharge when sleeping with an infected parent. On occasions, it may be the result of a sexual assault, which is often difficult to prove.

During birth, a baby passing through an infected cervix may acquire gonococcal conjunctivitis of the newborn (ophthalmia neonatorum): this condition is uncommon nowadays in this locality due to general improvements in antenatal care and the detection and treatment of gonococcal infection. Gonococcal conjunctivitis in older children and in adults is usually acquired by contact with fingers and/or moist towels contaminated with fresh pus.

Immunity to gonococcal infection

From the number of patients with well-documented, repeated infections, it is obvious that immunity to the gonococcus, sufficient to be protective, does not result from an earlier infection. Failure to develop effective immunity is probably not due to the rapid elimination of infection with antibiotics since repeated infections were common before these were available. Many infections in female patients are also asymptomatic for a long time.

Serum antibody to gonococci can be detected within a few days of infection but such antibodies are not protective. Since the gonococcus infects mucous surfaces, locally produced secretory immunoglobulin A (IgA) may be more important in immunity. Anti-gonococcal secretory IgA is found in secretions in many patients with gonorrhoea [22, 23], but its role in preventing or modifying infection is still to be elucidated. If local secretory IgA is an important defence against infection, its failure may be the result of rapid catabolism of IgA. *N. gonorrhoeae* has been shown to produce a protease which cleaves the IgA1 molecule [24]. Since there is considerable antigenic variation among gonococci, an individual may be immune to one strain but become infected with an antigenically different strain. In infected patients immune mechanisms, including cell mediated immunity, may be important in localizing the infection in the genito-urinary tract and in preventing systemic spread.

A degree of non-specific immunity to gonococcal infection probably exists, since not everyone exposed to an infection acquires the disease. The effectors of this immunity are at present poorly understood. It is possible that certain components of the normal endocervical flora are antagonistic towards gonococci and prevent the establishment of gonococcal infection [25].

The apparent lack of naturally acquired immunity to gonococcal infection makes it unlikely that an effective gonococcal vaccine will be available in the near future. In the infectious unit too the cocci are probably protected against humoral defence mechanisms and phagocytic cells will not recognize the cocci as long as the coating of granules is sufficiently dense.

Epidemiology

Gonorrhoea is a disease with world-wide distribution, and is the most prevalent infection after the exanthemata in the United Kingdom. As may be seen from Figure 10.1 the incidence of the disease fell after the Second World War, levelled off until the mid-1960's and rose sharply until about the early 1970's, since when the rate has been relatively constant. Similar trends have been reported from other countries but due to differences in methods of reporting, it is at present difficult to compare incidence rates from one country to another.

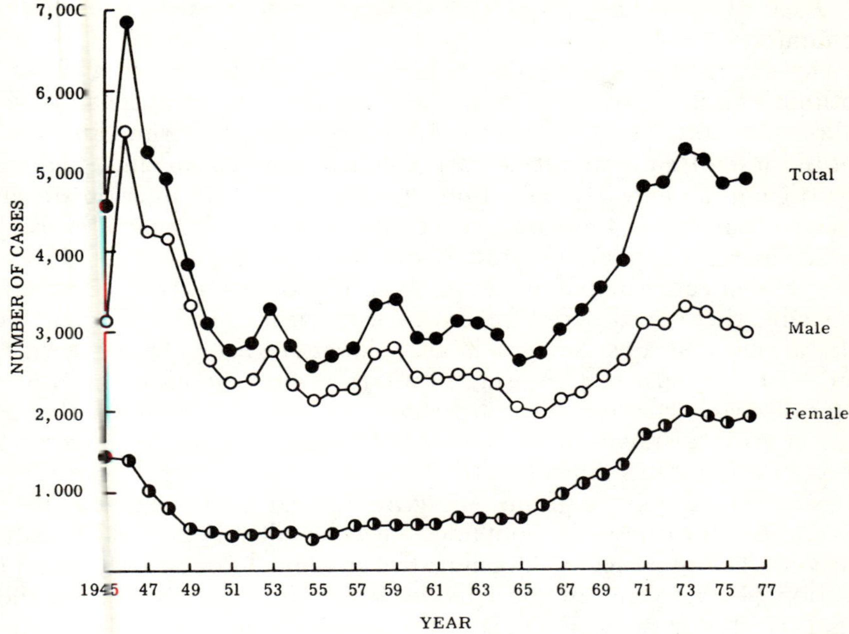

Figure 10.1 New cases of gonorrhoea in Scotland (1945–1976).

Gonorrhoea is mainly a disease of young adults, most cases being found within the 15–24 year age group. For example in the age group 20–24 the incidence per 100,000 population in 1973 was as follows (World Health Organization [26]):

Country	*Males*	*Females*
United Kingdom	751	451
Sweden	1724	1538
USA	2479	1406

Previously, the reported incidence in males was much greater than in females but the overall male:female ratio is tending to unity. In contrast, the rate for girls under 16 years is about four times that for boys of the same age group and reflects their earlier sexual maturation.

Some of the factors which have contributed to the increase in gonorrhoea seen in recent years have been discussed earlier (*see* Chapter

1). Lack of individual immunity also aids spread of infection within the community.

The emergence of strains of *N. gonorrhoeae* relatively insensitive to antibiotics has contributed to the world-wide increase in the infection. In certain areas, such as South East Asia, the indiscriminate use of antibiotics, often without proper medical supervision and in dosage insufficient to cure the infection, has led to the production of such strains. Isolates of gonococci completely resistant to penicillin due to penicillinase (β-lactamase) production were first reported in 1976 but have now been isolated in more than 15 countries [27]. Epidemiologically, these strains can be linked with either the Far East or West Africa: most strains isolated in or epidemiologically linked with the Far East are relatively resistant to tetracycline *in vitro*, are phenotypically wild-type or proline-dependent auxotypes and carry a plasmid* with a molecular weight of 5.8×10^6 daltons coding for β-lactamase production. Strains linked with West Africa are more susceptible to tetracycline, require arginine for growth, and their gene coding for β-lactamase synthesis is contained in a smaller 3.2×10^6 dalton plasmid. The presence of a conjugative plasmid,† found only in a proportion (43 per cent) of the Far Eastern strains and absent from those from West Africa may explain the relatively high prevalence of β-lactamase-producing strains (30–40 per cent among gonococcal infections) in certain areas of the Far East.

Clinical features in the adult male (Uncomplicated gonococcal infection)

URETHRAL INFECTION

The patient complains of urethral discharge and an often mild dysuria in about 90 per cent of cases. If infection has spread proximally to the posterior urethra there may be symptoms of frequency of micturition, urgency and painful erections. Clinical examination may reveal a reddened urethral meatus with a purulent or muco-purulent discharge. Inguinal lymph nodes may be enlarged on both sides. Examination of the urine by the two glass test (page 48) will show pus in the first glass if the anterior urethra is mainly affected, or in both glasses if the posterior urethra and/or bladder is involved. If the inflammatory process is less severe, evidence of urethritis may take the form of

*A plasmid is a small extrachromosomal piece of genetic material that can replicate autonomously and maintain itself in the cytoplasm of a bacterium for many generations; it is usually a circular piece of double-stranded DNA.

†A plasmid that contains the information for self-transfer to another cell by conjugation.

finding 'threads' (i.e. casts of urethral glands* composed of pus cells and descuamated tubular cells) in the urine.

It is now clear that a considerable number (possibly as many as 15 per cent in some localities) of males with urethral gonorrhoea have few symptoms if any [28].

Note: Post-gonococcal urethritis may occur in at least 20 per cent of males adequately treated with penicillin (Chapter 13).

OROPHARYNGEAL INFECTION

Infection of the pharynx results from transfer of organisms from the genitalia during fellatio or, less commonly, cunnilingus. Although there is a significant correlation between symptoms of pharyngitis and the practice of fellatio, the isolation of *N. gonorrhoeae* from the pharynx does not correlate with symptoms of pharyngitis [29]. Symptoms are present in only about 20 per cent of cases [30], when the patient's complaint is sore throat, perhaps with referred pain in the ear. Clinical examination may reveal no abnormalities, or a mild pharyngitis or tonsillitis.

ANORECTAL INFECTION

Infection in this site in the male is invariably the result of a homosexual act. The majority of patients (more than two-thirds) with anorectal gonorrhoea have no symptoms of infection [31]. In others there may be a history of pruritus and mucoid or muco-purulent anal discharge, anal pain, bleeding and tenesmus [32]. It is difficult to ascribe these symptoms to gonorrhoea, as they may also occur in uninfected homosexual patients, and possibly reflect a non-specific mucosal reaction to the trauma of intercourse.

Proctoscopic examination may show a normal appearance, or there may be either patchy or generalized erythema of the rectal mucosa with mucopus in the lumen of the anal canal and rectum. The inflammatory reaction does not extend into the sigmoid colon. In some cases the mucous membrane is friable, bleeding to the touch, and in others, may present a granular appearance. The anal canal, constructed of stratified cuboid or squamous epithelium, is not affected by the gonococcus.

Histologically there are areas of degeneration of the epithelium on the surface of the rectum and in the crypts. The underlying lamina

*Opening into the lumen of the penile urethra are the ducts of mucus-secreting glands located in the submucosa (Littré's glands). These glands are almost invariably inflamed in urethral gonorrhoea.

propria shows an intense inflammatory reaction with vasodilatation and infiltration with polymorphonuclear leucocytes, lymphocytes, plasma cells and monocytes [33].

The differential diagnosis of anorectal gonorrhoea includes ulcerative colitis, Crohn's disease, ischaemic colitis, radiation or drug-induced colitis, amoebic proctitis, giardiasis and lymphogranuloma venereum.

Local complications of untreated anorectal infection include peri-anal and ischio-rectal abscesses and anal fissures.

Local complications of gonorrhoea in the male

INFLAMMATION AND ABSCESS FORMATION IN THE PARAFRENAL GLANDS (TYSON'S GLANDS)

This is not common (less than one per cent) but, when it occurs, it usually produces painful tender swellings on one or both sides of the frenum. Pus may be expressed from the duct.

GONOCOCCAL BALANITIS

As the gonococcus tends not to attack the squamous epithelium of the glans penis this complication is uncommon.

INFLAMMATION AND ABSCESS FORMATION IN THE PARA-URETHRAL GLANDS ON EITHER SIDE OF THE URETHRAL MEATUS

This is rare now in areas where medical attention is easily available. A painful swelling develops on one or both sides of the urethral meatus. Pus may be expressed from the duct of the gland.

PERI-URETHRAL CELLULITIS AND ABSCESS FORMATION

This is rare except when medical help is delayed. The inflammatory reaction to the gonococcus in the subepithelial tissues of the urethra is particularly marked in the region of Littré's glands and ducts which may become obstructed resulting in the formation of small cysts and abscesses. Coalescence of these small abscesses results in the formation of peri-urethral abscess [14]. These abscesses may rupture into the urethra or to the exterior, or may heal with the formation of fibrous tissue.

There is pain and swelling at the site of the abscess and there may be some restriction in urine flow if it bulges into the urethra. If the corpus spongiosum is affected, painful erections will be experienced, and there may be ventral angulation of the penis. On examination there is a tender fluctuant swelling, most commonly at the site of the fossa navicularis or bulb.

If untreated the abscess may point; the overlying skin becomes inflamed and oedematous and the abscess may rupture, producing a fistula.

URETHRAL STRICTURES

Although rare in developed countries urethral strictures and fistulae as late complications are common in tropical countries [34]. Fibrous strictures develop from healing of areas of peri-urethral cellulitis or abscesses. Further peri-urethral abscesses may develop proximal to the area of the stricture and their rupture to the exterior results in the formation of urinary fistulae. Fistulae either single or multiple are most commonly found in the perineum or scrotum.

Strictures usually develop many years after infection, but may be found within 5 years of the initial infection [34]. Symptoms of urinary obstruction include straining at micturition, poor force of the urine stream, prolonged micturition with dribbling. Increased frequency of micturition occurs from incomplete emptying of the bladder or from cystitis. Urinary retention eventually develops and death can result from ascending urinary infection and renal failure.

INFLAMMATION AND ABSCESS FORMATION OF THE BULBO-URETHRAL GLANDS (COWPER'S GLANDS)

This complication is uncommon in developed countries. The patient complains of fever, throbbing pain in the perineum, painful defaecation and frequency of micturition. Reflex spasm of the sphincter urethra may produce acute retention of urine. An abscess, which is usually unilateral, may point in the perineum. The inflamed glands and abscess are palpable on rectal examination and are exquisitely tender.

PROSTATITIS AND SEMINAL VESICULITIS

Acute gonococcal prostatitis and seminal vesiculitis are rare. There are usually constitutional disturbances, fever, perineal discomfort, urgency of micturition, haematuria and painful erections. Occasionally acute retention of urine results from reflex spasm of the external sphincter of the bladder. A tender swollen gland is detected on rectal examination. With abscess formation, symptoms become more severe with painful defaecation and suprapubic pain. Pyrexia becomes more pronounced. Rectal examination shows a large, tense swelling bulging into the rectum. The abscess may rupture into the urethra or rectum.

Chronic prostatitis, inflammation of the bulbo-urethral glands (Cowperitis), and chronic inflammation of the seminal vesicles may be found in long-standing infections and can produce vague symptoms of local inflammation such as urethral discharge in the morning and perineal discomfort. Palpation of the glands may reveal irregular thickening, and the prostatic fluid expressed often contains large numbers of pus cells which may exhibit 'clumping' (Chapter 14).

EPIDIDYMITIS

This is usually unilateral, when the patient complains of a painful swollen testis. On examination there may be erythema of the scrotum on the affected side; the epididymis is enlarged and tender, and there is often a secondary hydrocele. Inflammation of the testis itself is rare (Chapter 14).

INFECTION OF THE MEDIAN RAPHE OF THE PENIS

This is rare but when it occurs a bead of pus may be expressed from a duct opening on to the skin on the ventral surface of the penis.

Clinical features in the adult female (Uncomplicated gonococcal infection)

Females with gonorrhoea usually have few, if any, symptoms (about 70 per cent or more). They may occasionally complain of vaginal discharge, but this may be attributable to concomitant vaginitis caused by *Trichomonas vaginalis.* Uncommonly, inflammation of the trigone of the bladder produces urinary frequency. The sites infected in the uncomplicated cases (*see* Figure 11.1) are:

Cervix	85–90 per cent
Urethra	65–75 per cent
Rectum	25–50 per cent
Oropharynx	2–5 per cent

The affected cervix may appear normal on inspection, or there may be signs of inflammation with mucopus exuding from the external os. There may be no clinical evidence of urethritis but occasionally pus may be expressed from the orifice. Rectal gonorrhoea in the female, as in the male, usually produces few symptoms. Oropharyngeal gonorrhoea in the female results from fellatio and the features are similar to those in the male.

Local complications of gonorrhoea in the female

INFLAMMATION AND ABSCESS FORMATION OF THE PARA-URETHRAL GLANDS INCLUDING THOSE LYING EXTERNALLY ON EITHER SIDE OF THE EXTERNAL MEATUS (SKENE'S GLANDS)

Abscess formation is not common but involvement of these glands by the gonococcus is probably present in urethral infection in the female.

INFLAMMATION AND ABSCESS FORMATION OF THE GREATER VESTIBULAR GLANDS (BARTHOLINITIS AND BARTHOLIN'S ABSCESS)

The glands may be involved on one or both sides. There may be few symptoms of Bartholinitis but, in the routine examination, on compressing the gland, pus may be expressed from the orifice of the duct. When an abscess forms, the patient may complain of pain in the vulva, and examination reveals a tender cystic swelling of the posterior half of the labium majus, the skin of which may be reddened. In less acute and partially treated cases a chronic inflammation may result, causing palpable thickening of the glands.

PELVIC INFLAMMATORY DISEASE AND SALPINGITIS

These complications are considered in Chapter 16. The incidence of salpingitis in untreated cases is generally given as 10 per cent.

Disseminated gonococcal infection, involving both sexes

This uncommon complication, occurring in less than one per cent of cases, is usually seen in women and in homosexual males in whom the infection has been asymptomatic and untreated [35]. Dissemination may occur from any infected site and more often during or just after menstruation and in pregnancy.

Gonococcal strains associated with disseminated infection are usually of the same auxotype ($Arg^-Hyx^-Ura^-$), extremely sensitive to penicillin G, and resistant to the complement-dependent bactericidal action of normal human serum [36]. Evidence indirectly indicating the importance of an intact, complement-dependent bactericidal system in protection from disseminated infection has been reported [37]. To what extent factors in the host or factors in the organism, or a combination of both, are responsible for causing disseminated gonococcal infections, is yet unknown.

The clinical manifestations of disseminated gonococcal infection usually take the form of fever, rash and arthralgia or arthritis. The spectrum of clinical features of this complication is fairly broad but two forms possibly represent successive stages of the disease.

In the initial bacteriaemic stage or form, symptoms are usually of short duration, the patient complaining of fever, rigors, joint pains and perhaps a skin rash. There are characteristic skin lesions and polyarticular arthritis involving usually the knees, wrists, small joints of the hands, ankles and elbows, without sufficient joint effusion present to allow aspiration. If obtained, the fluid from joints is sterile on culture but blood cultures are often positive for *N. gonorrhoeae* [38] if taken within 2 days of onset of the illness. There may be a tenosynovitis.

In the second form, involvement of one joint is usual, a considerable effusion is present and *N. gonorrhoeae* maybe recoverable from the synovial fluid, which contains many polymorphonuclear neutrophil leucocytes. This form sometimes called the 'septic-joint stage' occurs usually after symptoms have been present for at least four days. A large joint, especially of the upper limb, tends to be affected, e.g. shoulder, elbow. The sternoclavicular or temporomandibular joint may also be affected. Systemic features are usually milder than in the bacteriaemic form, skin lesions are seldom found and blood cultures are usually negative for *N. gonorrhoeae.*

Intermediate stages of the disease may be seen and in the 'septic joint stage' if untreated the articular surfaces of the joint may be destroyed and fibrous or bony ankylosis may follow.

THE SKIN LESIONS IN DISSEMINATED GONOCOCCAL INFECTION

These are usually associated with constitutional disturbance, including fever and polyarthritis. There are essentially two types of skin lesion [39]: (i) haemorrhagic lesions, (ii) vesiculopapular lesions on an erythematous base.

Both types of lesion begin as erythematous macules but in the haemorrhagic type the lesions become purpuric especially on the palms and soles. In the second type lesions become papular and progress through vesicles to pustules. Generally resolution occurs in 4–5 days, but cropping may occur during febrile episodes. The lesions, often painful, have an asymmetrical distribution over the body and are particularly noticeable on the extremities and around affected joints (Plate 7). Histological examination of a skin lesion [40] shows a small-vessel vasculitis in the dermis and subcutis and marked fibrinoid change. There is a perivascular infiltration of polymorphonuclear and mononuclear cells. Degenerating polymorphonuclear leucocytes and evidence of haemorrhage are commonly seen. Using conventional staining techniques, *N. gonorrhoeae* is rarely found in these skin lesions, although antigenic material may be found using direct immunofluorescent staining. It is possible that the skin lesions result from alternative pathway complement activation* by endotoxin [41].

The lesions of a disseminated gonococcal infection are clinically and histologically similar to those seen in meningococcal septicaemia.

MENINGITIS, ENDOCARDITIS AND PERICARDITIS

Meningitis is an uncommon manifestation of disseminated gonococcal infection and is usually found associated with arthritis and dermatitis [38].

Gonococcal endocarditis is also a rare complication [42]. The degree of severity of the condition lies between endocarditis due to *Staphylococcus aureus* and that produced by *Streptococcus viridans.* Most commonly the aortic valve is involved. Maculopapular skin lesions are common and appear in crops. Emboli to cerebral, renal and peripheral arteries may occur [43].

Myocarditis and pericarditis may occur more commonly than hitherto recognized. Transient electrocardiographic abnormalities appear to be common in disseminated infection [30, 38].

PERIHEPATITIS AND HEPATITIS

Acute perihepatitis usually occurs in association with pelvic inflammatory disease in women. This complication is very rarely found in men [44]. The patient complains of pain in the right hypochondrium and sometimes in the right shoulder from irritation of the right side of the diaphragm.

Hepatitis may occur following the bacteriaemia of disseminated infection [38]. The hepatic histology is not diagnostic, there being scattered foci of mononuclear and polymorphonuclear leucocyte infiltrates in the parenchyma, with enlarged portal zones infiltrated with lymphocytes.

Gonococcal conjunctivitis

This is rare except in the newborn and presents as a purulent conjunctivitis affecting one or both eyes. If untreated, keratitis or panophthalmitis with blindness may result.

*A pathway for the activation of the complement system which misses out the C1, C4 and C2 components and starts at the C3 step. The mechanism of activation does not depend upon the same part of the immunoglobulin molecule as the classical pathway and can be activated by aggregated immunoglobulins and various polysaccharides including bacterial endotoxin.

Gonorrhoea in infants and children under the age of puberty

GONOCOCCAL OPHTHALMIA NEONATORUM

This is a conjunctivitis with a purulent discharge in an infant which appears within 21 days of birth and it is a notifiable disease in the United Kingdom. Ophthalmia neonatorum was formerly caused chiefly by *N. gonorrhoeae*, but is now more commonly caused by other organisms including *Chlamydia trachomatis.* Gonococcal ophthalmia usually manifests itself within 48 hours of birth but it may be delayed for as long as a week and, if untreated, has dangerous consequences. The eyelids swell and pus collects in the conjunctival sac. Keratitis with corneal scarring may result if the condition is not treated.

ACUTE VULVO-VAGINITIS

This is uncommon in the United Kingdom nowadays. The parents usually notice discharge on the child's underwear and on examination a purulent vaginal discharge, with reddening and oedema of the vulva, may be found.

OROPHARYNGEAL AND RECTAL INFECTION

Recently workers in the United States of America have described the occurrence of gonorrhoea in these sites in a number of children from lower socio-economic groups [45] . Infection did not necessarily suggest sexual assault.

REFERENCES

1 Lucas, C T, Chandler, F, Martin, J E and Schmale, J D (1971) *Journal of the American Medical Association,* **216,** 1612

2 Brown, W J, Lucas, C T and Kuhn, U S G (1972) *British Journal of Venereal Diseases,* **48,** 177

3 Kellogg, D S, Peacock, W L, Deacon, W E, Brown, L and Pirkle, C I (1963) *Journal of Bacteriology,* **85,** 1274

4 Jephcott, A E and Reyn, A (1971) *Acta Pathologica et Microbiologica Scandinavica,* Section B, **79,** 609

5 Jephcott, A E, Reyn, A and Birch-Andersen, A (1971) *Acta Pathologica et Microbiologica Scandinavica,* Section B, **79,** 437

6 Swanson, J (1973) *Journal of Experimental Medicine,* **137,** 571

7 Heckels, J E, Blackett, B, Everson, J S and Ward, M E (1976) *Journal of General Microbiology,* **96,** 359

8 Ofek, I, Beachey, E H and Bisno, A L (1974) *Journal of Infectious Diseases,* **129,** 310

9 Novotny, P, Short, J A and Walker, P H (1975) *Journal of Medical Microbiology,* **8,** 413

10 Knapp, J S and Holmes, K K (1975) *Journal of Infectious Diseases,* **132,** 204

11 Johnston, J H, Holmes, K K and Gotschlich, E C (1976) *Journal of Experimental Medicine,* **143,** 741

12 Wang, S P, Holmes, K K, Knapp, J S, Ott, S and Kyzer, D D (1977) *Journal of Immunology,* **119,** 795
13 Sidberry, H D and Sadoff, J C (1977) *Infection and Immunity,* **15,** 628
14 Harkness, A M (1948) *British Journal of Venereal Diseases,* **24,** 137
15 Ward, M E, Robertson, J N, Englefield, P M and Watt, P J (1975) *Microbiology,* **2,** 188
16 Novotny, P, Short, J A, Hughes, M, Miler, J J, Syrett, C, Turner, W H, Harris, J R W and MacLennan, I P B (1977) *Journal of Medical Microbiology,* **10,** 347
17 Chipperfield, E J and Catterall, R D (1976) *British Journal of Venereal Diseases,* **52,** 36
18 Evans, B A (1976) *British Journal of Venereal Diseases,* **52,** 40
19 Barlow, D, Nayyar, K, Phillips, I and Barrow, J (1976) *British Journal of Venereal Diseases,* **52,** 326
20 Holmes, K K, Johnson, D W and Trostle, H J (1970) *American Journal of Epidemiology,* **91,** 170
21 Bhattacharyya, M N and Jephcott, A E (1974) *British Journal of Venereal Diseases,* **50,** 109
22 Kearns, D H, O'Reilly, R J, Lee, L and Welch, B G (1973) *Journal of Infectious Diseases,* **127,** 99
23 O'Reilly, R J, Lee, L and Welch, B G (1976) *Journal of Infectious Diseases,* **133,** 113
24 Plaut A G, Gilbert, J V, Artenstein, M and Capra, J D (1975) *Science,* **190,** 1103
25 Saigh, J H, Sanders, C C and Sanders, W E (1978) *Infection and Immunity,* **19,** 704
26 World Health Organization (1978) *Neisseria gonorrhoeae* and gonococcal infections. *Technical Report Series* 616, Geneva
27 Perine, P L, Thornsberry, C, Schalla, W, Biddle, J, Siegel, M S, Wong, K H and Thompson, S E (1977) *Lancet,* **ii,** 993
28 Neilsen, R, Sondergaard, J and Ullman, S (1975) *Acta Dermato-venereologica* (Stockholm), **55,** 499
29 Wiesner, P J, Tronca, E, Bonin, P, Pedersen, A H B and Holmes, K K (1973) *New England Journal of Medicine,* **288,** 181
30 Stolz, E and Schuller, J (1974) *British Journal of Venereal Diseases,* **50,** 104
31 Catterall, R D (1962) *Proceedings of the Royal Society of Medicine,* **55,** 871
32 Owen, R L and Hill, J L (1972) *Journal of the American Medical Association,* **220,** 1315
33 Harkness, A H (1948) *Proceedings of the Royal Society of Medicine,* **41,** 476
34 Osoba, A O and Alausa, O (1976) *British Journal of Venereal Diseases,* **52,** 387
35 Graber, W J, Sanford, J P and Ziff, M (1960) *Arthritis and Rheumatism,* **3,** 309
36 Schoolnik, G K, Buchanan, T M and Holmes, K K (1976) *Journal of Clinical Investigation,* **58,** 1163
37 Petersen, B H, Graham, J A and Brooks, G F (1976) *Journal of Clinical Investigation,* **57,** 283
38 Holmes, K K, Counts, G W and Beaty, H W (1971) *Annals of Internal Medicine,* **74,** 979
39 Ackerman, A B, Miller, R C and Shapiro, L (1965) *Archives of Dermatology,* **91,** 227
40 Seifert, M H, Warin, A P and Miller, A (1974) *Annals of Rheumatic Diseases,* **33,** 140
41 Scherer, R and Braun-Falco, O (1976) *British Journal of Dermatology,* **95,** 303
42 John, J F, Nichols, J T, Eisenhower, E A and Farrar, W E (1977) *Sexually Transmitted Diseases,* **4,** 84
43 Williams, R H (1938) *Archives of Internal Medicine* (Chicago), **61,** 26
44 Kimball, N W and Knee, S (1970) *New England Journal of Medicine,* **282,** 1082
45 Nelson, J D, Mohs, E, Dajani, A S and Plotkin, S A (1976) *Journal of the American Medical Association,* **236,** 1359

Further Reading

Roberts, R B (1977) (Ed) *The Gonococcus.* John Wiley and Sons, New York

CHAPTER 11

Diagnosis of Gonorrhoea: Laboratory and Clinical Procedures

Microbiological tests are mandatory in making a diagnosis of gonorrhoea. Because of the short incubation period and high infectivity, rapid diagnosis followed by immediate treatment is important in the control of infection within the community.

Neisseria gonorrhoeae is a very fastidious organism and very careful techniques are necessary for the collection of specimens and their transport to the laboratory for culture and investigation. Ideally the patient is seen at a clinic with an adjacent or closely-sited laboratory. Under these conditions the majority of infected patients (about 95 per cent of males and 60 per cent of females) can receive appropriate effective treatment on the first attendance after examination of Gram-stained smears. Cultural diagnosis of additional cases and confirmation of smear-positive cases can be made within 24 to 72 hours.

SPECIMENS REQUIRED FOR BACTERIOLOGICAL EXAMINATION

In *males,* material for examination is obtained by inserting a sterile bacteriological loop (page 47) into the everted urethral meatus and gently scraping the walls of the terminal part of the urethra. A loopful or less of the exudate obtained may be examined by microscopy of a Gram-stained smear and by culture. If recent anal intercourse is acknowledged or suspected a proctoscope is passed and mucus or mucopus obtained for microscopic examination and culture. Direct microscopy of rectal material is often unhelpful as there are large numbers of other organisms in this site, and interpretation of a Gram-stained smear may be difficult. If there has been oro-genital contact with a person who may possibly have been infected, material should be obtained for culture from the tonsillar crypts or bed and pharynx. Ideally, in every case of gonorrhoea or in known contacts, it is wise to take this test without seeking details of sexual practice which patients may be reluctant to discuss.

If the patient is known to have had sexual intercourse with an infected partner and he has no obvious signs of urethritis, it is often helpful to re-examine him when he has held his urine for several hours, preferably overnight. Any exudate which may have collected may then be massaged to the urethral orifice and examined by microscopy and culture. Even in the absence of an obvious discharge, specimens for culture should be obtained by gently scraping the urethral walls with a bacteriological loop (page 47). Occasionally examination of prostatic fluid may detect an asymptomatic infection.

Normally a single examination is sufficient to diagnose or exclude urethral gonorrhoea in men. However, if the patient is known to have had sexual intercourse with an infected partner or if rectal or pharyngeal infection are suspected, cultures should be repeated twice at weekly intervals if the first tests are negative.

In *female patients* specimens for cultural investigation should be taken from the urethra (Ur), cervical os and cervical canal (Cx), rectum (R) and throat (T). If pus is expressed from the orifice(s) of the ducts of the greater vestibular glands, this should be similarly examined (page 52). Smears should be taken from the urethra and endocervix for microscopic examination after Gram-staining.

If the first set of tests (Ur, Cx, R and possibly T) is negative they should be repeated one week later before reassuring the patient that she does not have gonorrhoea. A third set of tests is a justified additional precaution in the case of contacts of gonorrhoea who have given two negative cultures. The use of non-selective medium should be considered for second and third tests in gonorrhoea contacts (page 186).

When disseminated gonococcal infection is suspected routine tests and several blood cultures should be taken before commencing therapy. Microscopic examination of smears from skin lesions by immunofluorescent techniques, or Gram's stain may aid diagnosis. Cultural examination for *N. gonorrhoeae* should also be attempted. Fluid obtained by aspiration of a joint effusion should be similarly investigated. For these investigations a non-selective medium should be employed in parallel with a selective medium.

Importance of culture site and number of diagnostic tests

Repeated testing of multiple sites is necessary since not all infections in women will be detected on first attendance (Figure 11.1). The proportion of infected women detected at their first attendance has been variously reported as 66 per cent (Catterall [1]), 90 per cent (Thin *et al* [2]), 91 per cent (Chipperfield and Catterall [3]), 97 per cent (Barlow *et al* [4]) and 98 per cent (Young *et al* [5]). Provided that the microbiological service consistently reaches a high standard only two sets of investigations need to be performed to diagnose or exclude gonorrhoea in women [4, 5]. It is prudent to carry out a third set of tests in the case of gonorrhoea contacts.

A single endocervical culture can detect up to 90 per cent of infections although this will vary depending on factors such as the culture medium used (Figure 11.1). A figure as low as 40 per cent has been

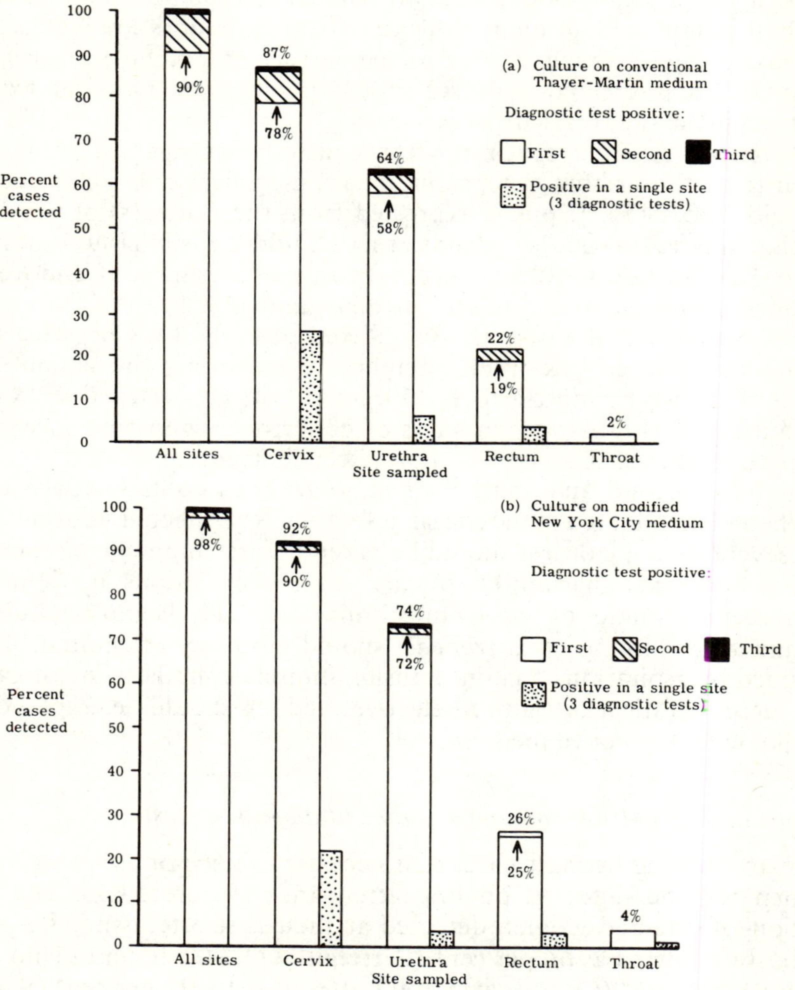

Figure 11.1 Importance of culture site and number of diagnostic tests in the detection of gonorrhoea in women. (Data from Young *et al* [5]).

reported [6]. In terms of a screening schedule more infections are detected by testing additional sites at the first attendance than by re-screening by endocervical culture [5].

A high vaginal swab is totally inadequate for diagnosing or excluding gonorrhoea and if this is the only specimen taken one in three infected women is likely to be missed [7]. The poor results with vaginal specimens are to be expected since this material detects only gonococci which may have contaminated the area, particularly from the cervix, a site of infection where gonococci are actively multiplying.

Rectal cultures are important in the female: approximately 25–50 per cent of patients have anorectal involvement and 5–10 per cent may be positive only in this site [8]. Since rectal infection is usually symptomless, and may be an important cause of treatment failure, rectal cultures are essential in screening for infection and assessing effectiveness of treatment.

Pharyngeal cultures are also important since in 2–5 per cent of infected females there is pharyngeal involvement [5]: such patients require higher penicillin dosage than those with uncomplicated infection (page 198).

Diagnostic methods

1. Microscopy

This is important as it enables a presumptive diagnosis to be made in the clinic so that appropriate treatment can be given immediately.

THE GRAM-STAINED SMEAR

A smear of secretion or discharge is prepared and Gram-stained by standard bacteriological technique [9] but 0.1 per cent neutral red is the preferred counterstain. The stained and dried slide is examined under a 2 mm oil immersion objective lens. A typical positive Gram-stained smear of urethral discharge from a male patient with gonorrhoea usually shows a large number of characteristic kidney-shaped Gram-negative diplococci (GNDC) lying within the polymorphonuclear leucocytes with few extracellular organisms (Plate 6). If pleomorphic extracellular Gram-negative diplococci and bacilli with rare extracellular GNDC with morphology typical of *N. gonorrhoeae* are seen the result of the smear examination is equivocal and not diagnostic. If no GNDC are seen the smear result is reported as negative.

Results in males

In patients whose Gram-stained smears of urethral discharge are unequivocally positive or negative this technique provides an immediate differential diagnosis between gonococcal and non-gonococcal urethritis in 85 per cent of patients [10]. When the Gram-stained smear shows typical intracellular GNDC the culture is positive in over 95 per cent of cases. Similarly when the smear is unequivocally negative the culture is also negative in over 95 per cent of cases.

A diagnosis should not be made on the basis of equivocal results. As a general rule, Gram-staining is less reliable in the diagnosis of long-standing or asymptomatic infections. Because of the complexity of the gut flora rectal smears are only of value if pus or mucopus can be collected by proctoscopy. Gram-staining has no place in the diagnosis of pharyngeal infection.

Results in females

Microscopic examination of Gram-stained smears of urethral and cervical secretions is less sensitive and only 55–65 per cent of infections are detected in patients who give positive culture results [3, 5].

In the asymptomatic infections commonly seen the number of gonococci are less than in the male. The bacterial flora of the female genito-urinary tract, also, is both qualitatively and quantitatively greater than in the male. Many of these organisms are small Gram-negative cocci and cocco-bacilli, sometimes appearing in pairs, and occasionally intracellularly, making interpretation of the smear difficult. Rectal smears are not examined microscopically as a routine in the female patient.

In a small percentage of both male and female patients typical positive smear results will be obtained but gonococci will not be isolated on culture. This could arise when patients have taken an antibiotic before coming to the clinic, or be due to the particular strain of gonococcus having a pronounced sensitivity to one of the antibiotics used in the selective medium (page 185).

IMMEDIATE IMMUNOFLUORESCENCE STAINING

Immunofluorescence staining* of secretion direct from the patient is referred to as 'immediate' immunofluorescence. This form of on-the-

*Immunofluorescence staining relies on the principle that antibody to *N. gonorrhoeae* when conjugated with the fluorescent dye, fluorescein isothiocyanate, produces a highly specific stain for gonococci.

spot diagnosis provides results similar to those obtained by Gram-staining but it is more time consuming and technically demanding and is not recommended for routine use [11]. 'Immediate' immunofluorescence may be useful in identifying gonococci from sites which normally give poor culture results, e.g., skin lesions or joint aspirates.

2. Culture

Immediate diagnosis must be supplemented as well as confirmed by culture if the maximum number of positive results is to be obtained. Cultures are obligatory in the diagnosis of rectal, oral, disseminated and asymptomatic infections in both sexes, and are also essential in order to determine antibiotic sensitivities and to assess treatment efficiency. In the married these cultures are advisable in case divorce proceedings arise.

CULTURE MEDIA

There are many variations of media in use but all contain a rich nutrient base supplemented with blood, either partially lysed by heat ('chocolate' agar) or completely lysed by the chemical saponin. Most laboratories now use some form of selective medium.

Thayer-Martin (TM) selective medium

In comparison with a non-selective medium the selective medium of Thayer and Martin [12], formulated to allow growth only of gonococci and meningococci, increases the proportion of positive isolations from all sites. It is particularly valuable in isolating the gonococcus from heavily contaminated sites such as the rectum of pharynx. The antibiotics (vancomycin, colistin and nystatin) present in the medium prevent other flora in the sample from overgrowing any gonococci present. *Proteus* spp. are resistant to these antibiotics and occasionally their spreading growth completely covers a culture plate: trimethoprim added to the medium can inhibit *Proteus* spp. [13]. Although gonococci are sensitive to the sequential action of sulphamethoxazole and trimethoprim when combined in co-trimoxazole they are much more resistant to trimethoprim alone than are most other bacteria.

Although widely used in many laboratories TM medium has been criticized because 3 per cent [11] to 10 per cent [14] of gonococcal strains are inhibited by vancomycin; growth is slow and colonies are small on TM medium. Superior isolation of gonococci and complete inhibition of *Proteus* was achieved with a modified Thayer-Martin medium [15] which differs from TM medium in containing double the concentration of agar (2.0 per cent), glucose (0.25 per cent) and trimethoprim (5.0μg per ml).

Modified New York City (MNYC) medium

This simply prepared modification of the original New York City (NYC) medium devised by Faur *et al* [16] to provide a luxuriant growth of pathogenic neisseriae after incubation for 24 hours contains lincomycin, colistin, amphotericin and trimethoprim: lincomycin is less inhibitory to gonococci than vancomycin while amphotericin is more inhibitory to yeasts than nystatin. MNYC medium is also enriched with yeast dialysate and glucose so that growth is more rapid and colonies larger. In comparison with TM medium, MNYC medium improves the overall isolation rate and enables a larger percentage of isolates to be identified at 24 hours [17, 18].

Combination of a selective and non-selective medium

Recently, a significant proportion of clinical isolates of *N. gonorrhoeae* have been shown to contain mutations which result in a markedly increased susceptibility to a variety of antibiotics [19]. Because of these findings, and the problem of vancomycin sensitivity referred to above, ideally the combination of a selective and a non-selective medium should be used. Such a procedure is too time-consuming and technically demanding and not cost-effective for routine use. However, a non-selective medium should be included in the subsequent examination of contacts of infected patients if their initial tests were negative. A non-selective medium can always be used in sampling sites, such as joint fluid or blood which are normally sterile.

INOCULATION AND TRANSPORT

Best results are achieved by *direct plating.* Culture plates, warmed beforehand to 37°C are inoculated directly with patient's secretions and immediately incubated at 36–37°C in a moist atmosphere containing 5–10 per cent carbon dioxide.

When direct plating and immediate incubation is impracticable several transport and culture systems are available. These consist of a selective medium, usually present in a small chamber containing CO_2 or a CO_2 generating system, e.g., Transgrow* [20]; Jembec† [21].

*Difco Laboratories, Detroit, Michigan, U.S.A.

†Gibco Bio-cult Ltd., 3 Washington Road, Sandyford Industrial Estate, Paisley, Scotland.

The media can be inoculated directly from the patient and transported to the laboratory, either before or after incubation. Unfortunately, such systems are very expensive and it is more usual to send a swab in a simpler transport medium, e.g., Stuart's or preferably Amies's modification of Stuart's medium [22]. Dry swabs should *not* be sent as the gonococcus is very susceptible to drying.

IDENTIFICATION

After 24 hours of incubation, plates are examined and any colonies suspected as being gonococcal are tested as follows:

The cytochrome oxidase test

This is a useful screening test since all neisseriae are oxidase positive, whereas many other organisms such as coliforms, staphylococci and lactobacilli are negative. The test is conveniently carried out by touching the colony with a cotton swab soaked in a one per cent (w/v) solution of tetramethyl-p-phenylenediamine dihydrochloride. A positive reaction is indicated by the colony turning purple within five to 15 seconds. This technique is so simple and quick that, when using a selective medium virtually all colonies can be tested, thus minimizing the risk of missing gonococci due to an atypical colonial appearance. Colonies with the same morphology must be examined by Gram-staining since other organisms, e.g., *Moraxella* spp. are also oxidase positive.

Gram-stained smear from colony

The various members of the genus *Neisseria* are indistinguishable by microscopy: all appear as Gram-negative cocci, usually in pairs but sometimes in clumps or singly. Although a presumptive diagnosis of gonorrhoea, from material taken from a genital site, can be made on the basis of oxidase-positive Gram-negative diplococci growing on selective medium, this is not entirely reliable since other neisseriae occasionally grow on selective medium and meningococci may also be found on genital sites. Further identification, therefore, is necessary to provide a precise diagnosis.

Delayed immunofluorescence

In contrast to the immediate immunofluorescence test described earlier, the immunofluorescence staining of a smear of suspect organisms obtained from the primary isolation plate is termed the delayed technique. Provided that the technique is well controlled delayed immunofluorescence provides a rapid and reliable confirmation of the gonococcus in the majority of instances [23]. When stained with the fluorescent antiserum gonococci from the culture give bright apple-green fluorescence when viewed with a suitable microscope. Other neisseriae do not normally fluoresce and carbohydrate utilization tests are necessary to identify these neisseriae.

Carbohydrate utilization

Gonococci produce acid from glucose only, whereas meningococci produce acid from glucose and maltose. *Neisseria lactamica,* an organism found mainly in the fauces, grows readily on selective media with a colonial morphology similar to the meningococcus. It utilizes lactose in addition to glucose and maltose.

1. Conventional tests for carbohydrate utilization

In conventional tests for carbohydrate utilization, a solid medium containing the appropriate carbohydrate and pH indicator is inoculated with the test organism. Although widely used, these tests are unsuitable since a positive reaction is dependent on adequate growth of the test organism which may take up to 72 hours.

2. Rapid carbohydrate utilization test (RCUT)

In the RCUT (page 192) pre-formed enzyme is measured by adding a suspension of the overnight growth of the suspect organism to a buffered, non-nutrient solution containing the sugar to be tested and a pH indicator [24]. Apart from rapidity, enabling identification of other neisseriae and confirmation of *N. gonorrhoeae* to be made within 24–72 hours of seeing the patient, the RCUT, in measuring pre-formed enzyme, has the advantage of being independent of growth. Results of the RCUT are usually available after one to three hours incubation at 37°C.

Negative cultures

Incubation is continued for 48 hours and the plate re-examined by the tests described before any culture can be reported as negative.

Coagglutination

This technique described by Danielsson and Kronvall [25] in which anti-gonococcal antibodies absorbed to the protein A component of staphylococci cause agglutination of gonococci may in future provide a valuable aid to identification.

ANTIBIOTIC SENSITIVITY TESTS

Once the gonococcus has been fully identified, antibiotic sensitivity tests are carried out. These are retrospective since the majority of patients will already have been treated on the basis of Gram-stained smear results. Nevertheless, they are important for epidemiological purposes and in planning rational therapy for use in the geographical area concerned.

Most laboratories carry out initial screening against several antibiotics using a disc technique. The minimum inhibitory concentration (MIC) of any antibiotic to which the strain shows decreased sensitivity can then be determined by testing the ability of the strain to grow on medium containing a series of antibiotic concentrations. The lowest concentration of antibiotic which inhibits growth is taken as the MIC. Occasionally IC50 values (50 per cent inhibitory concentration) are reported: the IC50 is usually about half of the MIC [26]. Penicillin is always included in the range of antibiotics tested which may also include streptomycin, kanamycin, tetracycline, a sulphonamide and occasionally spectinomycin; sulphamethoxazole and trimethoprim may also be tested separately and in combination.

The majority of reports define a less sensitive (or relatively resistant) strain as one requiring 0.125μg/ml or more of penicillin for inhibition [27]. In this country most strains (approximately 80 per cent) are fully sensitive to penicillin and of these many are sensitive to very low levels (less than 0.015μg/ml). Of the less sensitive strains (MIC $\geqslant$ 0.125μg/ml) only a few have an MIC as high as 1.0μg/ml: infections with such strains can still be cured with ampicillin and probenecid in the dosage recommended (Chapter 12).

SCREENING FOR PENICILLINASE

The recent discovery of strains of gonococci totally resistant to penicillin due to penicillinase (β-lactamase) production has increased the importance of laboratory antibiotic sensitivity tests [27].

All strains with decreased sensitivity to penicillin (MIC $\geqslant$ 0.125μg/ml) should be tested for penicillinase production. Several tests are available [28]: one test depends upon the release of a coloured product when a suspension of penicillinase-producing gonococci is incubated with a chromogenic cephalosporin. Other tests depend upon the bacterial breakdown of penicillin to penicilloic acid, which is detected by the ability of penicilloic acid to dissociate a starch-iodine complex, or by a pH indicator system. The latter method can be easily carried out alongside the rapid carbohydrate utilization test as part of the routine identification procedure enabling all strains to be tested. Using this method results for penicillinase production may be available before disc sensitivity tests [18].

3. Serology

The gonococcal complement fixation test (GCFT) is the only test which has been used to any extent in routine diagnosis. The test has fallen into disrepute over the years and it should not be relied upon either to detect or exclude uncomplicated infection.

There is a real need for a sensitive and specific serological test in order to screen large groups of individuals at risk as it is impracticable to carry out genital examination in such situations. Current research using radio-immunoassay (RIA) [29, 30]; and enzyme-linked immunosorbent assay (ELISA) techniques with highly purified antigens such as gonococcal pilus protein [31], or outer membrane protein [32] may eventually provide a suitable test. At present these tests are hampered by lack of both sensitivity and specificity; the positivity rate in infected women being respectively 85 per cent (Oates *et al* [30]), approximately 65 per cent (Low and Young [31]), and approximately 55 per cent (Glynn and Ison [32]), while the corresponding reactivity in controls was 13 per cent, 5 per cent and 11 per cent respectively.

Although not so convenient, the high sensitivity and specificity found in studies on the local humoral antibody response in gonorrhoea suggest that it may be feasible to develop a diagnostic test based on examining genital secretions. When secretions from the male urethra [33] and from the uterine cervix [34] were examined for antibody reactive with *N. gonorrhoeae,* using an indirect immunofluorescence technique, antibody was detected in the secretions of 98 per cent of 132 infected men and in 97 per cent of 75 infected women. All the men and 97 per cent of the women in whom antibody was detected had anti-gonococcal IgA: the majority of the IgA reacting with the gonococcus was of the secretory type. Successful treatment was associated with a rapid decline of specific IgA activity suggesting that the value of such a test would not be limited greatly by detecting adequately treated patients.

AN APPROACH TO THE DIAGNOSIS OF GONOCOCCAL INFECTION DEPENDING UPON LABORATORY RESOURCES AVAILABLE

Possible alternative approaches to the diagnosis of gonococcal infection depending upon clinical laboratory resources, as recommended by the World Health Organization [28], are shown in Table 11.1. Even where adequate facilities do exist, the most suitable culture and identification scheme for a particular locality will depend on factors such as the source of the specimens (hospital clinic, family planning clinic, general practitioner etc.) and the proximity of the microbiological laboratory. The culture and identification scheme outlined in Figure 11.2 has been found to work well in the Edinburgh Royal Infirmary where the clinic and laboratory are sited close to each other.

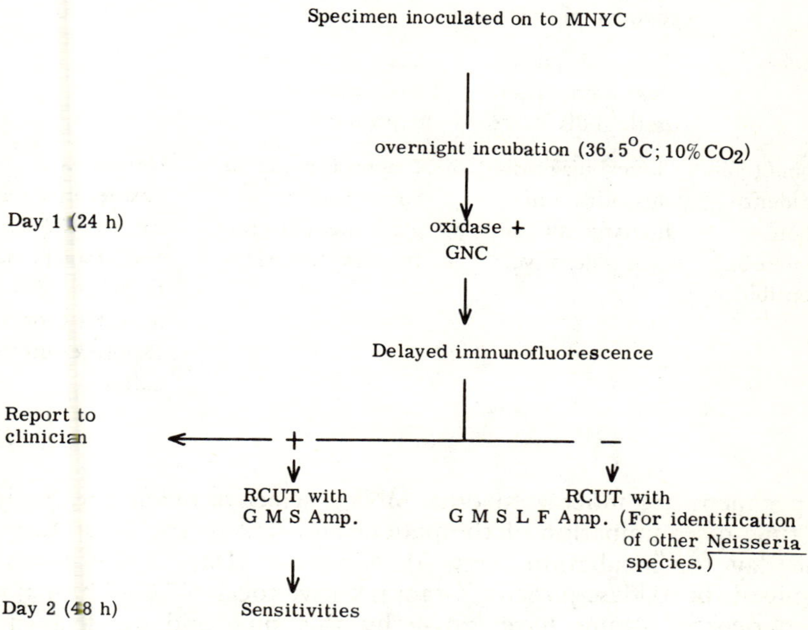

Figure 11.2 Culture and identification scheme used in the Royal Infirmary, Edinburgh (from Low and Young [28]). *Key:* + = positive; – = negative; GNC = Gram-negative cocci; RCUT = Rapid carbohydrate utilization test; G = glucose; M = maltose; S = sucrose; L = lactose; F = fructose; Amp = ampicillin.

Table 11.1 Possible alternative approaches to gonococcal infection depending upon clinical laboratory resources available

Clinical laboratory resources	*Men*		
	Symptoms of urethritis	*Symptoms of proctitis*	*Asymptomatic contact*
Absent	Clinical diagnosis (spontaneous purulent discharge suggests gonococcal urethritis; mucoid or clear expressible discharge suggests non-gonococcal urethritis).	Diagnosis made on basis of recent exposure.	
Minimal	Clinical diagnosis plus Gram stain of urethral discharge.	Diagnosis made on basis of recent exposure.	
Optimal (culture, identification, antimicrobial susceptibility)	Clinical diagnosis plus culture of discharge if Gram stain is negative.	Diagnosis made on basis of recent exposure; culture from anal canal.	Homosexual exposure: urethral culture, throat and/or anal culture from homosexual man. Heterosexual exposure: urethral culture.

Specimens are inoculated onto MNYC selective medium directly at the time of examination of the patient and sent to the laboratory the same day for incubation (Day 0). Next day (Day 1) the plates are examined for oxidase-positive, Gram-negative cocci (GNC). The majority of gonococcal strains have grown by this time and on delayed immunofluorescence testing they give an unequivocal bright apple-green fluorescence. The clinician can then receive a positive report 24 hours after seeing the patient.

Often there is sufficient growth on Day 1 to carry out the rapid carbohydrate utilization test (RCUT) on a suspension made directly from the primary isolation plate. An aliquot of the bacterial suspension

Clinical laboratory resources	Women: Symptoms of cervicitis, urethritis, or endometritis	Symptoms of salpingitis	Asymptomatic contact
Absent	Clinical diagnosis.	Clinical diagnosis based on lower abdominal pain, abnormal uterine bleeding, recent vaginal discharge, cervical motion tenderness.	
Minimal	Clinical diagnosis plus Gram stain of endocervical-urethral discharge.	Clinical diagnosis plus Gram stain of endo-cervical-urethral secretion.	Gram stain of endocervical-urethral secretion.
Optimal (culture, identification, antimicrobial susceptibility).	Clinical diagnosis plus culture from endocervix and anal canal and/or urethra.	Clinical diagnosis plus culture from endo-cervix and anal canal and/or urethra. *or* Culture of culdocentesis or laparoscopy specimen.	Culture from endocervix and anal canal and/or urethra.

(From *Neisseria gonorrhoeae* and gonococcal infections, *WHO Technical Report Series 616*, Geneva, 1978)

is added to a tube containing buffer, the appropriate sugar, and a pH indicator. Fluorescence-antibody-test-positive cultures are tested against glucose, maltose and sucrose whereas cultures giving weak or no fluorescence on the primary isolation plate, and all non-genital isolates, are also tested against fructose and lactose.

In the case of the gonococcus, acid production, detected by a change in the colour of the indicator from red to yellow, takes place in the glucose tube only; the meningococcus produces acid from glucose and maltose while *N. lactamica* produces acid from glucose, maltose and lactose.

If required, penicillinase production can be tested for by adding ampicillin in place of the sugar; penicillinase-producing strains break down ampicillin to penicilloic acid turning the indicator yellow. If there is insufficient growth on the primary isolation plate, a sub-culture is made on to MNYC medium and incubated overnight before carrying out the RCUT. All isolates of gonococci are sub-cultured on to sensitivity test agar containing 10 per cent (v/v) lysed blood and antibiotic discs added for determination of antibiotic sensitivities next day.

By combining a rapid carbohydrate utilization test with delayed immunofluorescence a reliable and rapid identification scheme is obtained. Gonococci antigenically distinct from those used to produce the anti-gonococcal conjugate are detected and there is a safeguard against cross-reaction with *N. meningitidis.*

The accurate differentiation of the gonococcus from the meningococcus and other neisseriae is important not only in medico-legal cases, but also in oral infections, in cases of disseminated gonococcal infection in which the gonococcus and the meningococcus may evoke identical clinical syndromes, and in the examination of conjunctival specimens. Rarely, *N. meningitidis* may also be implicated in urogenital infection [35] so that it is important for clinical and epidemiological purposes to distinguish these organisms carefully.

The scheme described [18], also provides rapid identification which is particularly important for detection and treatment of the 30 to 40 per cent of cases in female patients, missed by the first examination of Gram-stained smears. The patient is also more likely to attend when the time interval between the initial visit and subsequent appointment is short.

REFERENCES

1 Catterall, R D (1970) *British Journal of Venereal Diseases,* **46,** 122

2 Thin, R N, Williams, I A and Nicol, C S (1971) *British Journal of Venereal Diseases,* **47,** 27

3 Chipperfield, E J and Catterall, R D (1976) *British Journal of Venereal Diseases,* **52,** 36

4 Barlow, D, Nayyar, K, Phillips, I and Barrow, J (1976) *British Journal of Venereal Diseases,* **52,** 326

5 Young, H, Harris, A B, Urquhart, D and Robertson, D H H (1979) *Scottish Medical Journal,* **24,** 302

6 Norins, L C (1974) *Journal of Infectious Diseases,* **130,** 677

7 Bhattacharyya, M N, Jephcott, A E and Morton, R S (1973) *British Medical Journal,* **2,** 748

8 Bhattacharyya, M N and Jephcott, A E (1974) *British Journal of Venereal Diseases,* **50,** 109

9 Cruickshank, R, Duguid, J P, Marmion, B P and Swain, R H A (1975) in *Medical Microbiology,* Vol. 2, 12th edition. Churchill Livingstone, Edinburgh, page 34

10 Jacobs, N F and Kraus, S J (1975) *Annals of Internal Medicine,* **82,** 7

11 Reyn, A (1969) *Bulletin of the World Health Organization,* **40,** 245

12 Thayer, J D and Martin, J E (1966) *Public Health Report (Washington),* **81**, 559
13 Seth, A (1970) *British Journal of Venereal Diseases,* **46**, 201
14 Brorson, J E, Holmberg, I, Nygren, B and Seeberg, S (1973) *British Journal of Venereal Diseases,* **49**, 452
15 Martin, J E, Armstrong, J M and Smith, P B (1974) *Applied Microbiology,* **27**, 802
16 Faur, Y C, Weisburd, M H, Wilson, M E and May, P S (1973) *Health Laboratory Science,* **10**, 44
17 Young, H (1978) *British Journal of Venereal Diseases,* **54**, 36
18 Young, H (1978) *Journal of Clinical Microbiology,* **7**, 247
19 Eisenstein, B I and Sparling, P F (1978) *Nature,* **271**, 244
20 Martin, J E and Lester, A (1971) *Health Services and Mental Health Administration Health Report.* U S Department of Health Education and Welfare, Rockville, Maryland, **86**, 30
21 Holston, J R, Hosty, T S and Martin, J E (1974) *American Journal of Clinical Pathology,* **62**, 558
22 Amies, C R (1967) *Canadian Journal of Public Health,* **58**, 269
23 Lind, I (1975) *Annals of the New York Academy of Sciences,* **254**, 400
24 Young, H, Paterson, I C and McDonald, D R (1976) *British Journal of Venereal Diseases,* **52**, 172
25 Danielsson, D and Kronvall, G (1974) *Applied Microbiology,* **27**, 368
26 Reyn, A, Bentzon, M W and Ericsson, H (1963) *Acta Pathologica et Microbiologica Scandinavica,* **57**, 235
27 Wilkinson, A E (1977) *Journal of Antimicrobial Chemotherapy,* **3**, 197
28 World Health Organization (1978) *Neisseria gonorrhoeae* and gonococcal infections. *Technical Report Series* 616, Geneva
29 Buchanan, T M, Swanson, J, Holmes, K K, Kraus, S J and Gotschlich, E C (1973) *Journal of Clinical Investigation,* **52**, 2896
30 Oates, S A, Falkler, W A, Joseph, J M and Warfel, L E (1977) *Journal of Clinical Microbiology,* **5**, 26
31 Low, A C and Young, H (1979) *Medical Laboratory Sciences,* **36**, 275
32 Glynn, A A and Ison, C (1978) *British Journal of Venereal Diseases,* **54**, 97
33 McMillan, A, McNeillage, G and Young, H (1979) *Journal of Infectious Diseases,* **140**, 89
34 McMillan, A, McNeillage, G, Young, H and Bain, S S R (1979) *British Journal of Venereal Diseases,* **55**, 265
35 Beck, A, Fluker, J L and Platt, D J (1974) *British Journal of Venereal Diseases,* **50**, 367

CHAPTER 12

Treatment of Gonorrhoea

Since its introduction into medical practice in 1944, penicillin has been widely and successfully used in the treatment of gonorrhoea. More recently, semi-synthetic penicillins and other antimicrobial agents have been added to the therapeutic armamentarium. Although the percentage of strains demonstrating reduced sensitivity to penicillin has been rising slowly since the 1960's, the problem of resistance to penicillin has become more ominous with the recent discovery of β-lactamase-producing strains.

Principles of treatment

The aim of treatment is to eradicate the organism from the body as quickly as possible. Ideally the treatment used should be based on the pattern of sensitivity to antibiotic and chemotherapeutic agents observed amongst the strains of the organism in the population served. Regimens of treatment should be constantly reviewed, account being taken of the results of continuous monitoring of isolates for the emergence of drug resistance.

A course of almost any antimicrobial drug to which the organism is sensitive will cure the majority of patients with gonorrhoea. Patient compliance, however, is often unsatisfactory and tablets may be inadvisably shared with a consort. For example, within 24 to 48 hours of commencing oral treatment with ampicillin 250mg four-hourly, symptoms of urethritis in a man with urethral gonorrhoea may have almost completely resolved, misleading the patient into assuming that his infection has been cured. Failure to complete courses of antibiotic drugs may result in the emergence of strains of the organism with increased resistance.

For these reasons a single large dose of antibiotic, given orally or parenterally, is used in the treatment of uncomplicated infection and is given under supervision in the clinic. In most cases blood and tissue concentrations of drug are maintained at a high level and for a length of time sufficient to eradicate the organism. The oral administration of antibiotics is preferred to painful intramuscular injections.

Single-dose therapy has not proved satisfactory in the management of oropharyngeal, male anorectal or complicated infections.

Table 12 1 Drug regimens for single-dose treatment of uncomplicated gonorrhoea

Antimicrobial agent (and reference)		*Dosage*	*Cure rate %*	*Comments*
Penicillins				
Ampicillin + probenecid	(*a*)	2.0g, 1.0g } orally	98	Treatment of choice in areas where β-lactamase-producing strains are not prevalent
Talampicillin + probenecid	(*b*)	1.5g, 2.0g } orally	97	ditto
Amoxycillin + probenecid	(*c*)	3.0g, 1.0g } orally	94	ditto
Procaine penicillin + probenecid	(*d*)	2.4 million units intramuscularly 2.0g	97	No advantage over oral treatment since it may not consistently abort incubating syphilis
Tetracyclines				
Minocycline hydrochloride	(*e*)	300mg orally	95	Vertigo an uncommon side effect. Avoid in pregnancy. Cure rates in some localities much less (50 to 75 per cent)
Doxycycline hydrochloride	(*f*)	300mg orally	93	Nausea common
Macrolides				
Erythromycin stearate	(*g*)	2.5g orally	91	Marked regional variation in drug sensitivity and effectiveness
Cephalosporins				
Cefuroxime + probenecid	(*h*)	1.5g intramuscularly 1.0g orally	95	Not affected by β-lactamase. Reserve for infection with β-lactamase-producing organisms

continued overleaf

Table 12.1 *contd.*

Antimicrobial agent (and reference)	*Dosage*	*Cure rate %*	*Comments*
Miscellaneous			
Spectinomycin hydrochloride (*i*)	2g in male, 4g in female * (* intramuscularly)	97	Reserve for infections refractory to penicillin. Toxicity uncertain. Resembles aminoglycosides structurally

References:

(*a*) Bro-Jørgensen and Jensen [11]
(*b*) Al-Egaily *et al* [12]
(*c*) Thin *et al* [13]
(*d*) Taylor and Seth [14]
(*e*) Masterton and Schofield [1]
(*f*) Schofield and Masterton [15]
(*g*) Martini *et al* [16]
(*h*) Price *et al* [17]
(*i*) Finger [18]

Schedules

UNCOMPLICATED INFECTIONS IN MEN AND WOMEN

Table 12.1 shows various regimens of single-dose treatment currently used in the treatment of uncomplicated gonorrhoea and recommendations as to their uses and limitations. It must be understood that the sensitivity of the infecting organisms may vary geographically and that cure rates may not approach those cited. For example, although Masterton and Schofield [1] working in Glasgow, found that a single oral dose of 300mg of minocycline hydrochloride cured 95 per cent of infected patients, Duncan *et al* [2] in the USA reported only a 75 per cent cure rate and in Australia a 50 per cent rate has been recorded [3].

It is suggested that in patients who are not known to have penicillin hypersensitivity, ampicillin and probenecid provides an excellent first choice in the management of uncomplicated gonorrhoea. The other treatment schedules may then be reserved for patients with penicillin hypersensitivity and for treatment failures.

OROPHARYNGEAL AND RECTAL GONORRHOEA

Single-dose treatment is generally considered to be less effective in the treatment of oropharyngeal infection in both sexes and rectal infection in the male, than in uncomplicated genital gonorrhoea [4, 5].

Infection in these sites usually can be eliminated by a course of antibiotics given by mouth; either ampicillin (or talampicillin) 250mg four times daily for 5 to 7 days [6] or co-trimoxazole 2 tablets twice daily for 5 to 7 days [7].

POST-GONOCOCCAL URETHRITIS (PGU) IN THE MALE

The management of this complication is dealt with in the chapter on non-gonococcal urethritis. In an attempt to reduce the incidence of post-gonococcal urethritis, a five to seven-day course of oxytetracycline may be given starting on the day after giving treatment for gonorrhoea, to avoid the mutually antagonistic effects of penicillin and tetracycline.

COMPLICATED GONORRHOEA

1. Epididymitis

If severe, the patient should be admitted to hospital and kept in bed. A scrotal support should be worn to relieve pain. Antimicrobial therapy consists of either benzyl penicillin, one million units six-hourly intramuscularly, co-trimoxazole B.P. 2 tablets or doxycycline 100mg eight-hourly until the condition has resolved. It may be necessary later to aspirate a secondary hydrocele.

2. Bartholinitis and abscess

The patient may need admission to hospital if the inflammation is severe and she should be treated with penicillin in the dosage given for epididymitis. In less severe cases there is usually a response to a course of oral antibiotics. If an abscess persists, this is best treated by aspiration during antimicrobial therapy or by marsupialization if this fails.

3. Pelvic inflammatory disease including salpingitis

(*See* Chapter 16).

4. Gonococcal arthritis and skin lesions

The patient should be admitted to hospital, the affected joint(s) rested in a position of function and treatment with benzyl penicillin (one million units six-hourly intramuscularly) instituted. Usually within 48 hours the condition of the patient improves and oral treatment may be substituted and continued for 10–14 days. In such cases the gonococci have been found to be very sensitive to penicillin (page 175). In the case of those allergic to penicillin, co-trimoxazole may be suitable in a dose of two tablets twice daily by mouth. When vomiting is troublesome co-trimoxazole may be given, diluted as an infusion, intravenously. Two 5ml vials of co-trimoxazole (B.N.F; Septrin for infusion), each containing 80mg trimethoprim B.P. and 400mg sulphamethoxazole B.P. are diluted with 250ml infusion solution (e.g. sodium chloride injection B.P. 0.9%) and given intravenously over a period of approximately one and a half hours [8].

INFECTION WITH β-LACTAMASE PRODUCING *N. GONORRHOEAE*

The most appropriate treatment has yet to be determined, but the following have been suggested:

1. Spectinomycin (4g intramuscularly in females; 2g intramuscularly in males) followed next day by co-trimoxazole (two tablets twice daily for five to seven days).

2. Cefuroxime, a new cephalosporin, should be given intramuscularly in a dose of 1.5g with probenecid 1g orally.

TREATMENT OF PREGNANT WOMEN WITH GONORRHOEA

Care is needed in giving any drug in pregnancy. Penicillin is considered generally safe, and benzyl penicillin given intramuscularly in a dose of one million units six-hourly for 12 doses is effective. Erythromycin is also considered to be safe although cure rates may be low, say 70 per cent [9] and absorption uncertain (page 110); a dose of 500mg six-hourly orally for seven days is an alternative in patients hypersensitive to penicillin. Cefuroxime, a new cephalosporin, may be given by intramuscular injection in a dose of 1.5g and repeated in 12 hours.

CONJUNCTIVITIS OF THE NEWBORN (OPHTHALMIA NEONATORUM)

Combined local and parenteral therapy is necessary.

Local: Frequent, repeated instillations of sterile normal saline into affected eye. Topical antibiotic treatment may produce sensitization reactions.

Parenteral: Benzyl penicillin should be given in a dosage of 50,000 units per kg body weight per day in two or three divided doses by intramuscular injection until cure is obtained, generally within a week [10].

Note: Both parents must be examined and treated.

Tests of cure

After treatment every patient should be carefully examined to ensure that the infection has been cured.

FOLLOW-UP TESTS IN THE MALE

In any given area it is first essential to assess the cure rate of the treatment schedule adopted as a routine. In general these assessments are made by the rapid disappearance of signs and/or symptoms and their continued absence over 14 days. Persistence of urethral signs and/or symptoms necessitate urethral cultures taken preferably after the urine has been retained for three hours, or the immediate culture of exudate from the first urine voided. Such trials are possible only in some centres.

When confidence in a schedule has been obtained the following routines are satisfactory: any urethral discharge should be examined and the urine inspected for the presence of pus and/or 'threads' on the seventh day. These tests should be repeated three weeks later and serological tests for syphilis should be carried out then and again two months later.

To determine the efficacy of treatment of rectal and pharyngeal gonorrhoea, cultures should be taken from the affected sites until three consecutive cultures, taken at weekly intervals, are negative.

FOLLOW-UP TESTS IN THE FEMALE

Two consecutive series of cultures from the urethra, cervix and rectum should be taken at weekly intervals before assuring cure. If positive on first attendance the culture from the fauces should be taken twice, one and two weeks after treatment.

Note: It is often difficult to distinguish between treatment failure and re-infection. By convention, the finding of positive tests within two weeks of treatment is regarded as a failure of treatment if the patient does not admit to further sexual intercourse.

TREATMENT WHEN DIAGNOSIS OF GONORRHOEA IS SUSPECTED ON EPIDEMIOLOGICAL GROUNDS

Accurate diagnosis and treatment is the approach of choice when adequate facilities exist. Treatment before diagnosis is not desirable as a routine even in contacts, except when there are special problems. For example a female contact of a known case of gonorrhoea may be treated if she is unlikely to re-attend. In such a case a form of treatment known to produce high cure rates in that locality (say of 95 per cent) may be justified. In the case of contacts of patients with an infection due to a β-lactamase-producing strain of gonococcus then spectinomycin/co-trimoxazole treatment is justified. Follow-up is important also.

REFERENCES

1 Masterton, G and Schofield, C B S (1976) *British Journal of Venereal Diseases,* **52,** 43

2 Duncan, W C, Glicksman, J M, Knox, J M and Holder, W R (1971) *British Journal of Venereal Diseases,* 47, 364

3 Baytch, H (1974) *Medical Journal of Australia,* **1,** 831

4 Scott, J and Stone, A H (1966) *British Journal of Venereal Diseases,* **42,** 103

5 Ödegaard, K and Gundersen, T (1973) *British Journal of Venereal Diseases,* **49,** 350

6 John, J and Jefferiss, F J G (1973) *British Journal of Venereal Diseases,* **49,** 362

7 Waugh, M A (1970) *British Journal of Venereal Diseases,* **47,** 34

8 Data Sheet Compendium (1978) *Septrin (Co-trimoxazole) for infusion.* Pharmind Publications, London, page 1068

9 Brown, S (1978) quoted in *Neisseria gonorrhoeae and gonococcal infections, Technical Report Series 616.* World Health Organization, Geneva

10 McCracken, G H and Eichenwald, H F (1974) *Journal of Pediatrics,* **85,** 297

11 Bro-Jørgenson, A and Jensen, T (1971) *British Medical Journal,* **2,** 660

12 Al Egaily, S, Dunlop, E M C, Rodin, P and Seth, A D (1978) *British Journal of Venereal Diseases,* **54,** 243

13 Thin, R N, Symonds, M A E, Shaw, E J, Wong, J, Hopper, P K and Slocombe, B (1977) *British Journal of Venereal Diseases,* **53,** 118

14 Taylor, P K and Seth, A D (1975) *British Journal of Venereal Diseases,* **51,** 183

15 Schofield, C B S and Masterton, G (1974) *British Journal of Venereal Diseases,* **50,** 303

16 Martini, J, Halabi, J and Borgono, J M (1968) *Review of Medicine,* Chile, **96,** 525

17 Price, J D, Fluker, J L and Giles, A J H (1977) *British Journal of Venereal Diseases,* **42,** 103

18 Finger, A H (1975) *British Journal of Venereal Diseases,* **51,** 38

CHAPTER 13

Non-gonococcal Urethritis and Related Infections

Non-gonococcal urethritis (NGU), synonym, non-specific urethritis (NSU), is a convenient term to describe the very common condition seen in men and presenting clinically as a purulent or mucopurulent urethral discharge, associated often with the symptom of dysuria and occurring a few days to a few weeks after intercourse. The discharge of a patient with NGU contains pus cells but *Neisseria gonorrhoeae* cannot be detected by microscopy or culture (Chapter 11). The term non-specific genital infection (NSGI) has been introduced to include with non-specific urethritis in the male the clinically less clearly defined infection in the female, who may have neither symptom nor easily detected sign.

Non-gonococcal urethritis is the commonest sexually-transmitted disease in men and in the United Kingdom is more than twice as common as gonorrhoea. In 1973 there were 4508 cases recorded in Scotland and 70,440 in England and Wales. NGU varies widely in severity from the clinical point of view and asymptomatic infections are common. Other genital or ocular infections, likely to share the same aetiology, include epididymitis and chronic abacterial prostatitis in the male, and cervicitis and other pelvic inflammatory disease in the female. In some forms of non-gonococcal ophthalmia neonatorum (conjunctivitis of the newborn) the agent is transmitted from the genital tract of the mother during parturition. A similar inclusion conjunctivitis is seen also in all age groups and in male homosexuals a non-gonococcal proctitis may occur.

Aetiology

There is experimental evidence that at least two organisms, *Chlamydia trachomatis* and *Ureaplasma urealyticum* have a role in the aetiology of NGU although the extent of their involvement is not yet clear.

CHLAMYDIA

Organisms belonging to the genus *Chlamydia* are the cause of a variety of ocular, genital and systemic diseases in man. Two species are recognized, *Chlamydia trachomatis* and *Chlamydia psittaci:* both are obligate intracellular parasites forming inclusion bodies within the infected cell. The presence of glycogen (diagnostic of subgroup A chlamydia) in the inclusion of *C. trachomatis* distinguishes it from *C. psittaci* (subgroup B). The name *C. trachomatis* is at present applied to all subgroup A *Chlamydia* including TRIC (trachoma-inclusion conjunctivitis) agents, LGV (lymphogranuloma venereum) agents, and also certain *Chlamydia* of animal origin. Although both organisms contain a common group antigen they also possess a type-specific antigen and are further differentiated by the sensitivity of *C. trachomatis* to sulphadiazine and D-cycloserine.

The chlamydiae, because of their obligate intracellular growth, were formerly considered to be viruses, but many of their fundamental properties are akin to those of bacteria. The chlamydial particles contain both deoxyribonucleic acid (DNA) and ribonucleic acid (RNA), multiply by binary fission, possess enzymes, have a bacteria-like cell wall and are sensitive to certain antibiotics. As obligate intracellular parasites chlamydiae can only be isolated and grown in suitable host cells. Early workers used the yolk sac of the embryonated chicken egg, but a suitable tissue culture is a more convenient and sensitive method.

All chlamydiae undergo a unique developmental cycle in the cytoplasm of eukaryotic cells. The elementary body, the infectious form of the chlamydial agent, is a metabolically inert, rigid-walled particle about 0.3μm in diameter. Once within the cell, it becomes reorganized into a larger thin-walled form about 0.5 to 10μm in diameter, the reticulate or initial body, which is non-infectious but metabolically active. The reticulate body multiplies by fisson to form a microcolony of pleomorphic chlamydial forms which lie within a cytoplasmic vacuole, recognized by light microscopy as a basophilic cytoplasmic inclusion. Division is followed by reorganization of reticulate bodies into smaller intermediate forms and then into elementary bodies. Finally rupture of the mature inclusion releases a fresh generation of infectious chlamydial agents into the extracellular environment [1].

Chlamydia trachomatis

Two subgroups of *C. trachomatis* exist, one causing lymphogranuloma venereum (LGV) and the other capable of causing genital or ocular disease such as a non-gonococcal urethritis, trachoma and inclusion conjunctivitis. Immunologically these organisms can be divided into a number of serotypes by means of a micro-immunofluorescence test. There are 3 serotypes in LGV (Chapter 27), 4 serotypes (A, Ba, B and C) commonly associated with tropical trachoma and 7 (D, E, F, G, H, I and K) associated with sexually transmitted oculogenital and genital infection of western countries [2]. The sexually transmitted serotypes of *C. trachomatis* can cause a non-gonococcal urethritis in man, a cervicitis and salpingitis in women, a conjunctivitis in the new-born and a proctitis in the homosexual male.

In trachoma, the organisms are spread by eye-to-eye transmission particularly in unhygienic tropical conditions, affecting about 500 million people and causing blindness in some 2 million. *Chlamydia* require rapid transmission in moist conditions and hyperendemic trachoma occurs in conditions of 'ocular promiscuity'* – that is to say in conditions that favour the frequent, unrestricted and indiscriminate mixing of ocular contacts or of ocular discharges. The oculogenital infections of western countries tend to be seen where there is frequent mixing of genital contacts or discharges with occasional transfer to the eye [3].

Organisms causing trachoma and inclusion conjunctivitis have sometimes been referred to as TRIC agents: this term is best avoided, particularly in dealing with genital infections since confusion may arise with *Trichomonas vaginalis.*

Chlamydia psittaci causes a disease (psittacosis) in parrots and certain other birds. Psittacosis in man may arise when infected dust or droplets are inhaled; illness ranges from an 'influenza-like' syndrome with general malaise, fever, anorexia, rigors, sore throat and headache and photophobia, to a severe illness with delirium and a pneumonia with numerous well demarcated areas of consolidation.

UREAPLASMA

Ureaplasma urealyticum

Ureaplasma is the name proposed for a new genus of organism which is found in association with urethritis and which is distinguished from all other known mycoplasmas, whether found in the urethra or not, by its capacity to produce urease and hydrolyse urea: the name *Ureaplasma urealyticum* has been given to the single human species so far identified in this new genus in which there are at least eight serotypes [4]. These organisms were termed T-mycoplasmas since they formed tiny colonies on the media used by early investigators.

Mycoplasmas are common inhabitants of the oropharyngeal and

*The word promiscuous derives from *pro* – for, or in favour of; *miscere* – to mix: hence promiscuous conditions are conditions that favour mixing.

genital mucous membranes. They are variable in size (0.125 to 0.3μm in diameter), differ from other bacteria in that they lack a rigid cell wall, and are able to pass through bacteria-stopping filters. Although they are Gram-negative they stain poorly with the usual aniline dyes and are best observed in Giemsa-stained smears. Since mycoplasmas lack a rigid cell wall, they are not inhibited by antibiotics such as penicillin which act upon this component of the bacterial cell.

Mycoplasmas and *U. urealyticum* are alike in the physical properties just described and can grow on cell-free medium. All the human genital mycoplasmas require cholesterol or a related sterol for growth. The basic medium employed for the genital mycoplasmas, is a peptone-enriched beef-heart infusion broth containing also horse serum and yeast extract. Mycoplasmas grow best when the pH of the medium is about 7.5 but *U. urealyticum* prefers a pH nearer 6.0. Solid media are best incubated in a carbon-dioxide enriched atmosphere.

Clinical and microbiological studies on the aetiology of NGU

Results of studies in NGU in men have given overall isolation rates for *C. trachomatis,* varying from 23 to 57 per cent [5] while an isolation rate approaching 70 per cent was found in patients with a frank urethral discharge [6]. The isolation rate in patients with gonococcal urethritis is approximately 10 to 30 per cent [5] while in control groups it is usually less than 5 per cent. Significantly more pairs of sexual partners give the same chlamydial culture result than give different results and the chlamydial isolation rate is higher among men admitting a casual sexual contact than in men claiming only regular partners [6]. These findings provide evidence for sexual transmission of *C. trachomatis* and for its aetiological role in NGU.

Indirect evidence for the association of *C. trachomatis* with NGU is provided by serological studies. The micro-immunofluorescence test, used to demonstrate the existence of serotypes (three of LGV, four of tropical trachoma, and seven associated with sexually transmitted oculogenital and genital infections), can be used also to detect serum antibody [7]. With this technique the positivity rates in patients with NGU, gonococcal urethritis, and no urethritis were 55 per cent, 79 per cent and 38 per cent respectively; the corresponding isolation rates for *C. trachomatis* were 42 per cent, 19 per cent and 7 per cent respectively. The serotype of the chlamydial isolate correlated with the specificity of the serum antibody.

An increase in serum antibody gave good correlation with the isolation of *C. trachomatis.* When paired sera were examined, conversion from negative to positive was found in 54 per cent and a fourfold rise in titre in 30 per cent of patients from whom *C. trachomatis* was isolated, whereas only 4 per cent of patients with negative culture demonstrated sero-conversion or a fourfold rise in titre [7]. An IgM response is seen in patients with primary chlamydial infection [8].

Among patients, whose cultures failed to yield *C. trachomatis*, antibody prevalence correlated with the number of past sex partners and with previous NGU: this could, in part, account for the high prevalence of antibody in patients with gonococcal urethritis. There is also an association between *C. trachomatis* and the development of post-gonococcal urethritis as discussed on page 209.

Although these cultural and serological studies suggest that *C. trachomatis* is a significant cause of NGU its exact pathological role is difficult to establish unequivocally: it could be argued that chlamydiae normally lead a commensal existence in the genital tract but may, on occasions, act as opportunistic pathogens. Alternatively, their numbers may simply increase when another infection develops making their detection easier.

The same arguments can be applied to the role of *Ureaplasma urealyticum* in NGU. Studies on the isolation of *U. urealyticum* have given isolation rates ranging from approximately 20 to 80 per cent in patients with NGU, and approximately 10 to 50 per cent in control groups [9]. Antibody against *U. urealyticum* has not been shown to develop with any regularity in NGU [9].

The failure to provide unequivocal conclusions about the role of *C. trachomatis* and *U. urealyticum* in the aetiology of NGU is due, in part, to the impossibility of finding control groups whose sexual behaviour can be matched with that of the group of patients with urethritis being tested. Variations, also, in the efficiency of sampling and isolation techniques and the tendency of organisms to become latent or hidden are likely to be important considerations. For these reasons attempts have been made in recent times to come to a firmer conclusion about the role of these organisms by studying the effect of antibiotics in alleviating the clinical manifestations of the disease, and to determine whether there is a relationship between improvement and the disappearance of organisms from the urogenital tract. In one clinical trial there was statistically significant evidence that sulphonamides, with some activity against *C. trachomatis* but not *U. urealyticum,* were effective in treating chlamydia-positive cases of urethritis but ineffective in treating ureaplasma-positive cases whereas spectinomycin, active against *U. urealyticum* but relatively inactive against *C. trachomatis,* was successful in ureaplasma-positive cases but not in chlamydia-positive cases. These results [10] support the theory that *C. trachomatis* was an important cause of NGU and also suggest that *U. urealyticum* was implicated.

Experimental inoculation of humans with organisms is not to be undertaken lightly; even in NGU the problem of repeated relapses, Reiter's disease and other syndromes with less clear-cut effects associated with urethritis or conjunctivitis make experimental inoculation a matter for serious consideration from an ethical point of view. Notwithstanding such issues, two medical men, Dr Taylor Robinson and Dr Csonka inoculated themselves with two strains of *U. urealyticum.* In this experiment special precautions were taken to be sure that the inoculum contained *U. urealyticum* only, and that these were not in numbers of organisms in excess of what might be introduced during sexual intercourse.

In one subject, the ureaplasma multiplied in the urethra and dysuria developed soon. Pus cells were detected in the urine and an immunological reaction of short duration was detected serologically. Tetracycline given six days after inoculation brought about rapid clearance of organisms from the urine and a more gradual disappearance of symptoms and signs. In the second subject another ureaplasma 'strain' was inoculated and similar effects followed although there was evidence that prostatic involvement occurred. Although treatment with tetracycline a month after inoculation eliminated the organisms, urinary threads of epithelial cells and polymorphonuclear leucocytes persisted for at least six months [11].

As a result of their experiment it can be concluded that *U. urealyticum* is able to cause urethritis but whether it is responsible for a major or insignificant part of the naturally occurring NGU remains unanswered. Other mycoplasmas, *Mycoplasma fermentans* and *M. hominis* are not generally regarded as significant in the aetiology of NGU.

Urethritis may be caused by other organisms but these are very uncommon (less than 1 per cent) in relation to the mass of NGU. Herpes simplex virus, *Candida albicans* and *Trichomonas vaginalis* have been considered as causes. Cystitis due to *Mycobacterium tuberculosis* is now a very rare cause of urethritis in this country, but in urinary tract infections due to other bacteria a urethrocystitis is not uncommon. Both trauma and foreign bodies are occasional factors and hypersensitivity may be involved.

In summary, cultural, serological and therapeutic studies demonstrate that *C. trachomatis* and *U. urealyticum* are associated with a major proportion of cases of NGU although unequivocal evidence for their pathological role in this condition is not yet available. These studies must be evaluated against a background of improving methodology and it may be that in future, quantitative studies will help to provide unequivocal results. The aetiology of a proportion of cases of NGU is still far from clear as no organisms can be isolated.

Post-gonococcal urethritis (PGU)

After treatment for gonorrhoea with the penicillins or aminoglycosides up to about 50 per cent of men can be expected to develop post-gonococcal urethritis (PGU) [12], their urethral discharge recurs and an excess of polymorphonuclear leucocytes is seen on microscopy but *N. gonorrhoeae* cannot be found on microscopy or on culture.

The sexually transmissible serotypes of *C. trachomatis* have been implicated in the aetiology of PGU. *C. trachomatis* has also been isolated from urethral material in approximately 50 per cent of men who developed urethritis following treatment for gonorrhoea; the organism could not be demonstrated in the control group of patients who did not develop PGU [12]. Others [13] have noted that men with gonococcal urethritis who also have a chlamydial infection are more liable to develop PGU. It may be that *N. gonorrhoeae* and *C. trachomatis* are sexually transmitted at the same time. *U. urealyticum* or other mycoplasmas have not been shown to have a role in the aetiology of PGU [7, 12].

It has been suggested that defective cell wall forms of gonococci (L-forms) may be a cause of PGU, but the presence of such L-forms in clinical specimens has still to be proved [14]. L-forms of gonococci can be produced *in vitro* by treatment of cultures with penicillin and it has been suggested that sub-lethal levels of penicillin could cause this change *in vivo* [15]. L-forms are able to multiply in osmotically favourable surroundings and, because of their defective cell wall, are resistant to antibiotics which affect cell wall synthesis.

PATHOLOGY OF CHLAMYDIAL INFECTION

In conjunctivitis due to chlamydiae the formation of a follicle commonly occurs, but this is a tissue reaction to irritation and is not specific. In trachoma, cellular inclusions were first described by Halberstaedter and Prowazek in 1907 [16]. In histological sections of cervical mucosa similar inclusions appear as cytoplasmic vacuoles when examined by light microscopy and are most easily seen in columnar endocervical cells. The vacuoles may occupy nearly the entire volume of the cell and, on electron microscopy, are seen to contain numerous small spherical bodies about 1μm in diameter; these represent infectious elementary bodies, non-infectious reticulate bodies and transitional stages [17]. The pathology of the urethra and conjunctiva is not easy to study as biopsy is not justified. Changes are not necessarily attributable wholly to chlamydiae as other organisms commonly colonize the cervix. Neutrophil polymorphonuclear leucocytes are dominant in the early stages of eye infections and are similarly found in urethritis and cervicitis.

Clinical features of non-gonococcal urethritis

In the male NGU usually presents clinically as a mucopurulent urethral discharge associated with dysuria. The dysuria tends to be variable in severity with the discomfort or pain localized to the shaft of the penis or to the region of the meatus. The onset may occur within a few days to a month or more after the infecting intercourse. The urethral discharge may be small in quantity and mucoid, or it may be copious and frankly purulent. Sometimes the discharge may dry at the urethral meatus to form a greyish crust and the discharge may appear to be more copious in the morning than at other times. Occasionally dysuria is very severe and the urethral discharge blood-stained. When there is a urethrocystitis, frank haematuria may occur with blood dispersed throughout the urinary stream. In patients, particularly in those whose symptoms or signs are mild, it is important to examine the urethra for discharge before the patient has passed urine in the morning.

In acute haemorrhagic cystitis the patient may complain of malaise and of passing blood after urinating, when dysuria may occur at the end of micturition (terminal dysuria). There may be frequency, urgency and strangury.

The term non-specific genital infection (NSGI) in the male includes the commonest clinical presentation of non-gonococcal urethritis (NGU) as well as less common effects such as cystitis, epididymitis and prostatitis. Non-gonococcal proctitis is seen in male homosexuals; *C. trachomatis* may be isolated in about 10 per cent of male homosexuals.

Associated disease, complications of a generalized nature, or distant from the original genital site are uncommon (less than 1 per cent) and include acute follicular conjunctivitis, Reiter's disease, anterior uveitis and possibly ankylosing spondylitis. It has been suggested also that subfertility may be related to ureaplasma infection, the organisms attaching themselves to the spermatozoon and inhibiting fertilization [18].

Non-specific genital infection (NSGI) in women

Non-specific genital infection (NSGI) is a term that extends to the theoretically-expected involvement of the female, although it is a less precise clinical entity than NGU in the male. The diagnosis may be unsatisfactorily based on the existence of a non-gonococcal urethritis in the partner, symptoms of vaginal discharge or dysuria and the evidence of inflammation of the cervix, vagina, urethra or greater vestibular gland (bartholinitis). In chlamydial infection the cervix may have a follicular or 'cobblestone' appearance. Pelvic inflammatory disease, involving the fallopian tubes, can be found in some patients considered to have NSGI; infertility may result from tubal involvement. Non-specific vaginitis is not a clear cut entity and is discussed more fully in Chapter 17.

AETIOLOGY

It is likely that *C. trachomatis* is responsible for a proportion of cases of NSGI in women. *C. trachomatis* can be isolated from the cervix in 20 to 40 per cent of women who have gonorrhoea or who have been contacts of men with NGU [19, 20]. Clinical findings suggest that oedema, congestion and mucopurulent discharge are associated with chlamydial infection of the cervix in a proportion of cases, and that these signs regress after treatment [21]. These workers drew attention to the historical evidence for an association between chlamydial cervicitis and pelvic inflammatory disease, particularly in relation to maternal infection and neonatal chlamydial conjunctivitis. They conclude that *C. trachomatis* is a pathogen in the female genital tract and that it provokes, in some cases, a well-marked tissue response to infection of the cervix: it can be found in the fallopian tubes in salpingitis [22].

There is some evidence to suggest that *U. urealyticum* and *Mycoplasma hominis* may be implicated in a few cases of pelvic inflammatory disease, although the precise extent of their involvement is not clear [9].

Diagnosis of NGU in men and NSGI in women

C. trachomatis and *U. urealyticum,* the two main organisms implicated in the aetiology of NGU in the male and related infections in the female, can be detected by microbiological tests as outlined below, but this service is often not offered as a routine as resources are limited. In practice, a diagnosis of NGU in men and NSGI in women is made by considering the clinical presentation, relevant history and by exclusion of certain other conditions.

NGU IN MEN

In the case of urethritis in the male it is the clinician's prime duty to exclude the presence of the gonococcus, initially by careful microscopy of the Gram-stained smear but backed up by inoculation of a culture plate at the same time. If the laboratory is distant then a swab may be sent in Amies's transport medium (page 186).

If the initial examination of a good sample of pus from the urethra shows numerous pus cells but no Gram-negative diplococci then a presumptive diagnosis of non-gonococcal urethritis may be made.

This diagnosis of NGU of the anterior urethra is strengthened by finding of haziness with or without urethral threads in the first glass in the urine test and a clear urine in the second and third (page 48). In the case of a urethrocystitis, all specimens of urine in this test show a haze due to pus cells. A haze in urine due to precipitated phosphates may be differentiated from the haze due to pus cells by adding 10 per cent acetic acid to dissolve the phosphates.

Routine tests need not be taken to exclude *T. vaginalis* and *C. albicans* in the male, as cultures are frequently negative and the role of these organisms as a cause of NGU is probably not important. In the case of cystitis in the male, however, a midstream specimen should be taken for bacteriological investigation and plans must be made for an excretion urogram, as bacterial cystitis in the male is almost invariably associated with a functional or anatomical abnormality in the urinary tract (Chapter 19).

NSGI IN WOMEN

A diagnosis of NSGI in women implies that *Neisseria gonorrhoeae* has been excluded as a cause. Although attempts may be made to eradicate *C. trachomatis* and *U. urealyticum* it must be emphasized that other organisms such as *Bacteroides fragilis* may be pathogenic on occasions, such as after surgical procedures, and here treatment with metronidazole may be necessary. Streptococci, staphylococci, Gram-negative bacilli, anaerobes or facultative anaerobes, can be pathogens in the genital tract and antibiotic or chemotherapeutic treatment may be required, depending on the sensitivity of these organisms.

In the case of pelvic inflammatory disease, although it is common practice to define the aetiology by isolating potential pathogens from the endocervix, the aetiology is probably better defined by examining tubal flora when possible. The cervix and vagina of normal women may contain all the species of anaerobic bacteria capable of causing pelvic infection. Endocervical cultures are of limited value in suggesting the species of organisms responsible for tubal infections, although these may be due to mixed infections or anaerobes [23]. *N. gonorrhoeae* is the only pathogen for which recovery from the cervix is correlated with recovery from the fallopian tubes. Pelvic inflammatory disease is dealt with more fully in Chapter 16.

If facilities exist, *C. trachomatis* and *U. urealyticum* can be detected as follows.

Isolation of Chlamydia trachomatis

In the male an endo-urethral swab (Medical Wire and Equipment Co. Ltd.) is passed into the anterior urethra and withdrawn and agitated in a container of 2SP*. Excess fluid is removed by rotating the swab while gently pressing against the inside of the container. After moistening the swab can be passed gently along the anterior urethra for 5–10cm. On final removal the swab may be cut off with disposable scissors.

In the female, specimens may be obtained for testing by scraping the cervix and cervical canal with a cotton-wool swab, concentrating on any inflamed area or where 'follicles' are seen. Similarly, material may be obtained from the rectum or from the oropharynx. In the case of the conjunctiva in the neonate particularly, the lower lid of each eye should be everted and a specimen taken by drawing a cotton wool-tipped swab along it mucosal surface. Specimens should be taken from the upper lids also if possible.

Specimens should be sent to the laboratory within 2 hours where they can be stored at –70°C before inoculating monolayers. If this is not possible specimens should be transported in liquid nitrogen.

Methods for the laboratory diagnosis of chlamydial infection, summarized in Table 13.1, are as follows:

1. Detection of inclusion bodies by direct microscopy

In addition to Giemsa and immunofluorescence staining, iodine may

*2SP is a sucrose phosphate transport medium containing fetal calf serum and antibacterial and antifungal agents (i.e., streptomycin or gentamycin, 50μg/ml; vancomycin, 100μg/ml; amphotericin B, 2.5μg/ml) to prevent overgrowth by contaminants. Since penicillin interferes with the formation of elementary bodies within cultured cells used for isolation of chlamydiae, specimens should not be placed in a virus transport medium which contains penicillin. Chloramphenicol and tetracyclines must also be avoided.

Table 13.1 Laboratory diagnosis of chlamydial infections

Condition	*Sample*	*Test*	*Comment*
NGU (Male)	Urethral scraping	Microscopy	Time-consuming. Insensitive.
NSGI (Female)	Cervical scraping	Cell culture	Adequate facilities essential. Sensitive.
	Serum	Micro IF	Adequate facilities essential. IgM antibody in primary infection. Allows differentiation of serotypes. Applicable also to secretions.
LGV	Lymph node aspirate	Microscopy	Time-consuming. Insensitive.
		Cell culture	Adequate facilities. Sensitivity to be assessed.
	Serum	LGVCFT	4-fold rise in paired sera significant in acute infection. Commonly available.
		Micro IF	Allows differentiation of serotypes.

also be used to detect the glycogen-containing inclusion bodies of *C. trachomatis* in smears made from urethral, cervical and vaginal scrapings or swabs. Unfortunately, direct microscopy by any of these techniques is too insensitive to be of practical value.

2. *Culture*

Isolation of *C. trachomatis* on McCoy* cells irradiated to stop their replication is a sensitive method, whereas the isolation in the yolk sac of an egg is insensitive and prone to contamination [24]. As irradiation is inconvenient for some laboratories alternative methods of comparable sensitivity have been described, e.g., treatment of cells with the nucleoside analogue 5-iodo-2-deoxyuridine (IDU) or with the fungal metabolite cytochalasin B.

Treatment of the cells with these agents favours intracellular parasitism by preventing host cell replication and thus making more of the nutrients and precursors in the medium available to the chlamydiae. A simplified culture technique [25] uses cycloheximide, an inhibitor of protein synthesis in eukaryotic but not in prokaryotic cells, to favour the growth of chlamydiae. This technique is suitable for routine isolation of *C. trachomatis* on a large scale as it does not involve pre-treatment of the cells; cycloheximide is added after the chlamydiae have been taken up by the cells.

The clinical specimen is inoculated into flat-bottomed tubes containing the cell monolayers on coverslips and the tubes are then centrifuged for 1 hour at 1000 to 3000*g* at a temperature of 35°C to enhance the intracellular uptake of chlamydiae. The inoculated monolayers are then incubated for 48–72 hours, the coverslips fixed with methanol and stained with iodine or Giemsa's stain. Inclusions may be demonstrated in positive cases.

3. *Serology*

The microimmunofluorescence test [27] allows for identification of specific antibodies: sera are screened against several antigens, either singly or in groups, representative of the many chlamydial serotypes. Only a few laboratories offer this test at present. A simpler test using a single antigen (*C. trachomatis* serotype E) is capable of detecting antibodies to a group antigen as well as type-specific antibodies to

*The McCoy cell line, originally used because it was thought to be a line of human synovial cells, is now known to be closely related in karyotype and antigenic constitution to the mouse fibroblastic tumour cell line L929, used for the laboratory growth of *C. psittaci* [26].

C. trachomatis serotypes [28]. Using this test, single serum specimens from patients can be readily screened. Although the test may yield useful epidemiological information on the extent to which a particular population has been exposed to genital chlamydiae infections, it is of little value in the assessment of individual patients, since antibody could be due to a past infection.

A fourfold rise in titre or conversion from seronegative to seropositive correlates well with the isolation of *C. trachomatis,* but this does not provide rapid diagnosis.

Detection of quantitative differences in antibody by an objective test such as radio-immunoassay or enzyme-linked immunosorbent assay may prove of value in future, as may the investigation of secretory IgA. A single method to detect chlamydial antigen in genital secretions would also provide a useful diagnostic test.

Isolation of Ureaplasma urealyticum

In both sexes the centrifuged deposit from the first voided urine (40ml) provides a useful specimen. In males, urethral exudate can also be collected with a cotton-tipped swab or by scraping the anterior urethra with a bacteriological loop. If media cannot be inoculated directly, swabs should be sent in a suitable transport medium, e.g. Amies's medium lacking charcoal, since charcoal itself might interfere with the colour reaction in the growth medium. Urine specimens should be sent to the laboratory within four hours.

The isolation and identification of *U. urealyticum* is aided by its ability to hydrolyse urea. A liquid culture medium (e.g. U9) containing urea, a pH indicator, and penicillin* to inhibit bacterial contaminants is useful for the isolation of *U. urealyticum* from clinical material: accumulation of ammonia due to hydrolysis of urea raises the pH of the medium causing a change in the colour of the indicator [29]. When solid media are used colonies of *U. urealyticum* can be identified with a 1.0 per cent solution of urea containing 0.8 per cent manganous chloride in a direct test for urease: a positive reaction is obtained within 5–10 seconds.

The NYC medium, devised in the New York City Department of Health, primarily for the isolation of pathogenic neisseriae, also readily supports the growth of *U. urealyticum* and mycoplasmas. The medium permits direct isolation and identification of these organisms as well as *N. gonorrhoeae* without interference from contaminating saprophytes [30].

*The antibiotics used in gonococcal-selective media (Chapter 11) can be added to U9 medium and are of particular value in preventing overgrowth by contaminants in specimens from women.

Liquid cultures are normally incubated aerobically at 37°C, while solid media are incubated in an atmosphere containing 95 per cent nitrogen and 5 per cent carbon dioxide. Results are usually available within one to five days.

Chemotherapy of chlamydia and ureaplasma infections

The results of a laboratory evaluation of antibacterial agents against chlamydia suggest that oxytetracycline is most effective MIC, 0.06μg/ml) and erythromycin has a useful second place (MIC, 0.03μg/ml) [31]. Gentamicin, spectinomycin, trimethoprim/sulphamethoxazole are not likely to be effective and the effects of pencillin G and ampicillin are relatively poor.

The results of a laboratory evaluation of antibacterial agents against ureaplasma showed that minocycline was the most active antibiotic with a median MIC (0.03μg/ml), well below reported blood serum concentrations attained after therapeutic doses [32]. Doxycycline and demeclocycline, although not as active *in vitro* as minocycline against the majority of strains tested, still gave low median MIC values (0.125μg/ml). Tetracycline was less active than its analogues (MIC 0.25μg/ml). Erythromycin required the highest concentration, MIC 2.0μg/ml Approximately 10 per cent of ureaplasma isolated may be resistant to oxytetracycline and minocycline [33]. Resistance to erythromycin does not seem to be linked to tetracycline resistance [33] although strains resistant to both antibiotics have been isolated [32].

TREATMENT OF NGU IN THE MALE

The value of tetracycline in the treatment of NGU was investigated in patients, who were members of a 5500-man crew of a large aircraft carrier in the US Navy [34]. After six days of liberty in the Philippines the men returned for 30 consecutive days at sea where discipline was strong and opportunities for further sexual intercourse very remote. It was established that tetracycline was better than placebo and that a seven-day course was better than a four-day course, that is to say with a follow-up limited to 20 days or less.

In the long term, however, the effects are less clear and in a trial in Birmingham there was only about a ten per cent difference between placebo and a short course of tetracycline when an assessment was made over a ten-week period [35].

In the case of NGU treated with placebo, the patient will tend to suffer symptoms longer, so treatment with a tetracycline is justified on this ground alone. It is recommended that oxytetracycline is prescribed in a dose of 250mg four times daily for seven days. The patient may then be assessed after one week and two weeks, when a further week's course may be prescribed if symptoms or signs of urethritis persist or if numerous urethral threads containing pus cells are seen in the first glass in the urine test. As the value of a 21-day course has not been proved to be greater than a seven-day course it is not accepted routine practice to prescribe a long course.

In addition to the tetracycline treatment the patient is advised to abstain from alcohol for two weeks* and to abstain from intercourse for the same period. The former is advised on the basis that the inflammation appears to be aggravated by taking alcohol and to subside more readily with rest. Relapse after coitus and/or excessive alcohol consumption is often reported by patients with NGU.

A long-acting tetracycline, minocycline, is effective and blood levels of 2μg per ml can be maintained with a 12-hourly dose. A course of 200mg followed by 100mg 12-hourly for six days in one trial [36] produced a short-term cure in 89 per cent (41 patients) and failed to do so in 11 per cent (5) who had discharge after a six-day period. With minocycline the complaint of vertigo is a recognized complication which tends to resolve in spite of continued treatment. An isolated case of a hypersensitivity-like acute interstitial nephritis has been reported in a 43-year-old woman, occurring ten days after treatment with minocycline (250mg four times daily for five days) for an upper respiratory infection [37]. The patient recovered spontaneously, after withdrawing minocycline, which had been prescribed again before admission to hospital.

Doxycycline (Vibramycin (Pfizer Ltd.)) is sometimes effective in a dose of 200mg once on day 1 and 100mg daily for six days afterwards. The capsules should be taken immediately after meals to avoid abdominal pain which may occur when the stomach is empty and the possibility of photosensitivity has to be taken into account.

At present it is suggested that, when eradication of ureaplasma is deemed to be advisable, a tetracycline should be used. Isolation facilities for diagnosis, antibiotic sensitivity testing and tests of cure are not widely available.

TREATMENT OF NSGI IN THE FEMALE

In the case of a regular partnership, or where *C. trachomatis* or *U. urealyticum* have been isolated, treatment of both male and female partners is recommended. In females with signs or symptoms suggestive

*The time of two weeks is set as a policy with which the average man may be reasonably expected to comply.

of NSGI then treatment may also be justified even if isolations are not obtained. Treatments and dosages are similar to those for the male, except that erythromycin stearate should be used in women who are pregnant or lactating.

Non-gonococcal conjunctivitis of the newborn (Non-gonococcal ophthalmia neonatorum)

Mild inflammation of the conjunctiva is common a few days after birth and resolves generally without treatment. This may be due to trauma or a transitory infection acquired during birth. In the case of gonococcal conjunctivitis, acquired from the infected maternal cervix, blindness will result if no treatment is given, and diagnosis in the child will require also examination, diagnosis and treatment of the mother and her sexual contacts, whether consort or husband. The social consequences of this intervention are to be endured in all cases because the dangers of omission of treatment are very serious.

In non-gonococcal conjunctivitis not caused by bacteria the condition is commonly an inclusion conjunctivitis, caused by one of the sexually transmissible serotypes of *C. trachomatis.* The steps taken to ensure treatment of the mother and father or partner will not require insistence to the degree required in any gonococcal infection.

CONJUNCTIVITIS OF THE NEWBORN DUE TO *CHLAMYDIA TRACHOMATIS*

The increase in incidence in the United Kingdom of non-gonococcal urethritis in men by about 150 per cent over the last decade, associated with the isolation rate of certain serotypes of *C. trachomatis* of some 40 per cent in this condition, is likely to be also associated with a large number of women acting as carriers. As a chlamydial infection can be asymptomatic in men with minimal signs of urethritis, and is ordinarily so in women, conjunctival infections of the newborn are likely to be common.

Clinical features

The onset of signs tends to occur about a week after birth (three days–two weeks). The discharge may be only scanty and not obviously purulent but it is sometimes more copious and frankly purulent, or on occasions blood-stained [21]. In its more severe form there is also oedema of the eyelids and oedema of the palpebral conjunctiva, particularly of the lower lid. Signs may be minimal and the inflammatory reaction apparently transitory but in some cases conjunctival scarring develops [38].

Investigation of severe neonatal conjunctivitis

Discharge should be wiped gently away from the surface of the eyelids with a swab and the lower lids everted. A cotton-wool tipped swab should be passed gently along the mucosal surface of the lower lid to obtain the following necessary smears and cultures:

1. Smear for examination with Gram stain.
2. Direct inoculation of culture to exclude *N. gonorrhoeae.*
3. Swab in SP2 transport medium for isolation of *Chlamydia.*
4. Swab for isolation of other bacteria.

Treatment

Once *N. gonorrhoeae* has been excluded it is justifiable to treat a mild neonatal conjunctivitis with a 0.5 per cent (w/v) solution of neomycin prescribed as single dose sterile eye drops (Minims (Trade Mark) Neomycin Sulphate (Smith and Nephew Pharmaceutical Ltd. 20 units in each single dose), instilled into the eye every four hours. Neomycin is effective against most isolates of staphylococci and some strains of *Proteus vulgaris* and *Pseudomonas aeruginosa.* It has no action against fungi, viruses or intracellular chlamydia. If the conjunctivitis is marked and does not respond to neomycin then isolation of chlamydia should be attempted and if this organism is discovered one per cent tetracycline eye-ointment is applied (Achromycin eye-ointment) along the lower lid four hourly on four occasions daily for 21 days [39]. Short courses may suppress but not eradicate chlamydia. Further studies are required to determine the indications for treatment of chlamydial conjunctival infections and effectiveness of treatment.

REFERENCES

1 Stirling, P and Richmond, S (1977) *British Journal of General Microbiology,* **100,** 31

2 Darougar, S (1976) Immunology of Chlamydia. In *Sexually Transmitted Diseases.* (Ed) Catterall, R D and Nicol, C S (Proceedings of a conference of June 1975) Academic Press, London, page 111

3 Jones, Barrie R (1975) The prevention of blindness from Trachoma. *Transactions of the Ophthalmological Societies of the United Kingdom.* Vol. XCV Part I, 1975

4 Shepard, M C, Lanceford, C D, Ford, D K, Purcell, R H, Taylor-Robinson, D, Razin, S and Black, F T (1974) *International Journal of Systematic Bacteriology,* **24,** 160

5 Oriel, J D, Reeve, P, Wright, J T and Owen, J (1976) *British Journal of Venereal Diseases,* **52,** 46

6 Alani, M D, Darougar, S, Burns, D C MacD, Thin, R N and Dunn, H (1977) *British Journal of Venereal Diseases,* **53,** 88

7 Holmes, K K, Handsfield, H H, Wang, S P, Wentworth, B B, Turck, M, Anderson, J B and Alexander, E R (1975) *The New England Journal of Medicine,* **292,** 1199

8 Wang, S-P, Grayston, J T, Kuo, C-C, Alexander, E R and Holmes, K K (1977) Serodiagnosis of *Chlamydia trachomatis* infection with the micro-immunofluorescence test. In *Non-gonococcal urethritis and related infections.* (Ed) Hobson, D and Holmes, K K. American Society for Microbiology, page 237

9 McCormack, W M, Braun, P, Lee, Y H, Klein, J O and Kass, E H (1973) *New England Journal of Medicine,* **188**, 78

10 Bowie, W R, Floyd, J F, Miller, Y, Alexander, E R, Holmes, J and Holmes, K V (1976) *Lancet,* **ii**, 1276

11 Taylor-Robinson, D, Csonka, G W and Prentice, M J (1977) *Quarterly Journal of Medicine,* New Series, **46**, 309

12 Vaughan-Jackson, J D, Dunlop, E M C, Darougar, S, Treharne, J D and Taylor-Robinson, D (1977) *British Journal of Venereal Diseases,* **53**, 180

13 Oriel, J D, Reeve, P, Thomas, B J and Nicol, C S (1975) *The Journal of Infectious Diseases,* **131**, 376

14 Waitkins, S A and Geary, I (1977) *British Journal of Venereal Diseases,* **53**, 161

15 Holmes, K K, Johnson, D W and Floyd, P M (1967) *Journal of the American Medical Association,* **202**, 474

16 Halberstaedter, L and von Prowazek, S (1910) *Berliner Klinische Wochenschrift,* **47**, 661

17 Swanson, J, Eschenbach, D A, Alexander, E R and Holmes, K K (1975) *Journal of Infectious Diseases,* **131**, 678

18 Gnarpe, H and Friberg, J (1972) *American Journal of Obstetrics and Gynecology,* **114**, 727

19 Oriel, J D, Powis, P A, Reeve, P, Miller, A and Nicol, C S (1974) *British Journal of Venereal Diseases,* **50**, 11

20 Burns, D C, MacD, Darougar, S, Thin, R N, Lothian, L and Nicol, C S (1975) *British Journal of Venereal Diseases,* **51**, 314

21 Rees, E, Tait, A, Holson, D, Byng, R E and Johnson, F W A (1977) *British Journal of Venereal Diseases,* **53**, 173

22 Mardh, P-A, Ripa, T, Svensson, L and Westrom, L (1977) *New England Journal of Medicine,* **296**, 1377

23 Thompson, S E and Hager, W D (1977) *Sexually Transmitted Diseases,* **4**, 105

24 Darougar, S, Cubitt, S and Jones, B R (1974) *British Journal of Venereal Diseases,* **50**, 308

25 Ripa, T and Mardh, P-A (1977) New simplified culture technique for *Chlamydia trachomatis* (Eds.) Hobson, D and Holmes, K K in *Non-gonococcal urethritis and related infections.* American Society for Microbiology, Washington, D C, pages 323–327

26 Hobson, D (1977) Tissue culture procedures for the isolation of *Chlamydia trachomatis* from patients with non-gonococcal genital infections. In *Non-gonococcal urethritis and related infections.* (Ed) Hobson, D and Holmes, K K. American Society for Microbiology, Washington, D C, pages 286–294

27 Grayston, J T and Wang, S P (1975) *Journal of Infectious Diseases,* **132**, 87

28 Richmond, S J and Caul, E O (1977) Single-antigen indirect immunogluorescence test for screening venereal disease clinic populations for chlamydial antibodies. In *Non-gonococcal urethritis and related infections.* (Ed) Hobson, D and Holmes, K K. American Society for Microbiology, Washington, D C, pages 259–265

29 Shepard, M C and Lanceford, D C (1970) *Applied Microbiology,* **20**, 539

30 Faur, Y C, Weisburd, M H, Wilson, M E and May, P S (1974) *Applied Microbiology,* **27**, 1041

31 Ridgway, G L, Owen, J M and Oriel, J D (1976) *Journal of Antimicrobial Chemotherapy,* **2**, 71

32 Spaepen, M S, Kundsin, R B and Horne, H W (1976) *Antimicrobial Agents and Chemotherapy,* **9**, 1012

33 Evans, R T and Taylor-Robinson, D (1978) *Journal of Antimicrobial Chemotherapy,* **4**, 57

34 Holmes, K K, Johnson, D W, Floyd, T M and Kvale, P A (1967) *Journal of the American Medical Association,* **202**, 467

35 Fowler, W (1970) *British Journal of Venereal Diseases,* **46**, 464
36 Prentice, M J, Taylor-Robinson, D and Csonka, G W (1976) *British Journal of Venereal Diseases,* **52**, 269
37 Walker, R G, Thomson, N M, Dowling, J P and Chisholm, S O (1979) *British Medical Journal,* **1**, 524
38 Watson, P G and Gairdner, D (1968) *British Medical Journal,* **3**, 527
39 Charters, D W and Rees, E (1976) *New Zealand Medical Journal,* **83**, 82

CHAPTER 14

Inflammation of the Prostate, Testis and Epididymis

Prostatitis

In those with clinical features, particularly episodes of pain in the distribution believed to be characteristic of inflammation of the prostate, it may not be possible to confirm a diagnosis of prostatitis because histological findings and the results of examination of the prostatic fluid, including attempts to isolate organisms, are often inconclusive. Acute and chronic bacterial prostatitis due to organisms isolated by conventional bacteriological means (referred to as eubacteria in this discussion *see also* Chapter 19) are, however, more clearly defined as entities than in the case of 'chronic prostatitis', where no organisms can be isolated either by conventional bacteriological methods, or even by the special methods required for other organisms considered possibly to have an aetiological role. As the diagnosis of prostatitis tends, therefore, to be made on symptoms it is necessary to consider first 'prostatic pain', recognizing also that there will be overlap in symptomatology with non-gonococcal urethrocystitis on the one extreme and with dysnergic bladder neck obstruction on the other.

Prostatic pain

'Prostatic' pain occurs in inflammatory conditions of the gland and has its origins in the gland itself and in structures with which it is intimately related (urethra, the trigone and its urethral extension, the pre-prostatic sphincter and the musculature of the pelvic floor) [1].

The pain may be felt in the suprapubic region, the groins and the spermatic cord and testis of one or both sides, and may radiate to the inner thighs. It may radiate to the perineum and to the penis where it may be felt in the urethra and in the penile meatus usually at the beginning and completion of micturition. There may also be urgency, frequency, dysuria and painful ejaculation. Symptoms in prostatitis may include any one or all of these [1, 2].

In view of the common segmental autonomic innervation of the kidneys, urethra, bladder and prostate the distribution of pain may be the same in pathology of any part of the upper and lower urinary tract;

for these reasons excretion urography and cystourethroscopy will be necessary to exclude such pathology when the prostate itself, so far as can be ascertained, is not the cause of the pain [1]. Similar symptomatology is also seen in those with or without prostatitis but with dysnergic bladder-neck obstruction detected by investigation of urinary flow during micturition [3]. Prostatitis itself may cause intra-vesical obstruction, effects which could be explained by spasm of the external sphincter [4].

Prostatitis with demonstrable eubacterial infection

ACUTE PROSTATITIS

This is characterized by pyrexia, rigors, frequency and urgency of micturition and dysuria. There is pain in the distribution described, although perineal pain itself is uncommon in the acute phase, since the accompanying malaise encourages bed rest and relaxation of pelvic floor musculature [1]. Gentle palpation of the gland per rectum may show that it is tender, swollen, irregular and indurated. If untreated a prostatic abscess may develop and cause perineal pain of great intensity.

Bacteriological examination of the urine by conventional techniques generally demonstrates the causative organism, which may be *Escherichia coli*, *Klebsiella* spp., *Pseudomonas aeruginosa* or *Proteus* spp

CHRONIC PROSTATITIS

This is one of the most common causes of relapsing urinary tract infection due to eubacteria in any age group but, more commonly, in middle age. It may be associated with a variety of organisms, most commonly Gram-negative bacilli but occasionally Gram-positive organisms. Chronic bacterial (eubacterial) prostatitis is characterized by a relapsing urinary tract infection due to the same pathogen [2] and although some patients present with an asymptomatic bacteriuria, symptoms of 'prostatic' pain and dysuria also occur.

Prostatitis without demonstrable eubacterial infection

CHRONIC OR 'NON-ACUTE' PROSTATITIS WITH 'PROSTATIC' PAIN

Clearly this is the most common form of prostatitis seen today in western, developed, countries. In its clinical presentation it is chronic with recurrent episodes of pain and it may be referred to in terms such as abacterial prostatitis, non-acute prostatitis, prostatosis, or chronic prostatitis. Symptoms are those already described under the heading of 'prostatic' pain (page 223) but malaise pyrexia are absent, and the perineal pain particularly is not as severe as in acute bacterial prostatitis. In contrast to chronic eubacterial prostatitis recurrent episodes of cystitis and epididymitis do not tend to occur.

As *Chlamydia trachomatis* is probably the cause of acute 'idiopathic' epididymitis, occurring particularly in men under 35 years of age and as the organism may be isolated from material aspirated from the epididymis in such cases [5] a similar aetiology might be suggested for chronic or 'non-acute' prostatitis. In an investigation of 53 cases of non-acute prostatitis in Sweden, Mardh *et al* [6], however, isolated *C. trachomatis* from the urethra in only one case and failed to find this organism in any of the 28 specimens of prostatic fluid examined. From this and from microimmunofluorescent tests they considered that in their study *C. trachomatis* appeared to play only a minor role, if any, in 'non-acute' prostatitis: isolation difficulties might however be analogous to the situation of ocular hyperendemic trachoma where it is possible to isolate *C. trachomatis* from 70 per cent of acute cases but only 5 per cent of the chronic [7].

Prostatitis, chronic in form with a tendency to relapse and remission, is a difficult entity to define on criteria other than the presence of 'prostatic' pain as findings based on examination of the expressed prostatic secretion are not reliable; the overlap of its symptomatology with bladder neck dysnergia and sometimes with serious pathology of the urinary tract necessitate referral for urological advice and examination. When symptoms do not abate completely with antimicrobial treatment, given either speculatively or for what may be a coincidental infection with either chlamydia, ureaplasma or trichomonas, referral for urological examination is necessary.

The discovery of excess leucocytes in the expressed prostatic secretion (page 227) has been taken as the sole criterion in making a diagnosis of prostatitis in patients without prostatic pain. Using this finding 'prostatitis' has been diagnosed after treatment of urethritis, both gonococcal [8] and non-gonococcal [9], as well as in a number of conditions of uncertain aetiology, namely: in most (83 per cent) cases of ankylosing spondylitis [10]; in most (95 per cent) cases of Reiter's disease [10], compared with 33 per cent rheumatoid arthritis; and in many cases (64 per cent) of anterior uveitis [11].

For reasons given below under the heading 'Diagnosis of Prostatitis' there is doubt over the significance of both the diagnosis and of the findings of 'excess' pus cells in the expressed prostatic secretion.

Diagnosis of prostatitis

Younger patients with symptoms of 'prostatitis' will tend, rather than the older, to be seen in STD clinics together with those whose sexual habits may bring anxiety about venereal disease. The symptom of 'prostatic' pain will generally be the reason for initiating fuller investigation, although the finding of significant bacteriuria (page 303) usually with pyuria in men will also necessitate such examinations.

The diagnosis of prostatitis due to eubacteria may be made by quantitative bacteriological techniques [2, 12]. The following procedures are necessary:

INVESTIGATIONS IN PROSTATITIS [2]

Urethral smears, including early morning urethral smears and cultures, should have been taken to exclude gonococcal infection (Chapter 11); tests should also be taken when possible to exclude *Ureaplasma urealyticum, Chlamydia, Trichomonas vaginalis* and herpes virus.

Intercourse should be proscribed for at least 24 hours [13], say, as a routine, for 48 hours before testing; the patient should have a full bladder and a desire to micturate (e.g., after retaining urine overnight or for about eight hours).

1. Skin preparation is usually unnecessary in the circumcised male. The uncircumcised man is instructed to retract his foreskin and maintain retraction throughout collection of the specimens. The glans is cleansed with detergent, all soap is washed away with a swab soaked in sterile saline.
2. The first 5–10ml of urine passed is collected in a sterile tube (SPECIMEN 1).
3. A mid-stream specimen of urine (MSU) is obtained after the patient has urinated about 200ml (SPECIMEN 2).
4. The patient stops voiding and by gentle prostatic massage a few drops of prostatic fluid is collected in a wide mouth container (SPECIMEN 3: prostatic fluid).
5. The patient then voids and 5–10ml urine is collected (SPECIMEN 4, urine after prostatic massage).

Cultures for eubacteria should be quantitative.

The diagnosis of bacterial prostatitis (or, *sensu stricto*, eubacterial) is made when the bacterial counts in Specimen 3 (prostatic fluid) or Specimen 4 (urine after prostatic massage) are more than tenfold those in Specimen 1 and Specimen 2.

TECHNIQUE IN OBTAINING SPECIMENS OF PROSTATIC SECRETION

As a general rule it is best for the patient to be placed in the left lateral position, with the buttocks at the edge of the bed and the knees well drawn up, although some doctors prefer to have the patient in the dorsal or knee-elbow position. The patient should be asked to breathe freely through the mouth as this will relax the abdominal muscles and avoid the Valsalva manoeuvre [14] i.e., causing increased intrathoracic pressure by forcible exhalation effort against a closed glottis. The well-lubricated forefinger should be introduced *slowly.* Each lateral lobe of the prostate receives two or three gentle strokes with the palmar surface of the finger, commencing at the periphery of the gland and ending at the midline. This is followed by two downward strokes in the midline over the prostatic urethra. Finally the finger is withdrawn *slowly* through the anal canal. Slow insertion and withdrawal of the finger lessens discomfort considerably. If no secretion appears at the external urethral meatus even after gentle milking of the penile urethra, a further attempt may be made at a later date [15] .

A number of adverse reactions to prostatic palpation have been described. Bilbro [16] has recorded eight episodes of syncope or faintness, occurring within 30 seconds to two minutes, in 2500 prostatic examinations on US Army personnel in Korea during a 13-month period. The patients turned pale and had a bradycardia of 36–48 beats per minute. As the patients showed a sudden loss of consciousness, if they were not placed supine, it must be assumed they were not lying down when rectal examination was carried out [14] . In one case, a 30-year-old man complained of severe anal spasm after examination of the prostate and collapsed, striking his head on the edge of a desk and sustaining a scalp wound. While falling he had a mild tonic-clonic seizure and was subsequently apnoeic and pulseless. A sharp blow to the anterior chest produced a carotid pulse and a bradycardia of 46 beats per minute. The patient regained consciousness after 3 minutes and recovered uneventfully [17] . Again it seems that this patient was not lying down during the examination.

On direct examination of the expressed prostatic secretion (wet film) there is a raised leucocyte count to more than 10 per high power field (× 40 objective) and there may be aggregates of more than 10 per hpf. A change in the pH (measured by Biotest pH papers, Camlab Ltd., Cambridge, England) is related to the inflammatory response and not to the organisms isolated [18, 19] ; and this may be of value as a clinical test. To base a diagnosis on microscopy findings alone, however, is not reliable [2] ; counts of more than 10 leucocytes per high power field have been found in 6 per cent of healthy volunteers in the Royal Navy [13]. Cellular content varies from day to day and on occasions not enough may be found in a sample. As infection appears to be focal, prostatic needle biopsy is also thought to be an unsatisfactory method of examination [2, 13].

In those cases of prostatitis not due to eubacteria, when there has been a poor response to courses of treatment with oxytetracycline or doxycycline, even when a course has been continued for a three-week period, examination of the urine should be extended to include the examination of three specimens of early morning urine for *Mycobacterium tuberculosis* by microscopy and culture; a bloodcount, serum urea, creatinine and electrolytes are usefully obtained at this stage.

Consultation with a urologist is necessary in all men with a eubacterial urinary infection, whether or not there is also a prostatitis and whether or not the urinary tract infection has responded to a course of antibiotics. In prostatitis with 'prostatic' pain and without a demonstrable eubacterial cause a urological opinion is necessary particularly when organisms thought to be associated with non-gonococcal urethritis, namely *C. trachomatis* or *U. urealyticum* have been eradicated without a permanent change in symptoms.

On cystoscopy the urologist may find little more than erythema of the bladder trigone to back the diagnosis of prostatitis. In urinary infections, whether due or not to eubacteria, causes of persistent prostatic pain include neoplasm, urethral stricture, glandular prostatic hyperplasia, radiolucent or opaque bladder calculi and other causes of structural or functional obstruction to urinary flow. An excretion urogram may precede urethrocystoscopy. Because of the overlapping symptomatology with that of outflow obstruction the urologist may consider screening cases by a voiding flow record [3] although prostatitis itself may cause obstructive effects which can be explained by spasm of the external sphincter [4].

The pain of 'prostatitis' differs from that of proctalgia fugax which may be defined as pain, seemingly arising in the rectum, recurring at irregular intervals and being unrelated to organic pain [20]. Among the diagnostic features of this condition are:

1. unaccountable occurrence at very irregular intervals in the day or night in a patient in perfect health;

2. spontaneous disappearance of the pain;

3. localization of pain in rectal region above the anus always in the same place in the same patient but varying somewhat in different sufferers;

4. severity is variable but pain may be intense; and
5. the pain is described as gnawing, aching, cramp-like or stabbing [20].

Treatment in prostatitis

Treatment of eubacterial urinary tract infection has been considered in Chapter 19, but apart from doxycycline, erythromycin, oleandomycin, lincomycin and clindamycin, other antibiotics appear to diffuse poorly into prostatic fluid. For this reason co-trimoxazole has been suggested in a dose of two tablets twice daily for 2–12 weeks in eubacterial prostatic infections. In those who cannot tolerate co-trimoxazole long term suppressive therapy with nitrofurantoin, 50–100mg, once or twice daily may control the infection [2].

In those with 'non-acute' or chronic prostatitis with prostatic pain, not due to eubacteria there is a case to be made to eradicate *Trichomonas, Chlamydia* or *Ureaplasma,* if these organisms are to be found (Chapters 13 and 18).

An attempt should be made also to clear such an infection in the sexual partner(s) when the relationships are long-term rather than casual. In those with constant changes in partners this approach may not be justifiable. When the infection is believed to have been a sequel to non-gonococcal urethritis or to have arisen *de novo* after sexual exposure a course of doxycycline (200mg initially followed by 100mg daily for 14–21 days) which penetrates the prostate, may help when oxytetracycline or tetracycline have failed. If *T. vaginalis* is found in the patient or his partner metronidazole should be used in both (Chapter 18). Similarly, in vaginitis in the partner, whether due to *Candida* or of uncertain aetiology, attempts may be made to treat the vaginitis (Chapter 17).

When no organismal cause has been demonstrated and/or if the possibility of sexual transmission is only speculative, sexual intercourse should not be proscribed. There is no place for regular prostatic massage in the treatment of 'non-acute' or chronic prostatitis. Symptoms will tend to wax and wane regardless of therapy.

In the individual patient, if ingestion of alcoholic or other beverages, or of spicy foods, appear to have aggravated symptoms, restriction should be suggested. The same principle obtains regarding frequency of sexual intercourse [2]. Rest and reassurance may help when investigation has shown a disturbance of micturition and a deficient voluntary sphincter relaxation [1]. If there is evidence of bladder neck obstruction relief may be obtained by endoscopic bladder neck incisional procedures [3], although such surgical intervention will be restricted to those over 35 years of age to avoid possible interference with fertility in younger men, in whom symptoms may abate in time.

In cases when a diagnosis of prostatitis has been made on the sole basis of finding pus cells in numbers believed to be excessive (page 227) treatment is not indicated, unless a coincidental infection such as *N. gonorrhoeae* is also found or unless a positive attempt is being made to eradicate say a chlamydial infection for the benefit of a female sexual partner. In the case of diseases (page 225) in which excessive pus cells in the prostate is a coincidental finding there is no indication for treatment.

Inflammation of the testis and epididymis

Acute epididymitis occurs as a complication of a urinary tract infection, usually due to coliform organisms in the case of older men (over 35 years of age); in the case of younger men, in whom such a coliform infection is rare, epididymitis is usually due to sexually transmitted organisms, *C. trachomatis* or *N. gonorrhoeae.* In countries where medical attention and antibiotic or chemotherapy is readily available, gonococcal epididymitis is rare. Acute epididymitis due to coliform organisms tends to extend into the testis only in advanced disease, when there may be abscess formation.

In epididymitis complicating a general infection, as in leprosy and mumps and in the now rare late-stage syphilis, there is almost invariably substantial testicular involvement also [21]. It is therefore important to try to distinguish between acute epididymitis and orchitis by careful examination and to detect sexually transmitted infections. Patients who have a frank urethral discharge may tend to reach clinics for sexually transmitted disease, whereas those who do not have such a discharge or who may have only a slight discharge may be referred to surgical units. The approach to the diagnosis may therefore differ and there is a need for each discipline to collaborate in diagnosis and management of epididymitis as special microbiological facilities required for isolation of the organisms responsible are not always widely available.

Whenever there is uncertainty, however, as to the nature of any thickening, irregularity, nodule or enlargement of the testis or epididymis, referral to a surgeon is necessary as *surgical exposure is required for the exclusion or detection of malignant neoplasm.*

Acute epididymitis, a complication arising from infection of the urinary tract

AETIOLOGY

In the pre-antibiotic era of 1943, in US Army statistics, it was found that among 680 cases of epididymitis only 79 (11.6 per cent) were proved to be gonococcal, 19 were tuberculous and 582 (85.6 per cent) unspecified. Again in 1966 in a review of 610 cases an organism was identified in only a quarter of the series [21]. Histologically the microscopic changes of gonococcal epididymitis do not differ from the non-gonococcal form.

In countries where antibiotics are freely available acute epididymitis is an uncommon complication of gonorrhoea [21]. In a London STD clinic, Rodin [22] reported that in 1968 there was one case of epididymitis seen in 1214 cases of gonorrhoea and one case among 1691 cases of NGU. In young men, however, acute epididymitis is clearly associated with sexually transmitted organisms, as more recently in the investigation of a group of 18 men under 32 years of age with epididymitis, culture from the urethra yielded *N. gonorrhoeae* in six and *C. trachomatis* in six: both organisms were isolated in an additional patient. Isolations of herpes virus, cytomegalovirus and *U. urealyticum* were also made from urethral specimens in this group [23].

In a study of acute epididymitis (in clinics of the University of Washington hospitals) in 13 men under the age of 35 years and 10 over that age it was found that in the case of the younger men *C. trachomatis* was the likely cause, as this organism was found in the aspirated material from the affected epididymis in five of the six tested. In four of the five patients with chlamydia isolated from the urethra the organism was also obtained from the epididymis. In the older men only coliform organisms were found in material aspirated from the epididymis in five of the ten men examined [24]. In this investigation, also, in nine of fifteen men with epididymitis, not due to coliform organisms, *U. urealyticum* was found in the first voided urine (Chapter 13) but aspirated material from the epididymis provided no evidence that *U. urealyticum* reached the epididymis.

In older men in their thirties or later, when there may have been no risk of a sexually transmitted infection, epididymitis is usually associated with bacteriuria due to *Escherichia coli, Klebsiella* spp., *Pseudomonas aeruginosa* or *Proteus* spp. In such cases urological investigation is indicated and this should include an excretion urogram and urethrocystoscopy. When epididymitis is associated with a chronic cystitis there is always some predisposing cause of the infection such as obstruction, stone or neurological disorder and it is important to exclude pyelonephritis, renal tuberculosis or analgesic nephropathy. Chronic eubacterial prostatitis may also be a cause (page 224).

CLINICAL FEATURES OF ACUTE EPIDIDYMITIS, A COMPLICATION ARISING FROM AN INFECTION OF THE URINARY TRACT

The onset of acute epididymitis due to pyogenic organisms including *N. gonorrhoeae* or associated with non-gonococcal urethritis is usually acute, and the pain on the affected side severe. An associated purulent or mucopurulent urethral discharge is usual in this condition in young men and there may be malaise and fever. It tends to occur during the 2nd–3rd week of urethritis, affects the tail first then the whole of the epididymis which becomes painful, swollen and tender, while the overlying skin appears red and shiny. There may be an inflammatory hydrocele. After a few days the inflammation subsides but the epididymis may be left swollen and indurated.

After excluding the gonococcus as a cause, clinical findings may help to distinguish epididymitis due to coliform organisms from that due to chlamydia. Although a urethral discharge may be present in the majority of those with chlamydial infection the patient may not be aware of it; the first urine specimen voided will contain more pus cells than the second and threads may be present. In coliform urinary infection pyuria will be present in all urine specimens; there will often be visible turbidity in the first voided specimen as well as the second. Inguinal pain may be more pronounced in the chlamydia positive cases than in the coliform. Scrotal oedema and erythema may be more pronounced in the coliform infection [24].

DIAGNOSIS IN EPIDIDYMITIS

Gonococcal infections are recognized by the methods already outlined (Chapter 11). Non-gonococcal epididymitis may be associated with chlamydial infections although the diagnosis is usually reached by:

1. Detection or exclusion of the gonococcus as a cause.
2. Examination of urethral specimens for *C. trachomatis.* Epididymal aspirations are not advised as a routine procedure.
3. Detection or exclusion of *E. coli*, *Klebsiella* spp., *Pseudomonas* or *Proteus* spp., by bacterial examination of a midstream specimen of urine.

Blancy *et al* [26] advise that surgical exploration should be carried out in every apparent 'epididymitis' if there is no infection of the urinary tract, particularly when the swelling is not obviously confined to the epididymis. Acute inflammatory swelling of the testis is always a surgical emergency in a young man. The main differential diagnosis rests between epididymitis, torsion and tumour and, as clinical signs are not trustworthy, when urethritis, pyuria or bacteriuria are absent, surgical exposure is necessary.

Tuberculous epididymitis is rare but the examination of three consecutive early morning specimens of urine by microscopy of the consecutive deposit and by culture should detect *Mycobacterium tuberculosis*.

The diagnosis of infection with *W. bancrofti, W. pacifica* or *B. malayi* can be established with certainty only by identifying the microfilariae in the peripheral blood or by recovering an adult worm from an infected lymph node.

Once again it should be emphasized that in any undiagnosed thickening, irregularity, nodule or enlargement of the testis or epididymis, *surgical exposure of the testis is necessary for the exclusion or detection of malignant neoplasm;* in the case of an acute inflammatory swelling of the testis in a young man the *importance of excluding torsion is also emphasized.*

TREATMENT OF ACUTE EPIDIDYMITIS, A COMPLICATION OF URINARY TRACT INFECTION

Treatment will depend upon the cause. In the case of acute epididymitis the patient should rest in bed. A bandage or jock strap with a cotton wool pad supporting the testis will limit movement and prevent pain.

In gonococcal infections a course of benzylpenicillin (600mg or 1 million units) is given in six-hourly dosage intramuscularly for the first 2–3 days and may be changed later to ampicillin 500mg six-hourly given orally. Alternatively co-trimoxazole two tablets may be given by mouth thrice daily for 2–3 days initially and twice daily afterwards. Treatment should continue for one to two weeks. If a chlamydial infection is suspected or proved in the case of those without a coliform urinary infection, a course of oxytetracycline or doxycycline may be given after the specific treatment for gonorrhoea has been completed.

If the aetiology is thought to be that of non-gonococcal urethritis or if *C. trachomatis* has been isolated from the urethra, oxytetracycline (250mg six-hourly) or doxycycline (100mg twice daily) may be given for one to two weeks. Improvement is rapid but a cragginess or induration of the epididymis may persist for weeks or months. The tracing and treatment of contacts is essential in gonococcal infections and advisable in chlamydial infections as well as in those in which the organismal diagnosis is uncertain.

In urinary tract infections where there is a significant bacteriuria the investigations and management are discussed in Chapter 19.

Orchitis or epididymo-orchitis in generalized infections

Orchitis and epididymo-orchitis, secondary to generalized infections may be seldom seen in STD clinics but knowledge of their pathology [21], as well as that of other inflammatory lesions of the epididymis and testis, is necessary for differential diagnosis.

In syphilis the testicular lesion may be a diffuse chronic interstitial inflammation proceeding to atrophy or a gumma. Clinically this now rare late-stage effect presents as a painless smooth enlargement of the testis, which is characteristically not tender. Eventually the testis becomes hard due to fibrosis.

In leprosy, particularly lepromatous leprosy, involvement of the testis and to a lesser extent the epididymis is very common. *Mycobacterium leprae* proliferates freely in the testes and testicular atrophy is associated with sterility, impotence and gynaecomastia.

Tuberculous epididymitis may begin quickly and be indistinguishable from the infections described but it is usually insidious. The epididymis enlarges and becomes hard and craggy but is only slightly tender. The vas deferens may be elongated and beaded. Later the epididymis becomes fixed to the skin.

A tuberculous orchitis, generally accompanied by an epididymitis, is always secondary to lesions elsewhere especially in the lungs, bones, joints or lymph nodes. It is often preceded by tuberculosis of the prostate and seminal vesicles.

In mumps epididymo-orchitis complicates 20 per cent of cases in adults with one in six showing bilateral involvement. Scrotal swelling is usually noted within a week of parotid enlargement but sometimes only when the clinical signs of mumps have disappeared. Focal inflammatory changes in the testis become diffuse and there is suppuration in severe cases. The epididymis is involved in 85 per cent of cases and on rare occasions epididymitis occurs by itself. Bilateral orchitis followed by atrophy results in sterility or serious impairment of fertility. If there is no atrophy, even in bilateral cases, fertility does not appear to be impaired. The onset of orchitis is associated with fever and headache. The testis is extremely painful and tender

Appearing at any stage of the disease an orchitis is clinically more evident than an epididymitis in brucellosis. Morgan [21] cites reports on an incidence of 5–18 per cent, and records that it may be five times commoner in *Brucella melitensis* infections than in those due to *Br. abortus.* In *coxsackie virus B* infections orchitis is common, sometimes involving one-third of those infected.

A sperm granuloma is due to extravasation of spermatozoa into surrounding tissue, causing a characteristic cellular reaction followed by fibrosis. Sometimes such a granuloma may be seen in the spermatic cord, especially since vasectomy has become commoner.

A granulomatous orchitis is a chronic inflammatory lesion of uncertain aetiology leading to a hard swelling of the testis in those 50–60 years of age [21].

In an inflamed hydrocele proliferation of mesothelial cells in the inflammatory exudate is frequently seen, and is an observation of importance to the pathologist who wishes to differentiate this change from a true mesothelioma.

Hard non-tender masses of nodular periorchitis may be palpable through the scrotal wall. These may be 0.2–2cm in diameter, projecting from either or both layers of the tunica. Sometimes they form loose bodies and histologically they consist of concentrically laminated hyalin collagen [21].

In infestations with *Wuchereria bancrofti, W. pacifica, Brugia malayi* and related filariae, the clinical manifestations are slow to develop and change in each successive age group. As the infection develops, the adult worms in the lymph glands may be associated with an adenopathy and sometimes fever and an allergic inflammatory reaction in the catchment areas of the glands. A lymphangitis spreads centrifugally, down the spermatic cord and testis, for example from the affected lymph glands in the abdomen, producing a funiculitis and orchitis. An effusion may develop within the tunica vaginalis and eventually elephantiasis of the scrotum. Filariasis due to *W. bancrofti* will be seen in those from Africa and throughout the tropical world. In filariasis due to *W. pacifica* (from the islands of the Southern Pacific, particularly Samoa) clinical manifestations are more severe. In filariasis due to *B. malayi* (from coastal regions of India, from Malaya, Indo-China, Indonesia and New Guinea) genital involvement is rare [25].

Malignant tumours of the testicle

Reference has already been made to the importance of surgical exploration when there is doubt about the diagnosis of any swelling of the testis. The majority of testicular tumours are malignant although these are uncommon (annual incidence rates of 2.5 and 2.1 per 100,000 males for Scotland and England respectively; 4.5 and 3.6 for Denmark and Norway). The type of tumour found in over 90 per cent of cases is either a seminoma (about 40 per cent), teratoma (about 32 per cent), combined tumour (about 14 per cent), and malignant lymphoma (about 7 per cent). The surgeon has a difficult decision as the aim of inspection at surgery is to differentiate tumour from inflammatory disease and to decide whether orchidectomy is advisable as biopsy can lead to dissemination and has no place in the diagnosis of this disease, where 4–16 per cent or more of seminomas or teratomas may present as inflammatory lesions [26], and 74 per cent of testicular tumours occur in the age group 20–49 years [27].

REFERENCES

1 Blacklock, N J (1978) *British Journal of Hospital Medicine,* **20**, 80

2 Meares, E M (1978) *Drugs,* **15**, 472

3 Warwick, R T and Whiteside, C G (1976) A urodynamic view of clinical urology, in *Recent Advances in Urology.* (Ed) Hendry, W F. Churchill Livingstone, Edinburgh, pages 60–61

4 Buck, A (1975) *Proceedings of the Royal Society of Medicine,* **68**, 508

5 Berger, R E, Alexander, E R, Monda, G D, Ansell, J, McCormick, G and Holmes, K K (1978) *New England Journal of Medicine,* **298**, 301

6 Mardh, P-A, Ripa, K T, Colleen, S, Treharne, J D and Darougar, S (1978) *British Journal of Venereal Diseases,* **54**, 330

7 Darougar, S, Woodland, R M, Forsey, T, Cubitt, S, Allami, J and Jones, B R (1977) Isolation of *Chlamydia* from ocular infections. In *Nongonococcal urethritis and related infections.* (Ed) Hobson, D and Holmes, K K. American Society for Microbiology, Washington, page 295

8 Thin, R N T (1974) *British Journal of Venereal Diseases,* **50**, 370

9 King, A (1964) in *Recent Advances in Venereology,* Churchill, London, page 375

10 Mason, R M, Murray, R S, Oates, J K and Young, A C (1958) *British Medical Journal,* **1**, 748

11 Catterall, R D (1961) *Lancet,* **ii**, 739

12 Meares, E M and Stamey, T A (1968) *Investigative Urology,* **5**, 492

13 Blacklock, N J (1969) Some observations on prostatitis, In *Advances in the study of the prostate.* (Ed) Williams, D C, Briggs, M H and Standford, M. Heinemann, London, page 37

14 Leading Article (1970) *British Medical Journal,* **2**, 61

15 Harkness, A H (1950) in *Non-gonococcal Urethritis,* Livingstone, Edinburgh, page 362

16 Bilbro, R H (1970) *New England Journal of Medicine,* **282**, 167

17 Poleshuch, V A (1970) *New England Journal of Medicine,* **282**, 632

18 Blacklock, N J and Beavis, J P (1974) *British Journal of Urology,* **46**, 537

19 White, M A (1975) *Proceedings of the Royal Society of Medicine,* **68**, 511

20 Douthwaite, A H (1962) *British Medical Journal,* **2**, 164

21 Morgan, A D (1976) Inflammation and infestation of the testis and paratesticular structures. In *Pathology of the Testis.* (Ed) Pugh, R C B. Blackwell Scientific Publications, Oxford, pages 79–138

22 Rodin, P (1969) Incidence of epididymitis in a department of venereal diseases in the London Hospital. In *Tumours of the Testicle.* Blandy, J P, Hope-Stone, H F and Dayan, A.D. Heinemann Medical Books Ltd, London, page 69

23 Harnisch, J P, Berger, R E, Alexander, E R, Monda, G and Holmers, K K (1977) *Lancet,* i, 819

24 Berger, R E, Alexander, E R, Monda, G D, Ansell, J, McCormick, G and Holmers, K K (1978) *New England Journal of Medicine,* **298**, 301

25 Kershaw, W E (1978) Filariaris due to infection with *Wuchereria bancrofti, W, pacifica, Brugia malayi* and related Filaria. In *Diseases of Children in the Subtropics and Tropics,* 3rd edition. (Ed) Jelliffe, D B and Stansfield, J P. Edward Arnold, London, pages 915–919

26 Blandy, J P, Hope-Stone, H F and Dayan, A D (1970) *Tumours of the Testicle,* William Heinemann Medical Books Ltd., London

27 Pugh, R C B (1976) (Ed) *Pathology of the Testis. Testicular tumours–Introduction.* Blackwell Scientific Publications, Oxford, pages 139–159

Further Reading

Blandy, J P, Hope-Stone, H F and Dayan, A D (1970) *Tumours of the Testicle.* Heinemann Medical Books Ltd, London

Pugh, R C B (1976) (Ed) *Pathology of the Testis.* Blackwell Scientific Publications, Oxford

CHAPTER 15

Reiter's Disease: A Seronegative Spondarthritis

Introduction

Although Hans Reiter [1] described the disease which now bears his name in 1916, this disorder had been reported more than a century earlier by Stoll in 1776 and later by Sir Benjamin Brodie in 1818. Reiter described the occurrence of urethritis, conjunctivitis and arthritis in a young man. Since then, many cases have been recorded and it has become apparent that there is a spectrum of clinical features and not all three signs may be present.

Following the first acute attack, the patient may appear to recover completely, and may have no further episodes. Other individuals, however, may have multiple recurrences, with remissions varying from months to years. Generally, with each recurrence fewer features accompany the arthritis, which may be the sole indication of Reiter's disease in the later stages. Although rarely fatal *per se* Reiter's disease may lead to considerable pain, disability and anxiety.

There may be no acute initial episode and the disease may show itself in a patient as a subacute or chronic arthritis. In such circumstances it may be difficult, if not impossible, to say whether the individual has Reiter's disease or some other member of the group of non-rheumatoid diseases (seronegative spondarthritides).

Seronegative spondarthritides

Reiter's disease is one of a group of disorders known as the seronegative spondarthritides. Clinical and familial inter-relationships can be demonstrated between members of this group which must satisfy certain criteria [2].

1. Negative test for rheumatoid factor.
2. Absence of subcutaneous ('rheumatoid') nodules.
3. Inflammatory peripheral arthritis.
4. Radiological sacro-iliitis with or without classical ankylosing spondylitis.
5. Evidence of clinical overlap between members of the group.

6. Tendency to familial aggregation, that is, the presence of two or more examples of the same disease and/or two or more different diseases of the group within a single family.

Seven diseases fulfil these criteria and are called seronegative spondarthritides.

1. Idiopathic ankylosing spondylitis.
2. Psoriatic arthritis.
3. Reiter's disease.
4. Ulcerative colitis.
5. Crohn's disease.
6. Whipple's disease.
7. Behçet's syndrome.

Recent studies of the histocompatibility system have further strengthened the argument in favour of considering the above diseases together.

The HLA, human leucocyte antigen system, is a classification based on antigens found on the surface membranes of human cells, which are determined by two closely linked genes. The identification of these antigens is by the use of a test such as the microlymphocytotoxic test. Many antigens may be recognized in this way, and when accepted internationally, are given the prefix HLA and assigned to a subdivision A or B as in HLA-B27 [3].

The antigen HLA-B27

Brewerton *et al* [4] demonstrated that 72 of 75 patients with idiopathic ankylosing spondylitis possessed the antigen HLA-B27 in their tissues, whereas only three of 75 controls possessed this antigen. There was no correlation between this disease and other histocompatibility antigens.

The study of the association of a disease with a particular tissue type was extended; Table 15.1 shows the findings with regard to HLA-B27 in members of the seronegative spondarthritides. From these data the central position of idiopathic ankylosing spondylitis is obvious. Only when there is radiological evidence of spondylitis in patients suffering from psoriasis, Crohn's disease or ulcerative colitis, is there a significant difference from the control group in the possession of HLA-B27.

It should be remembered also that at least 80 per cent of individuals, who possess the tissue type HLA-B27, have no clinical or radiological evidence of any disease whatsoever.

Table 15.1 Results of investigation of patients with seronegative spondarthritides with respect to presence of HLA-B27 in their histocompatibility system

Disease	*Percentage of patients in whom HLA-B27 is identified*		*Reference*
Idiopathic ankylosing spondylitis	96	(72/75)	Brewerton *et al* [4].
Psoriasis			
(i) Peripheral arthritis only	18	(3/17)	Bluestone *et al* [18].
(ii) Peripheral arthritis with spondylitis	35	(8/23)	
Reiter's disease	71	(15/21)	An Edinburgh series, previously unreported.
Chronic inflammatory bowel disease (ulcerative colitis and Crohn's disease)			
(i) without arthritis	0	(0/19)	
(ii) with peripheral arthritis only	0	(0/14)	
(iii) with spondylitis	67	(8/12)	
Whipple's disease	*		
Behçet's syndrome	*		
Controls	6		

*Insufficient data

AETIOLOGY

The cause of Reiter's disease, as indeed of all the members of the group of seronegative spondarthritides, is unknown.

In the United Kingdom, and in the United States of America, urethritis (usually non-gonococcal) is the condition which most often shows itself before other manifestations of the disease. Reiter's disease is an uncommon complication of non-gonococcal urethritis (less than 1 per cent of cases). On the continent of Europe, it is an attack of *Shigella* dysentery which usually precedes the appearance of the disease. In the famous study in Finland by Paronen [5] the incidence of Reiter's disease was 0.2 per cent (344 cases) following an epidemic of dysentery due to *Shigella flexneri.* In most countries, however, it is likely that both venereal and post-dysenteric forms coexist. Rarely amoebic dysentery has been followed by Reiter's disease.

The possible role of *Chlamydia* in the aetiology of non-gonococcal urethritis has been discussed (Chapter 13) and this organism has been isolated from the urethra and the conjunctiva of men with Reiter's disease [6].

Chlamydia has been isolated from the synovial fluid during the acute episode on rare instances. *Chlamydia* may also be isolated from the conjunctiva of patients from whom the organism may be cultured from the urethra or cervix, but who have neither conjunctivitis nor arthritis. Presumably the conjunctiva is infected from the genitalia by contaminated fingers. The significance of the finding of *Chlamydia* in the urethra or conjunctiva in patients with Reiter's disease is therefore uncertain. Recent serological investigations using the micro IF test suggest chlamydial infection in many cases of Reiter's disease, but again the significance of this finding is not clear [7].

It is possible that Reiter's disease results when a patient with a certain genetic constitution is infected with a particular micro-organism, the combination of factors producing complex immunological reactions resulting in the appearance of the disease.

Infection with *Yersinia enterocolitica* usually produces a mild gastro-intestinal illness, but uncommonly may be complicated by arthritis, including sacro-iliitis. In a recent study [8] about 90 per cent of patients who had arthritis were found to have HLA-B27 antigen, compared with only 15 per cent of patients with diarrhoea but no arthritis. It may be that individuals who have this antigen are more likely to develop arthritis on challenge with a particular organism.

CLINICAL FEATURES

Reiter's disease is a disorder of young adults, the age of onset usually being between 18 and 50 years. Very rarely children under the age of 12 are involved. Males are affected some fifty times more frequently than females.

The pre-patent period is variable, but the disease usually manifests itself 10 to 30 days after sexual intercourse or after an attack of dysentery. The mode of onset is variable, but commonly urethritis precedes the appearance of conjunctivitis which is followed by arthritis. Any of the three features, however, may appear initially.

The duration of the first attack of Reiter's disease varies from between two weeks and several years. In general (more than 70 per cent) first episodes resolve within 12 weeks.

At least 50 per cent of patients develop recurrences, the interval between the initial episode and the recurrence varying between three months and up to 36 years. With regard to producing a recurrence, certain precipitating factors, apart from dysentery and urethritis, have been identified and include surgical operations on the urinary tract.

Inflammation of the genito-urinary tract in the male

1. NON-GONOCOCCAL URETHRITIS (NGU)

Non-gonococcal urethritis is the most common form of urinary tract inflammation in this disease. Non-gonococcal urethritis is associated with the post-dysenteric form of the disease in about 70 per cent of cases [5]. In a series of 144 cases of Reiter's disease associated with urethritis, the urethritis associated with the initial episode was gonococcal in 17 per cent; non-gonococcal in 43 per cent; both gonococcal and non-gonococcal in 36 per cent and undiagnosed in 4 per cent [9].

In patients who have a mixed gonococcal and non-gonococcal urethritis a urethral discharge usually persists following treatment of the gonorrhoea with penicillin. Occasionally a patient who has had gonorrhoea and has been adequately treated, develops Reiter's disease but shows no evidence of post-gonococcal urethritis even on careful examination.

The clinical features of the associated non-gonococcal urethritis are identical to those of uncomplicated urethritis. As in the latter condition, the severity varies considerably. If untreated, the urethritis usually subsides after some two to four weeks, but occasionally may persist for several months.

During the recurrent episodes of Reiter's disease, there may be no clinical evidence of urinary tract inflammation. Csonka [9], who studied 156 recurrences of the disease, recorded urethritis in about 58 per cent of these. When urethritis is associated with a recurrence, it is most often non-gonococcal in nature, and an integral feature of the recurrence, rather than the apparently initiating factor of the first attack. It is clear, however, that in some patients reinfection with gonorrhoea or with NGU following sexual intercourse, may precipitate a recurrence of signs and symptoms of Reiter's disease. Urethritis resulting from reinfection may not always be followed by a recurrence.

2. CYSTITIS

Cystitis may be associated with Reiter's disease. This may be mild with relatively little inconvenience. Csonka [10] reports an incidence rate of some 20 per cent.

A much more severe, but fortunately rare, form of cystitis is that of acute haemorrhagic cystitis. This condition is characterized by the rapid onset of frequency of micturition, nocturia, strangury, urgency, haematuria and suprapubic or perineal pain, which may radiate to the penis or testes. Occasionally the patient may be ill with pyrexia, malaise and a polymorphonuclear leucocytosis. In some patients there may be a preceding urethritis [11]. The urine contains many leucocytes and red cells, but is sterile by conventional bacteriological examination.

Cystoscopy ought to be avoided during the acute stage but it has revealed oedema of the bladder mucosa (including the trigone), superficial membranous sloughs, diffuse petechial haemorrhages, and multiple discrete ulcers.

Intravenous urography in most cases of acute haemorrhagic cystitis shows unilateral or bilateral dilatation of the ureters and renal pelves and calyces. This is probably due to obstruction of the ureteric orifices by mucosal oedema, although in a few cases, the inflammatory process may extend proximally from the bladder. Following resolution of the cystitis, the hydronephrosis usually, but not always subsides, generally within two months.

Without treatment, haemorrhagic cystitis may persist for long periods, often with exacerbations and remissions. Haemorrhagic cystitis may occasionally precede by weeks or months the appearance of other features of the syndrome or may be the sole feature of a recurrence.

3. ACUTE PROSTATITIS

Acute prostatitis which may be followed by the formation of prostatic abscesses, has been described in Reiter's disease, but is excessively rare.

The incidence of 'chronic prostatitis' is difficult to determine as there is controversy as to how such a diagnosis is made. Chronic prostatitis has been defined as being present when there are 10 or more pus cells per high power field in samples of the expressed prostatic fluid examined as a wet film. Using this criterion, chronic prostatitis has been diagnosed in 95 per cent of cases of Reiter's disease [12]; (*see also* Chapter 14).

4. EPIDIDYMO-ORCHITIS

Epididymo-orchitis, probably secondary to concomitant non-gonococcal urethritis, occurs uncommonly (*see also* Chapter 14).

5. RENAL PARENCHYMAL INVOLVEMENT

Renal parenchymal involvement in Reiter's disease is a rarity [5].

Inflammation of the genito-urinary tract in the female

In the female, evidence of inflammation of the urinary tract and/or reproductive system is less obvious and less easily defined. Urethritis rarely shows a definite discharge because the urethra of the female is shorter, relative to the male. The occurrence of non-specific inflammation may show by cystitis, which may on occasion be haemorrhagic and of intense severity, vaginitis or cervicitis [13].

Ocular inflammation

The most common ocular manifestation of Reiter's disease is conjunctivitis (occurring in about 30 per cent of cases) which may be unilateral or more frequently bilateral. There is wide variation in the severity of the conjunctivitis, which ranges from a mild irritation with few objective signs to a severe inflammation with subconjunctival haemorrhage. Conjunctivitis resolves spontaneously between 7 days and 4 weeks, although occasionally may persist for several months. Mild *episcleritis* may be associated with conjunctivitis.

During a recurrent episode of the disease, and occasionally late in the course of an initial severe acute episode, *anterior uveitis* may develop in about 8 per cent of patients. This complication is usually confined to one eye, when the patient complains of gradual onset of pain and blurring of vision in that eye. On inspection the affected eye is red, particularly at the margin of the cornea, because there is congestion of anterior ciliary blood vessels. As a result of oedema, the normal pattern of the iris is obscured, the pupil is small, reacting poorly to light, and is irregular due to adhesions forming between the iris and the anterior surface of the lens.

It has been demonstrated that anterior uveitis occurs more commonly when a patient has radiological evidence of sacro-iliitis than when he does not. In one study [14] of 15 patients with Reiter's disease who also had anterior uveitis, 12 had sacro-iliitis.

In a patient with Reiter's disease, uveitis is frequently recurrent, and is often the sole manifestation of a recurrence, objective evidence of arthritis being found infrequently. Indeed, it may be the presenting feature of the disease and hence all young people with uveitis should be fully examined to determine the aetiology of the ocular inflammation.

Arthritis and other connective tissue disorders associated with Reiter's disease

ARTHRITIS

During the acute initial episode of Reiter's disease, some 95 per cent of patients develop symptoms of joint involvement. Although a number of patients (about 15 per cent) may complain of arthralgia without objective evidence of inflammation such as joint swelling, the majority develop acute arthritis. The histological appearance of the synovial membrane does not present a characteristic pattern, being indistinguishable from that of rheumatoid arthritis.

There is rapid onset of pain in, and swelling of, the affected joint, and there is limitation of movement. The skin overlying the joint may be reddened. There is thickening of the joint capsule and evidence of effusion into the joint. Atrophy of the muscles adjacent to the joint develops rapidly.

Although occasionally only one joint, usually the knee, may be affected, Reiter's disease is most commonly associated with polyarthritis (more than 95 per cent of cases), with asymmetrical involvement of the peripheral large joints. The incidence of joint involvement during the initial episode of Reiter's disease in 50 cases is illustrated in Table 15.2. The joints of the lower limbs are predominantly affected. Usually the arthritis does not involve the joints simultaneously, as there is generally an interval of some days between one joint and another becoming inflamed. After reaching maximum severity, 10 to 14 days after its onset, the arthritis gradually resolves, but recovery may be punctuated by acute exacerbations, perhaps associated with recrudescence of other manifestations of the disease.

Table 15.2 Incidence of arthritis occurring during the initial episode of Reiter's disease (Data from 50 cases, 48 in men and 2 in women)

Joint involved	*Number (and percentage) of patients*	
Temporomandibular	1	(2)
Acromioclavicular	1	(2)
Shoulder	5	(10)
Sternoclavicular	2	(4)
Elbow	5	(10)
Wrist	12	(24)
Carpometacarpal	9	(18)
Metacarpophalangeal, Interphalangeal	14	(28)
Sacro-iliac	5	(10)
Hip	9	(18)
Knee	40	(80)
Ankle	32	(64)
Tarsometatarsal	10	(20)
Metatarsophalangeal	2	(4)
Interphalangeal	18	(36)

Following the acute arthritis of the initial episode, there may be no clinical evidence of joint damage. In some cases, with each recurrent episode of arthritis, permanent damage is done to the joint which may ultimately show the features of chronic arthritis. Uncommonly in less than 5 per cent of cases, following the initial episode of arthritis, resolution of the inflammatory process is incomplete, and chronic arthritis rapidly develops in the affected joints. The patient complains of pain, stiffness and swelling of the joint, the severity of symptoms being subject to exacerbations and remissions. Deformity is the ultimate fate of joints affected in this way. Most frequently it is the joints of the lower limbs, and the sacro-iliac joints which bear the brunt of chronic arthritis in this disease. Generally, as chronic arthritis develops, other manifestations of the disease become less obvious. with the possible exception of anterior uveitis.

In a disease in which there may be periods of activity separated by long periods of apparent quiescence, it is not possible to give an accurate prognosis after a single episode of Reiter's disease. In a study of 100 patients who had suffered from Reiter's disease some 20 years previously, 18 per cent had chronic arthritis [15] .

As a rare complication, *spontaneous rupture of a joint,* usually the knee joint, may occur. It is considered that joint rupture occurs from a cystic formation in the popliteal fossa. There is sudden onset of pain in the calf and examination reveals a swollen leg which feels warm, the signs resembling thrombophlebitis, which may also occur during the course of Reiter's disease (*see* below). Arthrography is of great value in differentiating between the two conditions [16].

Radiology of joints in Reiter's disease

In the early stages of an acute episode of Reiter's disease, no radiological abnormalities may be observed, or there may be non-specific, reversible changes such as thickening of the peri-articular tissues [17]. If the inflammatory process is mild, no further changes may occur, but as the disease progresses, radiological abnormalities develop in at least one joint in more than 40 per cent of cases. These changes are most noticeable in the joints and bones of the lower limbs, especially the feet and in the sacro-iliac joints.

Destructive lesions ('erosions') are found at the periphery of the articular surface of the affected joint, and appear as small well-demarcated areas of bone destruction. As the condition progresses, the area of destruction increases and the articular surface of the joint is eventually destroyed, with radiological narrowing of the joint space. Erosions are most commonly found in the metatarsal, tarsal and interphalangeal joints of the feet, and on the posterior aspect of the calcaneum.

In cases where radiological abnormalities are found, periostitis is frequent. Most commonly the periostitis affects the neck of the metatarsals and metacarpals, the distal parts of the tibia, fibula and the shafts of the proximal phalanges. It appears on X-ray as a thin linear opacity running parallel to the cortex of the bone. In the bones of the tarsus and carpus the sharp outline of the bone may be replaced by an irregular contour.

Periostitis affecting the calcaneum is a common radiological finding, occurring in more than 50 per cent of cases [17]. The changes involve the postero-lateral and plantar aspects of the bone. In chronic cases, as periosteal new bone is formed on the plantar surface of the calcaneum at the insertion of the plantar fascia, a 'spur' develops. This has a characteristic 'fluffy' appearance due to the diffuse nature of the periostitis.

Plantar spurs of a different character may be found in normal individuals, in those suffering from osteoarthrosis, in rheumatoid arthritis and in ankylosing spondylitis. These spurs representing ossification at the site of attachment of plantar ligaments are clearly defined and not associated with changes beyond the base of the spur.

Interpretation of radiographs of the sacro-iliac joints is often difficult, as some asymmetry of the joints is common, and leads to differences in appearance of the joints. Sacro-iliitis is found in about 50 per cent of cases, most frequently in recurrent cases, the incidence rising with duration of the disease. It is manifest radiologically as loss of the normal outline of the joint, irregularity of the joint margins due to erosions, and sclerosis beyond the area of the erosion. Although sometimes unilateral (less than 20 per cent), these changes are usually seen in both joints. Complete obliteration of the joint, as is seen in ankylosing spondylitis, is uncommon, but when it occurs, is indistinguishable from that condition. Occasionally, radiological changes, in the form of narrowing of joint-space, irregularity of the joint margin and ossification of joint ligaments, may be noted in the symphysis pubis.

Spinal changes may be noted uncommonly in Reiter's disease. Syndesmophytosis (i.e., the appearance of strips of bone joining adjacent vertebrae) occurs in cases of longstanding Reiter's disease. Rarely radiological changes indistinguishable from those found in ankylosing spondylitis are found in Reiter's disease.

In the chronic arthritis of Reiter's disease, joint deformities such as lateral dislocation of the proximal phalanges on the metatarsals may be noted on X-ray.

PLANTAR FASCIITIS

Clinical evidence of plantar fasciitis is found in about 20 per cent of patients suffering an acute episode of the disease. The patient complains of pain in the sole of the foot. In the most severely affected cases, the skin overlying the fascia is reddened and swollen. More commonly, there is only tenderness of the fascia, particularly close to the heel. Although usually involving both feet, one may be more severely affected than the other. Plantar fasciitis generally resolves within several weeks of its onset, but occasionally may be very persistent.

TENDONITIS AND BURSITIS

Although any tendon and its synovial sheath may become inflamed during the course of Reiter's disease, the tendo calcaneus most often produces clinical signs (about 10 per cent of cases in the acute stage).

Tendonitis is most often accompanied by adjacent bone or joint disease.

Rarely inflammation of bursae, especially the pre-patella bursa may occur during the acute stages of the disease. On a radiograph tendonitis and tenosynovitis may appear as a broad soft tissue shadow.

Lesions of the skin and mucous membranes

These lesions become manifest four to six weeks after the onset of the urethritis. Histological examination of the mucocutaneous lesions of Reiter's disease shows hyperkeratosis, acanthosis with elongation and hypertrophy of the rete pegs, and parakeratosis. Over the dermal papillae the epidermis is thinned. Polymorphonuclear leucocytes migrate into the epidermis and, with lysis of the superficial layers of the Malpighian layer, micro-abscesses form. The underlying dermis becomes infiltrated with lymphocytes and plasma cells.

This subacute inflammatory process is common to all the mucocutaneous lesions, but varying degrees of keratosis account for the different macroscopic appearances of these lesions. Hyperkeratosis is most prominent in lesions of the palms and soles, less so in dry penile lesions, and absent in oral and moist penile plaques [19].

SKIN LESIONS

Keratoderma blenorrhagica is the typical skin lesion found in Reiter's disease, occurring in about 10 per cent of cases. Although the soles of the feet are most commonly affected, keratoderma may also occur anywhere on the body (dorsa of the feet, palms, extensor surfaces of the legs and forearms, trunk, scalp, scrotum, shaft of penis, umbilicus) and occasionally presents as a generalized skin rash.

The initial lesion is a brown macule 2–4mm in diameter which rapidly becomes papular. The centre of the papule becomes pustular, and the roof becomes thickened. Increase in size occurs from the accumulation of parakeratotic scales on the surface of the lesion, and lateral growth of the base. This is the typical limpet-like lesion of keratoderma. Most commonly, the skin manifestations of Reiter's disease are less florid, and few typical keratoderma lesions are noted. In such cases, the occurrence of pustular lesions on the soles may be the only skin lesions found, and these subside generally within 3–4 weeks of their appearance. On the weight-bearing areas of the soles, lateral spread of the pustule produces a thick-walled bulla. Generally lesions on the trunk, arms, legs and shaft of penis are less typical, and consist of firm, dull-red papules (the hard parakeratotic nodule).

Keratoderma usually heals within 6 to 10 weeks from its onset, but may occasionally take much longer. 'Cropping' is characteristic during the course of an acute episode, various stages of development of the lesions of keratoderma being present at the same time.

Although the physical appearance of keratoderma may cause the patient mental distress, the lesions themselves do not usually produce discomfort, unless there is secondary bacterial infection.

The finger and toe nails may be involved in Reiter's disease. In mild cases, the nail plate becomes opaque, thickened, ridged and brittle. When the nails are more severely affected, in addition to the latter changes, sterile, subungual abscesses develop and as these dry out yellow debris accumulates under the distal half of the nail. As this process continues, the nail becomes elevated from its bed, turns brown and is often shed. The skin adjacent to the nail base, and the nail fold takes part in the reaction. These changes may be mistaken for fungal infection of the nails.

The Köebner phenomenon* has been described as occurring in Reiter's disease.

ORAL LESIONS

Lesions of the mucous membranes of the buccal cavity occur in about 10 per cent of cases of Reiter's disease. The most common site affected is the palate, followed by the buccal mucosa, gingiva, and tongue. Such lesions are asymptomatic and have to be looked for carefully. Generally they heal within a few weeks of their appearance.

On the palate the lesions usually appear as whitish slightly elevated macules, not covered by inflammatory exudate, and surrounded by a narrow erythematous zone. Occasionally, multiple purpuric spots may appear.

Similar lesions may be noted on the buccal mucosa. On the tongue, round or oval reddened areas appear ('bald' patches), sharply demarcated from the surrounding normal epithelium (Plate 8).

PENILE LESIONS

Reference has already been made to keratoderma of the shaft of the penis and the outer aspect of the prepuce. Lesions may also be found in

***Köebner phenomenon.* Non-specific trauma induces skin changes in the affected site of a type present at the same time elsewhere on the body. The Köebner phenomenon is found in many skin diseases e.g. psoriasis, lichen planus, warts [20].

about 25 per cent of cases on the glans penis and on the mucous surface of the prepuce, which usually precede other mucocutaneous manifestations.

On the glans, the appearance of the lesion depends on whether or not the individual has been circumcised. If he is circumcised, the lesions are dry and appear as slightly elevated scaling macules sharply demarcated from the surrounding skin. When a prepuce is present, scale formation is inhibited, and the lesions appear as moist, glistening, red, sharply-defined macules which become confluent, producing a polycyclic margin known as circinate balanitis. Unless there is secondary bacterial infection, which is a common complication, pain is absent, and healing tends to occur within 4 weeks of the appearance of the lesions.

Visceral lesions of Reiter's disease

Clinical evidence of involvement of organs of the body, other than those previously mentioned, is uncommon. It is quite possible that, in a disease with such a broad spectrum of symptoms and signs, many organs are involved in the inflammatory process, without producing obvious abnormalities clinically.

Cardiovascular system

1. PERICARDITIS

This occurs uncommonly (less than 5 per cent) during an acute episode of Reiter's disease. The patient may or may not have chest pain when there is pericarditis [21].

2. MYOCARDITIS

The incidence of myocarditis is difficult to determine, but is less than 5 per cent.

The most common finding is first degree heart block, i.e., a P-R interval of greater than 0.20 seconds. Rarely other conduction defects such as second degree heart block, left bundle-branch block and complete heart block, occur.

Although usually transient, these ECG abnormalities may persist unchanged for years, or one abnormality may supervene on another [22].

3. AORTITIS

This is a rare complication, having been adequately described in the literature in fewer than 30 patients. It is usually associated with recurrent episodes of the disease which has been present for at least eight years, with sacro-iliitis and with conduction defects [23]. Aortic incompetence is the usual presenting feature.

4. THROMBOPHLEBITIS OF THE DEEP VEINS OF THE LEG

This may be found during an acute episode of Reiter's disease in about 3 per cent of cases [24]. Patients complain of pain in the affected calf and there is tenderness, induration of the calf muscles, and oedema of the leg. Thrombophlebitis occurs within a few days of the onset of the arthritis and the knee joint on the affected side is always involved.

The most important condition to be distinguished from thrombophlebitis is spontaneous rupture of the knee joint (*see* page 247). Arthrography, ultrasonic examination of the veins of the calf, and venography are useful aids to diagnosis.

Respiratory system

Pleurisy has been described as occurring in the acute stages of Reiter's disease, having been found in about 8 per cent of cases described by Paronen [5]. Transient opacities may be observed on chest radiographs of patients, but their significance is uncertain [25].

Reticulo-endothelial system

Generalized enlargement of lymph nodes has been observed uncommonly in Reiter's disease (less than 1 per cent of cases). Histological examination reveals non-specific reactive hyperplasia. Rarely there is moderate enlargement of the spleen.

Nervous system

Various neurological abnormalities have been described in association with Reiter's disease, but these are seen in less than 2 per cent of cases. Meningo-encephalitis, multiple peripheral neuropathy, amyotrophic lateral sclerosis have been well documented as occurring during an acute episode of the disease, occasionally reappearing during recurrences [26].

In long-standing cases of Reiter's disease, the occurrence of Parkinsonism and other neuro-psychiatric abnormalities is difficult to evaluate, as these disorders also affect the general population [27].

Amyloidosis

This is a very rare complication of severe Reiter's disease, having been described in only two cases [28].

Laboratory tests in Reiter's disease

There is no diagnostic test for Reiter's disease, but the investigations given aid differential diagnosis:

BLOOD

1. Haemoglobin concentration, packed cell volume (PCV), mean corpuscular haemoglobin concentration (MCHC) and mean corpuscular volume (MCV)

In severe cases, the results of these tests indicate mild normocytic, normochromic anaemia, i.e., the haemoglobin concentration is less than 13.5g/dl but the MCV is normal (76–96fl; fl ≡ femtolitre ≡ μm^3) as is the MCHC (30–35g/dl).

2. White cell count

In the acute episode of Reiter's disease, there is a polymorphonuclear leucocytosis (i.e. a white cell count of greater than $11.0 \times 10^9/1$) in 25 to 30 per cent of cases.

3. Erythrocyte sedimentation rate (ESR)

This is elevated in more than 90 per cent of cases of acute Reiter's disease, being in the early stages greater than 50mm per hour (Westergren) in about 40 per cent of cases. The ESR falls slowly during the first month of the acute episode, and, although becoming normal by about the sixth to tenth week after the onset, may remain elevated in about 15 per cent of patients for much longer.

4. Plasma-protein changes

During the acute episode in about 30 per cent of cases the plasma albumin is lower than normal, and the alpha globulin fraction elevated. There is only slight elevation in the gamma globulin fraction. In the acute stage, serum IgM may be raised, but falls to normal as the inflammatory process resolves.

5. Rheumatoid factor

The incidence of rheumatoid factor in the normal population is about 4 per cent and in Reiter's disease the incidence is similar. The rheumatoid arthritis latex particle agglutination test and the sheep red cell agglutination tests are usually negative (96 per cent) in Reiter's disease. Although these tests for IgM rheumatoid factor are usually negative, IgG antiglobulin may be demonstrated in the serum of patients with Reiter's disease.

6. Anti-streptolysin O titre

The results of this test are within normal limits (less than 200 units per ml).

7. LE cells and anti-nuclear antibodies

These tests are usually negative.

8. Uric acid

The differential diagnosis from gout may be difficult in 2 per cent of cases of Reiter's disease when the serum uric acid is elevated.

9. Smooth-muscle antibody

This may be detected in about 50 per cent of cases, and it should be noted that this test is not specific for active chronic hepatitis.

SYNOVIAL FLUID

Joint aspiration need only be performed if the diagnosis is in doubt, or if there is considerable discomfort from a large effusion. Fluid aspirated from an affected joint is yellow and turbid, clotting spontaneously. The white cell count varies considerably from 1000 to 5000 × 10^6/l. The normal white cell count is less than 200 × 10^6/l. Although the inflammatory exudate is initially composed mainly of polymorphonuclear leucocytes, as the duration of the arthritis increases, lymphocytes predominate.

The protein content of the fluid is high, about 40 to 50g/l (normal–10 to 20g/l). Synovial fluid glucose concentration is low (about 4.2mmol/l) in about a third of patients. The total haemolytic complement activity in synovial fluid in Reiter's disease is normal or high (cf. rheumatoid arthritis where it is low). Recently, complement deposits have been demonstrated in the synovium.

STUDIES OF CELLULAR IMMUNOLOGY

When sensitive methods to detect alteration of cellular immunity are performed, aberrant immunity to IgG is shown in about 40 per cent of cases of Reiter's disease.

Reference has already been made to the results of tissue typing of patients with this disease (page 239).

Differential diagnosis of the acute episode of Reiter's disease

Although the diagnosis is clear when all three features of the triad are present, when there are only one or two signs, the following diseases must be considered in the differential diagnosis.

GONOCOCCAL ARTHRITIS

This is the disease with which Reiter's disease is most often confused. Both conditions have urethritis and arthritis in common. In any urethritis it is important to exclude the gonococcus, but it should be remembered that there may be dissemination of this organism from the pharynx or rectum, in the absence of urethral infection.

In gonococcal arthritis isolation of *N. gonorrhoeae* from the synovial fluid is often unsuccessful.

The skin lesions of the bacteriaemic stage of a disseminated gonococcal infection should not be confused with keratoderma.

Urethral gonorrhoea may be a precipitating factor in Reiter's disease and immediate differentiation may be difficult. Within two to three days of commencing antibiotic treatment, however, a gonococcal arthritis will have improved considerably, whereas improvement does not necessarily occur in Reiter's disease.

RHEUMATOID ARTHRITIS

This disease is more commonly found in females, and usually presents in middle age. In contrast to Reiter's disease, the onset tends to be insidious and joints are affected in a symmetrical fashion. Any synovial joint may be involved, but particularly the metacarpophalangeal (80 per cent), wrist (85 per cent), elbow (70 per cent), metatarsophalangeal (70 per cent) and knee joints (80 per cent). Although sacro-iliitis may be demonstrated radiologically, the appearances are rarely as striking as those found in Reiter's disease. Chronic prostatitis may be diagnosed in about 20 per cent of males with rheumatoid disease. Anterior uveitis may occur in about 20 per cent of patients. Rheumatoid factor is present in the serum in at least 80 per cent of patients. Subcutaneous nodules which occur in 30 per cent of cases of rheumatoid arthritis are never found in Reiter's disease.

RHEUMATIC FEVER

Although usually preceded by pharyngitis, a proportion (up to 30 per cent) of patients with rheumatic fever do not give this history. The onset of arthritis, which is usually polyarticular, is acute, when large joints are chiefly affected. Classically the arthritis is migratory, affected joints returning to normal within a few days of the onset. Joints, however, may remain inflamed for weeks.

Erythema marginatum is found in about 10 per cent of children affected, and in severe cases, subcutaneous nodules of various sizes may be found. Erythema nodosum may also be associated with rheumatic fever.

Ocular and urinary tract inflammation do not occur. Serum anti-streptolysin O titres rise above normal limits in 80 per cent of patients with rheumatic fever.

ACUTE SEPTIC ARTHRITIS (EXCEPTING GONOCOCCAL ARTHRITIS)

This may be caused by numerous organisms, e.g., *Staphylococcus aureus, Streptococcus pyogenes, Neisseria meningitidis, Salmonella* spp., *Streptococcus pneumoniae.*

Any joint may become inflamed, but most often the knee, wrist and elbow are affected. Aspiration of the effusion, with appropriate bacteriological examination of the aspirated fluid, is usually diagnostic.

YERSINIA ARTHRITIS

Infection with *Yersinia enterocolitica* usually produces mild gastro-intestinal tract disturbances, such as fever, diarrhoea and abdominal pain. It is uncommonly complicated by the appearance of a flitting polyarthritis, affecting most often the joints of the lower limbs. There may in addition be radiological evidence of sacro-iliitis. The majority of patients with yersinia arthritis have HLA-B27 in their tissue type. Diagnosis is by examining sera for antibodies against flagellar antigen [29].

TUBERCULOUS ARTHRITIS

In the United Kingdom this is a rare disease, encountered most commonly in the elderly. The onset is insidious and most often the arthritis is mono-articular. Synovial biopsy, with bacteriological and histological examination is necessary for diagnosis.

BRUCELLOSIS

Bone and joints are frequently affected in this disease. Peripheral arthritis, sacro-iliitis and spondylitis occur. The arthritis may affect any joint, but commonly the shoulders, knees, and elbows. Sacro-iliitis occurs in about 30 per cent of patients, and may affect one or both sides.

In a patient with arthritis, particularly if there has been contact with farm animals, the following serological tests for brucellosis should be done to exclude this infection: a standard agglutination test, the anti-human globulin (Coombs') test for non-agglutinating antibodies and the complement fixation test.

TRAUMA

Non-gonococcal urethritis is common in young men, and it is not uncommon to find urethritis in association with a traumatized joint.

ERYTHEMA MULTIFORME AND STEVENS–JOHNSON SYNDROME

Erythema multiforme is a self-limiting skin disease associated in many cases with some underlying condition, such as herpes simplex infection or drug idiosyncrasy. When severe, the condition is termed Stevens-Johnson syndrome and is associated with mucous membrane ulceration (oral and genital), bullous lesions of the skin, conjunctivitis and arthritis.

SYSTEMIC LUPUS ERYTHEMATOSUS (SLE)

Usually females are affected by this condition. LE cells and antinuclear factor are found in the blood.

OTHER SERONEGATIVE SPONDARTHRITIDES

Acute arthritis may be associated with ankylosing spondylitis, psoriatic arthritis, ulcerative colitis, Crohn's disease, Behçet's syndrome and Whipple's disease. The relationships of these conditions require separate consideration and may be important in the differential diagnosis, particularly of the chronic episode of arthritis.

Differential diagnosis of the chronic episode of Reiter's disease

IDIOPATHIC ANKYLOSING SPONDYLITIS

Ankylosing spondylitis and Reiter's disease share many features. Both are associated with a peripheral arthritis: about 98 per cent in Reiter's disease and about 60 per cent in ankylosing spondylitis. Sacro-iliitis is found in all patients with ankylosing spondylitis and in at least 50 per cent of cases of Reiter's disease in the chronic stages. Spinal involvement may occur in Reiter's disease, when the radiological appearance may be indistinguishable from ankylosing spondylitis. Rarely, those with all the manifestations of Reiter's disease develop the features of idiopathic ankylosing spondylitis later in life.

Evidence of inflammation of the urinary or reproductive system is found in all patients with Reiter's disease, and, as 'chronic prostatitis', in at least 80 per cent of cases of ankylosing spondylitis. Anterior uveitis, too, is a complication of about 20 per cent of cases of both conditions and aortitis is a rare complication of both.

Idiopathic ankylosing spondylitis is not usually associated with keratoderma or other mucocutaneous lesions.

PSORIATIC ARTHRITIS

This is the disease to which Reiter's disease bears a most striking resemblance. Psoriasis may uncommonly be associated with a sero-negative, radiologically-erosive polyarthritis (about 5 per cent of cases). Except in those patients with distal interphalangeal joint involvement the anatomical distribution of joints affected by arthritis is not a helpful factor in reaching a diagnosis. Radiological evidence of sacro-iliitis is found also in at least 20 per cent of patients with psoriatic arthritis.

There are close clinical and histological similarities between pustular psoriasis and keratoderma blennorhagica and also the occurrence of peripheral arthritis and sacro-iliitis is shared in the two conditions, so separation of psoriatic arthritis from Reiter's disease is not possible on every occasion. Not uncommonly, the features of one condition may predominate over the other. Sometimes, patients, diagnosed as suffering from psoriatic arthritis, may develop the later manifestations of Reiter's disease, and vice versa [30, 31].

ULCERATIVE COLITIS, CROHN'S DISEASE, WHIPPLE'S DISEASE AND BEHÇET'S DISEASE

These conditions share with Reiter's disease peripheral arthritis, sacro-iliitis, anterior uveitis and diarrhoea. The skin and oral lesions tend to be somewhat different clinically and histologically from keratoderma and the oral lesions of Reiter's disease. Table 15.3 shows the comparative incidence of these abnormalities in this group.

Table 15.3 Incidence of common features in Reiter's disease and four members of the group of seronegative spondarthritides

Disease	*Percentage incidence*					
	Peripheral arthritis	*Sacro-iliitis*	*Anterior uveitis*	*Diarrhoea*	*Skin lesions*	*Oral lesions*
Reiter's disease	97	50	8	*	10	10
Ulcerative colitis	10	20	5	80	2	15
Crohn's disease	5	20	5	50	2	10
Whipple's disease	65	20	0	90	†	†
Behcet's disease	45	†	70	40	80	98

*Incidence varies according to whether Reiter's disease follows urethritis or dysentery.
†Insufficient data.

Familial aggregation

WITHIN REITER'S DISEASE ITSELF

Familial aggregation has been observed in both post-dysenteric type Reiter's disease and the type associated with urethritis. It is difficult to be certain whether accumulation of cases within families is due to genetic factors or infectious agents or both.

BETWEEN REITER'S DISEASE AND OTHER MEMBERS OF THE GROUP

It has been shown that psoriasis is fourteen times more common in male relatives of Reiter's disease patients than in the general population. Clinical ankylosing spondylitis is eight times, and radiologically bilateral sacro-iliitis three times, as frequent in male relatives of patients with Reiter's disease, as in the general population [32].

Treatment

At present, treatment for Reiter's disease is not curative but is aimed at relieving symptoms. When the patient first attends, the course of the disease should be fully explained to him. He should be told particularly that the acute episode may last for at least six weeks, but that sometimes it may last for twice as long.

URETHRITIS

The management of non-gonococcal urethritis has already been discussed (page 217). The presence of the complication of Reiter's disease does not alter the general approach. Although of value in aiding resolution of urethritis, treatment with a tetracycline does not alter the course of the disease.

CONJUNCTIVITIS

This is a self-limiting condition, generally resolving within a few weeks of its onset. Although the use of topical steroid preparations may produce symptomatic relief, it is generally agreed that they should be withheld to prevent a possible viral keratitis.

IRITIS

In the management of this complication advice should be obtained from an ophthalmologist. Mydriasis is maintained by the use of atropine sulphate eye drops, BPC, 1 per cent w/v twice daily, with phenylephrine eye drops, BPC, three times daily. Dilatation of the pupil produces relief of pain and reduces the risk of the development of iris adhesions.

Steroids should be applied topically for example in the form of betamethasone eye drops, BPC, three or four times daily.

ARTHRITIS

During the acute stage of the illness when the joints are markedly inflamed, bed rest is advisable. It is of great importance to ensure that the correct posture is assumed during this period of rest [33]. The patient should be nursed on a firm mattress, with adequate support given for his back. A bed cage to keep the weight of the bed clothes off the lower limbs is useful. Pillows must not be placed behind the knees, as this favours the development of flexion deformities.

Local immobilization of an affected joint by means of a plaster of Paris splint, held in place by a bandage, may be a useful aid in relieving the patient's discomfort. Gentle active movement of the joint twice daily reduces the risk of stiffness developing in the splinted joint. By supervising these exercises, a physiotherapist can help with the patient's management.

Various analgesics and anti-inflammatory drugs have been used in the management of the arthritis of Reiter's disease. A few drugs with which the authors have had experience are mentioned below.

1. Aspirin and salicylates

The dosage of aspirin must be determined by trial and error, the minimum dose effective in relieving the pain being used. To maintain adequate blood levels of the drug, four-hourly oral administration is necessary. The total daily dose varies between 3g and 6g.

Side effects of aspirin are common, and dyspepsia is the most common complaint (at least 30 per cent of patients).

Aspirin administration may result in chronic gastrointestinal bleeding, and rarely acute massive haemorrhage. The use of salicylates should be avoided in all patients with a history of peptic ulceration.

Hypersensitivity reactions to aspirin are very rare.

2. Indomethacin

This is a powerful analgesic and anti-inflammatory agent. The dosage is 25mg three times daily by mouth. To relieve morning stiffness, a suppository, containing 100mg indomethacin may be useful.

The side effects of this drug are dose-related and include headache, especially in the morning, dizziness, tinnitus, drug rashes, nausea and anorexia. Occasionally gastrointestinal haemorrhage from a peptic ulcer has occurred and sometimes even perforation.

3. Phenylbutazone

This is also a powerful analgesic and anti-inflammatory agent. There are many side effects of this drug, including peptic ulceration with perforation, and gastrointestinal haemorrhage, blood dyscrasias, skin rashes and oedema. The usual initial dosage in Reiter's disease is 100mg three times per day orally. This can be reduced to 100mg twice daily after three to five days.

It is recommended that when a patient is seen with mild arthritis, aspirin should be used initially, and if there is a poor response to this drug, one of the other agents employed. In more severe cases, indomethacin or phenylbutazone may be required from the start, and continued until the inflammatory process begins to abate. Aspirin may then be substituted for these agents.

The use of corticosteroid preparations, such as prednisolone, is rarely necessary, most cases responding to the measures already outlined. When posterior uveitis or symptomatic pericarditis occur, specialist advice should be sought as steroids are indicated. The use of intra-articular steroids is not indicated in the majority of cases of Reiter's disease.

Unless considered necessary as an aid to diagnosis, or to relieve the symptoms of a tense effusion, aspiration of the joint is not usually necessary.

CIRCINATE BALANITIS

This condition usually resolves spontaneously within a few weeks of its onset, but healing may be facilitated by the use of a topical steroid preparation, combined with an antimicrobial agent, e.g. betamethasone ointment with clioquinol (Betnovate-C) applied twice daily.

When there is secondary bacterial infection, the use of local saline lavages, and dressings soaked in normal saline applied to the glans, are of value.

KERATODERMA BLENORRHAGICA

There is no specific treatment for this self-limiting manifestation. The skin should be kept dry.

THROMBOPHLEBITIS

The use of a supporting stocking and anti-inflammatory drugs (e.g., phenylbutazone) is sufficient to produce relief of symptoms. Patients with this complication should not be immobilized longer than necessary to reduce the possibility of phlebothrombosis developing in the deep veins of the calf.

REFERENCES

1 Reiter, H (1916) *Deutsche Medizinische Wochenschrift,* **42,** 1535

2 Moll, J M H, Haslock, I, MacRae, I F and Wright, V (1974) *Medicine,* **53,** 343

3 Oliver, R T D (1977) *British Journal of Hospital Medicine,* **18,** 449

4 Brewerton, D A, Caffrey, M, Hart, F D, James, D C O, Nicholls, A and Sturrock, R D (1973) *Lancet,* **i,** 904

5 Paronen, I (1948) *Acta Medica Scandinavica,* **131,** Suppl. 212

6 Gordon, F N, Quan, A L, Steinman, T E and Philip, R W (1973) *British Journal of Venereal Diseases,* **49,** 376

7 Dwyer, R St C, Treharne, J D, Jones, B R and Herring, J (1972) *British Journal of Venereal Diseases,* **48,** 452

8 Aho, K, Ahvonen, P, Lassus, A, Sievers, K and Tiilikainen, A (1974) *Arthritis and Rheumatism,* **17,** 521

9 Csonka, G W (1960) Recurrent attacks in Reiter's disease. *Arthritis and Rheumatism,* **3,** 164

10 Csonka, G W (1965) *Ergebnisse der Inneren Medizin und Kinderheilkunde,* **23,** 139

11 Berg, R L, Weinberger, H and Dienes, L (1957) *American Journal of Medicine,* **22,** 818

12 Mason, R M, Murray, R S, Oates, J K and Young, A C (1958) *British Medical Journal,* **1,** 748

13 Oates, J K and Csonka, G W (1959) *Annals of Rheumatic Diseases,* **18,** 37

14 Oates, J K and Young, A C (1959) *British Medical Journal,* **1,** 1013

15 Sairanen, E, Paronen, I and Mähönen, H (1969) *Acta Medica Scandinavica,* **185**, 57
16 Garner, R W and Mowat, A G (1972) *British Journal of Surgery,* **59**, 657
17 Murray, R S, Oates, J K and Young, A C (1958) *Journal of the Faculty of Radiologists,* **9**, 37
18 Bluestone, R, Morris, R I, Metzger, A L and Terasaki, P I (1975) *Annals of Rheumatic Diseases,* **34**, Suppl. pages 31
19 Kulka, J P (1964) *Arthritis and Rheumatism,* **5**, 195
20 Rook, A and Wilkinson, D S (1972) in *Textbook of Dermatology* 2nd ed. (Eds) Rook A, Wilkinson, D S and Ebling, F J G. Blackwell Scientific Publications, Oxford and Edinburgh, page 43
21 Csonka, G W and Oates, J K (1957) *British Medical Journal,* **1**, 867
22 Rossen, R M, Goodman, D J and Harrison, D C (1975) *American Journal of Medicine,* **58**, 280
23 Block, S R (1972) *Arthritis and Rheumatism,* **15**, 218
24 Csonka, G W (1966) *British Journal of Venereal Diseases,* **42**, 93
25 Gatler, R A and Moskowitz, R W (1962) *Diseases of the Chest,* **42**, 433
26 Oates, J K and Hancock, J A H (1959) *American Journal of Medical Sciences,* **238**, 79
27 Good, A E (1974) Reiter's disease: A review with special attention to cardiovascular and neurologic sequelae. *Seminars in Arthritis and Rheumatism,* **3**, 253
28 Caughey, D E and Wakem, C J (1973) *Arthritis and Rheumatism,* **16**, 695
29 Leading Article (1975) *British Medical Journal,* **2**, 404
30 Wright, V and Reed, W B (1964) *Annals of Rheumatic Diseases,* **23**, 12
31 Maxwell, J D, Greig, W R, Boyle, J A, Pasieczny, T and Schofield, C B S (1966) *Scottish Medical Journal,* **11**, 14
32 Lawrence, J (1974) *British Journal of Venereal Diseases,* **50**, 140
33 Boyle, J A and Buchanan, W W (1971) *Clinical Rheumatology.* Blackwell Scientific Publications, Oxford and Edinburgh

CHAPTER 16

Pelvic Inflammatory Disease

Pelvic inflammatory disease, in its acute form, is mainly a disease of sexually-active young women and usually results from an ascending microbial infection of the cervix and uterus. In pathogenesis and in prognosis with regard to fertility it differs from pelvic inflammatory disease arising as a sequel to previous surgical manipulation. Although inflammation of the uterine tubes (salpingitis) is clinically the most prominent feature, the supporting structures of the uterus share in the inflammation to a greater or lesser extent so pelvic inflammatory disease (PID) is strictly the more accurate term and may be used synonymously.

Aetiology

The complexity of the vaginal flora and the inaccessibility of the organs affected make it difficult to determine which organism(s) is (are) aetiologically responsible for pelvic inflammatory disease [1]. With the exception of *Neisseria gonorrhoeae,* it has not yet been possible to prove a causative relationship between organisms found in the cervical flora and those recovered from the fallopian tubes; for this reason it is convenient to classify the condition either as gonococcal or non-gonococcal PID, a diagnosis based on the presence or absence of *N. gonorrhoeae* in the cervical culture. It is not always possible to determine the aetiology because it would be necessary to obtain cultures directly from the uterine tubes at laparoscopy or laparotomy, or from the pelvic peritoneal fluid by culdocentesis.

GONOCOCCAL PELVIC INFLAMMATORY DISEASE

Salpingitis or, more strictly, PID is a complication in about 10 per cent of women with untreated gonorrhoea [2, 3], the exact figure for incidence depending on the criteria used for diagnosis, the population group studied and accessibility to medical care. As already stated, *N. gonorrhoeae* is the only pathogen for which recovery from the endocervix is correlated with recovery from the fallopian tubes [4]. Even in this case the correlation is not good since the gonococcus is isolated from the uterine tubes in only about 10 per cent of women with untreated gonorrhoea and salpingitis. This low recovery rate might be explained by a bactericidal action of the inflammatory exudate, or by a possibility that some other micro-organism is responsible. *Chlamydia trachomatis* may be isolated from the endocervix of about 40 per cent of women with untreated gonorrhoea [5], but, although *Chlamydia* may play a part in the aetiology of PID [6] the role of this organism in the aetiology of PID associated with gonorrhoea is not yet clear.

While recovery of *N. gonorrhoeae* from an endocervical culture of a patient with PID does not prove conclusively that the gonococcus caused the disease in the fallopian tubes, there is little doubt that, at least in some cases, the gonococcus is the primary pathogen. *In vitro* studies have shown that *N. gonorrhoeae* can infect tubal mucosa, and invade and destroy epithelial cells [7].

NON-GONOCOCCAL PELVIC INFLAMMATORY DISEASE

The aetiology of PID not associated with gonorrhoea remains enigmatic. The study by Rees *et al* [6], suggests a possible role for *Chlamydia;* a high incidence (16 of 24) of pelvic inflammatory disease, with an onset of pain between 13 and 38 days post partum, was found in mothers of babies with chlamydial conjunctivitis. Rees *et al* [6] also noted about 4 per cent of cases of PID in 127 women with a chlamydial cervical infection. Although this organism has only rarely been isolated from the peritoneal fluid of women with PID this may reflect a bactericidal action of the fluid, as in gonorrhoea, or lack of sensitivity of present sampling methods.

Mycoplasma hominis has been isolated from the uterine tubes of just under 10 per cent of women with acute salpingitis [8], and *Ureaplasma urealyticum* from 4 per cent, but once again the role of these organisms is not clear.

Anaerobic organisms, whilst possibly involved in the pathogenesis of recurrent PID [9], are unlikely to play a part in the aetiology of PID seen in sexually-active young women, who have not undergone surgery of the reproductive tract [10]. In the case of women with PID in the puerperal period and following surgery, including termination of pregnancy, anaerobes such as *Peptostreptococcus* and *Bacteroides* spp. may be implicated as can streptococci and occasionally enteric bacteria such as *Escherichia coli.* Often more than one organism is involved, particularly when anaerobes are isolated and trauma of surgery, residual blood clots, *in situ* sutures and vaginal packs are all predisposing factors.

Mycobacterium tuberculosis is now a rare cause of salpingitis, and is usually secondary to disease elsewhere, reaching the uterine tubes and uterus by means of the bloodstream [11].

The role of viruses in the aetiology of PID is not clear, although Eschenbach *et al* [12], demonstrated that *Herpesvirus hominis* and *Cytomegalovirus* were not causative in his cases.

Pathogenesis

Organisms reach the uterine tubes by ascending from the endocervix. Rarely (less than 1 per cent) tubal inflammation results from extension of inflammation from another pelvic organ, most commonly the appendix.

Several factors predispose to ascending infection. Surgical operations in the uterus, including hysterosalpingography, may lead to the development of PID in less than 5 per cent of cases. Women using an intra-uterine contraceptive device have a greater risk of developing salpingitis [13]. Previous episodes of PID predispose to subsequent recurrences [3]. In the absence of surgical procedures, PID in pregnancy is uncommon.

In gonococcal and in non-gonococcal salpingitis, not associated with surgical operations, the inflammatory process affects chiefly the endosalpinx, the organisms having ascended by way of the endometrium, where only mild inflammation may be induced. There is destruction of tubal epithelium and a purulent exudate fills the lumen. Pus may escape from the fimbriated end of the tube and track down to the rectovaginal pouch, where a pelvic abscess may form. With continued inflammation, the ostia become occluded by oedema, and pus collects in the cavity of the tube forming a pyosalpinx. If untreated, fibrous adhesions form within the tube, with relatively few external adhesions. Occasionally a hydrosalpinx (an accumulation of serous fluid in the tube) is found; its pathogenesis is uncertain, but it may result from recurrent episodes of subacute salpingitis [2].

Damage to the ciliated epithelium and the production of fibrous adhesions within the uterine tube, may delay the transit of a fertilized ovum to the uterus, and as a result, implantation may occur in the tube giving an ectopic pregnancy. Ectopic pregnancy is associated, in about half the cases, with changes suggestive of PID [14].

Infertility may result in about 20 per cent of women who have been treated for PID [15] the prognosis being better when salpingitis is mild. Women who have had gonococcal salpingitis have a significantly higher chance of conceiving than those who have had non-gonococcal salpingitis.

Salpingitis associated with minor gynaecological operations is usually brought about by infection which ascends by means of the lymphatics in the outer layers of the uterus and tubes. Such an 'exosalpingitis', if untreated, tends to be followed by extensive pelvic adhesions. The lumen of the tube is commonly little affected by the inflammatory process and, therefore, in such cases pyosalpinx and hydrosalpinx are uncommon, and fertility interfered with less often than in 'endosalpingitis' of gonococcal or non-gonococcal origin.

Clinical features

ACUTE PELVIC INFLAMMATORY DISEASE

The symptoms of acute PID usually occur during or shortly after menstruation or in the puerperium.

The patient complains usually of lower abdominal pain, often exacerbated by movement of the psoas muscle, fever, rigors, malaise, anorexia and vomiting. With the increased use of laparoscopy, it has become apparent that whilst abdominal pain is the most reliable symptom, it may be minimal in at least 5 per cent of cases [16]. Pyrexia (temperature of 38°C or greater) may be found in only about two-thirds of women with acute PID, and more commonly in cases due to *N. gonorrhoeae* [17].

There is usually tenderness, and a variable degree of muscular guarding over the lower abdomen. Pain is elicited by moving the cervix during bimanual examination. Palpation of the uterus and tubes is usually impossible on account of tenderness and guarding.

In about half the cases of acute PID, the white cell count is elevated [18]. The erythrocyte sedimentation rate is raised in about 75 per cent of cases [16], especially when the salpingitis is associated with gonorrhoea [17].

Paralytic ileus presenting with abdominal distension and vomiting may occur in 1 per cent of cases. In such cases fluid levels are noted on the plain X-ray film of the abdomen, taken with the patient in an upright position.

CHRONIC PELVIC INFLAMMATORY DISEASE

Chronic PID may be asymptomatic and undiscovered until the patient is investigated for infertility. Symptoms, when they occur, consist of intermittent lower abdominal pain or discomfort; discomfort in the groins; backache, malaise and frequent heavy menstrual periods. The tubes may not be palpable, or they may be irregularly thickened; the uterus may be retroverted and fixed.

Differential diagnosis

ECTOPIC PREGNANCY

There is usually sudden onset of pain in an iliac fossa or hypogastrium, often with syncope. Tracking of blood to the upper abdominal cavity may induce pain referred to the shoulder. Symptoms usually develop after a short period of amenorrhoea during which there may have been cramping discomfort in one iliac fossa. If intra-abdominal haemorrhage is severe, the patient presents a state of shock, with pallor, tachycardia and hypotension. There is tenderness over the lower abdomen, and on vaginal examination (which must not be performed in patients with signs of severe haemorrhage) there is irregular, tender enlargement of the tubes on the affected side. Pelvic haematoma may be detected in the rectovaginal pouch. Urine tests for pregnancy may be either positive or negative depending upon the secretory activity of the trophoblast (Appendix to Chapter 2).

ACUTE APPENDICITIS

Abdominal pain commences usually in the umbilical area and after some hours localizes to the right iliac fossa. Menstrual irregularities are unusual, but nausea and anorexia is more pronounced than in acute pelvic inflammatory disease.

RUPTURED OVARIAN OR ENDOMETRIOTIC CYST

There is usually sudden onset of lower abdominal pain, most commonly occurring about the time of menstruation. The patient is usually afebrile.

ACUTE PYELONEPHRITIS

There is generally a sudden rise in temperature, often with rigors, and pain in the loins and iliac fossae. Commonly there are urinary symptoms such as frequency of micturition, urgency, strangury, dysuria, nocturia and haematuria. The urine contains pus; there is a polymorphonuclear leucocytosis in most cases.

INTESTINAL OBSTRUCTION

Pain is colicky in nature and is felt in the umbilical or hypogastric areas. It is associated with vomiting and absence of passage of flatus. Bowel sounds are hyperactive. There may be a history of previous abdominal surgery.

SEPTIC ABORTION

A history of amenorrhoea is followed by symptoms and signs of abortion - either complete or incomplete. There is uterine bleeding, painful uterine contractions, pyrexia, tachycardia, offensive vaginal discharge, uterine tenderness and general systemic upset. The white cell count and erythrocyte sedimentation rate are raised. Vaginal examination may show a dilated cervix.

Diagnosis

A presumptive diagnosis of acute pelvic inflammatory disease may be made from the patient's history and the clinical and laboratory findings. Confirmation of acute PID requires the use of laparoscopy, except when a presumptive diagnosis of gonorrhoea has been made by smear examinations or confirmed by culture (*see* below). Jacobson and Westrom [16], demonstrated that only 60 per cent of clinically diagnosed cases of acute PID were confirmed by laparoscopy. In their series, acute appendicitis, pelvic endometriosis and intrapelvic haemorrhage were the conditions most commonly mimicking acute salpingitis.

Laparoscopy, however, requires the administration of a general anaesthetic, and is not without hazard. Rawlings and Balgobin [19] reported a complication rate of 6 per cent. Complications included perforation of the bowel wall, mesenteric haemorrhage, haematoma of the abdominal wall and pelvic abscess formation. Laparoscopy should only be undertaken by gynaecologists experienced in its use.

When a young woman attends a sexually transmitted diseases clinic complaining of lower abdominal pain whose onset has been within 10 days of the onset of menstruation, and when examination reveals tenderness in both fornices, the most likely diagnosis is acute pelvic inflammatory disease. Every effort must be made to identify gonococcal cases in the manner described elsewhere (Chapter 11). Where facilities exist, cultures from the cervix should also be taken for *Chlamydia trachomatis* and possibly *Ureaplasma urealyticum.* Treatment should be started on the result of examination of Gram-stained smears, and altered, if necessary, when culture reports become available.

Should there be any doubt about the diagnosis, particularly if symptoms fail to subside with treatment, advice from a gynaecologist should be sought as laparoscopy may be required.

Treatment

Cases of acute salpingitis with systemic disturbance should be admitted to hospital. The decision is not so straightforward in patients with less severe symptoms and signs. If there is any doubt as to the diagnosis, or about the patient's reliability in taking the antibiotic or chemotherapy prescribed, admission to hospital is indicated. In pregnancy women are best cared for as in-patients.

GONOCOCCAL PELVIC INFLAMMATORY DISEASE

In patients with acute salpingitis requiring admission to hospital, benzylpenicillin 1 million i.u. (600mg) by intramuscular injection every six hours results in improvement in the patient's condition generally within 48 hours. After this time, provided resolution of the salpingitis is occurring as judged by decreased tenderness in the iliac fossae and reduction in size and tenderness of the tubes, an oral antimicrobial agent may be substituted. Ampicillin given orally in a dose of 500mg six-hourly is satisfactory, and should be continued for at least 10 days. In patients with infections due to β-lactamase producing gonococci, cefuroxime (2.0g) intramuscularly in eight-hourly doses (or occasionally six-hourly) is suggested as an approach to treatment, possibly preceded by spectinomycin 4.0g as a single intramuscular dose.

In patients who fail to respond to penicillin treatment, reappraisal of the initial diagnosis must be made and a gynaecologist's advice sought as laparoscopy and possibly removal of an IUCD may be necessary. The development of pelvic abscesses, a very rare occurrence in the United Kingdom, but common in the lower socio-economic groups in certain urban areas of the USA, may require drainage through the posterior fornix of the vagina.

Other antimicrobial agents may be used in the management of acute salpingitis. Co-trimoxazole given orally in a dosage of two tablets eight-hourly for at least 10 days is effective. Doxycycline in an oral dose of 200mg eight-hourly for 48 hours followed by 100mg eight-hourly for at least 14 days is satisfactory in some localities. Therapy with a tetracycline has the advantage of being effective against the potential or actual pathogens *C. trachomatis, M. hominis* and *U. urealyticum;*

tetracyclines should not be used in pregnancy. In pregnant women who are hypersensitive to penicillin, erythromycin stearate orally, in a dosage of 500mg six-hourly may be used.

Although steroids may produce rapid resolution of the symptoms, there is no beneficial effect on future fertility or in preventing the later development of chronic abdominal pain [18].

NON-GONOCOCCAL PELVIC INFLAMMATORY DISEASE

Since non-gonococcal PID is now thought to be primarily a polymicrobial infection, broad spectrum antimicrobial cover is required. Tetracyclines should be the treatment of first choice in patients with non-gonococcal salpingitis. Doxycycline in the dosage given above has been found to be useful. In pregnancy, erythromycin stearate may be substituted.

In PID following surgical manipulation in particular, where trauma of the operation, residual bloodclots, *in situ* sutures, and vaginal packs are all predisposing factors, the possibility of anaerobic infection will require treatment with antimicrobial agents, such as metronidazole. An oral dose of metronidazole 2g immediately then 200mg thrice daily for 5–7 days has been found to be very effective [20]. In this report, also, a similar course of metronidazole, given as a prophylactic was dramatically effective in reducing vaginal carriage rate of non-sporing anaerobes such as *Bacteroides* spp. It is clear also that a bactericidal level of metronidazole in patients' blood sustained over the operative and immediate postoperative periods reduced the frequency of postoperative pelvic inflammatory disease. Metronidazole, in doses of 1g, can be given as a suppository at eight-hour intervals in those who cannot take oral drugs [21]. Currently it is advised that a 1g metronidazole suppository is inserted into the rectum eight-hourly for three days in the treatment of anaerobic infections in the adult and that oral medication with 400mg three times daily should be substituted as soon as this becomes possible. Treatment should not ordinarily continue beyond a seven day period (ABPI Data Sheet Compendium, 1978). A fuller discussion on metronidazole is given in Chapter 18 and on page 284 of Chapter 17.

The characteristics required in an antimicrobial agent to be effective in anaerobic infections include the ability to penetrate abscesses, resistance to inactivating enzymes in the infected site, activity against high inocula of organisms and activity under anaerobic conditions. Three drugs currently fulfil these criteria: clindamycin, cefoxitin and metronidazole. Emerging resistance has been seen with clindamycin which also carries a risk of pseudomembranous colitis (page 382), and some strains are resistant to cefoxitin. Metronidazole, although inactive against aerobic components of mixed infections [22] may render these organisms more susceptible to the phagocytic defence system by the elimination of anaerobes [23]; *see also* discussion on metronidazole in Chapter 18).

Prognosis

The earlier the patient is treated, and the milder the symptoms, the better is the prognosis with regard to fertility [15]. Patients with treated gonococcal PID are less likely to be infertile than women with non-gonococcal PID. Abdominal pain may persist for many months in about a fifth of women treated for acute PID [10].

REFERENCES

1 Lukasik, J A (1963) *American Journal of Obstetrics and Gynecology,* **87**, 1028
2 Rees, E and Annels, E H (1969) *British Journal of Venereal Diseases,* **45**, 205
3 Eschenbach, D A and Holmes, K K (1975) *Clinics in Obstetrics and Gynecology,* **18**, 35
4 Thompson, S E and Hager, D (1977) *Sexually Transmitted Diseases,* **4**, 105
5 Woolfitt, J M G and Watt, L (1977) *British Journal of Venereal Diseases,* **53**, 93
6 Rees, E, Tait, I A, Hobson, D and Johnson, F W A (1977) Chlamydia in relation to cervical infection and pelvic inflammatory disease. In *Non-gonococcal urethritis and related infection.* (Ed) Hobson, D and Holmes, K K. American Society for Microbiology, Washington, D C, pages 67, 76
7 Ward, M E, Watt, P J and Robertson, J N (1974) *Journal of Infectious Diseases,* **129**, 650
8 Mardh, P-A and Westrom, L (1970) *British Journal of Venereal Diseases,* **46** 179
9 Swenson, R M, Michaelson, T C, Daly, M J, Facog and Spaulding, E H (1973) *Obstetrics and Gynecology,* **42**, 528
10 Westrom, L and Mardh, P-A (1977) *Epidemiology, etiology and prognosis of acute salpingitis: a study of 1,457 laparoscopically verified cases.* (Ed) Hobson, D and Holmes, K K. American Society for Microbiology, Washington, D C
11 Jeffcoate, N (1975) in *Principles of Gynaecology.* Butterworths, London, pages 292–301
12 Eschenbach, D A, Buchanan, T M, Pollock, H M, Forsyth, P S, Alexander, E, Russell, Lin, Juey-Shin, Wang, San-Pin, Wentworth, B B, McCormack, W M and Holmes, K K, *New England Journal of Medicine,* **293**, 166
13 Westrom, L, Bengtsson, L P and Mardh, P-A (1976) *Lancet,* **ii**, 221
14 Harralson, J D, Van Nagell, J R and Roddick, J W (1973) *American Journal of Obstetrics and Gynecology,* **115**, 995
15 Westrom, L (1975) *American Journal of Obstetrics and Gynecology,* **121**, 707
16 Jacobson, L and Westrom, L (1969) *American Journal of Obstetrics and Gynecology,* **105**, 1088
17 McCormack, W M, Nowroozi, K, Alpert, S, Jackel, S G, Lee, Y-H, Lowe, E W and Rankin, J S (1977) *Sexually Transmitted Diseases,* **4**, 125
18 Falk, V (1965) *Acta Obstetrica et Gynecologica Scandinavica,* (Suppl.) **6**, 1
19 Rawlings, E E and Balgobin, B (1975) *British Medical Journal,* **1**, 727
20 Study Group, Luton and Dunstable Hospital (1974) *Lancet,* **ii**, 1540
21 Study Group, Luton and Dunstable Hospital (1976) *British Medical Journal,* **1**, 318
22 Tally, F P (1978) *Journal of Antimicrobial Chemotherapy,* **4**, 299
23 Ingham, H R, Sisson, P R, Tharagonnet, D, Selkon, J B and Codd, A A (1977) *Lancet,* **ii**, 52

CHAPTER 17

Candidiasis and Non-specific Vaginitis

I. CANDIDIASIS

Vulvo-vaginal and penile candidiasis

Candidiasis (syn. candidosis; thrush; moniliasis), is an infection caused mostly by the yeast *Candida albicans,* which varies in severity from a very common brief and trivial surface infection in the otherwise fit to a very rare and often fatal systemic disease. *C. albicans* is ordinarily a saprophytic fungus, existing as a common constituent of the microflora of body cavities of man and other warm blooded animals, but it is opportunistic and assumes the role of a pathogen under certain circumstances. It is the presence of factors in the host, which allows *Candida* to become pathogenic and to induce the clinical conditions known as candidiasis. Vulvo-vaginal candidiasis, characterized by pruritus with or without vaginal discharge, tends to be a minor condition in that its physical effects are not seriously damaging although it is a very frequent cause of irritation and annoyance in women. Men tend to be involved to a much lesser extent than women as the milieu of the glans and preputial sac is generally less favourable as a site to *Candida.*

AETIOLOGY

Candida albicans is the commonest species responsible for vaginal candidiasis (more than 80 per cent of infections although others such as *C. stellatoidea* or *C. tropicalis* may also cause disease. Sometimes *Torulopsis glabrata,* another yeast-like organism, may be a less common cause of a clinically similar vaginal mycosis [1, 2].

Normally, *C. albicans* grows as a thin-walled non-capsulated oval yeast (blastospore) 1.5–4.0μm in diameter, which reproduces by budding. It can give rise to a pseudomycelium by producing elongated filaments called pseudohyphae: these filaments result from one or two generations of buds remaining attached to each other. At temperatures below 26°C in nutritionally poor media, such as corn meal agar, it characteristically produces thick-walled resting cells 7–17μm in diameter called chlamydospores. No sexual forms are known. On blood agar or Sabouraud's medium colonies usually reach 0.5mm in diameter after 18 hours and develop into high, convex, cream-coloured colonies 1.5mm in diameter after two days. When the yeast is transferred from a peptone-containing medium to mammalian serum at 37°C curved elongated germ tubes are produced; this finding is virtually diagnostic of *C. albicans* although *C. stellatoidea* will also give a positive result in the germ tube test. If required *C. albicans* and other yeasts can be identified more fully by carbohydrate-assimilation patterns and other tests [3, 4]. For exacting work of a comparative taxonomic nature complete studies of the yeast are necessary. *C. albicans* and *C. stellatoidea* have been classified in a separate genus to which the name *Syringospora* has been given [5]; when diagnosis has to be made rapidly some limitation in taxonomic practice is unavoidable.

T. glabrata, a member of a genus similar to *Candida,* is a less common cause of clinically similar vaginal mycosis. *T. glabrata* does not produce pseudohyphae and is germ tube negative.

In infections with *Candida,* blastospores and pseudohyphae can be identified in the vaginal smear stained with Gram's stain, and it has been proposed that the relative proportions of these forms may be useful in making a clinical assessment. Although the predominance of pseudohyphae suggests pathogenicity and the predominance of blastospores suggests that *Candida* is saprophytic, the association is not constant and the appearance of the fungus will be determined by the equilibria reached between the growth of the yeast and the localized conditions in the vagina.

C. albicans can be either a saprophyte or a pathogen on the skin or mucosa. Conditions which favour the transition to a pathogen and are relevant to vaginal candidiasis include pregnancy, diabetes, damage or maceration of the tissue, immunosuppressive drugs, possibly also the oral contraceptive and oral antibiotics [6]. Pregnancy is an undisputed factor in pathogenicity possibly by virtue of changes in cell-mediated immunity, in glucose metabolism or by the provision of a glycogen-rich vaginal epithelium [7, 8]. In pregnancy there is a reduction of T-cell activity which may help to protect the fetus from rejection [9] and there are changes in carbohydrate metabolism [10], which may both favour the growth of *Candida:* a reduction in the incidence of *Candida* in the vagina takes place in the post-partum period [11].

The oral contraceptive produces, in the vaginal skin, a state analogous to that in pregnancy and therefore would be expected to provide a similar predisposition to vaginal candidiasis. There are differences, however, in the results of various studies and the situation is not yet clear [6]. The wider use of the oral contraceptive pill with a low oestrogen content makes certain evaluation more difficult.

Antibodies to *C. albicans* in patients' serum with vaginal candidiasis have been found to be secretory immunoglobulin in type. This confirms the importance of local stimulation and a regional response in mucocutaneous infections with a back flow into the systemic circulation of antibodies produced by permucosal immunocytes [12].

Candida is a common constituent of the microflora of vagina, rectum and mouth and this yeast has been found respectively in 28, 39 and 48 per cent of these sites in a series of 300 patients attending a clinic. It is possible that the mouth contributes to the continuing re-inoculation of the intestinal tract and is thus an indirect source of vaginal infection [13].

Oral antibiotics interfere with the normal balance of the gut microflora and make it easier for *Candida* to become established in large numbers.

Other conditions, less commonly encountered, which predispose to infection include any debilitating disease particularly malignancy, the nephrotic syndrome and hypothyroidism.

PATHOLOGY

Histological study of infected vulvar and vaginal tissue is not part of routine clinical practice and as a result reports are few. Gardner and Kaufman [14] noted mild to moderate inflammatory changes without invasion of vaginal tissue by the yeast. It has been shown, however, that in the mouth at least, in acute and chronic candidiasis there is invasion of the epithelium by hyphae, which grow downwards in more or less straight lines without respect for epithelial boundaries. In this site electron microscopy examination confirmed that the growth of *Candida* is intracellular and that the fine structure of the epithelial cytoplasm shows minimal change [15]. Certain changes in squamous cells such as radial clumping and emptiness of stained material in the cytoplasm as well as increased nuclear activity and perinuclear haloes have been described in cervical vaginal Papanicolaou smears [16].

CLINICAL FEATURES OF CANDIDIASIS

Signs and symptoms [14] have diagnostic significance and history-taking and examination are therefore important.

Candidiasis of the female genitalia

Vulvar *pruritus,* which may vary from slight to intolerable, is the cardinal symptom of candidiasis. When pruritus is intense vulvar erythema is pronounced. Sometimes patients complain of pruritus or burning after intercourse. On occasions, however, even when plaques or pseudomembrane involves the vagina widely there are no subjective symptoms or even evidence of vulvitis.

Burning is a common complaint, particularly upon micturition and especially when there is also local excoriation due to scratching. Sometimes complaints of dysuria and frequency can be erroneously attributed to cystitis.

Dyspareunia especially in the nulliparous may be severe enough to make intercourse intolerable. *Vulvar oedema* may cause ill-defined vulvar discomfort and worry and apprehension may add to the patient's distress. A vaginal discharge is seldom the presenting complaint but the majority of patients have a discharge at some time and some patients may complain of dryness.

Erythema of the vulva is the commonest sign of candidiasis and tends to be limited to the mucocutaneous surfaces between the labia minora. Although often limited to the vestibule, erythema may extend to the labia majora, the perineum, the peri-anal skin and occasionally to the mons veneris, the genito-crural folds, the inner thighs and even buttocks.

Oedema of the labia minora is commonly observed and is often more pronounced in candidiasis during pregnancy. Fissuring may occasionally be noted at the fourchette and at the anus. Traumatic excoriations from scratching are often found in patients with severe itching.

The vagina is abnormally reddened in about 20 per cent of cases. If adherent patches or plaques of 'thrush' or pseudomembrane are removed the vaginal skin underneath appears erythematous and superficial ulceration with bleeding may be seen. The vaginal contents may be apparently normal but a characteristic curdy material is found in 20 per cent of the non-pregnant and in 70 per cent of the pregnant. Although plaques may be small (1mm) in size, larger (1cm) and thick accumulations of exudate may be seen. A yeast odour is not thought to be characteristic in candidiasis [14].

In contrast, primary cutaneous candidiasis involves the outer parts of the labia majora and the genito-crural fold and not infrequently the mons veneris, the peri-anal region and inner thighs. Vulvar lesions tend to be reddened and moist with defined scalloped edges. Cutaneous lesions tend to begin as small papules on a red base with outlying small satellite vesicles or pustules and progress to form shallow ulcerated areas resulting from ruptured vesicopustules.

T. vaginalis or *N. gonorrhoeae* may coexist with the yeast infection and on occasions all three organisms are found together.

Candidiasis of the glans penis and prepuce

Characteristic symptoms of soreness and itching of the penis, accompanied sometimes by a discharge from under the prepuce, are seen in candidiasis of the penis. On examination there may be a balanoposthitis with superficial erosions and sometimes eroded maculopapular lesions and preputial oedema. *C. albicans* may be isolated from the subpreputial sac, but on occasions there may be a balanoposthitis with erosions without detectable yeasts which appears to develop 6–24 hours after intercourse with a partner who has vaginal candidiasis [17]. Such a balanitis may be due to sensitivity to yeast-containing vaginal discharge. The balanoposthitis associated with diabetes has a similar appearance and *Candida* may not always be isolated.

Neonatal candidiasis

Candidiasis in the newborn may involve the umbilicus, mouth and napkin areas. The maternal vagina is only one source as colonization may involve also the mouth and bowel. Attendants and environmental sources may also contribute to transmission.

DIAGNOSIS

Since *C. albicans* is a common inhabitant of the vaginal cavity (16 per cent or more in the non-pregnant), its mere detection by microscopic or cultural means, does not by itself provide proof of its clinical significance in a patient and there is no way of deciding in the laboratory whether a given isolate is or is not pathogenic.

Vaginal and sub-preputial exudates may be examined as either wet preparations or Gram-stained smears. Both yeast forms (blastospores) and pseudohyphae are Gram-positive. The relative proportions of yeast forms and pseudohyphae in the vaginal films may assist in making a clinical assessment, although, as already stated, this is not a reliable guide. Microscopic examination of exudates should be supplemented by culture on a suitable fungal medium (Sabouraud's agar). Patients with the most florid clinical manifestations may show evidence of candidiasis only on culture. The organism survives well in exudate collected on swabs but a swab in transport medium enables the laboratory to search for *T. vaginalis* as well.

The interpretation of a finding of *C. albicans* depends on the patient's symptoms and a comparison of the numbers of the organism, both in absolute terms and in relation to other organisms. As serological tests are insufficiently available to assess their clinical value in the diagnosis of vaginal candidiasis this method has little practical application at present. The antibody response is mainly local, consisting of secretory immunoglobulin IgA, some of which finds its way into the systemic circulation.

TREATMENT

In vaginal candidiasis, treatment is indicated on the basis of the symptom of pruritis, the finding of vaginitis and the detection of *C. albicans* or *T. glabrata,* and possibly other species of *Candida.* This mycotic infection can be an annoyance that is difficult to tolerate, but otherwise it is not serious in a patient who is otherwise fit. Its tendency to recur, however, necessitates on occasions fuller investigations as a cause of local irritation as well as disharmony in a personal sexual relationship.

The polyene antibiotics, nystatin and amphotericin B are effective antifungal agents and act by increasing the permeability of the fungal membrane and causing leakage of intracellular solutes. The sensitivity of the yeasts to polyenes has not changed perceptibly over the years although a slight increase in resistance would render them virtually useless as chemotherapeutic agents [18, 19].

Isolates made resistant to polyenes, however, are unlikely to survive in nature as they show profound differences in their morphology and are less pathogenic. The first amphotericin-resistant isolates reported as having arisen due to therapy in a patient, showed that the usual ergosterol in the membrane had been replaced by other unidentified sterols, a change which apparently protected the fungus against polyenes. These isolates showed slow growth, impaired pseudomycelia formation and loss of pathogenicity and therefore were unlikely to survive in nature [19, 20, 21]. The use of these polyenes in the short-term therapy of vaginal candidiasis is not likely, therefore, to give rise to resistance in nature. Resistance induced experimentally appears to be reversed on withdrawal of the polyene and there is no selective breeding or resistant strains [22].

Nystatin is prescribed as vaginal tablets, each containing 100,000 units, with instructions to insert one at night for 14 nights continuing during menstruation. The patient should wash her hands and vulva before bedtime, lie down on the bed and gently insert the tablet into the upper third of the vagina. She should be told not to worry about the appearance of a yellow discharge as the nystatin is itself yellow in colour. Nystatin cream (100 units per gram) may be applied to the vulvar skin if necessary. Should relapse occur retreatment and the administration of oral nystatin (500,000 units four times a day for a week) together with local treatment is justified.

The antifungal imidazoles, clotrimazole and miconazole inhibit yeasts and other species of fungi associated with human infection in this country. Topical applications are effective in candidiasis of the skin and vagina and their action appears to cause alterations to the structure and properties of the fungal cell membrane. Studies comparing the topical application of these imidazoles with nystatin are difficult to interpret, because the two drugs would have to be used for the same duration, therefore one or other drug would have to be given for a period that is not recommended [23]. As the *imidazoles have an antibacterial action clotrimazole or miconazole should not be used for vulvovaginal candidiasis when a gonococcal infection has to be excluded.* Clotrimazole concentrations in the vagina are very substantial; a mean value of ~47μg/ml has been obtained 6–9 hours after the last 100mg tablet of a 12-day course of once-daily vaginal tablets had been inserted [24]. The gonococcus is, however, very resistant to clotrimazole, with a minimum inhibitory concentration of 64 to >256μg/ml and minimum 'cidal' concentration of >256μg/ml [24].

Clotrimazole (Canesten) is supplied as a 1 per cent cream for topical use and as 100mg vaginal pessaries. Although early recommendations showed that one 100mg vaginal tablet inserted every night for six nights was an effective alternative to nystatin [25] and more pleasant to use, a shorter course of two 100 mg vaginal tablets inserted for three consecutive nights may be sufficient in the uncomplicated case [26].

Miconazole nitrate (Daktarin, Dermonistat) is supplied as a 2 per cent cream for topical use, as a 2 per cent intravaginal cream (Gyno-Daktarin, Monistat) and as vaginal pessaries, each containing 100mg. The intravaginal cream is effective when it is introduced into the vagina by means of an applicator which is filled to contain the required 5g of the cream (equivalent to 100mg miconazole nitrate). The pessary or cream, introduced into the vagina once nightly for 14 consecutive nights is effective treatment curing more than 80 per cent of cases [27, 28]. It is likely that shorter courses will prove to be effective in the uncomplicated case.

Although treatment failure may occur relapses are more frequent. It is possible that the mouth contributes to the continuing re-inoculation of the intestinal tract and is thus an indirect source of vaginal infection. Such cyclic re-infection from the bowel may require oral nystatin. The sexual partner may be examined and treated if there is evidence of candidiasis of the glans or preputial sac.

The vaginal absorption of the imidazoles, in the preparations used, appears to be limited and most is lost by vaginal leakage. About 2.5 per cent of the dose of econazole and 1.5 per cent of the dose of miconazole was recovered in the urine and faeces during a 96-hour period after the administration of a 5g intravaginal dose [29]. These drugs should be avoided during the fetal organogenetic period in the first trimester of pregnancy, even though teratogenic effects have not been seen in laboratory animals treated with the drug. As nystatin does not appear to be absorbed from mucosal surfaces it should be used in preference, when treatment of candidiasis in the first trimester is essential. Local hypersensitivity to imidazole is rare and other side effects are very rare with topical use.

Balanitis due to *Candida* will generally settle with saline lavage (approximately 0.9 per cent w/v being used) twice or three times daily; separation of the skin surfaces of the glans and inner surface of the prepuce is made by means of a strip of gauze (about 3.5cm × 12cm) soaked in saline which is renewed twice or three times daily. If such a measure fails nystatin, clotrimazole or miconazole cream is effective.

SYSTEMIC CANDIDIASIS

In life-threatening systemic candidiasis, 5-fluorocytosine is an extremely effective drug particularly when this condition is associated with organ transplant or cardiac prosthetic surgery, although not all 'wild' strains of yeast-like fungi are sensitive to it. It is likely that topical use of 5-fluorocytosine could induce an increase in the number of *Candida* strains with enhanced resistance to it and the drug could lose much of its therapeutic value [30].

II. NON-SPECIFIC VAGINITIS

The diagnosis of vulvo-vaginitis due to candidiasis (first section of this Chapter) or to trichomoniasis (Chapter 18) is often clear cut, leading to effective specific therapy. In many cases, however, a clinical diagnosis may not be confirmed by finding these organisms, the vaginitis remains unexplained, and an unsatisfactory diagnosis of non-specific vaginitis has to be made. The complexity of the vaginal microflora make it particularly difficult in a case of non-specific vaginitis to ascribe an exact pathological role to many of the organisms isolated.

AETIOLOGY

Bacteriological studies of the vagina in health and disease have been conducted for over a century and yet the pathogenic status of bacteria other than the gonococcus in the sexually mature cervix and vagina remains controversial. In a recent study of patients with vaginitis the micro-organisms deemed to be the predominant component of the upper vagina and which did not differ from those of the cervix, consisted of *Bacteroides, Candida, Trichomonas, Neisseria gonorrhoeae,* coliforms, *Streptococcus faecalis, Staphylococcus aureus* and *'Haemophilus' vaginalis* [31]. In this study anaerobes, particularly *Bacteroides* spp. were thought to be associated with non-specific vaginitis.

The problem of attributing a pathological role to individual organisms becomes particularly perplexing when taxonomic uncertainties arise, as in the case of the organism referred to as *Corynebacterium vaginale* or *Haemophilus vaginalis.* In 1954 Gardner and Dukes [32] published a brief report that the organism had been isolated from 81 of 91 cases of non-specific bacterial vaginitis, and assigned the name *Haemophilus vaginalis* to the bacillus [33]. Subsequent reports from independent and geographically diverse sources referred to this small Gram-negative bacillus, which could grow on blood agar and could be isolated from the genito-urinary tract [34]. Initially classified as a species of *Haemophilus* [33], it was later shown that the bacilli were Gram-positive, when grown on inspissated serum slopes [35] and that growth requirements did not include blood serum factor X, factor V or other definable co-enzyme-like substances [36].

These studies demonstrated that the bacterium could not be a member of the genus *Haemophilus* because all members of the genus require factors X or V or both. The proposal of Zinnemann and Turner gained substance and most of the recent literature refers to *C. vaginale.* Among the data against the inclusion in this genus, Dunkelberg [34] includes a finding that its cell wall lacks arabinose, a trait deemed to be characteristic of corynebacteria.

Vaginitis may not however be associated with *C. vaginale* as Frampton and Lee [37], working in London, isolated the organism in 23 per cent of 507 women investigated and found that its prevalence was similar in patients complaining of a vaginal discharge or vaginitis (25 per cent) as in the control group (21 per cent). Again, Robinson and Mirchandani [38], in Nova Scotia, isolated *C. vaginale* from 195 (32 per cent) of 610 women attending antenatal clinics but noted that almost never were there signs or symptoms when it occurred without *Trichomonas* or *Candida.* Only a small group (six cases out of 195) had mild symptoms, but no *Trichomonas* or *Candida,* and might be called *'Haemophilus'* vaginitis.

More recently, Pheifer *et al* [39] examined 97 women with a vaginal discharge. All had negative cultures for *N. gonorrhoeae, T. vaginalis* and

C. albicans. C. vaginale was isolated from a significantly higher proportion of symptomatic patients with clinical signs of vaginitis (39 of 43 cases; 91 per cent) than of normal controls who were symptom free (two of 20 cases; 10 per cent). In a further group of 10 women, without symptoms but with signs of vaginitis, *C. vaginale* was isolated in eight. *Mycoplasma hominis, Ureaplasma urealyticum* and *Bacteroides melaninogenicus* were found more often in those with abnormal than from those with normal results on vaginal examination.

C. vaginale is probably transmitted sexually: Pheifer *et al* [39] isolated the organism from 27 of 34 male sex partners of women with *C. vaginale* infection and none of three partners of women without infection. Earlier, in a survey of 200 women attending a venereal disease clinic in Atlanta, Georgia, USA, Dunkelberg *et al* [40] found that the incidence of *C. vaginale* (31 per cent) was no higher than that of populations not considered to be at high risk of contracting venereal disease; these workers thought that this was due to the low virulence of *C. vaginale,* the limited numbers of organisms in the infected male and the detrimental effect of the pH of the normal vagina on the bacillus.

Other bacteria of interest to the clinician dealing with sexually transmissible diseases include streptococci of Lancefield's group B and novobiocin-resistant micrococci. The latter organisms are associated with urinary tract infections in young women and are discussed in Chapter 19.

Group B streptococci are sexually transmitted [41] and have been found to occur in the vagina of approximately 20 per cent of females and the urethra of 16 per cent of males attending the venereal diseases clinic in Uppsala, Sweden [42]. These bacteria are unimportant with regard to symptoms of urogenital infection such as dysuria and urethral or vaginal discharge. Group B streptococci are however associated with puerperal and neonatal infections [41, 43] but the correct therapeutic approach to pregnant women harbouring group B streptococci is not yet clear.

CLINICAL FEATURES

Vaginitis is a term that may have a rather broad interpretation. The inflamed epithelium of the vagina that is painful on examination does not occur amongst the bulk of patients presenting with an obviously pathological discharge, yet both groups may be labelled vaginitis [37].

Figures of the incidence of *C. vaginale* obtained in one study cannot be readily interpreted, as it is impossible to know if the various series are strictly comparable from the clinical point of view.

Gardner and Dukes [33] have described clinical manifestations of vaginitis considered to be associated with *C. vaginale* infection. The discharge tended to be scanty rather than profuse; grey in colour in the majority (85 per cent), yellow grey in 5 per cent and green in 3 per cent (yellow-green discharges were considered to be almost invariably associated with *T. vaginalis* infection); the odour was disagreeable but less offensive than in trichomoniasis; frothiness was found in 27 per cent of *C. vaginale* infections and in 34 per cent of those due to *T. vaginalis.* Pheifer *et al* [39] described the discharge as homogeneous of low to normal viscosity, more yellow than normal with a pH of 5.0; the discharges were usually present at the introitus, were uniformly adherent to the vaginal walls and had a disagreeable odour.

It is difficult to assess the value of pH findings particularly as Cohen, in his careful study [44], came to the conclusion that 'In the absence of blood in the vagina, the average variation in pH in any one patient did not exceed 0.2 over a period of 3–6 months at any time of the menstrual cycle and irrespective of infection, treatment, type of contraceptive used, type of underclothing worn and nature of sanitary protection used'.

DIAGNOSIS

Attention has been drawn to the difficulties in making a diagnosis as assessment depends on subjective matters, namely impressions of colour, quantity, consistency of discharge and odour of discharge.

Gardner and Dukes [33] placed reliance on the appearance of wet vaginal films in their study of vaginitis attributed to *C. vaginale.* Leucocytes were not prominent and there was a conspicuous absence of lactobacilli. They found that the appearance of epithelial cells was a most valuable clue to the presence of *C. vaginale.* The cytoplasm was especially granular in appearance, *C. vaginale* being uniformly spaced upon the surface of the cells. Not all cells were involved and some cells showed only partial involvement. Frampton and Lee [37] described particularly a Type I 'clue cell' with a dense layer of bacilli, uniform in size, covering the cell surface; when Type I clue cells were found cultures were nearly always positive for *C. vaginale.* In Type II clue cells, however, bacteria of variable size and shape were unevenly distributed over the cell.

Isolation of *Corynebacterium vaginale* is not widely undertaken as its pathogenicity is low and its role in vaginitis not yet clear. Media and techniques for the isolation and identification of *C. vaginale* are reviewed in detail by Dunkelberg [34]. The most widely used medium is a peptone-starch-glucose agar. The selection of peptone appears to be critical since some peptones do not contain the five B-vitamins required or lack the necessary purines and pyrimidines. Lack of attention to such details could account in part for the widely differing conclusions reached in studies on the aetiology of non-specific vaginitis.

More of the complexities of *C. vaginale* and its possible role in vaginitis have been considered recently in fuller detail [34, 45, 46].

TREATMENT

In the majority of cases of bacterial vaginitis reversion of the abnormal flora to normal can occur spontaneously; recurrence can be similarly expected. In patients attending clinics for the detection or exclusion of sexually transmitted disease, no antimicrobial agents should be used which might interfere with tests for the detection particularly of *N. gonorrhoeae* or of syphilis.

Neither ampicillin nor doxycycline given orally were effective in Pheifer's study [39] in which *C. vaginale* was believed to be the pathogen responsible; topical sulphonamide cream was also ineffective. *C. vaginale* is sensitive *in vitro* to ampicillin but not to sulphonamides and resistance to tetracycline occurs.

In Pheifer's [39] cases, metronidazole in a dose of 500mg twice daily for seven days produced clinical improvement in 80 of 81 patients treated; a finding which was surprising as *C. vaginale,* a facultative anaerobe, was considered to be the pathogen. Serum levels greater than the inhibitory concentrations could have been achieved with the doses given but it is also possible that metronidazole acted by inhibiting obligate anaerobes against which it is very effective. A variety of obligate anaerobes, particularly species of *Bacteroides,* interfere with phagocytosis and killing of *Proteus mirabilis* and other aerobic bacteria *in vitro;* if this capability occurs *in vivo* the hypothesis would explain the rapid clinical and bacteriological response to metronidazole in patients with mixed infections when elimination of anaerobes would leave the aerobes much more susceptible to the phagocytic defence system. These observations of Ingham *et al* [47] suggest that the presence of obligate anaerobes may be fundamental to the pathogenesis of some types of infection.

Selwyn [31], in his study of bacterial vaginitis, found that *Bacteroides* spp. emerged as a leading group of organisms in severe vaginitis and cervicitis with *C. vaginale* relatively rare. For this reason, clotrimazole used topically as vaginal tablets was suggested as an appropriate therapy (page 279). Clotrimazole concentrations in the vagina were found to be very substantial; after insertion of the last 100mg tablet of a 12-day course of once-daily vaginal tablets the mean value after six to nine hours was 447μg/ml and after 10–30 hours 57μg/ml. With such high concentrations being obtained it is wise to avoid topical clotrimazole when the patient is being examined to exclude *N. gonorrhoeae* although this organism is relatively resistant to the drug (minimum inhibitory concentrations 64 to >256μg/ml; minimum bactericidal concentrations >256μg/ml).

Although neither the role of *C. vaginale,* nor of anaerobes such as *Bacteroides* spp. in the pathogenesis of non-specific vaginitis is yet clear, there is a good basis in choosing metronidazole for therapy, given orally in a dose of 200mg thrice daily. Consideration of the possible toxicity of metronidazole, which hangs like a 'small cloud' over its therapeutic use and which intrudes and influences practice in the USA particularly, has been considered on pages 271 and 295–298.

As an alternative, when *Bacteroides* spp. are present, clotrimazole may be used as vaginal tablets, 100mg to be inserted into the vagina once daily for six days.

Vaginal pessaries, each containing povidone-iodine (USNF), 200mg in a water-soluble base, may be effective. Each pessary should be wetted with water immediately before insertion. Patients with a history of iodine sensitivity should not use povidone-iodine (Betadine, Napp Laboratories; ABPI Data Sheet Compendium 1977). Neither clotrimazole nor povidone-iodine should be used when tests to exclude other sexually transmitted organisms are required.

REFERENCES

1 Oriel, J D, Partridge, B M, Denny, M J and Coleman, J C (1972) *British Medical Journal,* **4,** 761

2 Hurley, R, Leask, B G S, Faktor, J A and De Fonseka, C I (1973) *Journal of Obstetrics and Gynaecology of the British Commonwealth,* **80,** 257

3 Duguid, J P, Marmion, B P and Swain, R H A (1978) *Mackie and McCartney Medical Microbiology,* 13th edn., vol. 1. Churchill Livingstone, Edinburgh

4 Mackenzie, D W R (1966) Laboratory investigation of *Candida* infections. In *Symposium on Candida infections.* (Ed) Winner, H I and Hurley, R. Livingstone, Edinburgh, page 26

5 Lodder, J (1970) in *The Yeasts: A Taxonomic Study.* North Holland Publishing Company, Amsterdam, page 893

6 Ridley, C M (1975) in *The Vulva.* Saunders, London, page 120

7 Winner, H I and Hurley, R (1966) *Symposium on Candida infections.* Livingstone, Edinburgh

8 Carroll, C J, Hurley, R and Stanley, V G (1973) *Journal of Obstetrics and Gynaecology of the British Commonwealth,* **80,** 258

9 Finn, R, St Hill, C A, Govan, A J, Ralfs, I G, Gurney, F J and Denye, V (1972) *British Medical Journal,* **3,** 150

10 Lind, J and Harris, V G (1977) *British Journal of Obstetrics and Gynaecology,* **83,** 460
11 Spellacy, W N, Zaias, N, Buhi, W C and Birk, S A (1971) *Obstetrics and Gynaecology,* **38,** 343
12 Mathur, S, Virella, G, Koistinen, J, Horger, E O, Mahvi, T A and Fudenberg, H H (1977) *Infection and Immunity,* **15,** 287
13 Hilton, A L and Warnock, D W (1975) *British Journal of Obstetrics and Gynaecology,* **82,** 922
14 Gardner, H L and Kaufman, R H 1969) in *Benign diseases of the vulva and vagina.* Mosby Co, St Louis, page 149
15 Cawson, R A and Rajasingham, K C (1972) *British Journal of Dermatology,* **87,** 435
16 Heller, C and Hoyt, V (1971) *Acta Cytologica,* **15,** 379
17 Catterall, R D (1966) Urethritis and balanitis due to *Candida: Symposium on Candida infections.* (Ed) Winner, H I and Hurley, R. Livingstone, Edinburgh
18 Hamilton-Miller, J M T (1973) *Bacteriological Reviews,* **37,** 166
19 Franklin, T J and Snow, G A (1975) in *Biochemistry of antimicrobial action.* 2nd edition. Chapman and Hall, London, page 66
20 Drutz, D J and Wood, R A (1973) *Clinical Research,* **21,** 270
21 Woods, R A, Bard, M, Jackson, I E and Drutz, D J (1974) *Journal of Infectious Diseases,* **129,** 53
22 Hurley, R and Wright, J T (1978) *British Medical Journal,* **2,** 522
23 Milne, L J R (1978) *Scottish Medical Journal,* **23,** 149
24 Selwyn, S (1976) *Muenchener Medizinische Wochenschrift,* **118,** Suppl. 1, page 49
25 Highton, B K (1973) *Journal of Obstetrics and Gynaecology,* **80,** 992
26 Masterton, G, Napier, J R, Henderson, J N and Roberts, J E (1977) *British Journal of Venereal Diseases,* **53,** 126
27 Davis, J E, Frudenfield, J H and Goddard, J L (1974) *Obstetrics and Gynaecology,* **44,** 403
28 McNellis, D, McLeod, M, Lawson, J and Pasquale, S A (1978) *Obstetrics and Gynaecology,* **50,** 674
29 Vakovich, R A, Heald, A and Darragh, A (1977) *Clinical Pharmacology and Therapeutics,* **21,** 121
30 Holt, R J (1974) *British Medical Journal,* **3,** 523
31 Selwyn, S (1976) *Muenchener Medizinische Wochenschrift,* **118,** Suppl. 1
32 Gardner, H L and Dukes, C D (1954) *Science,* **120,** 853
33 Gardner, H L and Dukes, C D (1955) *American Journal of Obstetrics and Gynecology,* **69,** 962
34 Dunkelberg, W E (1977) *Sexually Transmitted Diseases,* **4,** 69
35 Zinnemann, K and Turner, G C (1963) *Journal of Pathology and Bacteriology,* **85,** 213
36 Dunkelberg, W E and McVeigh, I (1969) Growth requirements of *Haemophilus vaginalis. Antonie van Leeuwenhoek,* **35,** 129–145
37 Frampton, J and Lee, T (1964) *Journal of Obstetrics and Gynaecology of the British Commonwealth,* **71,** 436
38 Robinson, S C and Mirchandani, G (1965) *American Journal of Obstetrics and Gynecology,* **91,** 1005
39 Pheifer, T A, Forsyth, P S, Durfee, M A, Pollock, H M and Holmes, K K (1978) *New England Journal of Medicine,* **298,** 1429
40 Dunkelberg, W E, Skaggs, R, Kellogg, D S and Domescik, G K (1970) *British Journal of Venereal Diseases,* **46,** 187
41 Franciosi, R A, Knostman, J D and Zimmerman, R A (1973) *Journal of Pediatrics,* **82,** 707
42 Wallin, J and Forsgren, A (1975) *British Journal of Venereal Diseases,* **51,** 401
43 Bergquist, G, Hurvell, B, Malmborg, A S, Rylander, M and Tunell, R (1971) *Scandinavian Journal of Infectious Diseases,* **3,** 157
44 Cohen, L (1969) *British Journal of Venereal Diseases,* **45,** 241
45 Leading Article (1978) *Lancet,* **ii,** 459
46 Harris, J R W (1975) *Corynebacterium vaginale* infection. In *Recent Advances in Sexually Transmitted Diseases.* (Ed) Morton, R S and Harris, J R W. Churchill Livingstone, Edinburgh
47 Ingham, H R, Sisson, P R, Tharagonnet, D, Selkon, J B and Codd, A A (1977) *Lancet,* **ii,** 52

CHAPTER 18

Trichomoniasis

Trichomoniasis is a common and sometimes distressing condition in women resulting from infection of the genito-urinary tract by the protozoon, *Trichomonas vaginalis.* The parasite may be found in the vagina urethra, bladder, Skene's ducts, and occasionally in Bartholin's ducts. Although many women are symptomless, vaginal discharge, vaginitis, dyspareunia, dysuria and frequency are all common manifestations of infection with *T. vaginalis*.

Infection in men is often asymptomatic but the protozoon may sometimes be found in those with signs of a urethritis or prostatitis. The ratio of 1:13 for cases of trichomoniasis diagnosed in men and women respectively may be explained by the facts that the infection may be short-lived in men and the organism difficult to detect. With few exceptions, transmission is by sexual intercourse when the incubation period is in the range 4 days to 4 weeks. Neonates may occasionally develop a vulvovaginitis as a result of an infection acquired during passage through the birth canal.

Aetiology

The causative organism, *Trichomonas vaginalis* was first described by Donné in 1836 [1]. It is a motile pear-shaped protozoon approximately 10 to 30 μm in length (Figure 18.1) with four anterior flagella, which are about the same length as the body. Movement of the undulating membrane, a fin-like organelle lying along one side of the body, is vigorous and is controlled by the posterior flagellum which passes along its upper margin. The posterior flagellum is usually about one-third to two-thirds of the body length of the organism. The blepharoplast, a fibrillar apparatus, situated at the anterior end of the cell, has a direct connection with the flagella. The costa, a slender, chromatic, basal rod also arises from the blepharoplast and is situated beneath the undulating membrane. A hyaline rod, the axostyle, originates at the blepharoplast and passes down the centre of the cell and projects posteriorly as a small spine. A single oval nucleus lies near the anterior end of the cell. Multiplication is by longitudinal binary fission. Cysts are not formed [2].

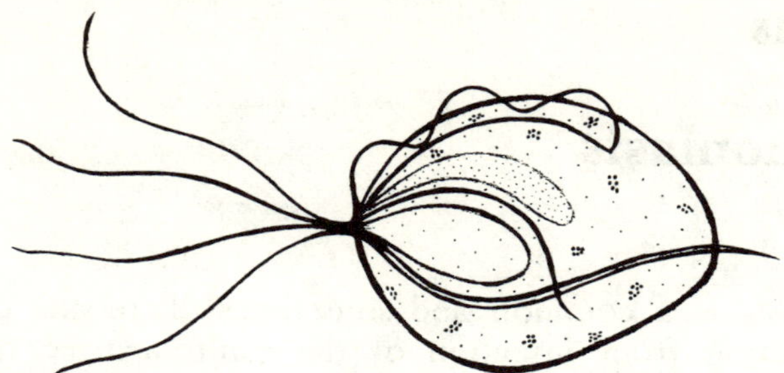

Figure 18.1 *Trichomonas vaginalis* approximately 10–30μm in length with four anterior flagella and a posterior flagellum along the upper margin of the undulating membrane.

T. vaginalis exhibits the characteristics of a micro-aerophile; in culture, anaerobic conditions prolong the period of population increase [3]. The principal mode of nutrition is by pinocytosis* and phagocytosis,† which may proceed in any part of the body [4]. First, an invagination appears in the cytoplasm and gradually its edges are drawn together. The wall of the vesicle thickens and acquires a villous pattern. Micro-organisms and large particles are usually caught by pseudopodia; large and small particles including entire cells may be engulfed. Some, but not all entrapped organisms seem to be altered but it is impossible to say whether they have undergone changes after engulfment or have been phagocytosed in a poor condition. They are usually located in phagosomes but may lie freely in the cytoplasm with no evidence of a limiting membrane.

Ovčinnikov *et al* [4] suggested that gonococci contained within trichomonads might be protected from the action of penicillin. Multiplication of gonococci within a phagosome could cause rupture and death of the trichomonad with release of the engulfed organisms. In their opinion, recurrences of gonorrhoea might be explained by ineffective treatment of a mixed infection; this situation, although possible in theory, has not been considered a problem in clinical practice.

A sexually transmitted trichomonad, *T. fetus,* is seen in cattle and found in the preputial sac and on the glans penis of bulls; the organism, transmitted to cows during sexual intercourse, may cause vaginitis, endometritis and abortion.

*Pinocytosis: 'cell-drinking' ingestion of large molecules and tiny particles by cells.

†Phagocytosis: 'cell-eating', a similar process to pinocytosis except that particles are large enough to be seen in the light microscope (Herbert, W J and Wilkinson, P C (1971) *Dictionary of Immunology,* Blackwell, Oxford).

Two other species of trichomonads, *Trichomonas tenax* and *Pentatrichomonas (Pt) hominis* occur in man [3]. Apart from *Pt. hominis* with its five anterior flagella, these organisms, although smaller (length 6 to 15μm compared to 10 to 30μm for *T. vaginalis*), are morphologically very similar to *T. vaginalis*. *T. tenax* is generally considered to be a harmless commensal of the mouth and is commonly associated with poor oral hygiene. It does not survive passage through the intestinal tract and cannot be established in the vagina. *Pt. hominis* is an inhabitant of the caecum and colon of man; a morphologically identical organism is found in other primates. Although it is considered to be a harmless commensal, it is often found in association with true pathogenic protozoa, e.g., *Entamoeba histolytica*. *Pt. hominis* does not survive in the mouth or vagina.

Pathology

In light and electron microscope studies of biopsies of the cervix in patients with trichomonal vaginitis Nielsen and Nielsen [5] found that trichomonads were gathered in small clusters on the stratified epithelium, but covered only a small area of the surface. Cells of *T. vaginalis* invaded superficial epithelial cells but did not penetrate to the deeper cell layer of epithelium. Epithelial damage tended to be located under clusters of trichomonads, but an intense vaginitis was present whether or not *T. vaginalis* cells were present on the epithelial surface. Their findings indicated that the interaction between cells of *T. vaginalis* and vaginal epithelium takes place primarily at a distance, probably by means of substances released into the vaginal fluid, and secondarily by a direct cell contact mechanism.

The biopsies showed chronic non-specific inflammation with subepithelial accumulation of plasma cells, lymphocytes and polymorphonuclear leucocytes. When inflammation was slight neutrophils were found superficially in the epithelium, and when more severe the neutrophils were in the deeper layers also. There was sometimes ulceration of the surface and all layers of the cervical epithelium showed some hyperchromasia and nuclear enlargement [5].

On colposcopy, when inflammation due to *Trichomonas* is severe, magnification reveals patches of higher vascular density, which on naked-eye inspection are usually described as forming a 'strawberry cervix'. The inflammation produces significant changes in the pattern of the original squamous epithelium as seen through the colposcope. The stromal papillae are higher and reach almost to the surface of the epithelium. In these papillae the vessels are clearly visible and form simple capillary loops running vertically to the surface, but at the top of the loop two or more crests may be found. The shape of the loops may be described as fork-like or antler-like [6]. As the capillaries are separated from the surface by only a few layers of epithelial cells contact bleeding is common [7].

Recently it has been reported that *T. vaginalis* causes striking retardation in motility of human spermatozoa when these were incubated *in vitro* [8]; the clinical significance of this observation has not been ascertained.

Epidemiology and transmission of infection

In adults, infection with *Trichomonas vaginalis* is generally regarded as being sexually transmitted [9, 10, 11]. Trichomoniasis is uncommon among children and virgins but most common between the ages of 16 and 35 years, which is usually the period of greatest sexual activity. Trichomoniasis is commonly associated with other sexually transmissible diseases and up to 40 per cent of women attending STD clinics with this infection may also have gonorrhoea [12].

A varying proportion, even up to 60 per cent, of male sex partners of infected women may harbour the parasite and the majority are asymptomatic [13]. In many instances, cure of women with recurrent trichomoniasis has only resulted after the parasite has been eradicated from the genital tract of their partner(s). There is often difficulty, at a single examination, in demonstrating the parasite in male patients who are contacts of women with *T. vaginalis* [9].

Trichomoniasis is mainly a sexually transmitted condition. Although direct female to female transmission, resulting from poor standards of sanitation and hygiene (e.g. contamination of baths, bidets, toilet seats, swimming baths and towels), has been proposed as a means of acquiring the infection, there is little evidence to support this view. Infection of a baby during delivery may result when the mother has vaginal trichomoniasis. Neonatal infestation followed by a long and variable period of latency could account for non-sexually acquired infection. However, neonatal infection in female babies, although a recognized clinical entity, is rare [10]. It has also been suggested that intestinal trichomonads could become adapted to the vagina. There is however, no evidence that these trichomonads can be successfully established in the human vagina.

There is an association between cervical carcinoma and infestation with *T. vaginalis* although a direct causal relationship is unproved (Chapter 31).

Clinical features in women

Although the precise prepatent period of trichomoniasis is difficult to determine, it has been estimated that clinical manifestations of the disease develop 4 to 28 days after sexual intercourse with an infected partner [14]. There is considerable variation in the clinical features of the infection, the most common symptoms being vaginal discharge (70 per cent), pruritus vulvae (20 per cent), vulval soreness (20 per cent), dysuria (15 per cent), frequency of micturition (8 per cent) and odour (10 per cent) [15]. Dyspareunia may be the presenting feature, and is perhaps commoner than appreciated. At least 10 per cent of infected women have no symptoms of infection, the diagnosis being made at the time of a routine examination.

The most common sign on examining a woman with trichomoniasis is a vaginal discharge, which varies in consistency from thin and scanty to thick and profuse. The classical sign of a frothy yellow discharge is found only in about one-third of cases. Vulvitis and vaginitis are often associated with the discharge, and the cervix is usually inflamed. When inflammation is severe patches of higher vascular density may give the appearance described as a 'strawberry cervix'. The tendency to contact bleeding from the surface is explained by the fact that only a few layers of epithelial cells separate capillaries from the surface. Urethritis is found in about a quarter of women. Bartholinitis is a rare complication, and is perhaps produced by bacterial infection rather than the protozoon. In above five per cent of infected women there are no abnormal findings on clinical examination.

Symptoms of trichomoniasis may be transitory, lasting for only one to two weeks even without treatment, but may persist for months or years, with varying severity. In patients treated with presumably adequate doses of nitroimidazole preparations, about one-third will have recurrence of the disease, possibly often due to reinfection.

Clinical features in men

Although *T. vaginalis* may be isolated from the urethra, urine or prostatic fluid of male contacts of women with trichomoniasis, more than 90 per cent of these men will have no symptom of infection. Urethritis, prostatitis, cystitis and epididymitis have been given as manifestations of trichomoniasis [16, 17] but the aetiology of these conditions may be more related to the aetiology of non-gonococcal urethritis and to pathogens, or potential pathogens, such as *Chlamydia trachomatis* and *Ureaplasma urealyticum,* undetected by conventional bacteriological examinations.

T. vaginalis may be isolated from the sub-preputial sac and may be associated with balanoposthitis, which may rarely be ulcerative.

Trichomoniasis and carcinoma of cervix

Infection with *T. vaginalis* is often associated with dysplasia and endocervical hyperplasia, changes which are reversible with treatment [18]. Although the incidence of trichomoniasis was found to be four times higher in patients with carcinoma of the cervix than in control patients in one study [19], there is no good evidence that the dysplasia observed in trichomoniasis is associated with malignancy. *T. vaginalis* may be associated with other sexually-transmissible agents such as herpesvirus (Chapter 20) and it is difficult to come to conclusions as to which organism, if any, plays the major role in the induction of cancer of the cervix.

Diagnosis

The diagnosis of trichomoniasis relies upon both microscopy and culture for the demonstration of *T. vaginalis* in the secretions of patients. Repeated testing from a multiplicity of sites, especially in males, may be necessary to establish a diagnosis.

In women, vaginal exudate is collected from the posterior fornix with a sterile cotton wool swab. If a urethral discharge is present in men this can be collected with a bacteriological loop, otherwise an early morning scraping should be taken gently from the urethra before the patient passes the first morning urine. If these tests are negative then a centrifuged deposit of urine and prostatic secretion should be examined.

Polyester swabs, which are gentler on the urethral mucosa have been recommended for taking specimens in men [20] while small rectangles of sponge (1cm × 1cm × 4cm) can be used for collecting vaginal exudate in women [21]; sponge is more absorbent than cotton wool and a larger inoculum may be collected in this way.

The following diagnostic techniques may be applied:

EXAMINATION OF A WET FILM

A fresh specimen of secretion may be examined rapidly as a wet preparation either directly, or after suspension in a few drops of isotonic saline or buffer. The actual technique of microscopy varies from clinic to clinic but dark-ground illumination, phase-contrast microscopy and ordinary light microscopy with reduced illumination are all used routinely. *T. vaginalis,* which is larger than a polymorphonuclear leucocyte but smaller than an epithelial cell, is readily recognized by its oval shape, its usually rapidly moving flagella, the rippling movement of the undulating membrane, and the jerky movements of the organism. Ideally, the specimen should be examined immediately but if this is impracticable the swab should be placed preferably in Amies's transport medium; *T. vaginalis* does not survive well in Stuart's transport medium beyond 24 hours [22].

EXAMINATION OF STAINED FILMS

Giemsa, Papanicolaou and Leishman's stains are commonly used for the diagnosis of trichomoniasis while other methods such as Gram-staining with safranin as counter stain and staining with acridine orange have also been applied. Diagnosis by stained smear has the advantage that, once fixed, the specimen can be sent to a laboratory for processing.

When sufficiently numerous and under good conditions of fixation and staining *T. vaginalis* is recognizable in cervical smears taken for cytological examination, although variations in morphology due to artefacts of smear making and staining and the eosinophilic appearance of the parasite found in blood stained smears, may make difficult a certain diagnosis. The protozoon nearly always loses its flagella during fixation and appears as a small sometimes pear-shaped cell 10–30μm in diameter, grey-blue in colour with multiple intracytoplasmic granules. Diagnosis depends on the recognition particularly of the small dark grey ovoid nucleus which can resemble degenerate nuclei of parabasal cells [23]. Opinion varies as to the value of staining techniques in general and to Papanicolaou-stained cervical smears in particular. In one study, errors in diagnosis due to false-positive and false-negative findings when the Papanicolaou smear was used as the criterion for diagnosing and treating *T. vaginalis* infestation reached almost 50 per cent [24]. When organisms are fewer in number the discovery of the motile protozoon with its flagella and undulating membrane in a wet film, examined preferably by phase-contrast microscopy or by direct light microscopy, is the method of choice. Details of cellular changes associated with trichomonal infection are given by Hughes *et al* [25].

False-negative results are not uncommon in diagnosis by microscopy, particularly if the numbers of trichomonads present are small. In such cases, *T. vaginalis* may be isolated by culture.

CULTURE

Many media are available for the cultural diagnosis of trichomoniasis but no one medium is consistently better than the others. These media are usually liquid and contain liver digest, serum and antibacterial and antifungal agents: commonly used media include cysteine-peptone-liver-maltose (CPLM) medium, Feinberg and Whittington's, and commercially available Oxoid trichomonas medium. Cultures should be inoculated directly with specimens taken from the same sites as those for microscopy. Cultures are incubated at 37°C for 48 hours and examined microscopically for trichomonads: incubation should be continued and cultures examined daily for up to one week.

Opinion varies considerably as to the relative efficiency of culture and microscopy. Techniques which work well in one area often give poor results in other laboratories. A combination of direct microscopic examination of a wet film of secretion and culture is recommended. However, culture need only be undertaken if the wet film is negative. In this way, heavy infestations may be detected more quickly by the wet preparation and lighter infestations detected within a few days by culture [26].

Accurate diagnosis of trichomoniasis followed by effective treatment is particularly important with respect to the interpretation of cervical cytology smears and biopsy specimens. Degenerative changes associated with trichomonal infection may mask the presence of dyskaryotic or malignant cells [25]. Because of the association of trichomoniasis with precancerous and cancerous states of the cervix, cervical cytology examinations are essential in women with persistent trichomoniasis.

Serological tests and immunity

Although serological techniques such as complement fixation, haemagglutination and indirect immunofluorescence have been applied to trichomoniasis these tests are not part of routine diagnosis. Trichomoniasis like other mucosal infections induces local production of secretory IgA in women [27], but this was seldom detected in men who harboured trichomonas or who were contacts of women who harboured the organism [28]. This antibody response is not capable of eliminating infection. Untreated trichomoniasis in women tends to subside into a chronic low-grade infection with occasional reappearance of symptoms. Also, immune response to infection with *T. vaginalis* does not prevent re-infection since repeated attacks of trichomoniasis are common.

Treatment with metronidazole

Trichomonads have been shown to be inhibited by nitroimidazole compounds such as metronidazole, which has been used widely since 1959. The morphological changes in *T. vaginalis* induced by metronidazole are consistent with those caused by an agent binding to DNA and inhibiting nucleic acid synthesis [29].

In vitro studies have shown that low concentrations of the drug are trichomonistatic, whereas higher concentrations are trichomonicidal. The exact minimal inhibitory concentration depends on the size of the inoculum of organisms. For an inoculum of 100,000 organisms per ml, the inhibitory and trichomonicidal concentrations of metronidazole are 1.0μg per ml and 3.3μg per ml respectively, levels which are obtained in serum and vaginal tissues after oral administration of standard doses of the drug [30].

Nitroimidazole preparations are well absorbed when given orally. About 60 per cent of these drugs are excreted, mostly in the unchanged form in the urine. Sometimes metabolites of metronidazole cause darkening of the urine. The serum half life of metronidazole is 7.3 hours. Nitroimidazole preparations not only inhibit trichomonads, but also other protozoa including *Giardia lamblia* and *Entamoeba histolytica* and some anaerobic bacteria.

DOSAGE

Several treatment schedules have been described, the most common being the oral administration of 200mg three times daily for seven days. Other schedules include using oral doses of 400mg three times daily for two days. The use of metronidazole in a single dose of 2g has been described but is not recommended; the failure rate was 18 per cent, compared with a failure rate of about 5 per cent when the drug is given in divided doses over a week [31].

TOXICITY

At the doses generally used for trichomoniasis (200mg thrice daily for a week), metronidazole is well tolerated and during the sixteen years of its widespread use, it has earned a reputation of being remarkably safe. Occasional side effects at these doses include nausea, an unpleasant taste in the mouth, furring of the tongue and gastrointestinal upsets; headache, dizziness, anorexia, depression and skin eruptions have been reported but rarely [32].

Metronidazole may produce a transient leucopenia in four per cent of cases [33] but this appears to be due to an accelerated disappearance of these elements from the blood, which temporarily exceeds bone marrow release, rather than to suppression of bone marrow [34] ; no serious blood dyscrasias have been reported.

In the case of pregnancy the drug should be avoided during the first trimester. This policy is adopted for all drugs which may possibly have teratogenic effects, whether these have or, as in the case of metronidazole, have not been reported. The first trimester includes the organogenetic period (Day 15–56) when any malformation that occurs will be related to the stage of development at which intervention took place. In the case of the nervous system the vulnerable age lies between 15 and 25 days; the heart between 20 and 40 days and the limbs between 24 and 26 days [35] .

As nitroimidazoles are excreted in breast milk, mothers who are breast feeding should not be given these drugs. Metronidazole, however, appears safe for use in children [36] .

DRUG INTERACTION (ALCOHOL AND METRONIDAZOLE)

In a study of 53 alcoholic patients on metronidazole in which one case in a male was described as representative of the results obtained in the others, a decreased tolerance for alcohol, a diminished compulsion to drink intoxicants and an apparent aversion to ethanol were described [37] . Mild to moderate disulfuram-like effects were also described (e.g., facial flushing, headache, nausea and sweating) with metronidazole, following alcohol ingestion. *In vitro* studies have shown that metronidazole can produce inhibition of aldehyde dehydrogenase and other alcohol-oxidizing enzymes, but a study in rats failed to substantiate the results of the *in vitro* studies [38] .

In recent well-controlled clinical studies the disulfuram-like reaction has not been reported, nor effects such as decreased craving for alcohol, described as occurring within one or two weeks of commencing metronidazole treatment [39] . Adverse effects of concurrent metronidazole and alcohol are apparently infrequent but patients should be advised about these possibilities in the event of alcohol being ingested during metronidazole therapy [38] .

MUTAGENICITY AND CAPACITY TO INDUCE TUMOURS IN EXPERIMENTAL ANIMALS

In some bacteria metronidazole can produce mutations and preliminary results from patients treated with long-term metronidazole (for 1–24 months) for Crohn's disease suggested a possible chromosome-breaking activity in human lymphocytes [40] . Recent observations by Hartley-Asp [41] on 12 patients, receiving metronidazole (200mg thrice daily for seven days) for trichomoniasis, showed no chromosome-breaking activity but Coulter [42] thought that the data from this experiment were insufficient to exonerate metronidazole. Coulter [42] indicated that the connection between mutation, a heritable change in DNA sequence, and gross changes in chromosome anatomy is not understood and that bone marrow cells, rather than peripheral, would be more likely to show effects of short exposure.

As a nitro compound in widespread therapeutic use, metronidazole has been investigated in regard to its capacity to induce tumours in some laboratory animals. In connection with the effect on tumour incidence in mice Roe [32], writes that 'the effect involved the administration throughout the lives of the animals of total doses, on a mg/kg body weight basis, equivalent to between 350–1000 times that given to patients in the form of a 10-day course for the treatment of trichomoniasis'.

A more subtle discussion has developed about possible effects arising from disturbance in the gastrointestinal flora by the selective killing of organisms such as *Bacteroides* which form a large proportion of lower intestine flora. As a result carcinogen-forming bacteria might be allowed to predominate and lead to a decrease in the capacity of intestinal flora to detoxicate potential carcinogens [43].

In his review Roe [32] writes that 'a small and indefinite cloud' hangs over the therapeutic use of metronidazole, as it does to many other drugs in relation to possible carcinogenicity and mutagenicity. Metronidazole, however, and another nitro compound, nitrofurantoin, have been in use for many years and in the United Kingdom for the years 1968, 1969 and 1970, more than 3 million prescriptions were written for the two drugs. So far no clinical evidence of carcinogenicity has been forthcoming [44]. The cure of trichomoniasis and the control of secondary non-specific vaginal infection is highly desirable and as a result may reduce the risk of cervical cancer itself [32]. The authors favour the use of metronidazole in the doses recommended for the treatment of trichomoniasis. More remote questions of carcinogenicity or effects on bowel flora cannot be completely answered yet: studies of populations with controls and data-linkage would be necessary for such an analysis.

At the Mayo clinic 767 women, given at least one prescription of metronidazole for *T. vaginalis* infections, between 1960 and 1969 have been followed up and no substantial increase in total cancer incidence, over that expected, has been found. In this study increased mobility, increase in divorces and remarriages with consequent name changes caused great difficulties in follow-up. The finding of 13 cases of *in situ* cancer of the cervix in this group and the discovery of four cases of cancer of the lung in heavy smokers [45], illustrate further difficulties in making comparisons.

AMERICAN MEDICAL ASSOCIATION'S EVALUATION OF METRONIDAZOLE

There is a body of responsible opinion in the United States which introduces a cautious note, but clearly does not propose that severe infections should be ignored. In the American Medical Association Drug Evaluations [46] it is proposed that metronidazole should not be used for trichomonal infections that can be made asymptomatic by the judicious application of locally acting agents; but because no carcinogenic effects have been reported in man the use of the drug seems justified in treating stubborn or severe infections.

Among other local applications suggested by the AMA Drug Evaluations [46] is the organic iodine-polyvinylpyrollidone complex which slowly releases iodine. The following advice is given:

'After swabbing the cervix and vagina with this povidone-iodine solution (Betadine), one application of the gel is inserted nightly followed by the use of the douche preparation the next morning. Daily applications of the gel and douche are advised throughout the menses, if necessary, for a minimum of 10–15 days. Therapy must be continued for the next two cycles. When extravaginal sources of re-infection are present local treatment is unlikely to clear the trichomoniasis.'

Objective assessment of the value of this elaborate local treatment, however, is lacking. There is a pressing need to resolve the fear of carcinogenicity as metronidazole is clearly a valuable and versatile drug (*see also* Chapter 16).

ANTI-TREPONEME ACTIVITY OF METRONIDAZOLE

Metronidazole has only weak anti-treponemal activity and it seems unlikely that the small doses of metronidazole used in the treatment of trichomoniasis would delay diagnosis in a patient incubating syphilis.

Nimorazole (Naxogin)

This nitroimidazole is similar to metronidazole. It is usually administered as three oral doses of 500mg at 12-hour intervals.

Treatment failure

Treatment is successful in eliminating *T. vaginalis* in about 95 per cent of infected women. Failure to achieve this may be due to poor absorption of the drug; inability to produce trichomonicidal concentrations of the drug in the vaginal tissues; inactivation of the drug by other micro-organisms in the vagina; failure to take the drug or to re-infection. Assuming that the patient has taken the nitroimidazole, and that she has not had sexual intercourse, the problems of inadequate absorption or distribution may be resolved by using the drug in high dosage, say 400mg three times per day for four to seven days. In cases of repeated treatment failure, admission to hospital to supervise treatment, particularly with regimens requiring higher dosage, may be advisable.

Although sensitivity of *T. vaginalis* to nitroimidazoles may be modified in the laboratory, proof of treatment failure due to nitroimidazole resistance has not been established. In one case, reported very recently, however, in Vienna [47], a 42-year-old woman was not cured by two courses of 500mg by mouth twice daily for five days, nor with a further 10-day course of 1000mg twice daily. A fourth course of 1000mg twice daily by mouth for ten days combined with 500mg vaginal pessaries once daily and an additional oestriol application finally produced clinical and parasitological cure. Reference sensitive isolates of trichomonas were killed by 1.6μg/ml metronidazole *in vitro*, whereas the isolate from this case, obtained after the third course of treatment, required a metronidazole concentration of 100μg/ml to inhibit motility. In clinical practice such tests have not been widely available in the United Kingdom and clearly a wider study of resistance would be valuable, particularly since the recording of the marked resistance described. The larger doses of metronidazole for the short periods of up to five or even ten days, which are required when the standard courses have failed, may cause vomiting. Neurological toxicity with fits or peripheral neuropathy does not seem to occur until the treatment period is prolonged, as in Crohn's disease, when courses with high doses have been extended for months [48].

Treatment of sexual partners of women with trichomoniasis

If the male partner(s) of women with *T. vaginalis* infection are not treated simultaneously, the re-infection rate is more than twice that found in women whose consorts have been so treated [49]. It is rational to examine and treat both partners if either is found by laboratory tests to have *T. vaginalis* infection, although the social upset caused by this approach may not be justified. A sense of balance is essential in clinical practice.

Microbiological tests should be carried out after treatment to ensure that trichomonads have been eradicated from the genito-urinary tract.

REFERENCES

1 Donne, A (1836) *Comptes rendus hebdomadaire's des Seances de l'Academie des Sciences,* **3,** 385
2 Adam, K M G, Paul, J and Zaman, V (1971) *Medical and Veterinary Protozoology,* Churchill Livingstone, Edinburgh
3 Lowe, G H (1978) *The Trichomonads.* Public Health Laboratory Service. Monograph Series 9, HMSO
4 Ovcinnikov, N M, Delektorsij, V V, Turanova, E N and Yashova, G N (1975) *British Journal of Venereal Diseases,* **51,** 357
5 Nielsen, M H and Nielsen, R (1975) *Acta Pathologica et Microbiologica Scandinavica,* Section B, **83,** 305
6 Kolstad, P and Stafl, A (1977) in *Atlas of Colposcopy,* Universtetsforlaget, London, page 37
7 Slavin, G (1976) in *The Cervix,* (Ed) Jordan, J P and Singer A. Saunders and Co, London, page 260
8 Tuttle, J P, Holbrook, T W and Fletcher, C D (1977) *Journal of Urology,* **118,** 1024
9 Catterall, R D and Nicoll, C S (1960) *British Medical Journal,* **1,** 1177
10 Bramley, M (1976) *British Journal of Venereal Diseases,* **52,** 58
11 Morton, R S and Harris, J R W (1975) *Recent Advances in Sexually Transmitted Diseases.* Churchill Livingstone, Edinburgh
12 Tsao, W (1969) *British Medical Journal,* **1,** 642
13 Catterall, R D (1977) The Sexually Transmitted Diseases. In *Recent Advances in Dermatology.* (Ed) Rook, W. Churchill Livingstone, Edinburgh
14 Catterall, R D (1972) *Medical Clinics of North America,* **56,** 1203
15 Wisdom, A R and Dunlop, E M C (1965) *British Journal of Venereal Diseases,* **41,** 90
16 Harkness, A H (1950) in *Non-gonococcal urethritis.* Livingstone, Edinburgh, page 224
17 Fisher, I and Morton, R S (1969) *British Journal of Venereal Diseases,* **45,** 252
18 Bertini, B and Hornstein, M (1970) *Acta Cytologica,* **14,** 325
19 Berggren, O (1969) *American Journal of Obstetrics and Gynecology,* **105,** 166
20 Oates, J K, Selwyn, S and Breach, M R (1971) *British Journal of Venereal Diseases,* **47,** 284
21 Robertson, D H H, Lumsden, W H R, Fraser, K F, Hosie, D D and Moore, D M (1969) *British Journal of Venereal Diseases,* **45,** 42
22 Nielson, R (1969) *British Journal of Venereal Diseases,* **45,** 328
23 Grubb, C (1977) in *Colour Atlas of Gynaecological Cytopathology,* H M + M Publishers, Aylesbury, England, pages 23, 28 and 29
24 Pert, G (1972) *Obstetrics and Gynaecology,* **39,** 7
25 Hughes, H E, Gordon, A M and Barr, G T D (1966) *Journal of Obstetrics and Gynaecology of the British Commonwealth,* **73,** 821
26 Hess, J (1969) *Journal of Clinical Pathology,* **22,** 269
27 Ackers, J P, Lumsden, W H R, Catterall, R D and Coyle, R (1975) *British Journal of Venereal Diseases,* **51,** 319
28 Ackers, J P, Catterall, R D, Lumsden, W H R and McMillan, A (1978) *British Journal of Venereal Diseases,* **54,** 168
29 Ings, R M J and Constable, F L (1975) *Journal of Antimicrobial Chemotherapy,* **1,** 121
30 Komer, B and Jensen, H K (1976) *British Journal of Venereal Diseases,* **52,** 404
31 Csonka, G W (1971) *British Journal of Venereal Diseases,* **47,** 456

32 Roe, F J C (1977) *Journal of Antimicrobial Chemotherapy,* **3,** 205
33 Lefebre, Y and Heseltine, H C (1965) *Journal of the American Medical Association,* **194,** 127
34 Taylor, J A T (1965) *Journal of the American Medical Association,* **194,** 1331
35 Mirkin, B L (Ed) in *Perinatal pharmacology and therapeutics,* New York, Academic Press, page 357
36 Rubridge, C J, Scragg, J N and Powell, S J (1970) *Archives of Diseases in Childhood,* **45,** 196
37 Taylor, J A T (1964) *Bulletin of the Los Angeles Neurological Society,* **29,** 158
38 American Pharmaceutical Association (1976) in *Evaluations of Drug Interactions.* 2nd edition, American Pharmaceutical Association, Washington D C, USA, page 158
39 Semer, J M, Friedland, P, Vaisberg, M and Greenberg, A (1966) *American Journal of Psychiatry,* **123,** 722
40 Mideman, F, Hartley-Asp, B and Ursing, B (1976) *Lancet,* **ii,** 802
41 Hartley-Asp, B (1979) *Lancet,* **i,** 275
42 Coulter, J R (1979) *Lancet,* **i,** 609
43 Wilson, R L (1974) *Lancet,* **i,** 810
44 Hamilton-Miller, J M T and Brumfitt, W (1976) *Journal of Antimicrobial Chemotherapy,* **2,** 5
45 Medical News (1978) *Journal of the American Medical Association,* **239,** 1371
46 American Medical Association (1977) in *A.M.A. Drug Evaluations.* Publishing Sciences Group Inc., Littleton, Massachusetts, page 857
47 Thurner, J and Meingassner, J G (1978) *Lancet,* **ii,** 738
48 Nir, I (1979) in *Anti-protozoal drugs. Side Effects of Drugs.* Annual 3. (Ed) Dukes, M N G. Excerpta Medica, Amsterdam–Oxford, page 246
49 Gardner, H L and Dukes, C D (1968) *American Journal of Obstetrics and Gynecology,* **44,** 637

CHAPTER 19

Frequency and Dysuria in Relation to Urinary Tract Infections in Adolescents and Young Adults

In this discussion the term urinary infection will be restricted to an infection caused by organisms isolated from the urine by conventional bacteriological methods and these organisms, not pathogenic when existing as bowel flora, will be referred to as eubacteria. The diagnosis of a urinary infection is based upon the discovery of these causative eubacteria in the urine and diagnosis should not be based on the presence or absence of symptoms or pyuria, or on the demonstration of a radiological abnormality of the urinary tract [1]. From the aetiological point of view urinary infection in the adult female may be related in part to sexual intercourse, an activity which by its mechanics encourages potentially pathogenic organisms, ordinarily in the gut but sometimes included in the flora of the vestibule and the introitus, to enter the bladder through the short urethra.

In patients who attend clinics for sexually transmitted disease and who complain of one or both of the symptoms of dysuria and frequency, routines required for the diagnosis of gonorrhoea (Chapter 11), and, in the male particularly, of non-gonococcal urethritis (Chapter 13) are always applied, whereas in general medical practice lack of facilities tends to favour omission of these procedures. Infections due to pathogens or potential pathogens, such as *Chlamydia trachomatis* or *Ureaplasma urealyticum,* are possible causes of urethritis leading to such symptoms and require special methods for their isolation (Chapter 13). *Trichomonas vaginalis* in the female particularly (Chapter 18) and herpes-virus (Chapter 20) sometimes also cause dysuria when an inflammatory reaction to infection involves the urethral meatus. These conditions tend to cause a urethritis whereas urinary infections will involve bladder, or kidney, or both.

INDICATIONS IN STD CLINIC PRACTICE FOR BACTERIOLOGICAL EXAMINATION OF THE URINE

In ordinary clinic practice the urine will not be examined routinely for eubacteria. In men, with gonococcal or non-gonococcal urethritis some degree of dysuria is common whereas frequency is often slight or absent. In patients with frequency or dysuria, when sexually transmitted organisms have been excluded as causes, this investigation is indicated. If, however, sexually transmitted organisms are discovered and symptoms do not disappear with the treatment normally effective in these infections, then this investigation is also indicated. Sometimes bacteriological investigation of the urine is necessary from the first when frequency of micturition, with or without dysuria, urgency or haematuria are prominent symptoms.

During the routine visual examination of urine of men, a turbidity due to pus cells in the second urine specimen (page 48) will often draw attention to cystitis. In women, with gonorrhoea or attending as contacts of men with urethritis from this or some other cause, both symptoms are uncommon. Bacteriological examination of the urine is indicated in men when frequency and dysuria appear to be unrelated to a sexual experience, that is to say, when it is too remote to be certainly relevant or when the sexual contact has been with a single partner exclusively. On occasions, a urethral discharge in the male, particularly in those over 35 years of age, may resemble a non-gonococcal urethritis but may prove to be an accompaniment of a 'eubacterial' infection of the bladder urine. In these cases, a clean catch mid-stream specimen of urine is necessary for diagnosis. Dip-slide and strip-culture techniques have made practicable the quantitative bacteriological examination of the urine required for a diagnosis of what is known as a significant bacteriuria. In the investigation of patients with symptoms of 'prostatitis' it is necessary always to examine the urine for eubacteria (Chapter 14).

Significant bacteriuria

The demonstration of 100,000 (10^5) or more of the same organism per ml in a freshly voided clean catch mid-stream specimen of urine is regarded as significant bacteriuria. For a firm diagnosis two consecutive samples, taken preferably first thing in the morning, particularly in the case of those who ingest large volumes of fluid, are necessary [1].

Aetiology of significant bacteriuria

Urinary infection is caused by *Escherichia coli* in 85 per cent of cases. Other causative organisms include micrococci, *Klebsiella* spp, *Streptococcus faecalis,* or *Staphylococcus albus.* Next to *E. coli,* one particular type of micrococcus is the second commonest cause of urinary tract infection in sexually active young women. The infecting micrococcus 'biotype' (subgroup 3 novobiocin-resistant) is only rarely found among the normal flora of the genito-urinary tract of young women, although other micrococci and staphylococci are commonly present [2]. Novobiocin-resistant micrococci are probably not sexually transmitted since the infecting biotype was rarely found in the male urethra or prepuce. The classification of *Micrococcaceae* has recently been revised and the novobiocin-resistant micrococci associated with urinary tract infection are now classified as *Staphylococcus saprophyticus* [3]. *Proteus mirabilis* is rare as a primary infection except in young boys (page 305) and in *Pseudomonas aeruginosa* infection instrumentation is generally responsible for its introduction into the urinary tract [1].

There is a common belief that there is an association between sexual intercourse and urinary tract infection in young women. 'Honeymoon cystitis' and pyelitis of pregnancy are dramatic events that are often preceded by a history of urinary infection and antecedent sexual activity but proof of association is lacking as physicians tend to see only patients with symptoms and generally have little information about sexually active women without symptomatic infection [4]. In the investigations of Kunin and McCormack [5], celibacy was associated with a lower frequency of infection: in this study bacteriuria was about half as frequent in the unmarried women of the 15–24 year age group (2.7 per cent) compared with the married (5.9 per cent) but the difference was only significant at the 0.1 level. It was more frequent among single women in this age group than among nuns of the same age (0.4 per cent).

In a study by Bran *et al* [6], the urethra was milked outwards 4–5 times during general anaesthesia and the urine obtained by suprapubic aspiration of the bladder. It was found that small numbers of bacteria may enter the bladder in association with urethral trauma, but in only four of the ten patients examined did the suprapubic aspirates contain bacteria that are commonly associated with urinary tract infection.

Bacteriuria in young girls and women is probably preceded by colonization of the vaginal introitus by the specific species of bacteria causing the urinary infection. This vaginal colonization is more frequent and more prolonged and characterized by a greater number of bacteria in women susceptible to recurrent urinary infections than in normal women [7]. *E. coli* adhere more avidly to the vaginal cells of women susceptible to urinary infections than those of normal women and this affinity may promote vaginal colonization by enterobacteria [7]. Host factors determining bacterial adherence are possibly more important than bacterial adhesive factors in determining susceptibility to urinary infection [8].

In a small proportion of women with a urinary tract infection serious morbidity is associated with recurrent frequency and dysuria and there is some risk of progressive renal damage. Infection may increase the risk of serious renal disease in diabetes, the abuse of analgesics and sickle-cell disease. Urinary infection and stones may also be associated with functional or anatomical abnormalities of the urinary tract. Urinary infection associated with chronic pyelonephritis is the result of disease acquired in childhood in which the kidneys are damaged as a result of a combination of infection and vesico-ureteric reflux [1].

In the case of males, as in children of any age, after only one proved attack of urinary infection all should be referred for excretion urography to exclude an obstructive abnormality of some part of the urinary tract or an underlying lesion of the kidney. In boys below the age of puberty urinary infections tend to be due to *Proteus* spp. in two-thirds of cases and to *E. coli* in one-third. In those referred it is not uncommon to find a normal urinary tract and the infection may be associated with colonization of the urethra and possibly the prostatic ducts. Recurrences however, in the absence of a radiological abnormality are rare [9].

In urinary tuberculosis the infection starts in the kidney and is secondary to tuberculosis elsewhere, although the primary focus may have healed.

Clinical features

Most cases of urinary infection (90 per cent) with cystitis and acute pyelonephritis occur in women and when severe the onset is abrupt with fever, malaise, nausea, vomiting and pain in the loin or hypochondrium. Frequency of micturition and dysuria occur also, although in children this may not be marked [10]. In many cases symptoms are not initially dramatic although the frequency and dysuria are not symptoms easily tolerated.

Pyuria may be absent in 25 per cent of patients with significant bacteriuria, although when persistent it is a sign of inflammation of the urinary tract at some point between the kidney and external urethral meatus. Tuberculosis is now a rare cause of pyuria in western countries. Proteinuria, similarly may be found in a urinary infection, but its absence does not exclude such a diagnosis. Less than half of all women, also presenting with frequency and dysuria, can be shown to have bacteriuria of the bladder urine. Haematuria may be associated with a non-gonococcal urethrocystitis in the male or in the female with an apparently coitus-related urinary infection. In countries where schistosomiasis is endemic terminal haematuria is often due to this infestation.

Diagnosis

Since urine specimens may be contaminated by bacteria from the area surrounding the urethra, a mid-stream specimen (MSU) is collected to reduce the risk of contamination. If the laboratory is accessible within three hours, a clean catch mid-stream urine collector (C.R. Bard International Ltd., Pennywell Industrial Estate, Sunderland, England SR4 9EW) may be given to the patient.

If the laboratory is not readily accessible examination by the dip-slide method (*see* below) is particularly useful. Normally, urine specimens more than four hours old will not be examined since the results may be misleading. Specimens are often contaminated with commensal organisms and since urine is a good culture medium these can soon reach numbers in excess of 10^5 organisms per ml. Often contamination of this sort results in the growth of a very varied flora and is fairly obvious. In acute urinary tract infection, growth is usually of a single bacterial species but in chronic infection there may be a mixture of organisms.

DIRECT MICROSCOPY

Part of the specimen is centrifuged and the deposit re-suspended in a small volume. A wet film of this deposit is examined for the presence of pus cells, erythrocytes, 'casts' of kidney tubules and bacteria. The Gram-stained smear may be examined routinely, or alternatively only when bacteria are present in the wet film. A Gram-stained smear of the deposit helps distinguish between infected specimens (pus cells with Gram-negative bacilli or Gram-positive cocci) and contaminated specimens (squamous epithelial cells with mixed organisms including Gram-positive bacilli often lactobacilli). In some true infections bacteria may grow in the urine without the production of pus cells.

CULTURE

The diagnosis of urinary tract infection relies principally upon quantitative culture of a mid-stream specimen of urine, i.e., the demonstration of 10^5 or more organisms per ml (usually of a single species). Although the bacterial viable count can be accurately determined by a surface count technique this is expensive in materials and technician-time and a number of simple alternative semi-quantitative methods have been developed.

One of the most popular semi-quantitative methods is the dip-inoculum slide method (Uricult, Gibco Bio-Cult, Washington Road, Paisley) This technique is popular, especially in general practice, because it removes the problem of transport of urine specimens. The dip-slide is of fixed area and coated with nutrient agar medium on one side and MacConkey agar on the other side. It is dipped in the fresh specimen, drained and then incubated. The density of growth in the medium is compared with standard charts to determine the bacterial count.

Following culture, identification of the organism and appropriate antibiotic sensitivity tests are carried out.

Management of urinary infection

SINGLE ISOLATED ATTACKS OF URINARY INFECTION IN ADULT WOMEN WHO ARE NOT PREGNANT

A high fluid intake without symptomatic treatment may clear the infection, but if the symptoms are acute and particularly if there are systemic symptoms or loin tenderness, antibacterial therapy is indicated. Although treatment cannot be withheld when there are acute symptoms culture of the urine should be taken before antibacterial treatment commences. Fluid intake should be high (2–3 litres daily) and the urine should be voided frequently and completely. The urine should be cultured also about 5 days after the start of treatment to ensure that the organism has been eliminated. More than half the patients treated for urinary infection will have a recurrence within 18 months.

Antibiotic and chemotherapy

Since treatment will be given, often before the sensitivity pattern of the infecting organism is known the choice in initial treatment should be based on the opinion of the local bacteriologist, who is familiar with the antibiotic sensitivity pattern of urinary pathogens encountered in the patient's locality [11]. Courses of treatment lasting for one week may be prescribed initially, as in the following examples:

1. Ampicillin capsules, BP, 250mg six hourly.

2. Co-trimoxazole tablets, BP, in a dose of 2 tablets (each containing 80mg of trimethroprim and 400mg of sulphamethoxazole) given twice daily.

3. Cephalexin capsules, BP, 250mg–500mg four times daily.

In the management of urinary infection it is important to have clear criteria or definitions of cure, re-infection and relapse [1] as further investigations or different forms of treatment may be necessary.

Definition of cure

Cure is attained with the elimination of bacteriuria after treatment; persistently negative cultures of urine are necessary before a cure is pronounced. Disappearance of symptoms is not acceptable as a criterion.

Definition of relapse

A relapse is considered to have occurred when there is a recurrence of bacteriuria with the same organism immediately on stopping treatment, although urine cultures have been sterile during treatment.

Such a relapse may be due to wrong choice of antibacterial agent or its inadequate concentration in the urinary tract, emergence of resistant strains, anatomical abnormality, stone, renal calcification, scarred kidneys or bladder diverticula. A feature of *Proteus* infections is that the organisms may be converted to spheroplasts, particularly by penicillins, which change back to the original form after withdrawal of the drug.

Definition of re-infection

A re-infection is considered to have occurred when there is bacteriuria in patients where initial treatment has eliminated bacteriuria for weeks or months and urine cultures have been sterile.

Indications for excretion urography

Intravenous urography (with a mortality rate of 1/20,000 examinations) is a means of detecting functional or structural abnormality of the urinary tract, impaired bladder emptying or stone disease. These abnormalities pre-dispose to recurrent urinary infection and intravenous urography is essential (1) in children and adult males of any age with a urinary infection; (2) in adult females with recurrent bacteriuria;

(3) in both sexes with haematuria, which demands also both cytological examination of the urine and cystoscopy after control of the infection, unless in the case of the female, the haematuria is clearly associated with a coitus-related urinary infection [12].

In children and adult women a micturating cystogram is required to detect evidence of reflux in cases of uncontrolled bacteriuria.

Recurrent urinary infections in women who are not pregnant

If there are less than three re-infections in a year and the intravenous urogram is normal, each attack is treated as if it were an isolated attack.

When the recurrence of the frequency and/or dysuria appear to be associated with the trauma of intercourse, lubricants (K-Y water soluble lubricating jelly, Johnson and Johnson Ltd., Slough. Code No. 41148) may be prescribed for use during intercourse and the patient should be encouraged to void urine within 15 minutes after coitus. It is best to avoid giving antibiotics in those with recurrent symptoms and consistently negative urine cultures, because bladder bacteriuria due to eubacteria cannot be the cause.

If re-infection with bacteriuria is more frequent than three times in a year, more prolonged therapy is indicated [1].

1. Encourage a high fluid intake.
2. Encourage post-coital micturition, preferably within 15 minutes after intercourse, and advise the patient to void her bladder frequently and completely.
3. Advise in the use of vaginal lubricants.
4. Discourage the use of antiseptics in the bath or of chemical douching
5. It is a reasonable precaution in such cases to check the husband or consort for urethral discharge or subpreputial infection.
6. In those in whom sexually transmitted disease is an infrequent risk, prescribe (*a*) co-trimoxazole two tablets twice daily, or (*b*) nitrofurantoin* tablets, BP 100mg four times daily for two weeks. The dosage may then be reduced by half at two-weekly intervals after ensuring that bacteriuria has not returned. Co-trimoxazole is reduced to one tablet on alternate nights and nitrofurantoin to a minimum dose

*Nitrofurantoin should not be used in those who suffer from an erythrocyte glucose-6-phosphate dehydrogenase deficiency as a haemolytic anaemia may be precipitated. This trait is very common, for example, in sephardic (eastern) Jews and in up to 20 per cent in East African Bantu. The trait is found also among some people from the Eastern Mediterranean. It is extremely rare in white Caucasians.

of 50mg to be taken at night after voiding. In up to one-half of patients there is a recurrence on prolonged low-dose treatment and there is the *potential hazard of drug resistance in long-term therapy* [13]. It is not possible to eliminate the organisms responsible from the bowel, where they are not pathogenic but can remain as a source.

Urinary infection in pregnancy

Some 30 per cent of pregnant women with asymptomatic bacteriuria in early pregnancy will develop acute pyelonephritis later and elimination of the bacteriuria can prevent this. Tetracyclines should be *avoided* since discolouration of the child's teeth may follow its use in pregnancy. Sulphonamides in the last trimester may precipitate or exacerbate kernicterus and nalidixic acid in the late stages may produce hydrocephalus even in low dosage [11]. Ampicillin or a cephalosporin such as cephalexin may be effective in about 75 per cent of cases, but here again consultation with the bacteriologist in the locality is important.

Urinary infection in men

When no anatomical or functional abnormality in the urinary tract has been found and when there is no renal lesion, there may be a focus of bacterial infection in the prostate in those who have perineal pain or epididymitis with a significant bacteriuria due to eubacteria. In those without bacteriuria, but with persistent or recurrent perineal discomfort and variable dysuria, chronic or non-acute prostatitis may be diagnosed (Chapter 14).

Frequent and complete voiding facilitates clearance of bacteria from bladder urine. At the end of micturition the urinary stream is halted about one-third of the way down the urethra, distal to the opening of the prostatic ducts. At each voiding the urine in the posterior urethra is returned to the bladder and prostatic secretion which has antibacterial properties, is injected into this part of the urethra and returned to the bladder where it may continue to exert its antibacterial action. This action serves as an antibacterial seal [1]. The antibacterial action of normal prostatic secretions is due to a zinc compound and its activity related to the amount of zinc present in the fluid [14].

Bacterial infection of the prostate is difficult to eradicate, because many of the commonly used antibacterial agents fail to penetrate prostatic fluid and, even if they do, they may not be fully effective in the acid prostatic fluid [12]. Erythromycin, co-trimoxazole, tetracycline, doxycycline or clindamycin produce effective concentrations but ampicillin, nalidixic acid, nitrofurantoin, oxytetracycline probably do not. In general, the investigation and management of bacteriuria in the male due to eubacteria falls within the province of a urologist and early referral for advice is encouraged.

Frequency and/or dysuria in men and women

In both sexes there may be intermittent or persistent frequency and dysuria in the continuing absence of bladder bacteriuria. In the male this may be attributable to non-gonococcal urethritis or chronic prostatitis with or without positive isolations for *Chlamydia trachomatis* or *Ureaplasma urealyticum. Trichomonas vaginalis* or herpesvirus may be occasionally thought to be responsible: sometimes bladder neck obstruction is the cause of dysuria, frequency and bladder awareness (Chapter 14).

In the female with frequency and/or dysuria the short urethra very seldom shows a marked discharge and the organisms already referred to cannot be always isolated. Attempts to resolve the condition may include the advice tendered (1–5) for re-infection with bacteriuria and trials with courses of doxycycline, oxytetracycline or erythromycin. The uncertain aetiology and the uncertain response to treatment leaves a number of patients with unrelieved or incompletely relieved symptoms.

REFERENCES

1 Cattell W R (1976) Urinary tract infection. In *Recent Advances in Urology,* (Ed) Hendry, W F, pages 232–244
2 Sellin, M, Cooke, D I, Gillespie, W A, Sylvester, D G H and Anderson, J D (1975) *Lancet,* **i**, 570
3 Baird-Parker, A C (1974) *Annals of the New York Academy of Sciences,* **236**, 7
4 Kunin, C M (1978) *New England Journal of Medicine,* **298**, 336
5 Kunin, C M and McCormack, R C (1968) *New England Journal of Medicine,* **278**, 635
6 Bran, J L, Levison, M E and Kaye, D (1972) *New England Journal of Medicine,* **286**, 626
7 Fowler, J E and Stamey, T A (1977) *Journal of Urology,* **117**, 472
8 Fowler, J E and Stamey, T A (1978) *Journal of Urology,* **20**, 315
9 Hallett, R J, Pead, L and Maskell, R (1976) *Lancet,* **ii**, 1107–1110
10 Newsam, J E and Petrie, J J B (1975) in *Urology and Renal Medicine.* Churchill Livingstone, Edinburgh, pages 131–153
11 Asscher, A W (1977) *British Medical Journal,* **1**, 1332
12 Higgins, P M (1978) *British Journal of Hospital Medicine,* **19**, No. 4, page 325
13 Franklin, J J and Snow, G A (1975) in *Biochemistry of antimicrobial action.* Chapman and Hall, London, page 19
14 Fair, W R (1977) Epididymitis and Prostatitis. In *Nongonococcal urethritis and related infections.* (Ed) Hobson, D and Holmes, K K. American Society for Microbiology, Washington, D C, USA, page 55

CHAPTER 20

Herpes Simplex Virus Infection

Herpes viruses consist of a number of agents with similar morphology. The virus particles consist of an icosahedral capsid with an approximate diameter of 100nm, the capsid being constructed of 162 hollow capsomeres which surround the viral genome (DNA). The capsids are enclosed in a loose outer envelope derived from the altered nuclear membrane of the host cell (Plate 11). The total diameter is between 150 and 200nm [1] in negative-stained preparations. The members of the group of importance to man are:

1. *Herpesvirus hominis* (HVH) comprising two main types, causing herpes simplex.
2. *Herpesvirus varicellae* (V-Z) causing varicella and zoster.
3. *Cytomegalovirus* (CMV) causing cytomegalic inclusion disease (Chapter 21).
4. *Epstein-Barr Virus* (EB) causing infectious mononucleosis (Chapter 22).

Herpes simplex

Herpes simplex, which is to be discussed in this chapter, is an acute infectious disease, characterized by a sometimes recurrent vesicular eruption, occurring anywhere on the skin, but most often on or near the lips or the genitals and sometimes involving the eye to cause a conjunctivitis with or without corneal involvement. The causative organism, HVH, can be divided into two types on the basis of certain antigenic, biochemical and biological differences. Type 1 HVH is usually isolated from lesions round the mouth or eye and transmitted by the direct contact of kissing or by droplet in cases or from carriers; Type 2 is responsible for the majority of genital tract infections and spread is by direct contact during sexual intercourse.

NATURAL HISTORY OF HERPES SIMPLEX

Herpes simplex, characterized by a vesicular eruption, is the commonest virus infection encountered in man. As a parasite herpesvirus has few equals. It is able to infect generally without causing serious disease, it is readily transmitted from person to person and can persist in its host.

The majority of the adult population, including women of child-bearing age, particularly in the lower socio-economic groups, carry neutralizing antibody to HVH. This antibody is transferred across the placenta and confers passive immunity to the newborn child, but anti-body will have disappeared by the age of six to eight months, when a primary infection can then occur in the non-immune infant. Primary infections are rare before the age of one year; the commonest time at which the infection is acquired, particularly in lower socio-economic groups, is between two and three years of age. The vast majority of primary infections are subclinical; in one study, only between 1 and 11 per cent of children showed some manifestation clinically, usually of stomatitis [2]. Following primary infection antibody appears and usually remains at a constant level for a prolonged period, although it may decline until re-infection or reactivation may bring about an increase and stabilization of the titre.

Distribution of herpesvirus types

HVH Type 1 may occasionally be recovered from saliva, tears and the genital tract between attacks and from lesions during attacks. In the case of HVH Type 2, asymptomatic carriers probably constitute the principal source of infection. The virus may be isolated in such cases from the cervix in the female or from the urethra in the male; symptoms may be absent and signs of urethritis slight.

Transmission occurs by direct or very close contact with a person who has a recurrent lesion. In the sexually active age-groups spread occurs by sexual intercourse or kissing. In the case of genital lesions, most are caused by HVH Type 2 but in some localities or social groups HVH Type 1 is not uncommon. In Edinburgh about 17 per cent of isolates from the genital area of both sexes belonged to HVH Type 1: among female patients almost one-third of genital isolates, including those from the cervix, were Type 1. HVH Type 1 is widely distributed in the community and transfer could occur by oro-genital contact or via saliva-contaminated fingers.

In higher socio-economic groups 40–90 per cent of people may have no antibody to either type of HVH whereas the corresponding figure in lower socio-economic groups is only 20 per cent. It seems that Type 1 HVH infection of the genital tract is more likely to occur in those without neutralizing antibody [3].

Complement fixation and neutralization tests can be applied to the serum of patients to determine their antibody status. Complement fixing antibody can be detected before neutralizing antibody and conversion from absence of antibody to its presence in serum will signify a primary infection, which can occur in the genital area with either Type 1 or Type 2.

Recurrent infection

After primary infection the virus remains latent, possibly in a non-infectious form, and not necessarily at the site of the primary infection. Although the cytotoxic mechanisms of the host may eliminate HVH from infected cells, the virus may be taken up in the neurons as a result of neurotropism of the virus or the inaccessibility of the nerves to mononuclear killer cells. HVH may enter the demyelinated nerve endings and migrate along the axon to the nerve cells in the trigeminal ganglion. There is a lot of evidence that the trigeminal or other sensory root ganglia are reservoirs for the latent HVH, although other sites (skin, oral mucosa, salivary and lacrimal glands and cornea) cannot be excluded entirely. Recurrent infections are thought to be due to reactivation of latent virus. Virus can be recovered from lesions at the time of recurrence, but not in the intervals between attacks, although isolations have been reported from saliva of patients without symptoms at the time of samplings.

THEORY OF HERPES SIMPLEX RECURRENCE

Ganglion trigger theory

This theory, most often proposed to explain reactivation, consists of three sequential events:

1. A stimulus acts on latent infection in the ganglion to ‘switch on’ virus.
2. Virus then travels down the peripheral nerve.
3. Epidermal cells are infected so that a skin lesion develops.

As local stimuli such as UV light or trauma can induce detectable virus in the skin and produce lesions possibly too quickly to be explained plausibly by the ganglion trigger theory, a ‘skin’ trigger theory has been proposed.

Skin trigger theory

In this theory it is proposed that the ‘reactivating’ stimulus acts on the skin rather than on the virus in the ganglion [4] and the sequence suggested is as follows:

1. Virus is often produced in the ganglion and as a result reaches the cells in the skin via the nerve, perhaps every few days.
2. Microfoci of infected epidermal cells develop, but are usually eliminated by defence mechanisms; some of these infections may be abortive. Sometimes HVH Type 1 is produced in saliva, tears or in the gum tissue without obvious lesions.
3. Changes in the skin occasionally allow these microfoci to grow into visible lesions either by stimulating virus replication or by temporary suppression of local defences.

Ultraviolet irradiation is one of the commonest reactivating stimuli and is known to produce several well-recognized changes in the skin (release of prostaglandins, delayed erythema, early depression of DNA synthesis in epidermal cells and later a burst of mitosis). Prostaglandins may themselves be involved in some reactivating stimuli. The observation that chlorpromazine reduces the incidence of herpes recurrence and also inhibits the release of prostaglandins may have therapeutic implications.

It has been suggested [5], that the clinical or subclinical primary infection, resulting in latency and recurrent infection of HVH, can be interpreted in terms of the cell-mediated immune and antibody responses to HVH. A deficiency of macrophage inhibition factor was found in patients with primary HVH infection who subsequently developed recurrence. T lymphocytes produce interferon, and decreased interferon production has also been correlated with an increased frequency of recurrent HVH infections. It is possible that the virus might infect or depress specifically T lymphocytes, thereby causing a transient cell-mediated immunodeficiency and permitting the virus to proliferate, until the cytotoxic reactions kill the virus and infected host cells. As already mentioned the cytotoxic mechanism may eliminate HVH by killing infected dermal cells but the virus may be taken up or persist in the neurons.

The significance of the immune responses becomes clinically evident in a variety of immunodeficiency states in which HVH infection or reactivation may lead to severe local or general disease, e.g., malnutrition, Wiskott-Aldrich syndrome,* lymphoma, and immunosuppressive therapy in renal transplantation.

*A familial disease, affecting boys, characterized by eczema, bloody diarrhoea, thrombocytopenia and abnormal susceptibility to infection [6].

PATHOLOGY

The basic lesion is one of localized necrosis. The nuclei of affected cells become swollen and the chromatin marginated. A dense basophilic mass fills the whole nucleus and later retracts from the nuclear margin. Finally an eosinophilic intranuclear inclusion appears (the Lipschütz or Cowdry type A inclusion); all stages may be found in any one section.

The lesions of the skin and mucous membrane are characterized by intra-epidermal vesicle formation. The earliest changes can be seen in epithelial cells in the middle epidermal layer. Intracellular and extracellular oedema leads to formation in the epidermis of a vesicle with a thin-walled roof. The inflammatory cells at this stage are mainly mononuclear. With rupture and maceration of the vesicles polymorphonuclear leucocytic infiltration follows. The margins of the vesicles are usually clearly demarcated showing a sudden transformation from normal epithelium to balloon degeneration and multinucleate epithelial cells containing basophilic and eosinophilic inclusions.

In severe disseminated infections visceral lesions consist of parenchymal lesions of coagulative necrosis with specific intranuclear changes. In the liver and adrenals, the areas of focal necrosis can be seen with the naked eye. In early encephalitis, necrosis is a marked feature and in the adult form, there is asymmetrical softening with numerous haemorrhages on the surface of affected areas. The temporal lobes and the posterior orbital gyri are most commonly affected [1].

CLINICAL FEATURES

The very common nature of inapparent infections, whether of HVH Type 1 or 2, is becoming better appreciated with increasing availability and improvement of isolation techniques.

Primary infections

Primary *herpetic gingivostomatitis* is the commonest clinical manifestation of primary infection of HVH Type 1 in children between 1 and 5 years of age. The stomatitis begins with fever, malaise, restlessness and excessive dribbling. Drinking and eating are very painful and the breath is foul. Vesicles appear as white plaques on the tongue, pharynx, palate and buccal mucosa. The plaques are followed by ulcers with a yellowish pseudo-membrane. Regional lymph nodes are enlarged and tender [7]. An identical clinical picture may be seen in adolescents and young adults who escaped infection in childhood but acquired the infection by kissing someone with a 'primary infection':

most often a reactivated lesion or cold sore is the source of the virus. The lesions usually heal in 10–14 days.

Primary *vulvovaginitis* (Plate 14) may be commonly seen in clinics for STD. There is sometimes fever and malaise; pain and dysuria can be severe. White plaques are present on the red swollen mucosae of the vulva, vagina and cervix; scattered vesicles are seen on the labia and these may extend to involve the peri-anal skin and the skin of the thigh. The regional lymphatic glands are enlarged and tender and there may be a vaginal discharge. Healing tends to take place over a period of 1 or 2 weeks, but new lesions sometimes continue to develop over a period of 6 weeks.

In primary cervicitis there may be only swelling and redness of the mucosa but sometimes there is a necrotic ulceration of the cervix which bleeds easily. The range of clinical effects is wide and asymptomatic cases are common.

In primary *herpes genitalis* in the male the lesions can involve the glans or coronal sulcus and, if severe, there may be a phimosis with accumulation of secondarily infected exudate and occasionally a resulting necrotizing balanitis. In rare instances a necrotizing balanitis [8] may develop without phimosis (Plate 16). In the circumcised, herpes genitalis is less common. Crops of vesicles may develop on the shaft of the penis, on the anterior aspect of the scrotum and on the skin nearby; in the homosexual the ano-rectum may be involved (Plate 15).

Herpesvirus may be acquired at other sites by contact, as in herpetic whitlow, seen in patients and medical personnel, or on the trunk as reported in an outbreak among wrestlers. Other forms include *keratoconjunctivitis* and *eczema herpeticum,* where infection has become superimposed on eczematous skin (Kaposi's varicelliform eruption).

In the rare disseminated infections in adults, HVH Type 2 can be isolated from vesicular or pustular lesions that may appear anywhere on the body. In such cases HVH meningitis or encephalitis does not necessarily occur.

Recurrent herpes infection

After the initial infection, whether obvious or inapparent, there may be no further clinical manifestations throughout life. Certain febrile illnesses, such as malaria and pneumonia, provoke attacks in those in whom the disease is latent. Exposure to sunlight, menstruation or emotional stress may have a similar effect [7].

In the commonest form of herpes of the face, lips or genitals, itching or burning precedes by an hour or two the development of small, closely grouped vesicles on a sometimes slightly raised erythematous base. Ordinarily healing is complete within a week or ten days. The shallow ulcers which develop may be very painful. Recurrences tend to be in the same region but not precisely on the same site.

Complications and sequelae are uncommon. On the penis there may be some depigmentation of the affected site, particularly when there have been multiple recurrences over months or years. In the eye, repeated attacks of ulceration may result in corneal opacity.

Uncommonly, acute retention may occur and persist for a week or more in association with an attack of anogenital herpes in women particularly, but sometimes also in the homosexual male. Although pain may be responsible, constipation, blunting of sensation over sacral dermatomes and neuralgic pains in the same area and sometimes absence of the bulbocavernosus reflex suggest involvement of sacral nerve roots [9].

Recurrent herpes genitalis can be more than a temporary annoyance. The involvement of sexual partners and anxieties, engendered by recurrences, are sometimes heightened by concern over the possible oncogenic effect in relation to carcinoma of the cervix (Chapter 31). Transmission to the fetus and newborn may have serious implications, which are discussed later in this chapter.

DIAGNOSIS

In herpes simplex involving the genitals, it is essential to exclude other sexually transmitted diseases, particularly syphilis and gonorrhoea, which may have been acquired concurrently. All genital lesions should be examined carefully to exclude syphilis. It is good practice to carry out at least two dark-ground examinations on all ulcers unless clearly due to HVH alone.

Isolations are first made from vesicular fluid, when present, and/or exudate; cellular debris is gently scraped from the lesions with a cotton wool applicator. The specimen obtained is then agitated in a bijou bottle containing Virus Transport Medium [10]. The virus is isolated in tissue culture of human embryo (lung) cells, which can support a wide range of viruses, including HVH and cytomegalovirus in particular.

As described below the virus isolates may be characterized in the laboratory by antigenic typing, pock size, the appearance of infected cells on electron microscopy and the cytopathic effect (CPE) in tissue culture cells [11].

Blood samples should be taken on first attendance and again after 10–14 days for a complement fixation test to determine whether the lesion is due to a primary or a recurrent infection. Antibody of the IgM class is produced during a primary infection, but is not detected often in recurrent states.

Typing herpesvirus isolates

1. Pock size on the chorio-allantoic membrane
Inoculation of the chorio-allantoic membrane (CAM) of 10–12-day-old embryonated eggs is followed by incubation at 35° C for seven days, when the CAM is excised, fixed in formol saline, and the diameters of at least six discrete pocks measured. HVH Type 1 produces pocks less than 0.75mm and Type 2 pocks of 1.0mm or greater (Plates 9 and 10). With care, this test can be useful in typing various isolates.

2. Cytopathic effect (CPE)
In BHK (baby hamster kidney) and fibroblast cells, HVH Type 1 produces a CPE characterized by the formation of rounded cells, whereas Type 2 HVH is characterized by the formation of fusiform syncytia in addition to round cells. This method of distinguishing the two types is rapid, 48 hours being sufficient in most cases and observations can be made on unstained preparations.

3. Filament production in nuclei
Monolayers of BHK, Vero or Hep-2* cells, are inoculated with sufficient virus to give complete cytopathic effect (CPE) in 24 hours. After fixation in glutaraldehyde and embedding in Araldite, sections are examined by electron microscopy. HVH Type 2 produces filaments in the nuclei of infected cells in addition to normal virions (Plates 12 and 13). This test, while possible in some laboratories, is time-consuming and unlikely to be applied routinely.

4. Typing by microneutralization
Virus isolates can be typed by a microneutralization test using rabbit antisera to HVH Type 1 and 2. Neutralizing potency values are established for each virus isolate tested against reference type specific antisera: the virus can then be allocated to either Type 1 or Type 2. Such procedures are possibly too time-consuming for a diagnostic laboratory.

5. Immunofluorescent antibody test
As human embryo lung cells may be used for isolation of HVH and as the CPE is variable in different strains of such cells, isolates of HVH are

*Vero – cell line initiated from kidney of a normal adult African Green Monkey (*Cercopithecus aethiops*). Hep-2 – Human epithelial cell line (epidermoid carcinoma, larynx) [12].

now typed by an immunofluorescence test. One variation of this test utilizes rabbit antibody against HVH Type 1, which has been absorbed with cells infected with HVH Type 2. If the absorption of the antibody to the shared antigen is complete, only Type 1 isolates react with this fluorescein conjugated antiserum.

TREATMENT

The character of HVH infection is such that proof of the value of topical treatment is difficult to secure and eradication of the virus unlikely to be achieved by this means. Difficulties in ensuring penetration of agents, in providing objective description of the mucosal or skin lesions, in making reliable measurement of the healing time and in obtaining the close supervision necessary, particularly in cases of genital herpes simplex, make organization and interpretation of clinical trials uncertain. The number of days during which virus may be isolated from lesions and the time taken for clinical healing are criteria which can be used to assess clinical value. The separation of primary from recurrent infection would be desirable in diagnosis and several months of follow-up are needed.

Therapy in viral disease is difficult because there is often a close relationship between the cellular processes required for virus multiplication and those needed for the integrity of the host cell. Some agents, which affect DNA synthesis in the virus, affect also the process in the host cell and have, therefore, given rise to anxieties, as yet insubstantial clinically, about possible mutagenic or carcinogenic effects. As lesions of HVH are often mild and the immediate surface effects self-limiting, topical agents with such uncertainties are not advocated in treatment on a routine basis.

In the male, in mild cases, when the lesion is sub-preputial particularly, cleansing with saline is sufficient. A gauze strip soaked in saline may be applied so that there is separation of the skin surface of the glans from the inner aspect of the prepuce, as this may aid healing and promote absorption of exudate. Sulphadimidine may be given (2g initially and 1g six-hourly for five days) to control secondary infection without interfering with tests, such as dark-ground illumination, necessary to exclude early syphilis. When superficial lesions are localized and painful or more widespread as in a generalized infection, local applications of an antiviral agent such as idoxuridine may be a means of securing more rapid healing or of diminishing the amount of virus present. In life threatening HVH infections systemic use of adenosine arabinoside is indicated, or possibly the new nucleoside, acycloguanosine.

Idoxuridine

Idoxuridine (5-iodo-2′-deoxyuridine, IDU), an analogue of naturally occurring thymidine, acts in HVH infection by its incorporation into viral DNA chains to produce malfunctioning molecules. IDU is very insoluble in water and its use as a 5 per cent solution in 100 per cent dimethylsulphoxide (DMSO) ensures penetration through the skin towards the affected cells. In herpes simplex of the face it was found that applying IDU (5 per cent in DMSO) with a paint brush three times a day for three days, using a total volume of 1ml, produced a shortening of the expected duration of the lesion from about two and a half days to less than one and a half days [13, 14]. The application of this form of treatment directly to the lesions of genital herpes can reduce pain but DMSO, the solvent, has itself anti-inflammatory effects, breaks down collagen and blocks conduction in peripheral nerves. It has been shown that in genital herpes simplex, treatment with 5 per cent IDU in DMSO was superior to the effect of the solvent, DMSO, in the controls in producing more rapid healing and shortening the period during which virus was shed [15]. Treatment may, however, do little to modify the natural incidence of recurrence. In localized primary infections of short duration or in recurrent infections at the initial stages its effectiveness is likely to be greater than where the lesions are diffuse or inaccessible. IDU, as a 20 per cent solution in DMSO, is more effective as a topical application in severe cases, but toxicity should be considered. In attempts to use systemic IDU in HVH encephalitis, toxicity, including bone marrow suppression with leucopenia and thrombocytopenia and elevated serum transaminase and alkaline phosphatase began to appear with a dose of more than 3g daily [16, 17]. Although systemic use of IDU has been abandoned, it was considered that a total systemic dose should not exceed 20g [18]. If toxicity begins to appear at 3.0g (7.5ml of 40 per cent IDU) daily, it would be wise to bear this limit in mind when using this substance topically in genital herpes and to limit its use to, perhaps, 0.25 to 1.0g, used over a three-day period.

There has been opposition to the topical use of IDU in sites other than the cornea, in which drug absorption is minimal, the area of infection limited and superficial cells only are exposed to effective drug concentrations [19]. Application to the skin and the use of penetrating agents such as DMSO may be expected to produce greater effects than in corneal applications. Halogenated pyrimidines are potentially mutagenic; other possible side effects include enhanced susceptibility of resistant cell types to infection by cytomegalovirus, adenovirus, enhanced replication of many other RNA and DNA viruses and induction of infectious virus production in cells with integrated virus genomes including viruses associated with human and animal neoplasia. It seems possible that undesirable activities of the HVH or of bystander or integrated viruses can result from topically administered IDU [19].

A single report of transitory premalignant changes following the use of IDU has been described in a patient with 'grouped papular lesions' on the glans penis and prepuce, which waxed and waned in severity over a year but never completely cleared. No virus was isolated from the lesion and serological tests gave negative results, but, as recurrent genital herpes simplex was suspected topical application treatment with 5 per cent IDU in DMSO was started initially, but, as no benefit was observed, the concentration was later increased to 40 per cent IDU. This treatment was continued over a three-week period when the penile lesion changed to a friable plaque; two weeks afterwards a biopsy was taken. As there were multiple bizarre mitoses in the epidermis and dysplasia, the lesion was thought to be premalignant but, after cessation of the IDU treatment, it regressed spontaneously and did not recur over a follow-up period of a year and no further action was required [20]. In this case HVH was not proven and the attribution of the premalignant epidermal changes observed in the papular lesions to IDU in DMSO is not beyond question. Benign-appearing indolent pigmented papules on the shaft of the penis, for example, with histological appearance of carcinoma *in situ* have been described recently [21].

Descriptions of contact dermatitis arising from topical applications [22], together with these potential risks, as yet unfulfilled clinically, place obligations to restrict the use of IDU in DMSO to more severe cases and perhaps also to limit the duration of applications to the three days recommended by MacCallum and Juel-Jensen [13] as for treatment of facial herpes simplex.

Adenine arabinoside

In the treatment of life-threatening HVH infections the pyrimidine nucleoside, cytosine arabinoside (Ara-C), has been replaced by a more effective and less toxic analogue, adenine arabinoside (Vidarabine Ara-A). Given intravenously in a dose of 15mg per kg per day for ten days, there was a dramatic response within 2–4 days of commencing treatment, followed by clinical cure even in immunosuppressed patients. No haematological, renal or hepatic damage was noted but nausea was common and phlebitis also occurred [23]. In life-threatening HVH infection the systemic use of adenine arabinoside is clearly justified.

The potential risks already discussed in relation to idoxuridine may also apply to the topical use of adenine arabinoside which has been used as a 3 per cent ointment applied thrice daily to produce more rapid healing than 0.2 per cent idoxuridine ointment [24].

Acycloguanosine

More recently a new nucleoside, acycloguanosine (9-(2-hydroxyethoxymethyl) guanine), has been synthesized and found to have a marked antiviral activity in animal models of HVH infection as well as very low toxicity. In plaque inhibition tests for various anti-herpes compounds it was found that the relative potencies of some substances were as follows: phosphonoacetic acid, 1.7; vidarabine, 6; idoxuridine, 100; cytarabine, 500; and acycloguanosine 1000 [25]. A single report of a dramatic therapeutic effect of acycloguanosine suggested that the drug should be considered as an alternative to adenine arabinoside [26].

Photo-inactivation

An intriguing observation in 1900 showed that low concentrations of methylene blue, which were without effect on *Paramoecia* in the dark, could lead to the rapid death of these organisms on exposure to light. This process of photo-inactivation has been shown to be effective against several viruses including HVH *in vitro*. It appeared that heterocyclic dyes, such as neutral red, proflavine and toluidine blue, had an affinity for the guanine base portions of the deoxyribonucleic acid (DNA) and that light caused excision of this guanine portion and disruption of the molecule [27]. There is some controversy about the importance of the experimental finding that the virus may be rendered oncogenic [28, 29] by this treatment, but because of this and because a well-conducted trial failed to demonstrate its value [30] this form of treatment has been abandoned by the authors. Among the recognized problems in conducting clinical trials, there are also difficulties in ensuring penetration of both the dye and light.

Phosphonoacetic acid

Phosphonoacetic acid (as the disodium phosphonoacetate), which inhibits viral DNA polymerase, has been proposed for clinical use [31], but there have been no clinical trials.

Ether

The topical application of ether has a logical basis because ethyl ether acts on the lipid-containing membrane of herpesvirus. When lesions are small ether may appear to have a beneficial clinical effect [32] but if larger areas are involved applications are painful.

Povidone iodine

In a small group of 10 female patients with herpes genitalis, povidone-iodine as a 10 per cent preparation (e.g., Betadine, Napp Laboratories Ltd., Watford, Herts.) appeared to reduce the expected duration of symptoms and hasten healing, but firm conclusions about its place or value in treatment cannot yet be made [33].

Steroids

Steroid preparations are ordinarily contra-indicated in acute HVH infections, even though there may be occasional justification if steroids are used in conjunction with specific chemotherapy [14].

Interferon

Interferon, promising in herpetic keratitis [34] is not yet available for testing in less critical sites. Interferon is a natural by-product of human viral infections, it is completely non-toxic and active against many viruses.

Chlorpromazine

Stimuli, such as hyperthermia, UV light and trigeminal neurectomy can cause lesions of herpes within a few days. It has been postulated that prostaglandins can induce these lesions and the suggestion made that known inhibitors of prostaglandin synthesis, such as chlorpromazine, might be usefully tested [4, 35].

COMMENT ON THERAPY IN HVH INFECTION

The problem of therapy in HVH infection is not yet solved and the difficulties inherent in clinical trials of treatment in herpes genitalis, in particular, have been commented upon. There are nucleosides, such as idoxuridine and adenosine arabinoside, which appear to be useful as topical agents, although fears of mutagenicity have made clinicians cautious in their use.

In the severe systemic and extensive HVH infections, which may be life-threatening, particularly in those on immunosuppressive therapy, adenine arabinoside [36] is effective parenterally although response in HVH Type 2 is poorer than in HVH Type 1 [37]. Acycloguanosine may prove as valuable as adenine arabinoside.

Diagnosis and treatment should be backed by laboratory identification of the virus. Anxiety over the possible causal relationship between HVH Type 2 to carcinoma of the cervix [38] can be mitigated by explanation, reassurance and cervical cytology with follow-up (Chapter 31).

Herpesvirus in neonatal infections and encephalitis

The very serious and often fatal infections with HVH are rare and occur as neonatal infections, acquired before or at birth, as sporadic encephalitis, acquired later in life, or as disseminated herpes simplex in the immunologically deficient. HVH is a rare cause of the aseptic meningitis syndrome. An understanding of the nature of these conditions is necessary for an appreciation of HVH infection, although this dimension will not be faced in clinics for sexually transmissible disease.

VERTICAL TRANSMISSION OF HVH

The importance of transmission by sexual intercourse and timing is illustrated by the case cited by Hanshaw and Dudgeon [39]. The report describes the exposure of a wife, one week before delivery, to her husband, who had an episode of penile herpes genitalis in a recurrent form at the time of intercourse. His wife had a primary genital herpes lesion at the time of delivery and the infant, born by Caesarean section six hours after rupture of the membranes, contracted a disseminated HVH infection and died at eight days of age.

NEONATAL INFECTION

Estimates of incidence of neonatal herpes in the United States vary between 1:30,000 and 1:3,500, with a frequency greater in the lower socio-economic groups. In some countries or social groups, a major source of virus to the infant is the mother's genital tract at the time of delivery and more than 80 per cent of HVH isolated from the newborn belong to Type 2, the common form of genital herpesvirus [40]. In the United Kingdom, in Manchester, however, in the period 1969 to 1973, the incidence of neonatal herpes was thought to be 1:30,000 live births; in one-third of the cases infection was acquired from a person other than the mother and in these cases HVH Type 1 predominated

[41]. Infection in the neonate can produce a wide spectrum of clinical effects from subclinical to disseminated forms or to those localized to the central nervous system, the eye or mouth. Increased application of virus isolation methods has shown that the incidence of subclinical infection is commoner than the serious clinical forms.

CLINICAL FEATURES IN NEONATAL INFECTIONS

Disseminated forms

The HVH infection affects usually the liver and adrenals, but other organs are commonly involved including the brain, trachea, lungs, oseophagus, stomach, kidneys, spleen, pancreas, heart and bone marrow. Low birth weight or prematurity are more common in this group than that expected in the population at large.

The illness may appear at birth or for as long as 21 days afterwards (average 6 days). There are a variety of clinical manifestations in disseminated infection including pyrexia or hypothermia, vomiting, loose stools, lethargy, convulsions, dyspnoea and jaundice. The illness is usually stormy, death occurring on average within 6 days.

Only six cases have been described linking HVH to the congenital defects of microcephaly, intracranial calcification, diffuse brain changes, chorioretinitis, retinal dysplasias and microphthalmia associated with vesicular rash at birth. HVH Type 1 was isolated in one case and Type 2 from the other five [42, 43].

Localized forms

1. Central nervous system

Signs of meningoencephalitis indicate the need for lumbar puncture which reveals a lymphocyte pleocytosis. In about half the cases, death follows in 1–3 weeks and in the remainder there tend to be sequelae such as microcephaly, porencephaly and varying degrees of psychomotor retardation. Eye effects will also be seen.

2. Eye

Conjunctivitis and keratitis develop early and occasionally chorioretinitis develops slowly about a month after birth.

3. Skin

Isolated vesicular lesions can occur as well as a more generalized rash. The vesicular lesions recur repeatedly up to 2 years after birth, becoming less extensive than the original eruption but tending to be found at the same site.

Although the skin lesions are sometimes benign, c.n.s. and ocular sequelae may follow so a prolonged follow-up is advised.

4. Oral cavity
Vesicular lesions in the mouth are very rare and cause a gingivostomatitis or involve the larynx. Diagnosis is dependent on recognition of the lesions and isolation of the HVH. Treatment is at present unsatisfactory.

Prevention of transmission to the fetus and the newborn

Men with penile herpes should be told about the dangers of communicating HVH and advised against intercourse with women who are pregnant. If herpetic penile lesions are present in the father, the mother's cervix and vaginal secretions should be cultured for HVH in the last month of gestation even if there are no symptoms of infection [39].

If HVH is present, even though inapparent clinically in the last six weeks of pregnancy, Caesarean section should be considered; if actual lesions are present, whether primary or recurrent, vaginal delivery is not advisable. If the membranes have already ruptured for up to four hours, Caesarean section is not likely to protect the fetus. These recommendations by Hanshaw and Dudgeon [39] are based on the hypothesis that the principal source of infection for the newborn is exposure to high titres of virus during passage through the birth canal. Uncertainties remain as the majority of infants born *per vaginam* to mothers with overt disease do not become clinically ill. In theory hyperimmune-anti Type 2 HVH gamma globulin, given to the neonate, would be expected to be useful in preventing involvement of an infant delivered vaginally in a woman with genital HVH Type 2 infection.

Exclusion of the infant from a mother with infectious lesions due to HVH Type 1 or 2 until these are healed and the exclusion of the nursery personnel with similar infections are warranted.

Like cytomegalovirus and rubella virus, herpesvirus is able to infect the fetus during the period of organogenesis and induce anomalies such as microcephaly and microphthalmia. It is probable, also, that *in utero* infection may not be compatible with continued life, and lead to abortion. For these reasons during critical periods of early pregnancy, women should avoid risk of a primary HVH infection.

SPORADIC HERPES ENCEPHALITIS

A tentative estimate of 25 to 50 cases per year has been made for the

United Kingdom and on the basis of an expected mortality of 60 per cent there will be about 25 deaths per year from this cause [44].

The patient, who can be of any age, will be admitted to hospital because of a disturbance of affect or consciousness; there may be loss of memory, mutism or a change in behaviour. Sometimes coma or epilepsy will focus attention on the brain and admission to a neurosurgical unit on suspicion of a space-occupying lesion is one classical presentation. Brain oedema and raised intracranial pressure are the cardinal problem in herpes encephalitis [44]. Fuller clinical descriptions are given by Oxbury and MacCallum [45].

ASEPTIC MENINGITIS

In the aseptic (or abacterial) meningitis syndrome characterized by fever, signs of meningeal irritation, an increased leucocyte count in the c.s.f., but no signs of frank encephalitis, HVH is a very rare cause among the wide array of other viruses which have been implicated in the aetiology of a varying minority of cases [46, 47].

DIAGNOSIS

An early and incontrovertible diagnosis of HVH encephalitis cannot be made without examination by brain biopsy material. The inferior aspect of the temporal lobe is the site of choice for biopsy in the absence of definite localization; recognition of the virus in brain tissue or firm histopathological evidence of acute necrotizing encephalitis is necessary for diagnosis. Except in HVH Type 2 infections, infectious virus can rarely be isolated from c.s.f., which may be normal or show a lymphocytic pleocytosis. The electroencephalogram is never normal. Neuroradiological techniques such as angiography, technetium brain scans and studies with the EMI scanner provide useful information. Antibody assays in the serum are of limited value by themselves and few patients can be investigated sufficiently early in their illness to determine a proper base line to their antibody response.

TREATMENT

In herpes encephalitis there is a disastrous and progressive necrosis of the brain. Treatment can be effective only if applied as early as possible during the destructive process. Treatment is based on antiviral chemotherapy and management of brain oedema with dexamethasone or by surgical decompression. Severe residual neurological crippling may be too high a price to pay for chemotherapeutic success [44].

REFERENCES

1 Dudgeon, J A (1970) Herpes Simplex. In *Modern Trends in Medical Virology.* 2. (Eds) Heath, R B and Waterson, A P. Butterworth, London, page 78

2 Spence, J, Walton, W S, Miller, F J W and Court, S C M (1954) *A Thousand Families in Newcastle-on-Tyne,* Oxford University Press, London

3 Smith, I W, Peutherer, J F and Robertson, D H H (1976) *Lancet,* **ii,** 1089

4 Hill, T J and Blyth, W A (1976) *Lancet,* **i,** 397

5 Lehner, T, Wilton, J M A and Shillitoe, E J (1975) *Lancet,* **ii,** 60

6 Soothill, J F (1978) Immunodeficiency. In *Textbook of Paediatrics.* (Ed) Forfar, J O and Arneil, G C. Churchill Livingstone, Edinburgh, page 1153

7 Rook, A, Wilkinson, D S and Ebling, A J C (1972) *Textbook of Dermatology,* Vol. 1. Blackwell, Edinburgh

8 Peutherer, J P, Smith, I W and Robertson, D H H (1979) *British Journal of Venereal Diseases,* **1,** 48

9 Oates, J K and Greenhouse, R D H (1978) *Lancet,* **i,** 691

10 Cruickshank, R, Duguid, J P, Marmion, B P and Swain, R H A (1975) In *Medical Microbiology,* 12th edition. Churchill Livingstone, Edinburgh, page 219

11 Smith, I W, Peutherer, J F and Robertson, D H H (1973) *British Journal of Venereal Diseases,* **49,** 385

12 Shannon, J E and Macy, M L (1972) (Ed) *The American Type Culture Collection.* Registry of Animal Cell Lines, 12301 Parklawn Drive, Rockville, Maryland, 20852

13 MacCallum, F O and Juel-Jensen, B E (1966) *British Medical Journal,* **2,** 805

14 Juel-Jensen, B E and MacCallum, F O (1972) *Herpes Simplex, Varicella and Zoster, Clinical Manifestations and Treatment.* Heinemann, London

15 Parker J D (1977) *Journal of Antimicrobial Chemotherapy,* Supplement A to Vol. 3, page 131

16 Boston Interhospital Virus Study Group and the NIAID-sponsored Co-operative Antiviral Clinical Study Group (1975) *The New England Journal of Medicine,* **292,** 599

17 Marshall, W J S (1967) *Lancet,* **ii,** 579

18 Nolan, D C, Lauter, C B and Lerner, A M (1973) *Annals of Internal Medicine,* **78,** 243

19 Green, J and Staal, S (1976) *The New England Journal of Medicine,* **295,** 111

20 Thomson, J and O'Neill, S M (1976) *Journal of Cutaneous Pathology,* **3,** 269

21 Katz, H I, Posalaky, Z and McGinley, D (1978) *British Journal of Dermatology,* **99,** 155

22 Nater, J P (1977) Drugs used on the skin. In *Side Effects of Drugs Annual.* 1. (Ed) Dukes, M N G, Excerpta Medica, Amsterdam–Oxford, page 132

23 Aronson, M D, Phillips, C F, Gump, D W, Albertini, R J and Phillips, C A (1976) *Journal of the American Medical Association,* **235,** 1339

24 Theodoridis, A, Sivenas, C, Vagena, A and Capetanakis, J (1978) *Archives of Dermatological Research,* **262,** 173

25 Schaeffer, H J, Beauchamp, L, de Miranda, P, Elion, G B, Bauer, D J and Collins, P (1978) *Nature,* **272,** 583

26 Goldman, J M, Chipping, P M, Agnarsdottir, G and Brigden, D (1979) *Lancet,* **i,** 820

27 Felber, T D, Smith, E B, Knox, J M, Wallis, C and Melnick, J L (1973) *Journal of the American Medical Association,* **223,** 289

28 Rapp, F (1974) *American Journal of Pathology,* **ii,** 85

29 Jarratt, M, Hubler, W R, Melnick, J L and Knox, J M (1974) *Archives of Dermatology,* **110,** 642

30 Myers, M G, Oxman, M N, Clark, J E and Arndt, K A (1975) *New England Journal of Medicine,* **293,** 945

31 Gerstein, D D, Dawson, C R and Oh, J O (1975) *Antimicrobial Agents and Chemotherapy,* **7,** 285

32 Sabin, A B (1975) *New England Journal of Medicine,* **293,** 986

33 Friederich, E G and Masakawa, T (1975) *Obstetrics and Gynecology,* **45,** 337

34 Jones, B R, Coster, D J, Falcon, M G and Centrell, K (1976) *Lancet,* **ii,** 128

35 Chang, J W (1975) *New England Journal of Medicine,* **293,** 153

36 Juel-Jensen, B E (1976) in *Sexually Transmitted Diseases.* (Ed) Catterall, R D and Nicol, C S. Academic Press, London, page 170

37 Ch'ien, L T, Cannon, N J, Charamella, L J, Dismukes, W E, Whitley, R J, Buchanan, R A and Alford, C A (1973) *Journal of Infectious Diseases,* **128**, 658

38 Nahmias, A J, Naib, Z M, Josey, W E, Franklin, E and Jenkins, R (1973) *Cancer Research,* **33**, 1491

39 Hanshaw, J B and Dudgeon, J A (1978) *Viral diseases of the fetus and newborn. Major problems in clinical pediatrics.* Vol. XVII. (Ed) Schaffer, A J and Markowitz, M. Saunders, Philadelphia, page 153

40 Nahmias, A J, Alford, C A and Koroner, S B (1970) *Advances in Paediatrics,* **17**, 185

41 Tobin, J O H (1975) *Proceedings of the Royal Society of Medicine,* **68**, 371

42 Hurley, R (1978) Antenatal Infections associated with foetal malformations. In *Towards the Prevention of Foetal Malformations* (Ed) Scrimgeour, J B. Edinburgh University Press, page 101

43 Florman, A L, Gershon, A A, Blackett, P R and Nahmias, A J (1973) *Journal of the American Medical Association,* **225**, 129

44 Longson, M and Bailey, A S (1977) Herpes encephalitis. In *Recent Advances in Clinical Virology* (Ed) Waterson, A P. Churchill Livingstone, Edinburgh, page 1

45 Oxbury, J M and MacCallum, F O (1973) *Postgraduated Medical Journal,* **49**, 387

46 Lennette, E H, Magoffin, R L, Longshore, W A and Hollister, A C (196[illegible]) *American Journal of Tropical Medicine and Hygiene,* **10**, 885

47 MacRae, A D (1961) Viruses as a cause of meningo-encephalitis. In *CIBA Foundation Study Group No. 7.* (Ed) Wolstenholme, G E W and Cameron, M P. Churchill, London, page 7

CHAPTER 21

Cytomegalovirus Infection

Cytomegalovirus infection is endemic in all human societies. If transmission is expedited by poor environmental conditions, as in some tropical countries, its acquisition in infancy or early childhood may confer a measure of protection [1]. Primary infection may, however, be delayed and become common in adolescents or young adults, aged 15–35 years, because of the requirement of close physical contact, such as kissing or sexual intercourse, for the effective spread of the virus. Although generally asymptomatic the infection becomes important mainly when it occurs as a primary infection during pregnancy, bringing with it a risk of placental passage of virus to the fetus and brain damage [2].

Aetiology

Cytomegalovirus (CMV) is a member of the herpesvirus family. When examined with the electron microscope, the virus particles, after negative-staining, are indistinguishable from other herpesviruses (Chapter 20). *In vivo* CMV produces striking cytomegaly with intranuclear inclusion bodies in epithelial cells. Under conditions of *in vitro* cultivation the characteristic cytopathology is predominantly manifest in human fibroblasts. Inocula of high infectivity may produce focal collections of swollen rounded refractile fibroblasts detectable in 24–72 hours, whereas inocula of low infectivity may take several weeks to produce sparse focal lesions [1].

Transmission

Congenital infection in babies is associated with primary CMV infection in the pregnant mother and it rarely follows reactivation of a latent infection in the mother, where pre-existing circulating antibody effectively prevents placental passage of the virus, although virus is usually cell-associated. Early postnatal infection of the baby tends to be mild possibly because of the presence of passively transferred maternal antibodies [2].

After a primary infection CMV persists in the body in a la
probably for life. Although antibody is present in the se

excretion due to reactivation occurs in pregnancy and in patients on immunosuppressive therapy. CMV has been recovered, for example, from the cervix in 18 per cent of pregnant Chinese in Taiwan and in 14 per cent of Navajo women, 5 per cent of Negro and 4 per cent of Caucasian women in Pittsburgh. If recovery of CMV from the cervix is the result of reactivation of a latent infection then a measure of the reactivation rate within these infected groups is provided by dividing the number with positive cervical cultures for CMV by the number with complement fixing antibody to CMV (i.e., latent infection) and, when these calculations are applied to the Pittsburgh and Navajo populations, the rates are about the same (about 14 per cent). Reactivation occurs more often in the third trimester than in the first or second and more often in the younger and primiparous, than in the older and multiparous patient [3].

In clinics for sexually transmitted diseases in Leicester CMV was isolated from the cervix in about 3 per cent of women and in Manchester antenatal clinics an isolation rate of 0.7 per cent was obtained [4]. Sexual intercourse, as a method for the spread of CMV, is supported by the finding of the virus, as extracellular aggregates, in the semen of asymptomatic men convalescent from heterophil-antibody-negative CMV mononucleosis [5, 6]. In one case, virus persisted in the semen for 14 months but, although the specimen was negative for CMV at two years, the urine still contained the virus; CMV was also recovered from the uterine cervix of a sexual contact three days after the most recent intercourse [5]. More than incidental reports of CMV in the semen have been given by Lang and Kummer [7] who obtained positive results in 2 of 18 men seeking fertility assessment, in 1 of 10 patients attending a clinic for sexually transmitted disease and in 3 of 54 young adults.

Persons acquiring a primary infection, perhaps those experiencing re-infection and some with activation of an existing infection may excrete virus in the urine or saliva for months. The urine may contain 10^6 infectious CMV units per ml so that widespread dissemination of infection occurs in closed institutions. Infection rates, in England, as determined serologically, rise appreciably in adolescents. CMV infection, like infectious mononucleosis, may be a 'kissing disease' [1].

Clinical features

A primary CMV infection in adolescents or young adults is almost invariably subclinical. A clinical syndrome may occasionally occur characterized by low-grade fever, diffuse lymphadenopathy, hepatomegaly and pharyngitis; a lymphocytosis develops with atypical lymphocytes in the peripheral blood. Paul-Bunnell-Davidsohn heterophil antibodies are not produced and the monospot test is therefore negative (Chapter 22).

Primary postnatal infections similarly are usually asymptomatic but hepatitis with hepatomegaly may occur with abnormalities of liver function tests. Serious ill-effects in previously healthy adults, as for example chorioretinitis [8] or thrombocytopenia [9] are exceedingly rare.

In the *post-perfusion syndrome,* named for its frequent association with the use of extracorporeal circulation and characterized by splenomegaly and heterophil-antibody-negative CMV mononucleosis, the infection is primary and the virus may be transmitted with fresh blood in the fraction rich in leucocytes [10].

Those with immunological deficiences, whether due to debilitating disease or due to therapy with suppressive drugs, particularly in organ transplant recipients, are also susceptible to CMV illness when the infection may be generalized or confined to one organ; interstitial pneumonitis is the most frequent form [11].

In the United Kingdom 40 to 60 per cent of women enter pregnancy without complement fixing antibodies to CMV and about 3 per cent of them suffer a primary infection at some time during the course of pregnancy. In about 50 per cent of cases, the fetus is infected. About 0.5 to 1 per cent of all babies are congenitally infected and are excreting virus in the throat and urine [2]. The consequences of fetal infection may range from inapparent infection to the classical syndrome of neonatal cytomegalic inclusion disease (hepatosplenomegaly, purpura, chorioretinitis, uveitis and microcephaly [12]. Less severe brain damage may also occur in symptom-free, prenatally infected babies. In a survey of congenital infection in London [2], CMV was isolated from urine collected on the day of birth from 16 of 4259 unselected babies screened. One of the infected babies died and of the 15 survivors, who were followed for at least one year, three were mentally retarded (20 per cent); one was severely retarded and microcephalic, the other two less severely affected. In the United Kingdom, on a national scale, it has been projected that about 2800 infants annually are congenitally infected with CMV and about 500 of them suffer severe brain damage. Possibly double or thrice this figure might suffer brain damage of a lesser degree [2]. These figures, which compare with an estimated frequency of 200 cases of congenital defects due to rubella in non-epidemic years [13], stress the need for prevention of primary infection during pregnancy.

Laboratory diagnosis

Specimens of urine, or mucus from the throat and cervix should be sent to the laboratory* for isolation of virus in cultures of human embryo lung fibroblasts [14]. On staining the cells with Giemsa, CMV is identified by characteristic intranuclear 'owl's eye' inclusions. Fluorescent antibody staining can also be used to identify CMV in tissue culture. Isolation of CMV from the urine is more likely to occur as a manifestation of primary infection. The CMV complement fixation test can be used to detect previous exposure to infection, although the indirect immunofluorescent antibody test is more sensitive, as is the ELISA technique (Peutherer, J F, personal communication).

In semen the presence of CMV may be demonstrable only when diluted specimens are inoculated into tissue culture. This fact may reflect toxicity of undiluted semen to the cell culture or may reduce the virus neutralizing capacity of any specific antibody present in the semen [7].

Prevention of congenital infection

CMV infection is much more difficult to deal with than rubella. Prevention, based on early diagnosis of primary infection in the pregnant woman followed by termination, is even less satisfactory than in the case of rubella. The primary CMV infection in the mother is almost always subclinical, making diagnosis difficult. Detection of primary infection would require routine monitoring of women throughout the greater part of pregnancy by complement fixing and CMV-IgM antibody tests. The fetus, also, can be severely damaged in the second trimester, making termination impracticable. Because of these problems vaccination of adolescent girls has been proposed by Stern [2], as a method of preventing primary CMV infection during pregnancy. Difficulties in matters of attenuation, antigenic differences among human strains of the virus, reactivation of latent infection and the oncogenicity of herpesviruses in general are considered in his discussion on vaccination, to which the reader is referred [2].

Increased morbidity and mortality due to fungal and bacterial infections in transplant patients with primary CMV infection has led to the suggestion that a prospective trial of CMV vaccine might be justified in this situation at the present time [15].

*Method as described for herpesvirus (Chapter 20). Specimens of mucus or urine should be kept at 4°C (not frozen) in the refrigerator.

REFERENCES

1 Weller, T H (1971) *New England Journal of Medicine,* **285**, 203, 267

2 Stern, H (1977) Cytomegalovirus vaccine. Justification and problems. In *Recent Advances in Clinical Virology.* (Ed) Waterson, A P. Churchill Livingstone, Edinburgh, page 117

3 Montgomery, R, Youngblood, L and Medearis, D N (1972) *Pediatrics,* **49**, 524

4 Harris, J R W (1975) Cytomegalovirus Infection. In *Recent Advances in Sexually Transmitted Diseases.* (Ed) Morton, R S and Harris, J R W. Churchill Livingstone, Edinburgh, page 361

5 Lang, D J, Kummer, J F and Hartley, D P (1974) *New England Journal of Medicine,* **291**, 121

6 Gill, P A, Milan, F, Schofferman, J, Byfield, R E and Gaze, L B (1977) *American Journal of Medicine,* **62**, 413

7 Lang, D J and Kummer, J F (1972) *The New England Journal of Medicine,* **287**, 756

8 Chawla, H B, Ford, M J, Munro, J F, Scorgie, R E and Watson, A R (1976) *British Medical Journal,* **3**, 281

9 Sahud, M A and McCabe, M (1978) *Archives of Internal Medicine,* **138**, 1573

10 Lang, D J and Hanshaw, J B (1969) *New England Journal of Medicine,* **280**, 1145

11 Krech, U, Jung, M and Jung, F (1971) *Cytomegalovirus Infections of Man.* S. Karger, Basel, page 76

12 Forfar, J O and Arneil, G C (1978) In *Textbook of Paediatrics.* Churchill Livingstone, Edinburgh, page 186

13 Dudgeon, J A (1973) in *Intrauterine Infections (CIBA Foundation Symposium 10)* (Ed) Elliott, K and Knight, J. Elsevier, Amsterdam, page 38

14 Timbury, M C (1978) *Notes on Medical Virology,* Churchill Livingstone, Edinburgh, page 75

15 Chatterjee, S N, Fiala, M, Weiner, J, Stewart, J A, Stacey, B and Warner, N (1978) *Journal of the American Medical Association,* **240**, 2446

CHAPTER 22

Infectious Mononucleosis

The aetiological role of the Epstein-Barr (EB) virus, as the causative agent of infectious mononucleosis, is established and its acquisition during adolescence or early adulthood as a result of kissing is an important facet of the epidemiology of this virus infection in the developed countries. The sore throat, the generalized lymph node hyperplasia and the typical blood picture occur in some 50 per cent of primary infections in the 15–25 year age group in contrast to the generally asymptomatic primary infection in childhood. The annual incidence of infectious mononucleosis in the United Kingdom is about 20–60 per 100,000 [1].

Aetiology

Epstein-Barr (EB) virus is named after the two virologists who discovered it by electron microscopy, when examining cultures of lymphoblasts from Burkitt's lymphoma (*see* below). EB virus is a herpes virus, morphologically identical, but serologically distinct from the other three human herpesviruses (herpes simplex, varicella and cytomegalovirus). It grows only in a suspension culture of human lymphoblasts and then only a proportion of cells tend to produce virions, although all cells carry the viral genome. The virus is detected by electron microscopy, immunofluorescence, or by its ability to 'transform' normal human lymphocytes into a continuously dividing line of cells [2].

The evidence that EB virus plays a part also in the aetiology of the African malignant disease, known as Burkitt's lymphoma, is substantial but not conclusive. Possibly, different human populations respond differently to EB virus infections [3] or possibly those involved are subjected to the immunosuppressive effects of malaria due to *Plasmodium falciparum.* In nasopharyngeal carcinoma EB virus may also have an aetiological role as replicating virus has been found in the malignant epithelial cells. This tumour is seen most often in patients of Southern Chinese origin.

Natural history of infectious mononucleosis

Inapparent primary infection with EB virus generally occurs in childhood and is always accompanied by seroconversion and immunity to infectious mononucleosis. If the primary infection is delayed, however, until late adolescence or early adulthood then this event leads to infectious mononucleosis in about 50 per cent of cases. As in herpes simplex virus infections, EB virus is most frequently acquired as a primary infection during childhood, particularly in the lower socio-economic groups and, in developing countries, almost all children before the age of ten are infected, so that very few young adults can develop a primary infection and infectious mononucleosis is therefore virtually unknown.

In previously uninfected adolescents, often from privileged classes, large doses of EB virus are ingested, when kissing; this virus is shed into the mouth by seropositive healthy carriers, who themselves have practically never shown signs of their original primary infection. In the case of young children indirect methods of spread probably operate and are responsible for the smaller infecting doses, which seem to play a part in determining inapparent infections without disease. Although infectious mononucleosis tends to occur within the 15–25 year age group, it may occasionally occur in those outside the group.

Once in the mouth of a susceptible person EB virus gains access to the body by infecting B lymphocytes, probably in the oropharyngeal ring of lymphoid tissue (Waldeyer's Ring). It is known that B cells have virus receptors and can carry the viral genome *in vivo.* In the oropharynx after an incubation period varying between 6 and 60 days a replicative virus cycle is set up and the virus must then be carried throughout the body by the peripheral circulation, either as a viraemia to infect B lymphocytes everywhere, or infected B lymphocytes, involved in the virus replication in the oropharynx, are themselves spread widely to liberate virus and infect other B cells at distant sites. Shedding of virus into the buccal fluid occurs as early as 8 days after the onset of symptoms and the finding of the virus at the orifice of the parotid duct suggests that salivary gland epithelial cells are also involved.

A virus-determined surface antigen is directly responsible for the disease manifestations, as it is recognized by killer T cells which are produced in great quantities and are responsible for the hepatosplenomegaly, jaundice, abnormal liver function tests, tonsillar and adenoidal changes as well as the typical blood picture. The characteristic mononucleosis and atypical cells have been shown to consist largely of T lymphocytes. Tissue necrosis, due to death of cells supporting a full replicative cycle, may also contribute to the sore throat.

Increase of virus-specific antibodies and T cell mediated responses brings the disease under control. T cell numbers are reduced as the mass of latently infected B cells are reduced. The infection of lymphocytes can result in a temporary depression of cell-mediated immunity response, e.g., the tuberculin skin test may become negative during the acute phase of the disease. After convalescence and for the rest of the patient's life virus production continues at a low level in a pool of cells somewhere in the oropharynx with intermittent release of extracellular virus into the mouth.

Transient IgM antibodies to viral capsid antigen reach high titres early in the disease; IgG antibody develops in two weeks and persists throughout life. Virus neutralizing antibodies reach a peak later and persist also for life. Other antibodies are recognized but none are related to the transient heterophil Paul-Bunnell-Davidsohn type whose association with EB virus is not understood [4]. This IgM antibody is almost always present when the patient develops symptoms and becomes negative within a few weeks or months. A significant proportion of infections in young children are not associated with a positive Paul-Bunnell-Davidsohn test.

Clinical manifestations

Infectious mononucleosis consists of an acute illness characterized by certain clinical and haematological criteria together with the presence of Paul-Bunnell-Davidsohn heterophil antibody in the circulation. The incubation period is difficult to determine as evidence in case-to-case infection is rarely clear cut. Figures are frequently quoted within the range of 6–60 days. The young adult presenting with malaise, fever with tachycardia, sore throat and skin rash, who is found to have lymphadenopathy and splenomegaly, is the classical clinical picture. There may also be headache, dysphagia and anorexia, myalgia, nausea, neck stiffness, photophobia and chest pain and even a mild jaundice in a few patients. Hyperplasia of the pharyngeal lymph follicles is common and a pharyngeal exudate is seen in about half the patients. In up to one-third of cases there are petechial lesions 0.5–1.0mm in diameter at the junction of the hard and soft palate near the midline. Discrete slightly tender lymph nodes are noted especially in the posterior cervical region.

Skin rashes, when present, usually consist of a faint diffuse erythematous or maculopapular eruption mostly on the trunk and proximal portions of the limbs. The rash is not diagnostic and may have been drug-induced as patients with infectious mononucleosis are particularly prone to hypersensitivity reactions of this kind.

Ampicillin will precipitate a rash in about eight per cent of individuals, but in patients with infectious mononucleosis or lymphatic leukaemia, a rash develops in more than 70 per cent of cases [5]. This may be due to alteration of the normal immune mechanisms resulting from the abnormal, but immunologically competent lymphocytes. Impurities of high molecular weight in ampicillin play a part and there is clinical support for efforts of manufacturers to remove these from antibiotics [6].

Other objective signs sometimes found include also hepatomegaly, periorbital oedema, arthropathy, cough and diarrhoea. Most of the unusual symptoms are associated with some rare complication and their undue emphasis tends to distort descriptions of the true clinical picture which, for the most part, is somewhat stereotyped. The most important and characteristic symptom is the sore throat which develops a few days after the onset of the illness [7].

Prognosis

The usual pattern is one of mild fever of about two weeks duration. Complications are rare although a wide variety, including haemolytic anaemia and thrombocytopenia, occasionally develop. Fatalities are very rare (less than 1 per 1000 cases) and may be associated with ruptured spleen, neurological complications, asphyxia and 'toxic' effects. A new syndrome has been recognized in which an X-chromosome-linked immunological deficiency has led to deaths as a result of primary virus infection. In this condition death seems to result from an unrestrained infection of B cells supporting virus replication throughout the body, as a result of the absence of humoral and T-cell-mediated immunological responses [4].

Haematological manifestations

The haematological features are characterized by an absolute lymphocytosis, 4,500–5,000mm^3 (4.5–5 $\times$ 10^9 per litre). A relative lymphocytosis of more than 60 per cent of total leucocytes is seen in 95 per cent of cases. The lymphocytosis tends to persist for two weeks unless bacterial infection supervenes. Twenty per cent or more of the lymphocytes are atypical and pleomorphic, varying in size, shape and staining qualities of the cytoplasm and chromatin configurations of the nuclei. Many lymphocytes show a tendency to flow round adjacent erythrocytes. Rapid changes in this picture may occur from day to day.

Serological manifestations

Non-specific cardiolipin tests for syphilis, such as the VDRL test and Wassermann Reaction may be positive: a great variety of other antibodies, such as rheumatoid and antinuclear factors may also develop [7].

PAUL-BUNNELL-DAVIDSOHN DIFFERENTIAL TEST

Sera from patients with many conditions other than infectious mononucleosis may agglutinate sheep red blood cells, but in such cases the heterophil antibodies are of the Forssman type, which can be absorbed by guinea-pig kidney cells. In infectious mononucleosis, however, the heterophil antibodies are not of the Forssman type and are not absorbed by guinea-pig kidney cells although the antibody is absorbed by ox cells. In the Paul-Bunnell-Davidsohn differential test, these properties are used to make the test highly specific for infectious mononucleosis. The test can also be made more sensitive by using horse erythrocytes. These principles have been used to provide rapid and specific screening tests, e.g., the monospot slide test (Ortho Diagnostics Inc., New Jersey, 08869, USA). In the monospot test, serum is mixed thoroughly with guinea-pig kidney stroma (GPK) on one spot and with beef erythrocyte stroma (BES) on another, and unwashed preserved horse erythrocytes are added immediately, to each spot. If agglutination of erythrocytes on the spot with GPK is stronger than that on the spot with BES, the result of the test is positive. If the agglutination pattern is stronger on the spot with BES the result is negative. The test is also negative if no agglutination appears on either spot, or if agglutination is equal on both spots.

Enzymic indicators of liver dysfunction (alkaline phosphatase, serum alanine aminotransferase) are positive in 85–100 per cent of patients with infectious mononucleosis.

Diagnosis

All cases of infectious mononucleosis characterized by the clinical and haematological criteria described, together with the presence of the Paul-Bunnell-Davidsohn heterophil antibody in the circulation, will be found to have antibodies against the Epstein-Barr (EB) virus. The diagnosis may be facilitated by serial laboratory studies; tests for heterophil antibody are readily available but not, however for antibody to EB virus.

There is a significant number of clinically and haematologically typical cases of infectious mononucleosis, which are Paul-Bunnell-

Davidsohn antibody negative, but which are due to EB virus as can be demonstrated by the presence of EB virus specific IgM antibodies.

In patients without EB virus antibodies and without Paul-Bunnell-Davidsohn heterophil antibodies, other diseases which may cause fever with lymph node enlargement, should be considered (cytomegalovirus infection, toxoplasmosis, listeriosis, tuberculosis, secondary syphilis and brucellosis). Viral or streptococcal pharyngitis, diphtheria, Vincent's infection or primary herpes simplex stomatitis may cause sore throat of similar severity to infectious mononucleosis.

A resurgence of heterophil antibody may occur in response to a non-specific respiratory tract infection [7] in patients who have had infectious mononucleosis months or years previously.

The following criteria may be accepted as definite evidence of recent EB virus infection [8] ; (1) the presence of IgM antibody, (2) the seroconversion of IgG antibody from negative to positive in paired sera. Single high or paired IgG antibody titres are not helpful in diagnosing recent EB virus infections, but a fourfold or greater rise in IgG antibody titre is regarded as suggestive evidence.

Treatment

Patients with uncomplicated infectious mononucleosis usually require rest in bed during the acute phase of the illness. Saline gargles and aspirin are useful for the relief of symptoms. As soon as the temperature is within normal range the patient may become ambulant and full activity is commonly resumed after about a month from the onset. Violent exercise should be avoided for at least three weeks after the spleen is no longer palpable.

Corticosteroids should be reserved for the rare case of a very ill patient, when there is, for example, significant thrombocytopenia, impending airway obstruction or acute haemolysis [7] .

REFERENCES

1 Pollock, T M (1970) in *Infectious Mononucleosis.* (Ed) Carter, R L and Penman, H G, Blackwell, Oxford, page 23

2 Timbury, M (1978) in *Notes on Medical Virology*, 6th Edition. Churchill Livingstone, Edinburgh, page 78

3 Wright, D H (1978) *The New England Journal of Medicine,* 298, 511

4 Epstein, M A and Achong, B G (1977) *Lancet,* ii, 1270

5 Cameron, S J and Richmond, J (1971) *Scottish Medical Journal,* 10, 425

6 Parker, A C and Richmond, J (1976) *British Medical Journal,* 1, 998

7 Finch, S C (1970) in *Infectious Mononucleosis.* (Ed) Carter, R L and Penman, H G. Blackwell, Oxford, page 23

8 CDS Unit (1978) *Communicable Diseases in Scotland.* Weekly returns and notifications of infectious diseases (7 January 1978) Ruchill Hospital, Glasgow, G20 9NB

CHAPTER 23

Genital Warts

Clinicians are now aware of the increasing prevalence of genital warts due to the human papilloma virus. Not only are they unsightly but their persistence and inconstant response to treatment give rise to anxiety and introspection in the patient as well as the inconvenience of multiple attendances. Their high infectivity and long prepatent period (average 3 months; range 2 weeks to 8 months) makes efficient control by therapy and contact-tracing possible only to a limited extent.

Aetiology and epidemiology

Papillomavirus, one of the Papovaviruses (pa = *pa*pilloma; po = *po*lyoma; va = *va*cuolating agent), is a DNA virus, icosahedral in shape and about 55nm in size [1]. It cannot be cultured. Examination of genital warts (condyloma acuminatum) and common skin warts (verruca vulgaris) show that both lesions contain morphologically identical virus. However, serological studies using immune electron microscopy have shown that the two viruses are not antigenically identical, the genital virus appearing to be a variant of the common wart virus [2].

Skin warts appear to be acquired from environmental sources, such as public bathing facilities or gymnastic apparatus, and occur primarily in children, while genital warts are mainly acquired by sexual intercourse. Vulvar and penile warts are more clearly associated with transmission by sexual intercourse, while anal warts are less clearly associated with anal intercourse and their origin remains speculative. In the case of the latter, tracing contacts is particularly difficult. Skin warts which are as common in cases of anal warts as in controls, seem not to be causally related. Wart virus may be a normal inhabitant of the anorectum in some patients and trauma may allow entry into the epidermis, but on the other hand warts are seldom a complication of anal fissures. The lack of a method of culturing the virus makes the study of its natural history very difficult [3].

The age incidence of genital warts shows a similarity to that of gonorrhoea, with the commonest age of onset being 22 years in the case of men and 19 years in the case of women. The incubation period varies between 3 weeks and 8 months with an average of about 3 months. About 65 per cent of consorts will be found also to have warts.

In England, for example, in the clinics for sexually transmitted diseases between 1971 and 1973 there was a 30 per cent increase in new cases of genital warts (increases from about 40 to 51 per 100,000 were reported in males and from about 20 to 26 per 100,000 in females) [4].

Immunology

The results of immune electron microscopy suggest that a one-way antigenic cross exists between the virus of the common skin warts and the virus of genital warts: sera from patients with common warts react with both the common skin and the genital wart virus, while serum from patients with genital warts appears to react only with the homotypic genital wart virus [2]. These studies show that patients with genital warts do produce humoral antibody to the homotypic virus. However, by itself, this may not be enough to produce resolution of the lesion and information on cell-mediated immunity is required. Studies on cell-mediated immunity would be facilitated by greater amounts of genital wart virus, but without a culture technique this cannot be obtained.

In pregnancy, when cell-mediated immunity is depressed, genital warts may enlarge and extend considerably, although they usually regress during the puerperium. Defective cell-mediated immunity is probably also the reason for florid genital warts which are sometimes seen in patients with Hodgkins disease [4] and occasionally in renal transplant patients.

Clinical features

Genital lesions

Various clinical types of wart can be distinguished. In men the fleshy hyperplastic wart (condyloma acuminatum) occurs most often on the glans penis and on the inner lining of the prepuce. The appearance depends upon the location, although moisture may enhance the size and the tendency to coalesce. Those in the terminal urethra have a bright red colour in particular. Hyperplastic warts occur also in women. Genital warts may occur at several sites in the same patient; the distribution, as recorded by Oriel [5] was as follows:

In men. Fraenum, corona and glans, 52 per cent; prepuce, 33 per cent; urinary meatus, 23 per cent; shaft of penis, 18 per cent; scrotum, 2 per cent and anus, 8 per cent. Genital warts are sometimes very extensive in the uncircumcised male.

In women. Posterior part of introitus, 73 per cent; labia minora and clitoris, 32 per cent; labia majora, 31 per cent; urethra, 8 per cent; vagina, 15 per cent; cervix, 6 per cent; perineum, 23 per cent and anus, 18 per cent. Most often warts appeared first at or near the posterior part of the vaginal introitus and on the adjacent labia majora and minora.

Other sexually transmitted diseases tend to be found as well as genital warts. In the case of men, urethritis, whether gonococcal or non-gonococcal, is common. In affected women trichomoniasis and candidiasis are seen much more frequently than in the affected male.

Sessile warts, resembling plane warts on the non-genital skin, tend to be seen on the shaft of the penis and although often multiple they do not coalesce. Sessile warts do not seem to occur on the vulva. Clear differentiation from the common wart is not always possible. Multiple *common skin warts* (verruca vulgaris) present as raised lesions; they occur only on the shaft of the penis and occasionally on the vulva and perianal skin.

Oral lesions

Papillomata of the larynx may sometimes appear within the first six months of life in babies born to mothers with genital warts at the time of delivery [6]. Mouth lesions may occasionally occur after orogenital contact with an infected partner.

Diagnosis

Identification of the virus in the lesion is seldom undertaken for diagnosis owing to the ease of recognizing a wart clinically. Very small lesions cause difficulty and to be certain that a wart has completely disappeared is often a problem, as minor changes in the skin surface often persist at its site.

Treatment

Before local treatment of genital warts is started it is important to attend to any other local infection, whether sexually-transmitted or not as warts tend to spread more readily in inflamed skin. In the case of men a balanoposthitis should be treated with frequent local saline washes. If necessary, gauze strips (3 × 15cm), soaked in saline, may be applied 2–4 times daily in such a way as to separate the inflamed inner surface of the prepuce from the glans. In such cases sulphadimidine 2g initially and 1g six-hourly by mouth for five days is a useful addition to therapy. In the case of women any cause of vaginitis or discharge must be discovered and eradicated, particularly candidiasis or trichomoniasis. Sometimes warts regress after local inflammation has been controlled. Treatment of genital warts is notoriously unsatisfactory and recurrences are common, although when warts are discrete and few, response to treatment may be rapid.

PODOPHYLLIN

A choice of local treatments is available, once local inflammation has been controlled. Podophyllin is a resin extracted from the rhizome of *Podophyllum emodi,* which grows in North India, or of *P. peltatum* of North America. In the United Kingdom it is the Indian variety which is usually obtainable. The chief active principle is podophyllotoxin [7]. A 25 per cent suspension in liquid paraffin is preferred but one in spirit of a similar strength may be used when smearing is to be avoided. Ordinarily, a few warts should be treated at a time, the adjacent skin being protected by Vaseline, powder, or both. It is good practice to treat at frequent intervals (every 3–7 days) with small amounts of 25 per cent podophyllin in liquid paraffin (not more than 0.3ml at a time). The patient should be instructed to wash off the podophyllin after an interval of about six hours. *N.B.* In pregnancy podophyllin should not be used as it has an antimitotic effect, which although mainly local, is better to avoid. In one case, where a very large amount (7.5ml) of 25 per cent podophyllin in tincture of benzoin compound, was applied to florid vulval warts, the patient developed a severe peripheral neuropathy and intrauterine death of the fetus (32 weeks) occurred [8].

In pregnancy it is often better to leave warts untreated as they frequently regress during the puerperium; if treatment is considered essential, liquid nitrogen or cautery may be used. Vertical transmission to the newborn appears to be rare, although laryngeal papillomata do occur.

ELECTROCAUTERY

This is an effective treatment in the case of genital warts, which are discrete. A one per cent solution of lignocaine is used as a local anaesthetic and the wart removed with the cautery. The aim should be to coagulate the wart down to the basement membrane and cause minimal damage to surrounding skin. In the case of intra-meatal warts, lignocaine gel (20mg per ml) may be instilled into the terminal urethra and the wart cauterized after 5–10 minutes. Occasionally removal of warts by diathermy or cautery will require general anaesthesia and circumcision is sometimes required, particularly when there is phimosis.

CRYOTHERAPY

The application of liquid nitrogen to discrete warts is sometimes effective. The aim should be to freeze the wart until a halo of frozen skin is just visible at the base. A cotton tipped applicator (Code No. 58404. Johnson and Johnson Ltd., Slough, Berks.) can be immersed in a vacuum flask of liquid nitrogen and then applied to the wart.

5-FLUOROURACIL

Dretler and Klein [9] reported on the successful use of this substance as a 5 per cent w/w cream in the treatment of intra-meatal warts in the male. The cream can be instilled into the anterior urethra with the aid of a nozzle or by using an applicator stick. On four occasions daily about 2ml of cream is instilled after the patient has emptied the bladder. Care is necessary to avoid contaminating the scrotal skin and treatment should be continued until the wart disappears or an intense inflammation develops (between six and 14 days after commencement of treatment). Careful supervision and follow-up with urethroscopy is important. Gentle dilatation of the anterior urethra is advisable after treatment to prevent the development of adhesions. A moderate meatitis after treatment is usual but this tends to settle. In our experience this treatment has been disappointing, as intra-urethral warts recurred in seven of eight cases treated, within six weeks to six months after cessation of treatment. The known tendency for warts to regress spontaneously makes assessment of treatment difficult.

Prognosis and contact-tracing

Where partners have a continued relationship, it is important to ensure that each partner is examined and treated. Contact-tracing, however, has a lower priority than in gonorrhoea or syphilis. With a possible prepatent period of as long as eight months a careful contact-tracing policy is difficult to secure. Treatment in the individual case is often prolonged and attendances may occasionally continue for a period as long as two years or more.

Malignant transformation of anal and genital warts

Malignant transformation of anal and genital warts is very rare. Carcinoma *in situ* occurring in one of a group of anal warts has been described in a homosexual: the warts had been recurrent over a two year period and were shown on electron microscopy to contain papillomavirus particles [10]. The authors have seen a case in which extensive recurrent hyperplastic warts became hyperkeratotic and were later replaced by a cutaneous horn near the fraenum, which was found on histological examination to be a well differentiated squamous cell carcinoma. Two cases have been recorded also in which cervical biopsy showed an invasive squamous cell carcinoma, associated with superficial cervical warts, ordinarily a common innocent lesion in young women [11] (*see also* Chapter 32).

The implications of such events may be more important in tropical Africa, particularly in Uganda where carcinoma of the penis is the commonest tumour in males representing 11 per cent of all tumours; in some tribes the proportion is 40 per cent [12, 13]. It is true that carcinoma of the penis is rare in those practising early circumcision, but in the uncircumcised, geographical location and tribal factors such as genital hygiene play a part [14]. In the case of women, carcinoma of the uterine cervix is the commonest tumour seen in some African cities [12]. Malignant transformation of warts may be one of the possible explanations of these cancers.

REFERENCES

1 Fenner F, McAuslan, B R, Mims, C A, Sambrook, J and White, D O (1974) *The Biology of Animal Viruses,* 2nd edition. Academic Press, New York and London

2 Almeida, J D (1976) Virological aspects of genital warts. In *Sexually Transmitted Diseases* (Ed) Catterall, R D and Nicol, C S. Academic Press, London, pages 179–186

3 Oriel, J D (1971b) *British Journal of Venereal Diseases,* **47,** 373

4 Oriel, D (1976) Genital warts–The clinical problems. In *Sexually Transmitted Diseases.* (Ed) Catterall, R D and Nicol, C S. Academic Press, London, pages 186–195

5 Oriel, J D (1971a) *British Journal of Venereal Diseases,* **47,** 1

6 Cook, J A, Cohn, A M, Brunschwig, J P, Butel, J S and Rawls, W E (1973) *Lancet,* **i,** 782

7 Bettley, F Ray (1971) *British Journal of Dermatology,* **84,** 74

8 Chamberlain, M J, Reynolds, A L and Yeoman, W B (1972) *British Medical Journal,* **2,** 391

9 Dretler, S P and Klein, L A (1975) *Journal of Urology,* **113,** 195

10 Oriel, J D and Whimster, I W (1971) *British Journal of Dermatology,* **84,** 71

11 Raftery, A and Payne, W S (1954) *Obstetrics and Gynaecology,* **4,** 581

12 Davies, J N P (1959) Cancer in Africa. In *Modern Trends in Pathology.* (Ed) Collins, D H. Butterworth, London, page 132

13 Dodge, O G, Owor, R and Templeton, A C (1973) Tumours of the male genitalia. In *Tumours in a Tropical Country. A Survey of Uganda 1964–1968.* (Ed) Templeton, A C. Heinemann, London, page 132

14 Schmauz, R and Jain, D K (1971) *British Journal of Cancer,* **25,** 25

CHAPTER 24

Viral Hepatitis

Hepatitis is a complication of infection with several different viruses, e.g., cytomegalovirus, Epstein-Barr virus, herpesvirus, varicella, rubella and yellow-fever viruses. The name viral hepatitis is applied to the most common forms of viral hepatitis, namely hepatitis A and hepatitis B; in some areas, however, the most common type of hepatitis, occurring after blood-transfusion, is clinically similar but antigenically unrelated to either type [1] and is called non-A, non-B hepatitis.

It is particularly the virus of hepatitis B (HBV) that may be spread by sexual intercourse; the exact mechanism of spread remains uncertain but viral antigens can be detected in blood and most body secretions.

Hepatitis A

The virus of hepatitis A (HAV) is transmitted by the faecal-oral route and undetected symptomless cases may be an important source of infection. The largest outbreak occurred in New Delhi during December 1955 and January 1956 when 29,300 cases resulted from the contamination of a major water supply with human sewage. Faeces of infected persons become infective 3–4 weeks after exposure and remain so for about 3 weeks. Symptoms develop up to 40 days after exposure. Patients are usually not infective when jaundice appears. In developed countries, infections occur at all ages with about 50 per cent of clinical cases being seen in children less than 15 years old In tropical and subtropical areas most infections are probably acquired in childhood and the majority are subclinical. The virus is excreted in the faeces and infection is acquired orally under conditions of poor hygiene and sanitation and overcrowding as in children's homes and camps.

HAV is a small virus (25–28nm) possessing cubic symmetry. Few or no hepatitis A virus particles are found in faecal extracts by the time most patients are seen by physicians and maximum shedding of virus occurs before the onset of jaundice [1]. While differences between the clinical syndromes of type A and type B hepatitis are apparent on analysis of large numbers of cases, these differences are not reliable for the diagnosis of individual patients with icteric disease. The prodrome of hepatitis A tends to be shorter than the insidious form seen in hepatitis B. Methods have been developed for assaying antibody to HAV but these are not yet widely available.

Hepatitis B

AETIOLOGY

Blumberg [2] described an antigen in blood, which reacted with serum from patients who had been given many blood transfusions. This antigen was found also most commonly in Australian aborigines and Asians and was termed 'Australia' antigen. The same antigen was subsequently discovered in the serum of patients with serum hepatitis [3]. It is now known as the hepatitis B surface antigen (HBsAg).

Later studies have shown that the antigen in the serum consists of three distinct particles, which may be present in variable concentrations:

1. Hepatitis B virus itself (HBV), a large (42nm) double-shelled spheroidal particle with a central core, approximately 27nm in diameter, known as the Dane particle [1, 4].
2. Small spherical particles with an average diameter of 22nm.
3. Tubular forms with a diameter of 22nm but varying in length up to 300nm.

The small spherical particles are always the predominant form. These structures are associated with several antigenic determinants.

The HBsAg is present on the surface of all three types of particle found in the serum of patients, and is the major component of 2 and 3. The HBsAg carries a common antigenic determinant *a* with other type specific antigens. These are mutually exclusive pairs, named *d* and *y*, and *w* and *r*. Thus the HBsAg can be typed as *adw*, *adr*, *ayw* and *ayr*: these findings are of epidemiological significance and have broad geographical associations. In Europe, the Americas and Australia, *adw* predominates, while in northern and western Africa, the eastern Mediterranean and the Indian subcontinent *ayw* predominates [1].

Detergent treatment of the HBV or Dane particle removes the outer HBsAg coat to release the core structure. The surface of this particle has a different antigenicity known as the HBcAg. The core also contains a circular piece of double-stranded DNA and a DNA polymerase enzyme.

The core particles can be detected in the nuclei of infected hepatocytes [5], whereas the HBsAg is found in the cytoplasm. It is likely that the core particles acquire an outer coat of HBsAg in the cytoplasm. It is not known why the HBsAg is produced in such great excess and released into the serum. Another antigen, the e antigen (HBeAg), is closely associated with hepatitis B infection and its presence in HBsAg carriers is correlated with a greater risk of transmitting infection. If present in patients with chronic liver disease [6] it is thought to be an unfavourable prognostic sign as regards the severity of the liver damage.

Epidemiology

THE CARRIER STATE

The persistent carrier state has been defined as the presence of HBsAg in the serum of the individual for more than six months. In the United Kingdom less than 1 per cent of the population are found to have HBsAg in the serum [7]. The prevalence in apparently healthy adults varies from 0.1 per cent in parts of Europe, North America and Australia to 15 per cent in several tropical countries. Within each country considerable differences in prevalence may exist between different ethnic and socio-economic groups. In homosexual men attending two major clinics for sexually transmitted disease in central London the prevalence of HBsAg was found to be about 5 per cent or about 50 times greater than that in unpaid blood-donors in the United Kingdom [8]. The carrier state may be associated with liver damage.

The carrier state is more common in males, more likely to follow infections acquired in childhood than those acquired in adult life and more likely in those with natural or acquired immune deficiencies. In countries in which HBV is common, the highest prevalence of HBsAg is found in children 4–8 years old with steadily declining rates among the older age groups. This decline in the HBsAg carriage rates with age suggests that the carrier state is not lifelong.

MODES OF SPREAD

In areas of low prevalence a major mode of spread continues to be the inoculation of blood and some blood products. Hepatitis B may be transmitted as a result of transfusion or by accidental inoculation of minute quantities of blood as may occur during surgical or dental procedures, intravenous drug abuse, mass immunization, tattooing, acupuncture and laboratory accidents. The sharing of razors, toothbrushes or bath brushes has been implicated as an occasional cause of hepatitis B.

Spread of HBV from carrier mothers to babies appears to be an important factor in some regions as well as the spread from those with an acute infection. In Taiwan, for example, where the prevalence of HBsAg is 5–20 per cent it was found that in about 40 per cent of cases, babies born to asymptomatic mothers became antigen positive within the first six months of life [9]. If an acute infection occurs in the second or third trimester or within two months after delivery there is a substantial risk that the baby will be infected. Women whose serum contains HBeAg will pass on hepatitis B virus to their babies whereas those with anti-HBe do not [10, 11]. The infection in the baby is usually anicteric and most children infected will become persistent carriers of the virus. The mechanism of perinatal infection is uncertain, but is probably by contact with maternal blood during birth or via breast milk.

HBeAg is associated with the acute illness and has been found more commonly in young, rather than adult carriers, while the prevalence of the antibody (anti-HBe) appears to increase with age. Since HBeAg is closely associated with infectivity, young carriers may be more infective.

The frequency of HBsAg and its antibody was found to be ten times greater in the sera of patients attending a clinic for sexually transmitted diseases, than in a control group of blood donors attending a blood transfusion centre. HBsAg and its antibody (anti-HBs) are also more commonly found in homosexual males than in heterosexual males [12] and there is a higher incidence in those who habitually adopt the passive role during sexual intercourse [13].

In 2612 homosexual males, who attended clinics for sexually transmitted diseases in central London, 129 (4.94 per cent) were found to be HBsAg positive. In 118 of the HBsAg positive individuals, who were tested for HBeAg, 45 (38 per cent) were found to be positive, suggesting that any of their sexual contacts would be likely to be at particular risk of infection [8].

In a sample of 293 women, registered as living by prostitution in Athens, there was evidence of hepatitis B infection (HBsAg or anti-HBs) in 61.1 per cent compared with 28.0 per cent of 379 controls; when the prevalence of HBsAg and anti-HBs were related to years in prostitution a substantially higher rate of HBsAg was noted in prostitutes in their first 5 years of prostitution (9.4 per cent), decreasing substantially in those who had been in prostitution for 5 years or more [14]. Sexually promiscuous persons clearly have a higher incidence of seropositivity in certain populations.

Clinical features

In the majority of cases, hepatitis, whether type A or B, is asymptomatic, being detected only by biochemical tests of liver function. In those who develop clinical manifestations of the disease, following a prepatent period of 30–50 days in the case of type A hepatitis, and 40–160 days in type B, there is a pre-icteric stage (prodrome) during which the symptoms of the disease develop. The patient complains of nausea, malaise, anorexia and discomfort in the upper right abdomen. Tender enlargement of the liver is found in most cases, and in about 20 per cent of patients the spleen is also enlarged. In less than five per cent of symptomatic cases manifestations of immune-complex disease appear, consisting of erythematous, maculopapular or urticarial skin rashes, and arthralgia.

Jaundice usually develops within a week of the development of the symptoms, and is preceded by the appearance of dark urine and pale stools. The onset of jaundice in hepatitis B may not always be associated with prodromal illness. With the development of jaundice, the patient's condition improves, and within two to four weeks most infections have resolved. Uncommonly, fulminant hepatitis develops, the majority of these patients having hepatitis type B infection.

Immune response and laboratory diagnosis

HBsAg AND ANTI-HBs (HEPATITIS B SURFACE ANTIGEN AND ITS ANTIBODY)

HBsAg is found 14 to 120 days following exposure to infection; the interval between exposure and appearance of detectable serum HBsAg is related to the infectivity of the inoculum. A rise in the serum titre of HBsAg occurs gradually, and, after reaching a peak falls rapidly. The serum aspartate transaminase level rises after the HBsAg peak, and by the time symptoms develop in uncomplicated cases, the transaminase levels are falling. In most cases, the disappearance of HBsAg and subsequent appearance of anti-HBs signal recovery from infection and the development of immunity to reinfection. Anti-HBs can appear at the time HBsAg disappears (Figure 24.1), or may not appear for several months. The persistence of HBsAg for more than three months, in some 5–10 per cent of cases, suggests the development of the carrier state. In fulminant hepatitis there is some evidence to suggest that an unusually strong and rapid immune clearance of HBsAg, associated with the early appearance of anti-HBs during the peak of liver damage, may be involved in the pathogenesis of this severe form of infection.

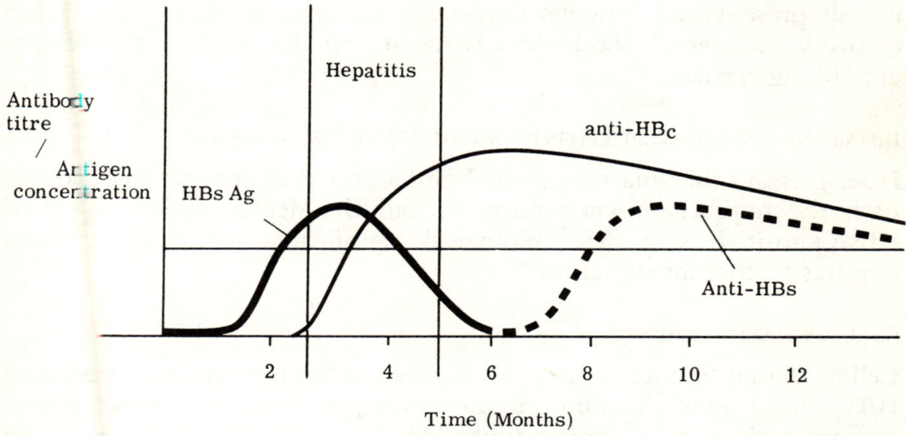

Figure 24.1 Hepatitis B antigen and antibody responses of value in the diagnosis of hepatitis B infection (Peutherer, J F, personal communication).

Several serological techniques are available for detecting HBsAg and anti-HBs but radio-immunoassay is the most sensitive [1]. The enzyme-linked immunosorbent assay technique (ELISA) has also been adapted to detect HBsAg: this technique was shown to have a sensitivity similar to that of radio-immunoassay (RIA) and has the advantage of stability, long shelf-life of reagents and simplicity of equipment. This method merits further appraisal in view of its potential wide application in laboratory practice.

The agglutination of erythrocytes coated with anti-HBs, termed reversed passive haemagglutination, is another convenient, although less sensitive method for detecting HBsAg. Anti-HBs can be estimated but a radio-immunoassay test is necessary. The detection of HBsAg is the main approach in the diagnosis of acute and chronic states. Other antigen and antibody tests are available for some individual cases, especially during the recovery from acute illness and to assess the carrier state.

HBcAg AND ANTI-HBc (HEPATITIS B CORE ANTIGEN AND ITS ANTIBODY)

Although HBcAg has been obtained from HBV-rich plasma and from infected liver tissue, free core antigen has not been detected in circulating blood. However, anti-HBc is found in the serum 2 to 10 weeks after the appearance of HBsAg and before the appearance of anti-HBs (Figure 24.1). It often appears during the acute infection while HBsAg is still present and remains detectable for a considerable time after recovery. In general, the highest titres of anti-HBc are found in persistent HBsAg carriers.

HBeAg AND ANTI-HBe (HEPATITIS B e ANTIGEN AND ITS ANTIBODY)

HBeAg is another marker of HBV infection that appears to correlate with the number of virus particles and the degree of infectivity of HBsAg-positive sera. The biological significance of these markers requires further investigation.

CELL-MEDIATED IMMUNITY

Cell-mediated immunity may be involved in terminating infection with HBV and, under certain circumstances, in causing hepatocellular damage and creating autoimmunity [1]. Normal T cell function may be a pre-requisite for the self-limited course of hepatitis; if the function is defective it may favour the development of chronic liver damage, and if it is absent altogether the result may be the asymptomatic carrier state.

Chronic hepatitis

There is an aetiological relationship between the persistence of HBsAg in the serum and chronic liver disease. In patients with hepatitis due to HBV, HBsAg remains persistently detectable in the serum in a proportion, as in the Copenhagen study, where HBsAg was found to persist in 11 of 112 patients with serum hepatitis [15]. Of these patients, eight developed chronic active hepatitis and two the benign, chronic persistent hepatitis, diagnoses confirmed pathologically by liver biopsy. The majority of cases of chronic active or chronic persistent hepatitis, however, are antigen-negative, and are said to progress more rapidly than those which are antigen-positive [16]. In the United Kingdom it was found that only 9 per cent of carriers had entirely normal liver histology although the changes were very minor in 38 per cent. All of 22 young Greek soldiers, on the other hand, had normal liver histology, or only mild non-specific changes. There seems little doubt that some individuals with persistent antigenaemia have no evidence of liver disease.

In chronic persistent hepatitis, the benign form, there is chronic inflammatory cell infiltrate in the portal tracts with marginal parenchymal cell involvement. In chronic active hepatitis there is an intense chronic inflammatory process, mainly lymphocytes but with variable numbers of plasma cells, involving the portal tracts and the lobules and spilling over to the neighbouring parenchyma. It may progress rapidly to hepatic cirrhosis [17].

In chronic active hepatitis the serum alanine and aspartate transaminase levels are raised to 300–500 i.u./l. Alkaline phosphatase is temporarily raised slightly. Serum immunoglobulin levels are elevated from the start to more than three times the normal and are mainly in the IgG class. Antinuclear factor and smooth muscle antibody may be also present in high titre [17].

In the investigation of homosexual males attending clinics for sexually transmitted diseases in London [8], already referred to, liver biopsy in 25 symptomless patients with HBsAg in the serum and disturbed liver function showed 11 with minor inactive liver disease (2 had minimal-change hepatitis, 9 chronic persistent hepatitis) and chronic active liver disease in 14 (10 chronic active hepatitis, 4 active cirrhosis). The higher than usual proportion with serious histological abnormalities might be a result of repeated exposure to the virus [8].

Primary hepatic carcinoma

In patients with primary hepatic carcinoma (PHC) antibody to hepatitis B core antigen (anti-HBc) was found to have a prevalence in the range of 70–95 per cent compared with 20–68 per cent in controls from Asia and Africa; it was present in the serum of 24 per cent of PHC patients and 4 per cent of controls from the USA.

These data support the hypothesis that chronic infection with HBV is aetiologically related to PHC, especially in Asia and Africa, although other factors must be involved [18, 19].

Indications for screening for virus markers in the serum of symptomless patients

Homosexual male patients are not always examined routinely for HBsAg in the serum, but those who have or have had hepatitis and those who may have had multiple contacts, particularly of a casual nature should be so examined. In HBsAg-positive patients, liver function tests (serum bilirubin, alkaline phosphatase and aspartate aminotransferase) are indicated. In those whose liver function tests remain abnormal for more than 6 weeks the opinion of a gastroenterologist is advised, as decisions are required about the necessity for a diagnostic liver biopsy and the means of securing follow-up. The necessity for treatment with corticosteroids in those with histological changes may have to be considered, although HBsAg-positive liver disease may respond less well than HBsAg-negative cases [8].

Patients who are persistent HBsAg carriers will need special care in the clinic, e.g., treatment of warts with electrocautery, with the possibility of dispersing virus to the risk of staff, might well be replaced by alternative methods. The taking of blood and the handling of such specimens will also require special precautions. Patients should be advised of their infectivity. The use of hepatitis B hyperimmune gamma globulin may be considered in HBsAg-negative sexual contacts, who have had a single such contact with a carrier within the previous 24–72 hour period and in whom a further risk is unlikely.

Hepatitis as an occupational hazard

Viral hepatitis is an occupational risk among health workers, who are at greater risk of contracting hepatitis B from their patients than vice versa. In clinics dealing with STD, staff have ample opportunity to be repeatedly exposed to HBV. The prevention of occupational hepatitis B is extremely important and those who routinely handle blood and other secretions should adhere scrupulously to sound hygienic measures for all specimen handling. They should, for example, avoid touching their mouth or eyes with their hands and the procedures for the safe handling of all clinical specimens should be meticulous. In addition rules, similar to the following, should be adopted in STD clinics to emphasize the special importance of hepatitis risk to doctors, nurses and technicians involved in taking blood samples.

Taking venous blood samples

1. The patient's arm should rest on a towel covered with a paper sheet.*

2. The paper sheet should be discarded, preferably every time or at least at intervals. If contamination with blood occurs both towel and paper sheet should be discarded; the former should be placed with the soiled linen and the latter with soiled dressings or in a bin similar to that for used syringes and needles.†

3. When a patient is known to be a carrier of hepatitis B, gloves must be worn by the person carrying out the venepuncture; the patient's

*e.g., 'Cestra' Clinical Sheets 45cm x 27cm. Code No. 69000: Robinsons, Chesterfield.

†BUR 'N' BIN, Metal Box Ltd., Labco, 54 Marlow Bottom Road, Marlow, Buckinghamshire, SL7 3NF, England. Bins can be incinerated.

arm should be laid on a plastic sheet. This plastic sheet should be discarded afterwards, whether contaminated or not. The blood sample should be emptied gently into the screw-capped container, to avoid spread by droplet and aerosol, and placed in a plastic bag labelled HEPATITIS, for transmission to the laboratory for serological testing. Screw-capped containers, preferably glass, should be used for all blood samples whether or not the patient is a carrier of hepatitis B.

4. A supply of Cidex* is to be kept in the clinic and activated when required. This activated Cidex is used for cleaning away any blood spillage from the floor or metal surfaces.

5. Any person who sustains a needle prick should inform the doctor and sister, who will record the event. A blood sample should be taken from the patient for an urgent examination for hepatitis B antigen. Arrangements for administration of hepatitis B hyperimmune immunoglobulin to the operator can then be made if antigen is found in the patient's blood.

6. Disposable needles should be returned to a rigid container to avoid risk of injury from the exposed point and placed in a BUR 'N' BIN with the disposable syringe for incineration later.

Care should be taken with all venepunctures and with every sample.

PREVENTION OF HEPATITIS B INFECTION IN HOSPITALS AND CLINICS

In units dealing with oncology and with chronic renal disease, where haemodialysis is practised, there has been an unusually high incidence of hepatitis B among patients and among medical staff. Screening of patients and staff for HBsAg, segregation of HBsAg-positive patients from susceptible patients and the employment of staff with anti-HBs in their serum for the care of HBsAg-positive patients are among the precautions which can be undertaken to reduce the infectious hazards [1, 20, 21].

If a member of staff pricks or cuts himself with an instrument contaminated with blood or contaminates a wound or scratch on the skin or mucous membranes of the mouth or eye, then the risk of the recipient acquiring hepatitis B must be assessed promptly. The HBsAg status of the donor must be tested. If he is found to be positive, or is

*Cidex (Ethicon). A 2 per cent solution of glutaraldehyde, to which an activating powder is added before use to make a buffered alkaline solution, which is stable for 14 days. The activator acts as a corrosion inhibitor and gives optimum activity to aqueous solutions. Alternatively strong hypochlorite – a solution yielding 10,000 parts per million of available chlorine – may be used to mop up spilled blood.

known to be positive in a recent test, then the recipient should be given an intramuscular dose of 500mg of hepatitis B hyperimmune immunoglobulin.

It is normal practice to test the recipient also for HBsAg; if he is already HBsAg positive no serum is given. Passive immunization should be undertaken as soon as possible after exposure and preferably within 24–72 hours. By this means a reduction in the risk of infection can be shown [22].

It is important to emphasize that hepatitis B virus carriers do present a definite hazard to medical personnel. However this must not lead to these patients being refused treatment as it has been established that they can be treated safely provided precautions are taken.

PREVENTION OF INFECTION IN INFANTS

Hanshaw and Dudgeon [23] have recommended, on the basis of preliminary studies, that high titred hepatitis B immune globulin or standard immune globulin should be given to HBsAg-negative infants born to mothers with hepatitis or with HBsAg in their serum. HBsAg-positive mothers, also, should be discouraged from breastfeeding, although there is no evidence to suggest that mother and baby should be separated while in hospital or afterwards. Although infected infants may be clinically well, they will be long-term carriers or may even have long-term hepatic sequelae from their 'silent' infections [23].

REFERENCES

1 World Health Organization (1977) Advances in Viral Hepatitis. *World Health Organization Technical Report Series, No. 602,* Geneva

2 Blumberg, B S (1964) *Bulletin of the New York Academy of Medicine,* **40**, 377

3 Blumberg, B S, Garstley, B J S, Hungerford, D A, London, W T and Sutnick, A I (1967) *Annals of Internal Medicine,* **66**, 924

4 Dane, D S, Cameron, C H and Briggs, M (1970) *Lancet,* **i**, 695

5 Huang, S (1971) *American Journal of Pathology,* **64**, 483

6 Eleftherion, N, Thomas, H C, Heathcote, J and Sherlock, S (1975) *Lancet,* **ii**, 1171–1173

7 Blumberg, B S, Sutnick, A I and London, W T (1968) *Bulletin of the New York Academy of Medicine,* **44**, 1566

8 Ellis, W R, Murray-Lyon, I M, Coleman, J C, Evans, B A, Fluker, J L, Bull, A, Keeling, P W N, Simmons, P D, Banatvala, J E, Willcox, J R and Thompson, R P H (1979) *Lancet,* **i**, 903

9 Stevens, C E, Beasley, R P, Tsui, J and Lee, W (1975) *New England Journal of Medicine,* **292**, 771

10 Schweitzer, I L, Edwards, V M and Brezina, M (1975) *New England Journal of Medicine,* **293**, 940

11 Okada, K, Kamiyama, I, Inomata, M, Mitsunobu, I, Miyakawa, Y and Makoto, M (1976) *New England Journal of Medicine,* **294**, 746

12 Fulford, K W M, Dane, D S, Catterall, R D, Woof, R and Denning, J V (1973) *Lancet,* **i**, 1470–1473

13 Lim, K S, Wong, V T, Fulford, K W M, Catterall, R D, Briggs, M and Dane, D S (1977) *British Journal of Venereal Diseases,* **53**, 190

14 Papaevangelou, G, Trichopoulos, D, Kremastinou, T and Papoutsakis, G (1974) *British Medical Journal,* **2**, 256

15 Nielsen, J O, Dietrichson, O, Elling, P and Christoffersen, P (1971) *New England Journal of Medicine,* **285**, 1157

16 Eddleston, A L W F (1976) in *Immunological aspects of the liver and gastrointestinal tract.* (Ed) Ferguson, A and MacSween, R N M. MTP Press, Lancaster, England, pages 291–317

17 MacSween, R N M and Berg, P A (1976) in *Immunological aspects of the liver and gastrointestinal tract.* (Ed) Ferguson, A and MacSween, R N M. MTP Press, Lancaster, England, pages 345–386

18 Maupas, P, Werner, B, Larouze, B, Millman, I, London, W T, O'Connell, A and Blumberg, B S (1975) *Lancet,* **ii**, 9

19 Eeckels, R and Desmyter, J (1978) in *Diseases of children in the subtropics and tropics.* (Ed) Jelliffe, D B and Stanfield, J B. Edward Arnold, London, pages 753–766

20 Rosenheim, Lord (1972) *Hepatitis and the treatment of chronic renal failure.* Report of the Advisory Group 1970–1972. Department of Health and Social Security. Scottish Home and Health Department, Welsh Office

21 World Health Organization (1973) Viral Hepatitis. *World Health Organization Technical Report Series No. 512,* Geneva

22 Final Report of the Veterans Administration Co-operative Study (1978) *Annals of Internal Medicine,* **88**, 285

23 Hanshaw, J B and Dudgeon, J A (1978) in *Virus diseases of the fetus and newborn.* Saunders, Philadelphia, page 226

CHAPTER 25

Molluscum Contagiosum

The lesions of molluscum contagiosum are benign virus-induced tumours affecting the human skin and conjunctiva exclusively. The lesions are manifested clinically by discrete papules, waxy in appearance, with a cornified centre which may be umbilicated or project as a plug. Close physical contact, often under moist conditions, appears to be necessary for transmission of the causative organism, a virus of the pox group.

Aetiology

The virus of molluscum contagiosum, although easily obtained in abundance from the skin lesions, cannot be grown in culture outside the human host. From its size (200–300nm), shape, fine structure, cytoplasmic site of replication and characteristic inclusion body, the virus is classed as a member of the poxvirus family.

The virus may possibly enter the epidermis not only from the exterior, but also by haematogenous spread from a more distant site or, more probably, by tissue fluid or lymphatic spread from a nearby portal of entry in traumatized skin [1].

Transmission

The contagious nature of the disease and its transmission by sexual contact has been long recognized [2, 3]. It has also been associated with outbreaks amongst those using communal facilities such as a swimming pool, where the virus was thought to have been transmitted by towels [4].

Although not proven, close physical contact, often under moist conditions, appears to be necessary for transmission, as is seen in spread from the external genitalia of one sexual partner to the external genitalia of the other, from masseuse to client and from sibling to sibling [5]. Infection of the newborn has been reported and raises doubts about the incubation period ordinarily said to be 14–50 days [6].

Immunology

Virion antigens are detectable from the time of appearance of the earliest lesion and are found in the stratum spinosum, granular and keratin layers. Virus-specific antibodies are present in the serum in nearly 70 per cent of patients, being of the IgG class in 58 per cent, IgM in 30 per cent and IgA in 10 per cent: the failure to detect antibody in 30 per cent of patients may be due to a lack of sensitivity of the fluorescent antibody technique used or to the fact that virion antigens are released from superficial lesions only after trauma and hence do not induce a humoral immune response. The relatively low incidence of virus-specific IgM in patients' sera in the presence of virus antigen within the lesion, is in contrast to the findings in wart-virus studies where there was a close correlation between the persistence of wart virus antigens and wart specific IgM [7].

Pathology

The lesion consists of a localized mass of hypertrophied and hyperplastic epidermis extending down into the underlying dermis, without breaching the limiting basement membrane and projecting above the surface as a papule. Beginning in the lower cells of the stratum spinosum, the intracytoplasmic inclusion bodies, growing larger as the infected cells migrate through the stratum granulosum, ultimately enlarge the host cells, pushing aside their nuclei and assuming dimensions varying between 24–27 microns in width and 30–37 microns in length [8]. The core of the lesion consists of degenerating epidermal cells with inclusion bodies and keratin.

Clinical features

In children lesions appear in a generalized distribution or may be localized to the face, forearms or hands, suggesting spread by direct contact. The lesions are pearly, flesh-coloured, raised, firm, umbilicated skin nodules, usually about 2–5mm in diameter. They may appear in most skin areas, singly or in groups, except for the palms and soles, where they are exceedingly rare. From the central pit, a white curdy material can be expressed. If the lesion is opened with a sterile needle the central core may not be easily detached. This core was described at the turn of the eighteenth century in Edward Jenner's notebook as a 'white body' equal in solidity to the 'boild crystalline humour of a fishes eye' [9].

Where transmission by sexual intercourse is the likely method of spread, lesions are seen on the inner aspect of the thigh and on the vulva in the case of the female [10] and on the penis (Plate 17), anterior aspect of the scrotum and pubic area in the male. Lesions often persist for many months or even for a few years, but most resolve spontaneously or following trauma or bacterial infection.

Diagnosis

Diagnosis is usually made by the characteristic appearance of the lesion. To identify the virus the surface of the lesion may be opened with the point of a disposable needle and the core extracted with forceps. The core is placed on the inner wall of a dry specimen tube and ringed on the outside for ease of identification. In the laboratory, after teasing out in saline, an electron microscope grid is dipped in the suspension. After drying and staining with phosphotungstic acid it is examined by electron microscopy.

Treatment

Lesions should be treated by destruction. Infiltration of the skin near the lesion with 1 per cent lignocaine and destruction by electrocautery is the preferred method.

REFERENCES

1 Postlethwaite, R (1970) *Archives of Environmental Health*, 21, 432
2 Henderson, W (1841) *Edinburgh Medical and Surgical Journal*, 56, 213
3 Paterson, R (1841) *Edinburgh Medical and Surgical Journal*, **56**, 279
4 Noble, W C and Somerville, D A (1974) in *Microbiology of the human skin* Saunders, London, page 228
5 Leading Article (1968) *British Medical Journal*, 1, 459
6 Mandel, M J and Lewis, R J (1971) *British Journal of Dermatology*, 84, 370
7 Shirodaria, P V and Matthews, R S (1977) *British Journal of Dermatology*, 96, 29
8 Van Rooyen, C E (1938) *Journal of Pathology and Bacteriology*, 46, 425
9 Woods, B (1977) *British Journal of Dermatology*, 96, 91
10 Wilkin, J K (1977) *American Journal of Obstetrics and Gynecology*, **128**, 531

CHAPTER 26

Marburg Virus Infection

This is a rare but dangerous infectious disease which is communicable by direct contact, usually blood contact, with a primary patient. Secondary infection can occur as a result of sexual intercourse during convalescence.

Marburg virus infection was unknown until 1967, when it appeared in circumscribed outbreaks among laboratory workers in the Federal Republic of Germany (Marburg and Frankfurt am Main) and in Yugoslavia (Belgrade). The virus had been introduced in a consignment of vervet monkeys (*Cercopithicus aethiops*) from Uganda. Altogether 31 people were involved and seven of them died. The illness was characterized by fever, a rash and haemorrhagic manifestations. The liver was particularly affected and there was evidence of involvement of the central nervous system.

The virus, unknown previously, had a filamentous structure (665nm in length) and contained RNA. The last case in the outbreak concerned a woman probably infected by the semen of her husband, which contained the virus, during his convalescence. Transmission is believed to have occurred in this way 83 days after the onset of his illness and involvement of his wife may have been favoured by her previous total hysterectomy for carcinoma of the uterus [1, 2].

A structurally similar but antigenically distinct virus has been isolated during epidemics in Sudan and Zaire, for which the name Ebola virus has been proposed. For these dangerous diseases attempts to isolate the virus must be carried out only in high security laboratories with optimum biocontainment facilities [2]. Patients should be warned of the serious dangers to partners should there be sexual intercourse during convalescence.

REFERENCES

1 Siegert, R (1970) The Marburg Virus. In *Modern Trends in Medical Virology*, 2. (Ed) Heath, R B and Waterson, A P, page 204

2 Simpson, D I H (1977) in *Marburg and Ebola virus infections:* World Health Organization Offset Publication No. 36, Geneva, page 5

CHAPTER 27

Lymphogranuloma Venereum

Lymphogranuloma venereum (LGV) is a sexually transmissible chlamydial infection found mainly in warm countries. In the cases seen in temperate climates the infection has been acquired in the tropics. The incubation period is short (2–5 days), after which an evanescent primary lesion occurs on the genitals or in the rectum or, rarely, elsewhere on the body. Two or three weeks after infection the draining lymph nodes enlarge, become matted together, fluctuant and eventually break down and discharge pus. If the disease is untreated the anogenital regional may become scarred, oedematous, and fistulae and strictures may develop. When pelvic nodes, which drain the cervix, upper vagina and rectum, are involved exudate may be discharged into the pelvic viscera and cause scarring; strictures may develop subsequently.

Aetiology

Lymphogranuloma venereum (LGV) is caused by *Chlamydia trachomatis.* The characteristics of chlamydiae have already been discussed in relation to the aetiology of non-gonococcal urethritis (Chapter 13). Inclusion bodies composed of aggregates of the organisms, may be identified in scrapings taken from primary lesions, in pus aspirated from buboes, and in histological sections of affected lymph nodes [1]. Using micro-immunofluorescence techniques, three serotypes of *C. trachomatis* associated with LGV (Type I, II and III) have been identified [2].

Lymphogranuloma venereum is mainly acquired during sexual intercourse with an infected partner. Accidental infections, for example, in doctors, are rare. Exudate from the primary lesion, discharging sinuses and the anus are infectious, as may be material from lesions which have persisted for years untreated.

Epidemiology

Lymphogranuloma venereum has a world-wide distribution; it is common in tropical and subtropical areas, but rare in temperate climates. In England and Wales in 1974, for example, only 46 cases were recorded (38 males and eight females). Infections diagnosed in the United

Kingdom have almost always been acquired abroad; seamen and other travellers are most frequently affected [3]. In tropical countries, prostitutes serve as an important source of infection. It seems that the global incidence of the disease is falling. LGV may be associated with other sexually transmitted diseases in the same patient.

Pathology and pathogenesis

The histological appearance of the primary genital lesion, a flat base of granulation tissue, surrounded by a narrow zone of necrosis, is not specific. The margins of the ulcer are undermined, and the adjacent epithelium may show pseudo-epitheliomatous hyperplasia. Lymphocytes and plasma cells infiltrate the underlying corium, where there may be necrotic foci.

The micro-organisms spread from the site of the initial lesion to the regional lymph nodes. Multiple necrotic foci appear within the parenchyma of the gland, followed by infiltration initially with polymorphonuclear leucocytes, and later plasma cells. Marked hyperplasia of the germinal centres occurs.

With the enlargement and coalescence of necrotic areas, abscesses develop. The gland capsule becomes inflamed early in the disease and perinodal tissues including skin become involved in this inflammatory process. Penetration of the abscess through the skin results in the formation of multiple sinuses.

In the female, inguinal lymphadenitis is less common than in the male. This is probably because lymphatic fluid from the upper vagina and cervix drain to the external and internal iliac nodes. The disease in females usually presents at a later stage by chronic vulvar ulceration and oedema of the labia (esthiomène, from the Greek meaning 'eaten away'). This results from obstruction of lymphatic vessels by fibrous tissue in the vulva and in the lymph nodes. Evidence of continuing inflammation is manifest as areas of granulomatous tissue in the genitalia [4, 5].

Rectal involvement, consisting essentially of ulceration of the mucosa with penetration of the muscular layer by inflammatory cells and subsequent stricture formation, is mainly seen in women, and in passive homosexuals.

Clinical features

The interval between exposure to infection and the appearance of the primary lesion, if this develops, is usually two to five days; longer intervals of up to five weeks have been described. A further interval of one to six weeks usually elapses before regional lymph node enlargement is detected. Untreated, the disease usually runs a course of between six and eight weeks and may resolve completely. In many cases (at least 70 per cent) there remain changes due to lymphatic obstruction; intermittent recrudescence of disease can occur. In the early stages, LGV may conveniently be divided into two syndromes: the inguinal and the genito-anorectal [6].

INGUINAL SYNDROME

This is the most frequent manifestation in the male; it is uncommon in females as the primary lesion is not commonly found in the lower vagina, or on the vulva. There are primary genital lesions, regional lymph node enlargement, and constitutional disturbances.

A history of a primary genital lesion, rare in females, is obtained in 20 to 50 per cent of male cases. The lesion, usually a painless papulovesicle, tends to occur anywhere on the penis and heals within a few days. Rarely a sore within the urethral meatus may mimic a non-gonococcal urethritis. Extragenital lesions are rare although oral infections are known.

There is regional lymph node enlargement within one to four weeks of the appearance of the primary lesion. In most cases (at least 75 per cent), there is unilateral involvement of the inguinal and/or femoral lymph nodes. The glands are painful, tender, and although initially discrete, become matted together as a result of periadenitis. Occasionally, multilocular abscesses develop within the lymph nodes which become fluctuant (bubo formation). Although, if untreated, buboes may resolve spontaneously within a few weeks, abscesses may rupture through the overlying adherent skin, producing multiple sinuses. Enlargement of lymph nodes, above and below the inguinal ligament produces a grooved appearance in the groin, 'sign of the groove', a sign almost pathognomonic of LGV. Healing with scarring eventually occurs, although there may be recurrent sinus formation.

In women, the inguinal syndrome is uncommon unless the primary lesion is on the vulva or in the lower vagina. Lymphatic drainage from these sites is to the inguinal nodes which may show the changes already described. The lymphatic drainage from lesions in the middle and upper vagina and the cervix is to the external and internal iliac and the sacral lymph nodes. Inflammation of these glands, may produce backache or symptoms of peritonitis. More commonly, there may be few symptoms in the early stage of the disease, which shows itself with later manifestations such as esthiomène.

Constitutional symptoms occur more commonly in the inguinal syndrome than in the genito-anorectal syndrome. Pyrexia, malaise, nausea, arthralgia and headache are frequent. Less commonly (about 10 per cent of female and 2 per cent of male patients) erythema nodosum or erythema multiforme may be seen.

GENITO-ANORECTAL SYNDROME

The clinical features of this syndrome are predominantly seen in women and in male homosexuals. Extension of the inflammatory process by the lymphatic vessels of the rectovaginal septum to the submucous tissues of the rectum is thought to be the principal factor involved in the production of the syndrome in females when the primary lesion has been in the vagina [7].

The patient usually complains of bleeding from the anus and later a purulent anal discharge. On proctoscopy, the rectal mucosa is found to be inflamed with multiple punctate haemorrhages and there is a mucopurulent discharge. There may be superficial ulceration and polypoid growths. Histological examination of rectal biopsy material shows a non-specific granulomatous inflammatory reaction [8]. Although the rectum is most severely affected, a more generalized colitis often coexists and can be demonstrated by barium enema examination [9].

In the later stages of both syndromes, if the disease is untreated, lymphoedema may affect the genitalia of both sexes. The interval between the appearance of the early manifestations of the disease and the development of the later features varies between one and 20 years. Women may develop considerable oedema (elephantiasis) of the vulva with the formation of polypoid growths, fistulae, ulceration and scarring (esthiomène). Elephantiasis less frequently affects males, but obstruction of the lymphatic drainage of the external genitalia may lead to oedema of the penis or scrotum and later to distortion of the penis. Strictures of the male and female urethra, with the formation of fistulae are rare late complications.

In the genito-anorectal syndrome late complications include tubular rectal stricture, with or without proctitis and colitis, peri-anal abscesses, perineal and rectovaginal fistulae. Intestinal obstruction may result from stricture formation and carcinoma may develop on a chronic rectal stricture [10].

Diagnosis

Diagnosis is based on the history, and clinical features of the disease, and backed by bacteriological and serological tests; intradermal tests such as the Frei test are obsolete.

CULTURE OF THE ORGANISM

Giemsa-stained smears of scrapings from a suspected primary lesion and pus aspirated from a lymph node may be examined by microscopy for inclusions. Attempts should be made to isolate the organism on tissue culture. Material, sent to the laboratory as quickly as possible on suitable transport medium, should be cultured on McCoy cells (Chapter 13). After incubation cell cultures are stained with iodine, Giemsa, or by immunofluorescence and examined microscopically for inclusions. Chlamydia are isolated only in about 30 per cent of cases.

SEROLOGICAL TESTS

Lymphogranuloma venereum complement fixation test (LGVCFT)

The chlamydial group antigen used in this test is prepared from the organism causing enzootic abortion of ewes. This test generally becomes positive during the initial 4 weeks of infection and the titre rises during this period in the untreated patient. Titres of 1:16 are regarded as significant, but as 3 to 4 per cent of the normal population will give a positive test at this titre, it should be repeated in doubtful cases after 2 to 3 weeks, to detect a rising titre.

If untreated, complement fixing antibodies may persist for years at high titre; there is a tendency, however, for these titres to diminish, and the results of the test sometimes become negative spontaneously.

In early LGV the LGVCFT titres fall after treatment and the test usually becomes negative after a variable period of months to several years. Treatment of chronic LGV rarely results in any change in the titre, which may remain high for the rest of the patient's life.

In infections with other serotypes of *Chlamydia trachomatis* or *Chlamydia psittaci* cross-reactions occur, but titres of the LGVCFT are usually low.

Radio-isotope precipitation test (RIP) [11, 12]

A group reactive antigen is used in this test which is some twenty times more sensitive than the LGVCFT.

Micro-immunofluorescence typing (micro-IF test) [2]

Using this technique, anti-chlamydial type-specific antibody can be detected in the serum and the particular serotype (I, II or III) of the infecting organism identified.

The latter two tests are available only in a few specialist centres.

Intradermal test (Frei test)

The Frei test is not used, because it not only has the disadvantages of a delayed hypersensitivity test in the evaluation of acute illness but also may be associated with false positive and false negative reactions [13]. The antigen for this test used to be prepared commercially from a growth of chlamydiae in the yolk sacs of chick embryos.

Other laboratory tests

During the course of untreated LGV, the erythrocyte sedimentation rate is usually elevated, particularly in chronic cases. This presumably reflects changes in the levels of plasma proteins. The gamma globulin fraction of the serum is usually elevated, the albumin being normal or low.

The total white cell count in the blood is often increased, with a relative lymphocytosis or monocytosis.

Differential diagnosis

Genital ulceration due to LGV must be carefully differentiated from syphilis by appropriate tests (Chapter 4). Other causes of genital ulceration may need to be excluded (Chapter 33).

Lymph node enlargement may occur in syphilis, herpes genitalis, granuloma inguinale, infectious mononucleosis, and in the reticuloses. Usually the onset of the glandular swelling in these cases is less acute and less painful except in herpes genitalis.

Pyogenic infection, cat-scratch disease and tuberculosis may produce painful swollen inguinal lymph nodes with, or without, a history of a preceding lesion on the genitals.

Treatment

The aim of treatment is to eradicate the infecting organism, as far as possible to prevent further damage, and correct any deformities caused by the disease. It is important to examine, if possible, sexual contacts of people with LGV.

To eradicate the organism, sulphonamides and tetracyclines have been most commonly used. The sulphonamides have the advantage of not interfering with the diagnosis of syphilis, particularly in the incubation period of this disease. Sulphadimidine 1g orally four times daily for at least 16 days may be used.

Oxytetracycline in a dosage of 500mg orally four times per day for at least 14 days is usually satisfactory for the treatment of early stage LGV. Therapy is guided by resolution of suppurating lymph nodes, reduction in size of the nodes, healing of sinuses, and improvement in the patient's general condition.

Response to antibiotic treatment is better in LGV in the early stage than in the late, when repeated prolonged courses may be required. At this stage improvement may not occur.

Buboes should be aspirated with aseptic precautions through a wide bore needle (No. 19 SWG) before they rupture spontaneously. Fluctuant glands should not be incised, as this delays healing. Clean surgical removal of the affected glands appears to be an effective treatment.

Surgical treatment, with simultaneous antibiotic therapy, is often required in the management of late LGV. Polypoid growths on the vulva require excision and fistulae need surgical repair. Rectal strictures will require regular dilatation, or excision and a colostomy. A stricture may cause acute intestinal obstruction.

REFERENCES

1 Jorgensen, L (1959) *Acta Pathologica et Microbiologica Scandinavica,* **47**, 113
2 Wang, S-P and Grayston, J T (1970) *American Journal of Ophthalmology,* 70, 367
3 Alergant, C D (1957) *British Journal of Venereal Diseases,* **33**, 47
4 Koteen, H (1945) *Medicine,* **24**, 1
5 Smith, E B and Custer, P (1950) *Journal of Urology,* **63**, 546
6 Abrams, A J (1968) *Journal of the American Medical Association,* **205**, 199
7 King, A J (1964) Lymphogranuloma venereum. In *Recent Advances in Venereology,* Churchill, London, page 311
8 Miles, R P M (1959) *Postgraduate Medical Journal,* **35**, 92
9 Annamunthodo, H and Marryatt, J (1961) *British Journal of Radiology,* **34**, 53
10 Morson, B C (1964) *Proceedings of the Royal Society of Medicine,* London, **57**, 179
11 Gerloff, R K and Watson, R V (1967) *American Journal of Ophthalmology,* **63**, 1492
12 Philip, R N, Hill, D A, Greaves, A B, Gordon, F B, Quan, A L, Gerloff, R K and Thomas, L A (1971) *British Journal of Venereal Diseases,* **47**, 114
13 Schachter, J, Smith, D E and Dawson, C R (1969) *Journal of Infectious Diseases,* **120**, 372

CHAPTER 28

Chancroid

Introduction

Chancroid is a sexually transmissible disease caused by infection with the bacterium *Haemophilus ducreyi.* There is a high incidence in tropical countries, particularly in areas where living standards are low. Prostitutes constitute an important reservoir of infection as the majority show no clinical evidence of disease.

After a prepatent period, usually less than one week, one or more ulcers develop on the genitalia, and are associated, in about half of cases, with inguinal lymphadenitis. Untreated, an abscess develops in the affected lymph nodes and this may rupture through the skin producing a sinus. Extensive tissue destruction is a distressing complication of the disease.

The diagnosis of chancroid is generally based on clinical findings, laboratory corroboration of the diagnosis being hampered by the fastidious nature of the organism on culture, and lack of specific serological tests.

Treatment with tetracyclines or sulphonamides is generally curative.

Aetiology

The causative organism, *Haemophilus ducreyi,* was first described by Ducrey [1] in 1889: it is a small Gram-negative cocco-bacillus which tends to occur in clumps or chains. In smears made from lesions, or material aspirated from swollen regional lymph glands, intracellular as well as extracellular bacteria may be noted. Although *H. ducreyi* is fastidious it can be cultured in media containing blood or blood products: it requires X factor (haematin) but not V factor (nicotinamide adenine dinucleotide).

Chancroid can be reproduced in man by inoculation with pure cultures. Ulcerative lesions have also followed the inoculation of monkeys and rabbits with pure cultures although virulence appears to diminish on repeated sub-culture [2].

Epidemiology

The incidence of chancroid is highest in tropical and sub-tropical countries. There is an association between chancroid, poverty and poor standards of hygiene [3]. Its incidence decreases as the standard of living improves. Chancroid is more prevalent in war-time and in American troops in the Korean war it was 14 to 21 times as common as gonorrhoea [4], while in the Vietnam conflict chancroid was second to gonorrhoea among venereal diseases [5]. In 1971 there were only 1507 cases of chancroid reported in the United States of America, compared with over 600,000 cases of gonorrhoea.

Chancroid is generally acquired as a result of sexual contact. There is a male:female ratio of approximately 10:1 in the reported numbers of cases. Some investigators have claimed to have isolated *H. ducreyi* from the vulva and urethra of healthy women, and the existence of such carriers may explain the small numbers of cases recorded in women [6]. In countries where chancroid is common, prostitutes probably constitute an important reservoir of infection. Chancroid is rare in the United Kingdom (less than 50 reported cases per year), where the majority of infections are seen in seafarers or recent immigrants.

Clinical features

The prepatent period of chancroid is short, usually two to three days, although it may vary from as little as 24 hours to longer than five days [7].

The earliest lesion is a papule which soon becomes a pustule and ulcerates as a result of thrombotic occlusion of underlying dermal blood vessels. Characteristically, the superficial ulcer so formed is painful and tender. A grey membrane covers its floor and removal of this membrane reveals glistening granulation tissue which bleeds easily. The edges are ragged and undermined, and a narrow zone of erythema surrounds the ulcer. Unlike the primary lesion of syphilis, the lesions of chancroid are not indurated. The size of the individual ulcers varies from 3 to about 20mm in diameter.

As a result of auto-inoculation of surrounding tissues, multiple ulcers are often produced and lesions at various stages of development are commonly seen in the same patient. Although single ulcers may occur, multiple ulcers are more common.

In the male, the lesions of chancroid most commonly occur at the preputial orifice, the resulting inflammation producing phimosis and commonly a paraphimosis. A suppurative balanoposthitis may result from the phimosis so produced, and necessitate surgical drainage of the preputial sac by a dorsal slit (page 415). Less frequently ulceration may occur on the glans penis, the shaft of the penis or the distal urethra. Chancroid of the anal region may occur in male homosexuals, and auto-inoculation from penile lesions may produce lesions of the scrotum and thighs.

The labia majora, introitus, vagina and peri-anal region are most commonly affected in the female. Rarely, cervical lesions have been described.

Extragenital lesions of chancroid are rare, and disseminated *H. ducreyi* infection is unknown.

In at least 60 per cent of patients with chancroid, inguinal lymph nodes become enlarged on one or both sides within days to weeks of the appearance of the genital lesions. Initially the nodes are discrete and not tender. In about half of those who develop lymphadenopathy, suppuration occurs in the nodes, which become tender, matted together and show evidence of unilocular abscess formation (bubo). The overlying skin, to which the inflamed glands adhere, becomes erythematous and if the inflammatory process continues, the bubo ruptures through the skin, forming a sinus. Bubo and sinus formation are usually unilateral [5].

Occasionally, ulceration becomes extensive, with considerable tissue destruction. In such cases, secondary bacterial infection, particularly with *Borrelia vincentii* and *Fusobacterium fusiformis,* probably plays an important role in the destructive process.

In some cases, ulceration may be more superficial, but cover a considerable area. Tissue destruction is minimal, but healing is slow, months or years elapsing before resolution is complete. Recurrent chancroid, although described, is a rarity.

Diagnosis

A diagnosis of chancroid is commonly made by finding organisms morphologically resembling *H. ducreyi* in stained smears prepared from material aspirated from a bubo or taken from the undermined edge of the ulcer: the lesion should be cleansed first with normal saline. Several staining methods can be used, such as Gram's or Giemsa. In preparing a smear, the swab should be rolled through 180° in one direction only, never back and forth, to maintain the arrangement of the organisms. The bacteria may exhibit bipolar staining and usually appear in chains, several of which may be in parallel with strands of mucus. Many cases previously diagnosed as chancroid have probably been examples of herpes genitalis, perhaps with secondary bacterial infection. Giemsa's stain may be helpful in identifying the giant balloon cells, frequently multinucleate, and the eosinophilic intracellular inclusion bodies characteristic of herpesvirus infections [2].

In general, cultural diagnosis of chancroid is unlikely to be successful unless there is ready access to a specialist laboratory [6]. *H. ducreyi* can be cultured with difficulty from chancroidal ulcers but more readily from material aspirated from a bubo. Various media, enriched with blood from a variety of animal species including man, have been used [8]. Hammond *et al* [9] found chocolate agar containing vancomycin (3μg/ml) an effective isolation medium; the organism was isolated in pure culture from 56 per cent of a group of patients with probable chancroid lesions seen in Winnipeg. The highest yield of positive cultures (88 per cent) was obtained by the use of heat-inactivated human serum obtained from the patient's own blood [10].

Immunological techniques which have been used in the diagnosis of chancroid include a skin test and a complement fixation test. The Ito-Reenstierna skin test involved the intradermal inoculation of a suspension of killed *H. ducreyi* into one site and a control suspension alone at another site. The value of this test as well as the complement fixation test is limited due to cross-reaction with other bacteria.

Biopsy is rarely necessary for diagnosis. It has been noted that beneath the ulcerated surface of the lesion there are one or two deeper layers recognizable histologically. The deep zone shows a dense infiltration of plasma cells and lymphocytes, above which there is a marked endothelial proliferation, palisading of blood vessels, degeneration of their walls and occasional thrombosis [11].

Differential diagnosis

In practice, a diagnosis of chancroid is often made on the basis of clinical presentation, history, and response to treatment. However, other conditions which produce ulceration of the genitalia (Chapter 33) must be considered in the differential diagnosis of chancroid, and syphilis must be excluded in all cases, as these diseases may coexist in the individual patient. Details regarding the tests required to exclude syphilis are found in Chapter 4, but it is important to stress the need for dark-ground microscopic examination of serum from the depth of lesions in searching for *T. pallidum*.

Infection with *Herpesvirus hominis* produces superficial multiple tender ulcers, which are not indurated, and this condition must be carefully excluded. In the absence of suitable laboratory facilities, it may be impossible to differentiate between the two diseases.

As the methods of cultural isolation of *H. ducreyi* are not efficient, it is possible that chancroid-like ulcers may be a non-specific host reaction to a variety of organisms rather than a single entity. Lymphogranuloma venereum may coexist with chancroid, as may other sexually transmitted diseases.

Treatment

Local treatment of chancroid consists of frequently repeated application of saline dressings to the ulcerated area to reduce the risk of development of secondary infection. A strip of gauze soaked in saline may be applied to separate inflamed surfaces. When a phimosis is present, and a balanoposthitis develops, the preputial sac should be gently irrigated with normal saline at hourly intervals. In more severe cases to secure drainage and to prevent phagedaenic ulceration of the glans a slit should be made extending dorsally along the prepuce from its orifice (dorsal slit) under general anaesthesia. Buboes should be aspirated with aseptic procedures before commencing treatment with antimicrobial drugs. Incision, however, is contraindicated as severe ulceration, resistant to treatment, may ensue [7].

Various antimicrobial agents have been used in the management of chancroid, but in most instances sulphonamides and tetracyclines are effective. Sulphonamides have the advantage that their use does not mask concomitant syphilis. Sulphadimidine may be used in a dosage of 2g initially and 1g orally every six hours for about 14 days until the lesions have healed.

Although tetracyclines have been widely used in treatment, recent experience in South-East Asia suggests that, at least in that area, drug resistance may have developed [5].

Streptomycin, given intramuscularly in a dose of 1g daily for five days has been used in treatment, but is not effective if buboes have developed [4].

Although penicillin is not used in the treatment of chancroid it is of interest that three of sixteen strains of *H. ducreyi* isolated in a local outbreak in Winnipeg, produced β-lactamase: further characterization is required to determine if the β-lactamase production is plasmid-mediated [12].

REFERENCES

1 Ducrey, A (1889) *Monatsschrift fur praktische Dermatologie*, **9**, 387

2 Gaisin, A and Heaton, C L (1975) *International Journal of Dermatology*, **14**, 188

3 Greenblatt, R B, Pond, E R, Sanderson, E G, Torpin, R and Dienst, R D (1953) Public Health Service Publication No. 255, Washington

4 Asin, J (1952) *American Journal of Syphilis, Gonorrhoea and Venereal Disease,* **26,** 483

5 Kerber, R E, Rowe, C E and Gilbert, K R (1969) *Archives of Dermatology,* **100,** 604

6 Alergant, C D (1972) *Practitioner,* **209,** 624

7 Harkness, A H (1950) Chancroid. In *Non-gonococcal Urethritis.* Livingstone, Edinburgh, page 182

8 Topley and Wilson's *Principles of Bacteriology, Virology and Immunity* (1975) Sixth Edition, Revised by Wilson, G S and Miles, A A. Edward Arnold, London, page 1035

9 Hammond, G W, Lian, C J, Wilt, J C and Ronald, A R (1976) *Journal of Clinical Microbiology,* **7,** 39

10 Borchard, K A and Hoke, A W (1970) *Archives of Dermatology,* **102,** 188

11 Sheldon, W H and Heyman, A (1946) *American Journal of Pathology,* **22,** 415

12 Hammond, G W, Lian, C J, Wilt, J C and Ronald, A R (1978) *Antimicrobial Agents and Chemotherapy,* **13,** 608

CHAPTER 29

Granuloma Inguinale (Donovanosis)

Granuloma inguinale is a chronic granulomatous infection caused by the bacterium *Calymmatobacterium granulomatis (Donovania granulomatis)*. The clinical effects are mainly in the anogenital region, and less commonly elsewhere. Most cases occur in tropical and subtropical countries, but in the United Kingdom it may be occasionally seen in immigrants and merchant seamen.

The mode of transmission is not clear, although in many cases sexual intercourse, whether heterosexual or homosexual, probably plays a major role.

After a variable prepatent period, an ulcer develops and slowly increases in size over the course of several months or even years until a considerable area of skin may become affected. The duration of the untreated disease varies from about a month to over thirty years; healing generally occurs, however, within two to three years. Recurrences after apparent healing are common and deformities of the anogenital region may result. Granuloma inguinale may be associated with carcinoma of the skin.

Aetiology

In 1905 in India, Major Donovan [1] noted the constant presence of intracellular bodies in smears from the ulcerated lesions of patients with granuloma inguinale. These bodies, which he described as 'gigantic bacilli with rounded ends', are usually referred to as Donovan bodies. Following successful culture of the causative organism on chick yolk sac, it was evident that the Donovan bodies were bacterial in origin and the name *Donovania granulomatis* was proposed [2, 3]. If, however, the bacteria failed to adapt by losing their associated capsular material, further passages were not possible. The organism can be grown in a synthetic medium, but it is fastidious and requires a low oxidation-reduction potential and a substance, probably a peptide, present in an enzymic digest of bovine albumin or soya meal [4].

Due to the problems associated with culture, complete characterization of the organism, which is now classified as *Calymmatobacterium granulomatis,* has not been accomplished, nor have Koch's postulates been fulfilled [5]. Clinical disease is not produced by injecting cultured organisms into man or by injecting animals with either cultures or tissue from lesions; injection of material from pseudo-buboes or suspensions of infected tissue, however, can produce clinical disease in man. The inability of cultured organisms to produce disease in man may be related to loss of virulence associated with loss of capsular material. Disease cannot be produced in laboratory animals [5].

C. granulomatis is a pleomorphic Gram-negative bacillus surrounded by a well-defined capsule which can be demonstrated by Wright's stain. The bacteria are intracellular parasites of the large mononuclear tissue cells: occasionally they are found inside polymorphonuclear leucocytes. In smears stained with Leishman or Giemsa stain the organisms usually appear as capsulate ovoid or bean-shaped bodies, varying in size from 1μm to 1.5μm in length and from 0.5μm to 0.7μm in thickness. A well-defined dense capsular material, pinkish in colour, surrounds the body of the organism, which shows bipolar staining of chromatin material. The bipolar staining gives the organism the appearance of a closed 'safety-pin'. The capsule of *C. granulomatis* shares antigens with various members of the genus *Klebsiella* [6]. Since bacteriophage material has been found in association with the organism in material from granuloma inguinale lesions, it is possible that *C. granulomatis* is a phage-modified bacterium.

The lack of an animal host and the inability to consistently culture organisms with complete capsular material have severely hampered more complete bacterial studies on this organism [5].

Epidemiology

Granuloma inguinale is found in tropical and subtropical countries. Cases occurring in temperate climates are imported usually by immigrants or seafarers. In 1954 it was considered to be endemic along the eastern seaboard of southern India, southern China, the East Indies, northern Australia, West and Central Africa, some countries of Central, South and North America and the West Indies [7]. The disease exhibits a male:female ratio of approximately 2:1 and appears to be also related to low socio-economic status and poor hygiene.

In 1971 there were 103 cases of granuloma inguinale reported in the United States giving an incidence of 0.1 per 100,000 population [8]. The disease is rare in Europe and only 11 cases were reported in the clinics of England and Wales in 1974 and in Scotland none were recorded during the period 1972–75.

The popular view that granuloma inguinale is usually sexually transmitted has been questioned [9]. The reported incidence of concomitant infection in sexual partners varies from infrequently [9] to over 50 per cent [10]. The main points presented in favour of sexual transmission of granuloma inguinale include: history of sexual exposure before the appearance of the lesion; increased incidence of the disease in age groups in which sexual activity is highest; lesions found on internal genitalia, such as the cervix, without any other lesions; lesions found only around the anus in passive homosexuals; and the genital or perigenital location of lesions. The occurrence of the disease in very young children and sexually inactive persons, its rarity in those engaged in prostitution and the rarity of the disease in the sexual partners of patients with open lesions are cited as evidence against sexual transmission [9].

As an alternative to sexual transmission it has been suggested that *C. granulomatis* occurs in the intestine and in conditions of poor hygiene, auto-inoculation of faecal material could establish it on skin made susceptible by trauma or bacterial inflammation: an organism resembling *C. granulomatis* has been isolated from faeces [11].

Our lack of knowledge concerning the organism and its interaction with its host and his environment make it impossible to be certain about the way it is transmitted. Transmission could occur by both sexual and non-sexual means: perineal contamination with faecal organisms might precede transfer by sexual means.

Clinical features

As the mode of transmission is uncertain the prepatent period is not known. In cases considered to have been acquired sexually, the period between exposure to infection and the appearance of the initial lesion has varied from 3 days to 6 months, but occurring between 7 and 30 days in more than two-thirds of patients [10].

The disease has a predilection for the moist stratified epithelium of the skin and the mucous membranes of the genital, anal, inguinal and oral regions. In more than 90 per cent of cases reported the initial, primary lesion is in the anogenital area [7].

In the male the prepuce, fraenum and glans are the usual sites in which the initial lesion develops. In the female the labia minora, mons veneris and the fourchette are the most commonly affected sites.

The earliest lesion may be a papule, a subcutaneous nodule or an ulcer. Such lesions are often intensely pruritic. The papule, which is usually between 5 and 15mm in diameter, is elevated above the surrounding skin, flat topped and covered by skin or mucous membrane. Within a few days ulceration occurs.

Less commonly the initial lesion may be nodular. This subcutaneous nodule, of varying size, is at first firm, but as the inflammatory process progresses, softening occurs with the production of an abscess. After several days the abscess ruptures through the skin, resulting in the formation of a granulomatous ulcer.

The lesion most frequently seen in clinical practice is the ulcer. It is of variable size, soft, velvety, bright pink in colour and has a serpiginous edge. The base of the ulcer is covered by a serosanguineous exudate or a thin transparent membrane. Despite the appearance the ulcer is generally painless unless there is secondary bacterial infection.

The disease spreads slowly along skin folds, taking months to involve a considerable area. In the female, the ulcerative process progresses posteriorly and downwards to involve the perineum and anal region. There is a tendency in the male for the disease to spread upwards and laterally to the inguinal region. Primary peri-anal lesions of granuloma inguinale most commonly occur in homosexual males [12].

Extragenital lesions have been described, usually secondary to longstanding genital disease. Most commonly these lesions are found in or around the oral cavity, but may occur anywhere in the body [13].

As the disease develops from the initial lesion, the base of the ulcer becomes elevated above the surface of the surrounding skin and the edge becomes thickened and greyish in colour. This hypertrophic type of disease is slow to progress and may remain stationary for years.

In some patients, most commonly female, there is a tendency, early in the disease, to extensive fibrous tissue formation. This often results in gross deformities.

Occasionally in patients with longstanding disease, acute inflammation develops which results in necrosis and destruction of extensive areas of skin and subcutaneous tissue. This uncommon event may be fatal.

Even in extensive granuloma inguinale, the regional lymph nodes are not enlarged, painful or tender. Histological examination of these glands shows only non-specific changes of endothelial hyperplasia and focal collections of mononuclear cells. Donovan bodies are not found [7]. Should the regional lymph nodes be enlarged the possible co-existence of other diseases such as malignant metastases, syphilis, lymphogranuloma venereum or secondary bacterial infection must be considered.

Systemic spread of infection from the primary site is said to be rare, although liver, spleen and bone may be affected [7].

The course of the disease is usually prolonged. Although in a few patients healing apparently takes place within a few weeks, the mean duration of the disease is about 18 months. There is a tendency for the disease to recur after apparent healing. Unless there is some concomitant disease such as pulmonary tuberculosis, the patient is otherwise generally well.

COMPLICATIONS

As a result of involvement of lymphatic vessels in the fibrosis associated with the disease, oedema of the genitalia may occur in 15 to 20 per cent of patients. Females are more commonly affected than males. In longstanding cases, genital deformities may occur; in the sclerotic forms of the disease there may be stenosis of the urethral, vaginal and anal orifices.

Malignancy has been reported in association with granuloma inguinale [12, 14] and either basal-cell or squamous-cell carcinoma may occur. As the pseudo-epitheliomatous hyperplasia associated with granuloma inguinale may be difficult to differentiate from early carcinoma, care is required in interpreting histological reports [15].

In the aetiology of carcinoma of the vulva or penis the role of *C. granulomatis*, as a predisposing factor, is suspected but not proven.

Diagnosis

A diagnosis of granuloma inguinale is based on the microscopic demonstration of the causative bacterium in tissue smears taken from the lesions. The lesions should be thoroughly and repeatedly cleansed with saline-soaked gauze, followed by gentle wiping with dry gauze. Since *C. granulomatis* is an intracellular parasite, granulation tissue must be examined: this is obtained either by biopsy punch from deep in the ulcer or from the edge of the lesion by means of a curette or a scalpel. The tissue is spread between two slides and the resultant smear stained with Leishman, Giemsa or Wright's stain. In 90–95 per cent of lesions of granuloma inguinale organisms with intense polar staining, resembling closed safety pins, can be seen within mononuclear leucocytes [7]. It may be difficult to demonstrate *C. granulomatis* in grossly infected lesions contaminated by other organisms. Repeated examinations are often necessary.

The difficulties associated with the growth of the organism exclude culture as a routine diagnostic procedure. Biopsy may be helpful in distinguishing the lesions from those of lymphogranuloma venereum: the ulcers of granuloma inguinale show a more subacute type of inflammation [16]. Skin tests and a complement fixation serological test have also been applied to the diagnosis of granuloma inguinale, although their use is limited due to lack of specificity and sensitivity and the limited availability of suitable antigen [17].

Since granuloma inguinale is associated with chancroid, syphilis and lymphogranuloma venereum, either alone or in combination in 10 to 20 per cent of cases [7], it is important to take serological tests and carry out dark-ground investigation of the lesions for *Treponema pallidum* to exclude syphilis, and to examine a Giemsa-stained smear for *Haemophilus ducreyi.* Granuloma inguinale differs clinically from lymphogranuloma venereum; the latter diagnosis is usually supported by a serological test (Chapter 27).

Treatment

Although tetracyclines are said to be of value in the treatment of granuloma inguinale [17], this was not the experience of physicians working in Vietnam [18] who found that this drug was not effective. In that locality, ampicillin in a dosage of 500mg orally six hourly for at least two weeks was effective in over 90 per cent of cases, complete healing occurring within one month of commencing treatment. Other workers have used ampicillin with good results [19].

Streptomycin given in doses of 1g daily by intramuscular injection for at least 20 days results in healing in about 85 per cent of cases. Higher and more frequent doses have been used, but otoxicity as a complication of therapy must be borne in mind.

Lincomycin has been used recently as an alternative to ampicillin in a small number of patients hypersensitive to penicillins [18] and given orally in a dose of 500mg six-hourly for two weeks. Like clindamycin, however, lincomycin brings a risk of antibiotic-induced colitis or pseudomembranous colitis [20], and should not be used except in serious or life-threatening conditions [21]. The colitis induced by these antibiotics appears to be due to *Clostridium difficile* and to respond to treatment with vancomycin [20].

In infections that are damaging, the problem of masking syphilis by treatment should not cause concern, provided sensitive and specific serological tests are carried out over a three month follow-up period and endeavours are made to ensure the examination of contacts.

REFERENCES

1 Donovan, C (1905) *Indian Medical Gazette,* 40, 414
2 Anderson, K (1943) *Science,* 97, 560

3 Anderson, K, DeMonbreun, W and Goodpasture, E (1945) *Journal of Experimental Medicine,* **81**, 25
4 Goldberg, J (1959) *British Journal of Venereal Diseases,* **35**, 266
5 Davis, C M and Collins, C (1969) *The Journal of Investigative Dermatology,* **53**, 315
6 Packer, H and Goldberg, J (1950) *American Journal of Syphilis, Gonorrhoea and Venereal Diseases,* **34**, 342
7 Rajam, R V and Rangiah, P N (1954) Donovanosis (Granuloma inguinale; Granuloma venereum). World Health Organization. Monograph, Series No. 24, Geneva
8 United States Public Health Service (1972) *V.D. Fact Sheet, 1971.* U.S. Department of Health Education and Welfare, Atlanta, Georgia
9 Goldberg, J (1964) *British Journal of Venereal Diseases,* **40**, 140
10 Lal, S and Nicholas, C (1970) *British Journal of Venereal Diseases,* **46**, 461
11 Goldberg, J (1962) *British Journal of Venereal Diseases,* **38**, 99
12 Davis, C M (1970) *Journal of the American Medical Association,* **211**, 632
13 King, A (1964) in *Recent Advances in Venereology.* J and A Churchill, Ltd., London, page 334
14 Goldberg, J and Annamunthodo, H (1966) *British Journal of Venereal Diseases,* **42**, 205
15 Beerman, H and Sonck, C E (1952) *American Journal of Syphilis, Gonorrhoea and Venereal Diseases,* **36**, 501
16 Stewart, D B (1964) *The Medical Clinics of North America,* **48**, 773
17 Wilcox, R R (1975) Granuloma inguinale (Donovanosis). In *Recent Advances in Sexually Transmitted Diseases.* (Ed) Morton, R S and Harris, J R W. Churchill Livingstone, Edinburgh, London and New York, pages 194–197
18 Breschi, L C, Goldman, G and Shapiro, S R (1975) *Journal of the American Venereal Disease Association,* **1**, 118
19 Thew, M A, Swift, J T and Heaton, C L (1969) *Journal of the American Medical Association,* **210**, 866
20 Pitman, F E (1979) *Adverse Drug Reactions Bulletin,* No. 75 (April). Adverse Drug Reaction Research Unit, Shotley Bridge General Hospital, Durham
21 Committee on Safety of Medicines (1979) *Adverse Reactions Series* No. 17 (June). Finsbury Square House, London

CHAPTER 30

Arthropod Infestations

Scabies

The condition known as scabies or 'the itch' is caused by the invasion of the stratum corneum of man by the mite *Sarcoptes scabiei* var *hominis.* Although promiscuous sexual behaviour may contribute to its spread among adolescents and young adults in some social circumstances, in most cases it is not spread by this means and domestic outbreaks within a household or family are more important within the community. Control may be achieved by early diagnosis and correct treatment of the patient and all members of the household, whether sharing beds or not. Individuals harbouring very large numbers of *Sarcoptes* may play an important part in the maintenance and spread of the disease in the community and waxing and waning of herd immunity may contribute to fluctuations in its incidence.

AETIOLOGY

Morphology and life cycle of the mite

The mite, *Sarcoptes scabiei* var *hominis* is translucent and hemispherical, measuring 0.4 × 0.3mm in the case of the female and about half of this in the male. Transverse corrugations are seen on its body and spines and bristles on its dorsal surface; the adult has eight legs. Fuller morphological details are given by Mellanby [1].

Mites can move rapidly on the warm skin (at a rate of about one inch per minute). The female, when fertilized, reaches its adult size and exercises some selection of the site into which it excavates a burrow in the stratum corneum. It extends the burrow daily by 2mm, lays 1–3 eggs each day and dies after 25 or more have been laid. Six-legged larvae emerge after 3–4 days and shelter in hair follicles where they undergo a moult to form an eight-legged nymph, which possibly moults again to form a second nymph. After another moult a mature adult male or an immature female is formed.

Mites are to be found in burrows at certain anatomical sites not influenced by the site of the initial infestation. The majority of mites (63 per cent) are found on the hands and wrists; the next most favoured site is the extensor aspect of the elbow, where about 11 per cent of the acari are found; the feet and genitals each may harbour about 9 per cent, the buttocks 4 per cent, the axillae 2 per cent and on the whole remaining surface of the body only 2 per cent of the mite population can be found [1]. The total population of mites is generally only about a dozen but in 3 per cent of patients there may be over 500. In the case of crusted scabies (Norwegian scabies) there may be very high counts both on the patient and in scale from the skin; in one such patient, washings from pyjamas and bed linen over a 48-hour period yielded 7640 mites [2].

EPIDEMIOLOGY

In Britain there appear to have been three epidemics, the first during the 1914–1918 war, the second beginning a few years before the second war and reaching a peak in 1943 and the third commencing about 1957. Peterkin [3], for example, recorded that 153 cases of scabies were seen in the Department of Dermatology at Edinburgh Royal Infirmary in 1932 and that the numbers increased to 306 in 1938, reaching a peak of 849 in 1941 and steadily declining to 31 in 1951. In the third epidemic, by 1967 scabies had increased sevenfold in Sheffield and threefold in London. From a recent study in Sheffield, where notification had been introduced in 1975, it was concluded that spread by sexual contact plays only a small part in the spread of the disease [4]. Infestation is introduced to households mainly by school children and teenagers, especially girls. The commonest sources are friends and relatives outside the home and schools do not play an appreciable part in spread. The high incidence in teenage girls is attributed to their greater contact with younger children and their habit of holding hands. Girls too may share a bed more often than boys [5]. In Sheffield, notification and contact tracing has led to the detection of cases of scabies in 17 per cent of the 873 contacts examined, but, although effective in this way, incidence of the disease in the community has not been reduced [4].

It is thought that about 15 years of widespread infestation is followed by a similar period when the disease becomes rare, although the cycle does not appear to be clear cut [6]. Some degree of immunity is induced by *Sarcoptes* and epidemics may be related to resurgence of the disease when 'herd immunity' has declined during a period of low incidence [1]. Normally in scabies there is an immune response up to the third month in which there is a marked reduction in parasite numbers. This is a delayed hypersensitivity due to a cell mediated immunity response, probably with some skin IgE [7]. The persistence of the acarus in asymptomatic patients and in cases of undiagnosed Norwegian scabies will form important sources of infection. Within hospital ward epidemics, isolation of the case of crusted scabies Norwegian scabies will form important sources of infestation. Within disinfestation, because cuticular fragments containing mites are abundant in the environment of such cases [2]. In scabies treated with topical steroids or immunosuppressants patients sometimes carry large numbers of acari [8].

Although family outbreaks are important in most communities it is important to exclude other sexually transmissible disease when scabies is found in an adolescent or young adult. Scabies is seen not uncommonly in STD clinics; in Edinburgh, for example, the diagnosis has been made about once in males for every 15 cases of gonorrhoea and in females once for every 30 cases. Gonorrhoea and syphilis are transmissible by brief sexual contact; scabies may require more prolonged skin contact than occurs in a casual intercourse.

CLINICAL FEATURES

The presenting symptom is itching which is worse at night. This appears to be due to sensitization and tends to develop about five weeks after a first infection, but earlier in the second and subsequent attacks. The reaction tends to be most intense on the genitals and buttocks where the acari may be destroyed by scratching.

Burrows and vesicles associated directly with the presence of the mite

The pathognomonic lesions are the burrows, appearing as serpiginous greyish ridges, 5–15mm in length, which may be difficult to find if hygiene is good. The mite is visible in the burrow as a raised whitish oval with dark pigmentation anteriorly.

Sarcoptes can be found mainly in burrows at specific sites, namely, on the anterior aspect of the wrist, along the ulnar border of the hand, between the fingers, on the extensor aspects of the elbows, around the nipples in the female and in the natal cleft. Mellanby [9] lists the frequency with which the different sites were affected in 886 cases (given as percentages): Hands and wrists, 85; Extensor aspect of the elbows, 41; feet and ankles, 37; penis and scrotum, 36; buttocks, 16; axillae, 15; knee, 6; umbilicus, 3; and hip, thigh, abdomen, arm, chest, nipples, back and neck as other sites less commonly affected.

Vesicles occur at the end of burrows and also separately from them, especially at the sides of the fingers. In infants bullae may form particularly on the palms and soles [10].

Urticarial papules not associated directly with the presence of the mite

Although papular lesions occur near the mite, an erythematous rash with urticarial papules is often most prominent in areas where mites are not necessarily found. Mellanby [1] has mapped these areas (Figure 30.1). Scratch marks, often with pin point blood crusts at the apices of follicles, may be numerous. In 30 per cent of patients there are penile and scrotal lesions [10].

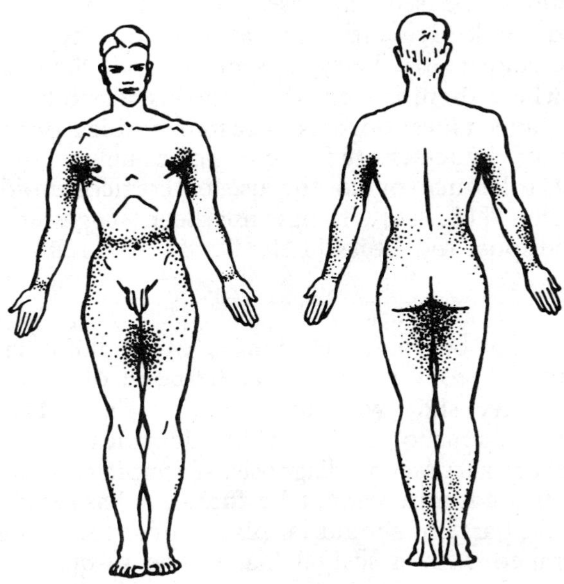

Figure 30.1 Sites affected by urticarial papular rash in scabies (note that the rash does not correspond with the sites of election of the acari) [1].

Indurated nodules

In about 7 per cent of cases itchy indurated nodules may be found. The commonest sites have been recorded as: axillae (50 per cent), scrotum (40 per cent), abdomen, sides of chest, groins (each about 30 per cent) and on the penis (about 20 per cent). The nodules may persist after treatment, but in only 20 per cent of cases do they persist for longer than three months [11].

Other changes seen in scabies

Eczematous changes may follow scratching and secondary bacterial infection may cause pustular lesions or even pyoderma. Colonization of scabetic lesions with streptococci is common; when these are nephritogenic acute glomerulonephritis may result, as in Trinidad in 1971, where the attack rate for acute glomerulonephritis reached 5.2 per 1000 children of 5–9 years of age [12].

Crusted scabies or Norwegian scabies, associated with vast numbers of mites, tends to be seen in cases of mental defect, as in Down's syndrome and senile dementia; in cases of debility as in leukaemia, beriberi, tuberculosis, bacilliary dysentery and rheumatoid arthritis and in cases where there is lack of cutaneous sensibility as in leprosy, syringomyelia and tabes dorsalis. Crusted scabies occurs also when there is lack of hypersensitivity due to a failure of sensitization, acquisition of tolerance or to the use of corticosteroid or immunosuppressive drugs [13, 14]. It has also been suggested that low IgE levels may predispose to scabies [15].

DIAGNOSIS

The mite can best be found by means of an illuminated magnifier and can be secured from a burrow on the point of a needle; it may be examined on a dry slide without mounting fluid. The burrows are pathognomonic lesions of scabies, but identification of the mite is desirable to secure accuracy in diagnosis. If scrapings are to be examined, because an individual mite cannot be found, it has been suggested that a drop of liquid paraffin should be placed over the suspected site and the lesion scraped with a scalpel blade. The suspended material can then be examined microscopically as an oily film covered by a coverslip [16].

In scabies of animal origin the clinical presentation is 'Scabies without burrows'. Irritable papules or papulovesicles, appearing at sites of close contact with the family pet, may be due to *Sarcoptes scabiei var canis.* Its feline counterpart, *Notoedres cati,* is rare in Britain but not uncommon in Czechoslovakia or Japan [11].

TREATMENT

Gamma benzene hexachloride (also known as lindane)

Since the successful use of a 1 per cent gamma benzene hexachloride cream in the treatment of scabies, recorded by Wooldridge [17] in 1948, this insecticide has been regarded as the most effective, safe and least irritant form of treatment. The preferred preparation is gamma benzene hexachloride BP, 1 per cent in a water-dispersible base (Quellada Lotion, Stafford Miller – 100ml). Although ill effects, apart from eczema on rare occasions, have not been found to occur clinically with the one or two applications required in treatment of the individual case, and although such treatment cannot be equated with risks in more intense or prolonged exposure, theoretical considerations of toxicity have led to the advocacy, in the medical literature of the USA particularly, of more caution in its use [18].

In the treatment of scabies with gamma benzene hexachloride lotion, according to Solomon *et al* [18], there are 'rare anecdotal communications' of toxicity (headache, nausea, transient seizures) which resemble the more serious effects of exposure to very high dosage. Brief consideration of the subject of toxicity is therefore justified here. Gamma benzene hexachloride can be absorbed percutaneously and the scrotal skin, for example, poses virtually no barrier to its penetration [19]. Early experimental work showed that although metabolized by the liver and stored in depot fat and other lipophilic tissues, the gamma isomer of benzene hexachloride was eliminated very rapidly and disappeared from fat depots in rats, for example, within 3 weeks [20]; there are, however, no data of this kind for man.

A study of pesticide workers in Hungary [21] showed a correlation between blood concentrations above 0.02 ppm and EEG abnormalities in 15 of 17 subjects; additional toxic effects such as depressed liver function and cardiac arrhythmia have been referred to by Solomon *et al* [18] in those suffering from chronic exposure. Although ill effects of a systemic nature resulting from the topical application of the 1 per cent gamma benzene hexachloride lotion in the limited manner used in the treatment of scabies, have not been recorded in the literature, Solomon *et al* [18] make certain observations regarding its use. Because percutaneous absorption may well be greater in those whose skin has been damaged by excoriation, or in infants, it is suggested that it might be better to apply the agent to the dry cool skin, or to allow the skin to dry and cool after any cleansing bath is taken, rather than to prescribe the bath with hot soapy water originally advised by Wooldridge [17]. Cannon and McRae [22] found the application to be quite effective without bathing. Other suggestions of Solomon *et al* [18] included a view that to leave the application on the skin for 24 hours before washing it off may be unnecessarily long and that a shorter contact time might be as effective; similarly the 1 per cent concentration might also be more than required. The substance should be avoided,

Solomon *et al* [18] suggest, in pregnancy, very small infants and those with marked excoriation. Retreatment, it is also advised, should not take place before 8 days and only if living acari are found.

Although the minimum dose needed to effect a cure in scabies has not been found, extensive clinical experience has shown that gamma benzene hexachloride 1 per cent is an effective sarcopticide, even when as many as 10 per cent of cases may be also secondarily infected [23]. The authors consider that it should be avoided in pregnant women during the organogenetic period within the first trimester, and in infants treatment should consist of one application only. Hospital staff should avoid regular contact with the substance.

Benzyl benzoate application

Benzyl benzoate application BP, a 25 per cent w/v emulsion, is effective and suitable for adolescents or adults when there is little excoriation. It is rather sticky to use and irritant to excoriated skins. As it causes stinging in children it should not be used for them.

Crotamiton lotion

Crotamiton lotion BP, 10 per cent w/v in an emulsified base (Eurax Lotion, Geigy Pharmaceuticals – 150ml; Eurax Cream is an alternative) is effective as a sarcopticide and relieves pruritus also from other causes than sarcoptes. It should not be used in infants or if there is excoriation of the skin.

The secret of success is that the sarcopticide selected should be applied to the whole body surface from the chin to the soles of the feet [24]. It is better to give the patient written instructions and for the nurse to give an explanation carefully. Details given below are suitable for the otherwise healthy adult; in the case of infants or in those with marked excoriation one application may suffice and there is a case for avoiding unnecessary exposure to the insecticide [18].

Instructions for treatment of scabies

(Gamma-benzene hexachloride, 1 per cent lotion).

1. Have a warm bath and scrub your skin gently but thoroughly; dry yourself with a towel and allow the skin to cool.
2. Apply the lotion to all the skin from below the neck to, and including, the soles of the feet, and allow it to dry.

3. Dress but retain the same clothing. (If you wash your hands again re-apply the lotion.)

4. After 12 hours have a second bath.

5. After an interval of 3 days apply the lotion again to all the skin from below the neck to the soles of the feet for the second and last time and allow to dry.

6. Change your clothing and bed linen.

7. After 12 hours have a third bath.

If benzyl benzoate application or crotamiton lotion is to be used the instructions may be modified to allow these scabiecides to act for longer. After applying as described, the medicament should be left for 48 hours before being washed off, when a second and last application is made and allowed to act for 48 hours once again. The patient should be told that although itching will diminish rapidly, it may not be completely relieved for some days or weeks.

Where the skin of the patient shows excoriation and in infants, one application of gamma-benzene hexachloride as a 1 per cent lotion may suffice. In infants or children the skin should not be scrubbed. All members of the household should be treated as well as the sexual contact and an attempt made to find the primary or source case. Ordinary laundering of clothes and bed linen will destroy the mites.

Pediculosis

The human louse, *Pediculus humanus,* is found in two forms, the head louse and the body louse, which can be considered as unstable environmental subspecies of the one species. The morphological differences between them are slight and variable and many specimens cannot be assigned to one or other subspecies [25]. The two forms are interfertile, with no evidence of type-specific mating choice [26]. The pubic louse is a different species, *Pthirus pubis.* All are obligate parasites of man and have mouth-parts adapted for piercing the skin and sucking blood [25].

Pediculus humanus as the body louse

The adult female is a greyish white insect 3–4mm long and the male a little smaller. The legs are adapted for grasping hairs. Both sexes suck blood and inject saliva while doing so. During a life span of about a month the female lays 7–10 eggs per day. Eggs hatch in eight days and the nymphs require a further eight days to reach maturity. The eggs are oval-lidded capsules, firmly cemented to a hair or to a thread, particularly along the inside of seams. Lice survive more than 10 days away from their hosts but eggs may survive in garments for a month.

EPIDEMIOLOGY

The infestation is occasionally seen in vagrants or mentally handicapped individuals who may attend clinics. The insects are spread by clothing or bedding, but the lice can travel short distances from the host.

The dimension to be faced in areas where a high proportion of the population carry *P. humanus,* and where louse-borne typhus is endemic or epidemic, is quite different to that faced by doctors treating a single patient [27].

CLINICAL FEATURES

In previously unexposed individuals the bite provokes only pin point red macules. After 7 days small weals or more persistent papules develop as pruritus becomes more troublesome.

TREATMENT

In the United Kingdom dicophane and gamma benzene hexachloride powders have been withdrawn from clinical use and powder containing pyrethrum, with its toxicity to insects enhanced by piperonyl butoxide, should be used for its quick knock-down effect, although its persistence is less (Cooper's Safe Insect Powder). Gamma benzene hexachloride 1 per cent in a detergent base (Quellada), should be applied over the skin surfaces and rubbed into dirty or hairy areas. Clothes should be disinfested [28].

The resistance of body lice to insecticides has been widely reported and may be determined by the use of the WHO standard test method. Where resistance has been found various alternative dusting powders may have to be used (e.g., 1 per cent gamma benzene hexachloride, 1 per cent malathion, 2 per cent temephos, 5 per cent carbaryl and 1 per cent propoxur) [27]. Malathion-resistant body lice have occurred in Africa and resistance ultimately threatens all types of control by conventional insecticides [26].

When a vacuum steam disinfestor is not available, as in overcrowded camps, the infested clothing may be treated with a fumigant, such as ethyl formate, by personnel trained in its use [27, 29]. In hospitals or where a large number of clothes have to be disinfested the clothes are placed in a cotton bag and disinfested by a vacuum steam method. An ordinary tumble dryer is effective and kills the lice and eggs on dry clothing, after which they may be sent quite safely to a conventional laundry if desired.

Pediculus humanus as the head louse

Head lice are almost confined to the scalp, but may be found on hairs in other parts of the body. Long fine hair and infrequent washing increase the chance of infestation.

EPIDEMIOLOGY

The incidence of head louse infestation was high in school children before 1939 but by 1960 it had been greatly reduced, until in 1969 it was again found that in some cities 10 per cent of school entrants were infested [11]. It is occasionally seen in clinics in female patients, although long-haired men may also be infested. Morley [30] notes that in Teesside 23 per cent of children in areas of poor and overcrowded housing were infested compared with 0.4 per cent in suburban areas; areas of local authority housing occupied an intermediate position with infestation rates of 13.4 per cent. The lowest infestation rates were in those under five years of age and highest in teenagers.

CLINICAL FEATURES

Pruritus is most severe around the back and sides of the scalp. Pruritus depends on hypersensitivity to the salivary antigens of the louse and in heavy infestation there may be no itching. Later the hair may become matted with pus. Impetigo of the scalp of the nape of the neck may accompany the infection.

TREATMENT

Lice resistant to DDT (dicophane) and gamma benzene hexachloride have been reported and the treatment of choice in infestation with these resistant lice is with malathion [11]. Malathion Scalp Application (0.5 per cent in an alcoholic base) is supplied as Prioderm, Napp Laboratories (55ml is sufficient for five treatments). Sufficient should be sprinkled on the scalp and rubbed well into the hair avoiding the eyes. It is allowed to dry and to remain untouched for 12 hours. After a shampoo the hair should be combed with a fine comb to remove the dead lice and egg cases. The treatment should be repeated in one week. If there is doubt about a patient's capacity to carry out instructions treatment should be given by a nurse who should wear rubber gloves when applying malathion. Contacts should be examined where possible as in some cities 20 per cent of children may be infested [28].

Pthiriasis pubis

The crab louse (*Pthirus pubis**) is greyish white; it measures about 1.2–2mm in length and is nearly as broad as it is long. There are three spiracles on its first abdominal segment [25]. It remains almost immobile on its host, the hind legs grasping two hairs. In this position it continues to feed intermittently for hours or days, rarely removing its mouth parts from their position in the host. The claws on the last two pairs of legs are adapted for grasping the widely spaced pubic hairs [26]. As it feeds it defaecates frequently, voiding blood and faeces intermixed.

Mating takes place on the host and some 26 eggs may be laid in 12 days. After a week the eggs hatch and the nymph attaches within a few hours. Three moults occur within 17 days. The nymphs and adults cannot survive more than two days when removed from their host [31].

EPIDEMIOLOGY

This louse is usually transferred by sexual contact but it can be spread by clothing. Pubic lice are becoming a more common infestation [32] and in Edinburgh, for example, in the years 1972–1976 a case was seen for every nine cases of gonorrhoea in males and for every eighteen cases in females.

The louse is mainly confined to the hairs of the pubic and peri-anal regions, but they may be found attached to the hairs of the abdomen, thighs and axillae. Very rarely they may be seen on the margin of the scalp, the eyebrows and eyelashes. In infants they will have reached such sites from the breast hairs of the mother.

CLINICAL FEATURES

Intense irritation is often the only symptom. Blue grey macules may be seen sometimes on the abdominal wall and upper thighs. In some patients irritation is minimal and the numbers of lice or eggs to be found are few.

TREATMENT

Gamma benzene hexachloride BP (1 per cent) in a detergent base (Quellada) or as gamma benzene hexachloride application BPC should be rubbed into the pubic, peri-anal, axillary and all other hairy parts below the neck. After being allowed to dry the patient may have a

*The correct name for the crab louse is *Pthirus pubis* (Phthirus is a widely dispersed error [26]).

bath after 24 hours. A second application after one week is generally sufficient. Malathion scalp application (0.5 per cent in an alcoholic base) can be used similarly.

Alternatively, malathion (1 per cent) shampoo (Prioderm Cream Shampoo, Napp Laboratories) should be rubbed into the wetted hair and worked up into a lather, rinsed out after five minutes and then the process repeated.

There are no reports of insecticide resistance in crab lice, but in view of the increased incidence and increased use of gamma benzene hexachloride and malathion, the future development of resistance cannot be excluded.

In eyelash infestations individual lice and eggs may be removed with forceps; an application of Vaseline may kill the lice by entering the spiracles. Other sites should be treated simultaneously with gamma benzene hexachloride or malathion.

REFERENCES

1 Mellanby, K (1972) *Scabies,* E W Classey, Hampton, Middlesex
2 Carslaw, E W, Dobson, R M, Hood, A J K and Taylor, R N (1975) *British Journal of Dermatology,* **92,** 333
3 Peterkin, G A, Grant (1959) *Archives of Dermatology,* **80,** 1
4 Church, R E and Knowelden, J (1978) *British Medical Journal,* **1,** 761
5 Christophersen, J (1978) *Archives of Dermatology,* **114,** 747
6 Orkin, M (1971) *Journal of the American Medical Association,* **217,** 593
7 Burgess, I (1973) *British Journal of Dermatology,* **87,** 519
8 MacMillan, A L (1972) *British Journal of Dermatology,* **87,** 496
9 Mellanby, K (1977) in *Scabies and Pediculosis.* (Ed) Orkin, M, Maibach, H I, Parish, L C and Schwartzman, R M. J B Lippincott Company, Philadelphia, page 14
10 Rook, A, Wilkinson, D S and Ebling, F J G (1972) in *Textbook of Dermatology.* Blackwell, Oxford, page 864
11 Bagnal, B and Rook A (1977) Arthropods and the skin. In *Recent Advances in Dermatology.* (Ed) Rook, A. Churchill Livingstone, Edinburgh
12 Porter, E V, Mayon-White, R, Svartman, M, Abidh, S, Poon-King, T and Earle, D T (1977) in *Scabies and Pediculosis.* (Ed) Orkin, M, Maibach, H I, Parish, L C and Schwartzman, R M. J B Lippincott Company, Philadelphia, page 39
13 Paterson, W B, Allen, B R and Beveridge, G W (1973) *British Medical Journal,* **4,** 211
14 Epsy, P D and Jolly, H W (1976) *Archives of Dermatology,* **112,** 193
15 Hancock, B W and Ward, A N (1974) *Journal of Investigative Dermatology,* **63,** 482
16 Muller, G H (1977) in *Scabies and Pediculosis.* (Ed) Orkin, M, Maibach, H I, Parish, L C and Schwartzman, R M. J B Lippincott Company, Philadelphia, page 100
17 Wooldridge, W E (1948) *Journal of Investigative Dermatology,* **10,** 363
18 Solomon, L M, Fahrner, L and West, D P (1977) *Archives of Dermatology,* **113,** 353
19 Feldman, R J and Maibach, H I (1974) *Toxicology and Applied Pharmacology,* **28,** 126
20 Davidow, B andnd Frawley, J P (1951) *Proceedings of the Society for Experimental Medicine,* **76,** 780
21 Czegedi-Janko, G and Avar, P (1970) *British Journal of Industrial Medicine,* **27,** 283
22 Cannon, A B and McRae, M E (1948) *Journal of the American Medical Association,* **138,** 557
23 James, B H E (1972) *British Medical Journal,* **1,** 172
24 Garretts, M (1972) *Prescribers Journal,* **12,** 32

25 Clay, T (1973) in *Insects and other arthropods of medical importance.* (Ed) Smith, K G V, British Museum, London, page 9

26 Busvine, J R (1977) in *Scabies and Pediculosis.* (Ed) Orkin, M, Maibach, H I, Parish, L C and Schwartzman, R M. J P Lippincott Company, Philadelphia, page 144

27 Gratz, N G (1977) in *Scabies and Pediculosis.* (Ed) Orkin, M, Maibach, H I, Parish, L C and Schwartzman, R M. J B Lippincott Company, Philadelphia, page 179

28 Garretts, M (1972) *Prescribers Journal,* 12, 16

29 Davies, F G and Bassett, W H (1977) *Clay's Public Health Inspectors Handbook,* 14th Edition, Lewis, London, page 493

30 Morley, W N (1977) *Scottish Medical Journal,* 22, 211

31 Matheson, R (1950) *Medical Entomology,* Constable and Co, London, page 194

32 Fisher, I and Morton, R S (1970) *British Journal of Venereal Diseases,* 46, 326

CHAPTER 31

Carcinoma of the Cervix Uteri

Cervical carcinoma has almost never been recorded in virgins. It increases in frequency the earlier the age of first coitus, and a history of multiple partners and increased sexual activity are features in the history of cervical cancer patients. It seems to be related to a sexually transmitted agent and antibody responses of women with cancer of the cervix lend some support to the belief that herpesvirus Type 2 (HSV2) is implicated in the aetiology [1, 2].

If HSV2 is an initiator of cervical cancer then the time between primary infection and malignant change must be long. It may be a promoter of cancerous change in already altered cells. In a survey of 871 women with HSV2 infection and 562 controls with no antibodies to HSV2, the rate of cervical dysplasia was found to be greater than two-fold and that of *in-situ* carcinoma eight-fold higher in the herpes group than in the control. There was also a two-fold higher rate of carcinoma *in-situ* in women who were pregnant at the time of their genital herpes infection [3].

Tentative implications of an uncompleted epidemiological study included also the view that certain males may venereally transmit a risk factor for cervical cancer in women [4]. HSV2 infection of the penis, chronic rather than latent, or a mutagenic action of the spermatozoon itself are among the possible explanations of the male role in cervical carcinogenesis.

Reference has been made already in Chapter 23, to two cases in which cervical biopsy showed an invasive squamous cell carcinoma, associated with superficial cervical warts, ordinarily a common innocent lesion in young women [5]. In some African cities carcinoma of the cervix is the commonest tumour seen, although the aetiology may also depend upon herpesvirus Type 2, rather than the papilloma virus. The observation too that carcinoma of the penis is the commonest tumour in parts of tropical Africa, as in Uganda, for example, where it forms 11–40 per cent [6] of all tumours in men, may have relevance also to the aetiology of carcinoma of the cervix, which is also common there (Chapter 23).

During the 1960s a downward trend in the mortality rates for uterine cancer as a whole was observed in all countries of Europe.

Although the data for the death rates from cancer of the cervix, specifically, are very unreliable it seems that a decline occurred and in Scotland for example, there was a decrease of 17 per cent in the mortality for uterine cancer as a whole during the 1960s. Some of this decline may have been due to better screening and some may have been due to better treatment of genital infections as a whole, including the recourse to hysterectomy for non-malignant uterine conditions [2].

A cervical cancer that would be otherwise fatal can be eradicated by excision at an early or precancerous stage; this curable stage is cytologically detectable and has usually, but not invariably, a long duration of 10–20 years. A cytological report 'positive cervical smear' means one containing cells from a severe dysplasia, carcinoma *in-situ* or invasive cancer of the cervix. The conversion from a negative to a positive smear is greatest in those aged 25–29, with a maximum prevalence at the ages of 35–39. Some of these lesions regress spontaneously, especially those classed as dysplasia, which are so common in the young. Careful follow-up is necessary to ensure their removal before becoming invasive or potentially so.

Invasive cervical cancer is a disease mainly of the second half of life and although there has been in England and Wales, as shown below, an increase in deaths in recent years from this cause in women under the age of 35 years, the percentage of all deaths from cervical cancer accounted for by this age group is less than 4 per cent (Table 31.1) [7].

The routine mass screening of women under 30 years of age has not, therefore, been considered to be an effective means of reducing the mortality [8], and the testing of young women on a large scale may be wasteful of resources, perhaps also inducing anxiety in those with dysplasia, unless used as a means of recruiting and identifying high-risk women [9]. Spriggs and Hussain [10] have made recommendations that cervical testing should begin well before the age of serious cancer risk; that the first cervical smear should be taken at any consultation for contraception, pregnancy or sexually-transmissible disease near to the age of 25 and any sexually-active woman who has not yet been tested should have a first smear at 30. They advise that the first smear should be repeated after one year to avoid a false negative error and again at three years if there is an opportunity for a pelvic examination. Follow-up screening should be done at 3–5 year intervals.

There is little doubt that it is among those who attend STD clinics that future sufferers of carcinoma of the cervix will be found. The age group attending is however younger than the main age group at risk from invasive cancer, so the value of screening in such clinics is limited, unless high risk patients or those with positive smears are encouraged

Table 31.I Deaths from cervical cancer in women under 35 years of age in England and Wales

	< 25 years		25–34 years		All ages
Year	*Numbers*	*Percentage of all deaths from cervical carcinoma*	*Numbers*	*Percentage of all deaths from cervical carcinoma*	*Numbers*
1970	5	0.22	34	1.52	2243
1971	2	0.09	41	1.77	2315
1972	4	0.18	46	2.07	2218
1973	7	0.31	39	1.73	2249
1974	5	0.24	50	2.42	2068
1975	9	0.42	68	3.17	2143
1976	9	0.41	60	2.72	2206

Significant improvement has been recorded for the death rates of those between 35 and 54 years of age [7]

to attend for follow-up [9] either at the STD clinic, their own general practitioner's surgery or at other clinics such as those for contraceptive advice. In those individuals who have had HSV2 infection, in those who have had intercourse at an early age and in those believed to be or to have been promiscuous, a lifelong follow-up is particularly important [11].

In educating the patient and public about the possible causal relationship of HSV2 to carcinoma of the cervix or about carcinoma of the cervix being a sexually-transmitted disease, anxiety can be mitigated by an explanation and reassurance about risks. It can be said in Scotland, for example, that the cervical cancer rate is about 18 per 100,000 for all ages and about twice this rate for those over 45 years of age. Furthermore it should be explained that this risk can be reduced by taking regular cervical smears and, probably even further with less morbidity by a colposcopy service.

Medical staff in clinics for STD, in cities in the United Kingdom for instance, are often in a position to ensure follow-up of high risk patients, some of whom will require continued medical care over a long period of time and other forms of assistance from the medical or social services. The recent increase in cervical cancer mortality, reported in England and Wales, in those under 35 years of age, reaching

69 in 1976, although tragic, represented only three per cent of the 2206 cervical cancer deaths at all ages. These changes foreshadow, perhaps, larger increases in later years unless these increases are forestalled by early detection and effective treatment of women with cervical cancer or its precursors [9].

The early lesions of squamous carcinoma of the uterine cervix are usually accessible and cytological examination of the area medial to the squamocolumnar junction [12] is possible by means of a specimen obtained with Ayre's spatula. Although screening techniques continue to pose problems in cost-benefit analysis, there is no doubt about the role of doctors in STD clinics in connection with this task. In 1975 our experience in a small sample of 819 patients showed a rate of 26 per 1000 with Grade II smears (doubtful cellular features) and four per 1000 with Grade III (cells suspected of being malignant). Identification of those with high risk or with abnormal smears and their close follow-up are responsibilities which should not be disowned. In the STD clinic the health visitor, or other staff trained similarly, can help by giving reassurance and explanations to patients, when the words of the doctor may have been incompletely remembered or understood, and by finding those who default.

Many more lesions in the dysplastic phase are now being identified as well as more borderline *in situ* carcinomas. For these lesions a cone biopsy with the attendant need for admission to hospital, morbidity and subsequent limitation of fertility seems a rather major procedure. The complications are sufficient to warrant a search for a better method of management of these young women with very early disease. In British Columbia, Canada, a colposcopy service has been developed with the expectation that the number of cone biopsies can be reduced by 70 per cent. It is also hoped [12] that cryosurgery or cautery can be used as treatment for the dysplastic lesions at an early stage in the evolution of the disease.

Diagnostic exfoliative cytology retarded the use of the colposcope. Training in colposcopy is time-consuming, but the magnification of the instrument allows evaluation of the striking changes in the surface pattern of the lesion and in the terminal vascular network. Areas from which biopsy may be taken can be accurately identified and changes which take place slowly over a long period of time may be recorded objectively by photography [13].

Preliminary results indicate that many lesions which would have been treated by diagnostic conization followed by hysterectomy or therapeutic conization have been evaluated and safely treated by cryosurgery, electrocautery, electrodiathermy or multiple punch biopsy on an outpatient basis or by a single admission to hospital. Study of laser techniques under colposcopic control suggests that these may prove ideal for the precise eradication of a focal lesion. The patient selected for this management is described as a young woman, desiring future pregnancy, who has a focal colposcopic lesion of a minor grade and columnar epithelium visible in the cervical canal [14]. Such patients will be discovered readily among those who attend clinics for sexually transmissible disease.

REFERENCES

1 Singer, A (1974) *Lancet,* **ii,** 41

2 Hill, G B (1976) Cancer of the uterus: mortality trends since 1950, *WHO Chronicle,* **30,** 188

3 Nahmias, A J, Naib, Z M and Josey, W E (1972) Genital Herpes and cervical cancer—can a causal relationship be proven? In *Oncogenesis and Herpes Viruses.* (Ed) Biggs, P M, de The, G and Payne, L N. Lyons, page 73

4 Kessler, I I (1976) *Cancer Research,* **36,** 783

5 Rafferty, A and Payne, W S (1954) *Obstetrics and Gynecology,* **4,** 581

6 Davies, J N P (1959) Cancer in Africa. In *Modern Trends in Pathology.* (Ed) Collins, D H. Butterworth, London, page 132

7 Yule, R (1978) *Lancet,* **i,** 1031

8 Knox, E F (1976) *British Journal of Cancer,* **34,** 444

9 Editorial (1978) *Lancet,* **ii,** 1029

10 Spriggs, A I and Hussain, O A N (1977) *British Medical Journal,* **1,** 1516

11 Editorial (1977) *Lancet,* **i,** 1297

12 Boyes, D A and Worth, A J (1976) Cytological screening for cervical carcinoma. In *The Cervix* (Ed) Jordan, J A and Singer, A. Saunders, London, page 404

13 Kolstad, P and Stafl, A (1977) Atlas of Colposcopy, Universitetslaget, Oslo

14 Coppleson, M (1977) Colposcopy. In *Recent Advances in Obstetrics and Gynaecology.* (Ed) Stallworthy, J and Bourne, G. Churchill Livingstone, Edinburgh, page 155

CHAPTER 32

Diseases due to Intestinal Organisms in Homosexual Males

The transfer of intestinal organisms between male homosexuals as a result of their sexual activity is being reported with increasing frequency [1]. Transfer may result directly by oro-anal, or indirectly by oro-genital contact and a wide range of organismal infections such as giardiasis, amoebiasis, shigellosis and enterobiasis has been reported. Although sexual activity probably plays a minor role in the spread of these infections, clinicians responsible for the medical care of male homosexuals should be aware of the possibility that gastrointestinal symptoms may be due to intestinal bacterial and other parasitic infections.

Diseases due to protozoa

GIARDIASIS

Giardia lamblia is a flagellate protozoon found in the small intestine. It has trophozoite (vegetative) and cyst stages. The trophozoites are usually found in the intestinal crypts at the duodenal level, where they are firmly attached to the epithelial surface. At times they are also found at lower levels of the intestine and in the common bile duct and gall bladder.

The protozoon is world-wide in its distribution and epidemics of the disease are associated with ingestion of contaminated water. It is estimated that in temperate climates, the prevalence of giardiasis varies from about 2 to 20 per cent [2]. Faecal–oral transmission probably accounts for some infections in homosexual males [3].

Although most infections are asymptomatic, clinical features of the acute disease include diarrhoea, abdominal distension, flatulence, abdominal colic, nausea, vomiting, fever and rigors [4]. Without treatment the symptoms subside after an interval of two days to three months. In some cases, however, symptoms persist for much longer and may be associated with features of malabsorption.

Diagnosis depends on the demonstration usually of cysts in the faeces: trophozoites, ordinarily located at the duodenal level, are not usually seen in stool specimens unless the patient has profuse diarrhoea. As excretion of cysts is intermittent, the examination of several specimens at intervals of two to three days is necessary [2]. In suspected cases where repeated examination of faeces fails to reveal the parasite, microscopy of duodenal fluid obtained by duodenal intubation has been valuable [4].

Mepacrine hydrochloride (mepacrine tablets BP) given orally in a dosage of 100mg three times per day for seven days [4], gives a cure rate of about 95 per cent in giardiasis [4]. Side effects include gastrointestinal upsets, and rarely exfoliative dermatitis, toxic psychosis; it should not be used in patients with psychotic illness or with psoriasis.

Metronidazole (metronidazole tablets, BP; Flagyl Tablets, May and Baker) 200mg three times per day for seven days is less effective (cure rate of less than 70 per cent) (Chapter 18).

AMOEBIASIS

Amoebiasis is caused by the protozoon *Entamoeba histolytica.* After ingestion by the host those cysts which escape the gastric juices pass into the small intestine where trophozoites are liberated to colonize the large intestine. Trophozoites may remain free-living in the intestinal lumen and in turn encyst and are excreted in the faeces; alternatively they may invade the mucous membrane of the intestinal wall, causing ulceration and sometimes producing the clinical features of amoebic dysentery. The amoebae may be carried from the intestine to the liver or, less commonly, other organs, where abscesses may develop.

The organism has a world-wide distribution with endemic areas usually in developing countries. Transmission in these areas occurs by ingestion of contaminated food or water.

Several recent reports draw attention to the occurrence of this infection in homosexual males, transmission probably occurring during oro-anal or oro-genital sexual contact [5, 6].

About 90 per cent of patients with amoebiasis are symptom free, and cysts of *E. histolytica* may be demonstrated in the faeces of about two per cent of healthy men in the United Kingdom [7]. In those who have symptoms the severity of the illness varies greatly. In symptomatic intestinal amoebiasis the patient complains of diarrhoea, abdominal discomfort, flatulence, blood and mucus in the stool, anorexia and weight loss. Sigmoidoscopy may reveal a normal rectal mucosal pattern or a mucous membrane which is red, oedematous and friable. The appearance may, however, be identical to that of non-specific ulcerative proctocolitis [8], when there may be multiple areas of ulceration, with individual ulcers, reaching up to a few millimetres in diameter, with a yellow base and an erythematous margin.

The development of hepatic abscess is associated with tenderness in the right hypochondrium, fever, and weight loss. Aspiration of the abscess produces a red-brown thick fluid, in which amoebae are rarely demonstrable. Cutaneous amoebiasis may rarely produce peri-anal or genital ulceration [9].

Diagnosis depends on the demonstration of trophozoites or cysts in the stool or material obtained from the base of ulcers in the rectum [2]. In acute amoebic dysentery, active unencysted amoebae (trophozoites) with ingested erythrocytes may be found in specimens of bloodstained stool if examined as a wet film prepared with saline within 15 minutes of the passage of the stool. Cysts are about 12μm in diameter (range 10–15μm) with characteristic chromidial bars–refractile rod-like structures with rounded ends; if stained with iodine cysts show 1–4 nuclei and a diffuse glycogen mass in the cytoplasm [10]. Cysts may be detected more frequently in the stool by the formol-ether concentration method [11]. Histopathological examination of biopsy material may not be helpful [8].

E. histolytica may be cultured on bacteria-containing media such as that of Robinson [12]. As the number of cysts necessary for viable cultures is large, these may be identified as readily by microscopy as by culture.

Serological tests for the diagnosis of amoebiasis have been available for many years; the most sensitive test at present is the indirect haemagglutination test. Serum antibodies against *E. histolytica* are found in most cases of invasive intestinal amoebiasis and hepatic abscess [13]. However, antibodies may persist for some months after successful treatment, and care is required in the interpretation of serological tests.

Not all strains of *E. histolytica* appear to be pathogenic, and there is controversy as to whether non-pathogenic forms of the protozoon can transform to pathogenic forms [14]. Sargeaunt *et al* [15] have identified four subspecies of *E. histolytica* on the basis of their content of isoenzymes and has shown that one subspecies, with a distinctive phosphoglucomutase, is regularly associated with organisms isolated from patients with invasive disease.

Where the entamoeba is invasive, as in intestinal and hepatic amoebiasis, metronidazole, given orally in a dosage of 800mg eight-hourly for five days, is an effective and relatively safe treatment (Chapter 18).

Emetine is also effective in invasive entamoeba infestations [2] but side effects such as electrocardiographic abnormalities occur and the patient should be treated as an inpatient.

Chloroquine is effective in the treatment of liver abscess but is ineffective against other forms of amoebiasis. It is given in a dose of 300mg twice daily by mouth for two days and then reduced to 150mg twice daily for seven days. It may be followed by a course of metronidazole (BNF 1976–78).

Diloxanide furoate (Furamide, Boots) in an oral dosage of 500mg eight-hourly for 10 days, is useful in the treatment of asymptomatic cyst carriers in temperate climates.

OTHER PROTOZOA WHICH MAY BE SEXUALLY TRANSMISSIBLE

Dientamoeba fragilis, Endolimax nana and *Iodamoeba buetschlii* may be transmitted similarly to *E. histolytica* [16].

Diseases due to bacteria

SHIGELLA DYSENTERY

Most cases of bacillary dysentery occur in children of pre-school or school age, when boys are more often affected than girls. Generally, in adults, the sexes are affected almost equally, with a slight preponderance of cases in females. Transmission of the organism is usually by hand to mouth contact; the infected individual contaminates toilet fixtures, which are then handled and the organisms transferred to the mouth of the new host. Occasionally infection results from contaminated water, food or fomites. In several recent outbreaks of the disease in the United States of America, more than two-thirds of adult cases were in young men; many of these men were homosexual, and transmission possibly a result of oro-anal and oro-genital sexual contact [1, 17]. Infectivity persists throughout the acute phase of the illness, and for a variable time, usually three to four weeks thereafter.

Shigella dysentery in homosexual males, may be accompanied by infection with other intestinal pathogens such as *Entamoeba histolytica* or *Giardia lamblia* and other sexually transmissible infections [6].

Clinical features

In the majority of cases bacillary dysentery is mild. After a prepatent period of two to seven days, frequent loose stools occur. The following day stools become more frequent, but less copious and the symptoms subside after a few days; there is usually no pyrexia, and only small quantities of mucus and blood may be passed.

In some cases the disease is more severe, beginning abruptly with frequent loose stools, blood and mucus; there is also fever, tenesmus and abdominal tenderness. Symptoms persist for about a week and then subside, the illness occasionally passing into a chronic phase.

Fulminating dysentery, with dehydration and electrolyte imbalance, is rarely seen in adults in developed countries.

Uncommon complications of bacillary dysentery include acute pyelonephritis, conjunctivitis and arthritis [18].

Diagnosis

Shigellae can be readily cultured from stool specimens, plated on to medium such as MacConkey agar, DCA (deoxycholate citrate agar), or XLD (xylose lysine decarboxylase) agar. The groups within the genus *Shigella* (e.g., *Sh. dysenteriae, Sh. flexneri, Sh. boydii, Sh. sonnei*) are identified by appropriate biochemical and serological tests.

Differential diagnosis

Dysentery due to *E. histolytica* and *Balantidium coli* is usually less acute in onset and trophozoites and/or cysts will be found in the faeces or in material obtained at sigmoidoscopic examination.

Dysentery due to schistosomes is often associated with eosinophilia and hypersensitivity reactions; ova are found in the stools and rectal mucosa. Serum antibodies against the schistosomes may be detected by fluorescent antibody methods in about 75 per cent of patients with schistosomiasis [19].

Giardiasis should be excluded by examination of the stools for cysts and trophozoites.

Ulcerative colitis and Crohn's disease require careful differentiation by sigmoidoscopy and barium studies.

Enteropathogenic strains of *Escherichia coli* may produce similar symptoms, but should be cultured from the stool. Salmonellosis may also be diagnosed by stool culture.

Treatment

In management of the patient bed rest and adequate fluid intake is necessary; careful attention to hygiene is important to prevent further transmission. Antibiotic therapy should not be given unless the illness is severe; the laboratory should confirm that the drug selected is active against the patient's isolate *in vitro.* In the past, antibiotic treatment has resulted in the emergence of resistant strains of the organism and clearance of the pathogen may not occur significantly earlier than when non-specific treatment has been given.

Diarrhoea may be controlled by the use of agents such as kaolin and morphine mixture, BPC, 10ml given orally every six hours. The use of diphenoxylate should be avoided, as its use in intestinal amoebiasis has resulted in the production of toxic megacolon [20]; infection with both *Entamoeba histolytica* and *Shigella* is not uncommon.

Nematode infestation

ENTEROBIASIS (THREADWORM INFESTATION)

The nematode *Enterobius vermicularis* is an intestinal parasite, usually transmitted from contaminated food or fomites, and most commonly found in children. After ingestion the ova hatch and develop within 6 weeks into adult worms, which inhabit the caecum and adjacent regions of the small and large intestines. The male worms are small, 2 to 5mm in length; the females larger, 8 to 13mm long. When fully mature the females emerge from the anus and deposit eggs on the peri-anal skin. It is this activity which produces pruritus ani, particularly at night. Uncommonly, threadworms enter the vagina and produce vulvo-vaginitis in young girls. Rarely ova may be found in cervical smears.

There have been several recent reports of threadworms in homosexual males [21], possibly acquired by oro-anal contact, a common practice in some homosexual men. Threadworm infestation should be excluded as a cause in pruritus ani.

In diagnosis, adult worms may be seen in the faeces or in the anal canal or rectum, or ova may be found on the peri-anal skin. Transparent adhesive tape (Sellotape), sticky side down, is applied to the peri-anal skin, preferably in the morning before the patient has defaecated. The tape is then applied to a slide for examination for ova by microscopy. Threadworm ova are 50 to 60μm long and 20 to 30μm broad; they are oval and flattened on one side.

Mebendazole is highly effective in eradicating *E. vermicularis* and cure rates of about 90 per cent may be obtained with a single oral dose of 100mg in both adults and children. Mebendazole may be given as orange-flavoured tablets (e.g., Vermox, Janssen Pharmaceutical Limited), which may be either swallowed whole or chewed and swallowed, or alternatively as a yellow banana-flavoured suspension (each 5ml spoonful containing mebendazole 100mg). No purging or laxatives are required.

Absorption of the drug is slight and levels of mebendazole and its metabolites in the plasma are extremely low with only about 5 to 10 per cent of the administered dose being eliminated in the urine within one or two days. Low doses of mebendazole act on the nematode by selectively and irreversibly blocking glucose uptake. Mebendazole has shown embryotoxic and teratogenic activity in pregnant rats, but no such findings have been reported in larger laboratory animals or observed in human pregnancy. Since the possibility of fetal damage exists, however, warnings have been given against its use in pregnancy and in infants under 2 years of age, where experience of its use is limited, mebendazole is not currently recommended (ABPI Data Sheet Compendium 1979–1980, page 450; Dukes, M N G (1979) *Side Effects of Drugs Annual 3,* Excerpta Medica, Amsterdam, Oxford, page 257; Martindale (1977) *Extra Pharmacopoeia* (ed) Wade, A, Pharmaceutical Press, London, page 106).

Piperazine acts within the gut by blocking the response of the nematode musculature to acetyl choline; the paralysed worms are then eliminated by normal bowel peristalsis.

Piperazine is readily absorbed from the gastro-intestinal tract and neurotoxic effects such as ataxia have occasionally been reported. Nausea, vomiting, diarrhoea, abdominal pain, headache, paraesthesia and urticaria may sometimes occur but disappear rapidly when treatment is stopped. Haemolytic anaemia among patients with G-6-PD deficiency, hypersensitivity phenomena and hepatitis are among rarities found in this widely used drug. In patients with liver or renal disease or with epilepsy or other neurological disturbances piperazine is contra-indicated.

Viprynium (e.g., Vanquin, Parke, Davis and Co.) often recommended, was withdrawn for commercial reasons in 1979.

Whatever drug is chosen it is advisable to treat members of the family simultaneously when a case is found; sexual contacts should be examined and be treated if infected. Personal cleanliness and regular changing of underclothing and bed linen are also essential. Retreatment with a second dose after two weeks is recommended in this infestation, so widespread, especially in school children (ABPI Data Sheet Compendium, 1979–1980, page 808; Dukes, M N G (1978) *Side Effects of Drugs Annual 2,* Excerpta Medica, Amsterdam, Oxford, page 262; Hamlyn, A N *et al* (1976) Piperazine hepatitis, *Gastroenterology,* 70, 1144).

Conditions of the ano-rectum and colon seen with unusual frequency in some male homosexuals

There is a group of ano-rectal and colonic conditions found with unusual frequency in male homosexuals [22], although these disorders are not confined to this population. Such conditions should be carefully excluded when investigating a man with a history of recent homosexual risk.

Table 32.1 indicates the ano-rectal conditions which may be encountered in the homosexual male. The data presented serve as a guide to the relative frequency of each condition in patients attending a clinic for the management of sexually transmitted diseases. More acute

Table 32.1 Colonic and ano-rectal findings in 194 homosexual men who consecutively attended a sexually-transmitted disease clinic in Glasgow during a 12-month period

Conditions diagnosed	*Number of men*
Ano-rectal gonorrhoea	31
Primary syphilis of anal canal	2
Secondary syphilis with condylomata lata and/or mucous patches at anus	5
Condylomata acuminata	15
Herpes simplex infection of anal margin	1
Molluscum contagiosum on peri-anal region	2
Bacillary dysentery	0
Proctocolitis due to *Entamoeba histolytica*	2
Giardiasis	1
Enterobiasis	9
Non-gonococcal proctitis*	7
Anal fissure	4
Anal fistula	1
Peri-anal abscess	1
Ischiorectal abscess	1
Traumatic lacerations	2
Rectal polyp	1
Anal incontinence	2
Lymphogranuloma venereum Granuloma inguinale Chancroid	0
No abnormalities detected	107
Total	194

**Chlamydia trachomatis* was isolated from the ano-rectum of two of these men colonic and ano-rectal problems would probably be managed *ab initio* by general physicians, gastro-enterologists and surgeons.

Non-gonococcal proctitis has been reported as being common in homosexual men [22]. Although amoebiasis and bacillary dysentery may produce proctitis, the aetiology is uncertain in most cases, although the role of *Chlamydia trachomatis* has not been adequately investigated. Histological examination of biopsy specimens shows only non-specific inflammatory changes [23].

In sexually transmitted disease clinics it is remarkable that so few traumatic lesions, either recent or past, are seen. Injury resulting from anal intercourse is usually manifest as anal fissuring or rectal laceration with haemorrhage. The less common, but dangerous practice of inserting the closed fist into the rectum has produced intra-abdominal perforation of the intestine, usually at the recto-sigmoid junction [24].

REFERENCES

1 Dritz, S K, Ainsworth, T E, Back, A, Boucher, L A, Garrard, W F, Palmer, R D and River, E (1977) *Lancet*, **ii**, 3

2 Markell, E K and Voge, M (1976) in *Medical Parasitology*. W B Saunders Company, Philadelphia, London, page 75

3 Meyers, J D, Kuharic, H A and Holmes, K K (1977) *British J. of Venereal Diseases*, **53**, 54

4 Wolfe, M S (1975) *Journal of the American Medical Association*, **233**, 1362

5 Schmerin, M J, Gelston, A and Jones, T C (1977) *Journal of the American Medical Association*, **238**, 1386

6 Mildvan, D, Gelb, A M and William, D (1977) *Journal of the American Medical Association*, **238**, 1387

7 Morton, T C, Neal, R A and Sage, M (1951) *Lancet*, **i**, 766

8 Pittman, F E and Hennigar, G R (1974) *Archives of Pathology*, **97**, 155

9 MacCallum, D I and Kinmont, P D C (1968) *British Journal of Dermatology*, **80**, 1

10 Crewe, W (1977) in Blacklock and Southwell (Ed), *A Guide to Human Parasitology*, 10th edition. Lewis and Co, London, page 18

11 Ridley, D S and Hawgood, B C (1956) *Journal of Clinical Pathology*, **9**, 74

12 Robinson, G L (1968) *Transactions of the Royal Society of Tropical Medicine and Hygiene*, **62**, 285

13 Juniper, K, Worrell, C L, Minshew, M C, Roth, L S, Cypert, H and Lloyd, R E (1972) *American Journal of Tropical Medicine and Hygiene*, **21**, 157

14 Leading Article (1979) *Lancet*, **i**, 303

15 Sargeaunt, P G, Williams, J E and Grene, J D (1978) *Transactions of the Royal Society of Tropical Medicine and Hygiene*, **72**, 519

16 Abrahm, P M (1972) *Journal of the American Medical Association*, **221**, 917

17 Dritz, S K and Back, A F (1974) *New England Journal of Medicine*, **291**, 1194

18 Woodruff, A W (1974) in *Medicine in the Tropics*. Churchill Livingstone, Edinburgh, page 251

19 Sadun, E H, Williams, J S and Anderson, R I (1960) *Proceedings of the Society for Experimental Biology and Medicine* (N Y) **105**, 289

20 Wruble, L D, Duckworth, J D, Duke, D D (1966) *New England J. of Medicine*, **275**, 926

21 Waugh, M A (1976) *Medical Aspects of Human Sexuality*, **10**, 119

22 Sohn, N and Robilotti, J G (1977) *American Journal of Gastroenterology*, **67**, 478

23 Kazal, H L, Sohn, N, Carrasco, J I, Robilotti, J G and Delaney, W E (1976) *Annals of Clinical and Laboratory Science*, **6**, 184

24 Sohn, N, Weinstein, M A and Gonchar, J (1977) *American Journal of Surgery*, **134**, 611

CHAPTER 33

Ulcers and Other Lesions of the External Genitalia

Acute ulcers

In the differential diagnosis of an acute genital ulcer, the cause to be considered first must be a sexually transmissible agent, particularly *Treponema pallidum:* within this group, ulcers found elsewhere, particularly in the oral and anal regions, must be included for consideration. In the context of general practice patients should be referred to clinics, where facilities for the necessary procedures are at hand. Antibiotics, which may obscure an important diagnosis, should not be prescribed blindly.

In all cases of a genital ulcer the first objective will be to diagnose or exclude early-stage contagious syphilis (Chapter 5) and to take steps to trace sexual contacts. Exclusion of other sexually transmissible diseases, particularly gonorrhoea (Chapters 10 and 11) and herpes genitalis (Chapter 20) is also necessary. In warmer climates, or in patients returning from them, possibilities of lymphogranuloma venereum (Chapter 27), chancroid (Chapter 28) and rarely donovanosis (Chapter 29) will require consideration, although in lymphogranuloma venereum the ulcer itself tends to be transitory and herpetiform.

The chancre of primary syphilis may often be a painless indurated ulcer with enlarged indurated non-tender lymph nodes, but its tendency to heal and to be modified by injudicious (e.g. topical steroid applications) and inadequate treatments makes it improper to base a diagnosis on clinical appearance alone. The importance of repeating serological tests for syphilis for a three-month follow-up period has been discussed.

In secondary syphilis moist eroded papules are seen in the mouth, on the genitalia or around the anus but the larger hypertrophic papules (condylomata lata) tend to be most obvious on the vulva in the female and in the anal region of both sexes (Chapter 5).

Although chancroid (soft sore) is rare in the United Kingdom and western Europe but common in the tropics and sub-tropics (Chapter 28), it is important to exclude syphilis by dark-ground examination and serological tests over a period of three months and to treat with a sulphonamide (e.g. sulphadimidine) to avoid masking the treponemal infection if it is present.

In the diagnosis of granuloma inguinale (Chapter 29) a small biopsy should be taken from the edge of the lesion and a tissue smear prepared and stained with Giemsa or Leishman stains to demonstrate the capsulate pleomorphic bacillus with bipolar staining.

Among other ulcers caused by infective agents are superficial herpetiform erosions at the introitus, associated with *Trichomonas vaginalis* vaginitis (Chapter 18). Some erosions, particularly at the fraenum in the male and at the fourchette in the female, may be traumatic from intercourse.

In *Candida* infection (Chapter 17) there may be erosions under the exudate in the vagina and fissuring, particularly of the fourchette. In the male contact a small proportion may show balanoposthitis with superficial ulceration of the glans and occasionally with fissures at the preputial orifice and a phimosis. *Candida* tends sometimes to flourish in the vagina in pregnancy, diabetes mellitus and in some patients taking contraceptive pills. Whenever there is a pruritus a search should also be made for pubic lice (Chapter 31) on the vulva, tinea in the groin, in the male, and threadworms or ova if the itch is peri-anal.

Non-gonococcal urethritis (Chapter 13) and the perhaps equivalent non-specific genital infection in the female is another possibility. In the male with non-gonococcal urethritis, superficial fissuring is sometimes seen in the fraenal and orifice portions of the prepuce. In Reiter's disease there is a circinate balanitis in 21 to 43 per cent of cases, and in the uncircumcised, these lesions on the glans may show maceration (Chapter 15).

Molluscum contagiosum (Chapter 25), with its small pearl-like umbilicated lesions, may be found on the penis in the male and on the vulva and inner aspect of the thighs in the female as well as elsewhere on the skin.

Condylomata acuminata (Chapter 23) are very common and neglect, coexistent vaginitis, urethritis or herpes infection may cause genital ulceration.

In scabies (Chapter 31), indurated papules, sometimes with pustulation and impetiginization are common on the shaft of the penis. The diagnosis rests on the history of pruritus, finding burrows and the recognition of *Sarcoptes scabiei.*

Even when furuncles and other pyogenic lesions are recognized, exclusion of syphilis remains a first consideration.

Chronic ulcers

Patients with oral aphthous ulcers have a 1 in 5 chance of having some haematological deficiency or malabsorption syndrome [1] so it is wise to extend the investigations (serum iron, iron binding capacity, serum folate, whole blood folate and serum B12) to cases with recurrent genital or orogenital aphthous ulcers.

In balanitis xerotica obliterans (BXO) (page 419), fibrotic, ivory-white areas are found on the margin of the prepuce, which shows fissuring and adhesion to the glans. This condition may affect the urethral meatus and lead to stenosis with a distinctive white peri-urethral collar. Ulceration can occur in chronic balanitis in the elderly, which may resemble BXO clinically. BXO may be equivalent to lichen sclerosus et atrophicus, essentially a disease of women, in which ivory papules and violaceous tissue-paper skin may be seen in the anogenital area. In the very rare Behçet's disease (page 424) there is also recurrent orogenital ulceration associated with iritis. Tuberculosis is now a rare cause of vulvar ulceration.

Crohn's disease (regional enteritis) can involve the anal region alone without apparent involvement of other parts of the gastrointestinal tract, presenting clinically as anal ulceration, anorectal fistulae or oedematous anal skin tags. Ulceration of the skin, separated from other areas of ulceration by normal skin, can occur and has been seen on the penis and on the vulva as well as elsewhere. Spreading ulceration of the skin of the perineum with linear extension into the groins and genitalia may occur after surgical treatment of an anal lesion [2].

In cases of chronic ulceration, malignant disease must also be excluded and particularly in erythroplasia of Queyrat (page 421), in which there is a raised bright-red well-demarcated plaque with a velvety surface to be seen on the glans, and in which a biopsy is necessary. Squamous-cell carcinoma of the penis is uncommon and, in the circumcised, extremely rare. The neoplasm develops within the preputial sac and it is usually wart-like rather than ulcerative. Other malignant tumours are very rare. Squamous cell carcinoma of the scrotum is associated with contamination of the skin with mineral oil and other carcinogens.

The characteristic symptom of vulvar leukoplakia is intense and persistent itch. Thickened white plaques tend to develop on the vulva, particularly around the clitoris, sometimes extending back to the anus; they do not encroach on the vestibule or vagina. Leukoplakia tends to occur in middle age and should be considered pre-malignant. Squamous carcinoma appears as a hard indurated swelling or an ulcerating lesion in the vulva with lymph node enlargement. In cases with pre-existing leukoplakia there is a long history of vulvar irritation.

Some other lesions of the genitalia and skin which may be seen in STD clinics

Balanoposthitis

The terms balanitis and posthitis refer respectively to inflammation of the glans and mucosal surface of the prepuce. As these conditions will ordinarily coexist the term balanoposthitis is strictly more correct than the commonly used shorter word balanitis. Acute and chronic forms may be due to traumatic, irritant or infective causes [3].

AETIOLOGY

Within the moist preputial sac an accumulation of smegma resulting from poor hygiene is an obvious predisposing factor in the aetiology of balanoposthitis. Irritation may also be due to friction of clothes, the unwise application of antiseptics or previous contact during sexual intercourse with pathogenic or opportunistic organisms within the vagina. Bacteria, yeasts or trichomonads may flourish in the moist environment, but sometimes balanitis may develop after intercourse, possibly as a result of sensitivity to a vaginal discharge containing *Candida* or substances derived from it (Chapter 17). With the restricting effect of phimosis, whether primary or secondary and due to inflammation, discharge may accumulate under pressure and if neglected may be associated with a necrotizing ulceration of the glans (phagedaena). Under these circumstances *Fusobacterium fusiforme* and *Borrelia vincentii* may be secondary invaders. Herpes simplex virus may be isolated from erosions.

Balanoposthitis may be associated with diabetes and occurs with debilitating disease particularly in the elderly and in urinary infections.

CLINICAL FEATURES

In infective forms of balanitis there is erythema of the glans, coronal sulcus and inner surface of the prepuce. It can be insidious in onset and pass unnoticed, but sometimes erythema and oedema is pronounced and a resulting phimosis may make inspection of the glans difficult or impossible. In the uncircumcised the affected surfaces become macerated and a purulent exudate accumulates, rapidly becoming malodorous. Erosion and ulceration may be painful.

In Reiter's disease (Chapter 15) a recurring circinate balanitis develops in 25 per cent of cases on the glans penis and mucous surface of the prepuce. In balanitis associated with or due to diabetes or candidiasis there may be fissuring of the prepuce, particularly at its orifice.

All forms of balanitis may become chronic or relapse frequently, particularly in the elderly, when fibrotic changes may resemble those seen in balanitis xerotica obliterans (page 419).

TREATMENT

Mild forms of balanitis are cleared readily by retracting the prepuce and bathing with physiological saline. This treatment should be repeated twice or thrice daily and, if inflammation is more than trivial, a strip of gauze (2.5cm × 15cm) soaked in saline should be applied to the glans and coronal sulcus in such a way that, on bringing the prepuce forward, the skin surfaces of the glans and the inner aspect of the prepuce are separated by gauze. The prescription of oral sulphadimidine (2g initially followed by 1g six-hourly) is useful when inflammation is pronounced and when local wide-spectrum antibacterial agents are to be avoided as in the diagnosis of early syphilis.

When inflammation is more chronic or unresponsive to the treatment outlined, a rapid response may follow the short-term (2–3 weeks) local application of a topical corticosteroid with an anti-infective agent (e.g. betamethasone valerate 0.1 per cent cream with 3 per cent clioquinol as Betnovate C Cream, Glaxo) which has both antibacterial and anticandidal activity. A small quantity should be applied gently to the affected area two or three times daily for a few days and then applications reduced to once daily for a limited period of 7–10 days. Betnovate C Cream may stain hair, skin or fabric (ABPI, Data Sheet Compendium, 1978, page 337). Alternatively, hydrocortisone and clioquinol ointment may be used. Topical steroid applications should not be used in herpes genitalis.

When phimosis is present, subpreputial lavage with saline three-to six-hourly is often sufficient to promote drainage and healing. As inflammation subsides the prepuce may become retractable and any ulcer inspected. When a necrotizing ulceration of the glans develops, rapid local destruction can occur. A swab of the subpreputial discharge should be examined microbiologically and if anaerobes are discovered antibacterial agents, such as metronidazole, may be prescribed. Subpreputial lavage may be carried out with a disposable hypodermic syringe or from a plastic container containing 0.9% saline; should this be unsuccessful in securing resolution streptomycin 0.5g may be given intramuscularly twice daily for 3–5 days, or the antibiotic or chemotherapeutic agent effective against the organisms isolated. When there is a dusky erythema of the penile skin with persistent phimosis and the inflammation is unrelieved by the saline lavage described and supplemented with an antibiotic, surgical exposure of the glans by a dorsal slit is necessary to secure the drainage of a necrotizing ulcer.

Some non-infective conditions

Psoriasis produces scaly lesions on the penis, peri-anal region or vulva. On the glans of the uncircumcised male, the lesions are bright red and sharply marginated. Psoriatic lesions will occur elsewhere and pits may be found in the finger nails. Lichen simplex with erythema, lichenification and fissuring in the anogenital lesion is associated with pruritus and affects a 'trigger-zone'. Lichen planus produces annular papular lesions which are pink or violet in colour and sometimes restricted to the genitals and mouth in young men. The surface of the lesions shows a network of fine lines.

Minor conditions sometimes causing anxiety in patients

Trichomycosis axillaris is a superficial infection of the axillary and pubic hairs with the formation of adherent yellow, black or red nodules on the hair shaft. These concentrations consist of tightly packed bacteria, which may also grow within the cells of the cuticle; more than one biochemical type of *Corynebacterium* is involved in the hair-shaft colonies [4].

Coronal papillae are dome-shaped or hair-like papules involving the corona of the penis, which may be mistaken for warts. The papillae are a normal variant. Small yellow papules (about 0.2mm) may be seen sometimes in clusters on the inner surface of the prepuce; these are seen also on the buccal mucosa and consist of sebaceous glands. Sometimes referred to as Fordyce's spots, they are normal sebaceous glands, which increase in number at puberty and continue to do so in adult life.

Tinea cruris

Tinea cruris is an infection of the groins by filamentous fungi, known as dermatophytes, which live only in the fully keratinized layers of the skin and, when established, may cause only minimal disturbance to their host. Although a variety of lesions occur, dermatophytes have been found in apparently healthy skin [4].

AETIOLOGY

In groin infections *Trichophyton rubrum* and *Epidermophyton floccosum* are usually implicated although *T. mentagrophytes* var. *interdigitale* may be detected on occasions. In Denmark it was found that in 17 per cent of *T. rubrum* infections in men, both the groin and feet were involved: this fungus species has become the most common dermatophyte in western Europe since the second world war [5].

Transmission takes place as a result of sharing towels and communal facilities. Tinea cruris is rare in females.

CLINICAL FEATURES

The affected skin is usually red and there is little tendency to central clearing. The surface is scaly, sometimes sufficient to mask the underlying erythema. The lesions due to *E. floccosum* tend to be sharply marginated and extend down the thighs on each side, usually lower on the left side. In *T. rubrum* infections, spread to the adjacent buttocks is common [6]. Involvement of the scrotal skin by the dermatophyte is common but the cutaneous reaction is often inconspicuous [7]. In one survey of Air Force recruits in the United States, 9 per cent yielded dermatophytes from the inguinal region or natal cleft [8], although the skin was apparently normal.

Material for mycological study may be taken by scraping outwards from the edge of the lesions; for the laboratory it is best to collect the specimens on to a folded slip of black paper. Alternatively, particles of keratin may be stripped from the skin with a vinyl adhesive tape (Scotch tape type 68), affixed to a microscope slide for transfer to the laboratory for culture [9].

For routine diagnosis, microscopic examination is most easily carried out by mounting skin scrapings in potassium hydroxide fluid (distilled water 80ml; potassium hydroxide 20g; glycerine 20ml). The process may be hastened by gentle heating. Alternatively the mounting fluid may be prepared with dimethylsulphoxide (40ml), potassium hydroxide (20g) and distilled water (60ml). Fungal elements can then be detected by microscopic examination of the unstained potassium hydroxide preparation covered by a coverslip [10].

Dermatophytes grow well on Sabouraud's medium and are distinguished principally by the nature of the spores. A key to their identification may be found in Rebell and Taplin [10].

TREATMENT

Imidazole derivatives [11] are a new generation of antifungal agents, which are effective as topical agents in the treatment of infections due to dermatophytes as well as in candidiasis (Chapter 17) [12]. Among many possible derivatives clotrimazole, miconazole and econazole [13] are effective in topical treatment. Used as a cream the various preparations should be applied 2–3 times daily as a thin film to the affected area and rubbed in gently (e.g. econazole nitrate 1 per cent as a cream – Ecostatin FAIR; miconazole nitrate 2 per cent as a cream – Dermonistat, Ortho; clotrimazole as a 1 per cent cream – Canesten, Bayer). Improvement occurs within 10–14 days and treatment may continue for 2–8 weeks and preferably for 2 weeks after disappearance of cutaneous signs. On occasions, reddening of the skin and pruritus may occur, but this is seldom severe enough for the patient to stop treatment. Eradication of the infection may not be achieved by topical agents, although clinical effects are controlled.

Griseofulvin may be used orally in more severe cases but accurate diagnosis by microscope and cultures is most desirable. It is taken up by keratin-forming cells and hair shafts, thus coming into intimate contact with the infecting dermatophyte [12]. In tinea of the groin, treatment may be required for a period of 6 weeks. It is prescribed as tablets (griseofulvin tablets BP 125mg; 500mg); the adult dose is 0.5g [6] which may be sufficient if taken once daily after a meal.

Erythrasma

Erythrasma is a mild chronic superficial infection of the skin, characterized by well demarcated flat lesions and probably caused by *Corynebacterium minutissimum* [3].

AETIOLOGY

C. minutissimum is a name which covers a complex of fluorescent diphtheroids, which may also be found on normal skin but which appear to be causative in erythrasma. The incidence is higher in boarding schools and in hospitals for the mentally handicapped [14].

CLINICAL FEATURES

The lesion is smooth and well demarcated from the surrounding skin. Initially red in colour, scaling develops as the lesion ages and it becomes brown. Commonly it involves the toe clefts, but the groin is frequently affected and the axilla or elsewhere occasionally. Usually there are no symptoms but, particularly in the groins there may be mild pruritus.

DIAGNOSIS

Under Wood's light erythrasma shows a characteristic coral-red fluorescence. Skin scales from the margin of the lesion should be examined mounted in potassium hydroxide solution (*see* previous section) to exclude tinea cruris. Exclusion of tinea from the diagnosis should, preferably, include culture of skin scales as well as examination by microscopy. Skin scrapings may be stained with Giemsa to detect the rods and filaments of *C. minutissimum* and cultured to confirm the diagnosis.

TREATMENT

Without treatment the condition persists indefinitely with exacerbations and remissions. *C. minutissimum* is sensitive to sodium fusidate *in vitro* and, in one small series, 2 weeks topical treatment with 2 per cent sodium fusidate ointment (Fucidin Ointment, Leo Laboratories Ltd) was curative [15]. Relapse appears to be more common when the toe web is affected.

Clotrimazole cream is effective in erythrasma and in tinea cruris [16] although tendency to relapse is a characteristic of both conditions.

Balanitis xerotica obliterans

Balanitis xerotica obliterans (BXO), as a term, has tended to be used to describe a naked-eye appearance of the glans penis with individual or confluent ivory white papules. There is sometimes involvement of the urethral meatus and sometimes fissuring and fibrosis of the prepuce [3]. As this macroscopic appearance can be brought about by different processes it is better to restrict the use of the term to those cases with the characteristic histological picture [17]. It resembles lichen sclerosus et atrophicus and may be a localized form of this condition, although other than penile lesions may be found in less than 20 per cent of cases.

PATHOLOGY

The diagnostic histological feature is oedema and homogenization of the dermal collagen, which occurs immediately beneath the epidermis in small islands or on a band of varying thickness. In these areas there is marked loss of elastic fibres. Similar changes occur in the dermal blood vessels. Immediately superficial to the altered collagen, the epidermis shows hyperkeratosis and atrophy of the stratum Malpighii, resulting in flattening or absence of the rete pegs. Deep to the abnormal collagen there is a variable band of chronic inflammatory cells, mostly lymphocytes [17]. The histological picture is similar to that of lichen sclerosus et atrophicus [3].

CLINICAL FEATURES

The condition occurs mainly in those of 30–50 years of age but it has been described between the ages of 11 and 83 years [18]. Patients may present with symptoms of a non-retractile prepuce, urinary obstruction, haematuria, pain and irritation of the penis or a subpreputial discharge [17].

Clinically the lesions of BXO are white, thickened plaques on the surface of the glans and prepuce, usually occurring around the corona and extending a short way into the urethral meatus. The glans and prepuce are thickened and fibrous; the latter may not be retractable. Involvement of the urethra is usually limited to the meatus and squamous epithelium of the fossa navicularis. Although lesions are usually restricted to the penis, unmistakable achromic papules of lichen sclerosus et atrophicus may on occasions be found elsewhere on the body (e.g., seen in four of 24 cases of BXO) [19].

DIFFERENTIAL DIAGNOSIS

It is important to make a diagnosis based on histological examination, because the macroscopic appearance may be similar to balanitis chronica circumscripta or due to non-specific inflammation. BXO usually occurs without skin lesions elsewhere although on histological grounds particularly it may be considered to be similar to lichen sclerosus et atrophicus, a skin condition which is most often seen in women [19, 20].

As in any penile lesion it is important to exclude syphilis and other sexually transmitted organisms which may cause balanitis and/or a urethritis.

TREATMENT

Anxiety about sexually transmitted disease should be relieved after having obtained the results of the tests taken.

When lesions are localized, attempts may be made to control non-specific inflammation of the glans and preputial sac (page 415). Short term applications of 0.1 per cent betamethasone valerate and clioquinol cream or hydrocortisone 0.1 per cent and clioquinol 1 per cent over a period of six weeks, with gradual reduction in the numbers of applications, sometimes produces improvement.

When lesions are extensive the diagnosis should be confirmed histologically and an assessment made at the time by a urologist. Circumcision may be needed when the prepuce is involved and retraction difficult.

Where there is meatal stenosis causing urethral obstruction, dilatations may be sufficient, when the meatal lesion histologically shows only non-specific inflammatory change, but if the navicular fossa and meatus show the changes of BXO, meatotomy or meatoplasty by a urologist may be necessary.

In lichen sclerosus et atrophicus, lesions may extend to involve the site of meatotomy, but this seldom appears to be a cause of further urinary obstruction.

PROGNOSIS

Balanitis xerotica obliterans tends to progress but sometimes this is at a very slow rate. Circumcision will only reduce the added effects of inflammation in the subpreputial sac and dilatation or meatotomy the effects of recurrent urinary obstruction. Carcinoma of the penis has been reported in some cases of BXO [19].

Erythroplasia of Queyrat

This is a premalignant condition of unknown aetiology, presenting most commonly between the ages of 50 and 60 years. It is rare on the penis of men who have been circumcised in infancy.

The condition appears as single or multiple well-defined red plaques on the glans penis or on the mucosal surface of the prepuce. They have a velvety, shiny appearance, and may occasionally ulcerate. Such lesions are commonly asymptomatic, although rarely pruritus or discomfort may be experienced.

The disease is slowly progressive, invasive change being manifest as induration, ulceration or warty growth. Psoriasis, lichen planus, fixed drug eruption, fungal lesions, syphilis and balanitis xerotica obliterans need to be carefully excluded in differential diagnosis. Histological examination is essential for diagnosis.

The appearance on microscopy is characteristic, the epidermis being acanthotic with focal parakeratosis, atypical epithelial cells with hyperchromatic nuclei, dyskaryotic cells and mitosis obvious in cells on the upper Malpighian layer. The dermis is infiltrated with lymphocytes and plasma cells.

Topical application of antimitotic agents such as 5-fluorouracil has produced excellent results in treatment. The subject of erythroplasia of Queyrat and its treatment has been recently reviewed by Goette [21].

Peyronie's disease (Plastic induration of the penis)

In Peyronie's disease a chronic localized fibrous induration involves the intercavernous septa of the penis, causing an angulation or curvature of the penis on erection. The disease, of unknown aetiology, was first described by Francois de la Peyronie, court physician to Louis XIV. In the majority of cases it occurs in the fourth and fifth decades of life although patients from eighteen to eighty years of age have been affected [22].

AETIOLOGY

The unpredictable occurrence of Peyronie's disease in patients who have been treated for eighteen months or more with beta-adrenoceptor blocking agents, such as propranolol [23, 24] and metoprolol [25], suggests that Peyronie's disease may have an association with other fibrous tissue abnormalities such as retroperitoneal fibrosis, which can also occur with these drugs [26]. Peyronie's disease was reported also in a patient with an unusual group of multi-system fibrotic disorders (sclerosing cholangiitis, portal cirrhosis and retroperitoneal fibrosis), who had also a serum alpha-1-antitrypsin deficiency, a finding which may be more than coincidental [26]. In the carcinoid syndrome, where there is an increase in serotonin, Peyronie's disease has also been described [27]. Urethritis, sexual problems and trauma have all been postulated as causes but no definitive cause has been discovered.

PATHOLOGY

There is a vasculitis in the areolar tissue sleeve separating the corpus cavernosum from the tunica albuginea. The inflammatory process, with perivascular lymphoid collections and sometimes cartilage and even bone, may extend into the corpus cavernosum [28].

CLINICAL FEATURES

The symptoms of this disorder are pain and curvature on erection, the sensation of a cord within the penis, the palpation of a lump in the penis, decreased erection distal to the plaque, interference with coitus and gradual impotence. Curvature of the penis is directed towards the lesion and a dorsal curvature is the most common.

The fibrotic plaque may range in size from a few millimetres to involve the entire dorsum of the penis. The plaque is usually located on the dorsum (about 70 per cent): the lateral aspect (about 20 per cent) and the ventrum (about 7 per cent) are less commonly affected.

Plaques may begin as multiple lesions and become confluent. There may be calcification on radiological examination in 20 per cent. The fibrosis tends to be self-limiting and capable of spontaneous remission [22].

TREATMENT

In those cases induced by beta-adrenoceptor blocking agents resolution occurred on withdrawal of the drug.

In the usual case, in which the lesion is an isolated finding, spontaneous remission may occur in half the cases over a period of a few years.

X-ray radiation, diathermy, ultrasound, Vitamin E, potassium para-aminobenzoate, dimethylsulphoxide, have all been used without proof of value. Intralesional steroids have been popular, but there is often great difficulty in getting the fluid into the hard plaque and the effectiveness of this treatment is uncertain [22]. Surgical intervention is unjustified.

Lymphocoele and localized lymphoedema of the penis (Sclerosing lymphangitis of the penis)

This is a benign, transitory condition, first described in a patient with gonorrhoea [29]. The aetiology is unknown, although trauma, in the form of frequent or prolonged sexual intercourse, frequently antedates the appearance of the lesion by an interval varying between a few hours and several weeks.

Histological examination of the lesion shows oedematous thickening of the wall of the affected lymphatic vessel, with minimal infiltration with lymphocytes [30].

Characteristically there is a wormlike swelling in the coronal sulcus, parallel to the corona of the glans penis, sometimes completely encircling the penis, and on occasion involving the dorsal lymphatic vessels of the shaft. Oedema of the prepuce may also be found. The swelling is neither painful nor tender, and on palpation it has a cartilaginous consistency. Within three weeks of its appearance, the lesion has usually resolved completely, and no treatment, other than reassurance, is required.

It is probable that there is wide variation in the presentation of this condition, varying between mild preputial oedema, and the 'classical' lesion described [31]. A similar condition may affect the vulva [30].

Behçet's disease

Behçet's disease is a systemic illness, of unknown aetiology, characterized by exacerbation and remissions of unpredictable duration, which affects mainly males aged 20–30 years. A vasculitis appears to be the common histological lesion and the clinical manifestations, present in most patients and considered to be diagnostic, are oral and genital ulcers, uveitis and a variety of skin lesions. Other common clinical manifestations are arthritis, thrombophlebitis and various neurological syndromes [32].

Behçet's disease has a world-wide distribution but the majority of reports tend to come from the Mediterranean basin, the Middle East and Japan. Although the true incidence is unknown a rate of 1 in 10,000 population has been reported for one district in Japan.

CLINICAL FEATURES

Painful recurrent oral ulcers 2–10mm in diameter occur in half to three-quarters of all patients and are the most frequent initial manifestation. The ulcers are shallow or deep with a central yellowish necrotic base and they occur as single lesions or in crops affecting the mucosa anywhere from the lips to the larynx. The ulcers tend to persist for one or two weeks and recur after intervals of several days to several months.

Genital ulcers resemble those of the mouth both in appearance and course. They are located on the scrotum or the penis in men and on the vulva or vagina in women. The ulcers are painful and disturbing to men but less troublesome to women.

Recurrent inflammation of the anterior segment of the eye usually shows itself as iridocyclitis and hypopyon. Posterior segment involvement may be found in about two-thirds of patients with lesions such as choroiditis, phlebitis, arteritis and optic papillitis. Serious sequelae with blindness may result. It is important to exclude syphilis by means of the necessary tests (Chapter 4), otherwise it may be overlooked.

A variety of skin lesions also occur. Arthritis with synovial changes, which appear to be characteristic histologically [33], develops in about 40 per cent. Thrombophlebitis and various neurological syndromes are also common. Neurological complications occur after some years and include intracranial nerve palsy, cerebellar and spinal cord lesions and meningoencephalitis, all conditions which tend to regress over several months.

Evaluation of treatment is difficult because of the naturally unpredictable course of the disease [32]. Corticosteroid therapy forms the basis of treatment for all manifestations [34].

REFERENCES

1 Wray, D, Ferguson, M M, Mason, D K, Hutcheon, A W and Dagg, J H (1975) *British Medical Journal,* **2,** 490

2 Morson, B C (1976) Regional Enteritis (Crohn's disease). In *Gastroenterology,* Vol. 2. (Ed) Bockus, H L. Saunders, Philadelphia, page 550

3 Rook, A, Wilkinson, D S and Ebling, F J G (1972) *Textbook of Dermatology.* Blackwell Scientific Publications, Oxford

4 Noble, W C and Somerville, D A (1974) *Microbiology of human skin.* Saunders, London, pages 100, 214

5 Rosman, N (1966) *British Journal of Dermatology,* **78,** 208

6 Beare, J M, Gentles, J C and Mackenzie, D W R (1972) Mycology. In *Textbook of Dermatology* (Ed) Rook, A, Wilkinson, D S and Ebling, F J G. Blackwell Scientific Publications, Oxford, Vol. 1, page 715

7 La Touche, C J (1967) *British Journal of Dermatology,* **79,** 339

8 Davies, C M, Garcia, R L, Riordon, J P and Taplin, D (1972) *Archives of Dermatology,* **105,** 558

9 Milne, L J R and Barnetson, R St C (1971) *Sabouraudia,* **12,** 162

10 Rebell, G and Taplin, D (1970) in *Dermatophytes: their Recognition and Identification.* University of Miami Press, pages 85 and 110

11 Sawyer, P R, Brogden, R N, Pinder, R M, Speight, T M and Avery, G S (1975) *Drugs,* **9,** 406, 423

12 Cartwright, R Y (1975) *Journal of Antimicrobial Chemotherapy,* **1,** 141

13 Holt, R J (1976) *Journal of Cutaneous Pathology,* **3,** 45

14 Somerville, D A, Seville, R H, Cunningham, R C, Noble, W C and Savin, J A (1970) *British Journal of Dermatology,* **82,** 355

15 Macmillan, A L and Sarkany, I (1970) *British Journal of Dermatology,* **82,** 507

16 Clayton, Y M and Connor, B L (1973) *British Journal of Dermatology,* **89,** 297

17 Bainbridge, D R, Whitaker, R H and Shepheard, B G F (1971) *British Journal of Urology* **43,** 487

18 Mikat, D M, Ackerman, H R and Mikat, K W (1973) *Paediatrics,* **52,** 25

19 Laymon, C W and Freeman, C (1944) *Archives of Dermatology and Syphilology,* **49,** 57

20 Ridley, C M (1975) *The Vulva.* Saunders, London, page 172

21 Goette, D K (1976) *Urology,* **8,** 311

22 Billig, R, Baker, R, Immergut, M and Maxted, W (1975) *Urology,* **6,** 409

23 Osborne, D R (1977) *Lancet,* **i,** 1111

24 Wallis, A A, Bell, R and Sutherland, P W (1977) *Lancet,* **ii,** 980

25 Yudkin, J S (1977) *Lancet,* **ii,** 1355

26 Palmer, P E, Wolfe, H J and Kostas, C I (1978) *Lancet,* **ii,** 22

27 Zarafonetis C J and Horrax, T (1959) *Journal of Urology,* **81,** 770

28 Smith, B H (1965) *American Journal of Clinical Pathology,* **45,** 670

29 Hoffman, E (1923) *Munchener Medizinische Wochenschrift,* **70,** 1167

30 Stolz, E, van Kampen, W J and Vuzevski, V (1974) *Hautarzt,* **25,** 231

31 Fiumara, N J (1975) *Archives of Dermatology,* **111,** 902

32 Chajek, T and Fainaru, M (1975) *Medicine, Baltimore,* **54,** 179

33 Vernon-Roberts, B, Barnes, C G and Revell, P A (1978) *Annals of the Rheumatic Diseases,* **37,** 139

34 James, Geraint J (1979) *New England Journal of Medicine,* **301,** 431

Index

Lines of Thought

Poems

by

Nicola Lindsay

KB

A Kestrel collection of poetry

First published 1997 by
Kestrel Books
48 Main Street
Bray
County Wicklow
Ireland.

ISBN 1 900505 10 X

Printed in Ireland by Falcon Print & Finish Limited
Bray, County Wicklow, Ireland.

For J.G.T. and C.D.
with fondest love

Contents

Just for you

I boldly searched
for lost words,
for mis-placed capitals
and punctuation gone astray.
Feeling hyphenated
after a fit of italics,
I reviewed my syntax.
I tripped over glottal stops
as I groped in the dim light
from illuminated manuscripts.
I even found some letters
hiding in the lower case.
I discovered quite a few
dropped H's and I fear
I flattened a vowel or two
in my search to please you.
I dusted my dots
and soothed the crossed T's.
I left the irregular verbs
conjugating in the corner
and I nearly had an apostrophe
because of trouble with my colon.
Now, out of this jumble
of interlocked alphabet,
I will carefully extract some words
to make a poem, just for you.

Ballad For Valerie

Valerie's varicose veins were a pain
and her clothes smelt of greasy, fried chips.
It seemed not to matter which diet she chose
- it all ended up on her hips.

The skin round her eyes was puffy and dark
from reading romances 'til late
- stories with men who were tender and kind
and who knew how to treat a loved mate.

Her voice had grown strident from shouting at kids
and nagging her lack-lustre spouse,
who seldom appeared in her common place life,
in that damp, battered, gerry-built house.

Sometimes, with a drink, to cheer herself up,
with her scrap book pulled from the shelf,
she would wistfully gaze at the beautiful girl
from the past, who had once been herself.

Noddy's Complaint

I'm buzzing around in my little red car.
I've polished it up so it shines like a star.
I've polished my bell and also my shoes,
pressed my short shorts - now he has to choose.

I'm really upset, I'm quite close to tears
- I haven't seen Big Ears for several years.
Some time ago he wasn't himself.
He had a breakdown - and married an elf.

He saw I adored him - why didn't he stay?
Enid knew very well that we were both gay.
And what makes things worse is, I don't get a look,
not even a mention in her latest book.

Imagine Toyland bereft of dear Noddy.
Her treatment of me is really so shoddy.
The story won't work - the whole thing's too odd.
I think I'll surrender to nice P.C. Plod.

Begonia

Here he comes
again
with that silly smile and coaxing voice.
He read somewhere that he should talk to plants
to get the best results.
Apparently, he was not warned
that most of us
are quite intelligent.

And so
he murmurs on,
stroking my leaves and squinting at my flowers,
checking me for bugs.
He pokes among my petals
to see if I have fungus.
Has he no shame?

I must admit
he never leaves me standing in cold water
and I quite like his choice of music.
But,
I could do without his pal
who drops his fag ends in my pot
when he thinks
no one is looking.

I have one major grumble;
he just can't read the instructions
on my Bio Feed.
He has a nasty habit of making up the mix
too strong.

Oh No,
he's filling the jug with water
and reaching for the measuring spoon.
If he could only get it right
- just once -
Oops, here we go . . . . .

Don't get me wrong,
I need feeding - just like you
but,
I c c c ome over
all dizzhy
an' I sshtart to
lean a li'lle
an'
I jush

can'

shink ennymore!....

sshraight

The ill-tempered Christmas Tree Fairy

She thought it not right, she thought it not fair,
left hanging around, ten feet up in the air,
with a dirty great chunk of tree up her skirt
that prickled her bottom so much that it hurt.

The fumes from the fire and the cigarette smoke
made her eyes fill with tears and she felt like she'd choke.
Her feet were entangled in tinsel and glitter
- no wonder the smile on her face was so bitter.

Her life on the tree top really was hell
- each time that she moved she bumped into a bell.
Her sequins were missing - they'd not cleaned her face,
her wand was all tarnished, her shoes a disgrace.

She hung on, determined to plan an attack
and worked out a way to get her own back.
She pondered and puzzled for a very long time.
What the place lacked, she thought, was the sweet scent of pine.

So, after the last drunken guest had departed
she lifted her skirts and she quietly farted.
And then, as an extra, she peed in her tights,
spoiled the tree's décor - and fused all the lights.

The Season's started Darling

This year's glitterati
were all at *my* party
- a social event
inside a large tent.

Every male in the place
had a handsome, bronzed face
and smelt - to a man
of Pacco Rabanne.

Though the weather was chilly
the dresses were frilly.
All the preening and prancing
meant you warmed up when dancing.

The wine was well chambréd,
the crêpe Suzette flambéd,
profiteroles all in a row
and young eyes starting to glow.

Girls flirted and smiled,
with sly glances beguiled
men, who later were led,
unprotesting, to bed.

The chat was of trips
to Lausanne, St. Moritz,
of clubbing and fun
in the snow and the sun,

of yachts and of cars
and chic aprés-ski bars
and small business perks
like Audis and Mercs.

Their talk's nothing new,
it's all quite déjà vu
and that is the reason
that I start the season

and throw my smart bash
- while I have the cash
and the whiskey and gin
and my waist is still thin.

While they all pretend
that *they're* setting a trend
and they're so worth inviting
- and it's new and exciting!

The Interview

"And what do you think you can offer us?"
the Personnel Manager said
as I desperately struggled to sort out
the disjointed ideas in my head.

She waited, so cool, poised and silent
for my articulate, informed reply.
The palms of my hands were all sweaty,
I couldn't talk, my mouth was so dry.

I gulped, then croaked out I was older
and wiser than most of the others
- not likely to flirt with the chaps in the suits
or join ranks with the unmarried mothers.

I said that I knew the ways of the world
and that no-one would start to complain
while I was in charge and running the show
in my Spanish [as spoken in Spain].

With manicured hands she smoothed back a hair,
and didn't seem over-impressed.
I tried hard to maintain equilibrium
but ended up badly depressed.

She let me see I was wasting her time,
was puzzled to know why I'd come.
I eventually crept from her presence
and slunk back to the ads feeling glum.

The Employer

"Nice doesn't count.
A will to win is what's wanted here.
She'll have to go." He said
as he picked up the 'phone
to ring a golfing pal.

A most successful man,
Armani suited, lightly tanned.
His priorities meant that employees
came way down on the list.
Somewhere after Property,
his stocks and shares
and glossy race horses
and appointments with Important People
- being seen
with personalities in exclusive restaurants.

Smart, gilt-edged cards
request his presence, to mingle
with the beautiful, desirable and rich.
They all agree with him
that nice - just doesn't count.

The Bus Stop

I'm standing at the bus stop
with the babby in the buggy.
I'm waiting for the 84
which is smoky, hot and fuggy.
Me four year old has taken off
and quite ignores me yells.
His clothes is all in tatters
an' - me Ma says that he smells.
The posh one right beside me
is looking down her nose
- O.K., I know we're scruffy
but I can't afford new clothes.
Me man's been made redundant
and he's gone back on the drink.
If I'd a known he'd change so much
I'd a had another think
before I let him sweet talk me
into climbing in my bed.
Me Ma said I would come to grief
- a no hoper's what she said.
Me carrier bag is bursted
and the spuds is spilling out
and if that kid don't come back soon
I'll give him such a clout.
I've waited here for half an hour
and not a bus in sight.

The babby's cross and crying
- it's his teeth - no sleep tonight!
Thank God, at last, I see a bus
- he's driving very fast.
I don't believe it - it's full up.
He *waves* as he drives past.
Me feet hurt and me back's in bits
and it's about to rain.
Next time we come into town,
we'll take the bloody train.

Funny Man

The kids watched
the funny man on TV.
He really was funny
as a man can be.
He juggled and joked
and tripped and fell.
And the children laughed,
for they couldn't tell
that after the show
he'd go home to his wife,
fire a bullet at her heart,
then take his own life.

Messing about in boats

"You will love it" he said
after he'd booked a cruiser for a week.
"Just wait and see - there's nothing else quite like it,
it makes all other holidays look very dull."

She wrote long lists to cover all their needs;
Box loads of food, plenty to drink,
clothing for hot, summer days ahead
and warmer gear, in case the nights were cool.
Dish cloths, brillo pads and soap, torches, rugs,
light reading for them both.
Medicines to cope with anything
from accidental drowning to a hangover.

The day came and they boarded the elegant craft
that was to be their home for seven days.
She learnt that ropes, at all times,
should lie coiled and ready fore and aft.
He deftly showed her how to tie them
around the bollards, so they would not slip.
She learnt what all the dials and switches meant
and came to grips with the strange sanitary drill,
accustomed herself to the tantalizing whiff
of sewerage which issued from a place called the bilges.
She was required to heave up a heavy trap and extract
river weeds and the occasional minced fish.

He impressed her by his cool handling
of this unruly thing that had no brakes
and a will of its very own.
She tried so hard to play the part
of able crew person to her suave captain
and leapt, gazelle like, the first time that they made land,
rope tightly clutched in white-knuckled fist,
only to fall with a dull thud onto the landing stage;
her performance noted by a large audience
of amused and highly vocal fellow floaters.
Her hands and knees, designer jeans and dignity
were badly battered by that first of many falls.
Her sense of balance never had been great
but she quite surprised to find, as she hung grimly on,
making her unsteady way from aft to stern,
just how terrified she felt.

And when he said he had a treat in store
- and would go off the advised route, drop anchor,
switch off the comfortably spluttering engine to have lunch,
she nearly died of fright because,
according to her map, rocks and reedy mud lurked beneath
the very spot where they, so slowly and so sickeningly
swayed, revolving to the left, then to the right, the horizon
gently spinning under dark grey clouds.

And supercilious swans ignored her offerings of stale crusts
from the tuna sandwiches.
He said he'd like a spot of fishing
but had to cut the line after his first cast.
The spinner no doubt, triple wrapped around
some deadly, submerged thing.
He was not pleased.

And then the rain began...

She wanly smiled, tried not to think
of soft, warm, comfortable beds back home
with electric blankets turned up high
and standing on flat surfaces that stayed quite still,
with ceilings at least six feet above her head.

Down in the depths of deep, dark locks, festooned with ferns.
she clung to rusty chains,
balanced on the uneasy, shifting boat
as water vomited through leaking gates
- great rivers of stout,
poured by some unseen, demented barman.
And he called out "Isn't this great fun?",
"Oh yes" she said through gritted teeth
as the rain trickled slowly down her neck
into her underwear.

To keep her sanity, she counted the days
to her release and dreamed sweet dreams
of static, sun-drenched holidays in future years,
if they survived this one.

And when they got back home,
he told their friends “The holiday was great.”
And she agreed
- and went to find the photographs.

Social Worker

Middle-aged, brown hair giving way to grey,
with tailored suit, good leather bag, she stands smiling
at the door. Her voice is pleasant, her accent,
educated. She says she is a Social Worker.

The girl asks her in. She steps with confidence
into the other's cosy home. Cold, grey eyes search
impatiently for the child she knows is there,
safe within the confines of his understanding.

Unobserved, she has watched and waited every day
for three, interminable, hungry weeks.

6 O'clock in the Supermarket

She was standing in the local supermarket,
peering at labels she could not see.
She looked old and crumpled and unsure.

As I pushed my wayward trolley past,
our eyes met and we smiled, began to talk.
Our conversation lasted a few, brief moments
and then I, pressed for time, said I had to go.

She put her hand on my arm and quietly said
"Thank you - I haven't spoken to a soul all day."

The Violin Player

The boy sat hunched, catching no one's eye.
Waiting his turn, violin on bony knees.
Half grown, with over-large ears, hands and feet.
Spiked hair, uncomfortably thin,
with features sharp-angled - like a young heron
- motionless and concentrated.
Alone amidst the sea of 'cello and fiddle cases
littering the dusty floor among the metal chairs.
A perilous musical assault course
to be undertaken only by the initiated.

His name was called. He clumsily unfolded
and walked nervously towards the pool of light,
to face the bored bunch of other people's relatives.

Then he began to play...
Violin tucked tightly underneath his chin,
with graceful bow hand and fingers dancing
on the strings. His eyes unseeing as he formed
the flood of notes that spilled around us - a cascade
of controlled sweetness that held us captive.

When he had finished
there was complete silence in that ugly, half-filled hall
before the thunder clap of applause
and he, head down, moved back into the shadows.

The Art Exhibition

Young men in velvet
with rings in their ears,
languidly chatting
to their social peers.
They pose by the paintings,
sip wine which is warm
and talk, rather loudly,
of colour and form.
They don't like the Cubists.
Mondrian is O.K.
They dismiss Picasso
and they're bored with Paul Klee.

They try to be clever
- and quick on their toes
and collar the artist
whom everyone knows
is terribly gifted
and ahead of his time.
They don't understand
why his paintings are fine,
know nothing about
the work that he does.
To be pictured beside him
is what gives them their buzz!

Request

I wish to start again
- with nothing.
To lose the clutter,
the unnecessary
and the ugly things
with which
our lives are
so insidiously filled.

I want smooth, empty walls,
doors open
onto sunlit space
with room to stretch
and mind untroubled,
clear-sighted,
spirit light as air.

All to be done anew,
in my own way.
All harm undone.
And all else better done
than I did before.

Sister Paul

She had made the journey many years ago,
when she was young and sure.
She had travelled, uncomfortably,
from a smoky, cold, grey world
to that hot, dusty place
where poverty and malnutrition lived,
unforgiving, hand in hand.
At first she had not understood their ways,
was irritated by the promises not kept.
She heard a different music in their language,
a faster pulse beat in the rhythms of their speech.
She grew to loathe the constant thieving,
the bribes, sly officials waiting
for their unearned extras.
The necessity of all things
having to be kept under lock and key.
The danger of not following the junta's rules.
She had shaken her fist at the hoards
of skinny, semi-naked boys as they ran,
scattering guava and mango in their wake.
Leaving the small, dry convent garden
denuded, yet again.

Without her noticing, the years went by.
She learned to speak their language haltingly
and laughed with them at her mistakes.

At Muslim and Christian festivals,
overflowing with palm wine and stout,
at births and baptisms and marriages,
excited children danced, like flocks of small,
chattering, ebony birds, they hopped and strutted,
singing with shrill, happy voices,
answering the call of the talking drums.
And she danced with them,
with dusty, sandalled feet slapping out the time
and flying rosary beads and sweat-stained habit,
she joined them in their joyful celebrations.

And she grew old and frail in that place
and was not careful for herself
because there was so much that needed tending.
She was the last of the Sisterhood
and was content to stay.

And when she died in that far place,
where death was everywhere and unremarkable,
they came in large numbers,
like a swarm of exotic butterflies,
dressed in their most sumptuous, flowing robes,
a shimmering confusion
of indigo, blood red and peacock blue,
embroidered with threads of gleaming gold.

They came to honour her
and the people sang and they rejoiced because
they knew that she was dancing to wild drum beats
with their ancestors, in a paradise
where God is black and accepts all creeds.

The small, wooden cross rots
in the overwhelming, damp, destroying heat
and creepers creep, their tendrils
closing over the small mound of baked, red earth
and termites build their spiked cathedrals.

Change

I was
my mother's child.

I was
his wife.

I was
their mother.

Now, it is time
to be me.

The Observer

So often
on the outside,
looking in.

Never truly
part of things.

Sometimes wistful,
sometimes glad
not to belong.

Perhaps
one sees more clearly,
standing apart.

Apprentice Writer

I'd like to write something of merit
but *things* seem to get in the way.
When I sit at my desk every morning,
sometimes I have nothing to say.

My mind is distracted by trivia
and my thoughts are muddled and grey.
How can I compose an ode to a rose
when door bells keep ringing all day?

I wanted to pen a poem or two
on finding myself quite alone.
I sat at my desk, determined to work
and defeat the burr of the 'phone.

I gritted my teeth and shut out all sounds
but the paper stayed totally blank.
Cats started mewing, stew needed stewing.
I just gave up and wrote to the Bank.

Pity the first-born

Pity the first-born;
their fate to be subject of experiment
with no trial run to test parent efficiency.
The apprentice mother, filled with blind panic
on returning home
with this small, perfect human being
who seems so fragile,
is non-returnable - and cries...

During the long months of waiting
she dreamed of a sweetly sleeping infant,
content and quiet at her breast.
Instead, this child who writhes in agony, grimacing,
whose contorted face
grows all of a sudden mottled red,
in deep concentration on internal phenomena
and then lies still - too quiet for comfort.
Whose body clock has gone quite mad,
who doesn't comprehend
the difference between the daylight hours and dark.
And she, as yet untutored in the art of motherhood,
suffering badly from self-doubt and overwhelming weariness,
struggles on.

She'll do it better, next time around.

Rebecca

It was as if black magic were at work
inside my daughter's small, limp frame.
Her fever burning more intensely
than the indifferent sun outside.
Her high-pitched cries grown weaker,
her skin sucked dry of moisture.

Suspended in a floating unreality,
we drove to the distant hospital.
An endless, time-stopped, nightmare journey.
We crawled our way over potholed, dirty roads,
past shouting traders and dust-laden, spiked palm trees,
fanned against a faded, heat-stewed sky.
The swollen, fly-spotted body of a bush dog lay,
back broken, teeth bared in a mirthless grin,
ignored, beside a dry storm drain.

And when we finally scrambled from the car,
sweat soaked clothes clinging to backs and thighs,
we found ourselves buried in a crowd
of other anxious, waiting people.
I stood in screaming silence and held her in my arms,
surrounded by noise, knowing that she was almost beyond rescue.
Then, shameless, I pushed my way to the front
and begged for help.

Cry Baby

It just wouldn't stop
- the terrible, persistent noise
of hiccoughing fury.
Demanding, needing,
never-ending,
enveloping, smothering.
Hammering
at the edges of her mind
until she was beyond fatigue.

Changing, suckling, winding,
rocking, walking
- nothing worked.
Terrified,
out of control,
she knew
that she would have to leave
because
she could think
of only one way
of silencing
that perpetual cry.

It's fun to go shopping . . . . Isn't it?

It's fun to go shopping with two year old James
and Emma, who's just about three.
You efficiently settle them inside the car
when James shrieks that he needs a pee.
When this has been sorted and all are strapped in,
the fun can really commence.
For Emma has just dropped her favourite doll
on it's head, in the mud, by the fence.
The doll is retrieved, all covered in slime
and smelling quite strongly of dung.
Sweet Jamie is singing a nursery rhyme
with a bead, up his nose, as a bung.
Your seat won't adjust and, after a search,
you discover the leaver's been jammed
by Lego and dismembered Barbie remains
- in fact - the whole car is crammed
with odd, missing socks and soft, building blocks
and sweets that have grown a strange fuzz.
And Emma has fished out the fly from her mouth,
to see if the thing will still buzz.
As we drive along this hellish, hot road,
my hearing's destroyed by a cry
for James has decided to suck his left thumb
and has missed and has poked his right eye.

We all three agree that we're sticky and hot,
so, James demands an ice-cream
but there's nowhere to park and the traffic's grid-locked
and James has started to scream.
They want to go home for Emma feels sick
- and Danger Mouse is on TV.
There's just no way that I'm shopping today.
Would you do it - if you were me?

A Good Luck poem for a child (For Mary Gallagher)

May magpies always come in twos,
black cats arrive unbidden.
Good fairies chase away your blues
and evil things stay hidden.

May your friendships last for life,
your secrets stay untold
and may you never cease to dance
though you grow very old.

Let gentle dreams be yours at night
- no nightmares come to fright you
and may you wake without a care
- and all the world delight you.

Shameless Seamus

Seamus O'Shaughnessy has nine lovely wives.
To keep them all happy he somehow contrives.
Most gentlemen manage with only one wife
- they say to have several would just lead to strife.
But Seamus adores them and says he'd like more,
thinks that sticking to nine would be rather a bore.
He has forty-six children and one on the way
and he'd quite like another one 'though he is grey.
He has to keep building to make some more room
as he tries to keep up with this wild baby boom.
The place is so crammed they fall over each other.
The children can't work out which one is their mother.
And the real trouble is, with the coming and going
he doesn't realise how much money he's owing.
He thinks it's alright but his reasoning's flawed
as he can't pay the premiums and he's underinsured.
It's really so shameless, the way he behaves.
It's enough to make wise men turn in their graves.
The ones who'd convert him are quite over-zealous
- the real reason being - they're terribly jealous!

The best days of their lives

Pale faced children
With tired
And over anxious eyes
Sitting behind
Preoccupied parents
Who are grim
In the early morning
And driving
Just a bit too fast
Because of leaving late
Sealed in their shiny cars
En route to deposit
Their sullen offspring
Who will
Without a backward glance
Heave their over-heavy bags
Onto their backs
And trudge silently
Towards the prepared day
Of expensive education
Peopled by adults
Who perhaps
Do not like children
All that much.

Puberty

Puberty was doing breast stroke in front of the mirror
to encourage the left breast to catch up with the right.
It was squeezing wicked spots and steaming blackheads,
crouched shivering in a cold bathroom, late at night.

Puberty was seeing Audrey Hepburn in the Nun's Story
and being dead set on becoming a nun.
Then, Florence Nightingale as a role model.
Then, a steamy heroine with her bodice undone.

Puberty was trying to look glamorous in beret and blazer.
It was pretending to know all about Literature and Art
and worrying, if a boy kissed you on the lips after a dance,
would he then tell all his friends you were a tart?

Puberty was about being chased by the truly awful
and being passed over by the one you adored.
It was not understanding calculus, being thought disruptive,
taught by teachers who were both boring and bored.

Puberty was trying to look mysterious - and failing.
It was having to play netball in cold January rain
when your hands and feet were frozen and your back ached
because you had the curse and you were in pain.

Puberty was trying to cope with anaemia and glandular fever,
hating your hair and knowing your legs were too short.
It was trying to read all the juicy bits in the naughty books
like Forever Amber and the Karma Sutra - without getting caught.

Puberty was being betrayed by your very best friend
and being embarrassed to death by your parent's failings.
It was sneaking out of school to overspend in the sweet shop
and then getting caught, climbing back through the railings.

Puberty was angling to stay with odd friends from dubious homes,
wanting lipstick, bouffant hair styles and a very short dress.
It was nagging and wheedling and demanding a party at home
that would leave the parquet floor in a stiletto-pocked mess.

Puberty was a mixture of misery, pleasure and pain.
I was told that it was preparation for real life
but when I emerged, I fear that I lacked credibility
as sensible woman, sane mother or dutiful wife.

The Fair Sex

Just watch the school girls as they pass,
with spotty faces, crooked ties,
untidy hair, socks at half mast,
with greasy bags of warm french fries.

They charge around the hockey pitch
and belt the ball with fearful force.
To win at all costs is their aim,
their methods rough, their language coarse.

Ungracious, noisy, often rude,
they feel they're so superior.
The other sex that has no breasts
they say, is quite inferior.

Then suddenly, things start to change,
school games lose their attraction
and men are high up on the list
and the ladies want some action.

And overnight, they've gained the skill,
worked out the right prescription
to find a man and hunt him down.
The Fair Sex beggars description.

Woman-Child

Over indulged, pretty and petulant
with flawless skin and glossy hair,
designer jeans hugging lovely curves.
She trails in her mother's elegant wake
- bored out of her mind.

Drifting from expensive shop to sleek boutique,
buying creams and lotions to take the place
of a whole pharmacy of half-finished jars.

Some day, this spoilt woman-child will search out
and hunt down a suitable mate
- one who will feed her extravagancies
and he, flattered and beguiled by two bright eyes,
will be trapped in that laser stare
- not realising, until too late,
the cold calculation behind their gaze.

He will pay dearly for the privilege of being snared
- and go on paying.

Che Bella!

I was just seventeen and visiting Rome,
savouring freedom, away from home.
The people were different, the food was divine
- long, drawn out meals with lashings of wine.

I studied the language as hard as I could,
frightened of being misunderstood.
I practised the art of gesticulation
- just as emphatic as the rest of that nation.

I basked in the sun which seemed always to shine
and visited galleries, when there was time.
I bought clothes that were classic, Italian and smart
and longed to be Roman with all of my heart.

The men they were handsome, attractive - and vain,
dressed in Gucci and Pucci and leather from Spain.
Adoring their mothers, despising their wives,
checking in mirrors for most of their lives.

They constantly watched you 'Che Bella!' they'd say,
kissing hands, rolling eyes, pinching bottoms all day.
They'd pay you wild compliments, make such a fuss
and then knock you flat to be first on the bus.

Cars driving on paths made me feel rather nervy
and living on pasta can make you too curvy.
The shouting and hooting and heat lost their charm
- I started to long to be home in the calm.

I needed to be in the cool and the rain,
take baths in bathrooms not reeking of drain.
I wanted to walk down the street unremarked,
not bump into cars, improperly parked.

I hoarded my Lira, then boarded the train,
just dying to be with my parents again.
It was good while it lasted - I learnt quite a lot
but at being Italian, I wasn't that hot!

Feet of clay

"You wouldn't understand." she said.
"It's another world, everything different,
better - and the people there
- they were special, not like here."

My young daughter back from her
first taste of group togetherness.

And in her exclusive isolation
she built an encircling wall,
a magic barrier, invisible,
unscaleable and with no door.

Indifferent, she let me know
that all I thought and did and said
was useless, without value.

Her head was way up in the clouds.
She made it plain that my own feet
were too well rooted to the floor.

Winter Garden

My numb hands are fused to the fork handle
as I slice through the crisp crust of earth,
sending crumbs of dark soil cascading
into the freshly dug furrows.

Bare branches rattle
in the chill, eye-watering wind
and there is a listless sighing of dry leaves,
lying cornered beside the old, brick wall.

All life suspended.
The dry, distorted limbs of plants
are ugly in their rigor mortis.
Rose buds are burnt and fractured by the cold.
Stiff wands of Dogwood glow amber and scarlet.
The comfortless, diffused sunlight
filters through waving fingers of shadow.

And the bitter sweet bonfire smoke
curls through the frozen air,
evoking countless winters past
and for an instant, I see you there,
hand raised in greeting.

Sour Spring

Oh Wow. It's Spring - if I'm not mistaken,
when all blossom from the trees is shaken
by icy winds and shrieking night time gales
and in between brief sunbursts, it then hails.
I'm right, for I have seen my first blue bottle,
head banging on the window at full throttle.

Soon, buxom girls who just will not be told,
will sport bare, unslim legs, mauve with the cold.
And tourists decked with cameras, maps and macs
will try to fend off vicious knife attacks.
The first few sleepy bees will spend long hours
tracking down pollen from defrosting flowers.

It's Spring. See all the snow drops lying flattened.
With sooty rain their fresh, new leaves are patterned.
I heard that damn dawn chorus earlier today
- all sung fortissimo with voices bright and gay.
Emerging soon, the ants and midges for some fun.
I've had enough of Spring. Where did I put my gun?

The Grumbling Gardener

I've an arthritic spine,
not near enough time
and the old arteries are hardening.
And I know very well
my back will be hell
when I've done three hours gardening.

I get things muddled see
- put slug bait in my tea
which gives me terrible gut ache.
But the worst thing I did
was poison husband Sid.
I fed him Super Grow by mistake.

There's creepy crawlies on the pear,
biting bugs are in the air.
The place is full of disease.
Every other day
I get out the spray
and that makes the old dog sneeze.

Would it be a sin
to chuck the lot in,
stop trying to keep it all neat?
Ah, but on the other hand,
today it looks just grand
and it *is* the best garden in the street!

There are earwigs in my roses

There are earwigs in my roses.
Leaves that were glossy and unblemished,
are freckled with innumerable soot-black spots.
Aphids, emerald green and snowy-white, sip their sap,
caterpillars crunch their crisp al dente lunch of stalk and bud.
Powdery mildew dusts the dahlia's pointed petals
and all fragrance has turned sour,
mingling with dark odours of slowly decomposing life
from the rotting compost heap, hidden in the shadows.
The worms have turned and left the soil,
compacted - hard as concrete.
Pernicious anaemia has struck down my silken-flowered azaleas
- the yellow, twisted leaves lie strewn at their feet.
The honey fungus casts its deadly web from stump to rotten stump.
Spores by the million rain softly down, pervading all
with an invisible and malign cloak of micro dots.
Giant spiders spin their untidy, sticky webs, biding their time,
waiting on the side line for the innocent and unaware.
In the damp, dark, secret places,
armadillo-plated wood lice creep and crawl,
with hurrying, scurrying, unseen feet and voracious appetites,
devouring the fallen strawberry's soft flesh.
Silent slugs and snails leave crystal trails, meandering
in a mad mazurka, crisscrossing the uneven, mossy lawn.

And mutant vegetables lie, club feet exposed,
riddled with an antique dealer's nightmare of small holes.

Sadly I see, the beauty that I thought was mine to keep,
dissolves before my eyes into decay.

Lament for a Christmas Tree

I was torn out by my roots.
White, sticky sap bled polka dot drops
on the sound-smothering bed of brown needles.
My limbs were twisted and hacked
and I was dragged over frozen, slippery rocks
by sweating, impatient men,
eager to have the job done.
I was gagged and bound,
thrown onto a heap of my brethren
on the back of a foul-smelling truck
that bounced and bucked
all the way into the city.

I was chosen from among many
and taken from the cool air
into the stifling heat.
Already my resined body scent
is fading.
I cannot breathe.
They festooned me with baubles
and hung me with fake icicles.
They heaped gifts at my feet.
I have never looked so splendid
as I do now,
slowly dying in the corner
of this laughter-filled room.

Morning has broken

Crooked street signs, swathed in shreds of wind-blown litter,
looking like a line of disreputable drunks,
waiting listessly outside the shuttered Off Licence
in the damp greyness of the early morning.
The pot-holed road shudders in protest as the first trucks
arrive to disgorge their cargoes, freezer units
roaring in competition with each other.

Last night's visiting vandals, a raiding party
from the hills, have left a telltale trail of broken bottles
and plants, uprooted from the raised flower beds.
The brick missiles lying, scattered where they fell
after a spot of midnight target practice.
The alarm still shatters the early morning air
with it's vibrating, insistent, non-stop call.
Shards of glass protrude from recently replaced shop fronts.
As you make your uncertain way over the path's
uneven paving slabs, you wonder if
the San Andreas fault hasn't shifted East a bit
and hope all good muggers are back, safe in their beds.

The yawning lads arrive on the building site,
their dragon breath curling in the cold, like smoke.
Their hard hats make them into Lego men
as they clamber up the multi-storey car park
in whose shadow your own house will soon be lost.

Lost too the evening sun and views of distant
brown-green, bracken-feathered mountain side.

A scrawny, mange-ridden cat slides through the railings
at your side and a bedraggled early bird warms up,
trying out a few, tentative notes, wondering if
his talents would be more appreciated in a quieter street.
He may as well sing, for his worm lies hidden underground,
cocooned in concrete.

Song of the Snowman

I understand the singing of the stars,
the music filled with ancient memory.
I watch their slow dance in the speckled night sky
which has no end. Sheathed in ice, I wait
in the whispering, frozen hours before the dawn.

I know my time here will be infinitely short.
The unkind wind will breathe on me less icily
as I am reabsorbed into the swirling mass of sky.

My melting molecules contain the universe.
As I vanish into nothingness, my crooked smile
will stay, distorted on the slush-grey, trampled ground.

A visit to the Zoo

Shall I take you to the zoo
to see the animals?

Look at the polar bears,
padding to and fro
across the concrete covered ground
that surrounds their scum-smothered pool.
See how they swing their heads
from left to right.
Do you think they miss
the cold, pristine whiteness
of their former life?

See over there,
a once silken coated otter
emerging from that tiny pond,
decorated with blown crisp packets
and floating cigarette butts.
Watch him as he paces out
a frantic figure of eight,
into the water,
through the length of plastic drain
and back again.
How many times do you think
he repeats that mindless journey,
day after day?

Let's go and see the ape house.
Look at that giant gorilla there.
See how he sits, motionless,
staring with sad, dark, empty eyes
at small boys who make faces
and bang on the glass box
which is his home, his jungle, his retreat.
Do you think he dreams of roaming free,
of climbing trees with his mother?
Forgetting that she is dead,
shot by poachers when he was small.

Why look so sad and say you have to go?
You do not want to stay and watch
these hostage animals losing the will to live
as madness slowly fills their minds?

The dying sea

They silence the soulful singing of the whale,
net and slaughter the life-saving dolphin.

They sluice out their oil tanks and soil
the ever-resourceful sea, rendering
all flying things flightless, binding bird's feathers
in a deathly, sticky coating of satanic black.

Dulled is the rainbow gleam of fish shoals
that once darted in shimmering curtains
and now float, mouths agape with staring eyes
in silent protest, tarnished silver bellies to the sky.

I remember a church

I remember a church, filled with the sweet scent of incense.
I remember the feeling of sanctuary and sanctity.
And there, I gravely made my first communion.
I remember the light which filled that place,
streaming through gem-studded, jigsaw windows
in bars of ruby, sapphire, emerald and gold.
I remember the beauty of responses sung in Latin
and the cream and white of cloth and vestment
when I stood, veiled in lace, beside the man I married.
I remember the uneven, stone flagged floor
and unforgiving, straight-backed wooden pews.
I remember my family and friends, watching
as my sleeping first-born child was baptised there.
I remember small children, dwarfed by large candles
which they held at perilous angles, kneeling at the altar steps.
I remember the lilac-blue drifts of flowers
at the service to commemorate a much loved father.
And I remember well the feeling of my being
in a special, holy place where people sang and prayed
and then went back into the troubled world, refreshed.

A Victorian glass

A Victorian glass with delicately frosted frieze,
engraved with images of gently curving foliage
like early morning frost on window pane.
A memory from times long past.
Rice paper thin with exquisitely tapered form,
once, perhaps, brim-full with cool, jade lemonade,
sipped by gentle women where quiet voices
murmured low in green shadowed conservatory.
Where pale shafts of mote-filled sunlight glinted
on elegant fern and half awakened flower.

And as I hold it carefully up to the light,
I wonder at it's history and how it came to be
in a dark corner of this dusty junk shop.

Newcastle Hospital

Crossing the sea of shiny lino I see her,
an isolated figure in the corner of the ward
sitting, fully dressed on the neat hospital bed,
an unopened novel beside her.
Stale flowers stand stiffly on the crowded locker.
Her dark hair is spread in a protective curtain,
half hiding her finely-lined, still young face.
She looks drained of all colour
except for blue smudges beneath her eyes.
Her hands lie, composed upon her lap.
She is unsmiling, barely talks,
enveloped in a drug-doped haze.
There is an unnatural stillness about her,
an unfocused quality that is deeply disturbing.
I see a woman in retreat from the world in which I live.
Clumsily, I search for the right words
but our lives, for the moment, have nothing in common.
She has suffered, is still suffering in a way I do not know.
How could I understand what she is feeling
as she struggles with this malady of the mind?
I want to hold her and hug away all that sadness
but that is the last thing that this stranger wants.
Powerless, I watch from a great distance.
I remember how she was not so long ago
as I wait and hope for her return.

This Place

This place, this wilderness, is beautiful.
It is perfumed and multi-textured.
Leaves spiked, rounded and frilled
in a hundred unnamed shades of green.
The blackbird's liquid song rising and falling.
And for a brief time, no discord.
A sense of spirit of place, all things in harmony.

For now, this small haven remains,
intact, inviolate and vulnerable.
And the softly shifting grains of sand
flow in the cracked hour glass
in the shadows on the dusty shelf.

Evening Africa

The damp, hot scents and smells of evening Africa.
Wet, warm vegetation and the odour of decomposition
with frogs, croaking out their hearts in hidden storm drains.
Stars, incredible in their unrealised number and intensity,
making the sky's velvet dark yet more beautiful.

Unceasing insect-thrumming night sound,
scent of jasmin drifting through door and window
and the ghostly frangiapani glimmering palely
in the depths of the garden. The omnipresent whine
of the ubiquitous mosquito and the quick flicker
of the gecko on the wall, watched by the prayerful mantis,
clothed in emerald. Colours and sounds collide,
bruising the senses in the evening's steamy heat.

A blood-red hibiscus flower lies trampled on the ground.

Eclipse of the Moon

27th September 1996

Floating fragments of torn clouds
hurry past,
shrouding the marbled disc
suspended there
with Saturn glinting at her side.
Briefly veiling
that magic eye of molten platinum
- a peep hole in the sky,
guarding entrance
to cold infinity.
The shadow slowly spreads
across the pock-marked beauty
of her face
and the moonlight dies.
It is as if
a celestial dimmer switch
had been turned off,
leaving the world
unlit
and unfamiliar.

Glendalough in Winter

Deserted, on a biting cold winter afternoon.
No voices echoing across steep valley sides.
No murmured chanting from the scattered ruins.

This was a place of wisdom and of learning,
of hardship, meditation, prayer and strife.
It enfolds the stranger with a potent mixture
of sanctity and old earth magic.
Here is total stillness and unheard sound.
Unseen eyes are watching.

No reflections lie in the bottomless, black lake
and dark, sentinel trees stand starkly motionless.
Large, feather-soft flakes of snow fall soundlessly
from sagging, heavy clouds and pervading all,
a chill, that numbs your limbs and soul.

Glendalough from a Chip Van

Unseen, they observe the passing people
as they brew the tea and fry the chips.

They see tired children at day's end,
their faces smeared with melted ice cream cones
- so sullen and so hard to please and queasy
after too much coke and chocolate.

They see irritated husbands and discontented wives,
bored to death with each other's company
but trying hard to make the best of things.

They watch young lovers, moulded at the hip,
sucking the passion from each other's lips.

And the skinny mongrel, with leg raised,
watering a Rover's fancy hub cap
then pelting back to find his scruffy, earinged owner
with guitar and strange, scented cigarettes.

They see pot-bellied, lager swilling lads,
pale skinned with shaven heads who splash
in the dark lake's icy water, right beside
the sign which reads 'Danger - do not swim.'

They see the thieves, the petty pilferers,
flitting from car to car, unnoticed,
searching for carelessly abandoned treasure.

They watch bus loads of visitors arrive,
obedient in well-marshalled groups,
heads aching as they try their best to take in
all this history. Jaded, their senses dulled,
sated with miles of green-filled scenery,
their eyes unbright and dying for some aspirins,
cool showers and long, refreshing drinks.

When everyone has left, they pack their gear,
pick up the wrappers and the trampled cans
and return home to count the day's takings.

Sea Sounds

Sea's silky sounds
and curling curlew call,
soft wind sighs
and sand grass rustles.
Gold light embroiders
the wave's edge
and torn shreds of mist
flow gently in
gliding over sliding,
water-polished pebbles.
Magic working silently,
emptying the body of itself
'til it becomes a husk
- a mere shadow, swaying
in the approaching night
that slowly spills
into the mouse-grey fields beyond.

Danger! Men at Work

It has come to my notice how often,
when a man tackles jobs round the place,
you may as well stop what you're doing
and join in with a smile on your face.

Perhaps they all long to be doctors
with reverent stooges in tow,
all dying to watch a master at work
in the house or outside in the snow.

They wait 'til they're right up a ladder
to discover the tool they have got
is not the right one and the other
is somewhere downstairs - but it's not.

You rummage around in the tool box
with the dim light from a torch.
He's turned the power off and it's freezing
- and the cat's got a mouse in the porch.

You finally track down the spanner
when the light dies and all is quite dark
and you stumble and bump into objects
- and the damn dog has started to bark.

Why do they need your attention?
You really don't want to disguise
the fact that you think that they're gifted
and incredibly clever, wise guys.

The one thing they don't seem to grasp
is that daily, hundreds of chores,
single-handed are quietly completed
by women, without being bores.

In the meantime, to boost their morales
as they show off their D.I.Y. skills,
we'll continue to play second fiddle
and hang onto their ladders for thrills.

The Drinks Party

All crammed together in this stuffy room.
Drawing near, then separating
- following the pre-ordained steps
of some strange, heathen ritual.
Gesticulating, mouthing half-heard exclamations
of pretended pleasure, delight
at meeting like this - yet again.

Half of the people in this place
have aching backs or feet
- or both,
as they juggle with their tepid drinks
and crumbling canapés;
their bosoms lightly dusted
with flakes of pastry
from exploding vol-aux-vents.
The asparagus escaping from its roll,
the unidentified mud-coloured dip,
the harpooned sausages
and the glistening, slippery olives,
lurking in the depths of proffered trays
- like some wild animal's droppings.

Stalking from group to group,
they circle one another, scenting the air
for a trace of scandal,
a hint of juicy gossip on which to feed.

He talks - she listens
and she knows his eyes
are searching in the room beyond
for sweeter prey than she.
Relinquishing her place,
she weaves her way
through the haze of toxic smoke,
choking on splinters
of half-swallowed peanuts as she goes,
leaving an uneven trail of foot prints,
marking the ash-strewn Axminster.

Love your Family - but don't overdo it.

Brothers and sisters - it has to be said,
should never be tempted to climb into bed.
It may seem very cosy but it's really not wise
- their children may prove a nasty surprise.

That also applies to first cousins too
- the offspring will only be fit for a zoo.
So, try to be careful at family doos;
don't get handy when randy and lay off the booze.

The girl in the painting

The painting of the girl hung
on my father's study wall.
I knew her name.

She stands, gazing out to sea
at cold, untidy, wind-tossed waves.
Brown drifts of seaweed limply lie
on the shiny sand and clouds scud
across a grey, uneasy sky.
Her small, brown, undistinguished dog
looks up - hopeful, tail erect.
She's unaware of her surroundings,
looks very young and innocent,
strangely intense, waif-like
on spindly, wool-clad matchstick legs.
Hands in pockets, face so pale
as if looking ten years ahead,
when she would give in to a friend
who was so desperate to forget
he overdosed - and died.

This girl would be considered culpable
and sent to prison - aged eighteen.

Remember, Nurses never run

"Remember, Nurses never run." said the starch stiff Sister
to the nervous newcomer, uncomfortable
in her crisp, unpliant uniform.
"No perfume will be worn, and Nurse,
no nail varnish, make-up or jewellery.
Nor must your hair touch the collar of your dress,
your stocking seams must be completely straight."

The squat, efficient Sister ruled the ward,
implacable and omnipresent.
Young nurses trembled in her wake,
shedding surreptitious tears in the sluice room,
between the bed pan washer and the sputum cups.
The new trainees would laugh behind her back.
'Sister Plod' they called her,
amused by her deliberate, flat-footed gait.
They missed the sharp intelligence
that lay behind the direct gaze of those brown eyes.
The junior Nurse was not sure if she liked
this super-calm, no-nonsense woman
who never seemed to be off duty.
And when she made mistakes and there were many,
she suffered silently the inevitable, icy rebuke,
firmly given in a quiet voice,
but always done when there was no one else
around to witness her embarrassment.

And when an old man died, falling backwards
in the bed so suddenly,
painfully choking on his last, snatched breaths,
to lie - like an abandoned glove puppet,
cast carelessly aside,
the young Nurse was there and did the things
she had been taught to do and gave comfort
to the distraught son.

And afterwards, she wept because
she never had seen Death at work before that day
and had been chilled by his proximity.
Nor had she ever heard a young man cry
so openly, great, unashamed tears of salty grief
that left her feeling alone and desolate.

It was the Sister who gently spoke to her
with such compassionate understanding
that the girl was both amazed and comforted.
And she was given time to dry her tears,
reminded that others needed her attention.
So, with quiet resolve, she went back to the ward,
following the older woman's steps.

Summer Afternoon

In the stippled sunlight,
lulled by the buzzing bees,
she dozes in the deck chair,
face, shadowed by the trees.

Young limbs leaden in the heat,
her weighted eyelids close.
Floating in and out of dreams,
filled with the scent of rose.

Green filigree of fern and leaf
stir in a gentle breeze.
An unread book lies open,
propped on her bony knees.

Chewed straw in a sticky glass
of unfinished lemonade.
A wooden flute lies on the ground
abandoned and unplayed.

Stains on her ripped shirt and shorts,
with tangled, sweat-soaked hair.
My wayward child - so fey and wild,
sleeps on, without a care.

Out of Place

I wake to find a dead bird with a broken wing
posted through my letter box.

I live where broken street lamps illuminate
the drug dealers and the teenage whores.
The baby-faced joy riders have made
the road outside a no-go zone after dark
and impatient mothers swear at their kids
who play in the dry patch of waste grass
where junkies feed on oblivion and drop
their needles, prized as play things
by the younger ones. They are unwilling
to return home to luke warm take-away
and flying fists when all the beer has gone.

The graffiti scrawled walls vibrate with unease
and the stench of rottenness is overpowering.
My neighbours avoid my glance and watch me
when they think I am not looking - their faces
sullen with distrust. They do not speak my language
and do not try, biding their time, knowing
that I am vulnerable because alone.

The Thieves have left no silver

There are cobwebs on the ceiling,
missing floor boards in the hall.
There's a cockroach by the cooker,
creeping dry rot in the wall.

The curtains smell of cigarette smoke.
Boiled cabbage scents the air.
The couch is deep in cat fluff
and mice frolic on the stair.

When she was young, she studied Vogue
and interior design.
She entertained with wit and style,
good food and fine old wine.

The thieves have left no silver,
nor gems, nor pearls, nor gold.
She can't remember when it was
that the Chippendale was sold.

And those who loved her company
are dead or gone away.
No one recalls her elegance
- for now, it's in decay.

She never sees her married son
and his cold, haughty wife.
A grandson sometimes comes to call
whose mind is full of life.

They talk about the friends she had
and the books that she has read
but every time he visits her
it's with a sense of dread.

He understands she's nothing left
- out of tune with modern ways.
He sees the sadness in the eyes
that watch the passing days.

It's for the best

"Listen, it's for the best" they said,
delivering her to the nursing home.

And she breathed in the acrid stench
of stale urine and heard low cries
of distress from another room.
Her startled eyes took in the row
of people with pale, vacant faces
- stripped of dignity, diminished.
And they in their turn looked at her,
blankly, while a trapped fly buzzed
against the frosted window pane
and the smiling game show host
gave away a car on the TV.

When several days had passed,
they came to see her with the news
that they had just dispatched
her terminally old, arthritic,
half blind dog - to put an end
to all his suffering.

"Listen, it's for the best" they said.

The manner of dying

I would choose the manner of my dying.
No sterile, long drawn out, unnecessary suffering.
Lingering, anonymous and silent in the noisy ward,
crowded with chatty visitors who, quite unaware,
jolt the bed end as they pass to joke and jostle round
the lucky ones who soon are going home.
Leaving behind the tasteless food - last meal at five o'clock.
Forgetting the hurrying nurse who wakes you
with a sleeping pill - then leaves you wakened,
desperate to sleep away the unquiet, long night hours.

I would reserve the right to say goodbye to those I love.
The choice of last companion should be mine.
One who will ease and calm me with a light heart and help me
make a quiet exit, with dignity and the minimum of fuss.

My Mother's Mother

My mother's mother died alone.
They promised to tell us
if there were any change.
We knew her heart was weak
- yet not so frail
that we should give up hope.
But she seemed not to care;
did all could to speed on death,
refusing to play the part
of dependent invalid.

Yet, did she want to die like that
- alone and frightened and in pain?
With no one there to hold her hand
or keep her company.

In the early morning
we were officially informed
that she had died,
in the cold hours of the dawn
when all things
are at their lowest ebb.

And when we went there
we were given,
with complete and chilling unconcern,
her rings and nightdress
in a dustbin bag.

The old man said...

The old man said ...

"My children left many years ago.
I would not know them now.
The few good friends I had
are dead and buried.
My working days are over.
My distorted hands
no longer obey my mind's commands.
My eyes have become too feeble
to re-read the books I love.
And she is long gone
- the one woman in the world
I ever loved.
Who never knew it
because I lacked the courage
to admit how much I cared.

I sit in the pale, unwarm, winter sunlight
with my vast store
of incomplete memories,
trying my best to fill in the gaps.
What is there left for me to do
but wait, impatiently
for indifferent Death?"

No Survivors

I was wakened by the screaming wind
hurling itself against the creaking door.
It tried to prise slate roof from old brick walls,
gain entry under rotten window sills.
It seemed relentless in its mad attack,
as it beat against all man-made things.

The roar of the hungry sea grew and I feared
for those who were tossed and buffeted
on its unfriendly, boiling surface
under the blind blackness of that sky.
Flying curtains of needle fine rain
flaying the hands and faces of men
as they fought to stay alive.
I saw pinpricks of light from the distant boat,
dancing wildly in the dark - then quenched
like a candle suddenly snuffed out.
Chilled to the bone I waited, but I knew.

And was their dying quick? Or was there time
for the unbelievers to repent their sins,
before clawing fingers of icy water
tugged them down, tumbling through cliffs of water
- to be sucked under, one last time.
Was there a brief moment of fearless calm
before Death came?

Gravity wins every time

I really resent growing older
and losing the battle with gravity.
On checking things out, I find there's a bump
where once was a nice, neat concavity.
It's a trial, when I peer through my glasses
at parts that *were* perky and proud.
I can't help but admit they they've shifted
but I'm damned if I'll sing it out loud.
I feel a bit grim when I look at my chin
and find that a second one's growing.
I've tried mouthing "Ooo Aaa" while driving my car
but it won't stop the dewlaps from showing.
I'm afraid all the wobble and sagging
must be seen as a sign of the times.
I'll just have to stop looking in mirrors
and forget about crinkles and lines.
And who will care, if they notice my hair,
I've not bothered to touch up the roots,
or when it's cold and I feel rather old
that I've donned my long johns and lined boots?
But people who love me and know me
would admit that I'm way past my best.
They agree that I still have my moments
and can look drop-dead gorgeous when dressed!

Nymph's Request

Oh, take me to bed and drive me quite wild.
I want to be bad - I want to be had.
I'm all woman you know, not a child.

I want you to take off my clothes 'til I'm bare
and bury your face in my tumbled down hair.
I want you to suck my fingers and toes
and tickle my neck with the tip of your nose.
I want you to lick me all down my spine,
sip wine from my navel - if you have time.
Cover my nipples with honey and cream
and massage my feet 'til I'm ready to scream.
I want you to suck ripe fruit from my lips,
rub sweet smelling oil onto my hips.
Coat my eyelids with kisses and fondle my thighs
and I promise, from me, you'll hear nothing but sighs,
low purrs of contentment, moans of delight.
That's if you pleasure me all through the night.

Oh, take me to bed and drive me quite wild.
I want to be bad - I want to be had.
I'm all woman you know, not a child.

Shepherd's Reply

Your amazing request came out of the blue
but, ravishing maidens is not what I do.
I fear my intentions are misunderstood;
my habits are chaste - I try to be good.
I hear what you're saying - I'm flattered to bits
but the things you're suggesting have me in fits.
Your terms of engagement will bring us one thing
- a whole load of grief, if you insist on a fling.
Taking your clothes off will just lead to trouble
- when your Dad finds out he'll be here at the double.
As for the bit about honey and cream
well, I think it's the answer to any man's dream
and I know where there's honey but I can't climb the tree
and can you imagine how sticky you'd be?
I think that you're lovely and shapely and nice
but I beg you to accept a piece of advice;
I really don't think I'd be right as your mate
- to bed you and please you is just not my fate.
There *are* other men for you to discover,
so I'll send you round my sex-crazed, younger brother.
I hope you're not hurt - I hope you don't mind,
for I know that your offer's incredibly kind.
To tell you the truth, I'm in love with another.
You really are gorgeous, but I fancy your mother!

A different way

We stripped our souls bare
and told each other
there would be no secrets.
We explored love
in great detail and were
intimate in every way.
A handful of years later,
love lay in shreds.

But they
always preserved their dignity.
Some things remained unsaid.
There was room for
a little mystery.
They valued the traditional ways
and made time
for measured conversation.
They showed each other
an exquisite courtesy.
And after forty years
of contained contentment
and pleasure in each other,
they parted only
when she died.

Sunday Breakfast

The sunlit kitchen is warm
and smells of coffee and fresh toast.
You, glasses perched on nose,
buried deep in your Sunday paper,
feed absentmindedly.
A scattering of crumbs lie on your dressing gown.
The programme we half listen to
murmurs an accompaniment
to the occasional "Did you read this?"

The cats sit as close to the fire
as it is possible to get.
They have already breakfasted
and groom each other with enthusiasm,
tails twitching, eyes half-closed.

You look up
and lean towards me,
brushing back my untidy, early morning hair
and kiss my mouth and neck.

I asked for Mozart and you gave me Brahms

Why, when I asked for Mozart,
did you promptly play me Brahms?
Why, when I said I'd like a hug,
did you gently fold your arms?

Why do you talk 'til two a.m.
when all I need is rest?
You're feasting on adrenaline
when I'm far from my best.

When we're invited out to dine,
why do you drive so fast?
I'd rather we turned up alive,
not minding if we're last.

When you know you'll mix your drinks,
- before the pain begins,
why are you not sensible
and take two aspirins?

Why hog the talk when friends drop in?
- you love to hold the floor.
You're witty, entertaining,
but sometimes, quite a bore.

Why do you, when you first awake,
start the day by moaning?
I'd like to hear the early News
without your non-stop groaning.

What makes you think you are *the* one
to ever really know me?
And to dictate which path I take
- just because you chose me?

Why, in the evenings, as I wait,
do I strain to hear your voice?
You drive me mad, perhaps we're doomed
but I'm happy with my choice!

Incantation

I have poured good wine as a libation,
been made pink-eyed and dizzy by the smoke
from a palisade of choking incense sticks,
offered up a fair-sized chicken [oven ready].
A supplicant in urgent need of help
to wreak my vengeance on you, make you see
the error of your wayward life.

I call upon all pagan Gods - Roman or Greek,
Indian, African, Norse or Celt.
It does not matter which, as long as they
are powerful, vexed and full of spleen.
I beg them to turn their malign gaze
to where you stand, oblivious.
May they hurl down great fistfuls of lightning
so the green grass scorches under your feet
and your (receding) hair catches fire,
burning with the acrid stench of sulphur.
I ask that plagues be visited on you
- not innocent frogs, leaf hungry locusts
but far worse and more spectacular.
May you sprout hives and boils unnumbered
in intimate, uncomfortable places.
May your house be filled with ticks and fleas
and bed bugs with voracious appetites,
impervious to your sprays and burning coils.

May noxious gas invade your room at night
and gruesome nightmares, too terrible to name,
visit each time your eyes are closed
and when you wake, the real world will seem
far worse than your most deadly dreams.
May your unlovely face be full of scabs and scars,
and creeping fungus fester on your feet.
I ask that your waistline further expands
so that no garment in your wardrobe fits
and moths will make a filigree of lace
from your remaining pin-striped suit.
May you never find a parking place in town,
all meters hooded and shut down.
And when you go on picnics to the beach,
may gritty sand coat all your sandwiches.
When washed, may your best socks refuse to match,
your underwear turn shocking pink and shrink.
And on the eve of your Hellenic cruise
you may well find that you have lost the key
to the steel safe in which there lies
your passport and your travel documents.

That's all for now - you may well tremble
for, 'though I am a novice at this game,
I have requested help from experts
and I have only just begun ....

Who do you party with?

When you are a woman
and are separated

female friends think
you will seduce their men.

Men friends think
you will subvert their wives.

Couples do not
ask you around because
you no longer are
half of a pair.

The only single people
that you know
are either mad, bad,
have suicidal tendencies
or totally engrossing jobs.

So... who do you party with?

Damage Limitation

My mouth is sour
with the after taste
of bitter words.
Now they lodge
like small, poisoned darts
in your memory.

The damage limitation
will be extensive
- no effort spared.
But we both know
the fragile fabric
tears so easily.

If only I had
the facility
to embroider
the frayed edges
with soft, silken thread
- to make it strong again

Good Intentions

I had hoped that, long before next year arrived,
a fresh code of practice could be contrived.
My new life of zeal and affirmative actions
and not getting side tracked by fatal attractions.
I know that I've done my fair share of sinning
but he who sins hardest ends up by winning.

I see that my habits are really quite shameless
but who wants a life that is totally blameless?
And Bucks Fizz for breakfast is really so nice,
with hot, crispy toast and caviar served on ice.
And making V signs at my troublesome neighbour
is not what I'd call really deviant behaviour.

I've tried making a list as everyone should,
to deal with my bad points and help me be good.
Drink, greed, lust, sloth, envy and turning up late,
I really can't help it - to sin seems my fate.
Getting my weight down, as everyone knows
means stretching and bending and touching my toes.
But I'd far rather sit with a gin and a book
and wear loose, floaty clothes and a seductive look.

By the time that I reach Deadly Sin No. 7
I fear I'll end up being blackballed from Heaven.
I really should try to revamp my existence
and if I work hard I'll get points for persistence.
As this bright New Year dawns I'll aim to improve
- I'll read all the Classics and visit the Louvre.

There are a vast number of things to be changed
but without all the fun times I'd get quite deranged.
I'll just tear up my list and slap on the make-up,
take to ciggies and booze - give the locals a shake up.
The best way to keep our imperfect world spinning
is by really enjoying some old fashioned sinning.

Now, don't be upset that your character's flawed.
Be a tiny bit bad and you'll never be bored.
There's no point at all one's pleasures denying
- there's serious living to do before dying.
So, finish the bottle, put on your best gear,
open your arms wide and embrace the New Year!

When she was young she fell in love

When she was young she fell in love
- and she was ignored.
She prayed that he would notice her
but, he just looked bored.

He was at university
- she was still at school.
He studied Modern Languages
- she learnt to play the Fool.

His clothes were very elegant,
his manner, charming,
his movements quick, his voice refined,
his smile, disarming.

But he was cruel and played a game,
amused to feel her pain.
It flattered him to see her grieve
- for he was very vain.

Now time has past - his image gone.
She's more wise than then
and she has learnt to stay well clear
of beautiful, young men.

Being apart

Now we're apart
I can make my new start.
Spread my cramped wings
and do all the things
that before were never allowed.

I will start life anew,
on my own, without you,
unafraid, unashamed and unbowed.

I'll be like an A.A.
and live day by day.
Find the courage to be
the person that's me
whom I lost in the life that we shared.

It will be a surprise
- it will open your eyes
when you see just how well I have fared!

Paradox

He fell in love with her beauty
and her differentness.
He admired her free spirit.
He adored her unexpected ways.

He wooed her with great passion
and determination.
He won - then broke her heart.
He insisted she conform
to his idea of ideal woman
and tried hard to erase
what had, at first,
seemed so desirable.

Sharing

Let me walk gently through your mind.
Show me the dark and secret places
where self-destroying doubt and anger lurk.
And crouching in the corners, half unseen,
your unnamed terrors and your fears,
waiting to invade at unexpected times.
Guide me carefully, let me know them all
and then, unlock the doors that hide
the brightness of your hopes and joys.

Monday morning

I remember
in the half-light of that early dawn,
your cool skin against my warmth.
Your body scent, so slight
- yet so arousing.
The feather touch of your finger tips,
unfocused, sultry eyes
beneath their sleep-heavy lids.
The softness of your lips resting on mine
as we breathed in each other.

And now,
I ache to be with you again.

Night Thoughts

At night,
when sleep will not come,
my head buzzing
like a honey bee
from one half-finished thought
onto the next.
I think of you
- so far away
beside the crumpled tin foil sea,
fortressed
by a semi-circle of green hills.
And on the heavy, midnight air
I hear
the pheasant's croupy cough
echo
across the flat fenlands
and wonder
if you lie awake
and sleepless there
and what thoughts
fill your mind.

Lullaby to a sleeping man

You lie here, who earlier were
so careworn, brim-full of troubles,
vexed with life.
Now you are at rest in my bed,
your even breathing almost inaudible,
like gentle sighs.
Features soft in sleep, unworried,
kissed mouth barely closed.
Eyes moving under crescent lids
as you dream your dreams,
tired limbs, motionless.
Sandpaper hands that craft
things of infinite delicacy,
lie quietly at your side.

May you rest peacefully,
untroubled by the worries
that tomorrow brings.
Sleep deeply while I keep watch
and in the morning, wake, refreshed.